The Priest, The Pope and The President

The True History of Abraham Lincoln's Fight Against the Jesuits and Pius IX

CHARLES T WILCOX

Benjamin Franklin's concept for the Great Seal… Moses, under the direction of God, destroys the army of Egypt in order to set up a government under God.

Wilcox, Charles T.

The Priest, The Pope and the President

The True History of Abraham Lincoln's Fight against the Jesuits and Pius IX

Most historical documentation previously published under the titles, *The Transformation of the Republic*, and *Perverting the Promised Land* has been reproduced

Chuckwilcox1@gmail.com

Graphics courtesy of The Chiniquy Collection Archives www.Chiniquy.ca , United States National Archives, Library of Congress, assorted universities and anonymous contributors

ISBN

978-0-359-14795-3

"I am a firm believer in the people. If given the truth, they can be depended upon to meet any national crisis. The great point is to bring them the real facts."

ABRAHAM LINCOLN

"We ought to be no less persuaded that the propitious smiles of Heaven can never be expected on a nation that disregards the eternal rules of order and the right which Heaven itself has ordained…it would be peculiarly improper to omit in this first official act my fervent supplications to that Almighty Being who rules over the universe, who presides in the counsels of nations, and whose providential aids can supply every human defect, that His benediction may consecrate to the liberties and happiness of the people of the United States a government instituted by themselves for these essential purposes, and may enable every instrument employed in its administration to execute with success the functions allotted to his charge."

GEORGE WASHINGTON – APRIL 30, 1789 - INAUGURAL ADDRESS AND DEDICATION OF THE U.S. TO THE GUIDANCE OF GOD - EXCERPT

"To the principles of our government nothing can be more opposed than the maxim of absolute [Catholic] monarchies. Yet from such we are to expect the greatest number of emigrants. They will bring with them the principles of the government they leave, imbibed in their early youth; in proportion to their numbers they will share with us the legislation. They will infuse into it their spirit, warp and bias its directions and render it a heterogeneous, incoherent, distracted mess. I doubt the expediency of inviting them by extraordinary measures."

THOMAS JEFFERSON – NOTES ON VIRGINIA

"Stop throwing the *Constitution* in my face. It's just a *goddamned piece of paper!"*

GEORGE W. BUSH, REPORTED BY AIDES IN NOVEMBER 2005

FROM JOHN ADAMS TO THOMAS JEFFERSON
6 May, 1816

I do not like the late resurrection of the Jesuits. They have a general now in Russia, in correspondence with the Jesuits in the United States, who are more numerous than everybody knows. Shall we not have swarms of them here, in as many shapes and disguises as ever a king of the gypsies, Bampfylde Moore Carew himself, assumed? In the shape of printers, editors, writers, schoolmasters, etc..? I have lately read Pascal's letters over again, and four volumes of the History of the Jesuits. If ever any congregation of men could merit eternal perdition on earth and in hell, according to these historians, though, like Pascal, true Catholics, it is this company of Loyola.

THOMAS JEFFERSON TO JOHN ADAMS
1 August, 1816

I dislike, with you, their restoration, because it marks a retrograde step from light towards darkness.

FROM JOHN ADAMS TO THOMAS JEFFERSON
9 August, 1816

My History of the Jesuits is not elegantly written, but is supported by unquestionable authorities, is very particular and very horrible. Their restoration is indeed "a step towards darkness," cruelty, perfidy, despotism, death and—! I wish we were out of danger of bigotry and Jesuitism. May we be "a barrier against the returns of ignorance and barbarism." What a colossus shall we be! But will it not be of brass, iron, and clay? Your taste is judicious in liking better the dreams of the future than the history of the past. Upon this principle I prophesy that you and I shall soon meet better friends than ever so wishes.

"When any church will inscribe over its altar the Saviour's condensed statement of Law and Gospel, 'Thou shalt love the LORD thy God, with all thy heart, with all thy soul, and with all thy mind, and thy neighbour as thyself,' *that* church I will join with all my heart."

Abraham Lincoln to a member of Congress as related by his intimate friend Hon. Isaac N. Arnold in reference as to why he did not join a denominational, politically involved creed-driven church

~

Ah sinful nation, a people laden with iniquity, a seed of evildoers, children that are corruptors: they have forsaken the LORD, they have provoked the Holy One of Israel unto anger, they are gone away backward.

Why should you be stricken any more? You continue to revolt more and more; the whole head [Washington, D.C.] is sick…the whole body [the people] is putrefied and full of open sores…your country is desolate, your cities are burned with fire: your land, strangers devour it in your presence, and it is desolate, as overthrown by strangers…Yet you will not repent…And when you spread forth your hands, I will hide mine eyes from you: yea, even though you make many prayers, *I will not hear:*

your hands are full of blood.

Isaiah 1: 4-5,7,15

"My people are destroyed for a lack of knowledge: because you have rejected knowledge, I will also reject you…As they were increased, so they sinned against me: therefore I will change their glory into shame"

Hosea 4:6,7

"AMERICA FOR AMERICANS"—We hold that all men are Americ

OMAHA, NEBRASK

AWAKES ONLY TO FIND HI

ND HIMSELF BOUND HAND AND FOOT.

ates who | rich himself by wringing money from | tion. We asked him what he thoug

Table of Contents

Photos: National Archives | HistoricCamdenCounty.com

WASHINGTON, D.C. (July 7, 1865) -- Convicted and hung as Lincoln assassination conspirators, Mary Surratt, Lewis Powell (a.k.a. Payne), David Herold and George Atzerodt were executed in Washington's Old Arsenal Prison yard. Four others were sentenced to life imprisonment. The leader of the gang -- John Wilkes Booth -- was killed by a Union Army soldier.

Photo: National Archives | HistoricCamdenCounty.com

Confederate spy John Surratt initially joined with John Wilkes Booth to be part of the Lincoln kidnapping plot. After Booth killed Lincoln, Surratt successfully evaded a national manhunt, caught a ship to England and made his way to Rome. There, he changed his name and joined the military unit that protects the Pope.

Introductory statement from the Author

The purpose for this book came to fruition in a rather roundabout way. My original purpose was to gather material for a definitive TV mini-series about the life and times of Abraham Lincoln, his influence on not only his own nation, but on the wider world in general. From 1993 to 2005, I worked in the film industry in Southern Alberta in Western Canada, working mostly on historical period films. In this capacity I was able to discuss history with a variety of people; actors, directors, producers and crew. The idea of a mini-series about the life of Lincoln came up.

After having acquired the sole publishing rights to a cache of documentation from the last surviving holder of the Chiniquy family archive, who had hidden it from public disclosure for some 120 years due to the fear of certain death threats received by that family if the contents were ever made public - and after much persuasion on my part to promise to give an honest historical account in my research in order to gain the trust of the proper handling of this file, I found myself so taken aback by the material, being filled with questions the material led me into, that I had to alter my focus to reveal the entire historical context of the life of Lincoln in juxtaposition to U.S history, from the years leading up to his birth in 1809 - to his murder in 1865, to show that the Civil War was engineered in great part by the globalist forces of Europe, the 'holy alliance', guided in large part by the Papacy and the Jesuit order and to then show the repercussions in the aftermath of his removal by the forces of globalism and how they still operate to this day. The goal to have this work adapted into a definitive and educational dramatic TV mini-series still stands.

Because my research led directly to into the realm of religion, I had no choice but to examine this specific angle of the history of the United States. In fact, religion is the linch-pin, the keystone of history. Without understanding this aspect, you can't make sense of the news. There is no historical grounding, no defining focus.

When I began to show various film producers what I had been made providentially privy to, the general consensus was to put it all into a book. I am not a professional writer by any means. This book is a 'first ever' effort, it has not been professionally edited and has been an ongoing project of refinement through a couple of pre-market versions to help the reader put the daily news into a very real historical context - that shows the formation of the U.S., as we know it, was not an accident of history; that the maliciousness and malignancy of the globalist powers of Europe would not sit by and see their 1,500 year old stranglehold on global power compromised; that the rule of the Almighty was still very much in the minds of certain selected men who were raised up to confront the powers of humanity that sought to establish a society under the rule of a man who places himself in the position of God on earth.

Lincoln was made privy to a material understanding of this malignant power during a court trial in 1856. He understood the historical fact that the United States was the only instance in history of a land founded and governed by a written code rather than through the will of a single man since the Hebrew's were given a written moral and legal code from Sinai. He understood that there were forces that were hell-bent on destroying the global influence of this 'new concept' of government. When he became president, he defeated these combined powers of what Samuel Morse, Thomas Jefferson, Samuel Adams, John Adams, John Quincy Adams, Benjamin Franklin, President Monroe and George Washington knew as the "Holy Alliance".

This "Holy Alliance" of European powers still exists in the great-great grandchildren of these same families. They now operate under the name, "Globalist" and "illuminati". They include in their company those corrupted and bought off politicians, journalists, bankers, industrial leaders and military officers who are in league with them. They wish to reverse the force and effect of the U.S. Constitution. They see this foundational legal stance of 1776 as a threat to their own dreams of Empire, specifically of resurrecting the bloody empire of Charlemagne, a feudalist/globalist union of church, finance, business and state, named a 'beast' by God; the "Holy Roman Empire". In short, they still desire the total destruction of the Anglo-American peoples, the offspring and inheritors of the promise to Jacob of national glory, given to Ephraim and Manasseh respectively, as any kind of world power.

This book is intended to put focus and clarity into the daily news; to give the lifetime of Lincoln a very real, vivid and contemporary historical significance, to show that the establishment of the United States was allowed by God for a reason; to show that the war between good and evil is, in reality, a war over the concept of government, to show why the Anglo-American peoples are about to undergo a moral and extreme societal correction not seen since the internal strife and eventual captivity of Ancient Israel - that came about beginning with their justifying the sacrifice and murder of their children.

Nearly every historian believes that George Washington and Abraham Lincoln were America's two greatest presidents. These men faced monumental crises—survival-of-the-nation problems. And if you look at their inspiring examples, you can see how they met and conquered those crises. In his book Our Sacred Honor, William J. Bennett writes: "What made this country different from all others was a prevalent belief that God played a direct and active hand in founding a people. Like the Jerusalem of old, America's 'New Jerusalem' was to become God's promised land to the oppressed—an example to all humankind."

Early Americans believed it was their destiny to set an example for the world!

Religion and Morality

In his inaugural address on April 30, 1789, George Washington said, "[T]he foundations of our national policy will be laid in the pure and immutable principles of private morality ...." In other words, private morality is not a peripheral issue; it is foundational.

In his farewell address in 1796, Washington said, "Of all the dispositions and habits which lead to political prosperity, religion and morality are indispensable supports." He knew that without religion and morality, America was doomed. Washington continued, "In vain would that man claim the tribute of patriotism who should labor to subvert these great pillars of human happiness, these firmest props of the duties of men and citizens."

Historians believe that America wouldn't even exist without the leadership of George Washington. God was with him, the first great American warrior.

President Washington believed, in essence, that character is everything. "We have now a national character to establish," he said. In political campaigns today, character isn't mentioned at all. Most Americans seem to think it has no bearing on a man's fitness to govern. Private morality and public duty are considered separate issues. Washington would have been appalled by that kind of thinking!

America's second president, John Adams, followed Washington's lead. He said that the foundation of national morality "must be laid in private families." He also said, "Our Constitution was made only for a moral and a religious people".

"Early American society was one built around the biblical sanctity of marriage and family," writes Angelo Codevilla in The Character of Nations. "Since the founders had no doubt that popular government is possible only among virtuous people, they revered marriage as few people before or since." Those early Americans were right: Strong marriages and families are crucial to national success! If you understand what the Bible teaches about marriage, you can see why their reverence for this institution was so important. Scripture shows that God designed marriage and family for many vital reasons. Marriage is a God-plane relationship—a type of the saints' marriage to Jesus Christ at His Second Coming!

French historian Alexis de Tocqueville wrote, "Religion and morality were indispensable to the maintenance of the American republic. While the constitutional law of liberty allowed Americans complete freedom to do as they pleased, religion prevented them from doing that which is immoral and unjust."

Tocqueville surmised, "Liberty could not be governed apart from religious faith, lest there be anarchy." America's founders knew that the Constitution allows humans tremendous freedoms, so there must be some kind of restraint to prevent lawlessness. That restraint is religion and morality.

Today, those restraints have been largely cast aside in American society! If the founders were correct—that these restraints were "indispensable" to our national survival—then this has grave implications for America's future! The abysmal state of America's character, its religion and morality, is putting the nation's survival in grave danger!

Ancient Israel's Poor Example

Early Americans considered themselves "new Israel" and looked to the example of biblical Israel. Anciently those Israelites were delivered from slavery in Egypt. At Mount Sinai, God delivered to them a moral code—the Ten Commandments, and a civil law, which they agreed to obey. However, they then rebelled and, as punishment, they were forced to wander in the wilderness for 40 years. When all the rebellious adults died, God used Joshua to lead the next generation into the Promised Land.

After Joshua died, Israel ran into real trouble, entering a period of unparalleled lawlessness and rebellion. You can read about this in the biblical book of Judges, which is the bloodiest book in the Bible! The general moral condition of the nation is summarized in this verse: "In those days there was no king in Israel: every man did that which was right in his own eyes" (Judges 21:25). When Israel lost its strong leader and cast aside character, it led to anarchy and, eventually, captivity! The book of Judges is part of the former prophets, which are prophecy mainly for today.

Is there any better description for what is happening in America today than everyone doing what is "right in his own eyes"? Immorality is rife within the American populace. And we have the government we deserve. Core institutions of American society can no longer be trusted because of a lack of strong religion and private morality—and institutional morality. Unsurprisingly, these institutions are held in contempt today. Congress has about a 17 percent approval rating. The Federal Bureau of Investigation and the Justice Department have betrayed the American people by trying to overthrow the fairly elected president. There is a war going on within the very highest levels of government! This is a curse on our nation!

Tocqueville wrote, "Any free society founded on liberty, yet without a sacred moral code to govern the actions of individuals, cannot stand." Look at the embarrassing spectacle in America today, and you have to say that it proves Tocqueville right!

A House Divided

Abraham Lincoln dealt with a nation that was ripped in two by civil war! He knew firsthand just how dangerous division within a nation can be. Surely Americans can recognize just how divided we have become. Should we not listen to what one of our greatest-ever presidents said on this subject?

"In my opinion, [national division] will not cease until a crisis shall have been reached and passed," he said in 1858. Why must we suffer through a crisis to learn these lessons? Lincoln continued, quoting from the Bible, "A house divided against itself cannot stand."

Attitudes among Americans today are similar to those of Americans before the Civil War! We are a house divided! And the division is going to have some terrifying consequences.

Here are the words Lincoln quoted—and they come from Jesus Christ: "And if a kingdom be divided against itself, that kingdom cannot stand. And if a house be divided against itself, that house cannot stand" (Mark 3:24-25).

America is on the brink of destruction! Do people really not recognize the danger? People are fighting each other over political differences, racial differences, ideological differences, and they don't even seem interested in coming to agreement—they just want to destroy each other! And in so many cases, they are telling and believing lies so rank and abominable you couldn't even impose them on a child ordinarily!

On March 30, 1863, Lincoln issued a proclamation designating a day of prayer and fasting. "We have been the recipients of the choicest bounties of heaven," he wrote. He was right! We enjoy what the Bible calls national "birthright blessings" from God! "We have grown in numbers, wealth and power as no other nation has ever grown," he continued. "But we have forgotten God."

Would a president today ever stand up and admit that we have forgotten God? The scorn and ridicule he would suffer for doing so would be beyond imagination!

"[W]e have vainly imagined, in the deceitfulness of our hearts, that all these blessings were produced by some superior wisdom and virtue of our own," Lincoln continued. "It behooves us, then, to humble ourselves before the offended power, to confess our national sins, and to pray for clemency and forgiveness."

Lincoln's national day of prayer and fasting healed the nation. This is the truth of America's history.

In a previous proclamation, on Aug. 12, 1861, Lincoln urged Americans to "humble ourselves before Him and to pray for His mercy—to pray that we may be spared further punishment, though most justly deserved." Who in America, Britain or the Jewish state in the Middle East could issue strong correction like this today and actually be heard?

As Lincoln left Illinois for the White House, he spoke to those gathered for his departure: "Unless the great God who assisted [George Washington] shall be with and aid me, I must fail. But if [He] shall guide and support me, I shall not fail, I shall succeed. Let us all pray that the God of our fathers may not forsake us now." In other words, the only way to succeed is to follow Washington's example and look to God!

Will America take this route today? Will we follow George Washington and Abraham Lincoln and go to God to heal our nation? Will we confess our sins?

This is America's own history—the greatest history you can imagine if you really understand it. Think on these examples, and you can see why these two presidents were so great. There was a reason, and it goes far beyond mere human ingenuity!

Lincoln did all he could to unify the nation. He called for all Americans to humbly seek God. He believed the words of Christ: "And Jesus knew their thoughts, and said unto them, Every kingdom divided against itself is brought to desolation; and every city or house divided against itself shall not stand" (Matthew 12:25).

Notice that: Every house—every family! That means private morality! A family must be united if it is to stand. You cannot be divided and have a beautiful family. A nation cannot remain strong if it is consumed by infighting!

The way America is weakening itself and consuming itself through discord is direct proof of the problems that result when the pillars of religion and morality are removed. We must have strong religion and morality on a grand scale to succeed collectively.

God will still look after you and protect you individually if you will obey Him. Establish that private morality and religion in your own life! The scriptures make it plain and show it gets right down to the family! That is where you must begin. Strong, moral families are the backbone of your entire nation! We must look to God and humble ourselves before Him. That is really at the heart of the magnificent examples that President Washington and President Lincoln set for us, and that is how we can solve all our problems!

These great men actually gave a warning that the American people should heed today. President Washington and President Lincoln showed us how to solve our nation's major problems. If we followed their examples, we could do the same today. That may seem astounding, but it is the inspiring truth of history!

Really, this applies to all the Western world and anybody who would apply these lessons. Even if our nations do not follow these examples, God says He will save us individually if we do so.

America's earliest settlers believed that America was the new Israel. They didn't know that this belief was literally true. And just as ancient Israel became polluted with the pagan religions that surrounded them, going so far as to incorporate these beliefs into their own lives and causing God to eventually use the warmongering Assyrians to punish them, the modern descendants of these same people have followed the same path. Prophecy shows that the descendants of those ancient Assyrians – the German nation, will be used by God one final time to punish those who God calls, "my people".

I, personally, do not belong to any particular religious denomination, however I firmly believe biblical truth and I am a political atheist – I place my trust in the government God will soon establish on this planet. Even though I come down hard on the Roman Church, this is not to be confused with any kind of what would be termed 'bigotry', as Samuel Morse pointed out and whom I quote on this particular assertion. Morse focused on the political aspects of Romanism, but the Papacy and the Jesuits particularly, conflated this into a religious argument; and, like Lincoln and so many others, I cannot help but be struck by or escape the cyclical realities of history, the duality and certainty of Hebrew prophecy and the understanding of Mankind's purpose of establishing and living by a universal code of righteous law on the earth; a government by, of and under God.

Another American Civil War is being engineered by the European enemies of righteousness and their lawless allies. This time, unless there is a national repentance, America will be destroyed and the elimination of America will usher in the period called, 'the times of the gentiles.'

May God the Father, through the leadership of King Jesus, the Christ, preserve and refine those He intends to keep alive [save] through the coming storm and fire of "Jacob's Troubles". Refer to Isaiah chapter 41 and Amos chapters 3-7

Chapter 1

America and ancient Israel compared; The oldest dictatorship on earth; Lincoln discusses role and limits of U.S. Government; Sworn statements of Jesuit priests regarding foreknowledge of Lincoln's murder; Private letters from U.S. army Col. Edwin A. Sherman, Brig. Gen. T.M. Harris, Louis Weichman and Robert Lincoln to Charles Chiniquy; The real U.S. chain of command; Then and Now – Jefferson and Islam compared to Obama and Islam; past history prophetically portends future disaster.

The Republic of the United States of America was borne out of a deep desire to establish a system of government that closely modeled ancient Israel. This desire arose from the centuries of murder and political intrigue practiced by the Church of Rome, very much like Islam is portrayed today, through its various members and adherents all over the Continents of Europe and South America.

In the 1700's in most of the American colonies the Church of England, or Episcopal Church, was established in law as the official state religion. It had as its head the King, rather than a pope. It had sole authority in civil matters and acted as the authority for the State, providing the judges, magistrates, constabulary and other civil authorities who were privileged members of that denomination and establishing and enforcing the law backed up by the British army. This included tax collection that was sent back to London and perpetuated and enriched a church/state union.

The Church of England was viewed by the Presbyterians, Calvinists, Methodists, Lutherans and Baptist Scots, Irish, Dutch, German, Northern Europeans and transplanted English as an off-shoot daughter of the Roman Catholic Church, whose influence was greatly expanded under the Quebec Act of 1774, clinging to the corrupt church/state model that had been practiced by Rome for over a millennia and therefore equally corrupt and abusive in its administration of law. This act was one of the several 'intolerable acts of tyrants' enumerated in the Declaration of Independence, as it ceded a large part of the central parts of the continent of the territories of Illinois, Indiana, Ohio, Michigan, Wisconsin and Minnesota to Catholic Quebec in retaliation and as punishment for the Boston Tea party. They sought, by revolution, temperate yet firm, to establish a Presbyterian form of government that was wholly answerable to the people and rooted in the principles outlined in the Bible. What they committed themselves to was, in effect, a blood oath to serve their God. If they kept to their oath, God would, on a national level, bless their industry and efforts and protect them from the hostility of the nations around them; if they reneged God would spank them, sometimes severely. These were national blessings and curses felt by one and all. The entire chapter of Deuteronomy 28 is directed at the United States. (compare Lev. 26; Ezek.5-7, 20, 23-24)

When William Bradford stepped off the Mayflower in 1620, he borrowed his New World proclamation from the Prophet Jeremiah: "Come let us declare in Zion the Word of God." For Bradford, Michael Oren writes in *Power, Faith, and Fantasy*, Zion "was not the old Promised Land of Canaan but its new incarnation, America."

William Bennett made a similar point in *Our Sacred Honor*: "Like the Jerusalem of old, America's 'New Jerusalem' was to become God's promised land to the oppressed—an example to all humankind."

In *Character of Nations*, Angelo Codevilla says there was a tendency for "Americans to equate themselves with the children of Israel."

The first American statesman to draw a parallel between the biblical Exodus and the establishment of colonial America was Benjamin Franklin. In *Joshua's Altar*, Milt Machlin said Franklin described early America as "God's new Israel." Franklin's grandfather had said the people of New England "are like the Jews—as like as like can be."

This New Israel concept became especially poignant during the Revolution, Oren wrote. "Yale president Ezra Stiles noted that the number of Israelites present at Mount Sinai—3 million—was precisely the population of the United States at the time of independence," he wrote. "Harvard's Samuel Langdon suggested that 'instead of the 12 tribes of Israel, we may substitute the 13 states of the American union.'"

The comparison between the birth of ancient Israel as an independent nation in the world led by Moses and guided by God through the vehicle of a new government founded on righteous principles and the birth of the United States as a nation, "Under God", the only other peoples to have done that in recorded history, was obvious on its face.

As Israel, the extended family of Abraham through the line of Jacob, was the first family of peoples in all of human history to have been given the chance to choose for themselves what type of government they desired, whether they should copy the systems of the nations that surrounded them or separate themselves entirely so as to provide an example to them, to establish Godly government on earth, so too were the peoples who founded the United States given this chance for only the 2nd time in history.

Who, *really*, is Israel? Many think that the Jewish nation is Biblical Israel, but the Bible says these people are called Judah. So, who are the modern descendants of ancient Israel? In Genesis 48:16, Jacob [Israel] laid his hands on the 2 sons of Joseph; Ephraim and Mannaseh, and said, "...let my name be named upon them,". So, according to the Bible, only these two brothers would carry the name of Israel. Then he blessed the two brothers saying that they should be a great nation and a company of nations, that they would be a colonizing peoples [Gen.49:20], and the "shepherd and stone of Israel". In other prophecies the descendants of these 2 brothers would rule over ¾ of the earth, they would control the gates of their enemies. These are sea-gates, controlling the global trade routes [Gibraltar, Panama canal, Suez, Falklands etc.] They would be guided by the power of God and be the most blessed peoples on earth, that the older shall serve the younger. Only the Anglo-Saxon peoples of England/commonwealth and the U.S. fit this description.

President George Washington gave his Inaugural address in New York on April 30, 1789 and then shortly thereafter, headed down to a chapel and leading the entire newly sworn government in prayer, dedicated the newly birthed United States Republic to the providential hand of God.

Almost immediately thereafter the Roman Catholic monarchies, banker families and Imperialist families of Europe, whose decendants we now call Globalists today, (inspired by the position laid out in the Council of Trent, that is, "Death to all heretics", which was the Vatican's official response to the Protestant Reformers), conspired with the Vatican to destroy the concept of popular government, which was got up under the inspiration of the principles and character of the Eternal God; the political, civil and economic fruits of which sprang from the revolt from the Church of Rome, as found in the experiment of the United States. In fact, the U.S. Constitution was a declaration of war against those degrading globalist-feudal principles of tyrants in the same way as the 10 Commandments was a declaration of war against the Chaldean church/state system, practiced by every nation that existed at the time.

This destruction, or transformation, was accomplished by means of infiltration, subversion and corruption. The tools used were the Leopold foundation, which was set up by Prince Metternich of Austria and the Jesuit Order, the Company of Jesus, referred to by its members as "The Company", the 'shock troops' of the Vatican; a military order that engages in asymmetrical warfare. They are the inventors of modern intelligence gathering and social engineering for, "The

Greater Glory of God" - Ad Majoram Dei Gloriam. Jesuits are not all priests in black but are composed as well of co-adjutors from all occupations and walks of life….all who have taken the years of training and an oath and all who are in sympathy.

The Great Unrecognized Dictatorship

Many people say that Islam is both a political and a religious ideology that seeks to rule the world. But, while this may be true, how many have realized these staggering facts: The oldest political dictatorship on Earth is the Vatican! The Roman Catholic Church is far more than a religion. It is also politically a world power. And how many people know that the real objective of the Catholic political power is precisely the same as the goals of communism and fascism—to gain dominance, control and rule over the whole world! … Of course it is generally known that most nations send ambassadors to the Vatican, and papal ambassadors are established in most world capitals. But it has not been generally grasped that this Roman system is much more than a church—it is a state, called in the Encyclopedia Britannica an Ecclesiastical World Empire—it is a political dictatorship—it is a world power whose influence in many respects outweighs that of any nation on Earth. The Vatican predates Islam by several hunderd years and Muhammed, while hiding in a cave and guided by his Catholic wife and her Catholic cousin, devoured and incorporated the degrading and war-mongering teachings of the Catholic St. Augustine into the hallucinations and babbling that, over time, became the collection called the Koran.

The Vatican is a dictatorship. It is literally a state, with political interests, foreign policy, sovereign independence, recognition under international law, official relations, diplomatic immunity, administrative departments, ambassadors, a central bank, a capital, a very centralized government—and a man who dictates. History cannot be examined properly without including the influence of this machine in the equation.

How many people really understand that? How many Catholics understand that? The Vatican governs 1.2 billion Catholics around the world, and it influences millions of other people, as well as national governments.

I'm not here saying anything about, or against, Catholic people, either in the United States or elsewhere, nor am I here saying anything about the Catholic religion, save that it is pagan, cloaking the original Chaldean mysteries in the garb of Christianity, falsely so labeled, and deceiving its own adherents, who are quite often sincere and devout, with its sense-appealing pomp, ceremony, mysticism and superstition.

But what I am here concerned with is Catholic political power—the papacy as a world power, a dictatorship, bent on conquering and ruling the world.

The people of the United States, compared to the rest of the world, are woefully ignorant of the world that surrounds them. This was not so in the 18th and 19th Centuries. This is due, in large part, to a compromised school system from top to bottom and a corrupt media serving corrupt politicians.

The American Civil War was several decades in the planning. As we witness today once again, the goal was to alter the demographics and spiritual foundation of America through primarily massive Catholic immigration, break up the United States into its component parts, to cause the election of those politicians who were in sympathy with these globalists, balkanize the US and reinstate European feudal monarchial rule.

Abraham Lincoln was well aware of the dangers the Vatican, monarchies and money men of Europe posed to the young republic. According to the Columbia Encyclopedia, Abraham Lincoln entered on the national scene by serving one term in Congress (1847-49). He remained obscure, and his attacks as a Whig on the motives behind the Mexican War (though he voted for war supplies) seemed unpatriotic to his constituents, and he lost popularity at home. Lincoln, in disgust, retired from politics and settled down to the practice of law. He grew, rather than diminished, in stature as a public figure. While serving in Congress, Lincoln carried on a correspondence with his law partner, William H. Herndon, back in Illinois. Here is the text of a remarkable letter from that period which could effectively be called, 'Lincoln on the Iraq War'.

Washington, February 15, 1848
Dear William:

Your letter of the 29th of January was received last night. Being exclusively a constitutional argument, I wish to submit some reflections upon it in the same spirit of kindness that I know actuates you. Let me first state what I understand to be your position. It is that if it shall become necessary to repel invasion, the President may, without violation of the Constitution, cross the line and invade the territory of another country, and that whether such necessity exists in any given case the President is the sole judge.

Before going further consider well whether this is or is not your position. If it is, it is a position that neither the President himself, nor any friend of his, so far as I know, has ever taken. Their only positions are first, that the soil was ours when the hostilities commenced; and second, that whether it was rightfully ours or not, Congress had annexed it, and the President for that reason was bound to defend it; both of which are as clearly proved to be false in fact as you can prove that your house is mine. The soil was not ours, and Congress did not annex or attempt to annex it. But to return to your position. Allow the President to invade a neighboring nation whenever he shall deem it necessary to repel an invasion, and you allow him to do so whenever he may choose to say he deems it necessary for such purpose, and you allow him to make war at pleasure.

Study to see if you can fix any limit to his power in this respect, after having given so much as you propose. If to-day he should choose to say he thinks it necessary to invade Canada to prevent the British from invading us, how could you stop him? You may say to him, "I see no probability of the British invading us;" but he will say to you, "Be silent: I can see it, if you don't."

The provision of the Constitution giving the war-making power to Congress was dictated, as I understand it, by the following reasons: Kings had always been involving and impoverishing their people in wars, pretending generally, if not always, that the good of the people was the object. This our convention understood to be the most oppressive of all kingly oppressions, and they resolved to so frame the Constitution that no one man should hold the power of bringing this oppression upon us. But your view destroys the whole matter, and places our President where kings have always stood. Write soon again.

Yours truly, A. Lincoln

[From Lincoln, Abraham; Nicolay, John G., ed.; Hay, John, ed. [1848], letter to William H. Herndon, February 15, 1848 in 'The Complete Works of Abraham Lincoln, v.2 {New York: Francis D. Tandy Company, 1894}]

After the successful murder of the 'saviour of the nation', President Lincoln, on that Good Friday Easter weekend of 1865, a date of which the symbolism was not lost, the Jesuit masterminds of that most evil crime, people such as Fathers Bernard F. Wiget, Charles H. Stonestreet, N.D. Young and a Father Walter counted among them, began to pressure President Johnson to implement the 14th amendment to the United States' Constitution. This amendment had a multi-fold purpose; it effectively altered the citizenship away from the states' proper, under state authority, and transferred this to the Union, under a centralized Federal authority. Before this change one was considered a citizen of the United States by reason of being the citizen of a particular state.

This change meant that for the first time in U.S. history the groundwork was laid for the establishment of a more European Monarchial system of government, one which could be corrupted and thus making possible the ability to direct and control all the people under the volition of a single man. This amendment, on top of altering the very nature of citizenship, also removed the right of sovereignty of the individual states' in areas, which were not previously under Federal authority and placed them under a single central government thereby removing the right of secession in the case of entrenched tyranny. It also turned the God given rights of humanity as outlined in the original Bill of Rights, based wholly on Bible principles, into mere privileges granted by the State, which can then be revoked. The final purpose of this amendment was to create a foundation for Empire. The reasoning of the Jesuits was that if they can corrupt the leader and those around him after having corrupted the Constitution, Bill of Rights and the judiciary, the people have no choice but to submit to his authority. Ecclesiastically supported and sponsored dictatorship through the back door could then be established.

It has been stated by several historians that the Jesuits plan well ahead, in most cases of political intrigue and national transformation 100 years or more ahead.

Lincoln had rebuffed this proposed amendment all through his term and this obstinacy to the goals of the Church was cited as one of the major reasons for his demise. Another purported reason to eliminate him issued from the fact that he had begun to print currency, called *Greenbacks*, and declare it the legal tender of the land, thereby shutting out the Rothschild bankers and preventing them from bleeding the financial life of the Nation, much in the same way as John F. Kennedy, a liberal Catholic who refused to allow the Vatican to influence him, had issued his Silver Certificates in an effort to close down the vultures of the *privately owned and operated* FEDERAL RESERVE BANK of New York.

"Give me control of a nation's money, and I care not who makes the laws."- Mayer Amschel Rothschild

Rothschild learned early on how incredibly profitable it was to lend to nations instead of individuals, and at times of war, profits soared even more. Wars were expensive. Troops had to be paid, munitions bought, and over a period of time, the expense of war drained a nation's treasury.

Being recognized as the source for available funding, kings and rulers readily turned to the Rothschild family for money. The Rothschilds always demanded gold and silver in repayment, and when that ran out, control over the issuance of a nation's money was then demanded. Long story short, with its unparalleled, and unfathomable by most to the extent of its accumulation, the Rothschild banking clan became almost the only source of money to run a country.

What may not be as widely known is that the English Rothschild bank funded the North in America's Civil War, while the French Rothschild bank funded the South. It did not matter who would win, the Rothschild's were going to increase both their wealth and, more importantly for them, their influence in US politics. That had always been their primary objective.

Lincoln did not want to pay the bankers up to 36% interest for loans to fund the war. He decided to issue Greenbacks by the US government, interest free so that the country was not burdened with any interest costs, a very big deal. Lincoln was assassinated, [draw your own conclusions], and after his death, Congress immediately repealed the Greenback law. It should be known that when Lincoln announced his use of interest-free money as a source of funding, bankers stormed to Washington D.C. to complain bitterly.

Simply put, he was standing directly in the way of the Papists and European Autocrats and therefore had to be removed. And not just him, the entire top end of the chain of command was the original target.

That the Jesuits had planned the deed is beyond question as evidenced by the sworn statements and personal letters, which are quoted in full below and housed in the Chiniquy Collection. www.Chiniquy.ca

Some material comprising this first chapter has never been made public, nor has it been made available to historians. Charles Chiniquy, a French Canadian priest of Rome who eventually left the church, had commissioned a lawyer to investigate and collect the sworn statements of individuals who were privy to this extraordinary circumstance of foreknowledge which speak for themselves.

State of Illinois
Cook County

> Rev. F.A. Conwell being sworn declares and says that he is seventy-one years old that he is a resident of North Evanston, in Cook County State of Illinois, that he has been actively in the ministry for forty-six years, and is now one of the chaplains of the Seaman's Bethel Home in Chicago- that he was the chaplain of the First Minnesota Regiment in the War of the Rebellion.
>
> That on the 14th day of April AD 1865 he was in St. Joseph, Minnesota and heard there as early as six o'clock in the evening in company with Mr. Bennett who was there and was a resident of St. Cloud, Minnesota. That on this date there was no telegraph nearer than Minneapolis, which is about 80 miles from St. Joseph and there was no railroad communication nearer than Anoka, Minnesota which was about 40 miles distant.

Charles Chiniquy – Ex-priest of Rome and friend of Lincoln

That when he reached St. Joseph on the 14th day of April AD 1865 one Mr. Linneman who kept the hotel at St. Joseph told affiant that President Lincoln and Secretary Seward were assassinated. That it was not later than half past six o'clock on Friday April 14th 1865 when Mr. Linneman told me this. Shortly thereafter Mr. Bennett came in the hotel and I told him Mr. Linneman said the President and Secretary Seward were assassinated and there Mr. Linneman repeated the same conversation to Mr. Bennett in my presence.

That during that time Mr. Linneman told me that he had the charge of furnishing the friary or college for young men under the priests who were studying for the priesthood at St. Joseph. That there was a large institution of that kind at St. Joseph at this time.

Affiant says that on Saturday morning April 15th 1865 he went to St. Cloud a distance of about 10 miles and reached there about 8 o'clock in the morning, that there was no railroad or telegraph communications to St. Cloud. When he arrived at St. Cloud he told Mr. Haworth the hotel keeper that he had been told at St. Joseph that the President and Secretary Seward had been assassinated and asked if it was true.

He further told Henry Clay with Charles Gilliman who afterwards was Governor of Minnesota, the same thing and inquired of them if they had any such news and they replied they had not heard anything of the kind.

Affiant says that on Sunday morning 16th of April 1865 he preached in St. Cloud and on the way to the church a copy of a telegram was handed to him stating that the President and Secretary were assassinated on Friday evening at about 9 o'clock. This telegram had been brought to St. Cloud by Mr. Garten who had reached St. Cloud by stage and this was the first intelligence that reached St. Cloud of the events.

Affiant says further that on Monday morning April 17th 1865, he furnished the press, a paper of St. Paul, a statement that 3 hours before the event took place he had been informed at St. Joseph, Minnesota that the President had been assassinated and this was published in the press.

Francis Asbury Conwell

Subscribed and sworn to by Francis A. Conwell before me a notary public of Kankakee County Illinois at Chicago, Cook County Illinois, this 6th day of September 1883 Stephen R. Moore, notary public

** ** ** ** ** **

State of Minnesota
Sterns County
City of St. Cloud

Horace P. Bennett, being sworn declares and says that he is aged sixty-four years old, that he is a resident of St. Cloud Minnesota, and has resided in this county since 1856. That he is acquainted with Francis A. Conwell who was chaplain of the 1st Minnesota Regiment in the War of the Rebellion. That on the 14th day of April, 1865, he was in St. Joseph, Minnesota, in company with Rev. Francis A. Conwell, that they reached St. Joseph about sundown of said April 14th.

That there was no railroad or telegraph communication with St. Joseph at that time no nearer than forty miles distant.

That affiant, on reaching the hotel, went to the barn, and Rev. Mr. Conwell went to the hotel kept by Mr. Linneman. Shortly afterwards affiant had returned to the hotel. Mr. Conwell told him that Mr. Linneman had repeated to him the assassination of President Lincoln. That Linneman was present and substantiated the statement.

That on Saturday morning April 15th, affiant and Conwell came to St. Cloud and repeated what they had been told at St. Joseph about the assassination of President Lincoln.

That no one at St. Cloud had heard of the event at the time, that the first news of the event which reached St. Cloud was Sunday morning, April 16th. When the news was brought there by Leander Gorten, who had just arrived, that they spoke to several persons of St. Cloud concerning the matter when they reached there on Saturday morning, but affiant does not now remember who the different persons were.

Mr. Linneman said, as affiant remembers the transaction, that he had learned of the President's assassination from a soldier who was passing through St. Joseph. And further affiant saith not.

Horace P. Bennett

Sworn to me and subscribed in my presence this 18th day of October, AD 1883 Andrew C. Robertson Notary Public, Minn.

** ** ** ** ** ** ** ** **

State of Illinois
Kankakee County

Stephen R. Moore, of lawful age, a citizen of Kankakee County for thirty five years and engaged in the practice of law, that Father Chiniquy sent me to the village of St. Joseph and St. Cloud, Minnesota to investigate and report the facts concerning the remarkable statement of facts sworn to by Rev. F.A. Conwell that the knowledge of the assassination of the President Abraham Lincoln and Secretary of State Seward, were proclaimed publicly as accomplished facts at St. Joseph, Minnesota several hours before their occurrence.

Affiant states that he devoted about six days in the investigation of the facts, by interviews with persons who heard it stated publicly that the President and his Secretary of State were assassinated several hours ahead of the time when it took place in Washington City! That he talked with Mr. Linneman, the same hotel keeper, mentioned by said Reverend F.A. Conwell, that there I heard from Mr. Linneman himself that he well remembered having made that declaration to Mr. Bennett and Reverend F.A. Conwell.

That Mr. Linneman repeated several times to me that it was a public rumour in the village of St. Joseph that President Lincoln and Secretary of State Seward were killed by the hands of an assassin that day, April 14th, 1865, and that the rumour was spread there several hours before the deed was accomplished in Washington.

I tried to learn from Mr. Linneman how the rumour was spread, where it originated and how it was known there that the President was assassinated hours before the event took place, but he always answered that he did not know, that he heard it from several persons as a public rumour.

Affiant says that after having fully investigated the facts, he made a report thereof to Father Chiniquy, and when my report was submitted to him, he, father Chiniquy, inquired of me, as a lawyer, if he was not justified from these facts, to believe and publish, that such a public rumour, spread several hours before the event, was a sure proof that the fact was known in that place, only by the accomplices. That he, Father Chiniquy, had the legal right to believe and say, that some of the many priests and monks of that village, being constantly going to and coming from Washington, had learned that fact from their co-conspirators, who were day and night in the house of Mrs. Surratt where the plot of the assassination was prepared.

After having myself spent many days in investigating all the facts of that rumour, I told Father Chiniquy that he was perfectly justified to believe and publish that ***the priests and monks of Rome had learned that fact from their co-conspirators in Washington.*** [emphasis added]

Affiant says that St. Joseph is the center of a large Catholic population, containing a college for the education of priests, and he repeated this also to Father Chiniquy, and affiant says that it was impossible for so unnatural and remarkable event to be talked of in St. Joseph Minnesota, hours before it occurred in Washington, unless the murderers had accomplices in St. Joseph and parties to the crime.

Affiant further states that he saw and conversed with Mr. Bennett who told affiant that on April 14th 1865, he had heard Mr. Linneman tell him and Reverend F.A. Conwell that Lincoln and Seward were killed that day, and that declaration was made 5 or 6 hours before the act occurred in Washington.

I obtained the affidavit of Mr. Bennett to this fact, taken before Judge Robertson, at the City of St. Cloud,

Sterns County, Minnesota, which said Mr. Bennett is a credible and highly respected citizen of St. Cloud.

Affiant further swears that he learned while at St. Joseph, that Mr. Linneman was the purveyor and confidential man of the many priests and monks of the village of St. Joseph, and further affiant saith not.

Stephen R. Moore

Subscribed and sworn before me this 29th day of December, 1884. Sid R. Durfee, clerk

** ** ** ** ** ** ** **

As we can see so far, the entire priesthood of the Catholic Church in Minnesota knew, hours in advance, that President Lincoln had been murdered and were so sure of their success that they could not hold back from celebrating. We can also be assured that only those who were accomplices, meaning the Catholic Church's priesthood as a whole, could have been aware, for if this news was already celebrated half way across the continent you can be certain it was known on the west coast in San Francisco.

Following is a letter from Stephen R. Moore, a junior partner in the law firm Osgood, Paddock and Lincoln, to Charles Chiniquy after he had investigated this coincidence.

Kankakee, October 30, 1883
Dear Father Chiniquy,

I had a successful trip and obtained the affidavit of Horace P. Bennett, who was with Reverend F.A. Conwell, where the assassination of President Lincoln was talked of before it had taken place. Mr. Bennett is a very responsible man and his evidence cannot be impeached.

I had quite a time trying to get the statement of Mr. Linneman. He is the person who first told the statement. After I had it prepared, he refused to swear to it, but simply signs it. He changed his version of the matter considerably after he learned I wanted him to swear to it.

He does not say that Lincoln was *assassinated,* but that he was dead. He pretends too, that some woman told him, but he cannot remember her name. Mr. Bennett says he first told them he learned it from a soldier. He corroborates Mr. Bennett and Conwell as to the fact of there being such a conversation. His statement is not the whole truth or else he would have sworn to it. But it is very valuable.

I saw myself the large Catholic institution at St. Joseph where Mr. Linneman is. He is a Catholic, and was supplying this institution with provisions, groceries etc. at the time of this conversation. It is almost wholly settled by Roman Catholics, and at that time the community were all Roman Catholic.

It is a most remarkable matter that away on the frontier, away from telegraphs and railroads, the assassination was known on Friday evening 4 hours before it took place. Nevertheless, here is the clear evidence of this matter.

Yours Truly,
Stephen R. Moore

** ** ** ** ** ** ** **

I now present the reader with the statement of Mr. Linneman, a man who was intimate with the priests and monks of St. Joseph. A man who could be confided in by them. A man who knew that if it ever got out that he pointed the finger at them as the source of the knowledge of Lincoln's assassination, they would most likely cut his throat as recompense and as a fulfillment of their murderous oath which will be quoted later.

State of Minnesota
Stern County
Village of St. Joseph

John H. Linneman [the words, "being sworn, declares and" struck out] says that he is a resident of St. Joseph, in said county and state, and has resided there for the past twenty-nine years. That he is in the merchandising business. [the word "affiant" struck out and replaced with the word "he"] says that he lived here in April 1865. That on the *Wednesday previous* to the death of President Lincoln, affiant heard that the President was dead. [This is at

> least 2 days beforehand] This was a common rumour in the village and it was also talked of at Cold Springs about ten miles from here.
>
> That he remembers the time that Mr. Conwell and Mr. Bennett came to his place on Friday evening before the President was killed and ["affiant" struck out] he asked them shortly after they came to his place if they had heard he was dead and they replied they had not. ["affiant" struck out] He heard this rumour in his store from people who came in and out, but he can ["not now" struck out] never remember from whom!
>
> That he heard at the time that the statement originated in St. Cloud, which is about eight miles from here. That of that date there was no rail or telegraph communication nearer than St. Paul, a distance of about eighty miles.
>
> J.H. Linneman
> October 20, 1883

** ** ** ** ** ** ** **

From these statements we can see that the Jesuits knew several days in advance that Lincoln was to be eliminated. The plan called for the assassination of the entire head of the country, the president, vice-president, secretary of state, and commanding General of the Army, in order to leave it leaderless. After Lincoln's murder there was a concerted effort by certain people to expose the true culprits of the crime, not only of the assassination, but of engineering the Civil War for the purpose of weakening and bleeding the country in order to replace the system of representative government with an ecclesiastically backed dictatorship.

Men such as Charles Chiniquy, Brig. Gen. Thomas M. Harris (a member of the commission which tried the conspirators) and Edwin A. Sherman (a Union officer) combined their resources with the intent of enlightening the public and giving a true history before it was re-written to cleanse the Catholic Church from all complicity.

The following letters, quoted in full, will give the reader an intimate insight into what was taking place at the time. These letters, housed in the *Chiniquy Collection Archives*, www.Chiniquy.ca, have never been seen by the public or historians and have only been recently released in 2002 after having been stored in a basement in the Protestant Eastern Townships of Quebec for over 120 years. They are in almost pristine condition and the reader can now fill in certain holes which have been left dark all these years.

This has special import for the world today as President George W. Bush was quoted in "*The Catholic News Service*" March 24th 2001 as saying, "The best way to honour Pope John Paul II, truly one of the greatest men, is to take his teachings seriously, to listen to his words and put his words and teachings into action here in America." The article, written by Patricia Zapoa, goes on to say, "From the beginning of his presidency, George Bush has been promoting the Jesuit agenda. Two months into his presidency, surrounded by Cardinals of Rome, the President dedicated a cultural center in Washington D.C. to the Pope." [Reuters]

Shortly after his first inaugural address President George W. Bush went to visit Pope John Paul II. The purpose of this meeting was to finalize the coming Crusade against Islam.

This can be verified by the world-renowned author of *"Voyage of the Damned"*, Gordon Thomas. According to Thomas, in response to a question this author posed to him, Pope John Paul II has stated several times since 1983 that the coming globalist war would not be between the superpowers but rather between the nations of Christendom and Islam, it will be a full-fledged religious, class and race war. The ultimate goal will be for the purpose of relocating the Papacy to Jerusalem and use religion to destroy America pursuant to the 1891 Christmas day order of Pope Leo XIII.

In an op-ed piece from the *Ottawa Citizen* dated October 20, 2004 we find this to be the case. It reads in part, "...while we in the West are uncomfortable calling it a religious war, the enemy is not. The unfortunate souls whose deaths are featured on the beheading videos now in circulation are typically referred to as infidels."

I now present to you the letters to Charles Chiniquy from Edwin A. Sherman, a Union officer, and Brigadier General Thomas M. Harris, a member of the Commission, which tried the assassins of Abraham Lincoln. Mr. Harris' bench mates included the name of General Lew Wallace, author of the great classic, "*Ben Hur*" which was turned into a feature film starring Charlton Heston. On an interesting note "*Ben Hur*" was inspired by the revelations which came out of that trial, namely the role the Church of Rome played in the overall theme, being portrayed as the bad guy, and the choice of the specific day of the assassination. This becomes crystal clear when juxtaposing the message of these letters with the events that inspired Wallace.

1016 West Street,
Oakland, Ca.
November 28th 1883

Dear Father Chiniquy,

Your favor of the 17th inst. came duly to hand, and it and its accompanying slips I put into a letter of introduction for a friend of mine Mr. Marcus S. Hill to Rev. George Sutherland of Sydney in Australia and he sailed in the Zealandia yesterday where he goes as a mercantile agent for several houses in San Francisco and will be gone for several years.

I send you my book by mail duly registered and which I trust will reach you in safety. My book is not for public sale, but is chiefly confined to members of my own order and to freemasons who are well known, and sound upon this great question in which we are arrayed. My book will prepare the way for yours, and whatever I can do to aid you in the circulation of yours I will do just as soon as I can get my guns in battery and well manned in opening fire upon and springing my mines under the

"Engineer Corps of Hell, or Rome's Sappers and Miners".

You will see that I do not argue at all upon theological matters; that I leave to true, thorough Protestant ministers to do. I simply unmask Hell, lift the cover off and let the trustworthy look in and see all the big and little devils at work, understand what they are doing and be prepared to meet them.

You will see that my book is not fit to be read by young, inexperienced people, hence the care taken to place it only in the hands of prudent and discreet men, who will become instructed how to deal with the *WHORE AND BASTARDS OF ROME.*

I thus send the work as it is, and dedicated to yourself that it may serve as a guidepost to yours, and should you still be of the same mind as you once were, that you would dedicate your work to me. I am satisfied that it would add greatly to its sale and circulation. I have several thousand dollars yet to raise to meet the expenses of the publication of my own, but the more of mine that are out, the more it will create a demand for yours.

I remain yours Truly and Sincerely,
In the Cause of Freedom, the Truth and the Light
Edwin A. Sherman

** ** ** ** ** ** ** ** **

1016 West Street,
Oakland, Ca.
December 29th 1883

Dear Father Chiniquy,

Yours of the 10th and also of the 18th have come to hand. I am glad to know that the book pleases you and nothing in it all has given me so much pleasure as to pay you a portion of that debt of gratitude (which every true lover of civil and religious liberty not only in America but throughout the world owes to you in your stripping the mask off from the face of the Harlot of Rome) in my dedicating my book to you and the first book that I ever published in my life.

Now in relation to the matters of which you speak.

1st I do not know where to find the letters of Pope Pius IX to Jeff Davis, unless they are among the Rebel Archives in Washington. It may be, however, that they may be found in some history of the Rebellion; but the letter of the Pope Dec. 3rd, 1863, acknowledged the independence of the Southern Confederacy and he called Jeff Davis his, "Dear Son". By the way I notice that Jeff Davis' sister recently died in Frankfort Kentucky and that she was a Superioress in a convent in that place which is another link in the great chain of the Papal Conspiracy against Lincoln and the Union. I will try if possible to get copies of the letters of Pope Pius IX.

2nd I was not present at the unveiling of the Statue of Abraham Lincoln at the Monument at Springfield. It is a sad and humiliating truth that on October 15th, 1874 the Statue of Abraham Lincoln at the Monument at Springfield was unveiled by two nuns, of the Order of St. Dominic, Mother Josepha and Sister Rachael from Jacksonville, who had been especially invited to perform that duty which should only have been done by Protestant Americans. The invitation to them I believe was sent to them by ex-Governor John A. Palmer, a political demagogue, and a Democrat who unfortunately is a member of the Abraham Lincoln Memorial Association.

While it was an outrage on the one hand yet on the other it was appropriate with this exception, the Statue of Lincoln, instead of being erect, should have been lying prostrate, and then the nuns upon unveiling it might have said, "BEHOLD OUR VICTIM SLAIN BY THE ORDERS OF THE POPE OF ROME AND THIS IS OUR ACCOMPLISHED WORK!"

3rd In regard to the attempt to steal the body of Abraham Lincoln an account will be found in the Springfield newspapers of November 1876. But as usual the truth is covered up. The plot was laid in an Irish Catholic Whiskey Saloon in Chicago, and the body was to be stolen on Tuesday, November 7th, 1876, and when the attempt was made, a paper called *The Catholic Telegraph* published in Liverpool England was found on the grounds near the Monument, and bore the name of the subscriber at this Whiskey Saloon in Chicago.

The pretext for stealing the body was to obtain a reward for the remains and thus make money out of it. This is what is given for the world to believe. But we know better. Rome, like the ghoul and worse than the jackal would destroy even the bones and cast even the ashes and dust of her victims upon the rivers and seas if she could, and as she has done in times past. The thieves were tried and sentenced to one years' imprisonment in the State penitentiary, which was the greatest punishment that could be inflicted upon them by the law at that time.

EVERY ONE OF THEM WAS A ROMAN CATHOLIC and faithfully carrying out his orders from the Jesuit Headquarters.

4th Mrs. Surratt, John Surratt (her son), Dr. Samuel Mudd, J. Wilkes Booth, Edward Spangler and Michael O'Laughlin were all Roman Catholics. Atzerodt and Herold and Payne were not anything but being of Protestant parentage, had Protestant Chaplains to attend them in their last moments before being hung.

Catholic priests who appeared as witnesses for Mrs. Surratt at the time of the trial for the murder of Lincoln were B.F. Wiget, Francis E. Boyle, Charles H. Stonestreet, Peter Hanihan and N.D. Young. {These are the actual murderers of Lincoln, for they put forth the plan, hired and trained the fanatics in the house of Surratt and gave them absolution and safe harbor –ed.}

5th You had better send to Washington or perhaps it may be found in some library, Ben Pitmann's report of the trial of the Conspirators; he was the recorder to the commission which tried them. The publishers were Moore, Wilstach and Baldwin 25 West Fourth Street, Cincinnati and 60 Walker Street New York City. By carefully scanning that report and analyzing the evidence in going through it you will find the strongest corroborative testimony confirming what I have stated in my book. In my next edition I shall do so. I obtained a loan of the report referred to after my book was printed, or it would have appeared in this first edition.

6th Owing to great pressure on my time at present, it will be impossible to write out at length all that I would like to; but you have matter above already cited, and being so near to Springfield and the scenes where Lincoln so conspicuously figured when alive and where his ashes now repose, you can readily run down there and quietly gather such further material as you require for your book. There are so many Roman Catholics there now, that men who think and would act as we do, if it were prudent for them, but they for policy's sake and for the safety for their lives and property or business are compelled to remain silent.

The city authorities who control the avenues to the cemetery at Oak Ridge and even the cemetery itself are against us, or rather are of the enemy or are in sympathy with them, and the shrine where the pilgrims even from foreign lands as well as those of our own land go to drop their tears of love and affectionate memory for Lincoln and the keys to the City of the Dead are held by Rome.

A few years ago the Protestant Portuguese colonists in Illinois who went there for that purpose and even Military Companies from other portions of the State were debarred entrance to the Cemetery by the Municipal Slaves of Rome the Authorities of Springfield. The Papists do not like the monument and the Statue of Lincoln at Oak Ridge and they would rob the casket of its gem if they could. BUT IT IS SAFE.

I have not time to write further. My wife and Eddie send love to you and yours and wishing you a happy New Year and many of them.

I remain truly and affectionately yours, Edwin A. Sherman

** ** ** ** ** ** ** **

1016 West Street,
Oakland
Feb. 3rd 1884

Dear Father Chiniquy,

Yours received when my hands were full with the funeral of one of my brethren, Captain James M. Moore, who was a fellow soldier with Abraham Lincoln in the Black Hawk War and also a veteran of the Mexican War as well as myself.

In answer to the question propounded to me by you as to the name of that gentleman who asked me that question referred to by you on page 129 of my book, his name I could not possibly give. There were several divisions of that great procession in New York, whose columns were headed towards Wall Street. My Division was formed on Nassau Street.

My impression was that he was the Marshal of one of the City of Brooklyn Divisions that was being massed in front of my own. We were both dismounted at the time, he leading his horse at the time he came up to me. The orders for moving my Division followed immediately that I had not time to question him further as I had desired. My opportunity was lost to gain further information, and the duty of ferreting this matter out devolved upon myself and others, and which still continue to this day, which has been greatly aided by the facts involved in your own dark hours of trial and sorrow in the past, as already related in my book to which you have contributed so much as corroborative proof.

My position was Division Grand Marshal of the Pacific Coast Division, composed of Citizens of the States of California, Oregon, Nevada and the Territories of Idaho, Montana, Utah, Wyoming and Arizona, as you will see by reference to page 128 at the bottom in my book.

I am greatly pressed for time or I would write more as I am now crowded in getting ready for the celebration of the Seventy Fifth Anniversary of the Birthday of Abraham Lincoln.

My Wife and Eddie sent our love to you and yours,

Yours Truly, Edwin A. Sherman

** ** ** ** ** ** ** **

These conclude the letters from Sherman. Following are the letters from T.M. Harris who, as stated earlier, was a member of the Commission, which tried the Conspirators.

Much has been said about the fact that Islam is both a religious and a political organism, a union, but one has to ask, in light of the insight of what is revealed in these letters and in light of the fact that Romanism existed several hundred years prior to the birth of Muhammed, whose adherents have taken a very militant position since it's creation, did the one beget the other for ulterior political purposes? Was Muhammed influenced by the ungodly teachings of Augustine and his adherents used as manpower to suit the ambitions of the pope? Is this the reason for the unusually extreme desire emanating from the Vatican to bring Islam under the fold and control of the Vatican, to intermingle among western society under the banner of 'unity'? After all, one cannot help but notice that both religions seem to be a carbon copy of each other on several levels.

1016 West Street Oakland Cal. Dec 29th/83

Dear Father Chiniquy

Yours of the 10th inst and also of the 18th inst have come to hand. I am glad to know that the book pleases you. and nothing in it all has given me so much pleasure as to pay you a portion of that debt of gratitude (which every true lover of Civil and religious liberty not only in America but throughout the World owes to you in your stripping the mask off from the face of the harlot of Rome) in my dedicating my book to you and the first book that I ever published in my life.

Now in relation to the matters of which you speak.

1st. I do not know where to find the letters of Pope Pius IX to Jeff Davis. unless they are among the Rebel Archives in Washington, It may be however that they may be found in some History of the Rebellion; but the letter of the Pope, Dec 3d 1863 acknowledged the independence of the Southern Confederacy and he called Jeff Davis his "dear son."

By the way I notice that Jeff Davis' sister recently died in Frankfort Kentucky and that she was a Superioress in a Convent in that place which is another link in the great chain of the Papal Conspiracy against Lincoln and the Union.

I will try if possible to get copies of the letters of Pope Pius IX

2d. I was not present at the unveiling of the Statue of Abraham Lincoln at the Monument at Springfield. It is a sad & and humiliating truth that on Oct 15th 1874 the Statue of Abraham Lincoln at the Monument at Springfield was unveiled by two nuns, of the order of St. Dominic, Mother Josepha and Sister Rachael from Jacksonville, who had been especially invited to perform that duty which should only have been done by Protestant Americans. The invitation

November 21st 1891
Ritchie C.H. W.Va.

Rev. C. Chiniquy,
My dear brother in Christ,

I wrote to you some time since informing you that I was preparing for publication a book entitled, *"Assassination of Lincoln – A History of the Great Conspiracy, and the Trial of the Conspirators by a Military Commission"*. I found I could not make my book complete without adding, "*And a Review of the Trial of John H. Surratt*." In the letter referred to, I asked for information on certain points about which I had providentially learned that you had information, and was kindly answered by you referring me to certain pages in your book, *"Fifty Years in the Church of Rome,"* as giving light on the matters about which I inquired. I was providentially led last spring to engage in writing my book. I was a member of the Court that tried the assassins; and feeling that the magnitude, scope and purpose of that conspiracy had never been fully realized by our people, I felt impelled to present, in a calm and dignified way, the evidence of these, as shown before the Commission.

My purpose was to show the political aspects of this plot; that it had its origin with the political leaders of the rebellion; the purpose being to aid them in their work of subverting our government.

The fact that I was writing such a book becoming known through the newspapers, I have received many letters of inquiry, and some of suggestions. One of these brought yourself, and your book above referred to, to my knowledge. I sent and got your book from its publisher; and also the kind permission to use it in my work, only on the condition that I should give you credit for what I might use.

I have from the first suspected that the Church of Rome was the ultimate source of the justification of that crime of the ages, [emphasis added] as the tools used for its accomplishment were all furnished by that Church, but your book throws a flood of light on the subject that ought to reach every American Citizen. So, without departing widely from my original plan, I shall quote enough from you to awaken a curiosity to know more, and thus give me an occasion to commend your book to my readers. I find however that it will be impossible for me to entirely avoid the religious aspect of this Great

Conspiracy; for I couldn't follow the fugitive, John H. Surratt in his flight, without reference to Priests Boucher and La Pierre; and that in such a way as to make them accomplices after the fact; and my quotation from your book must also throw a dark cloud of suspicion over Bishop Bourget. **I think I can also trace the fine hand of the Jesuit all through the trial**. [emphasis added]

Permit me to ask you, if you know, were not the council for his defense Bradley's Sr. and Junior, and Merrick all Catholics? I judge they were from the spirit they everywhere manifest, and from their line of defense.

In studying that trial, it seems to me I can see Fathers Walter and Wiget watching the testimony for the prosecution like hawks, and procuring rebutting testimony whenever it is thought to be needed. Mr. Pierpoint, I should have said Judge Pierpoint, who was employed by the government to assist the prosecution of the case, in showing up Father Boucher, predicts that he will hear from his bishop and the pope for his agency in the affair; and also says that he has learned since the trial commenced, that LaPierre had undergone discipline. I would like to know how much those priests ever suffered at the hands of their bishops for the aid they gave to Surratt. It was all a sham, to throw dust in the eyes of liberty loving Americans, if their bishop ever pretended to discipline them for their conduct in this. The same may be said of the action of the Pope in giving Surratt to the United States in advance of any demand for him.

And the story of Surratt's escaping from his guards by plunging down a precipice at the risk of his life, is, I have no doubt a fabrication. If the truth were known, I have no doubt his escape was a preconceived affair. There was never a more obvious miscarriage of justice than in the result of that trial. I have no doubt it was owing to political and religious prejudice that the jury failed to agree.

I have been greatly interested in your book. You have had an eventful life; and the hand of God is everywhere seen in the experiences through which He finally, in His great grace and love brought you out of darkness and into the marvelous light and liberty of His gospel; and few, amongst the sons of Adam, will have more stars in their crown in this great day. My faith has been greatly strengthened, and my love to the blessed Saviour intensified by the reading of your book.

Very affectionately and respectfully your brother,

T.M. Harris

** ** ** ** ** ** ** **

Ritchie C.H. W.Va.
March 24, 1892

Rev. C. Chiniquy,

My Dear friend,

I hasten to acknowledge the receipt of your kind reply to my inquiry to the obligation of the Father Confessor to keep the confession inviolably secret. In my book I shall have a chapter on "Father Walter" who has from the time of the execution of Mrs. Surratt made himself so obtrusive in efforts to pervert public opinion as to her guilt. He has frequently appeared in print, the last time, as far as I am informed, through a letter which was read to a large assemblage by a Mr. Sloan at a large meeting held at LaSalle Institution in New York in May last. These people had come together expecting Cardinal Gibbon and Father Walter to discuss Mrs. Surratt's case. Neither the Father nor the Cardinal appeared but a Mr. Sloan read a letter from Father Walter on the subject.

In an article in the *Catholic Review* he states two positive falsehoods as to the testimony in the case. On the trial of John H. Surratt Mr. Merrick, a Catholic attorney, who was Surratt's counsel, brought the Father onto the stand as a witness and went through a programme that had evidently been arranged between him and the Father, in which he asked him if he had heard Mrs. Surratt's last confession. The Father replied that "he did; that he gave her communion on Friday and prepared her for death." Mr. Merrick then asked him if she declared to him her innocence at that time, but told him not to answer until he directed him to do so. The Father nodded his head but did not answer. Of course the prosecution objected to the question, as it had not the slightest reference to any issue that was before the jury. Mr. Merrick, of course, knew this; but yet he got what he wanted; that was, a point to twist in his argument by way of appealing to the prejudices of the Catholic members of the jury.

Between the attorney and the Father the matter was put into such a shape that it would appear to the jury and to the public that Father Walter stood ready there to state most solemnly under his oath, that Mrs. Surratt, in her last confession to him, declared her entire innocence to the crime of which she had been convicted, and for which she was about to be executed. Now if the claim, which he had made several times in his newspaper articles, that his priestly vows did not permit him to reveal the Secrets of the Confessional were true, was he not perilously near breaking them on that occasion?

I have a correspondent whose brother is a priest in the Roman Catholic Church, who informed me that Father Walter had a right to require the permission of Mrs. Surratt to make public her declaration of her innocence; and that she had a right also to require him to do so. I submitted my chapter to him for revision; and he informs me that it will be necessary to make some modifications which will be indicated to me, but which I have not yet received. When I get the manuscript back as corrected by him I will be glad to submit it to you for your suggestions.

I want to make very sure that I am standing on solid ground in any statements I may make, or any position I may take in my book. You are at liberty to make any use you may desire to of my letter, except as to this part of it, where I state that I have the above information indirectly from a priest of that church. This was given to me in the confidence of a private friendship, and in sympathy with my cause, and so must be held inviolate. Please never make any reference to this part of my letter.

I see just as you do the danger to our institutions from the rising power of the Roman Catholic Church in our country. This does not come so much from her numbers, as from the deep schemes and political sagacity and cunning of the Jesuits. They have always been men of supreme devotion to a purpose; and that purpose is to establish the temporal power of the Pope, and make him the supreme civil ruler of the world. This makes them always and everywhere politicians; the fomenters of discord and revolutions. They want to overturn, overturn, overturn, until the Pope shall have been accepted as the rightful civil ruler of the world. ***Our government is peculiarly obnoxious to them because the very ideas on which it is founded are everywhere popular outside of Rome, and are directly antagonistic to their purpose.*** [emphasis added] You now see the superior political wisdom of the plan of these men to get control of this country to that of the plan that made you a citizen of Illinois.

They take the cities, and have already gotten control of most of them, insofar as they can make or break the fortunes of politicians and so they can accomplish any purpose they may have to build up the power of Rome.

Woe to the man who antagonizes their schemes. They are fierce as wolves and as relentless as tigers. They are making the common schools of our country the point of their attack, and will push the fight on this issue. The cunning of Arch Bishop Ireland in a proposition for compromise, which looks so fair to make the Parochial schools Common schools for so many hours of the day, is calculated to deceive many of our people.

The fact however that this has made him an individual who is to have his palace in Rome ought to open their eyes to see this Trojan Horse in its true light. In my book I have only attacked the church in the person of such of its priests as have come in my way, and in my comments of Mr. Merrick's laudation of the church in his arguments; but this puts the Roman Catholic Church in a very bad light.

1st Most of the assassins were members of that church.

2nd Priests of that church took Surratt under their protection as soon as he reached Canada after the assassination and kept him concealed for five months knowing him to be charged with being a member of the conspiracy and then helped him off to Europe, there making themselves accessories after the fact.

He finally found refuge under the wing of the Pope and became a soldier in his army. When captured and brought to trial Father Boucher appeared voluntarily as a witness in his behalf and before he got through with Judge Pierrepont's searching cross-examination stood before the jury as a self-confessed scoundrel. And

3rd The efforts of the priests and dignitaries of this church to make it appear that Mrs. Surratt was an innocent woman and to throw odium on the Government, on the Judge Advocate, the Secretary of War, the Commission and all who had anything to do with visiting justice upon the heads of the assassins in the hope of restoring to power the party that tried to destroy the Government.

But my dear friend God has His purposes in regard to our country and is able to carry them out and will find the proper agents and make the occasions for the overthrow of His enemies. You have done a great work in your exposition of the true inwardness of the Papal System. I trust your books may yet be read by all of our people. I am working in my humble way in that in which Providence seems to have made a call upon me and prepared the occasion. You and I are both getting old. God has in his mercy preserved us both far beyond the measure of our years. When we are gone He will raise up others who will take up the work and carry it to completion.

I am sorry to learn of your condition to be such as to require a painful and perhaps dangerous operation. Be assured of my sympathies and my prayers for the success of the operation and a perfect recovery.

Will you my dear friend be so good as to keep me advised of the prospects and result as I see you have a very competent doctor.

I am very truly your brother in Christ,
T.M. Harris

P.S. I enclose the title page of my book for which I now have the copyright.

TMH

** ** ** ** ** ** ** ** **

Ritchie C.H. W.Va.
July 18, 1892

Rev. C. Chiniquy,

My Dear Sir,

I write to acknowledge receipt of your kind favor of the past and to thank you for the pains you took in replying to my inquiries about the terms of publication of books. I am very happy to be able to inform you that I have been able to secure terms for the publication of my book that are entirely satisfactory to me and by which I shall be amply rewarded for my labor should my book command a large sale. I was providentially led to the writing of my book and I can as distinctly see the hand of providence in providing me a publisher. The way I came to write it was this; the editor of the *Evangelical Repository* asked me nearly two years ago to write for his periodical "a history of the trial of Mrs. Surratt." This set me to reflecting, "Does this educated man or editor of a church periodical know no more about this great State trial than to thus characterize it?"

I was forcibly impressed with the idea that the people did not know as much about the great crisis in our history which gave occasion to this trial as they ought. I engaged in the preparation of the article as requested and as I proceeded I felt more and more the necessity of a complete history of the assassination plot. I then commenced a careful study of the evidence produced before the commission and from this deduced the history contained in my book. Before I got through with this I saw that to make my book complete I must review the trial of John H. Surratt and so I procured the official report of this trial and gave it a thorough study; and in this way completed the history.

I presume my book will stir up all the Catholic papers in the country to denounce and bitterly criticize my work. The assassins were all Catholics with perhaps the exception of two. I am informed that Arnold was a Protestant and it is claimed that Atzerodt was a Lutheran. Fathers Walter, Boucher and LaPierre come in my way and catch it hard. I pray you may live to read my book. I will mail you a copy as soon as it is out.

I have now written another book in view and will be greatly obliged if you will put me in the way of procuring the papal allocutions and encyclicals that show the attitude of the Church of Rome toward the Protestant ideas of the rights of conscience and of private judgment of free speech, a free press, free schools etc. etc.

You know that Cardinal Gibbon claims that Roman Catholics are the very best friends of republican institutions and of our government. I want to show the claims of the papacy from official documents and that they are inconsistent with the claims of the Cardinal. I want to enter more distinctly than I could find occasion to do so in my book upon discussion of the Pope's pretensions and to show that the real aim and the purpose of his emissaries or priests in this country is the subversion of our liberties. I want to contrast the workings of Protestantism and of Popery in the New World as shown in the history of the United States and of Mexico, Central America and the South American States. The American people I mean the Protestant people of the United States need to be aware to the dangers that threaten us from Jesuitical schemes to Romanize this country.

I passed my 79th milestone yesterday but I am young in feeling and vigorous in mind yet and I feel I have a call to save my country further in the direction indicated above. God is mercifully lengthening out my life and preserving my faculties and I desire to consecrate myself to His service as long as I live. Please accept my congratulations on your restoration to health. God is verifying to you His promise that "In old age when others fade their fruit still forth shall bring, they shall be fat and full of sap and always flourishing." May He still preserve you and make you useful to His cause and the upbuilding of His kingdom is my prayer.

I am very sincerely your friend and brother in Christ, T.M. Harris

** ** ** ** ** ** ** **

Ritchie C.H. W.Va. June 20, 1892

Rev. C. Chiniquy

My Dear Sir,

I have just read yours of March 28th which had been returned to you through the dead letter office, for which accept my thanks.

I presume the reason that it was not delivered to me was that you have gotten my initials wrong. My name is Thomas M. Harris. My letters from persons who are acquainted with me are addressed Gen. T.M. Harris as I always sign my name T.M. Harris. Should you write again address as above and I will be sure to get it. As I wrote to you on Saturday in response to your most recent letter I only write now to make the above explanation.

In my last I said that I had been informed that Arnold and Atzerodt were Protestants. I will read again the chapters in your book to which you refer and if I find proof incontrovertible that they were Catholics I will make a correction when I get the proof sheets.

Very Truly Yours,
T.M Harris

** ** ** ** ** ** ** **

Ritchie C.H. W.Va. November 19, 1892
Rev. C. Chiniquy

My Dear Sir,

I am rejoiced to be advertised by the papers every now and again of your activity in labor and to know that God is giving you health and strength at your time of life to do the special work which in His providence He is calling you to do and for which you are so well qualified. I shall look forward with a great deal of anxiety for the appearance of your new book. I explained to you why I did not involve the R.C. Priests in the Surratt house meetings and plottings. My place was to introduce no matter that was not fully brought out on the trial; as my purpose was to give a faithful and true history of the conspiracy <u>deduced from the evidence.</u> I presume you will be able to expose the part which the priests took in that conspiracy as I have no doubt they were at the bottom of it whilst at the same time the proof before the commission did not justify me in making that charge in my book. The facts brought out by the evidence at the two trials Military and Civil and presented in my book indicate very clearly the attitude of the Roman Catholic priesthood both at home and in Canada held to the assassination plot and so will prepare the public mind for the further revelations which your book will make. How soon do you expect to have it ready for the press?

Very Truly Yours in the bonds of Christian love and fellowship,
T.M. Harris

** ** ** ** ** ** **

Ritchie C.H. W.Va. March 16 1895

Rev. C. Chiniquy,
Montreal, Canada

My Dear Friend,

I desire to congratulate you on your restoration to health at your advanced age after a severe illness. The ever merciful and all wise Father has further use for you on earth. I felt indignant at the rude and obtusive [sic] officiousness of the Jesuits – male and female who invaded your sick chamber with the obvious intent of publishing to the world in case of your death that you had recanted and returned to the church as a humble penitent and had accepted of her final rites. God, in His mercy, foiled their wicked plan by restoring you to health and giving you the opportunity to testify again for Him. This must be to you a great consolation and cause of rejoicing. May He keep your soul in perfect peace through the atoning blood of His son, our Saviour, and may your pathway to the end of life's journey be as the shining light which shineth more and more unto the perfect day.

I am now nearing my 82nd birthday and am still mercifully preserved in mind and body. I have but one difficulty and that is an infirmity of sight. I have just commenced to write a book entitled, "Rome's Responsibility for the Assassination of Abraham Lincoln" and I desire the privilege of using freely from your book, *"Fifty Years in the Church of Rome"* such matter as I may desire to use.

I could not make a direct charge against the Roman Catholic Church in my *"History of the Great Conspiracy"* as I had to confine myself to the charge and specifications as made by the Government on the trial. In my present book I shall be at liberty to use all the material I can find and shall be able to make out a strong case if my eyes will permit me to accomplish the task I have undertaken.

With the kindness of Christian regards I am truly your friend,

T.M. Harris

** ** ** ** ** ** ** **

Ritchie C.H. W.Va. March 25, 1895

Rev. C. Chiniquy
Montreal

My Dear Friend,

I write to acknowledge receipt of your kind favor of the 19th inst., and to thank you for your kindness in permitting me to use freely of the evidence contained in your book, *"Fifty Years in the Church of Rome*" incriminating Rome in the matter of the assassination of President Lincoln.

If my sight will permit me to carry out my purpose of writing another book I shall avail myself freely of this privilege. In regard to the documents you offer me they are of too important a character and too much historic value to be entrusted to the care of any individual and especially of a man who is old enough to die.

They should be deposited in the archives of some historical society. I would suggest that you offer them first to the Historical Society of Illinois. They should be safely preserved for future use by him who shall write up the final history of that sad episode in our national life. [Note: the material mentioned was, in fact, discovered by the Jesuits in Chiniquy's house in St. Anne, Il. and burned to the ground. This is why the material in Quebec was stored, until recently, without anyone's knowledge. - Ed.]

I have had to suspend my work for the present but hope to have my sight restored soon if it shall please my Heavenly Father. I cannot see to keep on the line more than a few minutes at a time. I write almost mechanically. You would not think to look at it that I had any deficit of vision but I have just now about exhausted my powers of vision in writing this letter. I trust in God. My hope is in His word. He says, "Look unto me and be ye saved." I look to him through the merits of Christ and He will save me.

Very truly yours in the bonds of Christian fellowship,

T.M. Harris

** ** ** ** ** ** ** **

Harrisville W.Va. Sept. 28, 1897

Rev. C. Chiniquy
Montreal, Can.

My Venerable dear Bro in Christ,

I write to congratulate you on your safe return from abroad. I feel to praise God for His goodness to you in sparing you so long to testify for Him at home and abroad. You can now say with the apostle Paul "I am ready to be offered up, and the time of my departure is at hand; I have fought the good fight, I have finished the course, I have kept the faith, henceforth there is laid up for me a crown of righteousness, which God the righteous judge will give me at that day." And Oh!, what a blessed hope to enter into association and companionship with such men as Enoch, Noah, Abraham, David, Isaiah, Paul, Luther, Knox and all of God's eminent saints and faithful ones and to be with Jesus, our elder brother and our God and Saviour Jesus Christ. I pray and trust that God will give you grace and trust to joy in that blessed hope and to trust with confidence unto the end.

"The sting of death is sin, and the thought of sin is the law, but thanks be to God who giveth us the victory through our lord Jesus Christ. He met all the demands of the law for us as fulfilling its precepts in His life and kept paying its penalty at His death and so being in Him, the law has no further claims upon us and "Being justified by faith we have peace with God." Oh! That God may give you a happy peaceful death, as I feel sure that He will. Having triumphed over all your other enemies, may you triumph over the last enemy – death, which to those who are in Christ is not an enemy but a friend.

I will mail to you today a copy of my pamphlet, "*Rome's Responsibility for the Assassination of Abraham Lincoln*" You will see that I have drawn freely on your book, "*Fifty Years in the Church of Rome*" and have given you due credit.

You will see that I take a different view of Weichmann from that taken by you in your book. I have had a great deal of correspondence with him and am satisfied he was innocent of any knowledge of the assassination plot. Even J.H. Surratt clears him in his Brockville lecture. He says that Booth consulted him about taking Weichmann into the conspiracy but that he told Booth he would be of no use to them as he could neither ride nor shoot. This shows two things.

1st They considered Weichmann to be in perfect accord with them politically, and 2nd That they did not let him into their secret. I feel sure that it was a great surprise to Weichmann when he found that those with whom he had been intimately associating with had been engaged in this wicked business; and that he testified truthfully and told all that he knew. He feels that you have done him a great injustice in your book and that you should repair the injury you have done him. It was very natural that you should have implicated him along with the others, but I am satisfied he is innocent of their crime. The persecutions he has endured at the hands of the R.C. priesthood has shaken his faith in the church and I have been endeavoring to bring him into the light and liberty of the children of God. The great drawback in his case is that he has a brother in the priesthood to whom he is greatly attached, and of course it is very hard for him to get rid of the impressions of his early education and associations. He is naturally a very religious man and can never be an infidel. He will probably write to you, and I have written this much that you may know how to deal with him. I trust you may be able to show him the way of life and salvation. I send him the "*Converted Catholic*" pretty regularly.

I am very Truly your Bro. in Christ,
T.M. Harris

In point of fact Louis Weichman did write to Chiniquy requesting him to correct the assertions he had made in "*50 Years*". In a letter dated July 8, 1898 Weichman wrote:

> Rev. C.I. Chiniqui
> Montreal, Canada
>
> Dear Father Chiniqui:
>
> I have your letter of the 25th inst., and I am exceedingly obliged for the same. It is more than a gratification to me to read that you intend to make the correction asked for by me in the proposed new edition of your book. It has lightened my heart.
>
> For some reason, ever since I took the stand in 1865, I have been subjected on the part of the people of the Catholic Church to lies and misrepresentations of the most infamous character. What they could not accomplish against me on the stand, they have tried to do since by newspaper defamation. This has gone on for over thirty years. They said that Stanton had cut his throat because of remorse; that the members of the Commission had died of dread diseases. In 1865 no one, not even the fairest lady of the land, had a better reputation and character than myself. The night that the President was shot I was in bed at ten minutes of ten o'clock and was sound asleep when the awful tragedy took place. I did not even know that the poor man had gone to the theatre, yet within three hours after his murder the city detectives came to that house and told me that the friend of my youth and my school days, J.H.S., had assassinated the Secretary of State. Some day I will tell you just how those men came to that house so soon. I can tell you now if you will incorporate it into your book, but please let me know at once.
>
> I was witness for my government in 1865, went before a Congressional committee in 1866; in the latter part of the same year I appeared before the grand jury at Washington, which indicted Surratt and was then a witness at his own trial. So you see that I have probably had more to do in the way of testifying than any other man in the country.

During John Surratt's trial in 1867, a committee of some of the loyal ladies of Washington waited on me on the part of Secy. Stanton and told me not to have any fear of bodily harm as the Secretary had made arrangements to have a large number of colored men attend the trial every day and that they would afford protection to me and all the government witnesses. This was done and was certainly very satisfactory to me.

One day when I was seated in one of the ante-rooms of the court-house, who should come and seat himself on my lap but little Tad Lincoln; he put his arms around my neck and kissed me on the cheek and thanked me for my testimony on behalf of his murdered father. That act of this little boy has been a balm to me for many a wound that I have since received. If he were living now he would be one of my best friends.

Hoping to hear from you soon, and with best wishes, I remain,

Yours very truly,
L.J. Weichman

P.S. Have you mailed those chapters of the reminiscences which I sent you? I have not received them yet.

Louis Weichman

These conclude the personal letters and sealed sworn statements in reference to the role that the Roman Catholic Church played in the assassination of Abraham Lincoln. After Charles Chiniquy had published his book, "*Fifty Years in the Church of Rome*" key elements of the Church Hierarchy were determined to squelch the revelations made. They even went so far as to claim that Robert Lincoln had expressly disavowed Chiniquy's charges. They hounded the man relentlessly and pressed him to state publicly that Chiniquy had lied. Robert Lincoln wrote the following letter to Mr. Chiniquy after having received a copy of Chiniquy's book and a letter directing Robert to review the pages, which refer to the beloved President. This letter has never been seen by historians nor the public since the day it was received by Chiniquy.

> 10 Sept. 1885
>
> My Dear Sir:
>
> I beg you to accept my thanks for sending me your book and especially for the expression you use in your note in regards to my father. He made many friends in his life but plainly *none were more than yourself.*
>
> Most Sincerely Yours,
> Robert Lincoln

** ** ** ** ** ** ** **

It was no mistake that President George W. Bush used the dreaded C word in his address to the U.S. people and the world after the attacks in New York. "A ***Crusade*** against terrorism" is how he termed it. This after he had just recently been in audience with Pope John Paul II. The entire country was deeply in shock and was starting to clamour for revenge. Every Muslim in the world was forced to look back 1000 years to the hordes of "Christian" soldiers who invaded them in times past. Can you imagine if a few Jewish men were the alleged perpetrators of the 9/11 strikes and the words used were that a ***Holocaust*** was about to be unleashed against terror? The choice of words was truly ominous, even if it was an innocent choice of words.

In the 2008 election we saw the emergence of a radically socialist/collectivist/dictatorial minded, mulatto, unknown, narcissistic Illinois Senator named variously as Barack Hussein Obama alias Barry Soetoro, alias Barry Davis, [father believed to be Frank Marshall Davis] who used the phrase "Fundamental Transformation" to characterize his plan for steering the U.S. among the political icebergs resulting from a reduced global influence and aggressive foreign policy through CIA, CFR and banker inspired oil and resource wars. His election was heavily choreographed and he was advertised with religious fervor as a savior by the fawning media. He immediately commenced to build and expand upon the ruinous policies created by G.W. Bush, creating the NDAA and establishing a separate internal civilian army thereby bypassing Posse Comitatus, issuing a blizzard of Executive Orders, circumventing Congress, making up laws and then breaking them and blowing the Republic of Washington, Jefferson and Adams into an ever growing financially and morally insolvent, grotesque, infected and malignant shadow of its former self. In fact, one must ask – if I honestly loved my wife, would I really want to '*fundamentally* CHANGE' her? Would not this be the precise opposite of love?

Washington's policies are a reflection of the loss of high morals and virtuousity of the people as a whole, that used to be held in high esteem, because the people vote for and tolerate those who act in their name.

Researcher Eric Phelps offers this – (2014)

"Barack Obama is truly not the President of the United States. He is not a powerful person at all. Rather, he is a front man for more powerful entities that hide in the shadows.

The real power in the world is not the United States, Russia, or even China. It is Rome. The Roman Catholic Church (Vatican) is the single most powerful force in the world.

However, the Vatican has been under the control of its largest all-male order, the Jesuits. The Jesuits were created in 1534 to serve as the "counter-reformation" — the arm of the Church that would help to fight the Muslims and the Protestant Reformers. However, they fought with espionage. The Jesuits were expelled from at least 83 countries and cities for subversion, espionage, treason, and other such things. Samuel Morse said that the Jesuits were the foot soldiers in the Holy Alliance (Europe and the Vatican) plan to destroy the United States (Congress of Vienna). Marquis Lafayette stated that the Jesuits were behind most of the wars in Europe, and that they would be the ones to take liberty from the United States.

The head of the Jesuit Order is Adolfo Nicholas. His title is Superior General of the Jesuits. The use of the rank "general" is because the Jesuits are, in reality, a military organization.

Nicholas, as the Jesuit General, is the most powerful man in the world. He ultimately issues the commands that are administered by drones like Obama.

The Jesuit General is nicknamed "The Black Pope" because he always wears black robes. Pope Francis I is, thus, the "White Pope".

Directly under the Jesuit General is Fr. James E. Grummer, S.J. — one of the five Jesuit priests who serve as direct "assistants" to the Jesuit General. Grummer is his American assistant, and controls the US Jesuit Conference. He is the controller of every American Jesuit university and every American Jesuit Provincial. The New York Provincial has the most contact with Grummer (as the top provincial).

Under Grummer is the President of the US Jesuit Conference, Fr. Thomas H. Smolich, S.J., who was the Jesuit Provincial of California during the reign of Governor Arnold Schwarzenegger. Smolich was the power behind Arnold during these years. Smolich is a key force behind the planned Sino-Soviet-Muslim invasion, which the Jesuit Order is planning to use to bring down the United States. He is also actively involved in the orchestration of the Chinese-Mexican invasion.

Under Smolich is Fr. David S. Ciancimino, S.J., the Jesuit Provincial of New York. He is the top Jesuit Provincial in the United States, as New York is the capital of the Jesuit Order's power (that's why it was chosen as the staging area for 9/11). Here, Ciancimino (and the Jesuits beneath him) control Wall Street, the NYSE, and the Federal Reserve Bank. Ciancimino controls Archbishop Timothy Dolan, the most powerful Roman Catholic official in the United States who is not a Jesuit. Ciancimino is an occultist, as are many other top Jesuits.

Directly under Ciancimino is Fr. Joseph M. McShane, S.J., who is the President of Fordham University — the Jesuit college of New York, and the Jesuits' military stronghold there. It is through McShane that the Jesuits (led by Ciancimino in New York) control Archbishop Timothy Dolan. He has become known as the "penholder" for Dolan. He wears a decorative necklace that features an equilateral triangle, a Masonic symbol of the Risen Horus.

Under the control of these powerful Jesuits is Pope Francis I and under him Pope Benedict XVI. Francis I is the Vicar of Christ (Horus) and the current Roman Papal Caesar. He represents Osiris in Babylonian mystery-school/occult mythology.

Below Pope Francis I is Timothy Dolan, the Archbishop of New York. Dolan is the "American Pope" and the "Archbishop of the Capital of the World". He heads the American branches of the Knights of Malta and Knights of Columbus. He is a likely occultist and the controller of American Freemasonry, the CFR, the ADL (B'nai B'rith), the Pentagon, and the intelligence community [based in Georgetown].

Joseph A. O'Hare, S.J. is the President Emeritus of Fordham University and the man directly under Dolan. He is a Knight of Malta and has presided over CFR meetings as Dolan's operative. He is an adviser to David Rockefeller (Knight of Malta), Henry Kissinger (Knight of Malta), and Mayor Michael Bloomberg of New York. He is, thus, the Jesuit who directly controls the city mayor. He is also the Jesuit who controls the Rockefeller-Kissinger apparatus, of which the CFR is a key part.

O'Hare is a devoted Zionist who supports the State of Israel, which was created in 1948 by the United Nations (UN) — (a creation of the Archbishop of New York's Council on Foreign relations). It was Archbishop Francis Spellman of New York who solicited votes at the UN for Israel. Spellman played a key role in Israel's founding. The founder of Zionism was Theodor Herzl, who had frequent meetings with the Pope and had once planned to lead the Jewish people in a "mass conversion" to Roman Catholicism. The true designers, financiers, and promoters of Zionism are the Rothschild's, who Encyclopedia Judaica describes as "guardians of the papal treasure". That's right — the Rothschild's are the banking agents of the Papacy. The State of Israel is just the revived Latin Kingdom of Jerusalem, and it's under the Vatican's thumb.

Below O'Hare is John J. DeGioa, the President of Georgetown University. DeGioa is also a Knight of Malta and a member of the CFR. He is one of the over-seers of the State of Israel.

Below DeGioa, we find Richard N. Haas — the Chairman of the CFR. Haas is ultimately simply a lowly agent of Archbishop Dolan. Haas is a Jewish Labor Zionist and oversees the American Israeli Public Affairs Committee (AIPAC). These Jewish Zionists are mainly just Papal Court Jewish people.

Below Haas is Zbigniew Brzezinski, who was a member of the CFR, Bilderberg Group, and Trilateral Commission. Brzezinski had co-founded the Trilateral Commission. He was a Knight of Malta, as was the other founder of the Trilateral Commission – David Rockefeller. Brzezinski is a Polish Roman Catholic and an adviser to Georgetown University.

Brzezinski was Barry Soetoro's professor at Columbia University, and recruited him for presidential grooming. Are we beginning to see the big picture?

Once Brzezinski created "presidential candidate" Obama, his campaign was financed and promoted by the multi-billionaire behind hundreds of organizations on the "political left" — George Soros. Soros is a high-ranking CFR member and a member of the Carlyle Group, an international corporation that served as a front for the Vatican. Soros, a Hungarian Jew, is a strong socialist-communist (like Brzezinski). Like Haas, Soros is a Papal Court Jew and a Labor Zionist. He is also a Freemason. He is a friend of Rupert Murdoch. Soros is a major stockholder in Halliburton.

Murdoch is the protector of Obama, controlling his opposition. Murdoch was knighted by the Pope in 1998 for making large contributions to the Roman Catholic Church. He has said that his corporation – News Corp – is "just like the Jesuits" while speaking at Georgetown University. Murdoch is a member of the CFR.

Joseph R. Biden is the Vice President, and is directly under the Vatican's big-wheel operatives (Soros and Murdoch). He is Roman Catholic and has been honored at two Jesuit universities. His son is a Jesuit volunteer and a lobbyist for a Jesuit university he attended.

Under the guidance of Biden, we find Barack Obama, a 32nd Degree Freemason who has been trained in Romanism"

THEN and NOW

Thomas Jefferson, Patron Saint of American Liberals, would not recognize his spiritual offspring in today's liberal President Obama and his handling of the Middle East.

Jefferson, as a trade commissioner and then ambassador in Paris for six years (1784-90), faced almost daily the tragedy of American hostages enslaved by violent Muslims and his own frustrating inability to liberate them.

However, what he learned served him well as the leading hawk for war a decade later when he became president and went to war against belligerent Islam.

In May, A.D. 1784, immediately after America's Continental Congress, gathered in Annapolis, had signed the final draft of the treaty with England that formally ended the American Revolution, Congress appointed Benjamin Franklin, John Adams, and Thomas Jefferson as "trade commissioners" in an effort to open European markets to American commodities -- not an easy mission with Europe's traditionally closed, mercantile economic system.

But when Jefferson reached Paris in August 1784 to join the other two already there, he discovered that one unanticipated reality posed the greatest and most immediate threat to their fledgling United States. Every state was swamped in Revolutionary War debt and the way to pay it off would be shipping to European markets their great natural wealth, e.g. lumber from their endless forests, the produce of their fertile soil, the skins of animals for clothing, etc. But with the thirteen ex-colonies now independent of England, when their merchant ships crossed the Atlantic Ocean now, they would no longer be protected by the Royal Navy, the greatest in the world and by the "tribute" that the King of England paid to the pashas of Tripoli, Tunis, Algiers, and the Sultan of Morocco. This was basically protection money given to North Africa's so-called "Barbary Pirate" states to keep them from preying on British shipping.

When Jefferson boarded his friend Mr. Tracy's private vessel in Boston Harbor in July 1784 for the month-long voyage, he took along for reading Don Quixote, Cervantes's classic novel in which several central chapters take place in the slave dungeons of Algiers episodes based on Cervantes' own five years as a Christian slave to the Muslims, so the subject of Barbary piracy could not have been wholly foreign to Thomas Jefferson, principle author of America's Declaration of Independence.

But what surprised him was that, contrary to popular usage, these North African predators were not common pirates out for loot -- who when ashore liked to hang out in taverns, get drunk, sing "yo ho ho" and paw at wenches. No, these "Barbary Pirates" were in fact just normal Middle Eastern Muslims -- or Mahometans or Mussulmen as they were then called -- who did not drink alcohol at all. Unlike real pirates, they also prayed to Allah several times a day. Not at all venal, independent freebooters, they were simply the crewmen in the official cruisers of the Mediterranean Sea's Islamic city-states. While their livelihood was capturing cargo and passenger vessels, their rationale for doing so was religious. They saw themselves engaged in a jihad and called themselves mujahidin/soldiers in the jihad. In the late 18th century, one man's pirate was another man's holy warrior.

Jefferson, like Franklin and Adams, expected that his principle work for Congress would concern trade with Europe, but saw right away the immediate danger to U.S. freighters no longer protected by warships flying the Union Jack. America's ships would now be flying the Stars and Stripes, which flag no Mussulman had ever seen.

Jefferson foresaw catastrophe and thus spent the fall of 1784 reading up on Islam and probing fellow diplomats in Paris on how their countries dealt with the problem. He discovered that for a thousand years the Muslims of North Africa had plagued Europe with their hijacking, hostage-taking, and enslaving. (In truth, Europe also engaged in capturing Muslims and selling them in slave markets too, but that practice had died out earlier in the century.)

Jefferson discovered that in practically every century some European country got fed up and ordered its navy to bombard these Muslim port cities where on any given day there were thousands of Christian enslaved.

But no bombardment ever succeeded in ending the menace. There was also, from Europe's perspective, a religious dimension to the relationship. Christians were themselves, for over a thousand years, locked no less in an eternal holy war with Islam that, according to Catholic doctrine, was not another religion but a heresy with which there could be no peace. The kings of Catholic Spain on their coronation oaths for centuries pledged eternal war against infidel Muslims. The Crusades may have ended centuries earlier but not the animosity between the two cultures or the low-level violence.

Jefferson learned as well of a major turning point in history that occurred in the 1680s when Protestant England of Max Weber's *The Protestant Ethic and the Spirit of Capitalism* became the first Christian state to dismiss religion and see the problem pragmatically. British merchants reasoned that it would be better to pay the tribute that the Mahometans were demanding to refrain from their barbaric attacks. It made better commercial sense to pay the "tribute" and free the Royal Navy for safeguarding their burgeoning global empire elsewhere. Why remain bogged down in the Mediterranean to protect the increasingly smaller percentage of their business?

Two years later, Louis XIV of France copied England and before long, every maritime trading country in Christian Europe was paying for the right to do business in the Middle East unmolested.

But Jefferson also learned that the purchase of peace was at best temporary. The Mussulmen would always find some excuse to break the agreement, claim it was the European country's fault, renew the hijacking, and force new negotiations for higher tribute.

Jefferson is remembered as the father of the American principle of a "wall of separation" between church and state and thus was appalled that in their enlightened age -- what friend Tom Paine nicknamed "The Age of Reason"-- there were still such people in the world as these Muslims who continued to kidnap and enslave people as part of their religion.

Jefferson also discovered that the 'tribute" was in reality less a demand for cash and jewels, spices and fine fabrics, and more about weapons. The "tribute" was largely a demand for arms shipments of ammunition and naval supplies without which the "pirates" could not be pirates at all. The Muslims were much too backward to have their own foundries capable of producing cannon and shot, iron spikes, gunpowder, and the nails required for wooden sailing ships.

And the Europeans, led by the English and the French, were only too happy to oblige. Sending weapons meant helping the Arabs arm themselves for their attacks on other Christians, meaning, fellow Europeans traveling on innocent sailing vessels. European states were routinely in a state of war with one another, so, for example, what cared the French if the weapons they supplied the Algerines (sic) and Tripolitans (sic) were used to hijack and enslave Englishmen and Spaniards?

So Trade Commissioner Jefferson, after three months in Paris and research into the history and menace of militant Islam, formulated a policy in opposition to his partners, both of whom had spent years as diplomats in Europe. Benjamin Franklin the Quaker reckoned that since most U.S. maritime business was conducted elsewhere, U.S. importers and exporters should just avoid that dangerous sea. He did not think the country did enough business there to warrant the risk.

But John Adams, a lawyer to Boston merchants well-versed in maritime commerce and the laws of piracy, knew that in fact the U.S. did enough business in the Mediterranean not to want to abandon that market. He too knew something of the history of the threat and reasoned that since the superpowers England, France, and Spain with their major navies had chosen the path of tribute rather than violence, America with no navy had no choice. After the Revolution, the U.S. had sold off or scrapped every armed vessel it owned.

But Jefferson, the future father of original American Liberalism, wanted to fight. He found it intolerable that their revolutionary and little-in-population, infant republic would join this corrupt European practice in which civilized nations gave arms and money to uncivilized "barbarians" -- his word -- who used the weapons to attack civilized people and enslave them as part of a "holy war," no less.

Within weeks of formulating his strategy for dealing with Islam, which included his prescription for the building of a fleet of American warships, news of a hijacking by Morocco reached him in Paris. In the following summer of 1785, two more American vessels were captured, this time by Algiers. The ten merchant seamen seized by the Moroccans would be ransomed after nine months by Congress for $40,000 which capitulation Jefferson protested against, but not the twenty-one others enslaved in Algiers.

Jefferson remained in Paris for another five years during which time he and Adams never succeeded in freeing the American slaves in Algiers. They were still there when in 1790 Jefferson returned home to become the United States' first Secretary of State and among his first acts was filing a report on the depressed status of American commerce in the Mediterranean and the plight of the hostages still in Algiers.

For the next three years, Secretary of State Jefferson was the No. 1 hawk for war in America pressing Congress and President Washington to build a navy to rescue the hostages and put an end to hijacking, hostage taking, and enslavement in the Mediterranean.

In 1792, he commissioned John Paul Jones, the great naval hero of the Revolution who was a fellow radical liberal, to sail for Algiers to see what could be accomplished diplomatically but also covertly, to size up the place as a possible target for a U.S. attack, though Jones died before he could execute the mission.

In late 1793, Secretary of State Jefferson wanted to retire, and in his last report to Congress on any subject he dealt again with the menace of militant Islam and the recent, dreadful news that Algiers had struck again, this time hijacking eleven more American merchant ships carrying over one hundred seamen and passengers. He outlined the blow to the American economy. When word reached New York of the mass hijacking, the stock market crashed. In the few days it took for the news to travel up and down the Atlantic seaboard, voyages were canceled in every major port; seamen were thrown out of work, ship stores merchants went out of business. What 9-11 did to the U.S. economy in 2001, the mass hijacking by Muslims in late 1793 did too.

So it is not surprising that four months later, on March 27th, 1794, Congress -- after debating the topic sporadically over a decade since the first hijacking to Morocco -- finally decided to build a fleet of warships: six extra-large frigates including the first Constellation, today a tourist attraction in Baltimore's Harbor Place and Constitution (the future "Old Ironsides") in Boston harbor. In a nutshell, the United States Navy was born in response to unprovoked Muslim aggression.

Congress's compromise was to build the ships and hope that the construction itself would frighten the Algerines while at the same sending negotiators to appease them by imitating Europe and offering to join the tribute system. The Naval Establishment Act tried to please both hawks and doves by ordering the building of a fleet while simultaneously sending negotiators, with the text specifying that if they succeeded, the building of the warships, immensely expensive in every generation, would stop.

And that is what happened. The U.S. wound up paying close to $1,000,000 in ransom and to atone for its tardy delivery in barrels of gold coins also agreed to build for free a brand new warship as a gift to the pasha of Algiers. It was built in Portsmouth, New Hampshire and christened "The Crescent," in honor of the Islamic flag.

Jefferson, understandably, objected to the national humiliation under his erstwhile friend President John Adams.

In 1796, eighty-five surviving American hostages, crippled and emaciated by the ordeal, were freed from slavery.

Eventually the shipbuilding resumed, but the menace of Barbary piracy remained. Not until 1801 was action taken when Jefferson became America's third president. After 17 years of calling for war, one of his first acts was dispatching a naval squadron of four warships to the Mediterranean, and what ensued was a four-year war "to the shores of Tripoli" memorialized in glory for generations of Americans to come, one of whose dashing heroes was Navy Lieutenant Stephen Decatur, Jr. after whom more than a dozen American towns and counties would be named.

** ** ** ** **

President of the United States of America Barack Obama had not been president for more than ten minutes when he slapped American Jews in the face (and by extension Israel and all Jews). Though he did it so subtly -- in plain sight and in front of the whole world -- no one noticed.

On January 21, 2009, about three-quarters of the way through his first inaugural address, after paragraphs of bromides about American greatness, he alluded to the menace of militant Islam:

> "For we know that our patchwork heritage is a strength, not a weakness. We are a nation of Christians and Muslims, Jews and Hindus, and non-believers. We are shaped by every language and culture, drawn from every end of this Earth..."

It has become customary in our time to speak of America as a Judeo-Christian civilization because the facts of history show that, so "a nation of Christians and Muslims, Jews and Hindus" as a new formulation of the melting pot meme was a major departure.

In fact, although the settling of the original Thirteen Colonies was almost exclusively the handiwork of Christians from northern Europe and Great Britain, by the time of the American Revolution there were already six Jewish communities, one in each of the major colonial cities. Jews fought and died in the Revolution, and in 1802, when the military academy at West Point opened its doors, one of the first two volunteer cadets was a Jew.

Jews have been part of American culture ever since in the Military, Medicine, Science, Technology, Literature, Theater, Music, Movies, Television, Academe, Law, Journalism and Business.

Jews invented the nuclear submarine providing the United States its greatest line of defense in the Cold War. A German Jew invented jeans, the quintessential American garment. Although always a tiny percentage of the population, they have always punched above their weight in contributions to America.

Christians and therefore Jews too built the country. In American cities every December, merchants decorate their shop windows with "Merry Christmas" & "Happy Hanukah" signs. The country has most definitely been a Judeo-Christian enterprise.

Muslims, by contrast, played no role in the making of America. There is no evidence of a Muslim presence before the 20th century. Yet here on that January day was the brand new American President orating that the U.S. was "a nation of Christians and Muslims, Jews and Hindus…"

In this formulation, the Jews have been bumped back to third place, elbowed, so to speak, aside by Muslims who take their place. This recalls what happened in the 7th century when their Prophet Muhammad told his followers that they had replaced the Jews as Allah's Chosen People.

Barack Obama during his campaign had vowed to "fundamentally change this country," and, in retrospect, this formulation was part of that effort. The fundamental change would include the dispossession of the Jews of their second place in American culture and even downgrade them to the ranks of Hindus, whose tradition, like Islam, played no role in formrative United States history.

Indeed, Obama's next sentence continued, "To the Muslim world, we seek a new way forward, based on mutual interest and mutual respect," and this new formulation was surely part of that "new way forward" in the matter of Islam's role in American life.

Another feature of Obama's desired transformation was on display two and one-half months later -- on April Fool's Day no less -- when he was videotaped obsequiously bowing down before the king of Saudi Arabia whose official title includes Guardian of the Two Mosques (alluding to the ones in Mecca and Medina). This was a gesture one cannot imagine Obama ever executing before any other national leader -- let alone the prime minister of Israel.

And that bow was an offense against protocol and custom -- the Revolution had been not only a war of national liberation but a rejection of the very institution of monarchy. American presidents do not bow down to kings and thus it was doubly an insult, for this was no ordinary monarch but the potentate of the country where fifteen of the nineteen skyjackers on September 11, 2001 were raised and shaped by this king's religion, including 9-11's evil mastermind Osama bin Laden.

What Obama might have done was demand that the king show "mutual respect" by bowing down to him to beg forgiveness that some of his subjects had engineered that eruption of Muslim Hell on earth perpetrated against his fellow Americans. In Israel in 1997, after a Jordanian soldier had murdered seven little Jewish girls, the king of Jordan crossed over the River to visit the grieving mothers and literally went down on his knees to express his sorrow and shame. Obama should have asked the Guardian of the Two Mosques to do that too. Instead, there on view for posterity on YouTube is the President's protruding posterior.

Two months later, in June 2009, Mr. Obama made his first trip to the Middle East but snubbed Israel, America's long-time and most faithful ally. He flew instead to Egypt where he delivered a speech at Al-Azhar, Sunni Islam's oldest seminary, where Osama bin Ladin, Haj Amin al-Husseini, Sheik Ahmad Yassin and many other Muslim priests who preach the virtue of terror studied Islam and wallowed in its classical, Muslim-style Jew-hatred.

In his speech, Obama praised this religion beyond the boundaries of historical truth:

> "As a student of history, I also know civilization's debt to Islam. It was Islam at places like Al-Azhar that carried the light of learning through so many centuries, paving the way for Europe's Renaissance and Enlightenment...And throughout history, Islam has demonstrated through words and deeds the possibilities of religious tolerance and racial equality. I also know that Islam has always been a part of America's story. The first nation to recognize my country was Morocco. In signing the Treaty of Tripoli in 1796, our second President John Adams wrote, "The United States has in itself no character of enmity against the laws, religion or tranquility of Muslims." And since our founding, American Muslims have enriched the United States. They have fought in our wars, they have served in government, they have stood for civil rights, they have started businesses, they have taught at our Universities, they've excelled in our sports arenas, they've won Nobel Prizes, built our tallest building, and lit the Olympic Torch. And when the first Muslim-American was recently elected to Congress, he took the oath to defend our Constitution using the same Holy Koran that one of our Founding Fathers, Thomas Jefferson, kept in his personal library."

This was the vandalizing of history. In no way is it true that "...since our [America's] founding, Muslims have enriched the United States..." As noted, their presence came quite late, and what enrichment could he have had in mind?

And as for the early treaty with Tripoli (Libya): John Adams's statement was made after the repeated hijacking of American merchant ships and the cruel enslavement of their passengers and crews by the mis-named "Barbary Pirates." That was a colloquial nick-name for them; in reality, they were not pirates but the official navies of recognized Muslim powers. Adams's statement had been an attempt to appease them in the hope they would honor the treaty they had just signed and thenceforth cease and desist from attacking Ameri-can merchant ships (which they did not).

Likewise, Obama's reference to Thomas Jefferson was false. The principle author of the Declaration of Independence and first Secretary of State purchased his Koran when in Paris in order to study the intolerable aggression being perpetrated against fellow Americans by these so-called "pirates" who Jefferson learned were in reality observant Muslims who justified their hijack-ing and enslaving of infidels with the jihad.

Jefferson spent five years in France after the Revo-lution as a trade commissioner, then ambassador. That is when he bought his Koran, because almost every day of these years there were American hostages enslaved in North Africa that he struggled to but failed to liber-ate. In this period, he even met in London with an am-bassador from the Bashaw (pasha) of Tripoli, a prede-cessor of Muammar Gaddafi who demanded $100,000 not to begin hijacking American ships and enslaving all the people aboard. Jefferson listened as the ambassa-dor cited the jihad as the justification for this behavior. That was in 1786.

Fifteen years later, as America's third president and still the country's No. 1 hawk for war with Islam, Jefferson went to war against Tripoli because he had no doubt that these "pirates" were not independent free-booters but self-described holy warriors/mujahideen who could only be subdued via military force majeure. They were beyond reason.

By contrast, America's forty-fourth president, early in his first term, ordered his administration never to use the words "Islam," "Muslim" and "terrorism" in the same sentence.

Then in November of his first year in office, on the Ft. Hood, Texas army base, a Muslim shouting "Allahu Akbar!" massacred thirteen fellow soldiers, which carnage Obama insisted had nothing to do with Islam.

And we have not even touched on his other, serial insults to Israel's Prime Minister Benjamin Netanyahu and by extension the people of the democratic State of Israel that elected him.

Barack Obama's affection for Islam and his Islamic habit of trashing historical truth have been right there from his first inaugural speech when he misdescribed American society by demoting the place of the Jews in it.

Finally, for any who doubt this critical portrait: remember, too, that the day after his first inaugural speech and that evening's series of inaugural balls and festivities, when he entered the Oval Office the next morning to begin work as president -- with the U.S. economy in a crisis not seen since the Great Depression of the 1930s -- he asked that his first phone call as president be put through not to some expert on economics but Mahmoud Abbas, the Holocaust Denier and international Muslim terrorist criminal.

President Obama has been aggressing against the Jews in America and Israel since his first minutes on the job. No wonder, then, in January 2015, he did not attend the mass demonstration in Paris after the massacres by Muslims of the Charlie Hebdo staff and four Jews buying food for the Holy Sabbath.

The question is: why do Americans not only sit silently while the lives of innocents are destroyed, but also actually support the destruction of the lives of innocents? Why do Americans believe "official sources" despite the proven fact that "official sources" lie repeatedly and never tell the truth?

The only conclusion that one can come to is that the American people have failed. We have failed Justice. We have failed Mercy. We have failed the US Constitution. We have failed Truth. We have failed Democracy and representative government. We have failed ourselves and humanity. We have failed the confidence that our Founding Fathers put in us. We have failed God. If we ever had the character that we are told we had, we have obviously lost it. Little, if anything, remains of the "American character."

At its birth the U.S., as a peoples, placed their full faith in God, their daily life revolved around giving God His due and as a result God gave them the preeminence in the world, blessed their commerce and the world feared their power. Due to the sense of moral right and godly charity by its peoples, in contrast to, or in spite of its political leaders' foibles, the world has, for the most part been blessed. Now, the U.S. is driving God from its midst. The leaders behave like spoiled, self-aborbed teenaged brats. The foreign policy is self-defeating. Europeans control the dollar; China, Russia and Germany are buying up U.S. real estate, *the population itself has been pledged as security to foreigners* [A birth certificate looks like a security instrument because it is. The government creates a strawman corporation by reversing your name and writing it all upper case and the government issues and sells bonds to nations like China using that corporation with your name as collateral. All against your will] and the civilian agencies are being militarized.

The U.S. has reneged on it's oath by George Washington to the Almighty on its behalf. We have legalized the murder of our babies. We have used the law to justify deviancy of all kinds and have even perverted the law itself. In return, God is removing His protection, allowing all kinds of serious problems and depriving it of strong leaders. If it doesn't act fast to reverse the trend it is set upon, it will not be in a position to stop or delay or even hope to resist this re-emerging superpower called, The Holy Roman Empire, the 4th World Empire recorded by Daniel the prophet and expounded on in the revealing message of Christ to His Church [Rev.13-14]. Also read Ezek. Chapters 5-7.

The Republic of the United States of America is being deliberately destroyed and weakened in preparation for collapse and invasion. This *One Nation under God*, like their ancient forefathers of the Assyrian [national birthright holder Israel] and Babylonian [Scepter holder Judah] Captivities, will be emptied by war, disease, crime, destruction and occupation with the survivors enslaved or carried off to another land.

You absolutely need to understand the truth about what is happening to America today. We have been protected in this country for a couple hundred years. We have not experienced the turmoil that many other nations have. Yes, we were involved in a civil war and two world wars, but God has given us a lot of peace. As a result, our people have kind of settled into an unreality about what is really happening around us. They don't understand how deadly dangerous this world is!

How has the United States been maneuvered into this situation? To discover this we must go back to the events of the early 1800's and trace it forward to the present.

Chapter 2

Secret Treaty of Verona; Senator Robert Owen discusses ramification of Treaty; Who are the Jesuits?; Jesuit Oath of the 4th vow; Example of putting oath into practice; Goals of Vatican in the U.S.; Origin of Moral Majority and Religious Right; The political nature of the Religious Right; Jesuit political interference; A proposal from Britain; Monroe Doctrine; Nation's Census confirms threat; Bishop Hughes confirms threat; political effect of pope's letter to Jefferson Davis; Baltimore-The Vienna of America

The Civil War was the result of European interference in the U.S. and the murder of Abraham Lincoln was but one step in the attempt to carry out the Secret Treaty of Verona of October 1822, a pact entered into by the "High Contracting Parties" of the former Congress of Vienna, which held its secret sessions during the entire year of 1814-15.

Simultaneously, with the calling of the Congress of Vienna in 1814, Pope Pius VII restored the Society of Jesus (Jesuits) that had been abolished by Pope Clement XIV, July 21, 1773, on the grounds that it was immoral, dangerous and a menace to the very life of the Papacy. (1) Clement was promptly poisoned for his act. It was during this 40 year period of Jesuit inactivity that the United States was founded.

With the restoration of this order, the execution of the Secret Treaty of Verona was placed in their keeping. I will be quoting copiously from several documents, books, letters, and other assorted material which will lay out in detail the fine spider's web which was constructed for the sole purpose of eliminating forever the influence of liberty and freedom as it is embodied in the United States Constitution and Bill of Rights.

The "Secret Treaty of Verona" was the ratification of Article 6 of the Congress of Vienna and was signed by the representatives of Austria, France, Russia, Prussia and the Vatican. The first three articles of this treaty laid out the blueprint for the perpetuation of Monarchial rule which adhered to the Council of Trent and which was intended to influence and direct all the peoples of the earth and to kill the "cancer" of freedom. I quote excerpts from that document below, as it appears on the Congressional Record of April 25, 1916, placed there by Senator Robert Owen and as it is recorded in the Diplomatic Code, by Elliot, page 179:

> "The undersigned specially authorized to make some additions to the treaty of Verona after having exchanged their respective credentials, have agreed as follows:
>
> Article 1 The high contracting powers being convinced that the system of representative government is equally incompatible with Monarchial principles as the maxim of the sovereignty of the people with the divine right, engage mutually, in the most solemn manner, to use all their efforts to put an end to the system of representative governments, in whatever country it may exist in Europe, and to prevent its being introduced in those countries, anywhere in the world, wherever it is not yet known.
>
> Article 2 As it cannot be doubted that the liberty of the press is the most powerful means used by the pretended supporters of the rights of the nations to the detriment of those princes, the high contracting parties promise reciprocally to adopt all proper measures to suppress it, not only in their own state, but also in the rest of Europe.
>
> Article 3 Convinced that the principles of religion contribute most powerfully to keep the nations in the passive state of obedience which they owe to their princes, the high contracting parties declare it to be their intention to sustain in their respective states, those methods which the clergy may adopt with the aim of ameliorating their own interests, so intimately connected with the preservation of the authority of the princes; and the contracting powers join in offering their thanks to the Pope for what he has already done for them, and solicit his constant cooperation in their views of submitting the nations of the world.

Article 4 The situation of Spain and Portugal unite unhappily all the circumstances to which this treaty has particular reference. The high contracting parties, in confiding to France the care of putting an end to them, engaged to assist her in the manner which may at least compromise them with their own people and the people of France by means of a subsidy on the part of the two empires of 20,000,000 of francs every year from the date of the signature of this treaty to the end of the war.

Article 5 In order to establish in the peninsula the order of things which existed before the revolution of Cadiz, and to insure the entire execution of the articles of the present treaty, the high contracting parties give to each other the reciprocal assurance that as long as their views are not fulfilled, rejecting all other ideas of futility or other measure to be taken, they will address themselves with the shortest possible delay to all the authorities existing in their states and to all their agents in foreign countries, with the view to establish connections tending toward the accomplishment of the objects proposed by this treaty.

Article 6 This treaty shall be renewed with such changes as new circumstances may give occasion for; either at a new congress or at the court of one of the contracting parties, as soon as the war with Spain shall be terminated.

Article 7 The present treaty shall be ratified and the ratifications exchanged at Paris within the space of six months.

Made at Verona the 22nd of November, 1822

For Austria; Mr. Metternich
For Russia; Mr. Nesselrode
For Prussia; Mr. Bernstet
For France; Mr. Chateaubriand (2)

Senator Owen then went on to elaborate on the meaning of the treaty. The Record shows his statement in part as follows:

"I wish to put in the RECORD the secret Treaty of Verona of November 22, 1822, showing what this ancient conflict is between the rule of the few and the rule of the many...It throws a powerful white light upon the conflict between monarchial government and government by the people. The Holy Alliance under the influence of Metternich, the Premier of Austria, in 1822, issued this remarkable secret document…

"This Holy Alliance, having put a Bourbon prince on the throne of France by force, then used France to suppress the condition of Spain, immediately afterwards, and by this very treaty gave her a subsidy of 20,000,000 francs annually to enable her to wage war upon the people of Spain and prevent their exercise of any measure of the right of self-government. The Holy Alliance immediately did the same thing in Italy, by sending Austrian troops to Italy, where the people there attempted to exercise a like measure of liberal constitutional self-government; and it was not until the printing press, which the Holy Alliance so stoutly opposed, taught the people of Europe the value of liberty that finally one country after another seized a greater and greater right of self-government, until now it may be fairly said that nearly all the nations of Europe have a very large measure of self-government."

"However, I wished to call the attention of the Senate to this important history in the growth of constitutional popular self-government. The Holy Alliance made its powers felt by the wholesale drastic suppression of the press in Europe, by universal censorship, by killing free speech and all ideas of popular rights, and by the complete suppression of popular government. The Holy Alliance having destroyed popular government in Spain, and in Italy, had well-laid plans also to destroy popular government in the American Colonies which had revolted from Spain and Portugal in Central and South America under the influence of the successful example of the United States."

"It was because of this conspiracy against the American Republics by the European monarchies that the great English statesman, Canning called the attention of our government to it, and our statesmen then, including Thomas Jefferson, who was still living at the time, took an active part to bring about the declaration by President Monroe in his next annual address to the Congress of the United States that the United States would regard it as an act of hostility to the government of the United States and an unfriendly act, if this coalition , or any power in Europe ever undertook to establish upon the American Con-

> tinent any control of any American republic, or to acquire any territorial rights." (3)

The "Society of Jesus" the members of which are referred to as the Jesuits, has absorbed the Papacy. The present Pope Francis is the first Jesuit Pope in history. He is a rabid anti-American, promoter of the Gaia religion known as the 'green' movement and according to a British government official, military advisor to Prime Minister Thatcher, Sir Michael Howard, the current Pope Francis, whose real name is Jorge Bergoglio, aided the brutal Argentinian military junta (led by General Videla) in 1981 by brokering a deal through Vatican banker Roberto Calvi to get them around 20 Exocet missiles for US$200 million. These missiles were later used by the Argentinian military against Britain in Falklands War in 1982.

This Society was founded by a fanatic, one Ignatius Loyola, in 1541; its object being to control Jerusalem for the Papacy and to combat Islamism and the Protestant Reformation of Martin Luther of 1517. The Council of Trent, which followed shortly after Luther's gesture, condemned anything related to the Reformation, particularly the political, social and economic blessings, and the birth of the middle classes which were referred to as the Age of Enlightenment.

Loyola was the son of a prominent Spanish family, who had distinguished himself as a soldier, and by the immoral excesses of his private life, but who, owing to an accident, which maimed him, was supposed to have become "converted", and during the illness, which followed, the Society of Jesus was conceived in his brain, fertile with deviltry.

As stated earlier, the Jesuit organization was integral in implementing this treaty. This can only be demonstrated by disclosing to you the entire oath of induction, which every Jesuit must take if he is to be brought up into the higher command ranks of the order. This oath is the sole motivating factor for the present pope, Francis I. This oath was entered into the Library of Congress, Washington D.C., Catalog Card # 66-43354, and was made public in 1883 (4). The oath is still in effect, and is still used today.

Before I show you this I wish to quote from Napoleon while he was exiled at St. Helena,

> "The Jesuits are a *military organization*, not a religious order. Their chief is a general of an army, not the mere father abbot of a monastery and the aim of this organization is POWER. Power in its most despotic exercise. Absolute power, universal power, power to control the world by the volition of a single man. Jesuitism is the most absolute of despotisms; and at the same time the greatest and the most enormous of abuses." (5)

It is, in fact, a firm supporter of collectivism, fascism/communisim and dictatorship.

In his book, "*Will: The Autobiography of G. Gordon Liddy*", Mr. Liddy states,

> "As much as I had admired the German Benedictines, I admired the Jesuits more...the Society of Jesus was something special; the shock troop of the Catholic Church. So effective an organization was it that...Heinrich Himmler [himself a Catholic] used it as the model for his own corps of Ubermenschen, (supermen), the Schutzstaffel (SS), whose hand-picked members swore a special oath of loyalty to the Fuhrer as the highest rank of Jesuits did to the Pope...These men [Jesuits at the Fordham University club] ran the world, and it was obvious that they enjoyed it." (6)

"The National Government will regard it as its first and foremost duty to revive in the nation the spirit of unity and cooperation. It will preserve and defend those basic principles on which our nation has been built. It regards Christianity [they mean wicked Catholicism] as the foundation of our national morality, and the family as the basis of national life" ('My New Order', Adolf Hitler, Proclamation to the Catholic German Nation at Berlin, February 1, 1933)

In the book, "*The Secret History of the Jesuits*" by Edmond Paris, Chick Publications, Chino Ca., the Roman Catholic Adolf Hitler, (brought into power by Father Faulhaber, the same man who ordained Pope Benedict XVI, Benedict himself being a Hitler Youth member who afterwards headed the Office of the Inquisition, aka. Holy Office, under Pope John Paul II,) and a dictator, who was never excommunicated, is quoted on page 164 thus:

> "I learned much from the Order of the Jesuits...Until now, there has never been anything more grandiose, on the earth, than the hierarchical organization of the Catholic Church. I transferred much of this organization into my own party..." (7)

In fact, many Jesuit priests had traded in their black robes for SS uniforms and their crucifixes for guns. Orthodox Serbs were some of the first to suffer their brutality.

On page 165 Paris quotes the Papal nuncio, Franz von Papen, who stated,

> "The Third Reich is the first world power which not only acknowledges but also puts into practice the high principles of the papacy."(8)

These "high principles" were in reference to the proposed construction of the death camps in which Jews, Gypsies and religious enemies of the Papacy suffered.

These, dear reader, are rather strong indictments. Are they without merit? Are the Jesuits truly the military enforcement arm, the *Gestapo* of the Catholic Church? Let the reader be the judge.

JESUIT Extreme Oath of Induction as recorded in the Journals of the 62D Congress, 3d Session of the U.S.

(House Calendar No. 397. Report No. 1523)

Congressional Record---House, 15 Feb. 1913, pp3215-3216

The Jesuit novice presents himself kneeling on a red cross before the Superior of the order. Before him are two flags, the familiar yellow and white flag of the papacy, and the flag of the Jesuits, a black flag with a red dagger and red cross, above a white skull and cross bones. On the Jesuit flag is written the words, IUSTUM, NECAR, REGES, IMPIOS. (It is just to exterminate impious or heretical rulers, kings or governments). This is the Jesuit interpretation of INRI, the letters you would find on a crucifix idol and which the Catholic Church insists means, "Jesus of Nazareth, King of the Jews", in Latin, Iesus, Nazarenus, Rex, Iudaeorum.

The Superior hands the novice a small black crucifix, which he holds to his heart, and the Superior then presents to the novice a dagger. The novice grasps the dagger by the bare blade and presses the point to his heart with enough pressure to draw blood. This same blood is later used as ink to sign his name. The Superior, still holding the hilt of the dagger then speaks.

Superior-

My son, heretofore you have been taught to act the dissembler: among Roman Catholics to be a Roman Catholic, and to spy even among your own brethren; to believe no man, to trust no man. Among the Reformers, to be a Reformer; among the Huguenots, to be a Huguenot; among the Calvinists, to be a Calvinist; Among the Protestants, generally to be a Protestant; and obtaining their confidence to seek even to preach from their pulpits and to denounce with all the vehemence in your nature our Holy Religion and the Pope; and to descend so low as to become a Jew among the Jews, that you might be enabled to gather together all information for your Order as a faithful soldier of the Pope.

You have been taught to insidiously plant the seeds of jealousy and hatred between communities, provinces and states that were at peace, and to incite them to deeds of blood, involving them in war with each other, and to create revolutions and civil wars in countries that were independent and prosperous, cultivating the arts and sciences and enjoying the blessings of peace. To take sides with the combatants and to act secretly in concert with your brother Jesuit, who may be engaged on the other side, but openly opposed to that with which you might be connected; only that the Church might be the gainer in the end, in the conditions fixed in the treaties for peace and that the end justifies the means.

You have been taught your duty as a spy, to gather all statistics, facts and information in your power from every source; to ingratiate yourself into the confidence of the family circle of Protestants and heretics of every class and character, as well as that of the merchant, the banker, the lawyer, among the schools and universities, in parliaments and legislatures, and in the judiciaries councils of state, and to "be all things to all people", for the Pope's sake, whose servants we are unto death.

You have received all your instructions heretofore as a novice, a neophyte, and have served as a coadjutor, confessor and priest, but you have not been invested with all that is necessary to command in the Army of Loyola in the service of the Pope. You must serve the proper time as the instrument and executioner as directed by your superiors; for none can command here who has not consecrated his labors with the blood of the heretic; for "without the shedding of blood no man can be saved." Therefore to fit yourself for your work, and make your own salvation sure, you will, in addition to your former oath of obedience to your Order and your allegiance to the Pope, repeat after me:

I_______________ , now in the presence of Almighty God, the blessed Virgin Mary, the blessed St. John the Baptist, the Holy Apostles, St. Peter and St. Paul, and all the saints, sacred host of Heaven, and to you, my Ghostly Father, the superior general of the Society of Jesus, founded by St. Ignatius Loyola, in the pontification of Paul the III, and continued to the present, do by the womb of the Virgin, the matrix of God, and the rod of Jesus Christ, declare and swear that His Holiness, the Pope, is Christ's vice regent and is the true and only head of the Catholic or Universal Church throughout the earth; and that by the virtue of the keys of binding and loosing given His Holiness by my Saviour, Jesus Christ, he hath power to depose heretical kings, princes, States, Commonwealths, and Governments and they may be safely destroyed. Therefore to the utmost of my power I will defend this doctrine and His Holiness's right and custom against all usurpers of the heretical or Protestant authority whatever, especially the Lutheran Church of Germany, Holland, Denmark, Sweden and Norway, and the now pretended authority and Churches of England and Scotland, and the branches of same now established in Ireland and on the continent of America and elsewhere and all adherents in regard that they may be usurped and heretical, opposing the sacred Mother Church of Rome.

I do now denounce and disown any allegiance as due to any heretical king, prince or State, named Protestant or Liberal, or obedience to any of their laws, magistrates or officers. I do further declare that the doctrine of the Churches of England and Scotland of the Calvinists, Huguenots, and others of the name of Protestants or Masons to be damnable, and they themselves to be damned who will not forsake the same.

I do further declare that I will help, assist, and advise all or any of His Holiness's agents, in any place where I should be, in Switzerland, Germany, Holland, Ireland or America, or in any other kingdom or territory I shall come to, and do my utmost to extirpate the heretical

Protestant or Masonic doctrines and to destroy all their pretended powers, legal or otherwise.

I do further promise and declare that, notwithstanding I am dispensed with to assume any religion heretical for the propagation of the Mother Church's interest; to keep secret and private all her agents counsels from time to time, as they intrust me, and not divulge, directly or indirectly, by word, writing or circumstances whatever, but to execute all that should be proposed, given in charge, or discovered unto me by you, my Ghostly Father, or any of this sacred order.

I do further promise and declare that I will have no opinion or will of my own or any mental reservation whatever, even as a corpse or cadaver (perinde ac cadaver), but will unhesitatingly obey each and every command that I may receive from my superiors in the militia of the Pope and of Jesus Christ. That I will go to any part of the world whithersoever I may be sent, to the frozen regions north, jungles of India, to the centers of civilization of Europe, or to the wild haunts of the barbarous savages of America without murmuring or repining, and will be submissive in all things whatsoever is communicated to me.

I do further promise and declare that I will, when opportunity presents, make and wage relentless war, secretly and openly, against all heretics, Protestants and Masons, as I am directed to do, to extirpate them from the face of the whole earth; and that I will spare neither age, sex or condition, and that will hang, burn, waste, boil, flay, strangle, and bury alive these infamous heretics; rip up the stomachs and wombs of their women, and crush their infant's heads against the walls in order to annihilate their execrable race. That when the same cannot be done openly I will secretly use the poisonous cup, the strangulation cord, the steel of the poniard, or the leaden bullet, regardless of the honor, rank, dignity or authority of the persons, whatever may be their condition in life, either public or private, as I at any time may be directed so to do by any agents of the Pope or Superior of the Brotherhood of the Holy Father of the Society of Jesus.

In confirmation of which I hereby dedicate my life, soul, and all corporal powers, and with the dagger which I now receive I will subscribe my name written in my blood in testimony thereof; and should I prove false or weaken in my determination may my brethren and fellow soldiers of the militia of the Pope cut off my hands and feet and my throat from ear to ear, my belly opened and sulphur burned therein with all the punishment that can be inflicted upon me on earth and my soul shall be tortured by demons in eternal hell forever.

That I will in voting always vote for a Knight of Columbus in preference to a Protestant, especially a Mason, and that I will leave my party so to do; that if two Catholics are on the ticket I will satisfy myself which is the better supporter of Mother Church and vote accordingly. That I will not deal with or employ a Protestant if in my power to deal with or employ a Catholic. That I will place Catholic girls in Protestant families that a weekly report may be made of the inner movements of the heretics. That I will provide myself with arms and ammunition that I may be in readiness when the word is passed, or I am commanded to defend the church either as an individual or with the militia of the Pope. All of which I,_______________, do swear by the blessed Trinity and blessed sacrament which I am now to receive to perform and on part to keep this my oath. In testimony hereof, I take this most holy and blessed sacrament of the Eucharist and witness the same further with my name written with the point of this dagger dipped in my own blood and seal in the face of this holy sacrament.

The Superior then speaks:

You will now rise to your feet and I will instruct you in the Catechism necessary to make yourself known to any member of the Society of Jesus belonging to this rank.

In the first place, you, as a Brother Jesuit, will with another make the ordinary sign of the cross as any Roman Catholic would; then one crosses his wrist, the palms of his hands open, the other crosses his feet, one above the other; the first points with his forefinger of his left hand to the center of the palm of his right, the other with the forefinger of his right, points to the center of the palm of his left; the first then with his right hand makes a circle around his head, touching it; the other, then, with the forefinger of his left hand touches the left side of his body just below his heart; then the first with his right hand draws it across the throat of the other, and the latter then with his right hand makes the motion of cutting with a dagger down the stomach and abdomen of the first. The first then says IUSTUM; the other answers NECAR; the first then says REGES and the other answers IMPIOS.

The first will then present a small piece of paper folded in a peculiar manner, four times, which the other will cut longitudinally and on opening the name JESU will be found written upon the head and arms of a cross three times. You will then give and receive with him the following questions and answers:

Q: From where do you come?

A: From the bends of the Jordan, from Calvary, from the Holy Sephulcure, and lastly from Rome.

Q: Whom do you serve?

A: The Holy Father at Rome, the Pope, and the Roman Catholic Church Universal throughout the world.

Q: Who commands you?

A: The successor of St. Ignatius of Loyola, the founder of the Society of Jesus or the Soldiers of Jesus Christ.

Q: Who received you?

A: A venerable man with white hair.

Q: How?

A: With a naked dagger, I kneeling on a cross beneath the banners of the Pope and of our sacred Order.

Q: Did you take an oath?

A: I did, to destroy heretics and their governments and rulers, to spare neither age, sex or condition. To be as a corpse without any opinion or will of my own, but to implicitly obey my superiors in all things without hesitation or murmuring.

Q: Will you do that?

A: I will.

Q: **How do you travel?**

A: In the bark of Peter the fisherman.

Q: **Whither do you travel?**

A: To the four quarters of the globe.

Q: **For what purpose?**

A: To obey the orders of my General and Superiors and execute the will of the Pope and faithfully fulfill the conditions of my oath.

Superior- Go then into all the world and take possession of all the lands in the name of the Pope. He who will not accept him as the Vicar of Jesus Christ and his Vice-regent on earth, let him be accursed and exterminated. (9)

THE PROPAGATION SOCIETY. MORE FREE THAN WELCOME

In the book, '***The History of Protestantism***' by James A. Wylie, published by Cassell & Company Ltd. in the mid eighteen hundreds, Mr. Wylie gives a graphic guided tour description of the methods used by the Jesuits to coerce 'heretics' into re-examining their spiritual stance, all in the name of a loving God who tenderly healed the lame, cured the sick, made the blind see and wept for the dead.

This was the preferred method used by the Office of the Inquisition, now called the 'Holy Office' that until recently was headed by the current Nazi indoctrinated Pope Benedict XVI. It is rather interesting that the Church prides itself in the fact that it 'never changes', however modern society has

Coveting the "Promised Land" [United States] – T. Nast

placed certain practices in check much to the chagrin of the Church. Various governments, however, still use similar, albeit altered techniques to interrogate those held in their custody, *often with the presence of the clergy.*

Writes Wylie,

"Turn we now to the town of Nuremberg, in Bavaria. The zeal with which Duke Albert, the sovereign of Bavaria, entered into the restoration of Roman Catholicism, we have already narrated. To further the movement, he provided every one of the chief towns of his dominions with a Holy Office, and the Inquisition of Nuremberg still remains an anomalous and horrible monument in the midst of a city where the memorials of an exquisite art, and the creations of an unrivalled genius, meet one at every step. We shall describe the Chamber of Torture.

The house, so called, immediately adjoins the Imperial Castle, from which its lofty site looks down on the city, whose Gothic towers, sculptured fronts, and curiously ornamented gables are seen covering both banks of the Pegnitz, which rolls below. The house may have been the guard-room of the castle. It derives its name, The Torture-Chamber, not from the fact that the torture was here inflicted, but because into this one chamber has been collected a complete set of the instruments of torture gleaned from the various Inquisitions that formerly existed in Bavaria. A glance suffices to show the whole dreadful apparatus by which the adherents of Rome sought to maintain her dogmas. Placed next to the door, and greeting the sight as one enters, is a collection of hideous masks. These represent creatures monstrous of shape, and malignant and fiendish of nature. It is in beholding them that we begin to perceive how subtle was the genius that devised this system of coercion, and that it took the mind as well as the body of the victim into account. In gazing on them, one feels as if he had suddenly come into polluting and debasing society, and had sunk to the same moral level with the creatures here figured before him. He suffers a conscious abatement of dignity and fortitude. The persecutor had calculated, doubtless, that the effect produced upon the mind of his victim by these dreadful apparitions, would be that he would become morally relaxed, and less able to sustain his cause. Unless of strong mind, indeed, the unfortunate prisoner, on entering such a place, and seeing himself encompassed with such unearthly and hideous shapes, must have felt as if he were the vile heretic which the persecutor styled him, and as if already the infernal den had opened its portals, and sent forth its venomous swarms to bid him welcome. Yourself accursed, with accursed beings you are henceforth to dwell. Such was the silent language of these abhorred images.

We pass on into the chamber, where more dreadful sights meet our gaze. It is hung round and round with instruments of torture, so numerous that it would take a long while to even name them, and so diverse that it would take an even longer time to describe them. We must take them in groups, for it were hopeless to think of going over them one by one, and particularizing the mode in which each operated, and the ingenuity and art with which all of them have been adapted to their horrible end. There were instruments for compressing the fingers till the bones should be squeezed to splinters. There were instruments for probing below the fingernails till an exquisite pain, like a burning fire, would run along the nerves. There were instruments for tearing out the tongue, for scooping out the eyes, for grubbing up the ears. There were bunches of iron cords, with a spiked circle at the end of every whip, for tearing the flesh from the back till bone and sinew were laid bare. There were iron cases for the legs, which were tightened upon the limb placed in them by means of a screw, till flesh and bone were reduced to a jelly. There were cradles set full of sharp spikes, in which victims were laid and rolled from side to side, the wretched occupant being pierced at each movement of the machine with innumerable sharp points. There were iron ladles with long handles, for holding molten lead or boiling pitch, to be poured down the throat of the victim, and convert his body into a burning cauldron. There were frames with holes to admit the hands and feet, so contrived that the person put into them had his body bent into unnatural and painful positions, and the agony grew greater and greater by moments, and yet the man did not die. There were chestfuls of small but most ingeniously constructed instruments for pinching, probing or tearing the more sensitive parts of the body, and continuing the pain up to the very verge where reason or life gives way. On the floor and walls of the apartment were other larger instruments for the same fearful end – lacerating, mangling, and agonizing living men; but these we shall meet in other dungeons we are yet to visit.

The first impression on entering the chamber was one of bewildering horror; a confused procession of mangled, mutilated, agonizing men, speechless in their great woe, the flesh peeled off from their livid sinews, the sockets where eyes had been, hollow and empty, seemed to pass before one. The most dreadful scenes, which the great genius of Dante had imagined, appeared tame in comparison with the spectral groups, which this chamber summoned up. The first impulse was to escape, lest images of pain, memories of tormented men, who were made to die a hundred deaths in one, should take hold of one's mind, never again to be effaced from it.

The things we have been surveying are not the mere models of the instruments made use of in the Holy Office; they are the veritable instruments themselves. We see before us the actual implements by which hundreds of thousands of men and women, many of them confessors of the Lord Jesus, were torn and mangled and slain. These terrible realities the men of the sixteenth century had to face and endure, or renounce the hope of eternal life.

We leave the Torture Chamber to visit the Inquisition proper. We go eastward, about half a mile, keeping close to the northern wall of the city, till we come to an old tower, styled in the common parlance of Nuremberg the Max Tower. We pull the bell, the iron handle and chain of which are seen suspended beside the doorpost. The cicerone appears, carrying a bunch of keys, a lantern and a half dozen candles. The lantern is to show us our way and the candles are for the purpose of being lighted and stuck up at the turnings in the dark underground passages which we are about to traverse. Should mischance befall our lantern, these tapers, like beacon lights in a narrow creek, will pilot us back safely into the day. The cicerone, selecting the largest from the bunch of keys, inserts it into the lock of the massy portal before which we stand, bolt after bolt is turned, and the door, with hoarse heavy groan as it turns on its hinge, opens slowly to us. We begin to descend. We go down one flight of steps; we go down a second flight; we descend yet a third. And now we pause a moment. The darkness is intense, for here never came the faintest glimmer of day; but a gleam thrown forward from the lantern showed us that we have arrived at the entrance of a horizontal, narrow passage. We could see, by the flickering of the light upon its sides and roof, that the corridor we were traversing was hewn out of the rock. We had gone only a few paces when we were brought up before a massy door. As far as the dim light served us, we could see the door, old, powdery with dust, and partly worm-eaten.

Passing in, the corridor continued, and we went forward another three paces or so, when we found ourselves before a second door. We opened it and shut it behind us as we did the first. And we began to thread our way: a third door stopped us. We opened and closed it in like manner. Every step was carrying us deeper into the heart of the rock, and multiplying the barriers between us and the upper world. We were shut in with the thick darkness and the awful silence. We began to realize what must have been the feelings of some unhappy disciple of the Gospel, surprised by the familiars of the Holy Office, led through the midnight streets of Nuremberg, conducted to Max Tower, led down flight after flight of stairs, and along this horizontal shaft in the rock, and at every few paces a massy door, with its locks and bolts, closing behind him. He must have felt how utterly he was beyond the reach of human pity and human aid. No cry, however piercing, could reach the ear of man through these roofs of rock. He was entirely in the power of those who had brought him thither.

At last we come to a side door in the narrow passage. We halted, applied the key, and the door, with its ancient mould, creaking harshly as if moving on a hinge long disused, opened to let us in. We found ourselves in a rather roomy chamber, it might be about twelve feet square. This was the Chamber of Question. Along one side of the apartment ran a low platform. There sat of old the inquisitors, three in number – the first a divine, the second a casuist, the third a civilian. The only occupant of that platform was a crucifix, or image of the Saviour still remaining on a cross. The six candles which usually burned before the "holy fathers" were, of course, extinguished, but our lantern supplied their place, and showed us the grim furnishings of the apartment. In the middle was the horizontal rack or bed of torture, on which the victim was stretched till bone started from bone, and his dislocated frame became the seat of agony, which was suspended only when it had reached a pitch that threatened death.

Leaning against the wall of the chamber was the upright rack, which is simpler, but as an instrument of torture was not less effectual than the horizontal one. There was the iron chain, which wound around a pulley, and hauled up the victim to the vaulted roof; and there were two great stone weights which, tied to his feet, and the iron cord let go, brought him down with a jerk, which dislocated his limbs, while the spikey rollers, which he grazed in his descent, cut into and excoriated his back, leaving his body a bloody dislocated mass.

Here, too, was the cradle of which we have made mention above, amply garnished within with cruel knobs, on which the sufferer, tied hand and foot, was thrown at every movement of the machine, to be bruised all over, and brought forth discoloured, swollen, bleeding, but still living. All round, ready to hand, were hung the minor instruments of torture. There were screws and thumbkins for the fingers and toes, spiked collars for the neck, iron boots for the legs, gags for the mouth, cloths to cover the face, and permit the slow percolation of water, drop by drop, down the throat of the person undergoing this form of torture. There were rollers set round with spikes, for bruising the arms and back; there were iron scourges, pincers, and tongs for tearing out the tongue, slitting the nose and ears and otherwise disfiguring and mangling the body till it was horrible and horrifying to look upon. There were cages, which were clamped around the head, into which a rat was inserted and chased by a red-hot poker until the terrified rodent had burrowed a hole through the skull and into the brain. There were other things of which an expert only could tell the name and use.

We shall suppose that all this has been gone through; that the confessor has been stretched on the bed of torture; has been gashed, broken, mangled, and yet, by power given him from above, has not denied his Saviour: he has been "tortured, not accepting deliverance." What further punishment has the Holy Office in reserve for those from whom its torments have failed to extrude and extort a recantation? These dreadful dungeons furnish us with the answers.

We return to the narrow passage, and go forward a little way. Every few paces there comes a door, originally strong and massy, and garnished with great iron knobs, but now old and moldy, and creaking when opened with a noise painfully loud in the deep stillness. The windings are numerous, but at every turning of the passage a lighted candle is placed, lest the way should be missed, and the road back to the living world should be lost forever. A few steps are taken downwards, very cautiously, for a lantern can barely show the ground. Here there is a vaulted chamber, entirely dug out of the living rock, except the roof, which is made of hewn stone. It contains an iron image of the Virgin; and on the opposite wall, suspended by an iron hook, is a lamp, which when lighted, shows the goodly proportions of 'Our Lady." On the instant of touching a spring the image flings open its arms, which resemble the doors of a cupboard, and which are seen to be stuck full on the inside with poniards, a cache about a foot in length. Some of these knives are so placed as to enter the eyes of those whom the image enfolded in its embrace, others are set so as to penetrate the ears, brain and breast. Still others to gore the abdomen.

The victim is bidden to stand right in front of the image. The spring would be touched by the executioner, the Virgin would fling open her arms, and the wretched victim would straightaway be forced within them. Another spring was then touched – the Virgin closed upon her victim; a strong wooden beam, fastened to one end of the wall by a moveable joint, the other placed against the doors of the iron image, was worked by a screw, and as the beam was pushed out, the spikey arms of the Virgin slowly and irresistibly closed around the man, cruelly goring him.

When the dreadful business was ended, it needed not that the executioner should put himself to the trouble of making the Virgin unclasp the mangled carcass of her victim; provision had been made for its quick and secret disposal. At the touching of a third spring, the floor of the image would slide aside, and the body of the victim drop down the mouth of a perpendicular shaft in the rock. We look down this pit, and can see, at great depth, the glimmer of water. A canal had been made to flow beneath the vault where stood the iron Virgin, and when she had done her murderous work, she let them fall, with quick descent and sudden plunge, into the canal underneath, where they were floated to the Pegnitz, and from there to the Rhine, and then off to the ocean to sleep there beside the dust of Huss and Jerome."

** ** ** ** ** ** **

In the political structure of the Vatican, the Papal Secretary of State was the agent for the Jesuit General, otherwise known as the "Black Pope", so named because of the black robes of the Order and their work in the darkness of shadows, having the ear and confidence of the political leaders in privacy. He advises the "White Pope", the one elected by conclave, on the details of how the Church should act in regard to political involvement in the affairs of the nations to the furtherance of the interests of the Church. In the eyes of the Catholic Church the concept of separation of Church and State is a non-starter. The two must be united in purpose and be in a symbiotic relationship. It is a direct copy of the Babylonian system that was established by Nimrod, Semaramis and Cush, down to the finest detail. The State becomes the hammer of the Pope. If this relationship were to go awry, the State must be made to submit to the Church using any and all means possible, going so far as to use the military and machinery of the State, or another State which is suitably pliable, to coercively press the goals of the Church. For this reason the United States Constitution is regarded as anathema by the Church. This stance has never been rescinded. (10)

The Austrian Prince, Von Metternich, was well acquainted with this relationship and upon the signing of the Treaty of Verona immediately pushed for the destruction of the movement for liberty and freedom in Spain, which had been inspired by the successful example in the United States, using the army of France to accomplish it. Simultaneously, Metternich launched the St. Leopold foundation for the Furtherance of Catholic missions in America, the goal of which was to, "Make America Catholic", by flooding the urban centers with Catholic emigration so as to overwhelm the vote and thereby alter the civil and criminal laws, make impotent the Constitution and Bill of Rights and change foreign policy in order to conform to the dictates of the Church. (11)

Metternich

The Reverend Charles Chiniquy, a French Canadian priest, honoured by the governments of Quebec and Canada, and honoured by the Pope, was instructed to move from Kamouraska, Quebec to Illinois and establish a Catholic colony along the rural and open areas of the Mississippi Valley and subsequently brought tens of thousands of Catholic French Canadians, Belgians and French emigrants to settle the land. He eventually left the Roman Church and became a close friend of Abraham Lincoln. He records in his book, "*50 Years in the Church of Rome*", a meeting which took place in Buffalo, N.Y. in 1852, which outlines the thinking of the Bishops and Jesuits in America at that time. I shall let him recount the statement,

> "We are also determined to take possession of the United States; but we must proceed with the utmost secrecy and wisdom. What does a skillful general do when he wants to conquer a country? Does he scatter his soldiers over the farmlands, and spend their energy in plowing the fields? No! He keeps them close to his flanks and marching toward the strongholds: the rich and powerful cities. The farming countries then submit and become the price of this victory without moving a finger to subdue them.
>
> "So it is with us. Silently and patiently, we must mass our Roman Catholics in the great cities of the United States, remembering that the vote of a poor journeyman, though he be covered in rags, has as much weight in the scale of power as the millionaire Astor, and that if we have two votes against his one, he will become as powerless as an oyster. Let us then multiply our votes; let us

call our poor but faithful from every corner of the world, and gather them into the very hearts of the cities of Washington, New York, Boston, Chicago, Buffalo, Troy Albany, Cincinnati.

"Under the shadows of those great cities, the Americans consider themselves a giant unconquerable race. Let no one awake those sleeping lions today. Let us pray God that they continue to sleep a few years longer, waking only to find their votes outnumbered, as we will turn them forever, out of every position of honor, power and profit! When not a single judge or policeman will be elected if he be not a devoted Catholic! What will those so-called giants think when not a single senator or member of Congress will be chosen, unless he has submitted to our holy father the Pope!

"We will not only elect the president, but fill and command the armies, man the navies and hold the keys of the public treasury. It will then be time for our faithful people to give up their grog shops, in order to become the judges and governors of the land.

"Then, Yes! Then, we will rule the United States, and lay them at the feet of the Vicar of Jesus Christ, that he may put an end to their godless system of education, and impious laws of liberty of conscience [could deliberate sabotage against any of these aforementioned areas, i.e. political office, judiciary, armed forces, public education and the economy, be in the offing in the near future? Or are we already witnessing it?], which are an insult to God and man!" (12)

Such was the implacable hatred towards the freedom enjoyed and fostered by the principles which caused the founders of the American colonies to flee religious oppression and persecution to establish a nation that was built on solid Biblical moral foundations codified into law and become the greatest country on earth and the inspiration for all freedom loving peoples.

The late ex-Jesuit, Dr. Alberto Rivera, who was murdered for betraying his Jesuit Oath by detailing the extent of political influence in the United States, stated as far back as the 1960's, that a signal, which would be recognized by the Jesuit Order worldwide, would indicate that the world's major Christian denominations and the Presidential office had been finally converted to Romanist influence. That signal was when a President took the Oath of Office while facing an obelisk, a phallic symbol of combined religious and political power. This was finally fulfilled when for the first time in U.S. history, the swearing in ceremonies were moved to the west front of the Capitol and President Ronald Reagan took that oath while facing the Washington Monument.

In 1984, after he was shot, President Reagan formally recognized the Sovereign State of Vatican City with Knight of Malta William Wilson being named the first legal ambassador to the Vatican since America severed all relations in 1867 as a result of the Jesuit hand in the assassination of Lincoln. The key Administration players were all devout Roman Catholics – C.I.A. chief William Casey [Knight of Malta], Allen, Clark, Haig [Knight of Malta], Walters and William Wilson, Reagan's first ambassador to the Vatican. They regarded the U.S. – Vatican relationship as a holy alliance.

Within a few years the Soviet Union ceased to exist. This was the result of the tag team effort of Pope John Paul II and Washington working in concert to force the fulfillment of one aspect of the Fatima prophecies. The global policy of the Vatican and the foreign and domestic policy of the United States had finally been unified. (13)

In *Imperialism and papal politics*, October *18, 1978:*"Pope John Paul II, co-operating with America's Zbigniew Brzezinski, used Opus Dei to help bring down the Communist government of Poland. Opus Dei has ties to the European aristocracy, and promotes privatization; it uses the tactic, pioneered by Jews from the time of the Marranos, of operating covertly." In his book, *"The Vatican Moscow Washington Alliance"*, published by *Chick publications, Chino Ca. 1986 pp. 353,354* Avro Manhattan had this to say,

"The appointment of the pope's nuncio (ambassador) to Washington could be compared to the installation of a foreign general, obeying orders of the head of an aggressive state. Upon his goodwill or hostility depends the tranquility, cooperation and general good behavior of at least one third of the American population. Thus a word from the nuncio can alter the disposition, attitude and even political opinion of millions of Catholics. The nuncio will also become the arbitrator between the two major political parties of America. Both Republican and Democratic parties from now on must be extremely attentive to the reaction of the papal nuncio. Political wooing will be done at the papal nunciature in Washington, the political centre of the Catholic Church in the U.S. Politically; she is looming ever larger at the White House. She is a power in the Senate, a force at the Pentagon, an invisible secret agent at the F.B.I., and the most subtly intangible prime mover of the U.S. wheel-within-a-wheel: the Central Intelligence Agency."

Knight of Columbus, Jim Towey – Director of White House Office of Faith Based Initiatives 2002-2006

From the *U.S. News and World Report*, March 19, 1984 pp. 60-61

An Inside Look At Those Elite Religious Groups

"Their ranks are small, but a handful of key societies count as members some of the most influential Americans.

While the Rev. Jerry Falwell's Moral Majority draws most of the public attention, other religious groups are quietly trying to influence the nation's elite.

Their names are unfamiliar to most Americans – the Knights of Malta, Opus Dei, Moral Re-Armament, the Christian Reconstructionists. Yet their principles, which included strict adherence to Christian values, are the guiding force in the lives of some of the most powerful people in the U.S.

5

The Curse of Rome.

"By the authority of God Almighty, the Father and the Son and the Holy Ghost, and the undefiled Virgin Mary, Mother of God, and all the celestial virtues, angels, archangels, thrones, dominions, powers, cherubim and seraphim, and of all the holy patriarchs, prophets and of all the apostles, evangelists, of the holy innocents who in sight of the holy lamb are found worthy to sing the new songs of the holy martyrs and holy confessors, and of the holy virgins, and of the holy saints, together with the holy elect of God—may he, Guiseppo Garibaldi and his followers, be damned!

We excommunicate them, we anathematize them, and from the threshold of the holy church of God Almighty we sequester them that they may be tormented, despised and be delivered over with Dathan and Abiram, and with those who say unto the Lord, "Depart from us, for we desire none of thy ways," as a fire is quenched with water, so let the light of them be put out for evermore, unless they shall repent and make satisfaction! Amen!

May the Father, who created man, curse them!

May the Son, who suffered for us, curse them!

May the Holy Ghost, who suffered for us in baptism, curse them!

May the holy cross which Christ, for our salvation, triumphing over his enemies, curse them!

May the holy and eternal Virgin Mary, mother of God, curse them!

May all the angels, principalities and powers, and all heavenly armies, curse them!

May the praiseworthy multitude of patriarchs and prophets, curse them!

May St. John the Precursor, and St. John the Baptist, and St. Peter, and St. Paul, and St. Andrew, and all other of Christ's apostles together, curse them! And may the rest of the disciples, and our evangelists, who, by their preaching, converted the universe, and the holy and wonderful company of martyrs and confessors, who by their holy works are found pleasing to God Almighty, may the holy choir of holy virgins, who for the honor of Christ have despised things of the world, damn them!

May all the saints from the beginning of the world to everlasting ages, who are found to be beloved of God, damn them!

May they be damned wherever they be, whether in the house or in the stable, the garden or the field, or the highway, or in the woods, or in the water, or in the church; may they be cursed in living and dying.

May they be cursed in eating or drinking, in being hungry, in being thirsty, in walking, in resting, in fasting, in sleeping, in slumbering, in sitting, and in blood-letting!

May they be cursed in all the faculties of their bodies!

May they be cursed inwardly and outwardly; may they be cursed in their brains and their vortex, in their temples, in their eyebrows, in their cheeks, in their jawbones, in their nostrils, in their teeth and grinders, in their lips, in their throat, in their shoulders, in their arms and their fingers! May they be cursed in their breast, in their heart and appurtenances, damned to the very stomach!

May they be cursed in their reins and their groins, in their thighs, in their genitals, and in their hips, and in their knees; their legs and feet, and their toe-nails!

May they be cursed in all their joints and articulations of their members; from the crown of their heads to the sole of their feet may there be no soundness!

May the Son of the Living God with all the glory of His Majesty, curse them! And may heaven with all the powers that move therein, rise up against them and curse and damn them, unless they repent and make satisfaction.

Amen! So be it! Be it so! Amen!

Oh, gentle, loving, Christ-like, humanizing Rome!

CONTEMPORARY PRACTICE OF THE UNITED STATES RELATING TO INTERNATIONAL LAW

MARIAN NASH LEICH*

The material in this section is arranged according to the system employed in the annual *Digest of United States Practice in International Law*, published by the Department of State.

INTERNATIONAL STATUS OF STATES

(U.S. *Digest*, Ch. 2, §1)

The Vatican (Holy See)

On January 10, 1984, the Department of State announced that the United States and the Holy See, in the desire to promote further their existing friendly relations, had decided by common agreement to establish diplomatic relations between themselves at the level of an embassy on the part of the United States and of a nunciature on the part of the Holy See.[1] On the same day, President Reagan announced his intention to nominate William A. Wilson, Personal Representative of the President to the Holy See, to be Ambassador Extraordinary and Plenipotentiary of the United States of America to the Holy See.[2]

In response to questioning at the news briefing, John Hughes, Assistant Secretary of State for Public Affairs and Department Spokesman, stated that the United States had for a long time recognized the Holy See as having an international personality distinct from the Roman Catholic Church and had had a Presidential Personal Representative to the Holy See since 1939, when President Roosevelt had appointed Myron Taylor to that office. Mr. Hughes pointed out that upgrading the U.S. representation at the Holy See, an international focal point of diplomatic contact, would place the relationship on a level with parallel U.S. relationships with other entities, and would also conform with the relationship maintained by 107 other countries with the Holy See.[3] Finally, he noted the recent congressional repeal of the 1867 statute prohibiting the use of federal funds for a diplomatic mission to the Vatican,[4] and suggested that Congress (i.e., the Senate) would also have another opportunity to express any views on the matter, since the nomination as ambassador would require its approval.[5]

* Office of the Legal Adviser, Department of State.

[1] Dept. of State Daily News Briefing, DPC 6, Jan. 10, 1984, at 1.

[2] 20 WEEKLY COMP. PRES. DOC. 22 (Jan. 16, 1984).

[3] In addition, a Permanent Observer from the Holy See was accredited to the United Nations in 1964. *See* UN Press Section Note to Correspondents, No. 3782, Nov. 24, 1972. On July 1, 1978, the General Assembly of the Organization of American States accorded to the Holy See "by virtue of its specific nature on the international scene the status of Permanent Observer to the Organization of American States, on an exceptional basis." OAS Doc. AG/RES.334 (VIII-0/78).

[4] Sec. 134 of the Department of State Authorization Act, Fiscal Years 1984 and 1985, Pub. L. No. 98-164, approved Nov. 22, 1983, 97 Stat. 1017.

[5] Daily News Briefing, *supra* note 1.

427

Despite coming from different faiths, members share a common belief that a small number of dedicated people can indeed change the world. Still, these groups aren't without their detractors.

Outsiders often question the recruiting methods and veil of secrecy surrounding some of these organizations. Critics contend, too, that these societies are as much bastions of conservative politics as they are religious in nature. Oldest of these groups is the Knights of Malta, a Roman Catholic organization that dates back to the time of the Crusades when members fought Muslims in the Holy Land.

With headquarters in Rome, the group is recognized by some 40 countries as the world's only landless sovereign nation. In that role the Knights mint coins, print stamps and issue passports to their diplomats.

American network.

The U.S. membership of about 1000 – 70% men – accounts for one tenth of the worldwide total. Nearly all are prominent in business, government or professional life and include such well-known figures as Chrysler Chairman Lee Iacocca and Central Intelligence Agency Director William Casey. At least two U.S. senators are also members: Republicans Jerimiah Denton of Alabama and Pete Domenici of New Mexico. Other members active in conservative politics include former Secretary of State Alexander Haig, former Treasury Secretary William Simon and columnist William F. Buckley.

The president of the Knights' American branch is J. Peter Grace, chairman of the W.R. Grace Company, which provides a national focus for the organization by including seven other Knights on its board.

The main purpose of the Knights is to honor distinguished Catholics and raise money for charity, especially hospitals. But the close personal ties among members contribute to what some observers call a potent old-boy network of influential decision makers dedicated to thwarting Communism.

The Annual induction ceremony for new members at St. Patrick's Cathedral in New York [overseen by Cardinal Archbishop Edward Egan, the most powerful Catholic in America and some say Puppet-master of Presidents] is the only function of the U.S. chapter open to the non-members. Because many Knights and recipients of the Order's honors have worked in or around the C.I.A., critics sometimes suggest a link between the two."

According to the world renowned Welsh author Gordon Thomas, with whom this writer has been in contact, Pope John Paul II had stated several times since 1983 that a war between Christendom and Islam has been in the planning for many years and is to be launched under the disguise of "co-operation" or "mutual understanding" between the two religions. The current mass forced migration of mostly young Islamic men of fighting age is a part of this plan. These are to be the swordsmen of the Jesuits against all of her enemies.

Pope John Paul II and Imam

The following excerpt from a Saudi Television interview on June 10, 2005 with Egyptian historian Abd Al-Aziz titled "*The Vatican's Mission of Destroying Islam delegated to the U.S.*" relates the fact that many are aware of this plan:

> **Abd Al-Aziz**: "The decision to impose one religion over the entire world was made in the Second Vatican Council in 1965."
>
> **Host**: "Huh?"
>
> **Abd Al-Aziz**: "Yes, it was a long time ago."
>
> **Host**: "They decided to Christianize the world?"
>
> **Abd Al-Aziz**: Yes. The decisions of the 1965 Vatican Council included, first of all, absolving the Jews of the blood of Christ. This decision is well known and was the basis for the recognition of the occupying Zionist entity – Israel. The second decision was to eradicate the left in the eighties. I believe we've all witnessed this. The third decision was to eradicate Islam, so that the world would be Christianized by the Third Millennium."
>
> **Host**: Why is America hostile to Islam, although we never had and never will have the same conflict with them we had with Europe?'

> **Abd Al-Aziz**: "Well, do you remember what we just said about the Second Vatican Council in 1965 and about Christianizing the world? It was agreed upon and prearranged. John Paul II prepared a five-year plan, on the eve of the millennium, to Christianize the world. His address in 1995 was based on the assumption that by the year 2000, the entire world would be Christianized. Since the plan was not accomplished, the World Council of Churches assigned this mission to the U.S. in January, 2001, since the U.S. is the world's unrivalled military power. They named the decade between 2001-2010 "The age of eradicating evil" – "evil" referring to Islam and Muslims." www.memritv.org/search.asp?ACT=S9&P1=708

The fact that Pope John Paul II appeared to have openly condemned the war in Iraq was duplicitous to say the least. This was done to appease the Islamic world [the late Yassar Arafat's wife is a devout Catholic] by appearing to maintain a neutral stance while at the same time holding consultations with the Bush administration through intermediaries such as Cardinal Egan of New York. Cardinal Egan was the most powerful Catholic cleric in the United States and controlled the voting power of millions as well as being the Vicar of the U.S Armed Forces, the F.B.I, C.I.A. and D.H.S. In fact, this station is reserved for anyone who holds the office of Bishop of New York.

The 'mutual understanding' mentioned by Mr. Thomas boils down to this one point, that the Vatican is planning on using the Islamic world as its sword to exact revenge against all who oppose her. Islamic clerics have made no secret of the fact that they believe they are called to kill all those they consider 'infidels'. They also have a deep hatred of the government of the United States and the spirit that set it up. This mirrors the position of Rome.

According to several authorities, such as NSA ex-pat Ed Snowdon and Dr. J. Willie, the Jesuit run CIA, MI6 and Mossad created the radical Islamic entities al

Qaeda and its new incarnation ISIS/ISIL/IS and related offshoots in order to 1/ keep the herion opium routes open from Afghanistan, through Turkey and into Europe 2/ maintain the strength of the petro-dollar 3/ interfere with the competing Russian pipelines running from Iran to the ports at Syria and 4/ create religious hatred and keep it on full boil in order to act as cover for controlling the oil by political destabilisation. Jihad John of beheading fame is a Mossad operative. All of the NSA raw data ends up in Tel Aviv, digested and transmitted to the Jesuit General.

As well, Europe does not have a very deep history of representative government, and will choose an autocrat when push comes to shove in a crisis and when the U.S. loses global credibility and influence European Imperialists and autocrats, anxious to rebuild another Holy Roman Empire from the ashes of a crashed Euro currency, will rush to fill the void. Asia, helped along with Jesuit political and financial interference, will form an alliance and follow suit. Thus the Vatican can sit back and play innocent while agitating and directing both sides against the middle, having their 'enemies' war against each other and come out smelling like a rose. They can kill in the background and denounce the murders in the foreground.

Paul Weyrich, founder of the Moral Majority, had this to say in the *Christian Voice – Religious Roundtable*,

> "If we didn't know the Pope agrees with us, we Catholics in the New Right would have serious conscience problems. I would never work counter to the hurch's official position."

Alleged Serial rapist and pedophile Bill and 4th degree witch and lesbian Hillary Clinton enthralled with a Papal presence after bombing Orthodox Serbs on behalf of the Vatican, Germany and Catholic Croatia. As of 2014 German tanks still patrol the Balkans.

The radical religious in the United States, the so-called New Right, religious right, religious conservatives, and the Moral Majority, according to Paul Weyrich, wouldl be guided by the policy established in the Vatican.

To ensure that the Moral Majority did not act in ways the pope would not approve, the opinion of Weyrich and other Catholics in the organization must bear considerable weight in decision-making by the Moral Majority.

The Vatican controls Weyrich and his colleagues and thus controls the Moral Majority. It is a fact that the American Catholic bishops described the Moral

Majority in their Pastoral Plan of Action of 1975, four years before Jerry Falwell was asked by Catholics to head it.

This drew the fundamentalists in under the guise of religion, *but for explicitly political purposes.*

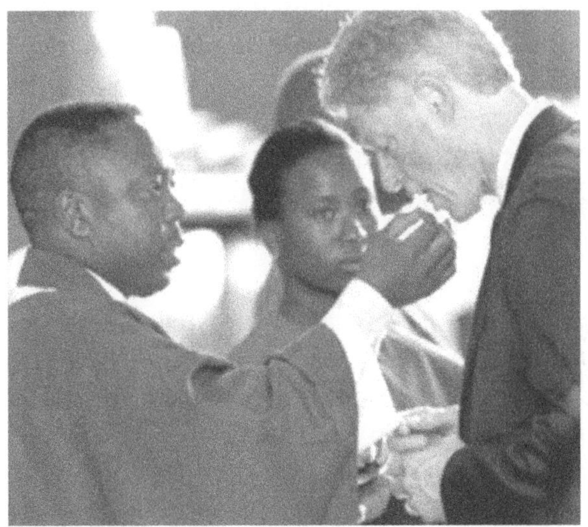

'Protestant' Bill Clinton at Catholic Mass

In the book, "*The Suppressed Truth About the Assassination of Abraham Lincoln*," which was published in 1923 by Burke McCarty, he had this to say regarding the Jesuit Oath as it pertains to instigating war between nations,

> "The next step in the Vatican's scheme is to make war between the United States and Japan after the latter country has been placed under the full dominance of the Jesuits. The priests, monks and nuns of the Roman Church have been pouring into Japan from all over the world now for many years with that purpose in view. The writer was told by a Christian Japanese minister in charge of a Protestant mission in Los Angeles in reply to the question as to why the Jesuits, who had been barred for years from Japan, had now been permitted to enter. He answered that the Roman Church had gotten into his country under the guise of Mohammedanism, (Islam), and that after it was well entrenched threw off its mask, and his country learned to its astonishment that it was to

the Roman Church and its monastic orders it had opened its doors." (15)

He then elaborates on how the Catholic politicians, under the control of the Jesuits, were engaged in anti-Japanese agitation in the United States and how the same method was being used in Japan to engender anti-American sentiment. When we understand that this was written a full twenty years before Pearl Harbor, and witnessed the mass suicides in the Marianas as a result of the intense propaganda they were subjected to over several years we cannot flippantly dismiss this information out of hand.

With the implementation of the Treaty of Verona towards the peoples of Spain the movement for democracy in that country had been effectively crushed. Considering that Spain had colonies in Latin and South America which were eyeing the situation of the mother country with apprehension and that the same fate awaited them at some point in time, this boded ill for those colonies as they also hoped to achieve some form of representative liberty. On top of that, the governments of both Spain and France were looking to regain the colonies and territories, which they had previously held in America. This was to be accomplished through massive emigration into the U.S.

Recently in the years 2000 - 2014 there has been an unprecedented influx of Mexican and Latin migrants, numbering some 15-20 million moving illegally across the border with the full blessing of Arch-bishop Cardinal Mahoney of Los Angeles. In September of 2007 the Mexican President Calderon created an uproar claiming that the authority of Mexico did not end at the border with the United States but rather extended north to include all those States where the majority of Mexican migrants have moved to. Some people have suggested that this is for the eventual purpose of creating another civil war which would allow Mexico to claim back all that she lost in the 19th Century.

Senator Robert Owen

Brig. Gen. Thomas M. Harris, a member of the military commission, which tried the co-conspirators of Lincoln's assassination, and bench mate of, "*Ben Hur*" author Gen. Lew Wallace, who served on the same commission, noted the resulting political quandary, which this represented to a system that built into its soul the concept of individual liberty with a government on a tight leash and set, well defined boundaries. He states in his book, "*Rome's Responsibility for the Assassination of Abraham Lincoln*",

"Every citizen, and every sojourner in this country, who is loyal to the Roman Catholic Church, is an enemy to our government, of necessity, for he yields his highest allegiance to the Pope of Rome, a foreign potentate, who has time and again anathematized every fundamental principle of our government. He has denounced liberty of the press, of conscience, of speech, and of worship and teaching, as pestilent and damnable heresies; destructive to order, and to the peace and welfare of society." (16)

Thomas M. Harris

Presidents Jefferson, Adams and Monroe also understood this same quandary. After the British statesman George Canning called a meeting with U.S. ambassador Rush to inform him as to the real implications of the Treaty and was met with some reluctance by the U. S. to understand the growing concern, he sent a communiqué to lay out the stark facts. In a proposed joint declaration with the United States on the Spanish Colonies in America, He stated:

> "Is it not the moment when our governments might understand each other as to the Spanish American Colo-

nies? And if we can arrive at such an understanding, would it not be more expedient for ourselves, and beneficial for all the world, that the principles of it should be clearly settled and plainly avowed?

For we ourselves have no disguise.

1/ We conceive the recovery of the Colonies by Spain to be hopeless.

2/ We conceive the recognition of them, as Independent States, to be one of time and circumstances.

3/ We are, however, by no means disposed to throw any impediment, in the way of an arrangement between them and the Mother Country by amicable negotiation.

4/ We aim not at the possession of any portion of them at any time ourselves.

5/ We could not see any portion of them transferred to any other Power, with indifference.

If these opinions and feelings are, as I firmly believe them to be, common to your government with ours, why should we hesitate mutually to confide them to each other, and to declare them to the face of the world?

If there be any European Power which cherishes other projects, which looks to a forcible enterprise for reducing the Colonies to subjugation, on behalf or in the name of Spain, or which mediates the acquisition of any part of them to themselves, by cession or by conquest; such a declaration on the part of your government and ours would be at once the most effectual and the least offensive mode of intimating our joint disapprobation of such projects.

It would at the same time put an end to all the jealousies of Spain with respect to her remaining Colonies, an agitation which it would be but humane to allay; being determined, (as we are), not to profit by encouraging it.

Do you conceive that under the power, which you have recently received, you are authorized to enter into negotiation, and to sign any Convention on this subject? Do you conceive that if you have not the competence, we can exchange ministerial notes upon it?

Nothing could be more gratifying to me than to join with you in such a work, and, I am persuaded that there has seldom, in the history of the world, occurred an opportunity when so small an effort, of two friendly governments, might produce such an unequivocal good and prevent such extensive calamities." (17)

President Monroe

Shortly after this declaration by Canning, President Monroe solicited the advice of Thomas Jefferson and John Adams. It was acknowledged by them all that the "Holy Alliance" was intent on the forcible interference between the Spanish government and South American Colonies, but more importantly, interference upon the soil of the United States in respect to the former Spanish holdings and those of others in Europe, most notably France. They were aware that England was giving the American government a chance to press their own interests to protect their own soil, and failing that, England would take the initiative by taking Cuba and the province of Texas. If this were allowed to occur, they reasoned, this would mean the forfeiture of any right of expansion. They knew that England had more than the means to carry out their intentions while the young Republic did not and if they could instead persuade the inhabitants of Texas or Cuba to enter into, or solicit a union with them an accommodation should be arranged.

The Spanish peoples would certainly not enter into a union with Britain. By joining with her in this proposed declaration, they would give her a substantial, and perhaps, inconvenient, pledge against themselves, and obtain nothing in return. They argued that they should at least keep themselves free to act as emergencies may arise, and not tie themselves to any principles, which might immediately be tied and brought to bear against themselves. To do so would make them appear to be subordinate to Britain and considering they were in negotiations with Russia over the North West areas of the Continent, and that the Russian Government was refusing to recognize any ministers from South America, this could be used to their advantage.

President John Quincy Adams

Adams made the point that this was the most suitable time in history to take their stand as a Nation against this, "Holy Alliance", and at the same time decline the overture of Great Britain. In this way it would be more candid and more dignified, to avow their principles explicitly to France and Russia than to come in as a cockboat in the wake of a British Man-O-War. So, on December 2, 1823, Monroe addressed Congress with the following:

> "... At the proposal of the Russian Imperial Government, made through the minister of the Emperor residing here, a full power and instructions have been transmitted to the minister of the United States in St. Petersburg to arrange by amicable negotiation the respective rights and interests of the two nations on the northwest coast of this continent. A similar proposal has been made by His Imperial Majesty to the government of Great Britain, which has likewise been acceded to. The Government of the United States has been desirous of this friendly proceeding of manifesting the great value which they have invariably attached to the friendship of the Emperor and their solicitude to cultivate the best understanding with his government. In the discussions to which this interest has given rise and in the arrangements by which they may terminate the occasion has been judged proper for asserting, as a principle in which the rights and interests of the United States are involved, that the American Continents, by the free and independent condition which they have assumed and maintain, are henceforth not to be considered as subjects for future colonization by any European Powers...
>
> It was stated at the commencement of the last session that a great effort was then making in Spain and Portugal to improve the condition of the people in those countries, and that it appeared to be conducted with extraordinary moderation. It need scarcely be remarked that the results have been, so far, very different from what was then anticipated. Of events in that quarter of the globe, with which we have so much intercourse and from which we derive our origin, we have always been interested and anxious spectators. The citizens of the United States cherish sentiments the most friendly in favor of the liberty and happiness of their fellow-men on that side of the Atlantic. In the wars of European powers in matters relat-

ing to themselves we have never taken part, nor does it comport with our policy to do so. It is only when our rights are invaded or seriously menaced that we resent injuries and make preparation for our defense. With the movements in this hemisphere we are of necessity more immediately connected, and by causes which must be obvious to all enlightened and impartial observers. The political system of the allied powers is essentially different in this respect from that of America. This difference proceeds from that which exists in their respective governments, and to the defense of our own, which has been achieved by the loss of so much blood and treasure, and matured by the wisdom of their most enlightened citizens, and under which we have enjoyed unexampled felicity, this whole nation is devoted.

We owe it; therefore, to candor and to amicable relations existing between the United States and those powers to declare that we should consider any attempt on their part to extend any of their system to any portion of this hemisphere as dangerous to our peace and safety. With the existing colonies or dependencies of any European power we have not interfered and shall not interfere. But with the governments who have declared their independence and maintain it, and whose dependence we have, on great consideration and on just principles, acknowledged, we could not view any interposition for the purpose of oppressing them, or controlling in any other manner their destiny, by any European power in any other light than as the manifestation of an unfriendly disposition toward the United States. In the war between those new Governments and Spain we declared our neutrality at the time of their recognition, and to this we have adhered, and shall continue to adhere, provided no change shall occur which, in the judgment of the competent authorities of this Government, shall make a corresponding change on the part of the United States indispensable to their security.

The late events in Spain and Portugal show that Europe is still unsettled. Of this important fact no stronger proof can be adduced than that the allied powers should have thought it proper, on any principle satisfactory to themselves, to have interposed by force in the internal concerns of Spain. To what extent such interposition may be carried, on the same principle, is a question in which all independent powers whose government differs from theirs are interested, even those most remote, and surely

> none of them more so than the United States. Our policy in regard to Europe, which was adopted at an early stage of the wars which have so long agitated that quarter of the globe, nevertheless remains the same, which is, never to interfere in the internal concerns of any of its powers; to consider the government de facto as the legitimate government for us; to cultivate friendly relations with it, and to preserve relations with it by a firm, frank and manly policy, meeting all instances the just claims of every power, submitting to injuries from none.
>
> But in regard to those continents circumstances are eminently and conspicuously different. It is impossible that the allied powers should extend their political system to any portion of either continent without endangering our peace and happiness; nor can anyone believe that our southern brethren, if left to themselves, would adopt it of their own accord. It is equally impossible, therefore, that we should behold such interposition in any form with indifference. If we look to the comparative strength and resources of Spain and those new governments, and their distance from each other, it must be obvious that she can never subdue them. It is still the true policy of the United States to leave the parties to themselves, in hope that other parties will pursue the same course..." (18)

This is what is commonly known as the, "Monroe Doctrine". In the winter of 2013-14, Secretary of State John Kerry proudly proclaimed that the US was putting an end to the Monroe Doctrine, thus telling European imperialists and everyone else that it is now perfectly all right to fill the power vacuum created by a receding US foreign policy.

The U.S. Government was well aware of the fact that if the political system forced upon Spain by the "allied powers" of the "Treaty of Verona" motivated by the Council of Trent was transferred to the Spanish Colonies in South America as well as Mexico, and that the population after being indoctrinated and corrupted by this forced system were then encouraged to emigrate en mass to occupy the Mississippi Valley from South to North, this would cut a wedge directly through the heart of America and effectively put an end to representative government by using the principles of democracy against it by means of overwhelming the vote. An ecclesiastical monarchy would then be established in North America. A monarchy subject to the Roman Pontiff.

The reality of this threat was confirmed by a dramatic shift in the nation's census statistics. By 1830 there were only 318,000 Roman Catholics in America, compared to a total population of 12,866,020. Just fifteen years later, over 100,000 immigrants were arriving annually. Within two years' time that figure was doubled. By 1850 the number of Catholic immigrants entering the country was up to 300,000 per year, and four years after that was pushing 500,000. On the eve of the Civil War the total number of Roman Catholics had mushroomed to 3,103,000, about ten per cent of the nation's total population. Eight years later the figure was standing at over five million. Whereas a mere 200 Catholic Churches existed in 1830, by 1860 over 2,400 Churches of Rome permeated the land of the Pilgrim's pride. (19)

During a sermon in 1850, Archbishop John Hughes of New York, the nation's leading Vatican spokesman, acknowledged that a conspiracy to subjugate free America did exist after all. An excerpt from *Shepherd of the Valley,* the official journal of the Bishop of St. Louis, declared,

> "If Roman Catholics ever gain a sufficient numerical majority in this country, religious liberty is at an end. So our enemies say, so we believe." (20)

Hughes' own paper, the *New York Freeman* announced, "No man has a right to choose his religion." (21)

John Hughes

The power of life or death hangs in the power of the state. This is the supreme power. If another power tries to claim that same supreme power on the same soil, a conflict occurs. No two supreme powers can co-exist on the same soil. Especially if the one is predisposed to annihilate the other.

After Lincoln's election in 1860, conditions moved from bad to worse with the advent of civil war. Despite declared neutrality, the Holy See was secretly aiding and abetting the Confederacy in the hope of dividing Protestant America. At the same time they were gaining control of the cities of the North.

The degree to which the Vatican could affect Lincoln's war measures was nothing short of astounding. Catholic citizens in the North aligned with their Southern brethren by voting Democratic, dodging or defending slavery and by opposing Lincoln on all fronts.

Irish federals deserted by the thousands after learning that Pope Pius IX had sent an official communiqué of support to Jefferson Davis, addressing him as *"Illustrious and Honorable President of the Confederate States of America."* (22)

In Brig. Gen. T.M. Harris' book an account is given from the Pension Dept. at Washington of the number of defections, which took place after the letter from the Pope as compared to the number of troops prior to it. It is here given:

Whole number of Troops..........................2,128,200
Natives of the United States.................... 1,627,267
Germans...189,817
Irishmen..144,221
British (other than Irish)...............................90,040
Other foreigners and missions.......................87,855

The “Dcscrtions” wcrc as follows:

Natives of the United States........................5 percent
Germans..10 percent
Irish Catholics..72 percent
British (Other than Irish).................. ....7 percent
Other foreigners...7 percent (23)

In other words: of the 144,000 Irishmen that enlisted, 104,000 deserted. Almost all of these desertions occurred after the recognition of the Confederacy by the Pope. It is also a fact that of the five percent of Native Americans rated as deserters, 45 percent of those were Catholics.

Harris went on to state that this was sufficient proof of the charge made that a good Roman Catholic could only be loyal to the Pope; and so could never be loyal to the government and its institutions. At the same time it is also true that there were some able and brave Roman Catholic officers in the Union Army, who were truly loyal to the cause; as also many in the ranks who were nominally members of the Roman Catholic Church; but these were they who had been educated in the free schools, and had thus become so imbued with the American Spirit, that they were no longer considered “good” Catholics.

When the retreating forces from Lee’s army at Gettysburg should have been eliminated on the banks of the Potomac, Lincoln’s Catholic commander, General George Meade, “conveniently” diverted one third of his army to securing New York City during the Draft Riots, perpetrated by the parishioners of Archbishop Hughes.

The papal church when expedient, follows the rule of pagan Rome to hold a conquered country in leash, and make it yield its pound of flesh, by placing over it native rulers, which is the easy way to approach the people on their blind side.

In 1753 an American born boy of eighteen, John Carroll, from Upper Marborough, Maryland, entered the College of the Society of Jesuits at Watteau, Flanders, to study for the priesthood of that Order. The time required ordinarily for that training is fourteen years. Since John Carroll was not ordained until he had served sixteen years in preparation, it would be safe to conclude that he was a well-grounded "cadaver" upon his return to the Colonies in 1769, and that his Society was justified in feeling that its interests would be competently administered.

It is interesting to note that John Carroll was a first cousin of Charles Carroll of Carrollton, the only Romanist who signed the Declaration of Independence.

The officials of Maryland Colony sent a committee, of which Benjamin Franklin was a member, to visit French Canada to see if he could solicit help from that source in the interest of the Colonies in the coming conflict with England.

It was recommended by Congress that Charles Carroll ask his cousin, John Carroll, the Jesuit priest, to accompany them, in the hope that he would influence the French priests in the Cause of the Colonies, an act which demonstrated the lack of understanding of the fundamentals and principles of the Jesuits, by the Colonists.

Archbishop John Carroll

Of course, the expedition utterly failed, owing to the fact that the French priests had influence over the French people of Canada, which Father Carroll was supposed to have had the power of persuasion. Though England was a "heretical" country, the increasing liberal and independent spirit of defiance in the American Colonies was a far more menacing prospect, in the eyes of the priests and the people of French Canada, and in the eyes of the divine righters of Europe. Priest Carroll's Jesuit oath precluded the possibility

SENATE
LIBERTY
HOME RULE
NO ALLEGIANCE TO ANY FOREIGN RULER.
FOREIGN RULE
FIRST ALLEGIANCE TO THE INFALLIBLE POPE OF ROME.
STATE
CHURCH AND STATE.
96

of his having any interest in his native country and consequently had to think in the same channel as his French brethren in religion. That he, a few years later, merited the distinction from his church to be made the first Archbishop of Baltimore, and was permitted to live to the age of eighty, is proof positive that he served his church faithfully by strictly adhering to his Jesuit Oath. He left his indelible stamp on that diocese. This was clearly demonstrated during the Civil War, for every plot to assassinate President Lincoln, and there were many, was formed in Baltimore, in fact Baltimore turned out to be the Vienna of America.

The first Archbishop of Baltimore must have been thoroughly cognizant of the fact that his society was having a rather rough time of it in Europe, for they were being kicked out of first one country and then another. The battle for political and intellectual freedom was being bitterly waged between the Jesuits on the one hand and the lovers of freedom on the other.

A group of French intellectuals, led by Jean Jacques Rousseau, had embodied a new concept of government, in which the central postulate was, that the only authority to govern was to come from the consent of the governed. This was shaped and published early in the eighteenth century and boldly proclaimed to the world by Rousseau in his, "Social Contract" of society. (24) Just eleven years later, Thomas Jefferson, Thomas Paine and other signators of the Declaration of Independence, incorporated it into the charter of liberty in Philadelphia in 1776. It was a grim Shakespearean joke indeed when Benjamin Franklin stated,

> "Gentlemen, we must now all hang together, for if we don't, most assuredly we will all hang separately." (25)

The success of the Revolution in the American Colonies gave the impetus to the French to revolt in 1789. In 1808 John Carroll was created the first Archbishop of Baltimore. Who would have thought that just a few months later an infant son would be born to a pioneer family in the backwoods of Kentucky, in a crude log cabin, and who was destined, fifty years later, to defeat the well laid plans of the Jesuits, the Vatican, the Romanoff's of Russia, the King of Prussia, Napoleon III, the feudalist Democrat party and the Hapsburg's of Austria.

A short time after the address by President Monroe, Professor Samuel Morse approached the President to tell him of his plan to go to Europe to uncover, as best he could, the designs of Rome to wreck the "experiment" of representative government. Monroe gave Morse his blessing.

Endnotes

1 The Footprints of the Jesuits, R.W. Thompson, (New York: Hunt and Eaton, 1894) pp. 227-8
2 The History of Romanism, John Dowling, (New York: Edward Walker, 1845) p.604
3 The Suppressed Truth About the Assassination of Abraham Lincoln, Burke McCarty, (Merrimac, Mass.: Destiny Publishers, 1973 by permission; originally published in 1924) pp. 8-9; Internet www.biblebelievers.org
4 Ibid. pp. 9-10
5 The Engineer Corps of Hell; Or Rome's Sappers and Miners, Compiled and translated by Edwin A. Sherman,(San Francisco, Ca.: Private subscription, 1883) pp. 118-124
6 Fifty Years in the Church of Rome, Charles Chiniquy, (Grand Rapids, Mi.: Baker Book House, 1968; originally published in 1886) pp. 487-488; quoting Memorial of the Captivity of Napoleon at St. Helena, General Montholon, Vol.II, pp. 62
7 Will: The Autobiography of G. Gordon Liddy, G. Gordon Liddy, (New York: St. Martin's Press, 1980) p.23

8 The Secret History of the Jesuits, Edmond Paris, (Chick Publications, Chino, Ca. 1975) Quoting Hermann Rauschning, former national-socialist chief of the government of Danzig: "Hitler m'a dit", (Paris, 1939, pp. 266, 267, 273)

8 Ibid. Quoting Robert d'Harcourt of the French Academy: "Franz von Papen, l'homme a tout faire" (L'Aube, 3rd of October 1946)

9 Double-Cross: Alberto Part Two, Jack Chick, (Chino, Ca.: Chick Publications, 1981) pp. 7, 12

10 Fifty Years in the Church of Rome, Charles Chiniquy, (by permission Chick Publications, Chino Ca.) Quoting "Catholic World", July, 1870; "Catholic Review", June, 1875; Father Hecker, "Catholic World", July, 1870; Pope Pius VII, Encyclical, 1808

11 Foreign Conspiracy Against The Liberties of The United States, Samuel F.B. Morse, under the name of Brutus, (New York: American and Foreign Christian Union, 1855) pp. 33-41; originally published in the "New York Observer", 1835

12 Fifty Years in the Church of Rome, Charles Chiniquy, (by permission Chick Publications, Chino, Ca.) pp. 281-282, originally published 1883

13 Vatican Assassins, Wounded in the House of My Friends. Eric Jon Phelps, Published by Halcyon Unified Services, Tehachapi, Ca. 2001; pp. 29-42; The Godfathers, Alberto part 3,p.26, Chino, Ca. Chick Publications; Newsweek, Jan. 26, 1981, p.32

14 Vatican Assassins, Wounded in the House of My Friends, Eric Jon Phelps, p. 633; "The Skulls" DVD Collector's Edition, secondary soundtrack commentary by director Rob Cohen; copyright 2000, Universal studios, Universal City, Ca.

15 The Suppressed Truth About the Assassination of Abraham Lincoln, Burke McCarty, p. 12

16 Rome's Responsibility for the Assassination of Abraham Lincoln, Thomas M. Harris, Brig. Gen. U. S. V., Published 1897, p.3

17 Sourced from the United States National Archives, Washington, D.C.

18 Sourced from the World Wide Web (internet) e-mail: watchmen@alphathruomega.com

19 Rome's Responsibility for the Assassination of Abraham Lincoln, Thomas M. Harris, Brig. Gen. U. S. V. , Published 1897, p.XI Foreword

20 Fifty Years in the Church of Rome, Charles Chiniquy, (by permission Chick Publications, Chino Ca.)) p. 285, quoting from "The Shepherd of the Valley", official journal of the Bishop of St. Louis, Nov. 23, 1851; originally published 1883

21 Ibid. p.285, quoting from, "New York Freeman", official journal of Bishop Hughes, Jan. 26, 1852

22 The Suppressed Truth about the Assassination of Abraham Lincoln, Burke McCarty, 1923, p.74 by permission Destiny publishers; Merrimac, Mass.

23 Rome's Responsibility for the Assassination of Abraham Lincoln, Thomas M. Harris, p.13

24 The Suppressed Truth About the Assassination of Abraham Lincoln, Burke McCarty, p.19 by permission

25 Ibid. p.20

Chapter 3

Metternich forms the Leopold Society; Samuel Morse investigates the threat; Young Lincoln; Concerns of priests of a "too free" government; Priests control the vote; Examples of religious antagonism; Morse gives an analogy; A new Crusade

Owing to the combination of circumstances in Europe just referred to, the autocrats did not dare to "wage open war" on the government of the United States since the warning of President Monroe as enunciated in the Monroe Doctrine. In 1828 an organization in Vienna was formed which was called the *"Saint Leopold Foundation for the Furtherance of Catholic Missions in America."* The plan was to operate under the mask of religion, which would insure its safety from any governmental interference and they hoped to accomplish by intrigue and innuendo what could not be performed by bullets and bayonets.

The Hapsburg family of Austria was the most powerful Roman Catholic ruling family in Europe and consequently the cruelest, despotic and reactionary. Professor Samuel F.B. Morse, the inventor of telegraphic code, thought it his patriotic duty to investigate further the religious overtones of the Treaty of Verona.

This was a man who used blunt logic and scientific reasoning to elucidate on a particular point. He eventually wrote a book on his findings entitled, "*Foreign Conspiracy against the Liberties of the United States*". So that I may not be accused of sensationalism, I quote exactly as it was written, including italics, in 1835 and as it appeared in installments in the New York Observer.

In chapter 1, on page 40-41 he stated,

> "Let us look around us. Is despotism doing anything in this country? It becomes us to be jealous. We have

cause to expect an attack, and that it will be of a kind suited to the character of the contest, the war of opinion. Yes! Despotism is doing something. *Austria is now acting in this Country.* She has devised a grand Scheme. She has organized a great plan for doing something here, which *she,* at least deems important. She has her Jesuit missionaries traveling through the land; she has supplied them with money, and has furnished a fountain for regular supply. She has expended a year ago more than *seventy-four thousand dollars* in furtherance of her design." On this particular point he adds a foot note which reads, 'From the best authority, I have just learned, (Dec.1834,) that $100,000 have been received from Austria within two years!'"

He then continues, "These are not surmises. They are facts. Some *official documents,* giving the constitution and doings of this *Foreign Society,* have lately made their appearance in the New York Observer, and have been copied extensively into other journals of the country. This society having ostensibly a *religious* object, has been nearly four years at work in the United States, without attracting, out of the religious world, much attention to its operations. The great patron of this *apparently religious* scheme is no less a personage than the *Emperor of Austria.* The Society is called the *St. Leopold Foundation.* It is organized in Austria. Its field of operations is these United States. It meets and forms its plans in Vienna. Prince Metternich has it under his watchful care. The Pope has given his apostolic benediction, and "His Royal Highness, Ferdinand V. King of Hungary, and Crown Prince of the other hereditary states, has been most graciously pleased, prompted by a piety worthy the exalted title of an apostolic king, to accept the office of Protector of the Leopold Foundation."

Now in the present state of the war of principles in Europe, is not a society formed *avowedly to act* upon this country, originating in the dominions of a despot, and holding its secret councils in his capital, calculated to excite suspicion? Is it credible that a society got up under the auspices of the Austrian government, under the superintendence of its chief officers of the state, supplying with funds a numerous body of Jesuit emissaries who are organizing themselves on all our borders, actively passing and re-passing between Europe and America; is it credible, I say, that such a society has for its object purely a *religious reform?* Is it credible that the manufactur-

> ers of chains for binding liberty in Europe, have suddenly become benevolently concerned only for the *religious welfare* of this republican people? If this society be solely for the propagation of the Catholic faith, one would think that *Rome,* and not *Vienna, should* be its headquarters! That the *Pope,* not the *Emperor of Austria,* should be its grand patron!"

One of the Hapsburg brothers, Prince Rudolph, was a member of the Roman Curia, the Cardinal Rudolph Hapsburg, of Olmutz. It was easy for the Jesuits of the Vatican to operate through him as the agent for the foundation funds, which poured into the United States. Nor did the Vatican furnish all the funds. The, "high contracting parties" of the Treaty of Verona furnished them. The money that was distributed amounted to nothing more than a gigantic political slush fund designed to corrupt and ultimately destroy the government and set up a monarchial one instead. Passage was paid for thousands of immigrants from all over Europe. They were quickly congregated in the major cities and scattered throughout the land to the Mississippi Valley.

Professor Samuel F.B. Morse

In chapter 2 of Morse's book he begins to cast a large amount of doubt upon the stated goals of this, "religious" mission. He asked the question,

> "Who, and what is Austria, The government that is so benevolently concerned for our religious welfare?"

This was an extremely valid question. Austria was one of that Holy Alliance of despotic governments, one of the "union of Christian princes," which was in league against the liberties of the people of Europe. Austria was one of the partitioners of Poland; the enslaver of the people of Italy. Morse went on to expound on the nature of the Austrian government, calling it

> "the declared and consistent enemy of civil and religious liberty, freedom of the press and of every great principle of which it is the glory and the privilege to inherit." (2)

The famous Thirty Years War was waged to extirpate those very principles of civil and religious liberty. Had Austria then triumphed, the Republic of the United States would never have been founded. The people were virtual slaves, in body and mind, whipped into shape and disciplined by priests who were not allowed to have any opinion of their own, and taught to consider their Emperor as their God.

Prince Metternich, whom the Germans called, "Mitternacht," German for midnight, referring to his efforts to cover Europe with political darkness, was on an equal footing with Napoleon as a despot. He persuaded the Emperor of Austria and the King of Prussia not to fulfill the promise to their subjects to give them free constitutions. It was Metternich who prevented [Orthodox] Czar Alexander from helping Greece and who lent ships to assist the Turks in the subjugation of the Greeks. He crushed the liberties of Spain by inducing Louis XVIII, against his wishes, to send 100,000 men, under the command of Duke d'Angouleme, to restore "public order." When Sicily, Naples and Genoa, in 1821, threw off the yoke of slavery, Metternich sent 30,000 Roman Catholic Austrian bayonets into Italy, and re-established his influence. Goaded into desperation by the extortion, tyranny, and bad faith of the Papal government, the Italian patriots made a noble and successful effort to remedy their political situation by a revolution firm, yet temperate and tolerant.

Metternich was an attacker, not of men, but of principles. This was the government and the people who had all at once manifested a deep interest in the spiritual condition of what they called a heretic land. The principles of Austria and the United States were as different as night from day. The fundamental principle of government, for example, would be a good place to illustrate this canyon of opinion. On the question from whom does the authority to govern arise, both sides agree-from God. It is on the next question where the fork occurs, To whom on earth is this authority delegated? Austria answered, to the Emperor- "I the Emperor do ordain..." The United States says to the people, "We, the people, do ordain, establish, grant..." In one principle is recognized the servitude of the people and in the other resides the supremacy of the people. The principles of liberty of conscience, opinion and of the press were also diametrically opposed.

It was to be through the slave-master mentality and influence of the Leopold Foundation in which the War of the Rebellion in the United States would first take root.

While the Society of Jesus was organizing its forces through the Leopold Foundation in Vienna, in 1828, two boys from Spencer County, Indiana, in their teens, guided their flatboat, which they had spent weeks making, toward the wharf in New Orleans, Louisiana.

One was a tall, awkward youth, with frank grey eyes, tanned skin and a shock of black hair topped off by a coonskin cap. When the boat was within reach of the pier, the taller lad tied it off and together, the two strode away, soon to be lost in the crowd.

They attracted no special attention and were busy taking in the sights and sounds of the great southern metropolis. There was one incident, however, which made a lifelong impression and proved to be the turning point in the taller boy's life. Their attention was directed to a large crowd by the loud voice of a man towering above it. He had long black hair, loose flowing tie, wore a large slouch hat, was dressed as a city man and was calling out in the language of an auctioneer. Every so often he would crack a black snake whip.

LINCOLN RECEIVES TWO SILVER HALF DOLLARS.

The boys moved over, pushing their way through the crowd and found their way to the inside of the circle around a large block upon which stood a young Negro, around the age of the two youths. The colored man was ordered to display his teeth and muscles, thereby demonstrating his strength and vitality.

The bidding was snappy; the auctioneer was facetious and garnering coarse guffaws from the crowd. Finally the hammer banged down and the deal was closed. A shrill cry suddenly pierced the air from a beautiful mulatto girl. She was one of the parcel of slaves who was to be auctioned off the next morning and was to be the bride of the boy who had just been disposed of. The crowd paid no attention to her and quickly dispersed. The show was over.

The two boys walked quickly away. Finally, as they were nearing the place where their boat was secured, our tall friend turned to his companion and said, "John, I swear, if I ever get a chance to hit that thing, by God I'll hit it and I'll hit it hard." That "thing" which was enunciated by the clergy and said,

> "Slavery does not constitute a crime before law, Divine or human. What reasons can we have for undermining the foundations of slavery with the same zeal that ought to always animate us into overcoming evil? When one thinks of the miserable state of degradation in which the hordes of Africa live, the slave trade may be considered a providential act and we must repudiate the philanthropy which sees in man one thing, material liberty." (3)

I would now like to explore the political character of this ostensibly religious effort, from the sentiments of the Austrian emissaries expressed to their foreign patrons. The following quotes betray expressions of antipathy to the free principles and to the government of the United States. Some hint at the subversion of the government and some carry acknowledgments of the political effects, which were to be expected from the operations of the society.

The Bishop of Baltimore, writing to the Austrian Society, lamented the state of the Catholic religion in Virginia. He said,

> "I sent to Richmond a zealous missionary, a native of America. He traveled through the whole of Virginia. The Protestants flocked on all sides to hear him; they offered him their churches, courthouses, and other public buildings, to preach in. In consequence of being spoiled by bad instruction, they will judge everything themselves; they therefore hear eagerly every new comer..." (4)

The Bishop, if he had the power, would of course loved to have changed this "bad instruction" for the better, and, as in Austria, would relieve them from the trouble of judging for themselves. Thus the liberties of private judgment and freedom of opinion, guaranteed by the institutions, were obstacles to the success of the Church.

A Catholic journal, called the *Register and Diary*, expressed the same sentiments. It stated,

> "We seriously advise Catholic parents to be very cautious in the choice of schoolbooks for their children. There is more danger to be apprehended in this quarter than could be conceived. Parents, we are aware, have not always the time or patience to examine these matters: but if they trust implicitly to us, we shall, with God's help, do it for them. Legimus ne legantur." (5)

We read, that they may not read. This was very kind. They would save the parents all the trouble of judging for themselves, but, "we must be trusted implicitly."

Bishop Flaget, of Bardstown, Kentucky, in a letter to his patrons abroad, had this plain hint at an ulterior motive, which was no less than the entire subversion of the republican government. Speaking of the difficulties and discouragements the missionaries had to contend with in converting the Indians, the last difficulty in the way he said was,

> "their continual traffic among the whites, which cannot be hindered as long as the Republican Government shall subsist." (6)

He said, in essence, that a republican government was unfavorable in its nature to the restrictions he deemed necessary to the extension of the Catholic religion. He was looking forward to the time when the government shall be sufficiently perverted to allow the hindrance of this traffic.

A German missionary named Mr. Baraga, who was living in Michigan, seemed impressed with the same conviction of the unhappy influences of a free government upon his church to make converts. In giving an account of the refusal of some people to have their children baptized, he laid the fault on this,

"Too free Government." (7)

In a more despotic government, in Italy or Austria, he would have been able to put in force compulsory baptism on these children.

Now, if some political effects were already avowed, as intended to be produced by this society, and that, too, immediately after reiterating its purely spiritual design, why may not that particular political effect be also intended, of far more importance, to the interests of the despotism of Metternich, namely, the subversion of the republican government of the United States?

What makes a mob turbulent? Ignorance- an ignorance in which it is for the interest of its leaders not to enlighten; for if you enlighten a man, and he will think for himself, and have some self-respect; he will understand the laws and know his interest in obeying them. Keep him in ignorance, and he is the slave of the man who will flatter his passions and appetites, or awe him by superstitious fears. Against the out-breakings of such men, society, as it is constituted in a free system, can protect itself only in one of two ways: it must either bring these men under the influence and control of a sound education, or it must call in the aid of the priests who govern them, and who may permit and direct, or restrain their turbulence, in accordance with what they may judge at any particular time to be in the interest of the church.

The same hands that can, whenever it suits their interests, restrain, can also, at the proper time, "let slip the dogs of war." In this mode of restraint by a police of priests, by substituting the ecclesiastical for the civil power, the priest led mobs of Portugal and Spain, and South America, in the early 1820's, are instructive examples. The civil and military powers were not able to restore order among them to the obedience of the laws without calling in the priests to negotiate and settle the terms on which they would cease from violating the laws.

On page 148 of Morse's book he wrote under the heading, *"Priests control the Mob,"*

> 'If no farther proof were wanting of the fact of the supreme influence of the Catholic priests over the mob, it is opportunely furnished in the testimony on the trial of the rioters at Charlestown, (Mass.) Mr. Edward Cutter testified that the Lady Superior, in an interview previous to the burning of the Convent, thus threatened him; she said, "the Bishop had 20,000 of the vilest (or boldest) Irishmen under his control, who would tear down the houses of Mr. Cutter and others; and that the selectmen of Charlestown might read the riot act till they were hoarse, and it would be of no use."
>
> But if any doubt is thrown over Mr. Cutter's testimony because he is a Protestant, hear what the Lady Superior herself testifies: "I told him," she says, "that the Right Reverend Bishop's influence over ten thousand *brave* Irishmen might lead to the destruction of his property and that of others."
>
> Here we have the startling fact, acknowledged in a court of justice by the Superior of the Convent, that the Bishop has such influence over a mob of foreigners, that he can use them for vengeance, or restrain them at pleasure. The question that occurs is, how much stronger is it necessary for this foreign corps to become before it may prudently act offensively against our obnoxious Protestant institutions? The fact is established, by Catholic testimony, that the Popish population is not an *unorganized* mob, but is moved by priestly leaders, Jesuit foreigners in the pay of Austria. They are ready to keep quiet, or to strike, as circumstances may render expedient. But, exclusive of other proof, another most important fact rendered certain by this singular confession of the Lady Superior, and that is *Roman Catholic interference in our elections.* Jesuits are not in the habit of slighting their advantages, and the Bishop who can control ten or twenty thousand, or five hundred thousand men, as the case may be, for the purpose of destruction and riot, can certainly *control the votes* of these obedient instruments! Will not American free men wake to the apprehension of a truth like this?" (8)

I found the point Morse made of, "keeping quiet, or to strike, as circumstances may render expedient." an interesting parallel under the present situation of "sleeper cells" in the "war on terrorism" or more accurately, the crusade on Islam we now are engaged in.

When Abraham Lincoln instituted the draft, at about the same time that Pope Pius IX recognized the legitimacy of the Confederacy, a riot occurred in New York among the Irish parishioners of Archbishop Hughes. In Charles Chiniquy's book, "*50 Years in the Church of Rome*", he recorded a conversation he had with Lincoln in which Lincoln stated,

> "The New York riots were evidently a Romish plot from beginning to end. We have the proofs in hand that they were the work of Bishop Hughes and his emissaries. No doubt can remain about the bloody attempts of Rome to destroy New York, when we know the easy way it was stopped. I wrote to Bishop Hughes, telling him that the whole country would hold him responsible for it if he would not stop it at once. He then gathered the rioters to his palace, called them his 'dear friends', invited them to go back home peacefully, and all was finished! So Jupiter of old used to raise a storm and stop it with a nod of his head!" (9)

On June 12, 1913, the Protestant people of Oelwein, Iowa, invited Jeremiah J. Crowley, ex-priest and author of the "Parochial School: A Curse to the Church and a Menace to the Nation," to address them in the theatre of that town on the subject of the public school question. At the instigation of the Roman Catholic priest of that town who delivered his sermon the Sunday before the Crowley lecture, some two thousand Romanists led by the Knights of Columbus and their cohorts, mobbed Mr. Crowley as he was leaving the theatre with some of his friends, and beat him severely. (10)

On April 14, 1914, the Rev. Otis Spurgeon of Iowa, who had been called to deliver a series of discourses by Protestant Americans at Denver, Colorado, was kidnapped from the Pierce Hotel in that city at 8 P.M., bound hand and foot, gagged and a strap placed around his neck, and was thrown into a car, parked in front of the hotel, whisked into the country and beaten into unconsciousness. En route his captors told him they were the Knights of Columbus and repeatedly during the trip when he refused to answer as they wished, he was choked by the strap. ("Strangulation Cord.") (11)

The Rev. Spurgeon was finally rescued, taken to a hospital where he was found to have sustained internal injuries and lay ill for three weeks. The Rev. Spurgeon was a "heretic."

On Feb. 4, 1915, Rev. William Black, ex-priest, was delivering a discourse of lectures, en route to the California coast, where he was to have testified that while he was a Roman Catholic priest and a Knight of Columbus he had taken the Jesuit Oath on the Congressional Record, cited heretofore. The Knight of Columbus oath is a modified version of that oath and written by Jesuits for them. The Rev. Black had reached Marshall, Texas, where he was to deliver two lectures. He gave his first lecture on the public school question in the auditorium of the City Hall at Marshall, Feb. 3. About 5 o'clock in the afternoon on Feb. 4, Mr. Black and his bodyguard, a Mr. J. A. Hall, ex-soldier and expert shot, were returning from a walk about the city. On reaching his door four men standing at the end of the corridor nearby approached him. They asked if he was Mr. Black and permission to come in and speak with him a few minutes. The Rev. Black opened the door and invited them in.

The visitors first of all informed him that they were members of the Knights of Columbus Council of Marshall; that they understood that he intended to deliver another lecture "against their church" that night. Mr. Black assured them that they were correct. Then the spokesman, a prominent attorney, Ryan by name, said, "No, you won't. We will give you just fifteen minutes to pack your suitcase and get out of town." Mr. Black coolly informed them that he intended to deliver his lecture; that he would relinquish his American constitutional rights for no man. On rising from a shoeshine box where he had been sitting, John Rogers, a leading architect of that vicinity who had drawn up plans of the hotel in which they now were, sprang toward him, pinned his arms and shot Black's body full of bullets.

Copeland, a leading banker and another Knight of Columbus, received a wound in the melee and also the consolations of his church. It is also of interest to know that the priest was in the lobby of the hotel when Black was shot. Through political influence, these K.C. participants in this assassination went free. (12)

April 6, 1915, the Rev. Dr. Joseph and Mary Slattery, ex-priest and ex-nun, of Boston, Mass., were called by Protestant Americans to deliver some lectures in Chicago, Ill. They were lecturing in a Masonic Hall on the south side of the city. In the early part of Dr. Slattery's talk a mob of Roman Catholics and members of the Knights of Columbus left their hall, which was just across the street, entered the Slattery meeting and proceeded to start a riot, by calling Mr. Slattery "a liar."

At a signal from a man wearing a Roman collar, from which he drew a handkerchief, which had been concealed inside, the riot started in earnest. Chairs and furniture were smashed, men and women were beaten indiscriminately and disfigured by the use of brass knuckles and blackjacks. The telephone wires in the hall and even the nearby drugstores had been cut and it was fully ¾ of an hour before they had any response from the Fourth degree Knights of Columbus policemen.

The speaker and his wife made a miraculous escape. The windows of the car in which they were driven were riddled with bullet holes. These Roman thugs entered streetcars and attacked the passengers who had not been at the lecture and knew nothing of the riot. They pulled the trolleys off the wires and derailed and demolished several cars. (13)

In Haverhill, Mass. April 4, 1916, The Knights of Columbus and their thugs were summoned for the occasion of entering the City Hall where a meeting was being held by Thomas E. Leyden, who was speaking upon the political activities of the Roman Church in American politics. The headlines read:

BIG RIOT RAGES IN HAVERHILL

MANY BEATEN, MILITIA IS CALLED

CITY HALL STORMED BY ANGRY MOBS

10,000 IN WILD HAVERHILL RIOTS - MILITIA CALLED OUT TO SUPPRESS MOB THAT GETS BEYOND POLICE

An editorial from the, *Christian Science Journal* Boston, April 21, 1916 read:

MOB LAW

"The question of free speech is one of such fundamental importance to humanity that it is easy to understand the commotion which has been caused in the State of Massachusetts, by the recent riots in Haverhill. The contention that a mob, with or without cause, is at liberty to usurp the prerogatives of the courts, and to substitute lynch law for official justice, constitutes, in deed, a precedent destructive of all popular liberty. The history of liberty is very largely the effort of authority to restrain license. When the human passions are roused license is always apt to come to the top.

There is no rhyme or reason in the attack of a mob. It is just as willing to smash a great invention like the spinning-jenny, for fear of the displacement of labor, as it is to stuff the mouth of a Foulon with straw. It is just this

> that makes the case of the mob in Haverhill so important. If its action is overlooked, if it is connived at, worse still if it is justified today, there is no length to which it may go tomorrow, and the example set, in Haverhill, may be repeated elsewhere at the expense of the very views which the Haverhill exhibition was intended to support.
>
> The simple fact is that the Haverhill mob outraged in the frankest and most indefensible way the common right of free speech. It is not of the slightest importance who Mr. Leyden was, what he was going to say, or what the effect of his words might be. He was entitled to speak, or he was not entitled to speak. If he was entitled to speak no mob had any right to decide the question and to enforce its own decisions. It outraged entirely the rights of free speech." (14)

These instances of Roman inspired mob rule document the norm rather than the exception. Insofar as documentation of clergy inspired mob rule and mob violence is concerned, another entire book could be written on the subject. Such is the extent of religious intolerance, hatred and insanity.

AMERICAN CITIZENS!

We appeal to you in all calmness. Is it not time to pause? Already the enemies of our dearest institutions, like the foreign spies in the Trojan horse of old, are within our gates. They are disgorging themselves upon us, at the rate of HUNDREDS OF THOUSANDS EVERY YEAR! They aim at nothing short of conquest and supremacy over us.

A PAPER ENTITLED THE

IN FAVOR OF

The protection of American Mechanics against Foreign Pauper Labor.

Foreigners having a residence in the country of 21 years before voting.

Our present Free School System.

Carrying out the laws of the State, as regards sending back Foreign Paupers and Criminals.

OPPOSED TO

Papal Aggression & Roman Catholicism.

Foreigners holding office.

Raising Foreign Military Companies in the United States.

Nunneries and the Jesuits.

To being taxed for the support of Foreign paupers millions of dollars yearly.

To secret Foreign Orders in the U. S.

We are burdened with enormous taxes by foreigners. We are corrupted in the morals of our youth. We are interfered with in our government. We are forced into collisions with other nations. We are tampered with in our religion. We are injured in our labor. We are assailed in our freedom of speech.

The PATRIOT is Published by J. E. Farwell & Co., 32 Congress St., Boston,

And for Sale at the Periodical Depots in this place. Single copies 4 Cents.

Interference in elections was nothing new to the Romanists with which Metternich, with the aid of the Jesuits, was flooding the United States. The Pope interfered in Poland in the revolution of that country, and, through the priests, commanded submission to the Czar. In Spain and Portugal, the priests led in the field of battle. Was there some strange metamorphosis by which the Church was modified by the institutions of the United States, seeking only the religious welfare of the people? Let us examine the history of the time.

384 HARPER'S WEEKLY. [May 8, 1875.

THE AMERICAN RIVER GANGES.

Thos. Nast cartoon addressing the infiltration of Rome into the public educational system of the U.S. This infiltration was alluded to in one of the letters from Brig. General T.M. Harris to Charles Chiniquy. 100 years later we see the results.

William Penn, while granting to all without distinction of creed, perfect religious freedom in his Colony, yet saw clearly the danger to the Commonwealth through the "blind obedience" of Papists to the commands of their priests, an obedience which has been manifest to the sagacious observer throughout the history of Pennsylvania. Later rulers of the Commonwealth thought they saw reason for curtailing the liberties which he in a spirit so different from that of the Romish Church, had granted to Catholics. The following proprietory instructions issued in 1738 and reiterated in 1766, will be interesting to our readers:

"Whereas the said province and counties were happily at first settled and afterwards subsisted without any considerable admixture of Papists, it is with concern that we now hear that of late times several Papists have resorted thither. Now, as their Political Principles, (which they ever inculcate as Religious Principles,) tend to the breach of public Faith, are destructive to morality and totally subvert every civil and Religious Right of a free people, we recommend it to you to prevent as much as in your lies, the coming in or settling of Papists within your Government, and that you do not extend any Privileges to them nor admit any of them into any office, post or employment whatsoever with your Government."

In Michigan, the Bishop Richard, a Jesuit, was several times chosen delegate to Congress from the territory, the majority of the people being Catholic. As Protestants became more numerous, the contest between the Bishop and his Protestant rival was more and more close, until, by the increase of Protestant numbers, the latter triumphed. The Bishop, in order to detect any delinquency in his flock at the polls, had his ticket printed on colored paper. Any who were so mutinous as not to vote according to orders, had penance inflicted on them. (15)

In Charleston, South Carolina, the Bishop, England was said to have boasted of the number of votes that he could control at an election. In New York, a priest, whose name remains obscured two hundred years later, in a late election for city officers, stopped his congregation after mass on Sunday and urged the electors not to vote for a particular candidate, on the ground that he was not a Catholic. The result was the election of the Catholic candidate. This is all documented in Morse's book. (16)

According to Morse, Popery, as he referred to it, is a political as well as a religious system. It embodies in itself the closest union of Church and State. In the Roman States the civil and ecclesiastical offices were blended together in the same individual. The Pope is the King. A Cardinal is Secretary of State. The Consistory of Cardinals is the Cabinet, the Ministry and they are Viceroys in the provinces. The Archbishops are Ambassadors to foreign courts. The Bishops are judges and magistrates and the road to all of the great offices of state is through the priesthood.

He then went on to provide an analogy.

> "Let us suppose", he said, "that the Emperor of Russia, in a conceited dream of divine right to universal empire, should parcel out our country into convenient districts, and should proclaim his intention to exercise his rightful sway over these states, now not owning his con-

trol; should we not justly laugh at his ridiculous pretensions? But suppose he should proceed to appoint his Viceroys and Grand Imperial Dukes, giving to one the title "*His Grace of Albany*", to another "*The Grand Duke of Washington,*" to yet another "*his Imperial Highness of Savannah,*" and should send them out to take possession of their respective districts, and subdue the people as fast as practicable to their proper obedience to his legitimate sway; and should these pompous Viceroys, with their train of sub-officers, actually come over from Russia, and erect their government houses, and commence by complaint matters and fair promises to procure lands and rentals to hold in the power of the Emperor, and under the guise of educating the rising generation should begin to sap the foundations of their attachment to the government, by blinding their reasoning faculties, and by the Russian Catechism instilling the doctrine of passive obedience, and the divine right of the Emperor; what should we say to all this? Suppose then, further, that the Emperor's cause, by Russian emigration, and the money supplied by the Emperor, had become so strong that the Viceroys were emboldened to try their influence upon some of the local elections; that the Russian party had become a body somewhat formidable; that its foreign leaders had their passive obedience troops so well under command as to make themselves necessary in the police of the country; that we feared to offend them, that the secular press favored them, Footnote: Is this a harsh judgment on the secular press? If a secular paper ventures to remonstrate against Catholics, is not the cry of intolerance or persecution at once raised and the editor scared away from his duty of exposing the secret political enemies of the republic, under the false notion that he is engaged in a Religious controversy? and the unprincipled courted them; to what point then, in the process of gradually surrendering our liberties to the Russian Czar, should we have come; and how near to their accomplishment would be those wild dreams of imperial ambition, which we had, in the first instance ridiculed?

What is the difference between the real claims, and efforts and condition of Popery at this moment in these United States, and the supposed claims, and efforts and condition of the Russian despotism? The one comes disguised under the name of Religion, the other, more honest, would come in its real political name. Give the latter the name of *Religion,* call the *Emperor, Pope,* and his *Viceroys, Bishops,* interlard the *imperial decrees* with *pi-*

> *ous cant,* and you have the case of pretension, and intrigue, and success too, which has actually passed in these United States! Yes, the King of Rome, acting by the promptings of the Austrian Cabinet, and in the plentitude of his usurpation, has already extended his scepter over our land, he has divided us up into provinces, and appointed his Viceroys who claim their *jurisdiction,* Footnote: "Indiana and Illinois, two states depending on my jurisdiction!"— [My Lord Bishop Flaget's letter.] from a higher power than exists in this country, even from his majesty himself, who appoints them, who removes them at will, to whom they owe allegiance, for the extension of whose temporal kingdom they are exerting themselves, and whose success let it be indelibly impressed on your minds, is *the certain destruction of the free institutions of our country.*" **(17)**

Morse had pegged it squarely. This was exactly the disguise used, under the inspiration of Metternich, the Jesuits and the Leopold Society, to achieve the goal of undermining the free institutions of the United States in the 1800's and transform the country into an ecclesiastically run tool to further Her empire.

Czar Nicholas

In Morse's second book on the subject titled, *"Imminent Dangers to the Free Institutions of the United States through Foreign Immigration and the Present State of the Naturalization Laws"* published in 1835 by E.B. Clayton, New York, 17 Hanover Street, for the Journal of Commerce, he expanded on his expose. After explaining to his readers that immigrants to virtually every country save the United States are *never* given the opportunity, even after being naturalized citizens, *to exercise the vote and thereby exert political influence*, he gets to the main thrust of the danger posed to the United States by quoting this confession from Prince Metternich,

> "**The Great Nursery** *of these destructive principles,* (the principles of democracy,) **The Great Revolutionary School for France and the rest of Europe, *is* North America!"** (p.8 Imminent Dangers to the Free Institutions)

Yes, the influence of the Republican government of the United States and the democratic system was vitally felt by Austria, the Roman Catholic autocrats and the Vatican. The remedy was to use the weakness inherent in the Naturalization Laws of the U.S. to exert political influence through massive immigration.

"Any", wrote Morse, "who dare to expose this weakness and change the law for the purpose of preserving the principles of freedom is to be branded as a bigot and hate-mongerer."

Morse had encountered a revealing aspect of a union of Church and State. In order to set it up, I will again quote from his book, italics being his,

> "A new experiment, another step forward in the march against our freedom has been tried in the West, at St. Louis, in the consecration of the Popish cathedral. The account is from a Popish journal, called the Catholic Telegraph. They shall have the benefit of their own recital.
>
> "'The cathedral of St. Louis is 134 feet long, by 84 wide. There are 8 rows of pews, 25 in each row, calculated to contain at least 8,000 persons. There are two mag-

nificent colonnades at opposite sides in the body of the church, consisting of five massive pillars of brick, elegantly marbled, and each four feet in diameter.

"The altar is of stone. It is only temporary, and will soon be superseded by a superb marble altar, which is hourly expected from Italy.

"The Church, it is said, has already cost $42,000. It is presumed that about $18,000 more will be required to finish it, according to the original and magnificent design of its founders; so that the entire cost of the building and its furniture cannot be less than $60,000.

"The consecration took place on the Sabbath, October 26, 1834.

"At an early hour, 7 A.M. on the day of consecration, four Bishops, twenty-eight Priests, twelve of whom were from TWELVE different nations, and a considerable number of young aspirants to the holy ministry, making the entire ecclesiastical corps amount to fifty or sixty, were habited in their appropriate dresses. As *soon as the procession was organized,* the pealing of three large and clear sounding bells, *the thunder of two pieces of artillery,* raised all hearts, as well as our own, to the Great Almighty Being.

"When the HOLY RELICS were moved towards their new habitation, where they shall enjoy an anticipated resurrection - the presence of their God in this holy tabernacle, *the guns fired a second salute.* We felt as if the soul of St. Louis, Christian, Lawgiver, and HERO, was in the sound, and that he again led on *his victorious armies* in the service of the God of Hosts, for the defense of his religion, his sepulcher, and his people.

"When the solemn moment of the consecration approached, and the *Son* of the *living God* was going to descend, for the *first time,* into the new residence of his glory on earth, the *drums* beat the *reveille, three of the star-spangled banners were lowered over* the balustrade of the sanctuary, the *artillery* gave a *deafening discharge.*

"The dedication sermon was preached by the Bishop of Cincinnati. *During the Divine* Sacrifice, two of the military stood with drawn swords, one on each side of the altar; they belonged to a *guard of honor,* formed *expressly* for the occasion. Besides whom, there were detachments from the four militia companies of the city, the

Marions, the *Grays,* the Riflemen, and the Cannoneers from Jefferson Barracks, stationed at convenient distances around the church.

"Well and eloquently did the Rev. Mr. Abell, pastor of Louisville, observe in the evening discourse, alluding to his own and the impressions of the clergy and laity, who were witnesses to the scene: Fellow Christians and Fellow Citizens! I have seen the flag of my country proudly floating at the mast head of our richly-freighted merchantmen; I have seen it fluttering in the breeze at the head of our armies; but never, *never* did my heart *exult* as when I this day beheld it for the first time bow before its God! Breathing from infancy the air which our artillery had purified from the infectious spirit of bigotry and persecution, it would be the pride of my soul to take the brave men by the hand, by whom these cannons were served. But for these cannons, there would be no home for the free, no asylum for the persecuted."

Morse then asks the question,

"What are the reflections of an American on an occurrence like this? What must they be to one who has ever felt his pride of country stir within him, when in foreign lands he has beheld the degraded slaves of despotism bow in like manner before the altars and idols of heathenish superstition, awed into seeming reverence by the *military array* which always accompanies the imposing ceremonial of the Popish church? But the military were only *a guard of honor!* Yes, this is the soft name given to this despotic chain, the musical sound to charm us away from scrutinizing it; and it will be sufficient, doubtless, to drown its harsher clanking in our torpid ears."

He then extrapolates,

"The *guard of honor,* that universal appendage of kings and sacred despots, is a serviceable band. It not only helps to swell a procession by its numbers, but with the glitter of its arms, and accoutrements, and gay banners, it adds splendor to the pageant of a heathen ritual. But, reader, it has an essential duty to perform. *Its duty is to* enforce the ceremonies of worship upon all present. Do you doubt this duty of the guard *of honor?* "The writer will give his own experience of the duties of the guard of honor. I was a stranger in Rome, and recovering from the debility of a slight fever; I was walking for air and gentle exercise in the Corso, on the day of the celebration of the Corpus Domini.

From the houses on each side of the street were hung rich tapestries and gold embroidered damasks, and towards me slowly advanced a long procession, decked out with all the heathenish paraphernalia of this self-styled church. In a part of the procession a lofty baldichino, or canopy, borne by men, was held above the idol, the host, before which, as it passed, all heads were uncovered, and every knee bent but mine. Ignorant of the customs of heathenism, I turned my back to the procession, and close to the side of the houses in the crowd, (as I supposed unobserved,) I was noting in my tablets the order of the assemblage. I was suddenly aroused from my occupation, and staggered by a blow upon the head from the gun and bayonet of a soldier, which struck off my hat far into the crowd. Upon recovering from the shock, the soldier, with the expression of a demon, and his mouth pouring a torrent of Italian oaths, in which *il diavolo* had a prominent place, stood with his bayonet against my breast. I could make no resistance, I could only ask him why he struck me, and receive in answer his fresh volley of unintelligible imprecations, which having delivered, he resumed his place in the *guard of honor,* by the side of the officiating Cardinal."

In conclusion Morse went on to say,

"Americans will not fail to observe in the precious extract of the discourse in which the priest gives vent to his feelings of exultation upon seeing our *national flag,* the star spangled banner, humbled in the dust before the Pope, that with the cunning of his craft he flatters the soldiery, and in a sermon professedly to the God of Peace, and in dedicating a temple to his name, he is inspired with no loftier feelings of the soul than this - "it would be *the pride of my soul* to take the brave men by the hand by whom these cannons were served." Why? Is it such a brave act to touch off a cannon? Or was the imagination of the priest reveling in the dream of seeing the military power of the country, at a future day, at the beck and call of the Pope, and his Austrian (Jesuit) master?" (18)

Consider, if you will, exactly how many Executive Orders have been issued since President Reagan officially reinstated diplomatic ties with the Vatican?

These orders are for all intents and purposes monarchy and autocracy through the back door and in every historical precept this has proven to be a dangerous development, providing the nutrients for a man to lend himself to despotism.

According to a Feb. 6, 2005 *Calgary Sun* newspaper article written by world affairs columnist Eric Margolis, former military intelligence analyst William Arkin revealed a previously unknown directive called "JCS Conplan 0300-97," authorizing the Pentagon to employ special, ultra-secret "anti-terrorist" military units on U.S. soil for what he claims are "extra-legal missions."

In other words, using U.S. soldiers to kill or arrest Americans, in much the same way as what took place in Nazi Germany, acts that have been illegal since the U.S. Civil War.

According to the same article Defense Secretary Donald Rumsfeld has recently created a new Pentagon special ops organization named "Strategic Support Branch," that will replace many of the CIA's tasks which include assassinations, rigging of elections [like Florida in 2000 and Ohio in 2004 resulting in the disenfranchisement of tens of thousands of black voters], 'terrorist' acts conveniently blamed on manufactured 'enemies' and sundry other operations.

This new SSB is headed by a notorious religious fanatic, Lt.-Gen. William Boykin, who calls the U.S. Army "the army of God in the house of God" in exactly the same manner as the Jesuits called Hitler's Panzer divisions, "the right arm of God," and Islamic insurgents "agents of Satan." He warned Muslims, "my God is bigger than your god, which is an idol." Boykin's command will now dispatch postmodern Christian 'crusaders' to cleanse the world of "Satanic Muslims" and other miscreants.

This 'black-ops' unit, staffed with militarized thugs and ultra-religious Rambo's, is largely excluded from Congressional oversight or media examination and answers directly to the President, who clearly believed he had been given a mandate from heaven after being re-elected by the less mentally active half of the American voters.

In response to a question this writer put to author Eric Phelps regarding the extreme nature of Lt.-Gen. Boykin's professed beliefs, Mr. Phelps said;

> "Boykin appears to be a true, Bible-believing Christian but I do not believe he is. [...to the Protestants generally to be a Protestant – Jesuit Oath] Black Ops has always been the function of agents of the Order, some of them professed coadjutors. Thus, the Order's present Crusade against Islam employs these assassins resembling Mussolini's Blackshirts and Hitler's Brownshirts, later the SS.
>
> Boykin is furthering the Order's purposed illusion that this war is being led by Protestants and Evangelicals. No wonder that RC-half Jewish John Kerry [another Skull and Bones member] was not appointed to be President and thus lead the Crusade! Roman Catholic Chris Matthews... called Bush "Oliver Cromwell" on inauguration day.
>
> Meanwhile, TV's most notorious Catholics are beginning to question the war including O'Reilly, Matthews, Buchanan and Russert –all Jesuits of the short robe. Notorious faux Protestants and Baptists Graham and Falwell are giving unreserved blessing to the Crusade. Thus the coming persecutions will be blamed on the Protestants, not Rome where the source of the murder has been planned and from where it will be executed."

Morse's nightmare scenario may have just finally come true.

Endnotes

1 Foreign Conspiracy against the Liberties of The United States, Samuel F. B. Morse, 1835, Ch.2 p.43

2 Ibid. Ch.2. p.43

3 The Suppressed Truth about the Assassination of Abraham Lincoln, Burke McCarty, 1923, p.71, quoting from, "Doctrine of the Jesuits" by Gury and translated by Paul Bert in 1879 by permission (Destiny Publishers, Merrimac, Mass.)

4 Foreign Conspiracy against the Liberties of the United States, Samuel F.B. Morse, 1835, Ch. 7, p.82

5 Ibid., p.83
6 Ibid. p.83
7 Ibid. p.84
8 Ibid. P.148-9
9 Fifty Years in the Church of Rome, Charles Chiniquy, (by permission Chick Publications, Chino Ca.) p. 299

10 The Suppressed Truth about the Assassination of Abraham Lincoln, Burke McCarty, 1923, p.246 by permission

11 Ibid. p.247
12 Ibid. p.247
13 Ibid. p.247-248
14 Ibid. p. 248-250
15 Foreign Conspiracy against the Liberties of the United States, Samuel F.B. Morse. P.93

16 Ibid. p.94

17 Ibid. p.95

18 Ibid. pp.168-173

Globalist President G.W. Bush and his puppet-master
Edward Cardinal Egan of New York

Chapter 4

Lincoln-Douglas debate; Lincoln states slavery is anti-biblical; Lincoln and the Bible; Abraham Lincoln's faith; Lincoln meets Charles Chiniquy; Chiniquy is framed by his church; Lincoln defends Chiniquy; Chiniquy warns Lincoln; The Bishop's testimony; The murder of five presidents

In 1854 a reporter from the *Boston Journal* covered the debates between Abraham Lincoln and Stephen Douglas, which made both of these men famous. The State Convention had nominated Mr. Lincoln for the United States Senate. The report was as follows:

> "The men are entirely dissimilar. Mr. Douglas is a thickset, finely built courageous man and has the air of self-confidence that does not a little to inspire his supporters with hope. Mr. Lincoln is a tall, lank man, awkward, apparently diffident, and when not speaking, has neither firmness nor fire in his eye. He has a rich, silvery voice, enunciates with great distinctness, and has a fine command of the language. He commenced by a review of the points Mr. Douglas had made. In this he shows great tact and his retorts though gentlemanly, were sharp and reached to the core of the subject in dispute. (Lincoln) "My distinguished friend says it is an insult to the emigrants of Kansas and Nebraska to suppose that they are not able to govern themselves. We must not slur over an argument of this kind because it happens to tickle the ear. It must be met and answered. I admit that the emigrants of Kansas and Nebraska are competent to govern themselves, but, (the speaker rising to his full height) I deny the right to govern any other person, without that person's consent."
>
> The vast throng was as silent as death; every eye was fixed upon the speaker. He then charged Mr. Douglas with doing nothing for freedom; with disregarding the rights and interests of the colored man, and for about forty minutes he spoke with a power we have seldom heard equaled. There was grandeur in his thoughts, comprehensiveness in his arguments, and binding force in his conclusions, which were perfectly irresistible. He was the tall man eloquent; his countenance glowed with animation, and his eye glistened with an intelligence that made it lustrous. He was no longer awkward and ungainly, but

graceful, bold, commanding. Mr. Douglas had been quietly smoking up to this time, but here he forgot his cigar and listened with anxious attention. When he arose to reply, he appeared excited, disturbed and his second effort seemed to us vastly inferior to his first. Mr. Lincoln had given him a great task, and Mr. Douglas had not time to answer him, even if he had the ability." (1)

Thus we see that Mr. Lincoln had made good on his promise to "hit that thing hard." As early as 1856, Mr. Lincoln availed himself of his opportunity to "hit that thing hard" when he entered the political campaign, after an absence of several years, which he had been devoting to his law practice and his family in Springfield, Illinois, with the intention of never leaving it again. The infamous Dred Scott Decision rendered by a strongly devout Romanist named Judge Taney, Chief Justice of the United States Supreme Court bench, drew him into the field. In 2016 this same government corruption led to the entrance of another private citizen into the political field, under very similar historical circumstances, Donald Trump. The Taney decision in a nutshell was, that the "Negro had no rights which the white man had to respect." This virtually placed the government endorsement on black slavery, and aroused Mr. Lincoln to action.

In the sixth joint debate held in Quincy, Illinois on October 13, 1858, Mr. Lincoln went further to hit it even harder. At the end of his part of the debate he was animated and emotional as he stated his position. I will quote from this part of his answer to Mr. Douglas.

> "...Perhaps that Democrat who says he is as much opposed to slavery as I am, will tell me that I am wrong about this. I wish him to examine his own course in regard to this matter a moment, and then see if his opinion will not be changed a little. You say it is wrong; but don't you constantly object to anybody else saying so? Do you not constantly argue that this is not the right place to oppose it? You say it must not be opposed in the free states, because slavery is not here; It must not be opposed in the slave States, because it is there; it must not be opposed in politics, because that will make a fuss; it must not be opposed in the pulpit, because it is not religion. Then where is the place to oppose it? There is no suitable place to oppose it. There is no plan in the country to oppose this evil over spreading the continent, which you say yourself, is coming. Frank Blair and Gratz Brown tried to get up a system of gradual emancipation in Missouri, had an election in August and got beat, and you, Mr. Democrat, threw up your hat, and hallooed "hurrah for democracy." So I say again, that in regard to the arguments that are made, when Judge Douglas says he, "don't care whether slavery is voted up or voted down," whether he means that as an individual expression of sentiment, or only as a sort of statement of his views on national policy, it is alike true to say that he can thus argue logically if he don't see anything wrong in it; but he cannot say so logically if he admits that slavery is wrong. He cannot say that he would as soon see a wrong voted up or down. When Judge Douglas says that whoever or whatever community wants slaves, they have a right to have them, he is perfectly logical if there is nothing wrong in the institution; but if you allow and admit that it is wrong, he cannot say that anybody has a right to do a wrong. When he says that slave property and horse property and hog property are, alike, to be allowed to go into the Territories, upon the principles of equality, he is reasoning truly, if there is no difference between them as property; but if

> the one is property, held rightfully, and the other is wrong, then there is no equality between the right and the wrong; so that, turn it any way you can, in all the arguments sustaining the Democratic policy, and in that policy itself, there is a careful, studied exclusion of the idea that there is anything wrong in slavery. Let us understand this, I am not, just here, trying to prove that we are right and they are wrong. I have been stating here where we and they stand, and trying to show what is the real difference between us; and I now say that whenever we can get the question distinctly stated- can get all these men who believe that slavery is in some respects wrong, to stand and act with us in treating it as a wrong-then, and not till then, I think we will in some way come to an end of this slavery agitation." (2)

He was applauded vigorously and walked off the stage to gain his composure. In the wing he was met by a Mr. Bateman, who was the Superintendent of Public Instruction for the State of Illinois. Lincoln was visibly shaking. Bateman invited Lincoln into a backroom to catch himself. He recorded a rather revealing conversation, which allowed him to see a side of Lincoln, which Lincoln had mostly kept to himself. While in the backroom Lincoln walked to a cabinet, picked up a bible and said,

> "I know there is a God, and that He hates injustice and slavery. I see a storm coming, and I know that his hand is in it. If He has a place and work for me, and I think He has, I believe I am ready! I am nothing, but truth is everything! I know I am right, because I know that liberty is right: for Christ teaches it.
>
> "I have told them that a house divided against itself cannot stand, and Christ and reason say the same thing. Douglas does not care whether slavery is voted up or down. But God cares, and humanity cares, and I care. And with God's help, I will not fail. I may not see the end, but it will come, and I shall be vindicated; and those men will see that they have not read their Bible's right! Does it not appear strange that men can ignore the moral aspect of this contest? A revelation could not make it plainer to me that slavery, or the government, must be destroyed. The future would be something awful, as I look at it, but for this ROCK (alluding to the Bible in his

> hand) on which I stand. It seems as if God had borne with slavery until the very teachers of religion had come to defend it from the Bible, and to claim for it a Divine character and sanction. And now the cup of iniquity is full, and the vials of wrath are to be poured out."

Mr. Bateman then relates that Lincoln for a while expounded on his belief in Divine Providence and the privilege of prayer for guidance and that he had sought guidance to lead his country out of the wilderness and into an era of untold well-being and prosperity. Bateman then replied,

> "I had not supposed that you were accustomed to think so much on this class of subjects; certainly your friends generally are ignorant of the sentiments you have expressed to me." Lincoln answered,
>
> "I know they are, but I think more on these subjects than upon all others, and am willing you should know it." (3)

About this same time the Whigs and Democrats were full of corrupt career politicians, much like today. People were becoming disenchanted. The result was that certain members from both parties left their respective parties to form the *American Party*, also known as the Know-Nothing Party. Another party forming was the Republican Party. As the issue of slavery was being tweaked the American Party became irrelevant at the onset of the Civil War and the remainder was folded into the Republican Party. Among the Know-Nothing's political platform was

1. A call to extend the five-year naturalization period to twenty-one years, as well as a proscription against the holding of elected offices by Catholics and foreigners. Like much of the country, however, the Know-Nothings soon divided over the explosive slavery issue, and the power of the party quickly waned. Their nominee for president in 1856, former President Mil-

lard Fillmore, received just twenty-one percent of the popular vote and won only the state of Maryland. Still disdaining urban foreigners, most of who were Democrats, many of the nowerstwhile Know-Nothings allied with the newly formed Republican Party.

2. Perpetuation of the Federal Union and Constitution, as the palladium of our civil and religious liberties, and the only sure bulwarks of American Independence.

3. *Americans must rule America;* and to this end *native*-born citizens should be selected for all State, Federal and municipal offices of government employment, in preference to all others. *Nevertheless*,

4. Persons born of American parents residing temporarily abroad, should be entitled to all the rights of native-born citizens.

5. No person should be selected for political station (whether of native or foreign birth), who recognizes any allegiance or obligation of any description to any foreign prince, potentate or power, or who refuses to recognize the Federal and State Constitutions (each within its sphere) as paramount to all other laws, as rules of political action.

6. The unqualified recognition and maintenance of the reserved rights of the several States, and the cultivation of harmony and fraternal good will between the citizens of the several States, and to this end, non-interference by Congress with questions appertaining solely to the individual States, and non-intervention by each State with the affairs of any other State.

7. The recognition of the right of native-born and naturalized citizens of the United States, permanently residing in any territory thereof, to frame their constitution and laws, and to regulate their domestic and social affairs in their own mode, subject only to the provisions of the Federal Constitution, with the privilege of admission into the Union whenever they have the requisite population for one Representative in Congress: *Provided, always*, that none but those who are citizens of the United States, under the Constitution and laws thereof, and who have a fixed residence in any such Territory, ought to participate in the formation of the Constitution, or in the enactment of laws for said Territory or State.

8. An enforcement of the principles that no State or Territory ought to admit others than citizens to the right of suffrage, or of holding political offices of the United States.

9. A change in the laws of naturalization, making a continued residence of twenty-one years, of all not heretofore provided for, an indispensable requisite for citizenship hereafter, and excluding all paupers, and persons convicted of crime, from landing upon our shores; but no interference with the vested rights of foreigners.

10. Opposition to any union between Church and State; no interference with religious faith or worship, and no test oaths for office....

13. Opposition to the reckless and unwise policy of the present Administration in the general management of our national affairs, and more especially as shown in removing "Americans" (by designation) and Conservatives in principle, from office, and placing foreigners and Ultraists in their places; as

> shown in a truckling subserviency to the stronger, and an insolent and cowardly bravado toward the weaker powers; as shown in reopening sectional agitation, by the repeal of the Missouri Compromise; as shown in granting to unnaturalized foreigners the right of suffrage in Kansas and Nebraska; as shown in its vacillating course on the Kansas and Nebraska question; as shown in the corruptions which pervade some of the Departments of the Government; as shown in disgracing meritorious naval officers through prejudice or caprice: and as shown in the blundering mismanagement of our foreign relations.
>
> 14. Therefore, to remedy existing evils, and prevent the disastrous consequences otherwise resulting therefrom, we would build up the "American Party" upon the principles herein before stated....

SOURCE: Greeley, Horace and John F. Cleveland. *A Political Text-book for 1860.* New York: Tribune Association, 1860.

Abraham Lincoln was well acquainted with the Bible.

When Abraham Lincoln visited his friend Joshua Speed in Kentucky in the summer of 1841, Speed's mother gave him an Oxford Bible. When Mr. Lincoln returned to the judicial circuit that fall, he wrote Speed's sister back in Kentucky: "Tell your mother that I have not got her 'present' with me; but that I intend to read it regularly when I return home. I doubt not that it is really, as she says, the best cure for the 'Blues' could one but take it according to the truth." Because Mr. Lincoln had suffered severe blues in January after breaking his engagement with Mary Todd Lincoln, an antidote was needed.

Mr. Lincoln may have had trouble taking the Bible as literal truth, but he had no trouble reading it. As President Lincoln said: "In regard to this Great book, I have but to say, it is the best gift God has given to man. All the good the Savior gave to the world was communicated through this book. But for it we could not know right from wrong. All things most desirable for man's welfare, here and hereafter, are to be found portrayed in it." But Mr. Lincoln was too honest a man to portray himself as conventionally pious. "A well-known picture of Tad and his father…represents the boy standing by his father's side, looking over the pages of a large book.," wrote journalist Noah Brooks. "Lincoln explained to me that he was afraid that this picture was a species of false pretense. Most people, he thought, would suppose the book a large clasped Bible, whereas it was a big photograph album which the photographer, posing the father and son, had hit upon as a good device to use in this way to ring the two sitters together. Lincoln's anxiety lest somebody should think he was 'making believe to read the Bible to Tad,' was illustrative of his scrupulous honesty."

But Mr. Lincoln's deep knowledge of the scriptures could not have come without regularly reading them. As Lincoln scholar Paul Angle noted: "There was one book…which left its mark on much of what he wrote. That was the Bible. Upon a familiarity which extended back to his youth he could always depend." Historian Michael Nelson wrote: "For all his mockery, Lincoln was consumed by religion as a subject, as well as by the Bible, a book that all of his biographers agree he had read and studied assiduously since his youth. Although disdainful of Christianity in its cruder, frontier forms, Lincoln seems to have been open to, even seeking, an account of the faith that rang true on grounds of reason and justice." Religious scholar

Earl Schwartz wrote: “Lincoln’s legacy, far more than any other president, has, over time, become inextricably bound up with the words and themes of the Bible. He has been endowed repeatedly with biblical features – sometimes cast as Moses, on other occasions as Father Abraham, and yet again as a fiery prophet or martyred savior. An aura of prophetic authority has accrued to his own words, heightened by his skillful use of literary devices that are also characteristic of biblical texts.”

For Mr. Lincoln, the Bible brought him a lifetime of education. Scholar Elton Trueblood wrote of Mr. Lincoln: “While it is generally recognized that young Lincoln heard many passages from the Bible both in his cabin home and in the Baptist meeting house, it is not equally known that he also encountered it in his fragmentary schooling. In this, as in so many aspects of his development, our most reliable evidence is that provided by the man himself. One day in the White House, as the President was speaking to Senator John B. Henderson, he was suddenly reminded of his early education. “Henderson,” he asked, “did you ever attend an old blab school? Yes? Well, so did I, and what little schooling I got in early life was in that way. I attended such a school in a log schoolhouse in Indiana where we had no reading books or grammars, and all our reading was done from the Bible. We stood in a long line and read in turn from it.” Thus, Lincoln read the Bible and heard it read before his father could afford to own a copy. According to his kinsman, Dennis Hanks, a family Bible was not purchased until 1819, when Abraham was ten years old.”

Julia Taft Bayne, a teenager who spent much of 1861 at the White House supervising her brother and their playmates, the two youngest Lincoln boys, recalled: “It is well known, of course, that

Mr. Lincoln was a great reader of the Bible, but I have a notion, without knowing exactly why I have it, that at the beginning of the war, he read the Bible quite as much for its literary style as he did for its religious or spiritual content. Perhaps I have this notion from his attitude when reading it. He read it in the relaxed, almost lazy attitude of a man enjoying a good book....Only once do I recall his saying anything about the Bible or religion and that was in reply to Tad's plea as to why he had to go to Sunday-school . 'Every educated person should know something about the Bible and the Bible stories, Tad,' answered his father."

Mr. Lincoln's knowledge of the Bible was impressive. After he heard that only 400 persons attended the Ohio convention nominating John C. Frémont for President in May 1864, Mr. "Lincoln took his Bible up from his desk and after a little search came upon the passage which told of David and the company which gathered about him at the cave of Adullam when he was pursued and persecuted by King Saul: 'And everyone that was in distress, and everyone that was in debt, and everyone that was discontented, gathered themselves unto him; and he became a captain over them; and there were with him about four hundred men.'(I Samuel 22:2.). Thus the president used his knowledge of the Bible to describe and ridicule the critics, complainers, and malcontents who had gathered about Fremont," wrote Clarence Edward Macartney in Lincoln and the Bible.

In his reply to Illinois Senator Stephen Douglas's criticisms at the beginning of their 1858 campaign, Mr. Lincoln said: "My friend has said to me that I am a poor hand to quote Scripture. I will try it again, however. It is said in one of the admonitions of the Lord, 'As your Father in Heaven is perfect, be ye also perfect.' The Savior, I suppose, did not expect that any human creature could be perfect as the Father in Heaven; but He said, 'As your Father in Heaven is perfect, be ye also perfect.' He set that up as a standard, and he who did most towards reaching that standard, attained the highest degree of moral perfection. So I say in relation to the principle that all men are created equal, let it be as nearly reached as we can.'"

During the 1860 campaign, a Springfield minister wrote a New Jersey colleague in defense of Mr. Lincoln: "From the frequency and readiness with which he is accustomed to quote from the Bible and the use he makes of such quotations it is clear that he has read and pondered its contents. I wish I could say that he is born of god." Clarence E. Macartney wrote: "The ordinary daily speech of Lincoln was salted with timely and apt quotations from the Bible." He cited President Lincoln's response to General George B. McClellan's complaints about the weather bogging down his army. Mr. Lincoln told aide John Hay that the general "seemed to think, in defiance of Scripture, that heaven sent its rain only on the just, and not on the unjust." Also during the presidential campaign, Mr. Lincoln had a long conversation with State Superintendent of Instruction Newton Bateman. Five years later, Bateman wrote that in October 1860, Mr. Lincoln "repeated many passages of the Bible, in a very reverent & devout way, & seemed especially impressed with the solemn grandeur of portions of revelation describing the wrath of Almighty God."

Mr. Lincoln himself said "the Bible is the richest source of pertinent quotations." Paraphrased biblical quotes were sprinkled through Mr. Lincoln's public and private speech. Theologian William Wolf wrote: "Lincoln enjoyed quoting a text as his immediate response to something said to him. He deflated the somewhat pompous Lord Lyons, the British ambassador, who made an official call to announce formally to the President in the name of his gracious sovereign Queen Victoria the betrothal of the Prince of Wales to the Princess Alexandra of Denmark. Said Lincoln to the bachelor ambassador when he had finished his communication, 'Go thou and do likewise.'

"Next to this type of repartee, he liked to quote Scripture in answer to Scripture. Hugh McCulloch, an official of the Treasury Department, once introduced a delegation of New York bankers with much deference. Speaking of their patriotism and loyalty in holding the securities of the nation, he clinched his commendation of them with the text: 'Where the treasure is there will the heart be also.' Lincoln, like a crack of the whip, rejoined, 'There is another text, Mr. McCulloch, which might apply, 'Where the carcass is, there will the eagles be gathered together.'"

Pennsylvania Republican leader Alexander K. McClure wrote: "President Lincoln was censured for appointing one that had zealously opposed his second term. He replied: "Well, I suppose Judge E., having been disappointed before, did behave pretty ugly, but that wouldn't make him any less fit for the place; and I think I have Scriptural authority for appointing him. "You remember when the Lord was on Mount Sinai getting out a commission for Aaron, that same Aaron was at the foot of the mountain making a false god for the people to worship. Yet Aaron got his commission, you know."

Presbyterian scholar Clarence Macartney wrote: "To a man who complained bitterly and carelessly against Edwin M. Stanton, the secretary of war, accusing Stanton of not carrying out the order that Lincoln had given two weeks before to have a man liberated from prison who was under sentence of death, but had been pardoned, Lincoln said: "If it had not been for me, that man would now be in his grave. Now, sir, you claim to be a philanthropist. If you will get your Bible and turn to the thirtieth chapter of Proverbs, the tenth verse, you will read these words: 'Accuse not a servant unto his master, lest he curse thee, and thou be found guilty.'" Macartney continued the story with the reminiscences of White House staffer Thomas N. Pendel:

"Whereupon the man got 'huffy' and went away. But as he went out, he said angrily, 'There is no such passage in the Bible.' 'Oh, yes,' said Mr. Lincoln, "I think you will find it in the thirtieth chapter of Proverbs and at the tenth verse.' This was late in the afternoon, and I thought no more of the occurrence. Next morning I was at Mr. Lincoln's office door as usual, about 8 o'clock, and heard some one calling out: 'O Pendleton! I say, Pendleton, come in here.' When I went inside Mr. Lincoln said to me, 'Wait a moment.' He stepped quickly into the private part of the house, through what is now the Cabinet Room, but which was then used as a waiting room, and soon reappeared with his Bible in his hand. He then sat down and read to me that identical passage he had quoted to the philanthropist, and sure enough it was found to be in the thirtieth chapter of Proverbs, and at the tenth verse."

William Wolf wrote: "Lincoln's knowledge of the bible was so thorough that his political opponents generally found themselves on dangerous ground when they quoted it against him. When Judge Douglas somewhat fantastically cited Adam and Eve as the first beneficiaries of his doctrine of 'popular sovereignty' Lincoln corrected him. 'God did not place good and evil before man, telling him to make his choice. On the contrary, he did tell him there was one tree, of the fruit of which he should not eat, upon pain of certain death.' Then added Lincoln pointedly, 'I should scarcely wish so strong a prohibition against slavery in Nebraska.'" The evidence of President Lincoln's religious faith is in the clearest possible location: his writings and speeches. Lincoln scholar Earl Schwartz wrote that his Collected Works are...peppered with biblical references, including several dozen direction quotations. These are taken, for the most par, from Hebrew bible narratives, including Psalms, Wisdom texts, and the Gospels." Mr. Lincoln's most famous works are studded with biblical quotations or references:

The "house divided" analogy from his 1858 Republican nomination speech for the Senate.

His reference in his First Inaugural Address to "a firm reliance on Him who has never yet forsaken this favored land".

His invocation in his First Annual Message to Congress that: "With a reliance on Providence all the more firm and earnest, let us proceed in the great task which events have devolved upon us."

The quotation in his Second Inaugural Address that "judgements of the Lord are true and righteous altogether."

The reference in the Gettysburg Address that this "Nation shall under God have a new birth of freedom."

Lincoln biographer William E. Barton wrote that Mr. Lincoln "read the Bible, honored it, quoted it freely, and it became so much a part of him as visibly and permanently to give shape to his literary style and to his habits of thought." When a delegation of African-Americans from Baltimore presented President Lincoln with a Bible in September 1864, he replied: "This occasion would seem fitting for a lengthy response to the address which you have just made. I would make one, if prepared; but I am not. I would promise to respond in writing, had not experience taught me that business will not allow me to do so. I can only now say, as I have often before said, it has always been a sentiment with me that all mankind should be free. So far as able, within my sphere, I have always acted as I believed to be right and just; and I have done all I could for the good of mankind generally. In letters and documents sent from this office I have expressed myself better than I now can. In regard to this Great Book, I have but to say, it is the best gift God has given to man."

All the good the Saviour gave to the world was communicated through this book. But for it we could not know right from wrong. All things most desirable for man's welfare, here and hereafter, are to be found portrayed in it. To you I return my most sincere thanks for the very elegant copy of the great Book of God which you present.

Rev. S. W. Chase spoke for the delegation that presented Mr. Lincoln with a Bible: "The loyal colored people of Baltimore have entrusted us with authority to present this Bible as a testimonial of their appreciation of your humane conduct towards the people of our race. While all others of this nation are offering their tribute of respect to you, we cannot omit suitable manifestation of ours. Since our incorporation into the American family we have been true and loyal, and we are now ready to aid in defending the country, to be armed and trained in military matters, in order to assist in protecting and defending the star-spangled banner."

"Towards you, sir, our hearts will ever be warm with gratitude. We come to present to you this copy of the Holy Scriptures, as a token of respect for your active participation in furtherance of the cause of the emancipation of our race. This great event will be a matter of history. Hereafter, when our children shall ask what mean these tokens, they will be told of your worthy deeds, and will rise up and call you blessed.'

"The loyal colored people of this country everywhere will remember you at the Throne of Divine Grace. May the King Eternal, an all-wise, Providence protect and keep you, and when you pass from this world to that of eternity, may you be borne to the bosom of your Savior and your God."

The Bible was the source of Mr. Lincoln's deep conviction of the role of "Providence" in human life. U.S. Marshal Ward Hill Lamon reported Mr. Lincoln recalling a dream that foretold his death. Mr. Lincoln read: "It seems strange how much there is in the Bible about dreams. There are, I think, some sixteen chapters in the Old Testament and four or five in the New in which dreams are mentioned; and there are many other passages scattered throughout the book which refer to visions. If we believe the Bible, we must accept the fact that in the old days God and His angels came to men in their sleep and made themselves known in dreams. Nowadays dreams are regarded as very foolish, and are seldom told, except by old women and by young men and maidens in love."

In a lecture delivered 15 years after Mr. Lincoln's death, Joshua F. Speed recalled a visit to President Lincoln at the Soldiers' Home: "As I entered the room, near night, he was sitting near a window intently reading his Bible. Approaching him I said: "I am glad to see you so profitably engaged.' 'Yes,' said he, "I am profitably engaged.' 'Well,' said I, 'if you have recovered from your skepticism, I am sorry to say that I have not.' Looking me earnestly in the face and placing his hand on my shoulder, he said: 'You are wrong, Speed. Take all of this book upon reason that you can and the balance on faith, and you will live and die a happier and better man.'" Lincoln scholar Wayne Temple wrote: "Lincoln had greatly modified his religious beliefs since Speed at Springfield in 1841. It appears, the longer Lincoln lived, the closer he felt to God and the more he relied upon God for sustenance.'"

Mr. Lincoln reportedly told Treasury Department official Lucius E. Chittenden: "Now, let us treat the Bible fairly. If we had a witness on the stand whose general story we knew was true, we would believe him when he asserted facts of which we had no other evidence. We ought to treat the bible with equal fairness. I decided a long time ago that it was less difficult to believe that the Bible was what it claimed to be than to disbelieve it. It is a good book for us to obey – it contains the ten commandments, the Golden Rule, and many other rules which ought to be followed. No man was ever the worse for living according to the directions of the Bible."

But Mr. Lincoln also approached the Bible with his customary humility. William Wolf wrote: "One of the greatnesses of Lincoln was the way he held to strong moral positions without the usual accompaniment of self-righteousness or smugness. He expressed this rare achievement provisionally in his humor and in an ultimate dimension in his religious evaluations. To the Pennsylvania delegation that congratulated him after the inauguration he said, urging forbearance and respect for differences of opinion between the states, 'I would inculcate this idea, so that we may not, like Pharisees, set ourselves up to be better than other people.'"

Abraham Lincoln's faith

In December 1864, President Abraham Lincoln wrote out a story for his friend, journalist Noah Brooks. It was entitled: The President's Last, Shortest and Best Speech. It read: "On Thursday of last week two ladies from Tennessee came before the President asking the release of their husbands held as prisoners of war at Johnson's Island. They were put off till Friday, when they came again; and were again put off to Saturday. At each of the interviews one of the ladies urged that her husband was a religious man. On Saturday the President ordered the release of the prisoners, and then said to this lady 'You say your husband is a religious man; tell him when you meet him, that I say I am not much of a judge of religion, but that, in my opinion, the religion that sets men to rebel and fight against their government, because, as they think, that government does not sufficiently help some men to eat their bread on the sweat of other mens faces, is not the sort of religion upon which people can get to heaven!"[1]

Abraham Lincoln was then and still is a religious enigma. Lincoln aide John G. Nicolay wrote: "Benevolence and forgiveness were the very basis of his character. His nature was deeply religious, but he belonged to no denomination; he had faith in the eternal justice and boundless mercy of Providence, and made the Golden Rule of Christ his practical creed."[2] Another aide, John Hay, wrote of Mr. Lincoln: "He belonged to no Church. Yet he was the uncanonized saint of all the Churches. He never uttered a prayer in public. Yet prayers for him fastened our cause daily with golden chains around the feet of God."[3] A third aide, Baptist William O. Stoddard, wrote: "President Lincoln was deeply and genuinely religious, without being in any way what may be called a religionist. His religion was in his faith and his life rather than in any profession. So far as I know, his religious belief or opinions never, at any period of his life, took the shape of a formal profession. His nature was not at all enthusiastic, and his mind was subject to none of the fevers which pass with the weak and shallow for religious fervor, and in this, as in all other things, he was too thoroughly honest to assume that which he did not feel."[4]

Connecticut Congressman H. C. Deming recalled that once when "the conversation turned upon religious subjects, and Mr. Lincoln made this impressive remark: 'I have never united myself to any church, because I have found difficulty in giving my assent, without mental reservation, to the long, complicated statements of Christian doctrine which characterize their Articles of Belief and Confessions of Faith. When any church will inscribe over its altar, as its sole qualification for membership,' he continued, 'the Saviour's condensed statement of the substance of both Law and Gospel, 'Thou shalt love the Lord thy God with all thy heart, and with all thy soul, and with all thy mind, and thy neighbor as thyself,' that church will I join will all my heart and all my soul."[5]

"His criticism of the churches of his day was that they neglected this fundamental love of God and of neighbor by too much introverted attention upon correctness in theological opinion. Prophetically Lincoln saw that concern for orthodoxy substituted for practical obedience," wrote religious historian William Wolf. "This perspective in Lincoln must not be confused, however, with another view that the churches themselves should not mix in politics. He took a dim view of preachers who used the pulpit for politics and said he preferred those who preached' the gospel.' By this, however, he meant that the layman's task was to put this gospel to work not merely in individual piety, although certainly there, but also in responsible political activity. As a biblical believer Lincoln saw God dealing with men not merely as isolated individuals with capacities for piety but as men in social orders that answerable to the Almighty."[6]

Mr. Lincoln's religious statements and supposed beliefs continue to confound. Historian Nicholas Parrillo wrote: "While Lincoln's statements on religion were at times profound, they were never lengthy or great in number. Some historians have tried to fill in the picture by using the reminiscences of people who knew Lincoln, but these sources entail problems of their own. Authors of reminiscences suffered from the tricks of memory. Further, they were especially tempted to bias their accounts when talking about religion, for after Lincoln was murdered and consequently canonized as a national saint, a heated controversy ensued over what religious group might claim him."[7] Nevertheless, noted church historian Mark A. Noll, "Lincoln's speeches and conversation revealed a spiritual perception far above the ordinary. It is one of the great ironies of the history of Christianity in America that the most profoundly religious analysis of the nation's deepest trauma came not from a clergyman or a theologian but from a politician who was self-taught in the ways of both God and humanity."[8]

In truth, Lincoln's religion was never conventional. He was as impious as a child as his parents were pious. While he accepted the antislavery dogma of the Pigeon Creek Baptist Church in which he grew up, he never adopted the fatalism of Calvinist predestination. He worshiped at the altar of reason and law. Reason for Mr. Lincoln was a refuge in an unreasonable world. Man's power was limited, but God was omnipotent. As a young man, he thought reason would solve everything. As a mature man, he grew to believe that only Providence could or would. Mr. Lincoln was open to revelation but skeptical of revelations delivered by self-appointed messengers. When a group of northern ministers pressed him on emancipation in September 1862, President Lincoln said: "I hope it will be irreverent for me to say that if it is probable that God would reveal his will to others, on a point so connected with my duty, it might be supposed he would reveal it directly to me; for, unless I am more deceived in myself than I often am, it is my earnest desire to know the will of Providence in this matter. And if I can learn what it is I will do it! These are not, however, the days of miracles, and I suppose it will be granted that I am not to expect for a direct revelation."[9]

Like his close friend Joshua Speed, Mr. Lincoln was a skeptic – he looked for proof for everything. Over the years, Herndon's allegation of Lincoln's heresy, although questioned and amended, has been largely adopted as historical gospel. It is generally admitted that Abraham Lincoln was a religious man, although an unorthodox one. About that there is little controversy. Harriet Beecher Stowe, the author of Uncle Tom's Cabin, interviewed the President prior to writing a profile for a Boston religious magazine. Mrs. Stowe, herself the sister of a famous New York abolitionist preacher, wrote: "In our times of our trouble Abraham Lincoln has had his turn of being the best abused man of our nation. Like Moses leading his Israel through the wilderness, he has seen the day when every man seemed ready to stone him, and yet, with simple, wiry, steady perseverance, he has held on, conscious of honest intentions, and looking to God for help. All the nation have felt, in the increasing solemnity of his proclamations and papers, how deep an education was being wrought in his mind by this simple faith in God, the rule of nations, and this humble willingness to learn the awful lessons of his providence." Mrs. Stowe recognized that Lincoln was not a conventional Christian, but "we see evidence in passing through this dreadful national crisis he has been forced by the very anguish of the struggle to look upward, where any rational creature must look for support."[10]

Lincoln's attitudes towards religion originally were formed by attendance at the Little Pigeon Creek Church near his boyhood home in Indiana. Lincoln scholar M. L. Houser wrote: "The members of the Little Pigeon Creek congregation were opposed to a paid ministry, and were also strongly anti-missionary."[11] Young Lincoln himself had a strong disposition that he could imitate the church's preachers. "I will tell you a circumstance about him. He would come home from church, put a box in the middle of the cabin floor, and repeat the sermon from text to doxology. I've heard him do it often," recalled one contemporary.[12] Young Lincoln did it well as a child. He did it better as an adult when his works like the Second Inaugural had a strong religious themes.

"When father and Mother would go to church, Abe would take down the Bible, read a verse – give out a hymn – we would sing," recalled stepsister Matilda Johnson. Young Abe "preached & we would do the Crying – sometimes he would join in the Chorus of Tears. One day my brother John Johnston caught a land terrapin – brought it to the place where Abe was preaching – threw it against the tree – crushed the shell and it suffered much and quivered all over. Abe preached against cruelty to animals, contending that an ant's life was to it, as sweet as ours to us."[13]

Religious scholar Ronald C. White, Jr., noted that "If Lincoln enjoyed spoofing the sermons of frontier preachers as a young boy, the mature man employed a form of speech resembling sermons as old as the New England Puritans and as contemporary as the discourses of the evangelical abolitionists."[14] As Mr. Lincoln grew older, he developed a reputation as a religious skeptic, but he also shared a profound respect for those with a deeper faith than he possessed. One Illinois contemporary, Gilbert Greene, recalled a side to young Lincoln that was seldom seen: "One day Mr. Lincoln said to me, 'Gilbert, there is a woman dangerously sick fifteen miles in the country who has sent for me to write her will. I should like to have you accompany me.' I cheerfully accepted the invitation. When we arrived the woman had but a few hours to live. After the will had been written, signed and witnessed, the dying woman said to Mr. Lincoln, – 'Now, I have my affairs in this world arranged satisfactorily. I have also made preparation for the life to come. I do not fear death. I am glad that I am soon to meet those who have gone before.' Mr. Lincoln replied, – 'Your faith in God is wise and strong. Your hope of a future life is blessed.' She asked him then if he would not read a few verses from the Bible. They offered him the Book; he did not take it, but began reciting from memory the 23rdrd Psalm. Then he quoted the first part of the 14th chapter of John, – 'In my father's house are many mansions; if it were not so, I would have told you.' After he had given these and other quotations from the Scriptures he recited several hymns, closing with 'Rock of Ages, Cleft for me.'" Gilbert recalled: "A little while after the woman passed to her reward. As we rode home in the buggy I expressed surprise that he should have acted as pastor as well as attorney so perfectly, and he replied, 'God and eternity were very near me today.'"[15]

Much of young Lincoln's time in New Salem was split between the small community's believers and its skeptics. Historian Michael Nelson wrote: "Working a variety of jobs and spending much of his free time at the general store, Lincoln was drawn to a crowd of cracker-barrel freethinkers who passed around well-worn copies of two popular works of the Enlightenment; Thomas Paine's The Age of Reason and Constantin-Francois de Volney's Ruins, or a Survey of the Revolution of Empires."[16]

Many contemporaries testified to his early skepticism. "When I knew him in early life, he was a skeptic," said friend Joshua F. Speed with whom Mr. Lincoln roomed in Springfield. "He had tried hard to be a believer, but his reason could not grasp and solve the great problem of redemption as taught. He was very cautious never to give expression to any thought or sentiment that would grate harshly upon a Christian's ear. For a sincere Christian he had great respect. He often said that the most ambitious man might live to see every hope fail; but, no Christian could live to see his fail, because fulfillment could only come when life ended."[17] Noted friend William Jayne, "I believe that Mr. Lincoln was by nature a deeply religious man. But have I seen no evidence that he ever accepted the formulated creed of any sect or denomination. I should say that all churches had his respect and good wishes."[18] President Lincoln told friend Joshua F. Speed: "Speed, you had better be without money than without religion." [19]

Mr. Lincoln's skepticism followed him to Springfield. James Matheny knew Mr. Lincoln in the mid-1830s and later charged that he "used to talk Infidelity in the Clerks office in the city about the years 1837-40. Lincoln attacked the Bible and new Testament on two grounds 1st from the inherent or apparent contradiction under its lids & 2dly from the grounds of Reason. Sometimes Lincoln bordered on absolute Atheism: he went far that way

& often shocked me."[20] But like Mr. Lincoln, Matheny's views also changed with time, noted Lincoln biographer William E. Barton.

Based on Matheny's testimony, William Herndon popularized the notion that Mr. Lincoln had written a shockingly irreverent tract as a young man in New Salem. Herndon wrote: "James H. Matheny tells me that from about 1854 to 1860 Lincoln played a sharp game here on the religious world, that Lincoln knew that he was to be a great man, was a rising man, was looking to the Presidency, etc., and well knowing that the old infidel, if not atheistic, charge would be made and proved against him, and to avoid the disgrace, odium, and unpopularity of it, trampled on the Christian toes, saying: 'Come and convert me.' The elders, lower and higher members of the churches, including ministers, etc., flocked around him and that he appeared openly to the world as a seeker after salvation, etc., in the Lord; that letters were written more or less all over the land that Lincoln was soon to be a changed man, etc., and thus was he used the Reverend James Smith of Scotland, old man Bergen, and others."[21]

Mr. Lincoln's early religious thinking is clouded by faulty and contradictory memories of his contemporaries. William Wolf wrote: "No one ever offered direct evidence that he had himself read or heard read this supposed essay on 'infidelity.' There is another theory about the lost book reputedly burned by Hill. This version holds that youngsters in the village found a sizable letter written by Hill but somehow dropped by him. They returned it to Lincoln, the village postmaster, and as he was reading it aloud, possibly for purposes of identification, Hill, wanting to keep its contents a private matter, snatched the letter away and threw it into the flames. This version, however, has obvious difficulties."

"Still another piece of testimony claims that Lincoln wrote an essay in defense of his own interpretation of christianity. It would be easy in that contentious atmosphere to see how the later story of an infidel book might have grown up. In the light of Lincoln's own denial of infidelity in the handbill of 1846 this explanation has more to commend it than Herndon's dramatic tale or the 'Hill letter' theory. It is further strengthened in coming directly from Mentor Graham, Lincoln's New Salem tutor and reputed helper in early speech writing."[22]

New Salem resident Mentor Graham had a very different story of Mr. Lincoln's tract-writing: "Abraham Lincoln was living at my house in New Salem, going to school, studying English grammar and survey, in the year 1833. One morning he said to me, 'Graham, what do you think about the anger of the Lord? I replied, 'I believe the Lord never was angry or mad and never would be; that His loving kindness endures forever; that He never changes.' Said Lincoln, 'I have a little manuscript written, which I will show you'; and stated he thought of having it published. Offering it to me, he said he had never showed it to anyone, and still thought of having it published. The size of the manuscript was about one-half quire of foolscap, written in a very plain hand, on the subject of Christianity and a defense of universal salvation. The commencement of it was something respecting the God of the universe never being excited, mad or angry. I had the manuscript in my possession some week or ten days. I have read many books on the subject of theology and I don't think in point of perspicuity and plainness of reasoning, I ever read one to surpass it. I remember well his argument. He took the passage, 'As in Adam all die, even so in Christ shall all be made alive,' and followed up with the proposition that whatever the breach or injury of Adam's transgressions to the human race was, which no doubt was very great, was made just and right by the atonement of Christ.'"[23]

Nevertheless, the evidence for skepticism on Mr. Lincoln's part during this period of his life is strong. Fellow attorney Milton Hay wrote: "Candor compels me to say that at this period, Mr. Lincoln could hardly be termed a devout believer in the authenticity of the Bible (but this is for your ear only)."[24] Law partner William H. Herndon forcefully argued that Mr. Lincoln was a religious skeptic. He wrote: "As already expressed, Mr. Lincoln had no faith. In order to believe, he must see and feel, and thrust his hand into the place. He must taste, smell, and handle before he had faith or even belief. Such a mind manifestly must have its time. His forte and power lay in digging out for himself and securing for his mind its own food, to be assimilated unto itself. Thus, in time he would form opinions and conclusions that no human power could overthrow. They were as irresistible as the rush of a flood; as convincing as logic embodied in mathematics. And yet the question arises: 'Had Mr. Lincoln great, good common-sense?' A variety of opinions suggest themselves in answer to this. If the true test is that a man shall judge the rush and whirl of human actions and transactions as wisely and accurately as though indefinite time and proper conditions were at his disposal, then I am compelled to follow the logic of things and admit that he had no great stock of common sense; but if, on the other hand, the time and conditions were ripe, his common-sense was in every case equal to the emergency. He knew himself, and never trusted his dollar or his fame in causal opinions never acted hastily or prematurely on great matters.[25]

Historian Richard J. Carwardine wrote: "Though James Matheny suggested that the only change to occur was in Lincoln's greater discretion, not his views, which Matheny thought remained skeptical (at least up to 1861), there are reasonable grounds for believing that the mature Lincoln of the 1850s was more receptive to Protestant orthodoxy than he had been twenty years earlier. Then the essential elements of Lincoln's religious outlook surely contributed to the new tone and substance of his speeches following his return to politics in 1854. For the first time he devoted whole speeches to the question of slavery, including its corrosive effect on individual enterprise and aspiration, and found a moral edge for which political opportunism provides only the shallowest of explanations."[26] Historian Allen C. Guelzo wrote; "Lincoln's own failure to establish a recognizable religious profile had long been, as he well knew, a major political liability; as early as 1837, he was aware that his political enemies were asking 'an old acquaintance of mine' whether 'he ever heard Lincoln say he was a deist,' and in 1843 he acknowledged that 'because I belonged to no church,' he had suffered 'a tax of considerable per cent, upon my strength throughout the religious community."[27] The problem was aggravated in his 1846 congressional campaign against Democrat Peter Cartwright, who was a well-known Methodist circuit-rider.

Historian Donald W. Riddle noted that Mr. Lincoln's religious orthodoxy was. "Peter Cartwright allowed his professional zeal to mislead him into making use of a campaign argument of questionable propriety, when he alleged that Lincoln was an 'infidel,' and no fit representative of Christian people. Report of Cartwright's campaign tactic was made to Lincoln, who took it seriously enough to cause a small handbill to be printed in which he refuted the charge. This was circulated in the northern part of the district, where Cartwright's charge appeared to be having some effect. Lincoln's friend, Dr. Robert Boal, some years later wrote to Richard Yates, recalling that 'Cartwright sneaked through this part of the district after Lincoln, and grossly misrepresented him.' Lincoln concluded, on the basis of the election returns, that because of Cartwright's raising of the religious issue he had lost some votes in the localities where he was less well known. He was the more exasperated because Cartwright had made his charges in a 'whispering campaign' almost on the eve of the election, so that Lincoln could not effectively counter them."[28]

In response to the rumors and criticism Lincoln wrote an unusual public statement: "A charge having got into circulation in some of the neighborhoods of this District, in substance that I am an open scoffer at Christianity. That I am not a member of any Christian Church, is true; but I have never denied the truth of the Scriptures; and I have never spoken with intentional disrespect of religion in general, or of any denomination of Christians in particular. It is true that in early life I was inclined to believe in what I understand is called the "Doctrine of Necessity' that is, that the human mind is impelled to action or held in rest by some power, over which the mind itself has no control; and I have sometimes (with one, two or three, but never publicly) tried to maintain this opinion in argument. The habit of arguing this, however, I have entirely left off for more than five years. And I add here, I have always understood this same opinion to be held by several of the Christian denominations. The foregoing, is the whole truth, briefly stated, in relation to myself, upon this subject."[29] During the congressional campaign Lincoln supposedly attended a revival meeting conducted by Cartright. When Cartright asked everyone in attendance who did not want to go to hell to stand, Lincoln stayed seated, so Cartright asked where Lincoln was going. "Brother Cartwright asked me directly where I am going. I desire to reply with equal directness," said Lincoln before walking out. "I am going to Congress."[30]

Historian Roy D. Packard wrote: "Lincoln resisted creeds and forms because he could not reconcile them with his own thinking of what religion should consist. His inquiring mind was never receptive to that which he could not reduce to essential elements. It has been said that he made no pretense to knowledge concerning those questions which 'theologians deal with so flippantly.' And he could not join the church, thereby subscribing to a belief in doctrines which he privately admitted were beyond his full understanding. A solitary reasoner, he would accept only his own decisions. 'If there were any traits of character that stood out in bold relief in the person of Mr. Lincoln,' wrote one of his associates, 'they were those of truth and candor. He was utterly incapable of insincerity or professing views on any subject that he did not entertain."[31]

Mr. Lincoln clearly had trouble with some religious doctrines. President Lincoln himself once told a visiting clergyman: "Elder Benjamn H. Smith, I understand your explanation of foreordination, election, and predestination; I understand your plea for a return to the apostolic order of things religious; but the way preachers have generally explained these things, the more they explained, the less I understood them, and my mind got more and more muddled. And I must confess that the latter story sometimes expresses a state of my mind that to me is dangerous. The preachers have preached and talked this 'miraculous conversion' and such other (to me) very absurd theories of religion and given such contradictory explanations of the Bible, that I have honestly at times doubted the whole thing."[32]

Mr. Lincoln's religious interest was intensified by the death of the Lincoln's second son, Eddie, a month short of his fourth birthday in 1850. Controversy surrounds a claim by Dr. James Smith that Mr. Lincoln subsequently had made a religious profession. Dr. Smith testified: "The Episcopalian rector, an excellent clergyman, being temporarily absent, could not be present to conduct the burial service, and I was called to officiate at the funeral. This led me to an intimate acquaintance with the family, and grew into an enduring and confidential friendship between Mr. Lincoln and myself. One result was that the wife and mother returned to her ancestral church, and the husband and father very willingly came with her, and ever since has been a constant attendant upon my ministry.[33] Brother-in-law Ninian Edwards testified: "A short time after the Rev. Dr. Smith became pastor of the First Presbyterian Church in this city, Mr. Lincoln said to me, 'I have been reading a work of Dr. Smith on the evidences of Christianity, and have heard him preach and converse on the subject, and am now convinced of the truth of the Christian religion.'" [34] Scholar William Wolf wrote: "Thomas Lewis, a Springfield lawyer and deacon of the church Lincoln attended, and John T. Stuart, his early law partner, both spoke of the impact of Dr. Smith's book on Lincoln. Ninian Edwards, his brother-in-law, reported Lincoln told him, 'I have been reading a work of Dr. Smith on the evidences of Christianity, and have heard him preach and converse on the subject and am now convinced of the truth of the Christian religion.'"[35]

John Todd Stuart later wrote: "Dr. Smith, then pastor of the First Presbyterian Church of Springfield, at the suggestion of a lady friend of theirs, called upon Mr. and Mrs. Lincoln and that first visit resulted in great intimacy and friendship between them, lasting until the death of Mr. Lincoln and continuing with Mrs. Lincoln until the death of Dr. Smith…I stated however that it was certainly true that up to that time Mr. Lincoln had never regularly attended any place of religious worship, but that after he rented a pew in the First Presbyterian Church, and that his family constantly attended the worship in that church until he went to Washington as president. This much I said at that time and can now add that the Hon Ninian Edwards, the brother-in-law of Mr. Lincoln, had within a few days informed me that when Mr. Lincoln commenced attending the Presbyterian Church, he admitted to him that his views had undergone the change claimed by Dr. Smith. I would further say that Dr. Smith was a man of very great ability and that on theological and metaphysical subjects, had few superiors and not many equals. Truthfulness was a prominent trait in Mr. Lincoln's character and it would be impossible for any intimate friend of his to believe that he ever aimed to deceive either by his words or conduct."[36]

Dr. Smith wrote to William Herndon in January 1867: "Your letter of the 20thth of December was duly received, in which you ask me to answer several questions in relation to the illustrious President, Abraham Lincoln. With regard to your second question, I beg leave to say it is a very easy matter to prove that while I was pastor of the First Presbyterian Church of Springfield, Mr. Lincoln did avow his belief in the divine authority and inspiration of the Scriptures. And I hold that it is a matter of greatest importance, not only to the present but to all future generations of the great Republic and to all advocates of civil and religious liberty throughout the world, that this avowal on his part and the circumstances attending it, together with very interesting incidents illustrative of the excellence of his character in my possession should be made known to the public. My intercourse with Abraham Lincoln convinced me that he was not only an honest man, but preeminently an upright man, ever seeking, so far as was in his power, to render unto all their due. It was my honour to place before Mr. Lincoln arguments designed to prove the divine authority and inspiration of the Scriptures, accompanied by arguments of infidel objectors in their own language. To the arguments on both sides, Mr. Lincoln gave a most patient and searching investigation. To use his own language, he examined the arguments as a lawyer who is anxious to reach the truth investigates testimony. The result was the announcement by himself that the argument in favor of the divine authority and inspiration of the Scriptures was unanswerable. I could say much more on the subject, but as you are the person addressed, for the present I decline. The assassin Booth, by his diabolical act, unwittingly sent the illustrious martyr to glory, honour, and immortality, but his false friend has attempted to send him down to posterity with infamy branded on his forehead, as a man who, notwithstanding all he suffered for his country's good, was destitute to those feelings and affections without which there can be no excellency of character."[37] Historian Allen C. Guelzo wrote: "Robert Todd Lincoln told Herndon years later that he never remembered 'Dr. Smith's having 'converted' my father…nor do I know that he held any decided views on the subject as I never heard him speak of it.' John Todd Stuart knew that Smith 'tried to Convert Lincoln from Infidelity so late as 1858 and couldn't do it.'"[38]

Mary Todd Lincoln joined Dr. Smith's church in 1852 while her husband was away on the circuit. She had been baptized and brought up an Episcopalian. Her husband had been brought up a Baptist but had never been baptized, a requirement for joining the Presbyterian Church. "Since Abraham Lincoln would have to follow the full process in order to join, he may have been reluctant or did not have the time for it. In any event, Abraham Lincoln donated and regularly paid his $50.00 per year rent for Pew No. 20 which was located on the East side of the center aisle, in the fifth row from the front. He attended when could," wrote historian Robert J. Havlik. Rev. Smith reported that Mr. Lincoln himself spoke to the Springfield Bible Society: "It seems to me that nothing short of infinite wisdom could by any possibility have devised and given to man this excellent and perfect moral code. It is suited to me in all conditions of life and includes all the duties they owe to their Creator, to themselves, and to their fellow men."[39]

Lincoln historian Wayne Temple wrote: "Mary Lincoln divulged to John Todd Stuart on December 15, 1873, that her husband's heart 'was naturally religious.' However, she carefully pointed out to William H. Herndon in the St. Nicholas Hotel at Springfield, Illinois, on September 5, 1866, that her husband had never joined any church. Gleefully, Billy Herndon announced in his lecture on Lincoln's Religion, published in the Illinois State Register as a supplement on December 13, 1873, that the sorrowing widow had admitted that Abraham Lincoln had not technically been a Christian. True enough; Lincoln had never joined any denomination, and that should have put the matter to rest, but it did not."

Perhaps an old Springfield friend and neighbor, Dr. William Jayne, gave one of the best answers when he declared that "Mr. Lincoln was by nature a deeply religious man. But I have no evidence that he ever accepted the formulated creed of any sect or denomination. I know that all churches had his profound respect and support." Lincoln, said Dr.

Jayne, had an "enduring and abundant religious faith in the relations between God and his immortal soul." "It is now beyond the realm of controversy," explained Dr. Jayne, "that Lincoln loved, honored, and revered Almighty God."[40]

Mr. Lincoln's deepening religiosity corresponded with his fervent anti-slavery sermons during the 1850s – which were delivered as political speeches. Historian Richard J. Carwardine wrote that Lincoln friend "Joseph Gillespie recorded the animation and almost Puritan earnestness with which Lincoln discussed the need to challenge slavery's moral and social evils: ostentatious wealth, enervating leisure and a view of injustice and an enormous national crime': the country, he told Gillespie, 'could not expect to escape punishment for it'. Surfacing here in Lincoln's thought was the Calvinist view of the political nation as a moral being. God punished wicked nations for their sins, just as he punished delinquent individuals." [41] Richard Yates, the wartime governor of Illinois, later wrote that "whatever may have been his religious views or convictions, yet nothing can be clearer than that from the day he left Springfield, until the day of his death, as all his proclamations, messages, and the testimony of many good men will show, he manifested an implicit reliance upon Divine Providence, and his faith was made sure and his arm strengthened by an unshaken conviction that the ever-living God was on our side and would preserve, unimpaired, our free institutions, a priceless heritage for ourselves and our children."[42]

Most observers agree that President Lincoln strongly believed in the rule of Providence in the world. "I know that Mr. Lincoln was a firm believer in a superintending and overruling Providence, and in supernatural agencies and events," noted Orville H. Browning. "I know that he believed the destinies of men were, or at least, that his own destiny was shaped and controlled by an intelligence and power higher and greater than his own, and which he could neither control nor thwart."[43] Jesse Fell wrote that Mr. Lincoln "fully believed in a superintending and overruling Providence that guides and control the operations of the world, but maintained that law and order, and not their violation or suspension, are the appointed means by which this Providence is exercised."[44] President Lincoln supposedly told Treasury Department official Lucius E. Chittenden:

"That the Almighty does make use of human agencies, and directly intervenes in human affairs, is one of the plainest statements of the Bible. I have had so many evidences of his directions, so many instances when I have been controlled by some other power than my own will, that I cannot doubt that this power comes from above. I frequently see my way clear to a decision when I am conscious that I have no sufficient facts upon which to found it. But I cannot recall one instance in which I have followed my own judgment founded upon such a decision, where the results were unsatisfactory; whereas, in almost every instance where I have yielded to the views of others, I have had occasion to regret it. I am satisfied that when the Almighty wants me to do or not to do a particular thing, he finds a way of letting me know it. I am confident that it is his design to restore the Union. He will do it in his own good time. We should obey and not oppose his will."[45]

Historian Nicholas Parrillo wrote that "though Lincoln always subscribed to the same technical definition of providence, the role that this concept played in his rhetoric under a gradual but dramatic change during his presidency."[46] Parrillo contended that "once Lincoln became president and began to prosecute war against the Confederacy, his statements on religion took on a different cast. The notion of God that appeared in his language gravitated ever closer to that of Calvinism: an activist, independent, and judgmental God whose designed informed every single earthly event but whose purposes often seemed inscrutable to human eyes. Linked to this notion was a Calvinist-like view of humanity as utterly sinful, deserving of retribution, and entirely dependent on God in all aspects of life."[47] Scholar Jacques Barzun connected Mr. Lincoln's belief in Providence to his consciousness of his own inadequacies: "What is clear is that Lincoln lived with the feeling of transcendence, that is, the awareness of something larger than his own consciousness and stronger than the visible acts of men. Such a feeling is not usual among those subject to depression, since depression feels like an outside power taking possession of one's own mind and will." [48] Historian Allen C. Guelzo observed that "Providence, in time, became a term of convenience for Lincoln: without committing him to any specific form of theism, it allowed him the psychological comfort of referring all events to an unseen control, a control that might also enjoy at least some form of recognizability as the God of his parents."[49]

Lincoln's religion was reflected in more than words. According to Secretary of Navy Gideon Welles, Lincoln's Emancipation Proclamation stemmed from a promise the President made that "if God gave us the victory in the approaching battle, he would consider it an indication of Divine will, and that it was his duty to move forward in the cause of emancipation." Mr. Lincoln said: "If it were not for my firm belief in an overruling providence it would be difficult for me in the midst of such complications of affairs to keep my reason on its seat. But I am confident that the Almighty has his plans and will work them out, and whether we see it or not, they will be the wisest and best for us."[50] Even William H. Herndon acknowledged that "Mr. Lincoln was a thoroughly religious man who was a strong believer in an overruling Providence, no man more so."[51]

In his unpublished, unspoken "Meditation on the Divine Will, President Lincoln wrote: "The will of God prevails – In great contests each party claims to act in accordence [sic] with the will of God. Both may be, and one must be wrong. God can not be for, and against the same thing at the same time. In the present civil war it is quite possible that God's purpose is something different from the purpose of either party and yet the human instrumentalities, working just as they do, are of the best adaptation to effect this." [52] President Lincoln believed in Providence but he never abandoned his presidential responsibilities. Lincoln's God was not Newtonian. He intervened in history. In a letter to Kentucky editor Albert E. Hodges in April 1864, Mr. Lincoln foreshadowed his own Second Inaugural 11 months later: "If God now wills the removal of a great wrong, and wills also that we of the North as well as you of the South shall pay sorely for our complicity in that wrong, impartial history will find therein new cause to attest and revere the judgment and goodness of God."[53]

Mr. Lincoln rarely talked about his religious beliefs to his friends. Mr. Lincoln seldom "communicated to any one his views on this Subject," wrote Jesse Fell. "Whilst he was practically, as I certainly think, one of the best of Christians, his views on these & Kindred topics were such as to place him, in the estimation of most believers, entirely without the pale of the Christian Church; tho' to my mind Such was not his true position, tho' he never attached himself to any religious Society whatever."[54] Senator Orville H. Browning stayed with the Lincolns at the White House during Willie's fatal illness in February 1862, but he later said: "What his religious views and feelings were I do not know. I heard no expression of them." Browning wrote: "To what extent he believed in the revelations and miracles of the Bible and Testament, or whether he believed in them at all, I am not prepared to say, but I do know that he was not a scoffer at religion. During our long and intimate acquaintance and intercourse I have no recollection of ever having heard an irreverent word fall from his lips."[55] Browning's statement came after a controversy erupted over a biography supposedly written by Lincoln friend Ward Hill Lamon but actually ghost-written by a young man who had never met Mr. Lincoln but who based his work on material collected by Lincoln law partner William H. Herndon. Sometimes, Chauncy F. Black used the truth. Often, he stretched it.

Biographer Joseph Holland also stretched testimony — in this case of State Superintendent of Instruction Newton Bateman. Bateman claimed that Mr. Lincoln discussed his faith in some depth during a lull in the presidential campaign in October 1860. In a conversation in the State Capitol, where Bateman had an office, they talked for "a long time" about religious matters. "In the course of the conversation he dwelt much upon the necessity of faith, faith in God, the christian's God, as an element of successful statesmanship, especially in times like these; said it gave that calmness and tranquility of mind, that assurance of ultimate success, which made one firm & immoveable amid the wildest excitements. He said he believed in divine providence and recognized God in History. He also stated his belief in the duty, privilege, and efficacy of prayer, and intimated in unmistakable terms that he had sought, in that way, the divine guidance and favor." As if anticipating the controversy that this conversation would raise in subsequent years,

Bateman said he told Mr. Lincoln “that I had not supposed that he was accustomed to think so much upon that class of subjects, and that his friends generally were ignorant of the sentiments which he had expressed to me. He replied quietly: ‘I know they are. I am obliged to appear different to them, but I think more on these subjects than all others, and have done so for years, and I am willing that you should know it.'”56

As Mr. Lincoln matured, so to did his religious thinking particularly during the Civil War in the 1860s. Religious historian Mark A. Noll wrote that “Lincoln, a layman with no standing in a church and no formal training as a theologian, nonetheless offered a complex picture of God’s rule over the world and a morally nuanced picture of America’s destiny.” Noll noted that in “1858, the future president meditated on God’s will with respect to slavery. This fragment included a sharp critique of Frederick A. Ross, whose Slavery Ordained of God (1857) had made the conventional biblical defense of slavery. Lincoln’s response pointed to the power of personal interest in determining biblical conclusions: ‘If he Ross decides that God wills Sambo to continue a slave, he thereby retains his own comfortable position; but if he decides that God will’s Sambo to be free, he thereby has to walk out of shade, throw off his gloves, and delve for his own bread. Will Dr. Ross be actuated by that perfect impartiality, which has ever been considered most favorable to correct decisions?’ But before he delivered himself of this judgment, Lincoln paused to confess a difficulty that few of his pious contemporaries could recognize: ‘Certainly there is no contending against the Will of God; but still there is some difficulty in ascertaining, and applying it, to particular cases.'”57 The Bible as well as the writings of America’s founders were Lincoln’s scripture which he reformulated with his own particularly genius. Psychohistorian Dwight Anderson wrote: “By reformulating this common fund of inherited meanings, Lincoln transformed American political history from an Old Testament story into a New Testament one, and thereby released the American Revolution from its Hebraic separatism so as to imbue it with a Christian universalism.”[58]

His faith was evident. Political scientist Joseph Fornieri wrote: “The early, private letters to Joshua Speed show that a core of biblical faith coexisted with Lincoln’s reservations about the frontier religion of his youthful days. In each case, Lincoln interpreted the events of his own life in reference to the unfolding of God’s providential design. Manifesting an openness towards to the promptings of grace, he conveyed his personal experience of the divine at work in his life. His articulation of biblical faith reveals a trust (fiducia) in the graciousness of a personal God whose mercy and benevolence guides individuals and nations toward some ultimate good. As a faithful servant (fidelitas), Lincoln bore witness to God’s providential design. God had made him an ‘instrument’ in bringing about good in someone else’s life.”[59]

Lincoln scholar David C. Mearns contended: “Dr. Smith Pyne, Rector of St. John’s Church across Lafayette Park from the White House, held him in ‘deep and affectionate regard and respect.’ He would not have used such phrases in addressing a notorious unbeliever. Once when interceding for an admiral, under a sentence of court-martial, Dr. Pyne wrote to Lincoln: ‘Let me hope that one more item will be added to the amount of obligation and attachment by which I have long felt myself bound to you both in your official and personal character.’ There were scores of gentlemen of the cloth who felt just as did Dr. Pyne about the strange tenant of the White House.”[60]

Mr. Lincoln's religious beliefs were a complex mixture that defied easy categorization, but that didn't stop contemporaries from trying. Even during his lifetime, people tended to view Abraham Lincoln through the lens of their own beliefs. Unitarian friend Jesse W. Fell recalled that "No religious view with him seemed to find any favor except of the practical and rationalistic order; and if, from my recollections on this subject, I was called upon to designate an author whose views most nearly represented Mr. Lincoln's on this subject, I would say that author was Theodore Parker." Naturally, Theodore Parker was a Unitarian like Fell. "If Lincoln's concept of God looked like anything else on offer, it was not the orthodox trinitarian God of Father, Son, and Holy Spirit described by the Old School theologians, but a truncated one with God the Father — remote, austere, all-powerful, uncommunicative — and neither Son nor Spirit," wrote Lincoln historian Allen C. Guelzo. "This seemed to some of his friends to place Lincoln as close to unitarianism as one could get, and Jesse Fell (himself a unitarian) believed that unitarians 'were generally much admired and approved by him.' Both Fell and Herndon, in fact, thought that Lincoln's nearest intellectual resemblance was to the radical Boston unitarian Theodore Parker. But unitarianism was, fully as much as it was a rejection of orthodox trinitarianism, a New England rebellion against the idea of predestination; and Lincoln could never reconcile his pervasive belief in 'necessity' with unitarianism's defiant assertions of human free will. 'In religious matters, Mr. Lincoln was theoretically a predestinarian,' wrote Joseph Gillespie. 'Mr. Lincoln once told me that he could not avoid believing in predestination.'"[61]

President Lincoln attended regularly on Sunday, but he did not allow church attendance to interfere with his official duties on the Sabbath. Baptist Stoddard wrote: "For all this, however, he was not what I think the controversialists call a 'Sabbatarian,' and while he preferred greatly to rest his body and mind, if he could, he never scrupled to give his attention to any necessary work on Sunday. This fact was generally well known, and some prominent men, of sufficient official or representative position to warrant them in disregarding the rules about 'receiving visitors,' were constantly in the habit of availing themselves of the chance offered by Sunday for finding the President disengaged, and this often to his extreme discomfort and dissatisfaction."[62]

Lincoln pyschobiographer Dwight Anderson wrote: "The references Lincoln characteristically made to divinity prior to assuming his presidential role were general and abstract. The God which found its way into his speeches was the God of the Declaration of Independence: Creator of the Universe, Almighty Architect, Ruler of the Universe, or, more simply, the Almighty. The manner in which he usually interpreted divine presence in secular affairs was equally abstract, as, for example, in the following: 'Our reliance is in the love of liberty which God has planted in our bosoms.' Occasionally Lincoln came close to identifying God with his cause without actually doing so. Of Republican party principles he once said: 'But I do hope that as there is a just and righteous God in Heaven, our principles will and shall prevail sooner or later.' He sometimes referred to the eventual disappearance of slavery as happening in 'God's own good time and way.' There was, then, nothing in Lincoln's typical usage to suggest the kind of theology he began to articulate immediately upon adopting the persona of impartial instrument of the nation's destiny."[63]

Mr. Lincoln made an interesting argument regarding sin shortly before the Civil War. "Isaac Cogdal, who had known Lincoln from the time of the New Salem period, recalled a discussion on religion in Lincoln's office in 1859. 'Herndon was in the office at the time. Lincoln expressed himself in about these words: 'He did not nor could not believe in the endless punishment of any one of the human race. He understood punishment for sin to be a Bible doctrine; that the punishment was parental in its object, aim and design, and intended for the good of the offender; hence it must cease when justice is satisfied. He added that all that was lost by the transgression of Adam was made good by the atonement; all that was lost by the fall was made good by the sacrifice, and he added this remark, that punishment being a 'provision of the gospel system, he was not sure but the world would be better off if a little more punishment was preached by our ministers, and not so much pardon of sin.'"[64]

Mr. Lincoln worked out his theology in the crucible of civil war. Few friends had real theological discussions with Mr. Lincoln, however brief. Because Mr. Lincoln didn't express his beliefs publicly, however, did not mean he didn't think deeply about religious questions. But it did mean his friends didn't know what he thought. Journalist B. F. Irwin wrote: "Though personally acquainted with Mr. Lincoln for twenty-eight years and often in his office, I never heard him say a word on the subject of his religious belief."[65] Biographer William E. Barton wrote: "His utterances on religious subjects were not made as dogmatic affirmations. He merely uttered as occasion seemed to him to demand such sentiments and principles as expressed those aspects of truth which he felt and believed to need expression at those times."[66] Jesse Fell wrote: "No religious views with him seemed to find any favor, except of the practical and rationalist order; and if, from my recollections on this subject, I was called upon to designate an author whose views most nearly represented Mr. Lincoln's on this subject, I would say that author was Theodore Parker."[67]

Historian Nicholas Parrillo wrote: "In April 1864, Lincoln completed the synthesis of religious ideas that had developed over the past two years. The synthesis appeared in a letter to newspaper editor Albert Hodges. Three major themes converged: 1) the war as a positive and purposeful instrument, 2) national sin, and 3) God's design to end slavery immediately."[68] The nation was sick, suffering and in need of redemption, as Mr. Lincoln suggested in his Proclamation Appointing a National Fast Day in March 1863, which concluded: "It behooves us then, to humble ourselves before the offended Power, to confess our national sins, and to pray for clemency and forgiveness."[69]

Historian Richard N. Current wrote: "As a boy, Lincoln doubtless came under the influence of the predestinarian Baptist doctrines of his parents and neighbors. As a young man, perhaps in response to the rationalistic literature he read, he favored a rather abstract and mechanistic conception – the 'Doctrine of Necessity' – which he argued with Herndon and which he mentioned in his campaign handbill of 1846. As he grew older, and especially after his elevation to the Presidency, Lincoln increasingly personified this moving force as God."[70] Whatever his religious beliefs, Mr. Lincoln was constitutionally unable to profess what he didn't believe. Honesty was too firmly engrained in his character. Attorney Henry C. Whitney wrote that "before he was run for the Presidency, he made frequent references to God in the same spirit of devoutness and trust; and, therefore, he was honest;

honest with his Father on his dying bed, honest in what he feared was (and which proved to be) his last affectionate farewell to his neighbors, honest to the many eminent bands of clergymen and Christian people who visited him, and honest with his cabinet in the most important consultation it ever held; then Lincoln, whether as man or as President, believed in God as the Ruler of the Universe, in a blessed hereafter, and in the efficacy of prayer. Mr. Lincoln believed himself to be the instrument of God; and that, as God willed, so would the contest be. He also be6lieved in prayer and its efficacy, and that God willed the destruction of slavery through his instrumentality, and he believed in the Church of God as an important auxiliary."[71]

Mr. Lincoln's faith deepened in the White House under the burden of the deaths of thousands of Americans and a few relatives and close friends. Biographer William E. Barton wrote: "Mr. Lincoln was not conscious of any radical change; but Mrs. Lincoln noticed a change in him after Willie's death, which grew more pronounced after his visit to Gettysburg, and his own faith, while undergoing no sudden and radical transformation, manifests a consistent evolution."[72] William Wolf wrote: "The acceleration in Lincoln's religious development that came with his assuming the burdens of the presidency in a time of civil conflict may be traced to two sources. The first was the personal anguish of the death of friends and the tragic loss of his beloved Willie. The second was the suffering and pain that tore at the nation's life in crisis after crisis and cried aloud for some interpretation. The erosion of these forces may be traced in the deepening facial lines of almost every subsequent photograph of Lincoln. The first pressure turned Lincoln toward a deeper piety than he had known before. The second inspired him to probe beneath the seeming irrationality of events for a prophetic understanding of the nation's history. The first was clearly reflected in the Farewell Address at Springfield and the second began to find expression in the First Inaugural."[73]

President Lincoln seemed particularly comforted by Quakers. Lincoln aide William Stoddard wrote: "Either his ancestors or some near relatives of his had been Quakers, and he always manifested great respect for and interest in that highly respectable religious community. I always thought, however, that his strong sense of the humorous and appreciation of the quaint and odd, had more than a little to do with this partiality. It would seem too, that the Quakers, as a rule, have an unusually large amount of quiet humor of their own; and it may be, moreover, that he had not entirely rid himself of the old popular delusion that the Quakers are more inclined to be honest than other men. His early associations with the Methodists, the religious pioneers and missionaries of the West, had impressed him with a high respect for the zeal and energy of that sect."[74]

As President, Mr. Lincoln clearly valued the faith and prayers of others. Mr. Lincoln wrote two Iowa Quakers at the beginning of 1863: "It is most cheering and encouraging for me to know that in the efforts which I have made and am making for the restoration of a righteous peace to our country, I am upheld and sustained by the good wishes and prayers of God's people. No one is more deeply than myself aware that without His favor our highest wisdom is but foolishness and that our most strenuous efforts would avail nothing in the shadow of His displeasure. I am conscious of no desire for my country's welfare, that is not in consonance with His will, and of no plan upon which we may not ask His blessing. It seems to me that if there be one subject upon which all good men may unitedly agree, it is imploring the gracious favor of the God of Nations upon the struggles our people are making for the preservation of their precious birthright of civil and religious liberty."[75] The letter was probably composed by John Hay, but it was approved and signed by the President. President Lincoln told Union army nurse Rebecca R. Pomroy, 'If there were more praying and less swearing, it would be better for our country; and we all need to be prayed for, officers as well as privates; and if I were near death, I think I should like to hear prayer."[76]

Journalist Noah Brooks recalled: "The honesty of Mr. Lincoln appeared to spring from religious convictions; and it was his habit, when conversing of things which most intimately concerned himself, to say that, however he might be misapprehended by men who did not appear to know him, he was glad to know that no thought or intent of his escaped the observation of that Judge by whose final decree he expected to stand or fall in this world and the next. It seemed as though this was his surest refuge at time when he was most misunderstood or misrepresented. There was something touching in his childlike and simple reliance upon Divine aid, especially when in such extremities as he sometimes fell into; then, though prayer and reading of the Scriptures was his constant habit, he more earnestly than ever sought that strength which is promised when mortal help faileth. His address upon the occasion of his re-inauguration has been said to be as truly a religious document as a state-paper; and his acknowledgment of God and His providence and rule are interwoven through all of his later speeches, letters, and messages. Once he said: 'I have been driven many times upon my knees by the overwhelming conviction that I had nowhere else to go. My own wisdom and that of all about me seemed insufficient for that day.'"

Just after the last presidential election he said: 'being only mortal, after all, I should have been a little mortified if I had been beaten in this canvas before the people; but that sting would have been more than compensated by the thought that the people had notified me that all my official responsibilities were soon to be lifted off my back.' In reply to the remark that he might remember that in all these cares he was daily remembered by those who prayed, not to be heard of men, as no man had ever before been remembered, he caught at the homely phrase and said: 'Yes, I like that phrase, 'not to be heard of men,' and guess it's generally true, as you say; at least I have been told so, and I have been a good deal helped by just that thought.' Then he solemnly and slowly added: 'I should be the most presumptuous block-head upon this footstool if I for one day thought that I could discharge the duties which have come upon me since I came into this place without the aid and enlightenment of One who is wiser and stronger than all others.'"[77]

Although President Lincoln was not certain of the will of Providence in the Civil War, he was certain that Providence was at work in the war and emancipation. Historian Kenneth M. Stampp wrote that in the Second Inaugural, President Lincoln "subordinated the struggle for the Union to the approaching end of slavery abandoned his secular view of history and resigned himself to serving as an instrument in the hands of his God."[78] William Wolf wrote: "One of the elements of perennial newness in Lincoln's statements about God is the abundant wealth of his titles and attributes in describing the Creator. They can all be summarized under a phrase in his Second Inaugural, 'believers in a Living God.' For Lincoln the 'givenness' of God and God's nearness to him in immediate relationship called forth a tribute of poetic praises. Mrs. Lincoln spoke of his religion as poetry. The devout St. Francis, who sang 'The canticle to the Sun' and imaginatively invested all creation with the breath of personal life, was paralleled by the President, who praised God in a wealth of concrete images. The following list has been selected from the Rutgers edition of his works:

"Almighty, Almighty Architect, Almighty Arm, Almighty Being, Almighty Father, Almighty God, Almighty Hand, Almighty Power, Almighty and Merciful Ruler of the universe, Beneficent Creator and Ruler of the Universe, Great Disposer of Events, Divine Being, Divine Guidance, Divine Power, Divine Providence, Divine Will, Father, Beneficent Father Who Dwelleth in the Heavens, Common God and father of All Men, Father in Heaven, Father of Mercies, Great Father of Us All, God of Hosts, God of Right, God of Nations, Most High God, Holy Spirit, Living God, Great and Merciful maker, Maker of the Universe, Most High, Supreme Being, Supreme Ruler of the Universe."[79]

God was more than a collection of proper names. The voice of God and the voice of the people were closely linked in Mr. Lincoln's mind. William Wolf wrote: "In the Puritan interpretation the people became aware that they were instruments of Providence. This was slowly transmuted into a reliance upon the people as the corporate bearer of God's wisdom. The people's wisdom would be expressed in the long run by means of majority rule. Here is the original root for the adage that the will of the people is the will of God. We have had numerous examples of Lincoln's confidence in the essential rightness and wisdom of the people. This explains his belief, expressed at Buffalo, that God's will is ultimately to be known through the people. 'I must trust in that Supreme being who has never forsaken this favored land, through the instrumentality of this great and intelligent people.'"[80]

Providence for Mr. Lincoln was also linked to patience. Mr. Lincoln developed a patience for circumstances. He didn't attempt to play God – rushing into situations and crises with an exaggerated sense of self-importance. He understood the limits of his own power – and the necessity to cede power to others in order to increase their effectiveness. As a military leader, he exercised power reluctantly – when he saw that military commanders were not acting with sufficient dispatch and foresight. Mr. Lincoln clearly thought God was at work during the Civil War. A just God could not abide slavery in Mr. Lincoln's view. Historian Allen C. Guelzo wrote: "Faced with a situation that turned right and wrong on their heads, Lincoln responded by turning his private meditations into a closer scrutiny of who God is. In the fall of 1862, he sketched the changing shape of his thinking on paper, beginning with this simple axiom: 'The will of God prevails.'"[81] When a Senator said "I believe that, if we could only do right as a people, the Lord would help us, and we should have a decided success in this terrible struggle," President Lincoln replied: "My faith is greater than yours. I am confident that God will make us do sufficiently right to give us the victory."[82]

Providence also required trust. President Lincoln's own pastor, Phineas D. Gurley of New York Avenue Presbyterian Church in Washington, D.C., eulogized Lincoln's "abiding confidence in God, and in the final triumph of truth and righteousness, through him, and for his sake." Some preachers went further in the post-assassination period and attempted to posthumously recruit the dead President for formal church membership. Such mistaken assertions were compounded in Joseph Holland's

1865 biography of Lincoln which cited and probably exaggerated the testimony of Lincoln friend Newton Bateman. All these religious proclamations proved too much for Lincoln's erstwhile legal partner, William Herndon, who proceeded to prepare a lecture to prove that Lincoln never abandoned the religious skepticism of his youth.

Shortly after Lincoln's death, friend Noah Brooks wrote that President Lincoln "was pervaded with a solemn sense of his obligations as a Christian Magistrate, which never forsook him. He was a praying man, and daily sought from God that aid which he had long since learned man could not give him. With great natural shrewdness and sagacity, he had a transparent simplicity which endeared him to all whom met him; and it is notable that those who knew him best loved him best, and those who had a distance been hostile to him were disarmed when they came to know the man."[83] Fellow attorney Leonard Swett wrote: "As he became involved in matters of the gravest importance, full of great responsibility and great doubt, a feeling of religious reverence, and belief in God, his justice and overruling power increased upon him. He was full of natural religion; he believed in God as much as the most approved Church member; Yet he judged of Providence by the same system of great generalization as of everything else."[84]

Providence was at work in America, President Lincoln believed. Oliver S. Munsell recalled a meeting a tired and depressed President, who told him: "I do not trust in the bravery and devotion of the boys in blue; God bless them though! God never gave a prince of conqueror such an army as He has given to me. Nor yet do I rely on the loyalty and skill of our Generals; though I believe we have the best Generals in the world, at the head of our armies. But the God of our fathers, who raised up this country to be the refuge and the asylum of the oppressed and downtrodden of all nations, will not let it perish now. I may not live to see it, and (he added after a moment's pause) I do not expect to live to see it, but God will bring us through safe."[85] President Lincoln was no doubt sure. "Lincoln identified himself at an early date with the purpose of God," wrote Lincoln scholar Roy G. Basler. "This fact is inescapable. The evidence is voluminous in his authentic public utterances as well as in the fervid accounts of those who later recorded conversations on the point with Lincoln. The Abolitionists had for years claimed divine assistance in their crusade. The slave oligarchy had claimed divine approval of slavery. It is not necessary to make theatrical or journalistic capital of Lincoln as a Jehovah Man or the Abolitionists as Hebraic-Puritan zealots in order to present an interesting picture of affairs as they stood at the time of Lincoln's election."[86]

Historian Nicholas Parrillo wrote: "Lincoln's religious transformation was closely interwoven with his policies regarding emancipation and war. He first departed from his old religious views because of the challenges of waging war, and he latched onto a Calvinist conception of providence when confronting his uncertainty over emancipation policy. He then discerned that freedom for the slaves and the redemptive bloodshed of war seemed to be features of providential design, and these realizations made it justifiable for him to stick by his emancipation policy and his relentless prosecution of the war, despite pressure to the contrary."[87]

Friend Leonard Swett wrote that "if his religion were to be judged by the line and rule of Church Creeds and unexceptionable language, he would fall far short of the standard; but if by the higher rule of purity of conduct, of honesty of motive, of unyielding fidelity to the right and acknowledging God as the Supreme Ruler, then he filled all the requirements of true devotion and love of his neighbor as himself."[88] Lincoln scholar Roy P. Basler wrote: "Whatever was Lincoln's religion, the fact remains that he became recognized upon his death as an authentic prophet. Some of the popular epithets of the poets writing his eulogy within a few days of his death illustrate the immediate recognition of his ordination, once he was dead. He was the 'Prophet of the West,' 'the Savior,' 'saint,' 'Freedom's martyr,' 'Philosopher, Saint, and Seer,' 'priest and savior,' 'hero, martyr, saint,' 'A Second Christ,' etc. Similar epithets abound in the sermons and funeral orations preached throughout the land on the prophet's death."[89]

In April 1862 President Lincoln told the Rev. Noyes W. Miner: " You know I am not of a very hopeful temperament. I can take hold of a thing and hold on a good while. But trusting in God for help, and believing that our cause is just and right, I firmly believe we shall conquer in the end. But the struggle will be protracted and severe, involving a fearful loss of property and life. What strange scenes are these through which we are passing. I am sometimes astonished at the part I am acting in this terrible drama. I can hardly believe that I am the same man I was a few years ago when I was living in my humble way with you in Springfield. I often ask myself the question, 'When shall I awake and find it all a dream?'"[90]

References

1.Roy P. Basler, editor, Collected Works of Abraham Lincoln, December 6, 1864, Volume VIII. pp. 154-155.

2.William E. Barton, The Soul of Abraham Lincoln, p. 280 (John G. Nicolay, Encyclopedia Britannica), ninth edition, Volume XIV, p. 662).

3.Michael Burlingame, editor, At Lincoln's Side: John Hay's Civil War Correspondence and Selected Writings, p. 117.

4.Michael Burlingame, editor, Inside the White House in War Times, p. 176 (White House Sketches #8).

5.Francis B. Carpenter, The Inner Life of Abraham Lincoln: Six Months at the White House,p. 190 (From Eulogy upon Abraham Lincoln, before the General Assembly of Connecticut, 1864, p. 42).

6.William Wolf, The Almost Chosen People, p. 92.

7.Nicholas Parrillo, "Lincoln's Calvinist Transformation: Emancipation and War," Civil War History, Fall 2000, p. 227.

8.Mark A. Noll, A History of Christianity in the United States and Canada, p. 326.

9.Roy P. Basler, editor, Collected Works of Abraham Lincoln,(Reply to Emancipation Memorial Presented by Chicago Christians of All Denominations), September 13, 1862, Volume V, p. 420.

10.Herbert Mitgang, editor, Abraham Lincoln: A Press Portrait, p. 378 (Harriet Beecher Stowe, "Abraham Lincoln," The Watchman and Reflector).

11.M. L. Houser, Lincoln's Education and Other Essays, p. 155.

12.Walter B. Stevens, A Reporter's Lincoln,(Dennis Hanks), p. 169.

13.Douglas L. Wilson and Rodney O. Davis, editors, Herndon's Informants,(Matilda Johnston Moore interview with William H. Herndon), p. 109.

14.Ronald C. White, Jr., Lincoln's Greatest Speech: The Second Inaugural, p. 151.

15.Ervin S. Chapman, Latest Light on Lincoln, Volume II, p. 524.

16.William E. Barton, The Soul of Abraham Lincoln, p. xxiii.

17.Joshua F. Speed, Abraham Lincoln, p.32.

18.Rufus Wilson Rockwell, editor, Lincoln Among His Friends, p. 81 (William Jayne, Springfield Chapter of Daughters of the American Revolution, February 12, 1907.

19.Don E. and Virginia E. Fehrenbacher, editors, Recollected Words of Abraham Lincoln, p. 414.

20.Douglas L. Wilson and Rodney O. Davis, editors, Herndon's Informants: Letters, Interviews, and Statements about Abraham Lincoln, p. 577 (James H. Matheny interview with William H. Herndon, March 2, 1870).

21.Emanuel Hertz, The Hidden Lincoln, p.577 (Letter from William H. Herndon to Ward Hill Lamon, March 6, 1870).

22.William Wolf, The Almost Chosen People, pp. 45-46.

23.William Wolf, The Almost Chosen People, pp. 46-47.

24."Recollections of Lincoln: Three Letters of Intimate Friends," Bulletin of the Abraham Lincoln Association, December 1931 (Letter from Milton Hay to John Hay, February 8, 1887).

25.William H. Herndon and Jesse W. Weik, Herndon's Life of Lincoln, pp. 479-480.

26.Richard J. Carwardine, Lincoln: Profiles in Power, p. 30.

27.Allen C. Guelzo, "Abraham Lincoln and the Doctrine of Necessity," Journal of the Abraham Lincoln Association, Winter 1997, p. 65.

28.Donald W. Riddle, Lincoln Runs for Congress, p. 173.

29.Roy P. Basler, editor, Collected Works of Abraham Lincoln,Volume I, p. 382 (Handbill Replying to Charges of Infidelity, July 31, 1846).

30.Stephen Mansfield, Lincoln's Battle with God: A President's Struggle with Faith and what it Meant for America, p. 70.

31.Roy D. Packard, The Riddle of Lincoln's Religion, p. 8.

32.Don E. and Virginia Fehrenbacher, editors, Recollected Words of Abraham Lincoln, p. 408.

33.William E. Barton, The Soul of Abraham Lincoln, p. 162.

34.William E. Barton, The Soul of Abraham Lincoln, p. 164.

35.William Wolf, The Almost Chosen People, p. 86.

36.Katherine Helm, Mary Wife of Lincoln,(Letter from John Todd Stuart to the Reverend J.A. Reed), pp. 117-118.

37.John Wesley Hill, Abraham Lincoln – Man of God, pp.291-292 (Letter from Dr. James Smith to William Herndon, January 24, 1867).

38.Allen C. Guelzo, Abraham Lincoln: Redeemer President, p. 156.

39.Robert J. Havlik, "Abraham Lincoln and the Reverend Dr. James Smith: Lincoln's Presbyterian Experience in Springfield," Journal of the Illinois State Historical Society, August 1999. William E. Barton, The Soul of Abraham Lincoln, p. 324

40.Wayne Temple: Abraham Lincoln: From Skeptic to Prophet, p. 358.

41.Richard J. Carwardine, Lincoln: Profiles in Power, p. 38.

42.John H. Krenkel, Richard Yates: Civil War Governor, p. 225.

43."Recollections of Lincoln: Three Letters of Intimate Friends," Bulletin of the Abraham Lincoln Association, December 1931 (Letter from Orville H. Browning to Isaac N. Arnold, November 25, 1872).

44.Douglas L. Wilson and Rodney O. Davis, editors, Herndon's Informants, p. 168 (Letter from Jesse W. Fell to Ward HillLamon, September 22, 1870).

45.Lucius E. Chittenden, Recollections of President Lincoln and His Administration, p. 448.

46.Nicholas Parrillo, "Lincoln's Calvinist Transformation: Emancipation and War," Civil War History, Fall 2000, p. 228.

47.Nicholas Parrillo, "Lincoln's Calvinist Transformation: Emancipation and War," Civil War History, Fall 2000, pp. 229.

48.Jacques Barzun, Lincoln's Philosophic Vision, p. 19.

49.Allen C. Guelzo, "Abraham Lincoln and the Doctrine of Necessity," Journal of the Abraham Lincoln Association, Winter 1997, p. 69.

50. Gideon Welles, Diary of Gideon Welles, Volume I, p. 143 (September 22, 1862). Allen G. Guelzo, "Holland's Informants: The Con-

struction of Josiah Holland's 'Life of Abraham Lincoln,'" Journal of the Abraham Lincoln Association, Volume 23, Number 1, Winter 2002, p. 51 (Letter of John V. Farwell to Josiah G. Holland, July 6, 1865).

51.Emanuel Hertz, The Hidden Lincoln, p. 409 (Letter from William H. Herndon to Truman H. Barlett), 1887).

52.Roy P. Basler, editor, Collected Works of Abraham Lincoln, September 1862, Volume V, pp. 503-504 (Meditation on the Divine Will).

53.Roy P. Basler, editor, Collected Works of Abraham Lincoln, (Letter from Abraham Lincoln to Albert E. Hodges), April 4, 1864, Volume VII, pp. 281-282.

54.Douglas L. Wilson and Rodney O. Davis, editors, Herndon's Informants: Letters, Interviews and Statements about Abraham Lincoln, September 22, 1870, p. 579 (Letter from Jesse W. Fell to Ward Hill Lamon).

55."Recollections of Lincoln: Three Letters of Intimate Friends," Bulletin of the Abraham Lincoln Association, December 1931, p. 9 (Letter from Orville H. Browning to Isaac N. Arnold, November 25, 1872).

56.Allen C. Guelzo, "Holland's Informants: The Construction of Josiah Holland's 'Life of Abraham Lincoln,'" Journal of the Abraham Lincoln Association,(Letter from Newton Bateman to Josiah G. Holland, June 19, 1865)., Winter 2002, p. 28. It appears in Josiah G. Holland, Life of Abraham Lincoln, pp. 236-239.

57.Mark A. Noll, The Civil War as a Theological Crisis, p. 88.

58.Dwight Anderson, Lincoln's Quest for Immortality, p. 138.

59.Joseph R. Fornieri, Abraham Lincoln's Political Faith, p. 40.

60.Henry B. Kranz, editor, Abraham Lincoln: A New Portrait, p. 106 (David C. Mearns, Lincoln, "Man of God").

61.Allen C. Guelzo, Abraham Lincoln: Redeemer President, p. 154.

62.Michael Burlingame, editor, Inside the White House in War Times, No. 8., p. 177 (Whte House Sketches #8).

63.Dwight Anderson, AL Quest for Immortality, pp. 128-129.

64.William Wolf, The Almost Chosen People, p. 104.

65.William E. Barton, The Soul of Abraham Lincoln, p. 187.

66.William E. Barton, The Soul of Abraham Lincoln, p. 291.

67.Ward Hill Lamon, Life of Abraham Lincoln, p. 492.

68.Nicholas Parrillo, "Lincoln's Calvinist Transformation: Emancipation and War," Civil War History, Fall 2000, p. 249.

69.Roy P. Basler, editor, Collected Works of Abraham Lincoln, March 30, 1863, Volume VI, p. 156 (Proclamation Appointing a National Fast Day).

70.Richard N. Current, The Lincoln Nobody Knows, p. 71.

71.Henry C. Whitney, Life on the Circuit with Lincoln, p. 268.

72.William E. Barton, The Soul of Abraham Lincolnp. 280.

73.William Wolf, The Almost Chosen People, p. 115.

74.Michael Burlingame, editor, Inside the White House in War Times, from William Stoddard,(White House Sketches,No. 8), p. 176.

75.Roy P. Basler, editor, Collected Works of Abraham Lincoln, Volume VI, pp. 39-40 (Letter from Abraham Lincoln to Caleb Russell and Sallie A. Fenton, January 5, 1863).

76.Don E. and Virginia E. Fehrenbacher, editors, Recollected Words of Abraham Lincoln, p. 362.

77.Michael Burlingame, editor, Lincoln Observed: Civil War Dispatches of Noah Brooks, pp. 209-210 (from Noah Brooks, "Personal Recollections of Abraham Lincoln," Harper's Monthly Magazine), May 1865).

78.James M. McPherson, editor, We Cannot Escape History: Lincoln and the Last Best Hope of Earth, p. 18 (Kenneth M. Stammp, "Lincoln's History").

79.William Wolf, The Almost Chosen People, pp. 179-180.

80.William Wolf, The Almost Chosen People, p. 151.

81.Guelzo, Allen C., "Lincoln's Sign," Illinois Issues, February 2005. http://illinoisissues.uis.edu/features/2005feb/purpose.html.

82.Don E. and Virginia E. Fehrenbacher, editors, Recollected Words of Abraham Lincoln, p. 261.

83.Michael Burlingame, editor, Lincoln Observed: Civil War Dispatches of Noah Brooks, p. 194 (April 16, 1865).

84.Douglas L. Wilson and Rodney O. Davis, editors, Herndon's Informants, p. 167 (Letter from Leonard Swett to William H. Herndon, January 17, 1866).

85.Charles Henry Collis, Religion of Abraham Lincoln, p. 23 (Letter from Oliver S. Munsell to Charles H. T. Collis, April 15, 1893).

86.Roy P. Basler, The Lincoln Legend: A Study in Changing Conceptions, p. 169.

87.Nicholas Parrillo, Lincoln's Calvinist Transformation: Emancipation and War, Civil War History, Fall 2000, p. 230.

88.Douglas L. Wilson and Rodney O. Davis, editors, Herndon's Informants, p. 168 (Letter from Leonard Swett to William H. Herndon, January 17, 1866).

89.Roy P. Basler, The Lincoln Legend: A Study in Changing Conceptions, pp. 168-169.

90.Don E. and Virginia E. Fehrenbacher, editors, Recollected Words of Abraham Lincoln, p. 330.

In November, 1855, Abraham Lincoln drew down upon him the fire of Rome when he answered a wire from the Reverend Charles Chiniquy, Catholic priest of Kankakee, Illinois, who had been engaged in a series of court suits with the Bishop of the Chicago diocese, of which he was a "subject," asking his professional services. Within twenty minutes the reply came to Chiniquy, "Yes, I will defend your honor and your life at the next May term of the court at Urbana. A. Lincoln."

Promptly on May 19th, 1856, Mr. Lincoln appeared at Urbana and consulted with Father Chiniquy, but I let him tell you of their meeting:

> "He was a giant in stature, but I found him more of a giant in the noble qualities of his mind and heart. It was impossible to converse with him five minutes, without loving him. There was such an expression of kindness and honesty in his face, such an attractive magnetism in the man, that after a few moments conversation, one felt as tied to him by all of the noblest affections of the heart.
>
> When pressing my hand, he told me: 'You were mistaken when you telegraphed that you were unknown to me. I know you by reputation, as the stern opponent of the tyranny of your bishop, and the fearless protector of your countrymen in Illinois. I have heard much of you from two friends, and last night your lawyers, Messrs. Osgood and Paddock, acquainted me with the fact that your bishop employs some of his tools to get rid of you. I hope it will be an easy thing to defeat his machinations.' He then asked me how I had been induced to desire his services. I answered by giving the story of that unknown friend, a lawyer, who had advised me to have Mr. Lincoln-for the reason that he was the best and most honest man in Illinois. He smiled at my answer with that inimitable and unique smile which we may call the 'Lincoln smile' and replied, 'That unknown friend would have been more correct had he told you that Abraham Lincoln was the ugliest lawyer in the country,' and he laughed outright." (***Fifty Years In The Church Of Rome***) (4)

The account given by Col. Edwin A. Sherman in his book, *"The Engineer Corps of Hell or Rome's Sappers and Miners"* is unique in that he gives the only account of Lincoln's disarming humour while at work and a very clear overview of the stakes involved where the survival of the country was concerned.

> "Suffice it to say in brief, that a general Roman Catholic colonization scheme for taking the possession of the Mississippi Valley had been determined upon by Pope Pius IX, in

1850, and a large emigration of people of that faith from the Continent of Europe and from Canada was put in motion, and under the leadership of Father Chiniquy, colonies were planted in various places, but chiefly in the state of Illinois, and under direct authority from Rome, subject to the rule of the Bishop of the Diocese. Father Chiniquy, partly with his own money and that of his fellow colonists, bought the land and laid out a town called St. Annes, in Kankakee County, built a church, established a school, and became at the same time pastor, teacher and manager of the affairs of his colony and exercised a truly paternal care over his entire flock, who were chiefly agricultural in their avocations and pursuits. While so engaged, he seems to have excited the envy and jealousy of some of his fellows in the priesthood, who were not pleased with his success and his indomitable perseverance, energy and industry, which was a standing rebuke to those who had less of piety in their composition, and who were more disposed to gratify their appetites and lethargy, than to cultivate the moral virtues of temperance and sobriety, or imitate the example of St. Paul, who laboured with his own hands rather than be a charge to others.

A portion of these colonists who were artizans settled in the city of Chicago, where they could obtain employment at their professions and trades. Here they bought a lot and erected a church, supplied the altar with the necessary adornments in the best of style, and with rich and costly vestments for the use of the priests. This neatness and elegance excited the envy of the Irish portion of the Roman Catholic population of that city and their priests, which extended even to the Bishop, their fellow countryman, who in the exercise of his arbitrary power, not only stripped the French Roman Catholics of their priests' vestments, but actually robbed them of the church itself. On a Sunday morning when they came to attend church, the Frenchmen found no church there. *It had been stolen bodily!* They followed up the tracks of the trucks upon which it had been hauled away, and found it in another part of the city, still on wheels, but occupied by Irish Roman Catholics and an Irish priest celebrating mass. Their indignation knew no bounds. They protested against these outrages, not only to their Irish brethren of the same faith, to the priests and lastly to the Bishop himself, but in vain. They were met by continuous insult and abuse. They called upon Father Chiniquy, who not only appealed to the Pope, but also to Emperor Napoleon III in nearly the following language:

"Sire: My grandfather was a Captain in the French Navy and for gallant services was in part awarded lands in Canada, by which the misfortunes of war was ceded by treaty to Great Britain. Upon retiring from the service of France he settled upon his estates in Canada, where my father and myself were born. I am thus with other Canadians who have come to this country a British subject by birth, an American citizen by adoption, but French still in blood and Roman Catholic in religion. I therefore, on the part of our people, humbly implore your Majesty to aid us by interceding with His Holiness Pope Pius IX, to have these outrages and wrongs righted."

The Emperor, Napoleon III, did intercede with the Pope, who sent out his Nuncio Bedini, who found things as stated. Bishop O'Reagan was removed, and another bishop who proved not to be much better, was appointed in his place. It was during these times of trial, abuse and tyranny when the machinery of the courts was abused to endeavour to force subjection of personal matters to Papal ecclesiastical law, in order to deprive American citizens of their just rights and free will [under the Constitution and Bill of rights] and to make them complete vassals and subjects of Rome. Having failed to accomplish this by many tedious, expensive and harassing lawsuits, then there was concocted one of the most damnable conspiracies that was ever hatched by devils to destroy the character of one of the noblest and fearless men that ever contended for the rights of man in any cause or anywhere on the face of God's earth. When the whole Papal power was united here in America against one man to crush and destroy him, and he was making the fight alone and single-handed in a cause which involved the rights of every American citizen; when they had exhausted his financial resources and he was overwhelmed in debt, to complete his ruin, if it were possible, they resorted to infamy of the blackest dye to rob him of his good name by falsely charging him with crime, confirming with perjured oaths, and damning their treacherous, cowardly souls forever. It was at this time in the darkest hour of gloom that he was given the services of that champion, whose voice and arm never lifted in vain to help the down-trodden and oppressed, **Abraham Lincoln**. The expense of the suit would be borne by the State, and the District Attorney and associate counsel would be aided by the power and influence of the Jesuits and Bishop O'Reagan.

His enemies, fearing that he might be acquitted if the trial were to be held in Kankakee, where Chiniquy was well and favourably known, caused a change of venue to be taken to Urbana, Champaign County, Illinois. Chiniquy was arrested in St. Anne's and taken by the Sheriff to the place of trial. Judge Norton, of Joliet, was the principle counsel on the part of the State against Chiniquy, while his defense counsel was Judge Osgood, of Joliet, Mr. J.W. Paddock, of Kankakee, and Abraham Lincoln.

Says Judge Osgood, also confirmed by Judge Norton: "Upon the trial of the cause against Father Chiniquy, the Roman Church had subpoenaed five Catholic priests as witnesses! They attended court dressed as priests, wearing long, black robes, looking very dignified, and presenting an air of great condescension on their part to have to appear in court, which they seemed to overawe by their presence and to give a sanctimonious air of truth to their false evidence to be given upon the stand when called for. Upon the convening of the court in the morning there came an awkward lull in business arising from the tardiness of a juror. The parties, lawyers and attendants were all in place ready to go on, and nothing could be done in the absence of the tardy juror. Judge David Davis sat on the bench, a jolly, fat, good natured person weighing about 300 pounds. Mr. Lincoln had angular features, long boney fingers, and presented a comical appearance at the bar, for he was ever joking with his brethren of the bar. Judge Jesse Norton was opposing counsel, a neat, tidy ministerial appearing person of the Presbyterian faith, who never joked, and his dignity was slighted by the faintest hint of "smutty" allusion. The eleven jurors were common country farmers. Honest, plain and blunt. The courtroom was densely packed with country folks who came to hear the distinguished array of counsel.

While this pause for the absent juror was continuing, the five priests emerged from a side door and marched down the room in a single, dignified procession and all took a seat in a row on a long bench that had been provided for witnesses. Of course, their appearance attracted much attention. They were dressed alike, sat very prim, looking neither to the right nor to the left; their hands were on their knees and their feet were in a straight line. For a minute a pin could have been heard to fall, so quiet was the room, and the audience seemed under a spell. At this moment, Mr. Lincoln seeing the effect they had produced, and quickly divining their purpose and determined to destroy it and their influence, which he conceived could be done at that point and in no other way, leaned over the bar table and toward Judge Norton, and with his hand to his mouth, as if to prevent his words being heard by anyone but Judge Norton, he spoke in a whisper voice (but a loud whisper voice that could be heard by every person in the room), 'Norton !', "Oh, Norton" (and pointing his long arm and fingers at the row of priests at the same time and making a quizzical expression of the face at the same time), 'I want to ask you a question in confidence.' 'What is it?' says Judge Norton. Says Lincoln, '*What has the g___d____fellers got peckers for anyhow?'* It was nearly a minute before the point to the question was seen by the people. But as soon as it was seen, the jury, the lawyer, crowd and court broke out into immoderate laughter. Norton was terribly shocked; the priests never smiled --- they looked a picture of disgust. Every few minutes thereafter someone would break out in laughter and soon after another round went about the courtroom and ran through the house. Judge Davis' sides fairly shook in the merriment. THE PRIESTS WERE TERRIBLY OFFENDED, AND THEIR EYES SHOWED A MALIGNITY OF INTENTION OF REVENGE TO BE GRATIFIED IN THE FUTURE WHICH THEIR TONGUES DARED NOT UTTER.

The defeat of Rome in this celebrated case by Mr. Lincoln; his terrific arraignment of the "perjuring gang of priests" who had left no stone unturned to ruin Mr. Chiniquy by a false accusation against him of rape, in which it was charged by the infamous priest, Lebel, that Mr. Chiniquy had made an attack upon his sister. On the night before the case was to go to the jury, Mr. Lincoln, himself, had almost given up hope of an acquittal, notwithstanding the fact that he was convinced of Father Chiniquy's innocence. He frankly told Chiniquy of his fears and his last admonition to the distressed and persecuted man was:

> "My dear Mr. Chiniquy, though I hope tomorrow to destroy the testimony of Lebel against you, I must concede that I see great danger ahead. There is not the least doubt in my mind that every word he has said is a sworn lie, but my fear is, that the jury thinks differently. I am a pretty good judge in these matters- I fear that our jurymen think you are guilty- I have never seen two such skillful rogues as those two priests. There really is a diabolical skill in the plan they have concocted to ruin you- The only way to be sure of a favorable verdict tomorrow, is that God Almighty would take our part and show your

innocence! Go to Him and pray, for He alone can save you." (5)

That very night Father Chiniquy spent almost the entire time on his knees interceding that his innocence might be established, when at three o'clock in the morning he answered a knock on his door, and as there stood Mr. Lincoln, "his face beaming with joy" as Chiniquy relates it.

"Cheer up, Mr. Chiniquy, I have the perjured priests in my hands. Their diabolical plot is known, and if they do not fly away before the dawn of day, they will surely be lynched. Bless the Lord, you are saved!" (6)

The following sworn statement supplied by the *Chiniquy Collection* archives, and never before seen by historians or the public until now, relates the story as it unfolded:

State of Illinois

Cook County} SS

I Philomene Schwartz, Being first duly sworn deposes and says that she is of the age of thirty three years and resides at 484 Milwaukee Avenue Chicago, that her maiden name was Philomene Moffatt. That she knew Father Lebel, Roman Catholic priest of the French Catholics of Chicago during his lifetime, and knows Reverend Father Chiniquy.

That about the month of May AD 1854, in company with Miss Sarah Chaussey, I paid a visit to Miss Eugenie Bossey, the housekeeper of her uncle, the reverend Mr. Lebel who was there living at the parsonage on Clark St. Chicago.

While we were sitting in the room of Miss Bossey, in the adjoining room, not suspecting that we were there hearing his conversation through the door which was partly opened. Though we could neither see him nor his sister, we heard every word of what they said together, the substance of which follows:

Reverend Mr. Lebel said in substance to Miss Bossey, his sister, "You know that Mr. Chiniquy is a dangerous man, and he is my enemy, having persuaded several of my congregation to settle in his colony. You must help me to put him down, by accusing him of having done a criminal action with you." Madame Bossey answered, "I cannot say such a thing against Mr. Chiniquy, when I know it is absolutely false."

Mr. Lebel replied: "If you refuse to comply with my request, I will not give you the 160 acres of land I intended to give you. You will live and die poor." Madame Bossey answered: "I prefer to never have that land and I like better to live and die poor than to perjure myself to please you."

The Reverend Mr. Lebel, several times urged his sister Miss Bossey to comply with his desires, but she refused. At last weeping and crying she said: "I prefer never to have an inch of that land than to damn my soul by swearing to a falsehood."

The Reverend Mr. Lebel then said: "Mr. Chiniquy will destroy our holy religion and our people if we do not destroy him" "If you think that the swearing I ask you to do is a sin, you will come to confess to me and I will pardon it, in the absolution I will give you."

"Have you the power to forgive a false oath," replied Miss Bossey to her brother, the priest. "YES", he answered, "I have that power for Christ has said to all his priests, "What you shall bind on earth shall be bound in Heaven, and what you shall loose on earth shall be loosed in Heaven."

Miss Bossey then said, "If you promise that you will forgive me that false oath and if you give me the 160 acres you promised I will do what you want." The Reverend Mr. Lebel then said, "All Right!"

I could not hear any more of that conversation, for in that instant Miss Eugenie who had kept still and silent with us made some noise and shut the door.

Affiant states that sometime later I went to confess to Mr. Reverend Lebel, and I told him that I had lost my confidence in him. I answered him: "I lost my confidence in you since I heard your conversation with your sister, when you tried to persuade her to perjure herself in order to destroy Father Chiniquy."

Affiant further says that in the month of October AD 1856 the Reverend Mr. Chiniquy had to defend himself before the civil and criminal court of Urbana Illinois in an action brought against him by Peter Spink. Someone wrote from Urbana to a paper of Chicago that Father

Chiniquy was probably to be condemned. The paper which published that letter was much read by the Roman Catholics who were glad to hear that that priest was to be punished. Among those who read that paper was Narcisse Terrien. He had lately been married to Miss Sarah Chaussey who told him that Father Chiniquy was innocent, that she was present with me when Reverend Mr. Lebel prepared the plot with his sister Miss Bossey, and promised her a large piece of land if she would swear falsely against Father Chiniquy. Mr. Narcisse Terrien wanted to go with his wife to the residence of Father Chiniquy, but she was unwell and could not go. He came to ask me if I remembered well the conversation of Reverend Mr. Lebel, and if I would consent to go to Urbana to expose the whole plot before the court, and I consented.

We started that same evening for Urbana, where we arrived late at night. I immediately met Mr. Abraham Lincoln, one of the lawyers of Father Chiniquy, and told him all that I knew of that plot.

That very same night the Reverend Mr. Lebel having seen my name on the hotel register came to me much excited and troubled and said: "Philomene, what are you here for?" I answered him: "I cannot exactly tell you that, but you will probably know it tomorrow at the courthouse."

"Oh, wretched girl!" he exclaimed, "You have come to destroy me." "I do not come to destroy you" I replied, "For you are already destroyed."

There drawing from his porte-money book, a big bundle of bank notes, which he said were worth 100 dollars. He said: "I will give you all this money if you will leave by the morning train and go back to Chicago". I answered him: "Though you would offer as much gold as this room can contain, I cannot do what you ask."

He then seemed exceedingly distressed and he disappeared. The next morning Peter Spink requested the court to allow him to withdraw his accusations against Father Chiniquy and to stop his prosecutions, having he said, found out that Father Chiniquy was innocent of the things brought against him, and his request was granted. There the innocency and honesty of Father Chiniquy was acknowledged by the court after it had been proclaimed by Abraham Lincoln, who was afterwards elected President of the United States.

Philomene Schwartz

I Stephen R. Moore a notary public in the County of Kankakee, in the State of Illinois, and duly authorized by law to administer oaths, do hereby certify that in this 21st day of October AD 1881, Philomene Schwartz personally appeared before me and made oath that the above affiant, by her subscribed, is true as therein stated.

Stephen R. Moore Notary Public

** ** ** ** ** ** **

The priests left town early in the morning, fearing the consequences as public opinion had been strongly against them, and Lebel's lawyer asked that the case be dismissed, which was granted.

Mr. Lincoln did not permit the priests to go unscathed, however, and in a most terrific scorching at their audacious attempt to corrupt the courts, he closed his rebuke as he towered above his auditors with these words:

"May it please your honor, gentlemen of the jury and American citizens, this conspiracy, I am aware, has failed in its efforts, but I have a few words which I wish to say."

He then went on and depicted the career of Father Chiniquy, how he had been unjustly persecuted, and in conclusion said:

"As long as God gives me a heart to feel, a brain to think, or a hand to execute my will, I shall devote it against that infernal power which has attempted to pollute the halls of justice and to use the machinery of the courts to destroy the rights and character of an American Citizen." (7)

That same year when he entered the political field, tearing to shreds, as no other man could, Roman Catholic Taney's Dred Scott Decision, in favor of black slavery, he fully understood the motive power behind it was Rome. From that time on the black clouds of Jesuitism were fast gathering about the life of Abraham Lincoln. These enemies followed his path as a shadow follows sunshine. From that moment his doom was written in letters of blood.

CHICAGO TRIBUNE IN LINE.

We clip the following from the Chicago *Tribune.* It is a sign of the times. A few months since the *Tribune* would not publish such matter as an item of news even. Today it not only publishes the news but comments upon it in true American fashion. When organs of the *Tribune* type, who run the risk of Rome's extreme boycott in their advertising department by daring to avow their sentiments it looks as if the berated and much-hated Orangeman and soundly-abused A. P. A. were getting in their work to some purpose:

SPECIMEN FOREIGN KNOW-NOTHINGISM.

There is much heated discussion in the Milwaukee papers nowadays concerning the recent utterances of a Polish priest named Gul-ki at a political meeting during the municipal and congressional contests in that city which ended last Tuesday. According to a correspondent of the Milwaukee *Sentinel* the words used by the Rev. Mr. Gulski at a meeting in St. Hyacinth Hall last Sunday were as follows:

"Every citizen and catholic who does not vote for Somers and Ludwig will not be allowed to come to church or be called a good catholic. In calling attention to this matter I am compelled to do my duty as a catholic priest and see to it that every candidate on the democratic ticket should and must be elected because he is a catholic."

Mr. Casimer Gonski, a member of the Rev. Gulski's congregation, objects to the report in the *Sentinel* and has written to defend his pastor against the criticisms of that paper based on the report furnished to it. Mr. Gonski asserts that:

"Not a word about ecclesiastical ostracism was said in case of non compliance with his [Gulski's] advice. He appealed to his hearers as Poles and catholics and asked them to support as such their religion and their cause by voting for Somers and Ludwig."

This report of the speech, it will be seen, mitigates to some extent the charge made against Gulski. He did not threaten his hearers with "ecclesiastical ostracism." Perhaps he feared that would bring him under ecclesiastical censure. But even on his friend Gonski's showing he went rather far. He appealed to his hearers to vote at the election not as American citizens but as Poles and as catholics for two candidates who happen to be catholics. And he finds an apologist in perhaps the most intelligent of his hearers for his outrageous, unjustifiable, bigoted, and intolerant harangue!

What a howl the Gonskis and Gulskis would have raised if some protestant clergyman had appealed to the majority of the citizens of Milwaukee to vote against Ludwig and Somers because they are catholics! Such bigotry as these two Poles have displayed might tempt unwise people to make such appeals.

But they are not alone. Last fall in this city a Polish priest in the ninth ward appealed to his congregation from the altar to vote the democratic ticket in the interest of the catholic church and the catholic schools. There has been no rebuke by the ecclesiastical authorities here as far as known. It is a notorious fact, too, that in the sixteenth ward in this city all the democratic meetings are held in the hall attached to the romish church, that the pastor attends those meetings and urges his hearers to vote for the democratic candidates, even for such democratic candidates as Peter Kiolbassa and Stanley Kunz, political changelings of the sorriest kind, for no other reason than because they are Poles and romanists.

Such outrageous intolerance is certain to meet with merited punishment before long. When Polish romish candidates appeal for American votes and American offices in Chicago and Milwaukee loyal American citizens, whether native born or foreign, romish or protestant, may have something to say on the subject.

A remarkable thing transpired, when, after the trial, Mr. Chiniquy asked Mr. Lincoln for his bill. Chiniquy had said,

> "Though I am not able to pay the whole of your bill at this moment, I will pay you to the last cent if you have the kindness to wait just a little while for the balance." At which Lincoln replied, "My dear Mr. Chiniquy, I feel proud and honored to have been called to defend you. But I have done it less as a lawyer than as a friend. The money I should receive from you would take away the pleasure I feel at having fought your battle. Your case is unique in my whole practice. I have never met a man so cruelly persecuted as you have been, and who deserved it so little. Your enemies are devils incarnate. The plot that was hatched against you is the most hellish one I have ever seen. Now, let us speak of what you owe me. What do you owe me? You owe me nothing! For I suppose that you are quite ruined. The expense of such a suit, I know, must be enormous. Your enemies want to ruin you. Will I help them finish your ruin, when I hope that I have earned the right to be considered among one of your most devoted and sincere of your friends?"

While he was drawing up a note for $50.00, as his client had requested, Mr. Lincoln said to him:

> "Father Chiniquy, what are you crying for? You ought to be the happiest man alive. You have beaten your enemies and come out triumphant; they have fled in disgrace."

To which the emotional Frenchman replied,

> "Dear Mr. Lincoln, allow me to tell you that the joy I should naturally feel for such a victory is destroyed in my mind by the fear of what it may cost you. There were in the court not less than ten or twelve Jesuits from Chicago and St. Louis, who came to hear my sentence of condemnation to the penitentiary. But it was on their heads that you have brought the thunders of heaven and earth! Nothing can be compared to the expression of rage against you, when you not only wrenched me from their cruel hands, but you were making the walls of the court house tremble under the awful and superhumanly eloquent denunciation of their infamy, diabolical malice, and total want of Christian principles, in the plot they had concocted for my destruction. What troubles my soul just now and draws my tears, is that it seems to me I have

read your sentence of death in their bloody eyes. How many other noble victims have already fallen at their feet? I am not weeping for myself, but for you, sir. They will kill you; and let me tell you this, if I were in their place and they in mine, it would be my sole, my sworn duty, to take your life myself, or find a man to do it." (8)

Chiniquy was right. They found their man.

This most celebrated court case also brought out the following facts as they are recorded in the revealing letter to the *Kankakee Times* by one of the lawyers of the defense team, which comes to the writer courtesy of "*The Chiniquy Collection*":

What the Church of Rome Understands by Liberty of Conscience -

The Romish Bishops Testimony

The Kankakee Times publishes the following communication from a member of the Illinois bar. Though perhaps containing nothing new or strange to those who have studied the matter, the statement made may convince such Protestants as imagine the Church of Rome to be a harmless institution of their great error. The principles of the Roman hierarchy remain unchanged. The wearer of the Tiara would as readily depose for simple heresy any temporal ruler of today, as his predecessor, six centuries ago, deposed and deprived of his estates, Count Raymond of Toulouse, for a like crime. ***Religious liberty is both hated and dreaded by the Church which claims the right of enforcing its spiritual decrees by the assistance of the secular arm.*** [Emphasis added]

In one of your past issues you told your readers that the Rev. Mr. Chiniquy had gained the long and formidable suit instituted by the Roman Catholic Bishop to dispossess him and his people of their church property. But you have not yet given any particulars about the startling revelations the Bishop had to make before the court, in reference to the still existing laws of the Church of Rome, against those whom they call heretics. Nothing is more important for everyone than to know precisely what those laws are.

As I was present when the Roman Catholic Bishop Foley; of Chicago, was ordered to read in Latin, and translate into English those laws, I have kept a correct copy of them, and I send it to you with a request to publish it.

The Rev. Mr. Chiniquy presented the works of St. Thomas and St. Liguori to the Bishop, requesting him to say, under oath, if those works were not among the highest theological authorities in the Church of Rome, all over the world. After long and serious opposition on the part of the Bishop to answer, the Court having said he (the Bishop) was bound to answer, the Bishop confessed that those works were looked upon as the highest authorities, and that they are taught and learned in all the colleges and universities of the Church of Rome as standard works.

Then the Bishop was requested to read in Latin and translate into English the laws and fundamental principles of action against the heretics, as explained by St. Thomas and Liguori.

1. "An excommunicated man is deprived of all civil communication with the faithful, in such a way that, if he is not tolerated, they can have no communication with him, as it is in the following verse: "It is forbidden to kiss him, salute him, to eat or do business with him." St. Liguori. Vol. 9, page 162

2. "Though heretics must not be tolerated because they deserve it, we must bear with them till, by a second admonition, they may be brought back to the faith of the Church. But those who, after a second admonition, remain obstinate in their errors, must not only be excommunicated, but they must be delivered to the secular power to be *exterminated*."

3. "Though heretics who repent must always be accepted to penance as often as they have fallen, they must not in consequence of that, always be permitted to enjoy the benefits of this life. *** When they fall again they are permitted to repent, *** but the sentence of death must not be removed. St. Thomas, Vol. 4, page 94

4. "When a man is excommunicated for his apostasy, it follows from that very fact, that all those who are his subjects are released from the oath of allegiance, by which they are bound to obey him." St. Thomas, Vol. 4, page 94

The next document of the Church of Rome brought before the Court was the act of the Council of Lateran, A.D. 1215.

We excommunicate and anathematize every heresy that exalts itself against the holy orthodox and Catholic faith, condemning all heretics, by whatever name they may be known, for though their faces differ, they are tied together by their tails. Such as are condemned to be delivered over to the existing secular powers, to receive due punishment. If laymen, their goods must be confiscated. If priests, they shall be degraded from their respective orders, and their property be applied to the use of the Church in which they officiated. Secular powers of all ranks and degrees are to be warned, indeed and, if necessary, compelled by ecclesiastical censure, to swear that they will exert themselves to the utmost in the defense of the faith, and extirpate all heretics denounced by the Church, who shall be found in their territories. And whenever any person shall assume government, whether it be spiritual or temporal, he shall be bound by this decree.

"If any temporal lord, after having been admonished and required by the Church, shall neglect to clear his territory of heretical depravity, the Metropolitan and Bishop of the province shall unite in excommunicating him. Should he remain contumacious a whole year, the fact shall be signified to the supreme Pontiff who will declare his vassals released from their allegiance from that time, and will bestow his territory on Catholics, to be occupied by them, on condition of exterminating the heretics and preserving the said territory in the faith.

"Catholics who shall assume the cross for the *extermination* of the heretics shall enjoy the same indulgence and be protected by the same privileges as are granted to those who go to the help of the Holy Land. We decree further, that all who may have dealings with heretics, and especially such as receive, defend and encourage them, shall be excommunicated. He shall not be eligible to any public office. He shall not be admitted as a witness. He shall neither have power to bequeath his property by will, nor to succeed to any inheritance. He shall not bring any action against any person but anyone can bring any action against him. Should he be a judge, his decision shall not have any force, nor shall any cause be brought before him. Should he be an advocate, he shall not be allowed to plead. Should he be a lawyer, no instrument made by him shall be valid, but shall be condemned with their author."

The Roman Catholic Bishop swore that these laws had never been repealed, and, of course, they were still the laws of his church. He had to swear that, every year, he was bound, under pain of eternal damnation, to say in the presence of God, and to read in his Brevarium, (prayer book) that "God Himself had inspired" what St. Thomas had written about the manner in which heretics shall be treated by the Roman Catholics.

I will abstain from making any remarks on these startling revelations of that Roman Catholic high authority. But I think it is the duty of every citizen to know what the Roman Catholic Bishops and Priests understand by liberty of conscience. The Roman Catholics are interested as the Protestants to know precisely what the teachings of their Church are on the subject of liberty of conscience, and hear the exact truth, as coming from such high authority that there is no room left for any doubt.

STEPHEN R. MOORE, Attorney

January 10th, 1871

In a private letter to Edwin A. Sherman, Mr. Moore gave an explanation as to how they were able to make the Bishop take the stand.

Kankakee, ILL. May 15, 1882

Mr. Edwin A. Sherman, San Francisco, Ca.

Dear Sir: You ask 'What judge was upon the bench at the time the suit (you mean trial) was brought when Bishop Foley was required to translate from the works of St. Thomas Aquinas etc.?'

"Judge Charles H. Wood: Chiniquy's lawyers were Judge Wm. Osgood, Paddock, Lincoln and myself."

"You ask me to give you the facts in regard to the examination of Bishop Foley when we made him make the translations.

We knew he was the head of authority in the church in Illinois. We knew he would not dare to deny the authority of the books as binding on the church. If Mr.

Chiniquy would swear and bear witness as to the authority of those books, it would be denied by all Catholics, when they could not deny it when the proof came from the Bishop.

We wanted to show, also, *that it was authority in the Church, to-day,* as well as at the time they were published. This could only be done by forcing the Bishop to appear as a witness. We knew he would go away from the jurisdiction of the court, so he could not be served with process if he knew what we wanted. Our statute allows any person, whether officer or not, to serve a subpoena. We got the process, and in my possession on the evening of the trial, and I took the evening train to Chicago. I found a friend in Chicago to go with me. I knew that if I sent up my name he would refuse to see me. My friend sent up his card, with request to see the Bishop. This was about nine o'clock at night. After a long delay, he came to the library. He was much astonished when he saw me, and looked at his card to ensure no mistake had occurred. I introduced my friend, who politely read the process, commanding him to appear upon the next day at Kankakee and testify in the case, at the same time tendering to him his witness fees, being five cents per mile and one dollar a day for his services. He indignantly refused the money, and *declared he would not attend.* ***He thought the courts had no power over him. He recognized no authority but the authority of the church.*** I assured him he must do as he thought best; but he must take the consequences. It would be a contest between him and the Court, *and I had never seen the Court fail to enforce the orders of the Court.*

He sent for the attorney for his diocese, Hon. B. G. Caulfield, and after the interview, *he had no difficulty obeying the order of the Court.* When it came down to it he made a good witness.

He never forgave me for it, however. He really felt that his high position had been lowered. *It was the first time any lawyer had ever done such a thing.*

Yours,

Stephen R. Moore

The murder of five presidents of the United States, by the enemies of Popular Government in less than sixty years, is a toll which is worthy of the most serious consideration of the American people. Five presidents of the Republic in 59 years were assassinated; two by the "poison cup" and three by the "leaden bullet."

Abraham Lincoln was the third president assassinated; two before him had been given the "Poison Cup." Indeed, poison had been administered to President Lincoln, according to the Charles Selby letter to Booth, which was a conspicuous government exhibit in the trials of Mary E. Surratt and the other conspirators, which stated:

"The cup failed us once, and might again."

There were two things the ultra-pro-slavery leaders of the South had been urging for years by which they expected to make the breach for their entering wedge. One was the invasion of Cuba. The other was the annexation of Texas.

An invasion of Cuba would have meant war with Spain, France, Austria, Belgium and Italy; all Catholic countries. The United States would never have stood a chance and the system of Popular Government would have seen total annihilation with the setting of a monarchial system with all of its institutions as was pledged at the Congress of Vienna and ratified at Verona.

Where Mexico was concerned, the plan was to wipe out the little Republic where the Liberals had succeeded, under the leadership of Juarez, the half-Indian, rebellious ex-priest, in throwing off the Spanish and Papal yokes. Juarez had been elected president of Mexico when Civil War broke out in the United States.

Benito Juarez

During this time the new popular government was progressing rapidly in Mexico. The first official act was the confiscation of all the Roman church property, which included over thirty-five percent of the most valuable and choicest land and holdings.

There was a certain line of policy which these monarchial plotters were pursuing in the United States through the Leopoldines. The slave question was becoming more acute all the time. The Jesuit-controlled leaders only, were aware of the plan. The masses of the Southern people had no real knowledge of it. They were not permitted to have, but their leaders had. The masses of any people cannot be corrupted. The strong sense of justice and right and fairness, which is planted in every human heart at birth by God, will invariably spring into action at a crisis, if they are permitted to have a clear understanding of the issue. As a matter of fact, their very instinct of self-preservation sharpens their judgment and strengthens their resolve. The only instances of wrong decisions, or actions at such times, comes from corrupted and wicked leaders.

In 1841 General William Henry Harrison of Ohio, was elected President by a large majority. The loyalty to the Union of General Harrison was above question, and it was out of the power of the Leopoldines to defeat him. It was with his election that the "Big Stick" of intimidation was first raised when political intrigue had failed.

In his inaugural address, which was a masterpiece, President Harrison clearly and finally cut any ground for hope from under the enemies to the Union of States when he said:

> "We admit of no government by divine right, believing that so far as power is concerned, the beneficent Creator has made no distinction among men; that all are upon an equality, and that the only legitimate right to govern, is upon the express grant of power from the governed." (9)

With these unmistakable words President Harrison made his position clear; he hurled defiance to the Divine Right enemies of Popular Government. As a matter of fact, he did more, for those were the words which signed his death warrant. Just one month and five days later from that day, President Harrison lay a corpse in the White House. He died from arsenic poisoning. The Jesuit oath had been swiftly carried out:

> "I do further promise and declare that I will, when opportunity presents, make and wage relentless war, secretly or openly, against all heretics, Protestants and Liberals, as I am directed to do, to extirpate them and exterminate them from the face of the earth...
>
> "That when the same cannot be done openly, I will secretly use the poison cup... regardless of the honor, rank, dignity or authority of the person or persons... whatsoever may be their condition in life, either public or private..."

I wish to quote for you from U.S. Senator Benton's "*Thirty Years' View*," volume 11, page 21, regarding the death of President Harrison:

> "There was no failure of health or strength to indicate such an event or to excite apprehension that he would not go through his term with the same vigor with which he commenced it. His attack was sudden and evidently fatal from the beginning." (10)

Vice President John Tyler, who had been approached by these assassins previous to the election of himself and Harrison, had replied to their interrogations on the annexation of Texas question:

> "If I should ever become president, I would exert the entire influence of that office to accomplish it." (11)

President Tyler made good on his promise and the annexation of Texas, which was tricked through, caused the resignation of every member of President Harrison's Cabinet, with the exception of Daniel Webster. Again I quote from Benton's "*Thirty Years' View*":

> "He (Webster) had remained with Mr. Tyler until the Spring of 1843, when the progress of the Texas annexation scheme carried on privately, not to say clandestinely, had reached a point to take an official form, and to become the subject of government negotiation, though still secret. Mr. Webster, Secretary of State, was an obstacle to that negotiation. He could not be trusted with the secret, much less conduct the negotiations. How to get rid of him was a question of some delicacy. Abrupt dismissal would have revolted his friends. Voluntary resignation was not to be expected...A middle course was fallen upon, that of compelling a resignation. Mr. Tyler became reserved and indifferent to him. Mr. Gilmer and Mr. Upshur, with whom he had few affinities, took but little pains to conceal their distaste to him...Mr. Webster felt it and told some of his friends. They said "resign." He did and his resignation was accepted with an alacrity which showed it was waited for. Mr. Upshur took his place and quickly the Texas negotiations became official, still secretly." (Thirty Years' View, pg. 562) (12)

William Henry Harrison – Murdered on the order of the Jesuits

Circumstances pointed to the Messrs. Gilmer and Upshur, as being the actual assassins of President Harrison. Thus, at last, they accomplished, after years of effort, one of their daring schemes - the annexation of Texas.

At the close of the chapter in Senator Benton's book, we read this significant bit of information, which should well be pondered regarding Harrison's family:

> "That the deceased President had been closely preceded and was rapidly followed by the deaths of almost all of his numerous family, sons and daughters."

That is "extirpation" with a vengeance. Wholesale extirpation. In fact, there was but one of his eight children, a son, permitted to live. Intimidation was the covert motive behind this wholesale assassination of the Harrison family of "heretics" whose father had been martyred for his belief in the Popular Government of which the people had made him the highest representative.

As these plotters against the Union had tried President Harrison out on the annexation of Texas, they used the invasion of Cuba as the test for Zachary Taylor, and had their plans ready to launch their scheme in the early part of his administration. From the very beginning President Taylor snuffed out all hope of its consummation during his term. In his first message to Congress, he said:

> "But attachment to the Union of States should be fostered in every American heart. For more than half a century, during which kingdoms and empires have fallen, this Union has stood unshaken...In my judgment its dissolution would be the greatest of calamities, and to avert that should be the steady aim of every American. Upon its preservation must depend our own happiness and that of generations to come. Whatever dangers may threaten it, I shall stand by it and maintain it in its integrity to the full extent of the obligations imposed, and power conferred on me by the Constitution." (13)

There was no quibbling in this. The pro-slavery leaders had nothing to count on in Taylor, therefore they decided on his assassination. While these politicians were not influential enough to name the President, they were cunning enough to be able to control the nomination of the Vice President, and it goes without saying that they always chose a man who was in full sympathy with their plans. They pursued this as the next best thing. It had become practically a "trade" between the two groups of politicians.

Millard Fillmore, a staunch pro-slavery man, strong for the things his party wanted, was chosen as Vice President for Taylor. The President, knowing the caliber of this running mate, had no sympathy, and as little to do with him as possible. The arch-plotters, fearing that suspicion might be aroused by the death of the President early in his administration, as in the case of President Harrison, permitted him to serve one year and four months, when on the Fourth of July, arsenic was administered to him during a celebration in Washington at which he was invited to deliver the address. He went in perfect health in the morning and was taken ill in the afternoon about five o'clock and died on the Monday following, having been sick in the same number of days and with precisely the same symptoms as was his predecessor, President Harrison. I quote again from Senator Benton's "*Thirty Years' View*":

> "He sat out all the speeches and omitted no attention which he believed the decorum of his station required...The violent attack began soon after his return to the Presidential mansion." (Vol. 11, pg. 763)

The Vice President, Millard Fillmore, was immediately sworn in as president, after the death of "Old Rough and Ready" as Zachary Taylor's friends affectionately called him.

The Presidential election of 1856 was a hotly contested one for the pro-slavery forces fully realized that never again would they be able to dominate or control the presidency. The newly awakened social conscience of the North had animated public sentiment to such an extent that this would be impossible, so they were ready to take the most desperate chances to elect James Buchanan as the only presidential possibility, in whom they could have any hope. Not being absolutely certain of his dependability, they resorted to their old policy of being doubly sure of his running mate and nominated John C. Breckinridge of Kentucky.

In order that the Dred Scott Decision should not in any way hazard the chances of Buchanan's election, these Jesuit schemers compelled Catholic Judge Roger E. Taney to withhold his decision until after the Inauguration, March 6, 1857.

The new President proved himself a decided "Trimmer." Although he was a Northern man, he had strongly courted the Southern leaders, and had given them to understand that he was "With them heart and soul," in short, he double-crossed them. He was invited to deliver an address on Washington's Birthday, and made a reservation at the National Hotel, (the headquarters for the Jesuits in Washington,) for himself and some friends. The Southern leaders immediately got in touch with him with the intention of testing him out and learning precisely whether he intended to make good on his pre-election promises or not.

Romanism in Washington.

TO THE EDITOR: I believe you are right in discrediting many of the foolish stories that are circulated about an intended uprising of the Romanists. But when all due allowance is made there are still some strange things that are unexplained. I am told that nuns are allowed free access to all the public departments in Washington, and to solicit regular contributions from every employee. Do you know whether this is true or false? It is reported that of 2,500 clerks employed in one department, more than 2,000 are Romanists; can this be so? Romanists number but one-eighth of our population, and would rightly be entitled to but 300 clerks in that department.

I understand that of the new Court of Appeals of the District of Columbia two of the judges are Jesuits, and the Chief Justice is the son of Romanist parents; do I understand correctly? I am assured that President Cleveland has Cardinal Gibbons come to the White House for political conferences; does he do this, or has he ever done it? There surely is no need of our long believing a falsehood concerning a matter so easily verified as this. Probably others of your readers have heard these reports; If you can tell us whether they are facts or fancies you will be doing us a favor. E. W. H.

We have no definite knowledge in regard to these matters. Roman Catholics are very apt to play into each others hands politically, and anyone who depends on Catholic votes for success on election day is likely to find himself very much under bondage to his Catholic constituents.

The gentleman had had his ear to the ground evidently and heard the rumble of the Abolitionists wheels, and when the committee asked for a conference, he coolly informed them that he was President of the North, as well as the South. This change of attitude was indicated by his very decided stand against Jefferson Davis and his party, and he made known his intention of setting the question of Slavery in the Free States to the satisfaction of the people in those States.

The following quotes from the *New York Herald* and the *Post* at the time chronicled what followed:

> "The appointments favoring the North by the Jeff Davis faction will doubtless be accepted, and treated as a declaration of war, and a war of extermination on one side or the other." (New York Herald Feb. 25, 1857)

> "On Washington's birthday, Buchanan's stand became known and the next day (23rd) he was poisoned. The plot was deep and planned with skill. Mr. Buchanan, as was customary with men in his station, had a table and chairs reserved for himself and friends in the dining room at the National Hotel. The President was known to be an inveterate tea drinker; in fact, Northern people rarely drink anything else in the evening. Southern men prefer coffee. Thus to make sure of Buchanan and his Northern friends, arsenic was sprinkled in the bowls containing the tea and lump sugar and set on the table where he was to sit. The pulverized sugar in the bowls used for coffee on the other tables was kept free from the poison. Not a single Southern man was affected or harmed. Fifty or sixty persons dined at the table that evening, and as nearly as can be learned, about thirty-eight died from the effects of the poison."

> "President Buchanan was poisoned, and with great difficulty his life was saved. His physicians treated him understandingly from instructions given by himself as to the cause of his illness, for he understood well what was the matter."

> "Since the appearance of the epidemic, the tables at the National Hotel have been almost empty. But more remarkable than the appearance of the epidemic itself, is the supineness of the authorities of Washington in regard to it."

> "Have the proprietors of the Hotel, or clerks, or servants, suffered from it? If not, in what respect did their diet and accommodations differ from those of the guests (Northern)?"

> "There is more in this calamity than meets the eye. It is a matter that should not be trifled with." (N.Y. Post, March 18, 1857)

The close call to death frightened and made James Buchanan the most subservient tool the Jesuits ever had. An old friend, who visited him in Washington a few months after, said he had "aged twenty-five years." He had been the picture of health, robust and straight as an arrow, when he arrived in Washington for his Inauguration. After he had gotten his dose he was emaciated and bent. Referring to the symptoms of such an attack, an item from the *Newark News Advertiser* of March 18, 1857, said:

> "A persistent diarrhea, in some cases accompanied by violent vomiting, and always with a most distressing loss of strength and spirits in the person. Sometimes the person for one day would be filled with the hopes of recovery, then relapse again to loss of spirits and illness."

> "Elliott Eskridge, the nephew of President Buchanan, died from the effects of the poisoning."

James Buchanan

During the Buchanan administration seven States seceded, headed by South Carolina, taking seven forts, four arsenals and one Navy Yard, and the United States Mint at New Orleans, with five hundred and eleven thousand dollars. The total value of the government property stolen at this time was twenty-seven million dollars and eight million dollars in Indian Trust Bonds.

The following graphic picture of the situation in 1850-1860 was taken from a eulogy, delivered on Wendell Phillips in Boston, April 9, 1884, by the Rev.

Dr. Archibald H. Grimke of Washington, D.C., one of the most scholarly and eloquent thinkers of his day:

> "But when the year 1850 came and the slave power hung its Black bill over the Free States, non-resistance had no longer any place in the conflict. The time for argument had passed; the time for arms had arrived. On the first wave of this momentous change Wendell Phillips mounted to leadership. His speeches were the first billows breaking in prophetic fury against the South. They were the first blasts of the tempest; the first shock on the utmost verge of the Civil War. Forcible resistance of the Black bill was now obedience to God.... The passage of the Bill was the actual opening of hostilities between two sections. The Union from that moment was in the state of war. Of course then, there were not any of the signs of war, no opposite armies, two belligerent governments...It was nonetheless real, however...The peaceable surrender of a fugitive slave becomes now treason to freedom. Wendell Phillips comprehended the gravity of the situation. He refused to cry peace when there was no peace. He answered the Southern manifesto with the thunder of his great speech on the anniversary of the rendition of Sims.... He is in command and has called for guns.... He saw clearly that the danger of the reform lay in the stupor and indifference, which repeated executions under the law, would produce.
>
> "The South was united and highly organized, impelled by a single purpose, and in possession of the whole machinery of government. He saw the North timid, irresolute, sordid, drugged by Whigs and Democrats, and frozen with the fear of disunion... Peace was slavery, and sleep was death. The only hope of freedom lay now in the finger that could pull the trigger. This might beat back the advancing apathy and save the citadel of liberty. It is the glory of Phillips that he saw this... He was an army in himself. His eloquence poured out month after month, and year after year, a kind of imminent presence... the very air of the Free States vibrated with the disembodied soul of his mighty invectives... Shock after shock has loosened the ice from the conscience and courage of the North. The Republican Party is born, and then comes the first political freedom. Abraham Lincoln has entered the White House, and Jeff Davis has turned his back upon Washington forever. The trial morning is rising gloomily upon the republic. The gray light is haunted with strange voices, winged portents, bloody apparitions. Right and

Wrong, Freedom and Slavery have reached the plains of '60." (14)

Thus we have been given a glimpse of the decade from the murder of Taylor to the Election of Lincoln.

Endnotes

1 The Suppressed Truth about the Assassination of Abraham Lincoln, Burke McCarty, 1923, p. 37-38 by permission Destiny Publishers, Merrimac, Mass.

2 Famous Speeches of Abraham Lincoln

3 Fifty Years in the Church of Rome, Charles Chiniquy, (by permission Chick Publications, Chino, Ca.) pp. 304- 305; Abe Lincoln's Yarns and Stories, Colonel Alexander K. McClure, 1901 p.379

4 Ibid. pp.262-263

5 Ibid. pp.274-275

6 Ibid. p. 276

7 The Suppressed Truth about the Assassination of Abraham Lincoln, Burke McCarty, 1923, p.41

8 Fifty Years in the Church of Rome, Charles Chiniquy, (by permission Chick Publications, Chino, Ca.) pp.280-281

9 The Suppressed Truth about the Assassination of Abraham Lincoln, Burke McCarty, 1923, p.44 by permission

10 Thirty Years' View; From 1820-1850, Thomas Benton, (New York: D. Appleton and Co., 1854)

11 The Suppressed Truth about the Assassination of Abraham Lincoln, Burke McCarty, 1923, p.46 by permission

12 Thirty Years' View, From 1820-1850, Thomas Benton

13 The Suppressed Truth about the Assassination of Abraham Lincoln p.47 by permission

14 Ibid. p.53

Chapter 5

Lincoln and Davis compared; European Catholic autocrats gear up; Lincoln reacts to Catholic monarchist interference; Letters from Austrian archives; Lincoln and Foreign Affairs

Both Abraham Lincoln and Jefferson Davis were cut from virtually the same cloth. They were of the same age and born about 100 miles apart. Both came from the same immigrant origin, Lincoln from England and Davis from Wales. Both families settled in the North and both eventually went to Kentucky for better opportunities. Both were born of pioneer parents and both were raised in a log cabin with the Davis house being larger.

Democrat and feudalist Jefferson Davis

Soon after their birth the differences began. The Lincolns moved north to Indiana and then to Illinois, the Davis family to Mississippi. The Lincolns remained poor but the Davis' rapidly became wealthy and prosperous cotton plantation owners. Young Jefferson was given a formal education and graduated from West Point in 1828. Abraham, on the other hand, had almost no formal education and worked on a Mississippi flatboat delivering produce all the way down to New Orleans.

In the Blackhawk War they both served fighting Indians, Davis as a commissioned officer and Lincoln as Captain of a local militia. In 1835 Davis resigned his commission and became a plantation owner whereas Lincoln worked at a number of menial low paying jobs which included being a store clerk, a rail splitter, a farm hand, an assistant at elections and a surveyor. During this time he ran for the State Legislature twice, winning in his second attempt in 1834. He studied law in his spare time and in 1837 opened his law office in Springfield, Illinois.

As politicians they represented opposing social groups and it was during this time that Davis became a strong supporter of states' rights, full sovereignty for the states and was a firm and fanatical believer in the Old Order of feudalism and used a distorted, cross-eyed misapplication of the Bible to justify the practice of slavery. He took the position that the Mexican War was a God-given blessing to extend the empire of slave-holding states all the way west to the Pacific.

Abraham Lincoln, on the other hand, became a Congressman in 1847 under the Whig banner and was antislavery. He believed in the supremacy of the Federal Union over the states and viewed the position of secession as the counterrevolution of a privileged minority. He denounced aggression in general and the Mexican War in particular. While his position was widely seen as unpatriotic and his law partner, William Herndon, warned him of the possible consequences, Lincoln replied,

> "Would you have voted for what you felt and knew to be a lie?" (1)

Davis was Secretary of War 1853-7 in Pierce's Democratic Cabinet and was strongly influenced by the pro-slavery faction of the South. At the same time Lincoln began to promote the idea of a Republican Party, a coalition of those who opposed slavery. The fact Davis, a war leader, met his match and was defeated by the pacifist Lincoln, is an irony which cost the lives of a half a million souls and five billion dollars.

With the election of Lincoln in 1860 the European monarchists and autocrats smacked their lips in anticipation of seeing the rift widen between the supporters of both sides and shared the hopes of the Southern masses to reverse the loss of influence they once held on the continent. They were holding on to the hope of a crown of a future confederate kingdom being placed on the head of a European prince.

In an August 1860 article of the *New York Times* we find that, "Commissioners of South Carolina and Mississippi," had requested help from Napoleon III and "held out to him the prospective of an American crown." In response, however, Napoleon, according to the same article is quoted as saying,

> "the Emperor shall have declared that 'in the nineteenth century no European government would ever dare to recognize a State based exclusively on slavery'."

This remark was most likely based on the fact that he viewed himself as a 'liberal' dictator. The Southern Commissioners in turn explained to His Majesty that as was stated in the *Times* report the

> 'South Carolinians were largely descended from French Huguenots and for this reason they felt a warm admiration of and affection for France as the 'Mother Country'. (2)

In another *New York Times* article it named "young Captain Bonaparte of Baltimore" as the proposed recipient of a future Confederate crown and was asked to

> "accept the position of a Military Dictator of the Southern Confederacy, with a crown at his disposal...fortunately for him, Captain Bonaparte...refused the unclean and unnatural proposition." (3)

Jerome Napoleon Jr. was born November 5, 1830 in Baltimore and was educated at West Point. He joined the army of his second cousin, Napoleon III in 1854 and it is more than probable that he played a significant role in Napoleon's American plans. The timing of these plans, however, was not right and Jerome Bonaparte had to decline this 'unclean' offer. Napoleon III thought the prospect of a premature conflict with the United States would endanger the family's American property with confiscation and he did not want to identify himself as a partner of the cabal against Washington.

Napoleon III

This proposal made virtually no impression on the other monarchs of Europe, as they were preoccupied with their response to the Monroe Doctrine and attempting to test the resolve of republicanism in America. They were also determined to choose their own candidate should any available crowns present themselves for the taking.

Eager to exploit the Civil War for their own purposes, the crowned heads of Europe gained encouragement by the early victories of the Confederacy. Bull Run had proved to them that the South had what it took to triumph. They overlooked, however, the fact that the Southern armies were ill-clothed and suffered from a substantial absence of industrial capacity. Promoters of outright military intervention by Europe's Atlantic powers gained influence and joint action in defiance of the Monroe Doctrine was considered. British shipyards started building war ships for the Southern Confederates and the French Generals were laying plans for stationing troops in Mexico. Spanish leaders mused about a recapture of Mexico and the Rothschild's and other financiers were eager to loan money to the Confederacy. Austria, under Metternich, took a wait and see approach.

Lincoln and Secretary Seward had no illusions of European intentions. It was evident that they were looking for the overthrow of republican Mexico and it was equally evident that a Mexican monarchy, supported by European crowns, would be a natural ally of the Confederacy and a permanent danger to the Union. Lincoln knew, as well, that he lacked a substantial naval power and that war with three European Empires simultaneously would be suicidal.

Seeing the European allies arraying themselves to launch a campaign in Mexico, Lincoln issued a warning knowing that it would result in conflicting reactions and discord among them. The note, signed by Seward, was addressed to Ambassador Dayton at Napoleon's court. It is kept in the Austrian archives and reads:

Washington 3rd March, 1862

Sir;

We observe indications of a growing opinion in Europe, that the demonstrations, which are being made by Spanish, French and British forces against Mexico, are likely to be attended with a revolution in that country, which will bring in a monarchial government there, in which the crown will be assumed by some foreign Prince.

This country is deeply concerned in the peace of nations, and aims to be loyal at the same time in all its relations, as well to the allies as to Mexico. The President has therefore instructed me to submit his views on the new aspect of affairs to the parties concerned. He has relied on the assurances given to this government by the allies, that they were seeking no political objects, and only a redress of grievances. He does not doubt the sincerity of the Allies and his confidence in their good faith, if it could be shaken, would be reinspired by explanations apparently made in their behalf, that the governments of Spain, France and Great Britain are not intending to intervene to effect a change in the constitutional form of government, now existing in Mexico, or to produce any political change there in opposition to the will of the Mexican people. Indeed he understands the Allies to be unanimous in declaring that the proposed revolution in Mexico is moved only by Mexican citizens now in Europe.

The President, however, deems it his duty to express to the Allies, in all candor and frankness, the opinion that no monarchial government, which could be founded in Mexico, in the presence of foreign navies and armies in the waters and upon the soil of Mexico, would have any prospect of security or permanence. Secondly, that the instability of such a monarchy there, would be enhanced, if the throne should be assigned to any person not of Mexican nativity. That under such circumstances the new government must speedily fall, unless it could draw into its support European alliances, which, relating back to the first invasion would in fact make it the beginning of a permanent policy of armed European monarchial intervention, injurious and practically hostile to the most general system of government on the continent of America, and this would be the beginning rather than the ending of revolution in Mexico

These views are grounded upon some knowledge of the political sentiments and habits of society in America. In such a case, it is not to be doubted, that the permanent interests and sympathies of this country would be with the other American republics. It is not intended on this occasion to predict the course of events, which might happen as a consequence of the proceeding contemplated, either on this continent or in Europe.

It is sufficient to say, that, in the President's opinion, the emancipation of this continent from European control, has been the principle feature in its history during the last century. It is not probable that a revolution in a contrary direction would be successful in an immediately succeeding century, while population in America is so rapidly increasing, resources so rapidly developing, and Society so steadily forming itself upon principles of Democratic American government. Nor is it necessary to suggest to the allies the improbability that European nations could steadily agree upon a policy favorable to such a counter revolution, as one conducive to their own interests, or to suggest that however studiously the allies may act to avoid lending the aid of their land and naval forces to domestic revolutions in Mexico, the result would nevertheless be traceable to the presence of those forces there, although for a different purpose, since it may be deemed certain that but for their presence there, no such revolution could probably be attempted or even conceived.

The Senate of the United States has not indeed given its official sanction to the precise measures, which the President has proposed for lending our aid to the existing government of Mexico, with the approval of the Allies, to relieve it of its present embarrassments. This however is only a question of domestic administration. It would be very erroneous to regard such a disagreement as indicating any serious difference of opinion in this government, or among the American people, in their cordial good wishes for the safety, welfare and stability of the republican system of government in that country.

I am, Sir

Your obedient servant, William H. Seward

This was a bold, plain, unveiled threat of support for the Mexican popular government as well as the antimonarchists in Europe. Both Lincoln and Seward had identified themselves with the revolutionists and defied the monarchists, emperors and by implication the feudalists in Mexico and Southern slaveholders.

Spain and Britain quickly bowed out. Napoleon III, however, united with the Catholic Hapsburg Francis Joseph I and launched an invasion into Mexico with the intent of placing a crown on the head of a Hapsburg Prince, namely Maximilian. This venture was given the active support and blessing of the Pope.

Secretary of State Seward

Maximilian's wife, Eugenie, hated the United States as a "hotbed of republicanism" and had constantly expressed the opinion that

> "sooner or later we will have to declare war on America"(4)

She spoke of Lincoln in a disparaging manner and was amused by the hostile cartoons in the newspapers. "Why is the French-American scientist DuChaillu searching Africa for the missing link when a specimen was brought from the American backwoods to Washington?"

Eugenie greeted the outbreak of civil war as a Godsend, which opened the gates to European monarchist intervention on behalf of the Confederacy, and the royalists of Mexico. It was, she insisted, a great opportunity to gain more power and glory for imperial France and her dynasty. It enabled Napoleon to offer the Mexican Crown to a Prince of the Hapsburgs as a gesture of conciliation with a view to a close alliance. Eugenie had envisioned a crusade of three Catholic Empires including Napoleon, Francis Joseph and Maximilian, to restore monarchy and the power of the Catholic Church, first in Mexico and then upon the smoldering ruins of a disintegrated United States.

Emperor Francis Joseph viewed the American republic as an assault against everything he held dear as far as the world order was concerned and one in which he represented by the grace and will of God. Therefore the concept of restoring monarchial principles to the North American Continent was an idea he fully supported. He had little interest in the United States but Mexico was a different story. Monarchist Mexico had been the jewel of his ancestor Charles V who ruled over a vanquished Aztec nation. Francis Joseph held firm to the idea that it was the first duty of his subjects to worship and obey him as they would God. Any subjects who were so impertinent as to challenge him were quickly executed or thrown into prison.

Maximilian was the only one who dared to raise his voice against this oppression. He criticized the police state, the military "pacification", the severity of justice and the almost inhumane court discipline. He became popular among the people but was soon shown his proper place by being removed far from Vienna, to Mexico. From this position he felt he was justified to consider himself as being chosen by divine providence to bring monarchic principles to a deviant America.

Emperor Maximilian

Near the end of 1861 the European principals made their bold move in a conspiracy against America. The goal was to completely destroy republicanism and bring the blessings of papal backed monarchy. In a letter to his son-in-law Maximilian, Leopold I wrote:

> **Augsberg, October 25, 1861**
>
> My dear son,
>
> I read with great interest the documents you transmitted to me. It was highly important and necessary for

me to learn *your* viewpoint, since, if you had declined the matter as too difficult a task, all further tasks would have become superfluous. The matter is of a difficult nature, because of the political demoralization, i.e., the lack of all loyalty and reliability [of the Mexicans] due to a constant change of authority. Two elements have not been quite destroyed, the large estates and the influence of the Clergy. The Indians are not an evil element and are better than the Creoles, although in the cities a part of the Leperos [Indian city-proletariat] may have become bad enough.

If England were following a farsighted policy, she would have a double incentive for supporting this project: first, to see Mexico productive once again; and, second, to raise a barrier against the United States and provide a support for the monarchial-aristocratic principle in the Southern states. Unfortunately, since the reform there are many influences obstructing a policy of real consequence, and discouraging old ministers from initiating such if it might cause personal trouble for them. They [the British Cabinet] are reluctant to pledge publicly their support for an expedition implying intervention in the internal affairs, [of Mexico] in order to establish a certain form of government. Should, however, Mexico *herself* choose monarchy, they would recognize the new form of state.

We face the question: Will the Conservatives [of Mexico] have the courage to undertake the necessary steps? They might be encouraged by the approaching help of Europe. On the other hand, I heard that the mob might massacre the Conservatives should it be faced with such an expedition. Thus the ultimate decision depends on what the country *itself* would do, since then we may have firm ground under our feet. Until these developments have taken place, it might be necessary to maintain freedom of action. Whether you should abandon your position in Austria in case of a favorable turn of events is a question that none but you alone can answer; unfortunately it cannot be denied that the beautiful monarchy is sick; whether you are able to contribute to its preservation can only be decided by you.

At the time that the independence of the Spanish colony was recognized by England, Mexico was a country excellently suited for a monarchy. Some Mexicans of influence had proposed to Canning that he persuade me to take over its government. England, however, was afraid that all out support would appear too self-interested and might be dangerous to Victoria. Thus the idea is not new.

The elements of a political life exist in Mexico. Had the secession not taken place in the United States, Mexico would have been seriously threatened from that quarter, since the idea of entirely absorbing her had taken firm root in the United States; but irrespective of the outcome of the war, there can be no longer any thought of further conquest south of the border. On the other hand, the South, as I said before, has an interest in the reorganization of Mexico.

Leopold I

So let us recapitulate: 1/ Mexico herself must enunciate the principle. 2/ Until this happens, you must insist on your freedom of action without, however, declining the offer. 3/ France is in favor of it, Spain is *not.* Yet they cannot propose aBourbon to Emperor Napoleon. Moreover, this would be regarded by the Creoles as a complete restoration, which they would not welcome. England will recognize the situation proclaimed by the majority of the Mexicans. Perhaps they will gradually realize that it will be of importance for the state of affairs in the North of America.

Charlotte gave me a well-rounded report of the situation; it could be a fine state if only Heaven were pleased to give guidance for the best. I shall dispatch today my message and hope that you are well.

And now, goodbye, I will keep you informed of whatever I can learn, as ever, my dear son,

Your Faithful Father,
LEOPOLD REX (5)

In analyzing this we can see that the clear purpose of involvement in Mexico was to, "raise a barrier against the United States and provide a support for the monarchial-aristocratic principle in the Southern States". They viewed the Southern States as a natural ally and were under the impression that the Union under Lincoln was not in a position to interfere with their plans to install a monarchial system in Mexico. In a memo by Maximilian he stated,

> "In the political respect: should Europe recognize the South as an independent State, we must demand – on a reciprocal basis – that the South should respect the integrity and independence of Mexico"(6)

This would have nullified the force and intent of the Monroe Doctrine by the Confederacy.

In an attempt to persuade England to join the crusade, a letter by Napoleon III to his London ambassador Count Flahaut we get a clearer insight to this conspiracy:

> "There is no need for me to enlarge upon the common interest which we in Europe have in seeing Mexico pacified…if it were regenerated it would form an impassible barrier to the encroachments of North America…The American war has made it impossible for the United States to interfere in the matter, and what is more, the outrages committed by the Mexican government [confiscation of Church property, expulsion of Catholic priesthood etc.] have provided England, Spain and France with a legitimate motive for interference in Mexico…According to the information I have received, as soon as the squadrons arrive off Veracruz, a considerable party in Mexico is prepared to seize the supreme power, summon a national assembly, and proclaim the monarchy…I put forward the name of Archduke Maximilian …The Prince's personal qualities, his connection through his wife with the King of the Belgians, who forms a natural link between France and England, and the fact that he belongs to a great non-maritime power appeared to me to meet all desirable conditions." (7)

The blueprint for the eventual conquest of America and a return to a monarchial system under European control soon gelled into five stages.

1/ The occupation of Mexico under the guise of a 'debt collection' against a defaulting Republic of Mexico

2/ Financial, moral and clandestine military support for the Confederacy

3/ Recognition of the Confederate States at the proper time

4/ Gradual introduction of a monarchial system of government in the Confederate States

5/ Suppression of all things antagonistic to the monarchy

This, of course, all hinged on the fact that the Confederacy would continue as it had begun and result in a divided America. This was not to be the case.

One of the most interesting documents that reached into the mind of Jeff Davis and his government in the summer of 1863 was written by Edward T. Hardy, Consul of the Austrian Empire in Norfolk, Va., and also a Confederate agent in the Consular service to Emperor Francis Joseph I. It is titled "*The Aspect of American Affairs*"

The Aspect of American Affairs*

As there must be some basis from which to start in the expression of opinion at such a period as now obtains, and as I am ignorant of the exact position of His Imperial Majesty, if indeed it be as yet definite, I have to assume a premise.

Nothing is more natural than that he should be, if not in "rapport," at least in sympathy with His brother the Archduke and elected Emperor of Mexico, and with all who are connected with the establishment of that Empire.

An Empire having been proclaimed, a war with the United States is inevitable; and next in importance to the pacification and reconciliation of the people of Mexico, is a recognition of the Southern Confederacy, an alliance offensive and defensive with it.

The people of Mexico are said to be a good tempered race; easily led by a promise of good. Their discords have proceeded out of the conflicting designs of ambitious leaders. Persons that have traveled through the interior make frequent allusions to the simplicity of their natures. Inquiries concerning the institutions of this country are often noted, and one writer mentions particularly their expressed desire to have a free school system like that of some of the United States. The high castes, as is generally understood, are of Spanish descent, mostly of pure blood. The Mexicans make fair soldiers, and with good leaders and a thorough discipline, might be formed into very effective armies. They fought better against the French, than they did against the Americans. The cause may lie in the fact that the French were from another continent; or from the fear of being reduced to the condition of a province of the French Empire. The stability of the government proposed for them, seems to insure it a congenial reception on all sides.

The programme of the new Imperial Government might be,

1st The establishment of the Throne beyond peradventure;

2nd The recognition of the Southern States;

3rd If it be necessary, war in conjunction with the South and other allies against the Northern States;

4th If war, then the recovery of the State of California, and, if the Southern States will allow, of the territory of New Mexico; both of which were necessarily ceded to the United States under the Treaty of Guadaloupe Hidalgo.

The State of Texas, which is a possible object with the Emperor of France, will be found impracticable. For 1st Its independence was acknowledged by Mexico before the war with the United States; 2nd it was an integral state of the Federal Union; 3rd it is now one of the Seceded States, all of which are pledged to the defence of its integrity; and 4th The people are of the most independent and jealous character, and would never consent.

The query occurs: If the Emperor of France after conquering Mexico and releasing it for ulterior designs, still purposes to retain for himself a foothold upon the continent, why is not the country to the South of Mexico suited to his views? It is as rich as Texas; is one of the most important on the continent as embracing the ithsmus of Darien; and would be found much more controlable. A stable government would be as great a blessing to the people of that region as to Mexico; and now is a fit opportunity to propose it. Mexico should be an integrity from Oregon to Honduras.

France is necessarily involved in any present war between Mexico and the United States.

England will not lose the opportunity of weakening and humbling so gigantic a rival, a neighbor, and moral antagonist. She has borne with subdued fury many insults during the last two years; but though the governnment has long been resolved on war, it is determined to provoke the declaration, not to make it. It cannot be long postponed. England and France will therefore probably be united with Mexico in the recognition of the Confederate States.

It is thought by many that Canada will not enter cheerfully upon a war with the United States. I know nothing of the present disposition of the Canadian population, except what is contained in the following extract from a letter written to me by a very intelligent and perfectly reliable man, who moved from here since the Federal occupation. He writes from Ottawa, the proposed capitol of Canada West, but has also resided in Port Hope and Toronto since leaving here. He says, "Here in Canada the English and Scotch part of the population and also of the French are decidedly on the Southern side. If you could hear the conversation on the streets as new despatches are received and witness the manifestations of sympathy and good wishes for the Southern cause, you would imagine yourself in a Southern city." My belief is that this represents the sentiment of the entire people of Canada. In all the British Provinces the inhabitants entertain a repugnance towards Northerners.

Others are of the opinion that if Canada were erected into a separate kingdom under a British Prince, the people would be inspired with a more special loyalty, than is at present accorded to the distant government. It might not be ineffectual; but with good leaders the people would fight well under either government. Nor is there any encouragement in the aspect of republican intstitutions on this continent at present, to taint the Canadians with the idea of rebellion, and a consequent alliance with the North. I regard this as out of the question under its present liberal institutions.

This is a fearful aspect for the North, but will be met, not unwillingly, by men, who are seeking power, and profess that they cannot escape from history.

There is a new sprung hope of an alliance with Russia. It will be pressed with vigour, but who can say with what success? Is Russia prepared to enter into an alliance offensive and defensive with a power having no interest in common with her, except that it is opposed to the Western Powers of Europe? Whose institutions are the antipodes of those of Russia? And every contact with which must leave contamination? As this is the most momentous question of the times, I trust to be pardoned for a few remarks.

I assume the Polish question is the only impediment to the impending action on this continent. It is not yet satisfactorily solved. And why not? It is plain to the outside world that the Czar has determined to extend the benign influence of liberal institutions to all his subjects, and will not be prevented by the mistaken demonstrations in Poland. But the difficulty, which keeps apart an amiable Sovereign and a loyal people, has sprung from, and is sustained by, misapprehension. The Poles do not understand the kind feelings of their noble Monarch, and the Czar, though willing, is fearful of condescending too far. Prince Gorchakov has already, in his first reply, signified the intent of his august Master to extend to the Poles a government as liberal as they are prepared to receive, and in spirit progressive.

Knowing from his acts the magnanimity of the Czar, I have never believed that the Polish insurrection could result in anything serious. And when the Czar shall so far condescend as to make manifest by his words and countenance, the benevolent intentions he entertains towards them, the Poles will lay down their arms and be happy to return to allegiance.

Since the first outbreak in Poland there has been a tenacious hope, that it would involve the Western Powers and inflame the republican sentiment all over Europe. The co-operation of all the restless elements was counted on: and then what a glorious opportunity to blot out forever the pretensions of England and France upon this continent. As the despatches of Earl Russell erected a firm attitude, the hearts of the Washington administration gloated with expectation. But now that it is too late to forebear the insults of Wilkes and others, or to retract the stand on on the subject of vessels built in England for the South, their hopes will be much embarrassed, if not paralyzed, by the recent developments in Polish affairs, to wit: the sending of Prince Nicholas Mouravieff to pacify the Poles; and also an embassador to Paris, to offer a separate constitutional government for Poland.

It is not to be supposed that the Czar would form an alliance with the United States simply to make war upon the Western Powers; for he really designs to pacify the Poles, and then what further object could he have? Nothing – except the ambition, pure and simple, of being engaged in war; or the desire of conquest. In his short but glorious reign, he has manifested no symptom of either sentiment. If mere war was an object, could he not have protracted the Crimean war indefinitely? If conquest; was not that as fair an opening for an expectation, as is now afforded?

I would rather suppose, that the transparent character of Mr. Clay, the United States Minister at St. Petersburg, being recognized, he has been cajoled with the flattering hope of an alliance, to hasten, in harmony with the animus of the rest of Europe, the catastrophe, to which the United States is palpably trending. There may be discovered some plausible evasion, only after it is too late for the Washington Cabinet to recall their action.

Long negotiations seldom result in war; and the Western Powers, so soon as they shall have recognized a manifest intent on the part of the Czar to comply with the treaty of 1815, may avoid any further complications with him. Thus they will be free to meet the views of the Washington Cabinet, whose great purpose is war. War, not peace, is their programme. So it do not exterminate the people of the North, they do not care how much war they have. Why? Because war keeps them in Dictatorial power, at the head of immense armies. I may here remark that I can imagine no possible combination, that can defeat them in the next Presidential election.

The reclaimation of the South into the Union is not so much an object, as to overrun the territory of the Southern States, and get soldiers to fight England, France and Mexico. They do get negroes, who, though of a most peaceable nature, may be drilled into tolerable soldiers. It requires a little time to awaken their faculties to a battle. They are first employed in digging entrenchments, and are gradually led on to enlistment.

Their hope is further, to so far reduce the Southern States, as to inspire the people with despair of sustaining the government; and then to inflame them with an appeal to their traditional animosity to England, to their common cause in the enforcement of the Monroe Doctrine, and also in the sentiment of republicanism. But white soldiers they will not get, even from these portions of the South that have long been in their possession. As for those within the Confederate lines, it is not to be thought of.

The enforcement of the recent conscription is a signal triumph of the administration. It is notorious that the riot in New York was constituted almost entirely of foreigners, principally Irish. Governor Seymour of New York is the only man that ever raised the expectation of opposition to the central power. Immediately after his inauguration, he showed that he lacked the spirit, and nothing further has been expected of him. Mr. Vallandigham, the only man that could raise an opposition, is banished. He may, or he may not be, elected governor of Ohio. If he be, on the alarm of foreign war, he will side with the Administration. Although there is a strong and growing party in favor of peace, they do not, and for the present will not, resist.

The difficulty in the development of the Democratic Party, lies in the impracticability of the assertion of states rights, without falling into the imputation of treason to the Union, for the preservation of which the North purports to be fighting. In a foreign war the North will be united, and under good generals their soldiers are formidable.

The plan for procuring soldiers from the Southern people, is to exact of all who fall within their reach an oath of allegiance to the central power, to the exclusion of states rights. But though, by cruelty and threats, they have registered a great many oaths, they have enlisted but a few men: and those who have taken the oath will disregard it, when there is encouragmment of permanent reoccupation by the South. A few take it voluntarily to gain favor; others to attain places, of which they never before had a dream. Such are the present civil authorities of Norfolk.

The programme of the South is 1st Freedom; 2nd Under States rights, that is, the sovereignty of the individual state; 3rd Their territory; all the seceded States, including Tennesee, Missouri, and the Territoy of New Mexico; 4th The offer to Kentucky and Maryland of their free choice to unite with South or North. It will be observed that I omit slavery, of which a few words presently.

The first and greatest states rights man in this country was Patrick Henry of Virginia. He was an extraordinary intuitive genius, who, reared a peasant, and without training, became the most distinguished orator amongst a galaxy of acknowledged great men. It was Henry, that precipitated the revolution, which led to a separation from Great Britain. He was the typical spirit, the representative man of the people, conscious by instinct of their rights, and jealous and restive of any encroachment upon them. With all his magnificent powers, for twenty days, he argued, wrestled, debated, protested and besought, in the name of the people, against the combined talent of the land, for the perpetuation of the *Constitution of Confederation,* under the auspices of which the war of liberation had been carried on: and bitterly opposed the present constitution, which, he forsaw, tended to the establishment of a central power and to the evolution of sectional oppressions. His points were unanswerable, but his voice failed of its usual effect. His warnings were prophetic, and are now realized. It is misfortune that the arguments and entreaties of this great man were never published among the other state papers, most of which are full of solicitude for the Union. He did write his speeches, and his power over an audience is said to have been such, that no man could report them. Only fragments are preserved.

An essential argument on this subject, and not one usually marshalled to its defense, is in this wise: Montesquieu, in his "Spirit of Laws," asserts the principle that a republican form of government cannot be long sustained in any territory larger than a *city.* "Quoad hoc," the state of Virginia, or any individual state of the former Union, what with 1st the modern advances in enlightenment; 2nd the progress in arts, whereby distance is neutralized and short separations disappear; 3rd the scanty population; and 4th their harmony of interest; might be regarded as representing the speculative embodiment of the "city" of Montesquieu. But, waiving nice points, the gist lies in that when a territory is so great as to cause antagonism of interest, or even of moral sentiments, there can be, under a republican government, no supreme head, independent of party or sectional prejudices and passions; who can afford to be as indifferent to the clamours of the strong, as sensitive to the cries of the weak; and able from extended experience to interpose with prudence and firmness between the fanatic and his victim, the plunder and his quarry, or to balance the injustice of equal antagonisms. An elected president must necessarily carry out the policy and designs of his party; 1st in gratitude for his election, 2nd to sustain the party and thereby his own authority; and 3rd to secure the next election. He cannot, therefore, be impartial. When the platform of the party is purely sectional, the election of its candidate is tantamount to a declaration of war. Such was the nature of Mr. Lincoln's election. How can an individual thus circumstanced prevent oppression to the section opposing him? Nay! Instead of interposition for the weak, he is exponent of their cruel foes. Hence the need, if the people are supposed to be Sovereign, of recognizing, in any Confederate association, that form of sovereignty, which approaches nearest to the people, and proceeds most immediately from them; and of providing such safeguards, that the smallest neighbourhood may enforce its own rights, or refuse its relations.

The greatest champion of the opposite sentiment, of consolidation, based on the sophistry that the authority delegated to the general government was a direct emanation from the people, instead of the States, was the prodigious Webster, a man, to whose name every public man involuntarily gives place, but who gained a not less hollow and ephemeral triumph for his argument on this subject in reply to the elegant and brilliant addresss of Mr. Hayne of South Carolina, than he did for his answer to the dignified note of the Chevalier de Hulsemann remonstrating against the act of President Taylor in the establishment at Vienna of a "quasi" Hungarian Legation.

The people of the South have shown that they are in earnest. They hate their insane oppressors with an invincible malice. Nothing short of extermination will conquer them. Their unanimity has never been fully realized abroad, and has been constantly misrepresented in the Northern press. Since the proclamation of President Lincoln in April, 1861, the people have been literally a unit. There is some division only in Northern sections of the Border States. The character of the people may be worth noting. As a mass, they are not so well educated as the people of the North, but are of a brighter nature and quicker instinct. They are not so shrewd in business but more honorable. This difference was notorious in reference to the members of congress from the opposite sections. From my little field of observation, I believe they are equal in tone and morality with the like number of any agricultural population in the world. Slavery has assuredly in that respect been no bane. It has been in other respects, and so has the policy of the South in several particulars, to which allusion need not now be made.

The South is willing to make concession in commercial negotiations, and in anything else that does not diminish her territory. This would as a rule apply to all republics, which with notions of freedom, would be reluctant to consign any of their population to opposing institutions. I know nothing of the animus of the government in this respect, but my own idea would be that if it could be spared, it would be New Mexico, an interior territory, thinly populated by emigrants and adverntureers, and therefore in a more transferable form. It is thought to be as rich in minerals as any part of Mexico. I think the South would rather see California in possession of the Empire than of the Northern States. It would be a rich acquisition. It is not improbable that definite and liberal terms offered to the Mormon population, would secure their co-operation. It would be a powerful aid in the rear of California. The Mormons are deeply exasperated against the United States, and when they emigrated to their present locality, did not dream that the United States would have so large a population to the West of them in so short a time. The population is estimated as between 70-80,000, with a preponderance of females. The fighting element is probably as good as any in the country.

The subject of slavery is so difficult of representation to one who has not witnessed its operation in our Southern States, that it would be avoided if possible.

The Constitution of the United States solemnly santions and guarantees the institution, and recognizes slaves as property. It could not have been formed without such provisions.

The Southern people are of the same races as the Northern, and are fully their equals in humanity, morality, and piety. Slavery was not of their seeking, but was fored on them, much against their will, by the government of Great Britian. Neither was it an object with the most intelligent of the population. They regard the negro as a great responsibility, forced on them thus perhaps for some wise purpose. The race has certainly been very instrumental in clearing malarious lands in the South, that would have been fatal to any white race. The leaders in the border states have been anxious for 30 years to initiate schemes for emancipation; but have been prevented by the sustained pressure of fanatical admonitions and threatenings from the North. The institution has therefore been a source of the keenest solicitude to our most sagacious statesmen, of whom Henry clay was the fairest exponent. It has not been the bent and pride of the South but her inevitable incubus.

Yet regarding affairs in their present attitude, reason as I may, I cannot escape the consciousness that, in the event of negotiations between the Powers of Europe and the Confederate States, if a pledge for gradual emancipation could be embodied, it would not only be a satisfaction to the people of Europe, high and low, but positive service to the South. It is a mistake to compare the Southern States with the West Indies in reference to emancipation. There, the abundance of indiginous productions enables the free black to live without work. But he cannot subsist in any portion of the south without labor. If freed therefore he would naturally fall into the usual custom in agricultural districts, of hiring himself by the year or month. Their condition might be for a time worse than formerly, but would gradually assume a difficult character. Some by industry would attain property and comforts, whilst others would sink into idleness and squalor. Southern negroes are not irreclaimably indolent. The better people of the South, and such are the slaveholders, would easily reconcile themselves to the new state of things, and to conform to circumstances with cheerfulness.

Though it was the immediate cause of the present war, the South is not fighting for the perpetuation of slavery. She only desired, in the Union or out of it, to be left alone to control her own affairs: merely assuming that her people are as intelligent as those of the North, and are capable of making as wise a disposition of their institutions, as those who have nothing to do with them.

The war, so far as relates to the North itself, will terminate upon the doctrine of states rights, or end in a Sovereignty. Practically it is the latter now, but there is a powerful opposition, and though the Democratic Party appear to have been split, there is much ground to judge that they will eventually unite on the peace platform, and will be the cause of peace, if not the actual negotiators. When the people awake to a sense of their position, they will be extremely restive under a Dictator, and will struggle hard for a renewed constitution based on states rights.

Mr. Lincoln will probably be the re-elected next President. It is usual to regard him as inferior in intellect to some members of his cabinet, at the head of whom Mr. Seward is supposed to stand. But Mr. Lincoln wears well. As he is more honest, so he is more logical than the Secretary of State; as he is more original, so are his turns more unexpected; and notwithstanding his quaint manners and expressions, he is very shrewd and pointed in his observations and acts. I should regard him as a more formidable antagonist in any encounter than the Secretary, whose specious plausibilites are not always discreet.

The South is certainly much reduced and is taxed to her utmost resources. The late reverses, some by bad management, others by supposed treachery, have had a very serious effect on the people at large, who cannot understand the position of affairs as the President and commanding Generals do. But though disheartened they still respond to the calls for men, and the elders are now filling the ranks that have been hallowed by the blood of their offspring. They will hail therefore with joy and gratitude the early announcements of a recognition from an alliance with their neighbours and natural friends. If therefore it has been determined on, saving all prudent delay in view of preparations for inevitable hostilities, the sooner the fact is signified to them, the better effect will it have on their affairs; not that they are likely to succumb, for they will not, but to cheer them and spare some suffering.

Respectfully submitted,

E.T. Hardy, V.C.

Vice Consulate of Austria

Norfolk, Va, Sept. 19th, 1863

*Sourced from the book *Lincoln and the Emperors*, A.R. Tyrner Harcourt, Brace & World Inc. 1962 pp. 91-102

After the losses at Gettysburg and Vicksburg, however, the Western Powers of the Holy Alliance backed off from the idea of a direct invasion. Jefferson Davis's last desperate attempt to invoke the help of the "European Protectors" became a dismal failure.

Abraham Lincoln and Foreign Affairs

On May 11, 1863 Lord Richard Lyons, the British Minister visited President Abraham Lincoln to present a formal announcement "that her son, his Royal Highness the Prince of Wales, is about to contract a matrimonial alliance with her Royal Highness the Princess Alexandra of Denmark." The President's response to the bachelor minister was brief: "Lord Lyons, go thou and do likewise."[1] Usually, diplomacy was a very serious business for President Lincoln. In his message to Congress on July 4, 1861, President Lincoln wrote: "On the side of the Union, it is a struggle for maintaining in the world, that form, and substance of government, whose leading object is, to elevate the condition of men – to lift artificial weights from all shoulders – to clear the paths of laudable pursuit for all – to afford all, an unfettered start, and a fair chance, in the race of life."[2]

President-elect Lincoln's experience in foreign policy was very limited. He had never been out of the country and intended to rely on his designated Secretary of State, William H. Seward, to handle foreign relations. In the first months of his administration, Lincoln admitted that he had "given so little attention to foreign affairs and being so dependent upon other people's judgment, and that he felt the necessity of 'studying up' on the subject as much [as] his opportunities permitted.'"[3] Seward's son, Frederick W. Seward, wrote about an incident in February 1861: "On his home from St. John's Church, the first Sunday after his arrival in Washington, Mr. Lincoln had said to my father: 'Governor Seward, there is one part of my work that I shall have to leave largely to you. I shall have to depend upon you for taking care of these matters of foreign affairs, of which I know so little, and with which I reckon you are familiar."[4] Seward biographer John M. Taylor wrote that Seward's background well fitted him for his new responsibilities: "Seward…had an alert and facile mind, skilled both in assessing people and in analyzing political developments. He had a deep knowledge of history and was well versed in the writings of America's statesmen, especially Jefferson….His two extended trips to Europe and the Middle East were two more than most men – Lincoln included – had made in his day." Taylor, noted however that Seward also had some deficiencies as the nation's top diplomat: "He liked to talk and was not always discreet in conversation."[5] Seward's self-confidence sometimes was interpreted as bluster.

Former New York Senator Seward had a tough job – at home and abroad. The Union's relationships with Europe during the Civil War were as much a function of Europe's internal problems and the ambitions of its leaders as it was the problems of diplomacy. Those relations were also a function of Republican leaders who thought they deserved a prestigious diplomatic postings to Europe. President Lincoln and Secretary Seward needed to act quickly since there were still in place many Buchanan-era diplomats of questionable loyalty to the Lincoln Administration. Seward biographer Thornton Kirkland Lothrop wrote: "To purge our diplomatic and consular service of all persons whose loyalty was uncertain was, however, his most urgent duty; in many cases it was not enough that our representatives abroad should 'speak only the language of truth and loyalty, and of confidence in our institutions and destiny,' but it was of the utmost consequence that they should be persons selected with especial regard to their ability and fitness for the posts assigned."[6]

In a power play Seward briefly tried to reject his appointment shortly before President Lincoln's inauguration. Having accepted it, Seward took hold swiftly. Frederick W. Seward wrote: "On the morning after his appointment to be Secretary of State, my father sent for Mr. Hunter, and requested that a complete list of all the officers, clerks, and employees should be brought to him. Then inquiry was made as to which ones were trustworthy and loyal to the Union and which were disaffected or openly disloyal. It was not difficult to select them, for Washington had so long been a Southern city and so many of its officials were in sympathy with the Secessionists, that outspoken disunion sentiments were freely avowed. In fact all the departments contained many whom it was believed only remained in order to use their positions to give aid or information to the opponents of the Government."[7]

Finding a Job for Carl Schurz

One of the most troubling dilemmas for the Lincoln Administration was what to do with German-American leader Carl Schurz who expected a prominent job in a European capital – probably in Sardinia. "Confidently expecting news of his nomination, Schurz did not allow Lincoln to forget him," wrote Schurz biographer Hans L. Trefousse. "On the day after the inauguration, as one of the spokesmen for the radicals, he came to the White House at seven o'clock in the morning to make sure of [Salmon P.] Chase's inclusion in the cabinet, a visit unquestionably designed to remind the President of his own claims as much as those of the Ohioan. He received congratulations on the supposed appointment and was confidently looking forward to a trip to Italy." But Schurz had opposition from fellow German-American Gustave Koerner, a close Lincoln ally who had served as lieutenant governor of Illinois. So Lincoln and Seward stalled Schurz for domestic and international political reasons.[8]

The wait was painful for the would-be diplomat. Schurz wrote his wife in mid-March: "Yesterday I received congratulations from all sides upon my appointment as minister to Sardinia. The news was even telegraphed to the newspapers, but I have had no official information. Yet I do know that evening before last Lincoln said to Horace Greeley and Senator Grimes that he considered the appointment a very fitting one and that he was strongly disposed to make it. The only necessary preliminary would be a consultation with Seward. He also told others that he would give me what I desired."[9] On March 13, Schurz wrote his wife that he was also being considered for Minister to Brazil: "If Lincoln brings the matter up I shall insist upon Sardinia, without however definitely refusing the other mission. The salary is $12,000 and Rio de Janeiro is said to be very beautiful. Still, I am sure that Lincoln designs me for Sardinia. He will at least not dispose of that mission without first consulting me."[10]

Secretary of State Seward thought that Schurz's radical background as a young man in Germany would make him unwelcome in European capitals and thus tried to shift Schurz's focus to Latin America. Schurz was adamant and tried to use anti-Seward Republicans to support his diplomatic nomination. The President wanted to keep both German-Americans and the Secretary of State happy by offering a diplomatic posting to Latin America. The dilemma became a political embarrassment for the president; the New York Herald observed that "next to the difficulty about Fort Sumter, the question as to what is to be done about Carl Schurz seems to bother the administration more than anything else." Schurz insisted on a first-class posting in a meeting with Secretary Seward and President Lincoln on the evening of March 20.[11]

Schurz tried to "speed up matters," according to biographer Hans L. Trefousse. "He became ever more friendly with Charles Sumner, the chairman of the Senate's Committee on Foreign Relations, and was a welcome guest at the White House. Sitting with Lincoln the balcony while the Marine Band was playing on the south lawn, he watched the President kiss numerous babies. After Lincoln retired, he went into the library to play the piano until the President came down and took him to tea." Schurz kept threatening to leave town and the President kept urging him to stay. With Postmaster General Montgomery Blair's help, the posting of Kentucky abolitionist Cassius Clay was shifted to Russia and Schurz was duly awarded the Spanish post. Schurz was overjoyed; the Spanish government was not, but Spain did not protest the appointment in time to block it. Trefousse wrote that President Lincoln had to balance pacification of Schurz with the risks of aggravating a major European power: "Anxious to placate his supporter and the German-Americans, he finally sent him to Spain, the one European country which, because of its ever-increasing involvement in the Caribbean, could not afford to create additional complications with the United States."[12]

Schurz returned to Washington after visiting Wisconsin – with new ambitions. "Carl Schurz was here today," Lincoln aide John Hay wrote in his diary on April 26. "He spoke with enthusiasm of his desire to mingle in this war. He has great confidence in his military powers, and his capability of arousing the enthusiasm of the young. He contemplates the career of a great guerilla chief with ardent longing. He objects to the taking of Charleston & advises forays on the Interior States."[13] After meeting with Secretary Seward to confirm his appointment to Madrid, "Schurz stepped across to the White House to call on his friend the President. Lincoln offered him a chair," wrote Lincoln scholar Jay Monaghan. "The tall, near-sighted German sat down and shook back his long hair. Lincoln looked at the hatchet-faced man with the stooped shoulders of a scholar and an ambition to lead light horse. The President smiled, then began the conversation by apologizing for his own ignorance. He had been able to devote 'so little attention to foreign affairs' and felt the necessity of 'studying up.' Lincoln hoped that the German would watch public opinion abroad and 'whenever anything occurs to you that you want to tell me personally, or that you think I ought to know, you shall write me directly.'"[14]

Loyal Republican politicians and journalists received many of Lincoln's important diplomatic postings. Massachusetts Congressman Charles Francis Adams was posted to England, former New Jersey Senator William L. Dayton went to France and Kentucky abolitionist Cassius Clay to Russia. Seward biographer John Taylor wrote; "The new diplomatic appointees were the standard mix of men of ability and political hacks….Although the more important posts were filled with able men, many a political debt was paid off in the State Department."[15] The able Adams himself noted: "The Republican party had been so generally in opposition that but few of its prominent members had had any advantages or experience in office. And, in the foreign service especially, experience is almost indispensable to usefulness. Mr. Seward himself came into the State Department with no acquaintance with the forms of business other than that obtained incidentally through his service in the Senate. He had not had the benefit of official presence abroad, an advantage by no means trifling in conducing the foreign affairs. A still greater difficulty was that, with the range of selection to fill the respective posts abroad, hardly any person could be found better provided in this respect than himself. Moreover, the President, in distributing his places, did so with small reference to the qualifications in this particular line. It was either partisan service, or geographical position, or the length of the lists of names to commendatory papers, or the size of the salary, or the unblushing pertinacity of personal solicitations, that wrung from him many of his appointments. Yet, considering the nature of all these obstacles, it must be admitted that most of the neophytes acquitted themselves of their duty with far more of credit than could have been fairly expected from the commencement."[16]

Problems with Europe

Secretary Seward soon had bigger problems than ambitious Republicans. Foreign intervention was critical to the success of the Confederacy. European governments were ambitious to intervene in the American Civil War. Historian James M. McPherson wrote: "Most European observers and statesmen believed in 1861 that the Union cause was hopeless. In their view, the Lincoln administration could never reestablish control over 750,000 square miles of territory defended by a determined and courageous people."[17] Assistant Secretary of State Frederick W. Seward later wrote: "Early in the war, we learned through the Legation at St. Petersburg that an understanding had been effected between the governments of Great Britain and France that they should take one and the same course on the subject of the American war, including the possible recognition of the rebels....This alliance for joint action might dictate its own terms. From a joint announcement of neutrality, it would be but a step to join mediation or intervention; and it was hardly to be anticipated that the Washington Government, struggling with an insurrection which had rent the country asunder, would be willing to face also the combined power of the two great empires of Western Europe. To the mind of the French and English statesmen the project was even praiseworthy. It would stop the effusion of blood and increase the supply of cotton. It would leave the American Union permanently divided; but that was a consummation that European statesmen in general would not grieve over."[18] As McPherson noted: "The principal goal of Confederate foreign policy in 1862 was to win diplomatic recognition of the new Southern nation by foreign powers."[19]

The cotton trade was a mutual concern for the Confederates and the British. About four-fifths of England's cotton came from the South. In hopes of prompting European intervention, the Confederacy quickly began an informal cessation of cotton exports but their embargo was ill-timed. "When the Civil War began in April 1861, most of the bumper 1860 crop had already been exported," noted historian Dean B. Mahin. "The only way to accelerate the arrival of a diplomatically useful 'cotton famine' in Europe was to restrict cotton exports from the Confederacy in 1861 and 1862."[20] When the Confederacy tried to reverse course and export cotton, the Union navy was better positioned to blockade the South and continue to starve Europe of southern cotton.

In March 1861, the Confederacy dispatched three would-be diplomats to Europe. "There was a basis for believing cotton diplomacy would be effective," wrote Lincoln scholar Charles Segal. "Trade was a key factor in British-American relations and cotton was vital to England's economy. British aristocracy, reflecting the bent of Europe's ruling classes, sympathized with the Confederacy; they believed the war between the states would sever permanently the American Union. British and French manufacturers looked to their respective governments to protect their interests."[21] While the Confederacy was determined to open diplomatic relations with Britain and France, Secretary of State Seward was determined to prevent it. On May 13, Britain proclaimed its neutrality in the American Civil War – a possible prelude to recognition. Segal wrote: "What was at issue in this international rumpus was that Lincoln and Seward wanted the British to be neutral for the Union and not against it."[22]

British Foreign minister John Russell looked for an opportunity to inject himself into the American conflict. Historian Howard Jones wrote that "the threat of slave insurrections in the South emerged as a major factor encouraging British intervention in the war. Russell had shown interest in a mediation, if invited, even before the fighting had begun. A civil war, he and other British contemporaries knew, usually left the divided nation so vulnerable that outside powers often yielded to temptation and intervened out of self-interest. In the United States, the danger loomed as particularly real because of the war's racial underpinning. Not only would a servile war undermine the cotton economy for years, but it could develop into a racial conflict that shook the foundation of the entire republic and even spread beyond American borders to hurt other nations."[23]

British journalist William Howard Russell wrote on April 8, "On returning to my hotel, I found a note from Mr. Seward, asking me to visit him at nine o'clock. On going to his house, I was shown to the drawing room, and found there only the Secretary of State, his son, and Mrs. Seward. I made a parti carre for a friendly rubber of whist, and Mr. Seward, who was my partner, talked as he played, so that the score of the game was not favourable. But his talk was very interesting. 'All the preparations of which you hear mean this only. The Government, finding the property of the State and Federal forts neglected and left without protection, are determined to take steps to relieve them from that neglect, and to protect them. But we are determined in doing so to make no aggression. The President's inaugural clearly shadows out our policy. We will not go beyond it – we have no intention of doing so – nor will we withdraw from it. After a time Mr. Seward put down his cards, and told his son to go for a portfolio which he would find a drawer of his table. Mrs. Seward lighted the drop light of the gas, and on her husband's return with the paper left the room. The Secretary then lit his cigar, gave one to me, and proceeded to read slowly and with marked emphasis a very long, strong, and able dispatch, which he told me was to be read by Mr. Adams, the American minister in London, to Lord John Russell. It struck me that the tone of the paper was hostile, that there was an undercurrent of menace through it, and that it contained insinuations that Great Britain would interfere to split up the Republic, if she could, and was pleased at the prospect of the dangers which threatened it."

"At all the stronger passages Mr. Seward raised his voice, and made a pause at their conclusion as if to challenge remark or approval. At length I could not help saying, that the dispatch would, no doubt, have an excellent effect when it came to light in congress, and that the Americans would think highly of the writer; but I ventured to express an opinion that it would not be quite so acceptable to the Government and people of Great Britain. This Mr. Seward, as an American statesman, had a right to make but a secondary consideration. By affecting to regard Secession as a mere political heresy which can be easily confuted, and by forbidding foreign countries alluding to it, Mr. Seward thinks he can establish the supremacy of his own Government, and at the same time gratify the vanity of the people. Even war with us may not be out of the list of those means which would be available for re-fusing the broken Union into a mass once more. However, the Secretary is quite confident in what he calls 're-action.' 'When the Southern States,' he says, 'see that we mean them no wrong – that we intend no violence to persons, rights, or things – that the Federal Government seeks only to fulfill obligations imposed on it in respect to the national property, they will see their mistake, and one after another they will come back into the Union.' Mr. Seward anticipates this process will at once begin, and that Secession will all be done and over in three months – at least, so he says. It was after midnight ere our conversation was over."[24]

Seward's belligerent attitude toward England was well noted abroad.

Historian Richard N. Current noted: "There is, to begin with, the Duke of Newcastle incident. According to the Duke, Seward told him at a Washington dinner party in November 1860: If I am to be secretary of state, it will 'become my duty to insult England, and I mean to do so.' When the British took this as a threat, Seward denied having said it. Then, two years later, he remembered having said something like that, but insisted he had only meant that he must somehow counteract the Democratic charge that the Republicans were pro-British."[25] Lincoln reined in Seward when necessary. He had Seward notify the British that "the President is solicitous to show his high appreciation of every demonstration of consideration for the United States which the British government feels itself at liberty to make. He instructs me, therefore, to say that the prompt and cordial manner in which you were received…is very gratifying to this government.'"[26]

But there may have been method in Seward's madness toward Britain. Historian Brian Jenkins wrote that "especially in his attitude toward the crucially important British, Seward was governed by three considerations. First, as a politician, he recognized the need to retain the confidence of his countrymen. One well-traveled way was to parade an 'energetic and vigorous resistance to English injustice.' In short, and not to put too fine a point on it, he intended to appeal to that large reservoir of anglophobia in the United States. Second, he was determined to exhibit absolute confidence in the permanence of the Union." And, third, Jenkins believed that dissolution of the United States was a dangerous precedent for the British union.[27] Seward looked for audiences before which to parade his belligerence, but British attitudes toward Americans tended to be negative. Historian Gordon H. Warren wrote: "While some Britons thought well of the United States – and lauded its high literacy rate, humane laws, small standing army, and the practicality and generosity of its people – offensive opinions still dominated public thinking. British travelers, who were generally well-to-do, did not differentiate between Northerners and Southerners except by attributing to them varying degrees of rudeness."[28]

One key to U.S.-British relations was the experienced and able British minister in Washington, Lord Richard Lyons. Historian Craig L. Symonds wrote: "Lyons was not particularly impressed by the new administration, reporting privately in London that 'Mr. Lincoln has not hitherto given proof of his possessing any natural talents to compensate for his ignorance of everything but Illinois village politics.'"[29] Historian Gordon H. Warren wrote of Lyons: "The minister had flaws, but he was not incompetent and he was at least as qualified as his recent predecessors...Unfortunately for relations between the two countries, Lyons's dispatches produced deep unrest and a sense of impending disaster within the London cabinet, and persuaded high civilian and military officials that war with the United States was almost a certainty."[30] In an August 12, 1861 dispatch to British Foreign Minister Lord Russell, Lord Lyons wrote:

"Considerable embarrassment has been felt by the Government of the United States in determining what do, during the war, with slaves captured by the United States armies, or taking refuge with them. The uncompromising Abolitionist Party desired that Slaves should be declared ipso facto free; and that every encouragement should be held out to the Slaves in the South to fly from their masters to the protection of Northern troops. The opposite Party maintained that, notwithstanding the war, the law should be maintained, and fugitive Slaves be in all cases restored to their masters. A temporary solution of the difficulty was devised by General Butler and very generally acted upon. This officer declared 'Slaves' to be 'contraband of war,' and as such, liable to seizure by the army."

"Congress passed an act, which was confirmed by the President on the 6th instant, confiscating all Slaves employed by their masters against the Government of the United States; and the Secretary of War on the 8th instant, issued instructions to the army on the subject." 31

The Trent Incident

Belligerence took a concrete form in the early fall 1861. On October 12, two would-be Confederate diplomats left Charleston for Havana, Cuba. On board were James Mason of Virginia, bound for England, and John Slidell of Louisiana, bound for France. At Havana, the two boarded a British ship, the Trent while at another port Captain Charles Wilkes heard about the two diplomats and resolved to capture them. On November 8, Captain Charles Wilkes and his ship, the U.S. San Jacinto stopped the Trent on November 8 and the Confederate emissaries were taken into Union custody. Historian John Taylor wrote: "The location of the Confederate commissioners was no secret, and an American naval officer made plans to do something about them. Capt. Charles Wilkes of the San Jacinto was a veteran of the Old Navy; after more than four decades of service, his reputation was that of an insubordinate, impulsive, overzealous, and yet fairly efficient' officer.". 32

Lincoln scholar Charles Segal wrote: "While Wilkes under international law, had the belligerent right to search the Trent for contraband, he had no right to make an arrest at sea. He could have ordered the Trent into port for adjudication by a prize court, but this he did not do. Instead, he violated the rights of a neutral nation by seizing Mason and Slidell." 33 Historians Larry Schweikart and Michael Allen wrote: "Wilkes's unauthorized (and unwise) act threatened to do what the Rebels themselves had been unable to accomplish, namely, to bring in Britain as a Confederate ally."34 Slidell and Mason were imprisoned at Fort Warren in Boston and the Trent continued on to England where news of Wilkes' actions caused a diplomatic storm. American public opinion was strongly supportive of Wilkes' unauthorized acts.

Historian Michael Burlingame wrote: "Lincoln may have briefly shared his constituents' glee, but within hours of receiving the news, he realized that Mason and Slidell had to be surrendered."35 President Lincoln had to balance public opinion with private diplomacy. Lincoln scholar William Lee Miller observed: "Although avoiding war was mandatory, it was also quite important to let the air out of the balloon of truculent American jubilation slowly – not to puncture it abruptly. American pride could be assuaged by showing that seen as we yielded, we achieved something at the same time – we brought Great Britain over to our view on freedom of the seas."36 Whether or not the Lincoln Administration authorized the actions of Captain Wilkes was crucial to resolving the crisis. In a letter to Charles Sumner, British leader John Bright proposed a moderate American approach to his country: "You would not have authorized such an act against a friendly nation, calculated to rouse hostile feelings against you; you repudiate any infraction of international law; the capture of the Commissioners is of no value when set against the loss of that character for justice and courtesy which you have always sustained; and you are willing to abide by the law as declared by impartial arbitration."[37]

The British government reacted to Wilkes' action with great seriousness. Historian Philip Van Doren Stern noted Prime Minister Palmerston and Foreign Minister Russell were the architects of Britain's policies toward the United States: "The fact that they were part of a Coalition Government, which could easily be turned out of office, made them wary about taking chances. This, of course, worked for the benefit of the North. Both had been born in the eighteenth century; both brought to their work a lifetime of experience in getting along with the men who ruled the nations of the world; both had held practically every high post in the British Government."[38] Palmerston was anti-slavery and anti-intervention but that was not the perception in America where Russell was perceived as more inclined to the North than Palmerston.

In the Trent crisis, both governments acted deliberately, but English newspapers were less restrained than the Palmerston government. "Abraham Lincoln," editorialized the London Morning Chronicle, "has proved himself a feeble confused, and little minded mediocrity. Mr. Seward, the firebrand at his elbow, is exerting himself to provoke a quarrel with all Europe, in that spirit of senseless egotism that induces the Americans, with their dwarf fleet and shapeless mass of incoherent squads they call an army, to fancy themselves the equals of France by land and of Great Britain by sea. If the Federal states could be rid of these two mischief-makers, it might yet redeem itself in the sight of the world."[39]

Still, the risk of war was great. Historian Richard Carwardine wrote: "Only slowly, while Britain ordered naval and military reinforcements to Canada and the eastern Atlantic, did Lincoln come to appreciate the depth of the crisis. Once more he benefited from regular discussions with Sumner, whose friendship with the English Liberal reformers, John Bright and Richard Cobden, made the senator a barometer of British opinion. There was real risk, Sumner knew that the hysteria of the 'Rule Britannia' political class might force Palmerston to act in defense of British honor."[40] Lincoln scholar Jay Monaghan wrote: "Lincoln listened to the popular acclaim of Charles Wilkes and decided that it would be unwise to release the prisoners. Yet William H. Russell, Lord Lyons, all the diplomats, insisted among themselves that the men must be given up or England would fight."[41]

President Lincoln had already dispatched several private emissaries to Europe, including New York Cardinal John Hughes, General Winfield Scott, and Albany editor Thurlow Weed, all of whom were close to Secretary Seward. Weed was anxious to help but ignorant of American policy. His grandson, Thurlow Weed Barnes, wrote: "Despatches concerning the Trent affair which were to go out to Lord Lyons for transmission to our government were forwarded by Lord John Russell to the Queen, at whose request Prince Albert, though then dangerously ill, reviewed them carefully. In an unofficial conversation with Lord Lyons, before any message reached this country, Mr. Seward intimated that everything would depend upon the wording of it; and it is easy to see that this was the literal truth; for, had England called for the release of Slidell and Mason in insolent or aggravating language, it would have been impossible for the American Secretary of State, acting for a proud, sensitive, and excited nation, to comply."[42]

Prince Albert's prudence was vital in achieving a resolution of the conflict. Lincoln scholar Jay Monaghan wrote that mood in Britain grew belligerent: "Both parties in Parliament were against war now the crisis had come, but popular clamor could not be ignored. Seward had talked so long and so belligerently that the average Englishman believed, without waiting for confirmation, that the American government sanctioned the capture. This belief increased with a rumor from France. Old General Scott was reported as saying that the American cabinet had planned the capture to excite a war. He, Scott, had come to enlist France on the Northern side, humiliate England, and take Canada."43

President Lincoln needed to defuse the diplomatic situation without demoralizing northern opinion, which strongly approved of the affront to the British government. Historian Philip Van Doren Stern observed, "The Trent Affair did not become explosive until news of it reached England. Adams, who was out of town on November 27, when word arrived, hurried back to London. He could learn nothing except what he read in the papers, for the State Department had not sent him any information and did not do so for days. When Russell called upon him for an explanation, he had to admit that he had not yet heard from Washington. Perhaps, he intimated hopefully, the fact that he had not been advised meant that Wilkes had acted without orders."44 Meanwhile, Secretary Seward was working behind the scenes to mollify the British government. Seward biographer Frederic Bancroft noted: "In a confidential despatch of November 27th Seward informed Adams that Wilkes had acted without instructions, and that, as Lord Lyons had not referred to the incident, 'I thought it equally wise to reserve ourselves until we hear what the British government may have to say on the subject.' Three days later he wrote that 'we think it more prudent that the ground taken by the British government should be first made known to us here, and that the discussion, if there must be one, shall be had here.'"45

American Minister Charles Francis Adams recalled, "Four dispatches were drawn up on the same day, the 30th of November, three of them addressed to the British minister at Washington, Lord Lyons, and one to the Lords Commissioners of the Admiralty. All of them distinctly anticipated an immediate rupture, and made provision for the event. One of these, very carefully prepared, instructed Lord Lyons to protest against the offensive act, and in the case the Secretary of State should not voluntarily offer redress by a delivery of the men, to make a demand of their restoration. The second directed Lord Lyons to permit of no delay of an affirmative answer beyond seven days. Should no such answer appear within that time, his lordship was formally instructed to withdraw with all his legation and all the archives of the legation, and to make the best of his way to London. The fourth letter, address to the Admiralty, contained instruction to prepare all the naval officers stationed in America for the breaking out of hostilities."[46]

The President wanted freedom to resolve the crisis peacefully. Congress, which returned to work at the beginning of December, presented a problem for President Lincoln. Historian David P. Crook wrote: "A respectable number of Congressmen were willing to give the administration a free hand over Trent, but a majority preferred that Congress should not abdicate its high functions during a war crisis. For his part Lincoln did not welcome a contentious debate in Congress which might embarrass negotiations, and Sumner labored successfully to stall discussion in the Senate. Nor did the President desire unnecessary cabinet deliberations."[47] The Lincoln administration response inevitably played out in the public. Historian Philip Van Doren Stern wrote: "When Americans saw how violent British opinion was, stock prices went down and gold went up. Apprehension replaced the wild enthusiasm that had originally greeted Wilkes' action."[48] Historian Gordon H. Warren wrote: "American officials, at every level, like their Canadian and British counterparts, worried over the condition of Atlantic coastal defenses. Every available gun was an obsolete smoothbore, not help against ironclad warships. The largest and most important commercial city, New York, lay open to a hostile fleet."[49]

Canadian foreign minister Alexander T. Galt came to Washington and met with President Lincoln and former Massachusetts Congressman George Ashmun on December 4. Galt "said that while we held the most friendly feelings to the U[nited] S[tates], we thought from the indications given of the views of the Gov-ern[nmen]t & the tone of the press, that it was possibly their [the American] intention to molest us, & that the existence of their enormous armed force might be a serious peril hereafter. [The] P.[resident] replied that the press neither here nor in England, as he had the best reason to know, reflected the real views of either Gov[ernmen]t." Galt concluded his memorandum: "The impression left on my mind has been that the President sincerely deprecates any quarrel with England, and has no hostile designs upon Canada, and his statement that his views were those of all his Cabinet is partly corroborated by the statement made to me by Mr. Seward that he [Seward] should be glad to see Canada placed in a position of defence."[50]

Historian Gordon H. Warren wrote: "Galt said Ottawa saw the administration's actions and the tone of the press as indicating a desire to molest his country. Answering that the press did not reflect his opinion, Lincoln denied ever hearing a cabinet member express hostile sentiments toward Canada. He pledged as 'a man of honor' that neither he nor any of his cabinet had any desire to disturb Britain's rights in North America. When Ashmun interrupted to say that the Trent affair might cause difficulty, the president replied vaguely that the 'matter could be arranged.'"[51] Galt left the White House optimistic that war could be averted.

On December 15, Seward received word from the British government that it regarded the Trent affair a serious violation of international law. That day, Illinois Senator Orville H. Browning recorded in his diary that while he was visiting President Lincoln. "Mr Seward came in with despatches stating that the British Cabinet had decided that the arrest of Mason and Slidell was a violation of International law, and that we must apologize and restore them to the protection of the British flag. I don't believe England has done so foolish a thing and so told the Prest: & Secy, but if she is determined to force a war upon us why so be it. We will fight her to the death."[52] Lincoln scholar Jay Monaghan wrote: "For ten days the British crisis kept Washington in suspense. People forgot McClellan's inactivity to predict fabulous victories over the British navy. Other people were sure that the nation was on the verge of collapse."[53]

On December 19, Britain formally presented its complaints and on December 23, a Cabinet meeting discussed the American response. The tone of the British demands – which had been softened by Queen Victoria's husband, Prince Albert, shortly before he died – helped encourage a conciliatory response from the Lincoln Administration. Albert had drafted the Queen's comments to her government. The Queen wrote; "This draft was the last the beloved Prince ever wrote; he was very unwell at the time, and when he brought it in to the Queen he said: 'I could hardly hold my pen."[54] President Lincoln recalled: "Seward studied up all the works ever written on international law, and came to cabinet meetings loaded to the muzzle with the subject. We gave due consideration to the case, but at that critical period of the war it was soon decided to deliver up the prisoners. It was a pretty bitter pill to swallow, but I contented myself with believing that England's triumph in the matter would be short-lived, and that after ending our war successfully we would be so powerful that we could call her to account for all the embarrassments she had inflicted upon us."[55] Seward managed to position the American response as an acknowledgment of neutral rights which the United States had always espoused. Historian Phillip G. Henderson wrote: "Seward noted that by siding with Britain in this affair, he was actually defending traditional American doctrines of the freedom of the seas that had been set forth in protest against British violations of neutrality at sea during Madison's administration. Although Secretary Chase and other members of the cabinet were unhappy with the prospect of heeding Seward's advice to release the envoys, they conceded that Seward had made such a powerful argument in favor of such action that they were in agreement that it should be carried out."[56]

On December 21, Senator Browning recorded that he "went to the Presidents and had a long private interview with him in relation to the affair of the Trent with England He told me that the despatches from England had not yet been delivered by Lord Lyons, but were with held for a few days at Mr Sewards request, but that he had an inkling of what they were, and feared trouble. I told him I was anxious a rupture should be avoided at present if it could be done without humiliation and dishonor, in which he expressed his full concurrence, and we both agreed that the question was easily susceptible of a peaceful solution if England was at all disposed to act justly with us, and suggested that it was a proper case for arbitration. I also said that as some of the rights of neutrals according to the principles of international law have long been in dispute between us and England say to England to make here statement of what the law of Nations is which shall govern this case, and all cases similarly circumstanced now, and forever hereafter, and we will agree to it. The President replied that the same thoughts had occurred to his mind and that he had reduced the propositions to writing He then took from his desk and read me a very able paper, which he intends, at the proper time, shall go as a letter from the Secretary of State to Lord Lyons (it now has that form) and in which both the foregoing propositions are stated with great force and clearness, and very much more in detail than I have given them."[57]

On December 23, Massachusetts Senator Charles Sumner wrote English politician John Bright: "The President himself will apply his own mind carefully to every word of the answer, so that it will be essentially his; & he hopes for peace."[58] Historian Burton J. Hendrick wrote: "As chairman of the Senate Committee on Foreign Relations, Sumner had considerable claims to Lincoln's confidence, and spent a part of nearly every day with him discussing the Trent question. Sumner saw clearly the issues involved. From the first he was for a peaceful settlement, not only because England has justice on its side, but because he knew that a military conflict would sink his country in disaster."[59]

Historian David P. Crook wrote: "Press rumors in the days before Christmas gave considerable publicity to 'the Lincoln Play,' but its fatal defects were becoming increasingly obvious. It proposed a policy of procrastination which would, at the least, have caused high exasperation in England. Russell, who had been going over in his mind 'the possible evasive answers of Mr. Seward,' had written to Lyons on December 7 to emphasize that 'What we want is a plan Yes, or a plain No to our very simple demands, and we want that plain Yes or No within seven days of the despatch." The British, however, were trying to give the Lincoln administration space to maneuver. Crook wrote: "Lyons had been carefully briefed. He was not to present the formal demand at his first interview, but to 'prepare' Seward unofficially, and to ask him to settle with the President and his cabinet what course they would pursue."[60]

Events came to a head on a bright and cool Christmas day that was best chronicled by Attorney General Edward Bates. Historian Burton J. Hendrick observed that the Cabinet was considering "the future of the United States. A stark alternative confronted the council: refusal to accept the British demand meant that, in addition to subduing the South, American army and naval forces would be compelled to add the British Empire to its foes."61 Seward had decided on his course of action but it was still unclear whether the rest of the cabinet would agree with him. Revelations of British feelings about the Trent crisis came as a revelation to hard-line members of the Lincoln cabinet. Bates recalled the four-hour cabinet meeting on December 25: "The instructions of the British Minister to Lord. Lyons were read. They are sufficiently peremptory, and without being very specific as to the precise elements of the wrong done, the 'affront' to the British flag, the point on which the British confidently claim that the law of Nations was broken by us, is that Capt Wilkes did not bring in the Trent, the Steamer for adjudication, so that the matter might be judged by a prize court, and not by the Capt, on his quarter deck."

"Then was read a draft of answer by the Secretary of State -"

"But before treating of that, I wish to note down several matters of interest that occurred in the session, tending to explain and give color to various parts of the transaction."

"Genl Cameron said that his Assistant Mr. Scott had rec'd a letter from Mr. Smith (our agent in England for bringing soldiers' to the effect – i.e. that Mr. Smith had rec'd information from respectable sources in London, that Commander Williams, the British mail agent on board the Trent, had declared that the whole matter, and measures of the capture had been arranged at Havanna by the Commissioners, Slidell and Mason themselves, and our Capt Wilkes'."

"This might seem incredible, if it stood alone, but that something of the sort was variously reported and believed, in well informed circles in England, is a fact, shown by other corroborative facts. For during the session, Senator Sumner (who as chairman of the Committee of Foreign relations) was invited in, to read some letters which he had just rec'd from England – from the two celebrated M. Ps. John Bright and Richard Cobden – One of those letters – Bright's I think – states, as news of the day, that at Havanna sic Slidell and Mason dined with Capt Wilkes on Board his ship San Jacinto and then and there arranged for the capture, just as it was, in fact, done!…"

"I must doubt the truth of this statement in as much as it seriously implicates Capt. Wilkes."[62]

Bates continued: "But, on the part of Mason and Slidell the policy is obvious and they could bring on a rupture between us and England – actual war or even a threatening quarrel – they would gain by a single stroke more than they could hope to accomplish by years of negotiation."

"These letters tend to show that in England there is about one feeling – all against us – about the capture. The passions of Mr. Bull are thoroughly aroused about his dignity and the honor of his flag."

"The opposition Lord Derby relied upon it, as a fit occasion, to force a ministerial crisis, and the administration. Lord. Palmerston, Russell were, or had to be, quite as warm in assuming to be the special guardians of the national honor! So the whole nation is of one mind and must have satisfaction."

"The French government fully agrees with England that seisure of Slidell and Mason, as made (i.e. without bringing the Trent, for adjudication) was a breech of the laws of nations. And this appears by the instructions sent to Mr. Mercier, the minister here, who has furnished Mr. Seward with a copy.

"Partly by the letter of instructions, but mainly by letters our own minister, Mr. Dayton, and divers private letters, it appears that France is in a very bad condition in regard to trade and finance, oweing in a large measure as the French suppose, to our blockade which besides the cotton trade cuts off the whole commerce of Boardeaux in wines, fruits, and silks with New Orleans, Mobile and Charleston – In short, if England can pick a quarrel with us, on the pretence of this seisure, France will join with England in forceiably opening the blockade and consequently acknowledgeing the Confederate States of America and that is war. And we cannot afford such a war."

"The first and immediate effect would be, to withdraw all our forces, land and naval from the southern coast – The suspension of all our revenue from customs. The destruction of our foreign commerce. The probable capture of our sea ports – and ills innumerable – The scene would be reversed! The southern coast would be open and the northern blockaded."

"In such an event, it would be small satisfaction to us to believe, as I do, that it would be sure to light up the torch of war allover Europe, the effects of which upon christendom I am no wise enough to forsesee."

"In such a crisis, with such a civil war upon our hands, we cannot hope for success in a super added war with England, backed by the assent and countenance of France. We must evade it – with as little damage to our own honor and pride as possible. Still we must avoid it now and for the plain reason that now we are not able to meet it. Three months hence if we do half our duty upon the sea coast and upon the Mississippi, the case may be very different. And happily for us it is that in yielding to the necessity of the case we do but reaffirm our old principles and carry out into practice the tr[a]ditional policy of the country, as is clearly shown by Mr. Seward in quotations from Mr. Sect. of State, Madisons instructions to our minister to England, Monroe, in 1804."

"In his comprehensive but disjoined report, Bates wrote: "Mr. Seward's draft of letter to Lord Lyons was submitted by him and examined and criticised by us with (apparently, perfect candor and frankness;) all of us were impressed with the magnitude of the subject and believed that upon our decision depended the dearest interest, probably the existence of the nation."

"In waiving the question of legal right – upon which all Europe is against us, and also many of our own best jurists urged the necessity of the case: that to go to war with England now, is to abandon all hope of suppressing the rebellion: as we have not the possession of the land nor any support of the people of the South. The maratine superiority of Britain would sweep us from all the southern waters! Our trade would be utterly ruined and our treasury bankrupt – In short, that we must not have war with England."

"There was great reluctance on the part of some of the members of the cabinet – and even the President himself – to acknowledge these obvious truths: but all yielded to the necesity, and unanimously concurred in Mr. Sewards letter to Lord. Lyons, after some verbal and formal amendments. The main fear I believe, was the displeasure of our own people – lest they should accuse us of timidly truckling to the power of England."

"I know not how it happened, but a rumor is currant and pretty extensively believed, that I had much more to do with bringing about the arrangement than the facts would warrant! For instance – as soon as Mr. Sewards letter was published, came Baron Geolt, Prussian minister, with his congratulations upon the result, and in, terms almost direct imputed to me the main views and arguments of Mr. Sewards letter – for which, by the way, he had no better warrant than some similarity of thought expressed by me in previous conversations with him – And since then, the Bremen minister Mr. Schleiden, has talked to me in the same way. Both of them expressed great satisfaction at what they called the honorable settlement of the affair, and said that was the general feeling of the foreign ministers."

"Some representatives of the press also, have gotten the erroneous idea of my supposed influence in the matter. They say that I had difficulty in bringing over two or three members. Coffey tells me this. He heard a prominent letter writer talking in that way to Gov Curtin of Pa. Of course I make no attempt to correct or explain these things the attempt would make the matter worse, and would be a bad precedent.63

Secretary of the Treasury Salmon P. Chase reported his own observations in his diary that night: "In my judgment, the case stands precisely thus: In taking the rebel Envoys and their Secretaries from the 'Trent,' without invoking or proposing to invoke the sanction of any judicial tribunal, Capt. Wilkes clearly violated the Law of Nations, and in that very principle which the United States have ever most zealously maintained. Great Britain, therefore, has a right to ask from us a disavowal of the act, and the restoration of the person to the condition in which they were taken; and, if this right be insisted on, it is our duty, however disagreeable, to do what is thus asked…"

"It is gall and wormwood to me. Rather than consent to the liberation of these men, I would sacrifice everything I possess. But I am consoled by the reflection that while nothing but severest retribution is due to them, the surrender, under existing circumstances, is but simply doing right; simply proving faithful to our own ideas and traditions under strong temptations to violate them; simply giving to England and to the world the most signal proof that the American Nation will not, under any circumstances, for the sake of inflicting just punishment on Rebels, commit even a technical wrong against neutrals."64

Illinois Senator Orville H. Browning, a longtime friend of President Lincoln, went to the White House for Christmas dinner and recorded in his diary: "After the Company had all left the Prest told me they had a cabinet meeting about British affairs to day, and had agreed not to divulge what had occurred, but that there would be no war with England. That whilst the cabinet was in session the French Minister sent them a letter he had just received from his government saying that the European powers were against us on the question of international law, and desired that we should settle the Controversy amicably. Also Sumner sent three letters which he had just recvd from England, one from Bright and two from Cobden, both of whom are our friends, and both urging a settlement, and both saying that the dispositions of the English are friendly – that England does not want war with us, and that if this trouble is settled they will not interfere in our domestic troubles, but leave us to deal with the rebellion as we think proper – "65

Frederick Seward recalled: "After the other gentlemen had retired, the President said: 'Governor Seward, you will go on, of course, preparing your answer, which, as I understand, will state the reasons why they ought to be given up. Now I have a mind to try my hand at stating the reasons why they ought not to be given up. We will compare the points on each side."

"My father heartily assented. The mutual confidence between the two had now grown so great, that each felt the other would ask approval of nothing that was not sound. On the next day [December 26] the Cabinet reassembled. The Secretary of State again read his reply. There were some expressions of regret that the step was necessary, but it was adopted without a dissenting voice. The council broke up reassured on the point that war with England was averted, but not without misgivings as to the temper in which the people would receive the decision. The President expressed his approval."66

The Cabinet approved the release of the Confederate diplomats. Ferris wrote: "As Bates stated, everyone present 'yielded to the necessity, and unanimously concur[r] in Mr. Sewards letter to Ld. Lyons, after some verbal and formal amendments.' Then after clerks had worked overnight in the State Department to produce copies of his lengthy revised note, Seward called Lyons to his office early on December 27."67 Frederick Seward recalled: "When the others were gone, my father alluded to their conversation of the day before. 'You thought you might frame an argument for the other side?' Mr. Lincoln smiled and shook his head. 'I found I could not make an argument that would satisfy my own mind,' he said, 'and that proved to me your ground was the right one.'" Young Seward added: "This was characteristic of Lincoln. Presidents and kings are not apt to see flaws in their own arguments. But fortunately for the Union, it had a President at this time who combined a logical intellect with an unselfish heart."68

Senator Sumner wrote to one of his English friends on December 31: "On reaching Washington for the opening of Congress, I learned from the Presdt. & from Mr Seward, that neither had committed himself on the Trent affair, & that it was absolutely an unauthorized act. Seward told me that he was reserving himself in order to see what view England would take. It would have been better to act on the case at once & to make the surrender in conformity with our best precedents; but next to that was the course pursued. Nothing was said in the message, – nor in conversation. Lord Lyons was not seen from the day of the first news until he called with his Letter from Ld Russell. The question was not touched in the cabinet. It was also kept out of the Senate, that there might be no constraint upon the absolute freedom that was desired in meeting it. I may add, that I had cultivated with regard to myself the same caution."69 Sumner quoted President Lincoln as saying: "I never see Lord Lyons. If it were proper, I should like to talk with him that he might hear from my lips how much I desire peace. If we could talk together he would believe me."[70]

President Lincoln himself later recalled: "Seward studied up all the works ever written on international law and came to cabinet meetings loaded to the muzzle with the subject. We gave due consideration to the case, but at that critical period of the war it was soon decided to deliver up the prisoners. It was a pretty bitter pill to swallow, but I contented myself with believing that England's triumph in the matter would be short-lived, and that after ending our war successfully, we would be so powerful that we could call her to account for all the embarrassments she had inflicted upon us."[71]

Two days after Christmas, noted Frederick Seward, "there were several guests at dinner at our house, among them Mr. and Mrs. [John J.] Crittenden, and Anthony Trollope, the novelist. Afterward came friends who, hearing rumors of a decision in the Trent matter, desired to have them verified, and to thank the Secretary for extricating the country from its dilemma. Coupled with their compliments, however, were many regrets, that the act must inevitably doom him to unpopularity, since the people would resent the loss of their prisoners, and would deem themselves humiliated by their surrender. 'It was too bad that he must sacrifice himself.'"[72] The senior Seward briefed key senators and they agreed on the course taken by the Lincoln Administration. Those included New York Senators Ira Harris and Preston King, Illinois Senator Browning and Massachusetts Senator Sumner. Ferris wrote that Seward "read them the documents pertaining to the Trent affair which he was about to release to the newspapers. Included among those documents were the British ultimatum, his own reply thereto, Thouvenel's dispatch on the subject, Seward's reply to that, and, finally, the secretary's conciliatory instruction regarding the seizure of Mason and Slidell which he had sent on November 30 to Adams at London. When Seward finished reading all these papers, the assembled senators apparently 'all agreed with him' that the captured Southern diplomats 'should be given up.'"[73]

On December 28, the Confederate diplomatic duo were handed over to British officials. Historian Phillip G. Henderson noted "As the Trent affair makes clear, while Lincoln was clearly in charge of his cabinet, he was willing, indeed eager, to draw upon the talents and good ideas of those who served in the cabinet, often refining and improving their contributions."[74] Historian Richard J. Carwardine wrote: "It was in the strategic interests of neither [country] to be swept into war. But rational action follows only from rational thought, and for that the decision-makers on both sides can take credit. Of these, none was more responsible than Lincoln for the preservation of a wary peace. Throughout he was a restraining influence, dampening rather than stoking the fires of chauvinism....He readily listened and deferred to those from whom he could learn, notably Sumner and a now statesmanlike Seward, who well knew when and when not to be bellicose, and who enjoyed good personal relations with Lord Lyons."[75] Historian Michael Burlingame noted: "The Palmerston government waived the demand for reparations and an apology, viewing the release of Mason and Slidell as a gesture sufficiently conciliatory to end the crisis."[76]

Seward clearly knew when to threaten war and when to make peace. Historian Burton J. Hendrick wrote: "The Trent episode made clear that Seward had other resources of diplomacy than menacing threats against the most powerful nations of Europe. Perhaps his skillful behavior when confronted with the contingency he had apparently so long hoped for sheds a new light upon the motives which had inspired these explosive moments."[77] Seward promoted a belligerent image of the United States, which was in turn accepted in the top councils of Britain. Hendrick noted that Confederate Secretary of State Judah P. Benjamin complained about "the thorough conviction entertained by the British ministry that the United States are ready to declare war against England…it is impossible not to admire the sagacity with which Mr. Seward penetrated into the secret feelings of the British cabinet and the success of his policy of intimidation, which the world at large supposed would be met with prompt resentment, but which he, with deeper insight into the real policy of that cabinet, foresaw would be followed by submissive acquiescence in his demands."[78] Seward's belligerence and Lincoln's prudence effectively kept France and England out of the war.

They also knew how to massage communications. Communications scholar Richard B. Kielbowicz wrote that "the State Department learned that telegraphic speed combined with journalistic enterprise could disrupt diplomacy's deliberative pace and formal protocol."[79] He wrote: "When the administration finally crafted an answer, the state Department embargoed all telegraph reports mentioning the Trent affair until the formal correspondence was safely on its way to England. On Friday, December 27, the United States agreed to surrender the Confederate emissaries and gave the British diplomat a letter, written by Seward and debated by the cabinet, for transmission to London."[80]

"Amidst the wild excitement created by this international interlude, the President alone maintained an imperturbable calmness and composure," wrote U.S. Marshall Ward Hill Lamon, a close Lincoln friend. "From the very first moment he regarded the capture of the Commissioners as unwise and inexpedient. He was heard to say repeatedly that it would lead to dangerous complications with England. 'Unfortunately,' said he, 'we have played into the hands of that wily power, and placed in their grasp a whip with which to scourge us.'

He went on to say further that the 'Trent' affair had occurred at the most inopportune and critical period of the war, and would greatly tend to its prolongation by creating a genuine bond of sympathy between England and the insurgent States."[81]

Historian David P. Crook wrote: "One long-term result of the Trent crisis was to stimulate northern propaganda campaigns abroad. Efforts were made in particular to counteract the enmity of the upper classes in England by appeals to middle and working class opinion. The affair also lent weight to the emancipation program of the Radical Republicans. The war must have a clearer character, that of an antislavery crusade, if overseas opinion was to support it."[82]

Cotton and the Confederacy

Both Union victories and the Union blockade helped stymie English support for the Confederacy.

The blockade, though leaky at first, strengthened and slowed Confederate trade. Historian James M. McPherson noted that Union military victories at the beginning of 1862 led France and England to back off their planned intervention in the conflict. McPherson wrote: "Charles Francis Adams, American minister to Britain, reported that, as a consequence of Union victories, 'the pressure for interference here has disappeared.' His son Henry Adams, private secretary to the minister, added that 'the talk of intervention, only two months ago so loud as to take a semi-official tone, is now out of the minds of everyone."[83]

Secretary Seward tried to pacify Europe on the subject of cotton exports. Historian Dean B. Mahin wrote: "During the winter of 1861-62 Seward assured Britain and France that a significant volume of cotton would soon be exported to Europe through Confederate ports captured by Union forces. Lincoln thought that the United States should 'show the world we were fair in this matter, favoring outsiders as much as ourselves.; Although he was 'by no means sure that [the planters] would bring their cotton to the port after we opened it, it would be well to show Europe that it was secession that distressed them and not we.'" [84] Historian Hendrick noted: "The Declaration of Paris, to which Great Britain and the United States subscribed, had declared that a blockade to be respected, must be 'effective.'"[85] Historian Richard Striner wrote that "the cotton embargo of the South was beginning to succeed in the summer of 1862: the British warehouse supplies were exhausted and a major 'cotton famine' was creating unemployment in the British textile industry. Pro-Confederate sentiment was growing in parliament, and one thing alone held it back: the long-standing anti-slavery feelings of the British electorate. Lincoln's Emancipation Proclamation – so politically risky at home – could bring tremendous benefits abroad. But, would the moment arrive soon enough to avert a Confederate diplomatic coup?."[86]

Historian Christopher J. Olsen wrote: "Without British intervention, the Union blockade slowly strangled Southern exports and imports, and eventually crippled the Confederacy's ability to pay for the war and meet some basic needs. The blockade was a daunting task, of course, given the Confederacy's size and long coastline..."[87] Fortunately for the Union, British officials abided by inventive constructions of admiralty law that supported American seizures of vessels breaking the blockade. [88] The British foreign ministry assented to the American interpretation of "continuous voyage." Burton Hendrick noted that although the loose and leaky Union blockade technically violated the Treaty of Paris, it was a convenient precedent for the British in case they needed in wartime to declare a loose blockade of Europe.[89]

British-American relations faced another crisis in the summer of 1862 when Confederate victories seemed to tip the war in their favor. Britain and France seemed on the verge of some kind of intervention. In September, the Confederate defeat at Antietam and President Lincoln's Draft Emancipation Proclamation a few days later stalled the British from making any formal moves to help the Confederacy. Once Britain and France saw the Civil War as a war against slavery, intervention was improbable even though France continued to entertain such possibilities during the fall of 1862. Historian James M. McPherson wrote: "The French asked Britain to join in a proposal for a six-month armistice in the American war during which the blockade would be lifted, cotton exports would be renewed, and peace negotiations would begin. France also approached Russia, which refused to take part in such an obviously pro-Confederate scheme. On November 12 the British cabinet also rejected it after two days of discussion in which Secretary for War Sir George... Lewis led the opposition to invention."[90] Such intervention would have less violent but equally injurious to Union interests.

Secretary of State Seward consistently rebuffed any suggestions of European involvement in setting the Civil War. Historian Hans L. Trefousse noted: "The repeated setbacks of Union armies strengthened pro-Confederate movements abroad, and Great Britain especially seemed to be edging closer to recognition of the Southern Government. Only July 18, Confederate sympathizer William Lindsay's motion for mediation was discussed in the House of Commons. Although it was not acted upon, when on August 4 Lincoln received news of the debate, he could hardly overlook the fact that friends of the Confederacy had cited his disallowance of Frémont's and Hunter's orders as proof of their contention that slavery was not an issue in the American Civil War. Long standing arguments for antislavery measures to prevent foreign interference were reinforced."[91]

Emancipation Proclamation

After President Lincoln issued the Final Emancipation Proclamation on January 1, 1863, the note from the British Charge d'Affaires, William Stuart,to the British Foreign Minister was brief: "I have the honor to enclose a Proclamation of the President of the United States, which was dated yesterday and published this morning, declaring the prospective emancipation of slaves on the 1st of January next, 'within any state, or designated part of a state, the people whereof shall then be in rebellion against the United States." Stuart was much more voluble four days later in describing an order of suspension Habeas Corpus, which he called an "unprecedented usurpation of power." Two days later, he reported that Secretary of State Seward "authorized me to inform Your Lordship that the United States Government would be ready to conclude a convention with Great Britain for the purposes of enabling Her Majesty's Government to transport from this country such of the Negroes who have lately been, or who may become, emancipated, as may be found willing to emigrate to Her Majesty's West Indian or other tropical possessions."[92]

In London, the response was mixed. "British officials reacted in predictable fashion to the Emancipation Proclamation; they expressed alarm over the ever-heartening fierceness of the war and supported intervention as an act of humanity," wrote historian Howard Jones.[93] Lord Palmerston, Britain's Prime Minister, disdained the Emancipation Proclamation. "It is not easy to estimate how utterly powerless and contemptible a government must have become which could sanction such…trash.'"[94] The London Morning Post took a similar position: "Abraham Lincoln, finding his authority waning, even where it is still nominally recognised, has determined to vindicate it where it is entirely ignored. He has failed to subjugate the Southern States by his legions, and in his extremity has decided on effecting his purpose by a scratch of his pen."[95] Historian Richard Allen Heckman concluded that "British newspapers with conservative and moderate persuasions were generally hostile to the Emancipation Proclamation. Liberal newspapers, although more sympathetic to anti-slavery forces, manifest[ed] serious objections to the methods and motives of the Union government in its attempt to end slavery....Many of the reactions to the Proclamation took the form of personal attacks upon the Chief Executive." [96] Certainly, the London Times was not persuaded of President Lincoln's wisdom. It called the Emancipation Proclamation Mr. Lincoln's "last card." The Times warned that a slave uprising might ensue. It editorialized that "when blood begins to flow and shrieks come piercing through the darkness, Mr. Lincoln will wait until the rising flames tell that all is consummated, and then he will rub his hands and think that revenge is sweet."[97]

Lincoln understood that the Emancipation Proclamation would be a two-edged sword in relations with the British government. Historian Allen C. Guelzo wrote that "the idea that the Proclamation would work as a kind of talisman to ward off the unwelcome attentions of the British and the French had far less importance for Lincoln than is often assumed. 'It would help somewhat,' he admitted to the Chicago clergymen, 'though not so much I fear, as you and those you represent imagine.' If anything, Lincoln had to fear more that the British would intervene because of an emancipation proclamation than they would without one."[98] Nevertheless, the impact in England was significant. 'The Emancipation Proclamation has done more for us here than all our former victories and all our diplomacy," wrote the son of the U.S. Minister in England. "It is creating an almost convulsive reaction in our favor all over this country."[99] Lord Russell and Lord Palmerston pushed a French proposal for intervention, but at a British cabinet meeting on November 11, 1862, they were virtually alone in their support. And even Palmerston's support was half-hearted; the proposal was rejected. Historian Howard Jones wrote of the British decision not to intervene: "The key consideration was British concern over antagonizing the Union. Indeed, neither side on the intervention issue in England highly opposition to slavery as its chief motive. But even though slavery did not emerge as a moral consideration in the heated British deliberations over intervention, it nonetheless remained a dominant force in the background by threatening to stir up a major political fallout from any ministerial decision supporting the slaveholding South and by encouraging the ever-present fear of slave uprisings caused by emancipation."[100]

Historian Dean B. Mahin wrote: "Lincoln and Seward would certainly have rejected any offer of British or joint mediation as summarily as they subsequently rejected a unilateral offer of French mediation. There was no chance that Lincoln would have accepted an armistice. Suspension of the blockade for six months would have eliminated all the advantage the Union had derived from its massive blockade efforts in 1861 and 1862."[101] In early December 1862, Charleston Consul Robert Bunch had written to Lyons: "Your Lordship is aware that the measure indicated by the so-called Emancipation Proclamation of Mr. Lincoln is to go into full effect on the 1st of January next. There are those who apprehend a rising of the Negroes in the seceded states at or about that time. Personally I do not share these apprehensions, which I believe to be chimerical, at any rate so far as cities or large towns are concerned. But there is always a possibility of insurrection, whether remote the possibility may appear."[102]

The machinations of the British government were hard to follow. Historian Burton J. Hendrick wrote "the publication of Spencer Walpole's Life of Lord John Russell in 1889....made clear a hitherto unknown fact; that Lord John Russell was the prime mover for recognition of Southern independence in August-November, 1862." Although Palmerston often did favor the South, Hendrick wrote, "Russell, from the firing of the first gun, looked upon the American Union as a thing of the past....To bring the struggle to a close as quickly as possible and end the useless shedding of blood, as well as toe end the suffering in England directly caused by it, was, in Russell's mind, his chief duty as a statesman."[103] Russell, like Palmerston, came to understand that continued efforts to meddle in the Civil War would have the fall of their government."[104]

Throughout the Civil War, President Lincoln was careful to cultivate official and private opinion in England and elsewhere in Europe. "Lincoln recognized more and more the potential positive impact of emancipation on foreign affairs. In September 1861 the Union minister in Spain, Carl Schurz, assured Seward that a White House declaration against slavery would unite Europe against the South. Early the following year Schurz returned to the United States and talked with the president about using an antislavery pronouncement to block foreign intervention," wrote historian Howard Jones.[105] "Lincoln carefully selected careful agents to work on public opinion in England. Thurlow Weed, prominent journalist, was one; Robert J. Walker, financier and governor of Kansas, another; Henry Ward Beecher, famous clergyman, and brother of Harriet Beecher Stowe of Uncle Tom's Cabin fame, a third," wrote historian Roy F. Nichols.[106] President Lincoln told New York Tribune editor Horace Greeley in February 1863 that "the emancipation policy" was "not having yet effect so much good here at home as had been promised or predicted." The President noted, however that the Emancipation Proclamation "had helped us decidedly in our foreign relations."[107]

Although the British government and British press acted badly toward the American government, Mr. Lincoln had his supporters in the London Emancipation Society formed in the winter of 1862-63. Mr. Lincoln also had prominent political admirers in England, including John Bright and Richard Cobden. New Jersey Congressman James M. Scovel recalled traveling to England in 1863: "By a sea-coal fire, late in a November night, Mr. Cobden gave me his opinion of Abraham Lincoln: 'This century has produced no man like Lincoln. Here is a man who has risen from manual labor to the presidency of a great people. To me he seems to be the man God has raised up to give courage and enthusiasm to a people unused to war, fighting what seems to me to be a doubtful battle in the greatest conflict of modern times. I like Mr. Lincoln's intense veneration for what is true and good. His conscience and his heart are ruled by his reason."[108]

President Lincoln found common cause with England in restraining the slave trade. A treaty of cooperation against the slave trafficking was passed by the U.S. Senate on April 24, 1862. Lincoln biographers Nicolay and Hay wrote of the anti-slave trade treaty with Britain: "No less to fulfill the dictates of propriety and justice than for its salutary influence on the opinion of foreign nations…[the president] secured the passage of 'An act to carry into effect the treaty between the United States and Her Britannic Majesty for the suppression of the African slave trade,' approved July 11, 1862. That this action betokened more than mere hollow profession and sentiment is evinced by the fact that under the prosecution of the Government, the slave-trader Nathaniel P. Gordon was convicted and hanged in New York on the 21st of February, 1862, this being the first execution for such crime under the laws of the United States, after their enforcement had been neglected and their extreme penalty denied for forty years."[109]

This treaty was an important event in Anglo-American relations and an important event in the eradication of the slave trade. Historian David P. Crook wrote: "By providing for a peacetime right of search under strictly prescribed conditions, the treaty resolved a problem which had bedevilled Anglo-American relations for half a century: how to permit the Royal Navy to destroy the slave trade on the high seas while preserving immunity for American neutral rights."[110] Historian Howard Jones noted: "The pact was primarily attributable to the White House effort to block British intervention on behalf of the South, but it also fitted nicely with the rapidly developing shift in the Union's policy toward slavery...The British had long sought such a treaty from the United States, and now the moral basis of the projected move had meshed with the realistic needs of the war to necessitate a sharper definition of the Union's position on slavery."[111]

The treaty also involved an elaborate charade on Seward's part, according to historian A. Taylor Milne, in which Seward appeared to lead the negotiations and then quibble with the British: "It was made to appear that Seward opened the negotiation on March 22 [1862] by writing to Lyons inviting him to sign a Slave Trade treaty, a draft of which he enclosed. Actually this was the identical, printed, British draft, with the formal headings reversed in red ink Lyons played his part by replying with an objection to a clause limiting the duration of the treaty to ten years, but did not desire 'to obstruct or retard the progress of the negotiation.'" Seward and Lyons engaged in a show of contentious negotiation to demonstrate that they were aggressively protect each country's interest rather than collaborating to achieve a common objective.[112] The charade made the treaty more palatable with Congress where Radical Republicans were suspicious of Seward's handling of foreign relations. When the Senate ratified the treaty, Seward exclaimed: "Good God! The Democrats have disappeared. This is the greatest act of the administration."[113] Seward's enthusiasm was justified. By allowing British warships to board American ships to search for slaves, the treaty had a dramatic effect on the importation of slaves in Cuba where newly imported slaves dropped from 30,473 in 1859-1860 to 143 in 1864-1865.[114]

British public opinion was not monolithic. Lincoln's policies had important grass roots supporters. President Lincoln commented in February 18th that "there were three parties in England: an aristocratic party, which cannot be sorry to see the Republic break up; a class allied to the South through trade relations; and a third, larger, or if not larger, of more import, which sympathizes warmly with the cause of the North."[115] At the end of December 1862, the working-men of Manchester, who had been disastrously affected by the shortage of cotton, addressed a petition to President Lincoln: "As citizens of Manchester, assembled at the Free-Trade Hall, we beg to express our fraternal sentiments toward you and your country. We rejoice in your greatness as an outgrowth of England, whose blood and language you share, whose orderly and legal freedom you have applied to new circumstances, over a region immeasurably greater than our own. We honor your Free States, as a singularly happy abode for the working millions where industry is honored."

"One thing alone has, in the past, lessened our sympathy with your country and our confidence in it; we mean the ascendancy of politicians who not merely maintained Negro slavery, but desired to extend and root it more firmly."

"Since we have discerned, however, that the victory of the free north, in the war which has so sorely distressed us as well as afflicted you, will strike off the fetters of the slave, you have attracted our warm and earnest sympathy. We joyfully honor you, as the President, and the Congress with you, for many decisive steps toward practically exemplifying your belief in the words of your great founders: 'All men are created free and equal.' You have procured the liberation of the slaves in the district around Washington, and thereby made the centre of your Federation visibly free. You have enforced the laws against the slave-trade, and kept up your fleet against it, even while every ship was wanted for service in your terrible war. You have nobly decided to receive ambassadors from the Negro republics of Hayti and Liberia, thus forever renouncing that unworthy prejudice which refuses the rights of humanity to men and women on account of their color. In order more effectually to stop the slave-trade, you have made with our Queen a treaty, which your Senate has ratified, for the right of mutual search. Your Congress has decreed freedom as the law forever in the vast unoccupied or half unsettled Territories which are directly subject to its legislative power. It has offered pecuniary aid to all States which will enact emancipation locally, and has forbidden your Generals to restore fugitive slaves who seek their protection. You had entreated the slave-masters to accept these moderate offers; and after long and patient waiting, you, as Commander-in-Chief of the Army, have appointed to-morrow, the first of January, 1863, as the day of unconditional freedom for the slaves of the rebel states."

"Heartily do we congratulate you and your country on this humane and righteous course. We assume that you cannot now stop short of complete uprooting of slavery. It would not become us to dictate any details, but there are broad principles of humanity which must guide you. If complete emancipation in some States be deferred, though only to a predetermined day, still in the interval, human beings should not be counted chattels. Women must have the rights of chastity and maternity, men the rights of husbands, masters the liberty of manumission. Justice demands for the black, no less than for the white, the protection of law – that his voice be heard in your courts. Nor must any such abomination be tolerated as slave-breeding States, and a slave market – if you are to earn the high reward of all your sacrifices, in the approval of the universal brotherhood and of the Divine Father. It is for your free country to decide whether any thing but immediate, and total emancipation can secure the most indispensable rights of humanity against the inveterate wickedness of local laws and local executives."

"We implore you, for your own honor and welfare, not to faint in your providential mission. While your enthusiasm is aflame, and the tide of events runs high, let the work be finished effectually. Leave no root of bitterness to spring up and work fresh misery to your children. It is a mighty task, indeed, to reorganize the industry not only of four millions of the colored race, but of five millions of whites. Nevertheless, the vast progress you have made in the short space of twenty months fills us with hope that every stain on your freedom will shortly be removed, and that the erasure of that foul blot upon civilization and Christianity – chattel slavery – during your Presidency will cause the name of Abraham Lincoln to be honored and revered by posterity. We are certain that such a glorious consummation will cement Great Britain to the United States in close and enduring regards. Our interests, moreover, are identified with yours. We are truly one people, though locally separate. And if you have any ill-wishers here, be assured they are chiefly powerless to stir up quarrels between us, from the very day in which your country becomes, undeniably and without exception, the home of the free."

"Accept our high admiration of your firmness in upholding the proclamation of freedom."[116]

President Lincoln responded to the petition several weeks later: "I have the honor to acknowledge the receipt of the address and resolutions which you sent to me on the eve of the new year."

"When I came, on the fourth day of March, 1861, through a free and constitutional election, to preside in the government of the United States, the country was found at the verge of civil war. Whatever might have been the cause, or whosoever the fault, one duty paramount to all others was before me, namely, to maintain and preserve at once the Constitution and the integrity of the federal republic. A conscientious purpose to perform this duty is a key to all the measures of administration which have been, and to all which will hereafter be pursued. Under our form of government, and my official oath, I could not depart from this purpose if I would. It is not always in the power of governments to enlarge or restrict the scope of moral results which follow the policies that they may deem it necessary for the public safety, from time to time, to adopt."

"I have understood well that duty of self-preservation rests solely with the American people. But I have at the same time been aware that favor or disfavor of foreign nations might have a material influence in enlarging and prolonging the struggle with disloyal men in which the country is engaged. A fair examination of history has seemed to authorize a belief that the past action and influences of the United States were generally regarded as having been beneficent towards mankind. I have therefore reckoned upon the forbearance of nations. Circumstances, to some of which you kindly allude, induced me especially to expect that if justice and good faith should be practiced by the United States, they would encounter no hostile influence on the part of Great Britain. It is now a pleasant duty to acknowledge the demonstration you have given of your desire that a spirit of peace and amity towards this country may prevail in the councils of your Queen, who is respected and esteemed in your own country only more than she is by the kindred nation which has its home on this side of the Atlantic."

"I know and deeply deplore the sufferings which the workingmen at Manchester and in all Europe are called to endure in this crisis. It has been often and studiously represented that the attempt to overthrow this government, which was built upon the foundation of human rights, and to substitute for it one which should rest exclusively on the basis of human slavery, was likely to obtain the favor of Europe. Through the actions of our disloyal citizens the workingmen of Europe have been subjected to a severe trial, for the purpose of forcing their sanction to that attempt. Under these circumstances, I cannot but regard your decisive utterance upon the question as an instance of sublime

Christian heroism which has not been surpassed in any age or in any country. It is, indeed, an energetic and reinspiring assurance of the inherent power of truth and of ultimate and universal triumph of justice, humanity, and freedom. I do not doubt that the sentiments you have expressed will be sustained by your great nation, and, on the other hand, I have no hesitation in assuring you that they will excite admiration, esteem, and the most reciprocal feelings of friendship among the American people. I hail this interchange of sentiment, therefore, as an augury that, whatever else may happen, whatever misfortune may befall your country or my own, the peace and friendship which now exist between the two nations will be, as it shall be my desire to make the, perpetual."[117]

In early April 1864, Mr. Lincoln visited with British anti-slavery activist George Thompson, whom he told: "Mr. Thompson, the people of Great Britain, and of other foreign governments, were in one great error in reference to this conflict. They seemed to think that, the moment I was President, I had the power to abolish slavery, forgetting that, before I could have any power whatever, I had to take the oath to support the Constitution of the United States, and execute the laws as I found them. When the Rebellion broke out, my duty did not admit of a question. That was, first, by all strictly lawful means to endeavor to maintain the integrity of the government. I did not consider that I had a right to touch the 'State' institution of 'Slavery' until all other measures for restoring the Union had failed. The paramount idea of the constitution is the preservation of the Union. It may not be specified in so many words, but that this was the idea of its founders is evident; for, without the Union, the constitution would be worthless. It seems clear, then, that in the last extremity, if any local institution threatened the existence of the Union, the Executive could not hesitate as to his duty. In our case, the moment came when I felt that slavery must die that the nation might live! I have sometimes used the illustration in this connection of a man with a diseased limb, and his surgeon. So long as there is a chance of the patient's restoration, the surgeon is solemnly bound to try to save both life and limb; but when the crisis comes, and the limb must be sacrificed as the only chance of saving the life, no honest man will hesitate."[118] As President Lincoln was constrained by both law and public opinion to conduct the necessary surgery precipitously. Historian David P. Crook noted: "Fashion now denigrates the view that moral outrage against slavery significantly qualified the calculations of power politics." But, argued Crook, "Moral outrage against slavery strongly affected public sentiment in Britain, and cannot be lightly dismissed in an age when public sentiment exerted unprecedented sway over weak executives in foreign policy."[119]

Seward's focus continued to be avoiding any European intervention. Historian Dean B. Mahin wrote that in the summer of 1863, "Lincoln and Seward continued to worry about the possibility that some incident would shatter the fragile structure of U.S.-British accommodation. Welles thought the orders restricting the Navy's use of Saint Thomas resulted from Seward's 'constant trepidation lest the Navy Department or some navy officer shall embroil us in a war, or make trouble with England.'"[120] In the early autumn of 1863, Seward took Washington diplomats on a tour of the New York State to demonstrate the Union's economic struggle. Lincoln scholar Jay Monaghan wrote: "Each day's ride disclosed new wonders of wealth, rich farms, factories with whirring wheels, miles and miles of railroad trains trundling freight, rivers, lakes and canals filled with vessels…"[121] According to Seward's son Frederick, "They visited New York and its vicinity, they went up the Hudson, then through the Valley of the Mohawk, then over the hills into Otsego County. They saw Albany, Schenectady, and Little Falls, visited Sharon Springs and Trenton Falls; they spent a night at Cooperstown and sailed on Otsego Lake. They went to

Utica, Rome and Syracuse. They stopped at Auburn, visited Seneca Falls and Geneva, traversed Cayuga and Seneca Lakes, saw the mills and factories of Rochester, and the harbour of Buffalo swarming with lake craft, and having its elevators in full operation." Frederick Seward noted that "everyday's ride was a volume of instruction. Hundreds of factories with whirring wheels, thousands of acres of golden harvest fields, miles of railway trains laden with freight, busy fleets on rivers, lakes, and canals, all showed a period of unexampled commercial activity and prosperity."[122] Secretary Seward charmed the diplomats and they ended the trip with a better appreciation of the secretary of state and the Lincoln administration.

Compared to his British counterparts, French Emperor Napoleon III was more anxious to intervene in the American conflict, but unwilling to do so alone. His conflict with Russia over Poland in early 1863 pushed Britain even farther away from intervention in the Civil War. Instead, Napoleon himself intervened in Mexico, installing the puppet Maximilian as the Emperor of Mexico, supported by French troops. Before Maximilian departed for Mexico, he visited Emperor Napoleon "to learn from Napoleon just what French support he could depend on in Mexico. M. Mercier hurried to Paris with a last-minute report of Lincoln's attitude. The Frenchman had talked with the President immediately before departing. Lincoln, according to Mercier, had intimated that Maximilian would be recognized by the United States, if Napoleon made no negotiations with the Confederacy. The Emperor beamed with pleasure," wrote Jay Monaghan.[123]

The Lincoln administration had good reason to distrust Napoleon; the English distrusted Napoleon as well. The Russians mistrusted everyone. The Lincoln administration successfully prevented the French government from further cooperation with Confederate diplomats and from immediate cooperation with Britain regarding intervention in the conflict. Meanwhile, the Lincoln government postponed a confrontation with France over Mexico until after the Civil War had been concluded. Historian Howard Jones wrote: "The threat of war with the Union…acted as a decisive restraint on Napoleon. Paradoxical as it seems," Napoleon "feared that recognition of the Confederacy meant a war with the Union in which he would have no allies. In late November 1863 he had told a British diplomat that such a war 'would spell disaster in the interests of France and would have no possible object.'"[124]

In Washington, the diplomatic corps did not have a high opinion of the President or the Union. The French minister was an undisguised proponent of the Confederacy. Baron Eduard de Stoeckl, the Russian minister in Washington during the entire Civil War, was contemptuous of President Lincoln, his supposed weakness and his unwillingness to compromise with the South. Lincoln biographer Benjamin Thomas wrote: "Throughout the war Stoeckl considered Lincoln well-meaning but weak, honest but under the dominance of others. May 11, 1861, Stoeckl wrote: "The more complicated the situation becomes the more feeble and undecided he [Lincoln] appears. He admits himself that his task is beyond his powers. Fatigue and anxiety have broken him down physically. As for Mr. Seward, he has not justified, since he has occupied the post of Secretary of State, the reputation that he enjoys. He is completely ignorant of international affairs, while his vanity is such that he does not wish to hear advice from anyone. His arrogance does more harm to the administration than the nullity of most of his colleagues."[125]

American foreign policy had its own rifts. Throughout the Civil War, Secretary Seward and Massachusetts Senator Charles Sumner vied for supremacy in the field of foreign affairs – especially where England was concerned. Journalist Ben Perley Poore wrote of Sumner: "Having been abroad himself, he knew the necessity for having, especially at that time, the country represented by educated gentlemen, and Mr. Seward often found it a difficult matter to persuade him to consent to the appointment of some rural politician to a place of diplomatic importance. Objection was made to one nomination, on the ground that the person was a drunkard, and a leading Senator came one morning before the Committee to refute the charge. He made quite an argument, closing by saying: 'No, gentlemen, he is not a drunkard. He may, occasionally, as I do myself, take a glass of wine, but I assure you, on the honor of a gentleman, he never gets drunk.' Upon this representation the appointment was favorably reported upon and confirmed by the senate, but it was soon evident that the person was an incorrigible sot, and when it became absolutely necessary to remove him, it leaked out that he had retained and paid the Senator for vouching for his temperate habits."[126]

During 1861, noted historian Richard J. Carwardine, President Lincoln "benefited from regular discussions with Sumner, whose friendship with the English Liberal reformers, John Bright and Richard Cobden, made the senator a barometer of British opinion."[127] Lincoln biographer Carl Sandburg wrote: "A curious friendship it was between these two strong men, having as many differences and contrasts as the remarkable and continued affection between Robert Toombs and Alexander H. Stephens. Having said, 'Sumner thinks he runs me,' Lincoln had no fear of evil resulting from the Bostonian's so thinking, and even encouraged the thought. Very slowly had the President during '61 and '62 moved toward what Sumner urged at the beginning, emancipation of the slaves. To John Bright and to the Duke and Duchess of Argyll, Sumner wrote that the President was slow, and conveyed the impression that under Sumner's steady prodding, which never ceased, the President in the end, would take the right action."[128]

Seward did not appreciate rivals for power and influence. Once when Seward was informed of the President quoting an opinion of Charles Sumner and favoring it as against Seward, Seward said, 'There are too many secretaries of State in Washington.'"[129] Sumner was more stiff-necked, more self-righteous, more proper than Seward. He saw most issues through a moral lens whereas Seward was more pragmatic. He saw his connections to the English and his understanding of them superior to those of Seward and Charles Francis Adams, the envoy who had long been a political competitor of Sumner. Ironically, whereas Seward tended to favor compromise with the South and Sumner opposed it, Sumner favored compromise with England while Seward favored confrontation.

Navy Secretary Gideon Welles, himself no admirer of Seward, worried about Sumner's influence in foreign affairs regarding an issue of maritime laws concerning the seizure of international mail. He wrote in his diary in April 1863: "Sumner called this evening at the Department. Was much discomfited with an interview which he had last evening with the President. The latter was just filing a paper as Sumner went in. After a few moments Sumner took two slips from the pocket, – one cut from the Boston Transcript, the other from the Chicago Tribune, each taking strong ground against surrendering the Peterhoff mail [in January 1863]. The President, after reading them, opened the paper he had just filed and read to Sumner his letter addressed to the Secretary of State and the Secretary of the Navy. He told Sumner he had received the replies and just concluded reading mine. After some comments on them he said to Sumner, 'I will not show these papers to you now; perhaps I never shall.' A conversation then took place which greatly mortified and chagrined Sumner, who declares the President is very ignorant or very deceptive. The President, he says, is horrified, or appeared to be, with the idea of a war with England, which he assumed depended on this question. He was confident we should have with England if we presumed to open their mail bags, or break their seals or locks. They would not submit to it, and we were in no condition to plunge into a foreign war on a subject of a little importance in comparison with the terrible consequences which must follow our act. Of this idea of a war with England, Sumner could not dispossess him by argument, or by showing its absurdity. Whether it was real or affected ignorance, Sumner was not satisfied.

I have no doubts of the President's sincerity, and so told Sumner. But he has been imposed upon, humbugged, by a man in whom he confides. His confidence has been abused; he does not – frankly confesses he does not – comprehend the principles involved nor the question itself. Seward does not intend he shall comprehend it. While attempting to look into it, the Secretary of State is daily, and almost hourly, wailing in his ears the calamities of a war with England which he is striving to prevent. The President is thus led away from the real question, and will probably decide it, not on its merits, but on the false issue, raised by the man who is the author of the difficulty.[130]

Senator Sumner had one distinct advantage over Secretary Seward – he had a far better relationship with Mrs. Lincoln than did Secretary Seward, who was despised by the first lady. "The Senator in his early fifties, was still austerely handsome and still a bachelor, the latter condition intriguing in itself. The fact that he allowed Mary Lincoln to enter his limited circle of confidants enhanced her image of herself as a cultivated woman," observed historians Justin G. Turner and Linda Levitt Turner. "It was gratifying to her that Sumner so readily laid aside his momentous concerns to join her at the opera; flattering that he came so often to relax in her drawing room, where he entertained her with anecdotes of his acquaintances in government and diplomacy, read her letters from foreign statesmen, or engaged her in earnest discussion of the works of Whittier, Longfellow, Emerson and the other New England savants who were his personal friends."[131]

Sumner's disadvantage was that President Lincoln could not relax in his presence without feeling Sumner's keen disapproval. With Seward, however, President Lincoln could relax completely. But with England, Seward was more publicly belligerent than was Sumner. Pennsylvania journalist Alexander K. McClure wrote: "The War of the Rebellion revealed to the people – in fact, to the whole world – the many sides of Abraham Lincoln's character. It showed him as a real ruler of men – not a ruler by the mere power of might, but by the power of a great brain. In his Cabinet were the ablest men in the country, yet they all knew that Lincoln was abler than any of them. Mr. Seward, the Secretary of State, was a man famed in statesmanship and diplomacy. During the early stages of the Civil War, when France and England were seeking an excuse to interfere and help the Southern Confederacy, Mr. Seward wrote a letter to our minister in London, Charles Francis Adams, instructing him concerning the attitude of the Federal government on the question of interference, which would undoubtedly have brought about a war with England if Abraham Lincoln had not corrected and amended the letter. He did this, too, without yielding a point or sacrificing in any way his own dignity or that of the country."[132]

Seward's bluster concerned and annoyed the British. British Prime Minister Lord Russell decided that Seward was "a vapouring blustering ignorant man."[133] However, historian Norman B. Ferris denied that Seward was jingoistic or that President Lincoln had to restrain him. He noted that "it was Seward's 'ordinary habit' to read his most important diplomatic instructions 'to the president before sending them.' Even as Lincoln frequently sought Seward's advice about the wording of such documents as his inaugural addresses and emancipation proclamation, so Seward welcomed the President's concurrence before issuing important state papers." Seward, argued Ferris, has been maligned by contemporaries like Navy Secretary Gideon

Welles and Postmaster General Montgomery Blair, who were jealous of his influence with President Lincoln. Historians have built on the "myth of Seward's jingoism." Ferris wrote that "Seward realized that a war between the United States and a European power would not only 'set the world on fire,' but would probably also wipe out democracy forever."[134]

Historian James A. Rawley wrote that Sumner took his criticisms public in 1863: "In Cooper Union, where Lincoln had won fame, he delivered a turgid address, lecturing England upon her duties with respect to intervention in a foreign war and slavery. Two days before this severe, schoolmasterish lecture, the British government had ordered detention of the powerful ironclad rams designed to break the blockade. Sumner had not known of the order, and when the news did reach American shores, he was subjected to a good deal of criticism." Rawley wrote: "Sumner both feared that Seward might provoke a war with France and hoped that Seward might be dismissed from the cabinet."[135]

American Minister Charles F. Adams had been relentless in pushing the British government to crack down on the manufacture in British ports of warships for Confederate use. Belatedly, the British cracked down and stopped the transfer of the Alexandra to Confederate hands. Seward's threat against England were actually a "masterpiece" of saber-rattling and quiet diplomacy, according to historian Burton J. Hendrick Seward instructed Adams to present a protest to the British foreign minister which ended that "it would be superfluous in me to point out to your Lordship that this is war" if the ram Alabama were allowed to sail. Hendrick wrote: "It was not Adams's threat, but the more subtle maneuvering of Seward that had persuaded the British government to change its policy." Hendrick wrote: "In addition to knowing when to threaten, when to bluster, when to prod, to hint, to instill suspicions and fears, Seward had another gift equally serviceable in diplomacy. He knew when to conciliate and when, without any loss in dignity, to yield."[136]

Seward's relations with Congress were never good but they worsened when his diplomatic correspondence was published and revealed some undiplomatic observations. While Senator Foreign Relations Chairman Sumner was at least cordial with President Lincoln, House Foreign Relations Chairman Henry Winter Davis was not. Davis was a major critic, saying "We are on trial before the nations of the world. Every despot in Europe curled his lips when the rebellion broke out, at the feeble, wretched vacillating, dilapidated government that undertook to restore its authority over this immense and magnificent region."[137] Historian William C. Harris wrote that: "Davis and many other members of Congress were livid when they read the correspondence between Seward and Dayton, documents that were supplied to the House by Lincoln upon its request. Denouncing Seward's action as a sellout to France, Davis wanted his committee to make a blistering report to the House floor on the issue. But with the election campaign of 1864 beginning and the war at a critical juncture in Virginia and elsewhere, members of his own party blocked Davis's effort to embarrass the Lincoln administration." Davis lost the vote and voluntarily lost his position as House Foreign Affairs chairman. Harris wrote: "Davis' victory was short-lived. The Republican press overwhelmingly denounced the House's action, charging that the resolution had more to do with Davis's malevolence toward Lincoln and Seward, combined with bitter Democratic partisanship, than with the conduct of foreign affairs or the issue of the French in Mexico."[138]

Union problems with Europe continued through the end of the war. William C. Harris wrote: "Troubles with Great Britain and France in late 1864 and early 1865, after a two-year period of relative quiet, raised the specter of an American armed conflict with one or both of these European powers. Controversies flared up with Britain over Confederate raids from sanctuaries in Canada and with France over that country's intervention in Mexico."[139] A particular concern were the increasingly desperate actions taken by Confederate agents operating out of British-held Canada. In dealing with the English, the French and Congress, President Lincoln and Secretary Seward were an effective team. Lincoln's "calm judgment, judicious view of U.S. priorities and interests, and extensive previous experience as an advocate and negotiator complemented Seward's greater knowledge of foreign countries and diplomatic practices and restrain Seward's initial tendencies to be indiscreet, impetuous, and temperamental," wrote historian Dean B. Mahin. "These two men of very different backgrounds and personalities forged one of the most effective partnerships in the history of U.S. diplomacy."[140] Historian James A. Rawley wrote: "Growing in stature as the war persisted, the wily Seward became an effective and even distinguished diplomatist."[141] Lincoln biographer David H. Donald overstated the case when he wrote: "It is a charming fancy to think of Lincoln as a 'diplomat in carpet slippers, applying homely common sense and frontier wisdom to the preservation of international peace. In fact, however, after curbing Seward's belligerent tendencies early in 1861, the President willingly left diplomacy to his able Secretary of State. In Lincoln's Collected Works there is notably little about foreign affairs, aside from routine diplomatic communications, which were of course written by Seward..."[142]

Historian Mahin observed: "Most of Abraham Lincoln's foreign policy was necessarily negative – to prevent or minimize foreign interference and to avoid foreign entanglements. But he also established a very positive international objective – to maintain and expand the role of the United States as a successful example of democratic government for all men everywhere."[143] Indeed, the conduct of foreign relations was a subject often on President Lincoln's mind as was the American example of democracy for the world. When a British girl visiting the White Hosue expressed her support of him in 1863, he replied: "We have a good deal of salt water between us. When you feel kindly towards us we cannot, unfortunately, be always aware of it. But it cuts both ways. When you, in England, are cross with us, we don't feel it quite so badly."[144]

References

1.Francis B. Carpenter, The Inner Life of Abraham Lincoln: Six Months at the White House, p. 245.

2.Roy P. Basler, editor, Collected Works of Abraham Lincoln (CWAL), Volume IV, p. 438.

3.Michael Burlingame, Abraham Lincoln: A Life, Volume II, p. 119

4.Frederick W. Seward, Reminiscences of a War-time Statesman and Diplomat, 1830-1915, p. 144.

5.John M. Taylor, William Henry Seward, Lincoln's Right Hand, pp. 144-145.

6.Thornton Kirkland Lothrop, William Henry Seward, p. 287.

7.Frederick W. Seward, Reminiscences of a War-time Statesman and Diplomat, 1830-1915, p. 144.

8.Hans L. Trefousse, Carl Schurz: A Biography, p. 99.

9.Joseph Schafer, editor and translator, Intimate Letters of Carl Schurz, 1841-1869, p. 250.

10.Joseph Schafer, editor and translator, Intimate Letters of Car l Schurz, 1841-1869, p. 251.

11.Hans L. Trefousse, Carl Schurz: A Biography, p. 101.

12.Hans L. Trefousse, Carl Schurz: A Biography, pp. 105, 1-3.

13.Michael Burlingame and John R. Turner Ettlinger, editors, Inside Lincoln's White House: The Complete Civil War Diary of John Hay, p. 12 (April 26, 1861).

14.Jay Monaghan, Diplomat in Carpet Slippers: Abraham Lincoln Deals with Foreign Affairs, p. 110. (See Carl Schurz, Reminiscences, Volume II, pp. 242-243.

15.John M. Taylor, William Henry Seward, Lincoln's Right Hand, p. 143.

16.Charles Francis Adams, An Address on the Life, Character and Services of William Henry Seward, p. 30.

17.James M. McPherson, This Mighty Scourge: Perspectives on the Civil War, p. 66.

18.Frederick W. Seward, Reminiscences of a War-time Statesman and Diplomat, 1830-1915, pp. 178-179.

19. James M. McPherson, This Mighty Scourge: Perspectives on the Civil War, p. 65.

20.Dean B. Mahin, One War at a Time: The International Dimensions of the American Civil War, p. 84.

21.Charles Segal, editor, Conversations with Lincoln, pp. 141-142.

22.Charles Segal, editor, Conversations with Lincoln, p. 143.

23.Howard Jones, Abraham Lincoln and a New Birth of Freedom: The Union and Slavery in the Diplomacy of the Civil War, pp. 49-50.

24.William Howard Russell, My Diary, North and South, pp. 70-71.

25.Richard N. Current, "Comment," Journal of the Abraham Lincoln Association, 1991, pp. 44-45.

26.George E. Baker, editor, The Works of William Henry Seward, Volume V, p. 261

27.Brian Jenkins, "The 'Wise Macaw' and the Lion: William Seward and Britain, 1861-1863" University of Rochester Library Bulletin, Autumn 1978.

28.Gordon H. Warren, Fountain of Discontent: The Trent Affair and Freedom of the Seas, p. 50.

29.Craig L. Symonds, Lincoln and His Admirals, p. 40.

30.Gordon H. Warren, Fountain of Discontent: The Trent Affair and Freedom of the Seas, p. 55.

31.James J. Barnes and Patience P. Barnes, The American Civil War through British Eyes Dispatches from British Diplomats , Volume I: November 1860-April 1862, p.154 (Dispatch from Lord Lyons to Lord Russell, August 12, 1861).

32.John Taylor, William Henry Seward, p. 182.

33.Charles Segal, Conversations with Lincoln, p. 141

34.Larry Schweikart and Michael Allen, A Patriot's History of the United States, p. 318.

35.Michael Burlingame, Abraham Lincoln: A Life, Volume II, p. 222

36.William Lee Miller, President Lincoln: The Duty of a Statesman, p. 204.

37.David P. Crook, The North, the South and the Powers, p. 157.

38.Philip Van Doren Stern, When the Guns Roared: World Aspects of the American Civil War, p. 21.

39.Dean B. Mahin, One War at a Time: The International Dimensions of the American Civil War, p. 66. (London Morning Chronicle, November 28, 1861).

40.Richard Carwardine, Lincoln, Profiles in Power, p. 178.

41.Jay Monaghan, Diplomat in Carpet Slippers: Abraham Lincoln Deals with Foreign Affairs, p. 172.

42.Thurlow Weed Barnes, Life of Thurlow Weed including His Autobiography and a Memoir, p. 376.

43.Jay Monaghan, Diplomat in Carpet Slippers: Abraham Lincoln Deals with Foreign Affairs, pp. 174-175.

44.Philip Van Doren Stern, When the Guns Roared: World Aspects of the American Civil War, p. 90.

45.Frederick Bancroft, The Life of William H. Seward, p. 233.

46.Charles Francis Adams, An Address on the Life, Character and Services of William Henry Seward, pp. 66-67.

47.David P. Crook, The North, the South and the Powers, p. 152

48.Philip Van Doren Stern, When the Guns Roared: World Aspects of the American Civil War, p. 93.

49.Gordon H. Warren, Fountain of Discontent: The Trent Affair and Freedom of the Seas, p. 171.

50.Charles Segal, editor, Conversations with Lincoln, pp. 146-147.

51.Gordon H. Warren, Fountain of Discontent: The Trent Affair and Freedom of the Seas, pp. 170-171.

52.Theodore Calvin Pease, editor, Diary of Orville H. Browning, Volume I, p. 515 (December 15, 1861).

53.Jay Monaghan, Diplomat in Carpet Slippers: Abraham Lincoln Deals with Foreign Affairs, p. 189.

54.Philip Van Doren Stern, When the Guns Roared: World Aspects of the American Civil War, p. 92.

55.Horace Porter, Campaigning with Grant, pp. 408-409.

56.Kenneth L. Deutsch and Joseph R. Fornieri, Lincoln's American Dream: Clashing Political Perspectives, p. 319 (Phillip G. Henderson, Abraham Lincoln and His Cabinet").

57.Theodore Calvin Pease, editor, Diary of Orville H. Browning, Volume I , pp. 516-517. (December 21, 1861).

58.Charles Sumner: The Selected Letters of Charles Sumner , Volume II, p.87 (Letter from Charles Sumner to John Bright, December 23, 1861).

59.Burton J. Hendrick, Lincoln's War Cabinet, p. 244.

60.David P. Crook, The North, the South and the Powers, pp. 158, 152.

61.Burton J. Hendrick, Lincoln's War Cabinet, p. 245.

62.Howard K. Beale, editor, The Diary of Edward Bates, pp. 213-214 (December 25, 1861).

63.Howard K. Beale, editor, The Diary of Edward Bates, pp. 214-217 (December 25,1861).

64.David H. Donald, editor, Inside Lincoln's Cabinet, p.53, 55 (December 25, 1861).

65.Theodore Calvin Pease, editor, Diary of Orville H. Browning, Volume I, pp. 518-519 (December 25, 1861).

66.Frederick W. Seward, Reminiscences of a War-Time Diplomat, pp. 189-190.

67.Norman B. Ferris, The Trent Affair, p. 187.

68.Frederick W. Seward, Reminiscences of A War-Time Statesman and Diplomat, 1830-1915, p. 190.

69.Charles Sumner: The Selected Letters of Charles Sumner, Volume II, p. 93 (Letter to from Charles Sumner to Richard Cobden, December 27, 1863).

70.Charles Sumner, The Selected Letters of Charles Sumner, Volume II, p. 94 (Letter from Charles Sumner to Richard Cobden, December 31, 1861).

71.Don E. and Virginia E. Fehrenbacher, editors, Recollected Words of Abraham Lincoln, p. 370 (Horace Porter).

72.Frederick W. Seward, Reminiscences of A War-Time Statesman and Diplomat, 1830-1915, p. 190.

73.Norman B. Ferris, The Trent Affair, p. 188.

74.Kenneth L. Deutsch and Joseph R. Fornieri, Lincoln's American Dream: Clashing Political Perspectives, p. 319 (Phillip G. Henderson, Abraham Lincoln and His Cabinet").

75.Richard J. Carwardine, Lincoln: Profiles in Power, p. 179.

76.Michael Burlingame, Abraham Lincoln: A Life, Volume II, p. 227.

77.Burton J. Hendrick, Lincoln's War Cabinet, p. 248.

78.Burton J. Hendrick, Lincoln's War Cabinet, p. 240.

79.Richard B. Kielbowicz, "The Telegraph, Censorship and Politics at the Outset of the Civil War," Civil War History, Spring 1994, p. 111.

80.Richard B. Kielbowicz, "The Telegraph, Censorship and Politics at the Outset of the Civil War," Civil War History, Spring 1994,

81.Ward Hill Lamon, Recollections of Abraham Lincoln 1847-1865, p. 228.

82.David P. Crook, The North, the South and the Powers, p. 164.

83.James M. McPherson, "No Peace without Victory, 1861-1865," The American Historical Review , February 2004. See http://www.historians.org/about-aha-and-membership/aha-history-and-archives/presidential-addresses/james-m-mcpherson

84.Dean B. Mahin, One War at a Time: The International Dimensions of the American Civil War, p. 85.

85.Burton J. Hendrick, Statesmen of the Lost Cause p. 272.

86.Richard Striner, Father Abraham: Lincoln's Relentless Struggle to End Slavery, p. 172

87.Christopher J. Olsen, The American Civil War: A Hands-On History, 182.

88.Burton J. Hendrick, Statesmen of the Lost Cause, p. 273.

89.Burton J. Hendrick, Statesmen of the Lost Cause, pp. 274-275.

90.James M. McPherson, This Mighty Scourge: Perspectives on the Civil War, pp. 73-74.

91.Hans L. Trefousse, Lincoln's Decision for Emancipation, p. 41

92.James J. Barnes and Patience P. Barnes, editors, The American Civil War through British Eyes: Dispatches from British Diplomats, April 1862-February 1863, Volume II, p. 189 (Letter from William Stuart to Lord Russell, September 28, 1862).

93.Howard Jones, Abraham Lincoln and a New Birth of Freedom: The Union and Slavery in the Diplomacy of the Civil War, p. 116.

94.Allen C. Guelzo, "How Abe Lincoln Lost the Black Vote: Lincoln and Emancipation in the African American Mind," Journal of the Abraham Lincoln Association, Winter 2004, p. 3.

95.Richard Allen Heckman, "British Press Reaction to the Emancipation Proclamation," Lincoln Herald, Winter 1969, p. 150.

96.Richard Allen Heckman, "British Press Reaction to the Emancipation Proclamation," Lincoln Herald , Winter 1969, p. 153.

97.A. Curtis Wilgus, "Some Views of President Lincoln Held by the London Times," 1861 to 1865," Journal of the Illinois State Historical Association, April-July, 1924, p. 163.

98.Allen C. Guelzo, Lincoln's Emancipation Proclamation: The End of Slavery in America, p. 225.

99.Hans L. Trefousse, "First Among Equals" Abraham Lincoln's Reputation During His Administration, p. 62.

100.Howard Jones, Abraham Lincoln and a New Birth of Freedom: The Union and Slavery in the Diplomacy of the Civil War, pp. 156-157.

101.Dean B. Mahin, One War at a Time: The International Dimensions of the American Civil War, p. 138.

102.James J. Barnes and Patience P. Barnes, editors, The American Civil War through British Eyes: Dispatches from British Diplomats, April 1862-February 1863, Volume II, p. 266 (Letter from William Stuart to Lord Russell, December 9, 1862).

103.Burton J. Hendrick, Statesmen of the Lost Cause, pp. 277-278, 279-280.

104.Burton J. Hendrick, Statesmen of the Lost Cause, pp. 277-278, 279-280.

105.Howard Jones, Abraham Lincoln and a New Birth of Freedom: The Union and Slavery in the Diplomacy of the Civil War, p. 63.

106.Roy F. Nichols, The Stakes of Power, 1845-1877, p. 126.

107.Don E. and Virginia Fehrenbacher, editor, Recollected Words of Abraham Lincoln, p. 182.

108.Rufus Rockwell Wilson, editor, Intimate Memories of Lincoln, p. 522 (James M. Scovel, Lippincott's Monthly Magazine, August 1889, February 1893, February 1899).

109. John G. Nicolay and John Hay, Abraham Lincoln, Volume VI, p. 99.

110.David P. Crook, The North, the South and the Powers, p. 193.

111.Howard Jones, Abraham Lincoln and a New Birth of Freedom: The Union & Slavery in the Diplomacy of the Civil War, p. 65.

112.A. Taylor Milne, "The Lyons-Seward Treaty of 1862, The American Historical Review, April 1933, p. 513.

113.A. Taylor Milne, "The Lyons-Seward Treaty of 1862, The American Historical Review, April 1933, p. 514.

114.A. Taylor Milne, "The Lyons-Seward Treaty of 1862, The American Historical Review, April 1933, p. 516.

115.Don E. and Virginia E. Fehrenbacher, editors, Recollected Words of Abraham Lincoln, p. 308.

116.CWAL, Volume VI, pp. 63-65 (Petition of Workingmen of Manchester, December 31, 1862).

117.CWAL, Volume VI, pp. 63-65 (Reply to the Workingmen of Manchester, England, January 19, 1863).

118.Francis B. Carpenter, Six Months at the White House, pp. 76-77.

119.David P. Crook, The North, the South and the Powers, p. 195.

120.Dean B. Mahin, One War at a Time: The International Dimensions of the American Civil War, p. 193.

121.Jay Monaghan, Diplomat in Carpet Slippers: Abraham Lincoln Deals with Foreign Affairs, p. 323.

122.Frederick W. Seward, Reminiscences of a War-Time Diplomat, p. 237.

123.Jay Monaghan, Diplomat in Carpet Slippers: Abraham Lincoln Deals with Foreign Affairs, p. 354.

124.Howard Jones, Abraham Lincoln and a New Birth of Freedom: The Union and Slavery in the Diplomacy of the Civil War, p. 183.

125.Benjamin Thomas, "A Russian Estimate of Lincoln," Bulletin of the Abraham Lincoln Association, June 1931.

126.Ben Perley Poore, Perley's Reminiscences, Volume II, pp. 98-99.

127.Richard J. Carwardine, Lincoln: Profiles in Power, p. 178

128.Carl Sandburg, Abraham Lincoln, The War Years, Volume IV, p. 193.

129.Carl Sandburg, Abraham Lincoln: The War Years, Volume II, p. 238

130.Gideon Welles, Diary of Gideon Welles, Volume I, pp. 286-287 (April 28, 1863).

131.Justin G. Turner and Linda Levitt Turner, editors, Mary Todd Lincoln: Her Life and Letters, p. 185.

132.Alexander K. McClure, Lincoln's Own Yarns and Stories, p. 329

133.Norman B. Ferris, Desperate Diplomacy, p. 17.

134.Norman B. Ferris, "Lincoln and Seward in Civil War Diplomacy: Their Relationship at the Outset Reexamined," Journal of the Abraham Lincoln Association, 1991, pp. 35-37.

135.James A. Rawley, The Politics of Union: Northern Politics During the Civil War, pp. 103, 102.

136.Burton J. Hendrick, Lincoln's War Cabinet, pp. 253-255.

137.Bernard C. Steiner, Life of Henry Winter Davis, p. 230.

138.William C. Harris, Lincoln's Last Months, pp. 163, 165.

139.John Y. Simon, Harold Holzer, and Dawn Vogel, editors, Lincoln Revisited, p. 281 (William C. Harris, "After Lincolns' Reelection Foreign Complications").

140.Dean B. Mahin, One War at a Time: The International Dimensions of the American Civil War, p. 258.

141.James A. Rawley, Abraham Lincoln and a Nation Worth Fighting For, p. 158.

142.Norman A. Graebner, editor, The Enduring Lincoln, p. 54 (David H Donald, "Abraham Lincoln: "Whig in the White House").

143.Dean B. Mahin, One War at a Time: The International Dimensions of the American Civil War, p. 262.

144.Don E. and Virginia Fehrenbacher, editors, The Recollected Words of Abraham Lincoln, p. 308.

Endnotes

1 Sourced from the Library of Congress, Washington D.C.
2 Huelsmann to Rechberg Feb. 7 1861 Austrian National Archives
3 Ibid
4 Henry Salomon, Paris ambassador for Metternich, Austrian archives
5 Austrian archives
6 Ibid
7 Ibid

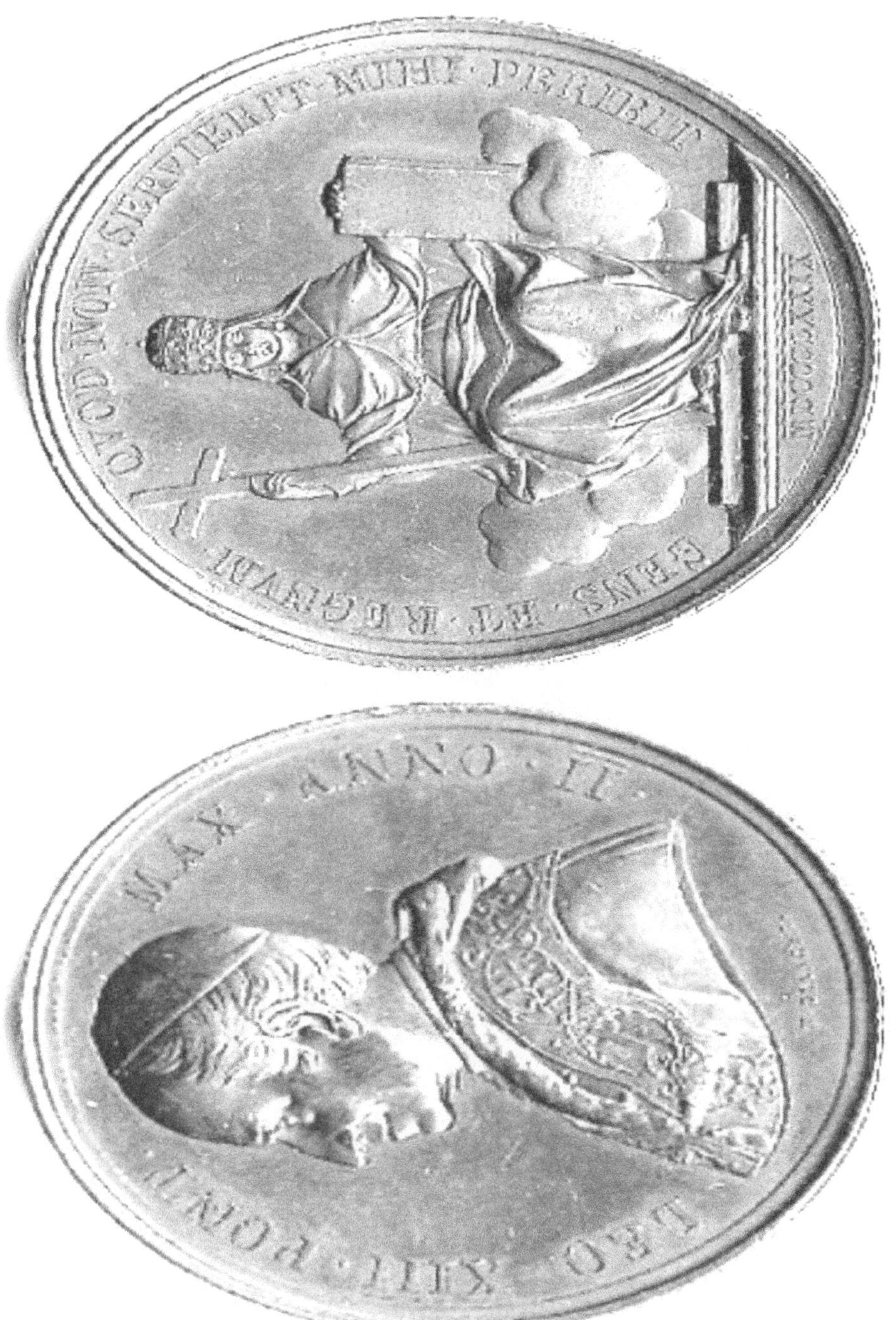

Medal of Pope Leo XIII Latin inscription reads:
"The Kingdom or Nation that refuses to serve me will PERISH"
Dec. 25, 1891 he issued an eternal order to launch a religious war on U.S. soil

Pandering to the Irish Catholic Vote

Chapter 6

Pius IX and the Catholic monarchs maneuvering in the U.S.; a study of Cardinal Antonelli; The Papal States; Catholic justification of slavery; Lincoln is faced with war; Lincoln shares his concerns with Charles Chiniquy

That Pope Pius IX conspired with Napoleon III to take advantage of the conflict between the North and the South in the United States and to with one blow destroy both Popular Governments of Mexico and the U.S. is beyond question.

During the years from 1864 to '65 the activity of these Jesuits in Europe was redoubled. There is no doubt that they were not in close touch with every step and phase of the Rebellion in the United States. In 1856 Prince Maximilian of Austria, was called to Rome where a marriage had been arranged through ecclesiastical and royal intrigue between himself and the Princess Carlotta, daughter of King Leopold II of Belgium, thus uniting two of the strongest Catholic powers in Europe.

The next step was the marriage of this royal couple in the Cathedral at Vienna. In April 1864, by the orders of the pope, they were crowned Emperor and Empress of Mexico at Pontifical High Mass and amidst great rejoicing. On April 14, 1864, just one year to the day, previous to Lincoln's assassination, this royal couple set sail in an Austrian ship of war for Mexico. They put in at Cevita Vecchia, the port in the Papal States, and were received at the Vatican by the most elaborate ceremonies, which had ever been extended by a pope to royalty. After several days of these honors and being loaded down with the papal blessings they again resumed their journey across the Atlantic.

Maximilian had been, during a previous visit to Napoleon III and his Empress Eugenie, assured of the assistance of thirty thousand French and Belgian troops for his invasion into Mexico, the specific object of which was the destruction of the young Republic already established under Juarez. These troops were poured in and were being supported by the Mexican people. It had been impressed upon Maximilian at the Vatican that his first official act must be the complete restoration of all the Church property and ecclesiastical rights of the clergy, which had been confiscated by the Liberal government.

After the conquest of Mexico the plan was for this imperialistic commander "Emperor" Maximilian, to join Jefferson Davis and Confederate troops at Richmond where they would sweep north and capture Washington.

Davis had made a strong appeal in 1863 in a letter to the Pope, and after the reply, which he promptly received from 'His Holiness' a wholesale desertion of the Irish Catholic troops of the North to the Confederacy followed as was shown earlier. I would now like to take a survey of conditions, which existed in the Papal States prior to and during the Civil War where the popes of Rome had been in supreme command for over fourteen hundred years. Certainly, fourteen hundred years ought to be sufficient for a thorough test of the merits of a system. Pius IX was elected in 1846. There had been three popes in the interim between him and Pius VII who had restored the Jesuits and called the congress of Vienna in 1814. There was no change in policy however, nor any laxness in regard to the attitude of the church towards its obligations to the "high contracting parties" of the Holy Alliance and their Treaty of Verona.

Of all his predecessors Pius IX was one of the most reactionary, and in his notorious Syllabus, which was proclaimed to a startled world in December 1864, he anathematized every fundamental principle upon which the United States is based. The historians are inclined to place all of the blame of his mistakes, and there were many, upon his Secretary of State, Cardinal Antonelli, who was beyond doubt "the power behind the throne", the agent for the "Black" pope. Antonelli is far more interesting as a character study than the "White" pope, inasmuch as he was so deeply interested in the affairs of the United States during the war.

I will take the liberty of reproducing some graphic pen pictures by the distinguished French journalist, M. About, who made a personal visit to the Papal States to learn, firsthand, if the astounding reports from the Italian Revolutionists, which had been pouring into the European press for several years, were correct, M. About's book "*The Roman Question*" is intensely interesting and written in the peculiarly piquant style of the brilliant Frenchman. It has been out of print for almost two hundred years, as has most of the material I reference in this book, and is difficult and expensive to secure as the Leopoldines had bought up every copy at the time.

His visit to the Papal States was made in 1859, the same year that Abraham Lincoln was making his political campaigns for the presidency, and immortalizing himself by his debate with Judge Douglas, on the Dred Scott Decision of Judge Roger E. Taney.

May 17, 1893. **The Presbyterian.**

LAFAYETTE'S PROPHECY.

BY JULIA W. DE WITT.

"If the liberties of the American people are ever destroyed they will fall by the hands of the Romish clergy." These words were uttered by General Lafayette, who, although a Romanist by birth and education, proved his love for this country and her institutions by his deeds, and has left on record his admiration for, and faith in, its civil and religious freedom.

It is our boast, as a nation, that the Constitution of the United States guarantees liberty to each of its citizens, and yet we have recently witnessed the arrival of a Papal Delegate at our National Capital, not only invested with supreme authority, but the Pope has caused to be published, throughout the land, that this Pontiff has the power to inflict any sentence he may see fit on certain of our citizens, "notwithstanding *constitutions*, apostolic ordinances, or any other, to the contrary."

We might lay the flattering unction to our souls that there is some ambiguity in the phraseology of this mandate, did we not recall the denunciations of a preceding Pope upon the "absurd doctrines in defense of liberty of conscience," which he characterized as "pests of all others most to be dreaded," and the still more pointed assertion of one of his bishops, that "religious liberty is merely endured until the opposite can be carried into effect without peril to the Catholic world."

Page after page of similar utterances might be quoted, but a glance at Europe during the Dark Ages will prove how, realizing that knowledge was power, Rome kept that power within her grasp by preventing the diffusion of learning, and used the ignorance and superstition of the masses for the furtherance of her interests and increase of her wealth. These ages form too dark a page of history for Americans to close their eyes to the growth of principles of which they were the legitimate sequence; but with prosperity we have grown luxuriously indolent, and it is easier to float with the tide than to stem it.

The enthronement of Satolli at Washington with the pomp and insignia of power has added to, rather than detracted from the fascination of our capital; and the Pontiff and his attendants, radiant in purple and scarlet, and flashing with diamonds, are central figures at elegant dinners and gorgeous assemblies. The admiring crowds that gather around him think little of how his gems were purchased, or who supports his regal magnificence, and the glittering pageant goes on, while republican simplicity and liberty move toward the grave, as the French warrior predicted long years ago.

While hope was dying within us during the late Civil War our commander-in-chief was planning the most masterly strategy the world has ever known, and when the enemy was unitedly attacked at all points the end of our protracted struggle was at hand.

A single glance at the North, West, South and East of our land will give us some idea of the progress of the hierarchy, which is massing its forces of wealth and learning at Washington.

Last summer I saw how rapidly convents and Roman Catholic schools were springing up along our side of the St. Lawrence river; and receiving an invitation to join a party of six hundred pilgrims on their road to the shrine of St. Ann de Beaupre, my curiosity became excited; and upon inquiry, I learned that from fifty to sixty thousand devotees visit this church annually, and a large proportion are from our northern counties, and from New England.

Rome has been adding to her missions on our Western border to supply the spiritual wants of its rapidly-increasing population; and Miss Drexel's millions, together with the labors of the self-sacrificing women she has gathered around her, are not now confined to the Indians, but are extending to the representatives of all nationalities, who are cordially welcomed into the Church of which she is so devoted a member.

Among the descendants of the French and creole families of the South there are women who are developing characteristics similar to those of Miss Drexel, and devoting both their time and talents to the work that Rome is so vigorously pushing among the Freedmen, as well as the whites, of the South.

Turning from these pictures to New England, we are not a little surprised to hear, from one of her sons, how, as if by magic, cathedrals and pro-cathedrals are springing up in close proximity to her mills and manufactories, and that the welcome that is extended to employers and employees is being responded to, even by those who once boasted their Puritan blood.

Patiently and persistently Rome and her children are working for the increase of Papal power; are we, who profess to be followers of Christ, working as faithfully to lead souls into the liberty wherewith he makes his children free? In the light of the Saviour's example, our duty is a plain one, for he sent his disciples "into every city and place whither he himself would come." There was no spot so dark and degraded that he did not go into it, and no being so wretched and despised that he had not a share in the love and pity of the Master; and down through the ages his words come to us in tones of mingled command and compassion, "Lift up your eyes, and lo[ok] on the fields, for they are white already to harves[t]

The great Italian poet and patriot, Mazzini, was an exile, living in a London attic, pouring out his soul's most noble appeals to the Liberals of Europe. The Pope's government had confiscated his large property holdings in Italy. The Carlysles had visited him in his attic and through their friendship he was brought from the miserable surroundings and ensconced in comfortable quarters, where the most distinguished literati of London and Paris visited him and were captivated by his remarkable talents and his sincere patriotism and completely won over by his irresistible arguments for a free and united Italy.

THAT CATHOLIC UPRISING.

TO THE EDITOR: There is quite an excitement about the Catholics rising and taking possession of the Government. I see that neither your paper nor other leading papers say much about it. I would be glad if you would give your views on the subject in your paper. Yours truly, JAMES W. YOUNG.
DELAVAN, Faribault Co., Minn.

We have seen a good many very strong statements in a certain class of papers to the effect that Catholics are arming and drilling all over the country in preparation for an uprising this Fall, when the Protestants are to be slaughtered without mercy and the sovereignty of this country is to be transferred to the Pope. This glorious act of Catholic emancipation is to take place, according to these papers, in pursuance of a command issued by the Pope last year in an encyclical letter, which is published in support of the statement that the rising is to take place.

All this sounds very dreadful, but the really dreadful thing about it is that men who claim to be servants of Christ are capable of circulating so monstrous a slander against millions of their fellow-citizens. The whole story is so preposterous as to be unworthy of the slightest attention on its own merits.

The spirit of persecution exists to-day as much as ever it did in the claims of the Roman Catholic Church, but the wide circulation of the Bible among the people has chained that spirit, as John Bunyan tells us, so that it has no longer the power to incite men to do such deeds. If the Pope should issue such an encyclical the great body of the Roman Catholics of America would indignantly refuse to obey, and the Pope would not be so stupid as to throw away his influence by turning his own supporters against him, even if he would like to see such a movement carried out.

The editors who are industriously circulating this slander should be compelled to prove their words or suffer the penalty imposed on slanderers, but they are careful not to place themselves within reach of the law by accusing indviiduals.

The exile Garibaldi, with his "Redshirted Legion," had answered the call of his country after a sojourn in the United States where he had also lived in an attic in New York City, following the humble profession of a candle maker, saving up his money.

One day he suddenly closed his attic door and disappeared as mysteriously as he had come. The great soldier patriot returned to Italy by the way of London and one of his most brilliant conquests was the capture of the hearts of the people of London. The red-blooded staunch Protestants not only of the city itself, but from all over England, came to welcome the man who had returned to offer his sword against the Papal yoke. They went wild with delight. Garibaldi, with his yellow flowing hair under his big slouch hat was lifted up to the shoulders of the crowd, mad with joy which surged about him, and carried as though his great form was but the weight of a feather.

This was an insult and an unforgivable sin in the eyes of the Jesuits, and the Vatican, which aroused the hatred for the English Protestant nation, a hatred which was to last for many decades.

One might presume under the circumstances that the Pope would have been too occupied with his own affairs to have meddled with the politics of the United States, at such a time.

The clever Frenchman, M. Dupin, has said:

> "Le Jesuitism est un epee dont la poingee est a Rome, et la point partout" –
>
> Jesuitism is a sword whose hilt is in Rome and it points everywhere. (1)

Gladstone had visited the Papal States in 1850 and on his return to England, had reported to his government and the London Press that the Papal government was "The negation of God."

In the preface of this book, M. About says:

"It was in the Papal States that I studied the Roman Question. I traveled over every part of the country; I conversed with men of all opinions, examined things very closely, and collected my information on the spot."

"The pressing condition of Italy has obliged me to write more rapidly than I could have wished; and this enforced haste has given me a certain air of warmth, perhaps of intemperance, even to the most carefully matured reflections... I fight fairly and in good faith. I do not pretend to have judged the foes of Italy without passion; but I have calumniated none of them."

"If", he continues, "I have sought a publisher in Brussels, while I had an excellent one in Paris, it is not because I feel any alarm on the score of the regulations of our press, or the severity of our tribunals. But as the Pope has a long arm that might reach me in France, I have gone a little out of the way to tell him the plain truths in these pages." (2)

And now for the "plain truths" about his Secretary of State, the Cardinal Deacon, Antonelli.

"He was born among thieves. His native place Sonnino, is more celebrated in the history of crime, than all Arcadia, in the annals of virtue. This nest of vultures was hidden in the southern mountains, toward the Neapolitan frontier. Roads, impractical to mounted dragoons, winding through brakes and thickets; forests impenetrable to the stranger; deep ravines and gloomy caverns-all combine to form a most desirable landscape for the convenience of crime.

"The houses of Sonnino, old, ill built, flung pell-mell, one upon the other, and almost uninhabitable by human beings, were, in point of fact, little else than depots of pillage and magazines of rapine. The population, alert and vigorous, had for many centuries practiced armed robberies, and depredation had gained its livelihood at the point of the carbine."

"Newborn infants inhaled a contempt of the law with the mountain air, and drew in the love of others goods, with their mother's milk. Almost as soon as they could walk, they assumed cioccie, or moccasins of untanned leather, with which they learned to run fearlessly along the ledge of the giddiest mountain precipices. When they had acquired the art of pursuing and escaping, of taking without being taken, the knowledge of the value of different coins, the arithmetic of the distribution of booty, and the principles of the rights of nations, as they are practiced among the Apaches or the Comanche's, their education was deemed complete...

"In the year of grace 1806, this sensual, brutal, impious, superstitious, ignorant and cunning race, endowed Italy with a little mountaineer, known as Giacomo Antonelli. Hawks do not hatch doves. This is an axiom in natural history, which has no need of demonstration. Had Giacomo Antonelli been gifted with simple virtues of an Arcadian shepherd, his village would have instantly disowned him. But the influence of certain events modified his conduct, although they failed to modify his nature."

"If he received his first lessons from successful brigandage, his next teachers were the gendarmerie. When he was hardly four years old, the discharge of a high moral lesson shook his ears; it was the French troops who were shooting brigands in the outskirts of Sonnino."

"After the return of Pius VII, he witnessed the decapitation of a few neighboring relatives who had dandled him on their knees. Under Leo XII, it was still worse. The wholesome correctives of the wooden horse were permanently established in the village square...St. Peter's Gate, which adjoins the house of Antonelli, was ornamented with a garland of human heads, which...grinned dogmatically enough in their iron cages... Young Giacomo was enabled to reflect upon the inconveniences of brigandage, even before he had tasted its sweets...He hesitated for some time as to the choice of a calling. His natural vocation was that of the inhabitants of Sonnino...to live in plenty, to enjoy every sort of pleasure, to rule others, to frighten them if necessary, but above all to violate laws with immunity."

"With the view of obtaining so lofty an end, without endangering his life, for which he had ever a most particular regard, he entered the great seminary of Rome."

That is a beautiful picture of the next highest prelate to the Pope, is it not? So much for the early years of Antonelli. But permit me to quote again from the pen of the author of "*The Roman Question*," who, as we know, was an eyewitness:

"No country in Europe is more richly gifted, or possesses greater advantages, whether for agriculture, manufacture or commerce...

"Traversed by the Apennines, which divide it about equally, the Papal dominions incline gently, on one side the Adriatic, on the other the Mediterranean. In each of the seas they possess an excellent port: to the east, Ancona; to the west, Civita Vecchia...If Panurge had had these ports in his kingdom, he would have infallibly built himself a navy...The Phoenicians and Carthaginians were not so well off.

"A river tolerably well-known under the name of the Tiber, waters nearly the whole country to the west. In former days it ministered to the wants of internal commerce. Roman historians describe it as navigable up to Perugia. At the present time it is hardly so far as Rome; but if its bed were cleared out, and the filth not allowed to be thrown in, it would render greater service and would not overflow so often.

"In 1847, the country lands subject to the Pope were valued at about 34,800,000 pounds sterling...the Minister of Public Works and Commerce admitted that the property was not estimated at above a third of its real value. If capital returned its proper interest, if activity and industry caused trade and manufactures to increase, the national income, as ought to be the case, it would be the Rothschild's who would borrow money from the Pope at six percent interest."

Empress Carlotta

As a matter of fact the Papacy was heavily indebted to the Rothschild's upon which About throws a high light further on.

> "But, stay," he continues, "I have not yet completed the catalogue of possessions. To the munificence of nature, must be added the inheritance of the past. The

poor Pagans of great Rome left all their property to the Pope who damns them.

"They left him gigantic aqueducts, prodigious sewers and roads which we find still in use, after twenty centuries of traffic. They left him the Coliseum, for his Capuchins to preach in. They left him an example of an administration without equal in history. But the heritage was accepted without the responsibilities."

That is a bird's eye view of the Papal States in the early eighteenth century, when the United States was having their blind struggle with the Papacy for the national existence of their country.

In his chapter on Plebeians, M. About had this to say:

"The subjects of the Holy Father are divided by birth and fortune into three very distinct classes - nobility, citizens, and people, or plebeians.

"The Gospel has omitted to consecrate the inequality of men, but the law of the state – that is to say, the will of the Popes - carefully maintains it. Benedict XIV declared it honorable and salutary in his Bull of January 4, 1746, and Pius IX expressed himself in the same terms at the beginning of his Chirografo of May 2, 1853"

Add to this a quote from *The New World*, the official organ of the Roman Catholic Church in the Archdiocese of Chicago, Ill., which was a comment on the Federation of Catholic Societies held at New Orleans in 1910:

"Human society has its origin from God and is constituted of two classes of people, rich and poor, which respectively represents Capital and Labor. Hence it follows that according to the ordinance of God, human society is composed of two classes, superiors and subjects, masters and servants, learned and unlettered, rich and poor, nobles and plebeians." (3)

Diomede Falconio, the Pope's Legate to the United States, who uttered the above divine right stance on that occasion, was at the time a naturalized citizen of the United States. Falconio was instructing the subjects of the Pope in the United States, at the New Orleans

Convention, that a government based on popular support is not worthy of "favor or support." (See Leo XIII Great Encyclicals, pg. 126.)

The Roman Church in the United States taught its subjects a separate citizenship inimical to American citizenship that the sole authority to rule must come from the consent of the ruled.

Cardinal Antonelli

This was the same Divine right idea, which rent the country from stem to stern in 1860, which gashed its fair face with the Mason-Dixon line. This was the same teaching that swept Abraham Lincoln from the face of the earth at the most critical time in his nation's history. This was the "Roman Question" which Lincoln understood and defined so thoroughly in his campaign with Douglas, the Leopoldine, the defender of slavery, who was chosen, whether consciously or unconsciously, to champion the cause of class distinction in the country, which they sought to destroy.

> "That is the issue that will continue in this country when the poor tongues of Judge Douglas and myself shall be silent.
>
> "It is the eternal struggle between these two principles - right and wrong - throughout the world. They are

> the two principles that have stood face to face from the beginning of time, and will ever continue to struggle.
>
> "The one is the common right of humanity and the other, the divine right of kings...it is the same spirit that says: 'You work and toil and earn bread and I'll eat it,' no matter in what shape it comes...it is the same tyrannical principle." (Lincoln's Speech at Alton, Ill., October 15, 1858)

Abraham Lincoln was the living embodiment of "the common right of humanity." In his life the perfection of the "New Idea" had been materialized, had become a living, breathing fact, which was unconquerable and unassailable.

Lincoln knew the struggle would go on, after "these poor tongues of Judge Douglas and myself shall be silent." Listen to the words of Lincoln as Charles Chiniquy recorded them in his "*Fifty Years in the Church of Rome*":

> "I do not pretend to be a prophet. But though not a prophet, I see a very dark cloud on our horizon. That dark cloud is coming from Rome. It will be filled with tears of blood. It will rise, and increase, till its flanks will be torn by a flash of lightening, followed by a fearful peal of thunder. Then a cyclone such as the world has never seen will pass over this country, spreading ruin and desolation from north to south. After it is over, there will be long days of peace and prosperity; for popery with its Jesuitism and merciless Inquisition, will have been forever swept away from our country. Neither you, nor I, but our children will live to see these things." (4)

Certainly, no president of the Republic of the United States was ever beset with so many staggering problems as President Lincoln. The more we study those perilous years, the more we wonder at his great wisdom, firmness and boundless patience and charity.

The Ultra-Pro-Slavery leaders had sworn to prevent the seating of Abraham Lincoln in the Presidential chair. So certain were they of the success of their plans that just as Buchanan was leaving the White House, before the arrival of Mr. Lincoln, he turned and said,

"As George Washington was the first President, so James Buchanan will be the last President of the United States." (5)

Roman Catholic General George Meade – After entertaining a Jesuit in his camp after the Battle of Gettysburg, according to C. Chiniquy, allowed his allegiance to the Pope to supersede his allegiance to the country and refused to chase after Lee. He diverted a full 1/3 of his army to go to New York to quell the draft riots perpetrated by Archbishop John Hughes. This allowed Lee to wage war for 2 more years.

Mr. Lincoln had no idea of the rottenness and treason that were there to face him in Washington. A traitor to the Government headed almost every department in Washington, for the plotters had been placing their tools preparatory to the final blow.

The first months of his administration were spent in investigating these national assassins, and replacing them with men who were true. This, in itself, was a task that only the judgment of Lincoln could have accomplished.

Mr. Lincoln had no idea of the dimensions of the Secession plot. He was later to find that his first call for 75,000 volunteers was inadequate and was amazed when the Governors of three Southern States refused to send their quota.

Another disillusionment came when he noted that as he increased his calls for troops, Jefferson Davis did not send out any call. From then on Lincoln began to realize something of the seriousness of the situation and his last call was for "three years or during the war." Southern leaders also realized the fact that they were up against the real thing.

When President Lincoln reached Philadelphia for his first inauguration, there was a plot discovered and disclosed to General John Hancock at Washington to assassinate Mr. Lincoln at Baltimore, where he was to have stopped to address the citizens on his way to the Capitol. The full details had been planned. An Italian barber well known in Baltimore, a Catholic, was to have stabbed him while he was seated in his carriage, when he started from the depot.

The son of William H. Seward, who was at that time Senator and afterwards Lincoln's Secretary of State, was sent post haste to Philadelphia to warn Mr. Lincoln of his danger. It was a difficult matter at first to convince him of the seriousness of it. He flatly refused to go to Washington immediately, as was suggested by his friends, but promised after he had raised the flag on Independence Hall in Philadelphia, and delivered an address to the members of the Legislature at Harrisburg, he would take an earlier train to Washington, which he did, accompanied by only one friend, Wade C. Lammon, one of his law partners, and William H. Pinkerton, head of the Detective Agency of that name in Chicago. The party took the six o'clock train out of Philadelphia, quietly without attracting any publicity, and as Mr. Lincoln was soundly sleeping, the train whizzed through Baltimore, and got him to Washington early in the morning, where he was taken in charge by the largest military and Secret Service escort a president ever had.

The awakening of the president and the North came on the morning of April 12, 1861 with the firing on Fort Sumter. General Beauregard, Jesuit leader of the military operations, sent this opening shot of the rebellion. Beauregard was a professed Romanist and sprung from a distinguished family of Jesuits.

The North was wholly unprepared for war. They seemed not to have been able to realize that there could ever be a conflict between the citizens of the United States. This delusion was shot to pieces on April 12, and amidst the greatest consternation and excitement preparations began in earnest.

That President Lincoln fully realized it was not a Protestant South with which he was contending, is evidenced from his own words on the subject in his conversation with the Reverend Charles Chiniquy, ex-Catholic priest of Kankakee, Illinois, who called once each year during the administration of Lincoln to warn him of his danger of assassination by the enemies of Popular Government and their agents.

Again I quote from Chiniquy's book "*Fifty Years in the Church of Rome*" in which Lincoln, while touring the field hospitals with his dear friend, states;

> "This war would never have been possible without the sinister influence of the Jesuits. We owe it to Popery that we now see our land reddened with the blood of her noblest sons. Though there were great differences of opinion between the North and the South on the question of slavery, neither Jeff Davis nor any of the leading men of the Confederacy would have dared to attack the North had they not relied on the promises of the Jesuits, that, under the mask of democracy, the money and the arms of the Roman Catholics, even the arms of France, were at their disposal, if they would attack us. I pity the priests, the bishops and the monks and nuns of Rome in the United States, when the people realize that they are, in large part, responsible for the tears and the blood shed in this war. I conceal what I know, for if the people knew the whole truth, this war would turn into a religious war, and at once, take a tenfold more savage and bloody character. It would become merciless as all religious wars are. It would become a war of extermination on both sides.
>
> "The Protestants of both the North and the South, would surely unite to exterminate the priests and the Jesuits if they could hear what Professor Morse has said to me of the plots made in the very city of Rome to destroy this Republic, and if they could learn how the priests, the monks and the nuns, which daily land on our shores under the pretext of preaching their religion and instructing the people in their schools, are nothing else than the emissaries of the Pope, of Napoleon, and the other despots of Europe, to undermine our institutions, alienate the hearts of our people from our Constitution, and our laws, destroy our schools, and prepare a reign of anarchy here as they have done in Ireland, in Mexico, in Spain, and wherever there are any people who want to be free.
>
> "Many things I have learned in these last few years, both from Mr. Morse and from you, Charles. That is, it is with the Southern leaders of this civil war as with the big and small wheels of our railroad cars. Those who ignore the laws of mechanics are apt to think that the large, strong, and noisy wheels they see are the motive power, but they are mistaken. The real motive power is not seen; it is noiseless and well concealed, in the dark, behind its iron walls. The motive power are the few well concealed

pails of water heated into steam, which is itself directed by the noiseless, small, but unerring engineer's finger.

"The common people see and hear the big, noisy wheels of the Southern Confederacy's cars: they call them Jeff Davis, Lee, Toombs, Beauregard, Semmes and others and they honestly think they are the motive power, the first cause of our troubles. But this is a mistake. The true motive power is secreted behind the thick walls of the Vatican, the colleges and schools of the Jesuits, the convents of the nuns and the confessional boxes of Rome.

"There is a fact which is too much ignored by the American people, and with which I am acquainted only since I became president; it is that the best, the leading families of the South have received their education in great part, if not in whole, from the Jesuits and the nuns. Hence those degrading principles of slavery, pride and cruelty, which are as second nature among many of those people. Hence that strange want of fair play, humanity; that implacable hatred against the ideas of equality and liberty as we find them in the Gospel of Christ. You do not ignore that the first settlers of Louisiana, Florida, New Mexico, Texas, South California and Missouri were Roman Catholics, and that their first teachers were Jesuits. It is true that those states have been conquered or bought by us since. But Rome had put the deadly virtues of her anti-social and anti-Christian maxims into the veins of the people before they became American citizens. Unfortunately, the Jesuits and the nuns have in great part remained the teachers of those people ever since. They have continued in a silent, but most effectatious way, to spread their hatred against our institutions, our laws, our schools, our rights and our liberties in such a way that this terrible conflict became unavoidable between the North and the South.

"Charles, I would have laughed at the man who would have told me that before I became president. But Professor Morse and to a large extent, you, have opened my eyes on that subject. And now I see that mystery, I understand that engineering of hell, which though not seen nor even suspected by the country, is putting in motion the large, heavy and noisy wheels of the state cars of the Southern Confederacy. Our people are not yet ready to learn these dark mysteries of hell; it would throw oil on a fire, which is already sufficiently destructive."

> "You are almost the only one with whom I speak freely on that subject. But sooner or later the nation will know the real origin of those rivers of blood and tears, which are spreading desolation and death everywhere. And then those who have caused those desolations and disasters will be called to give an account of them." (6)

Surely, no clearer conception of the masked enemy with which that great man was contending was ever glimpsed. While other men studied books, Lincoln studied men, and the above interpretation of the terrible conflict in which he was the Commander-in-Chief is startling in its accuracy. It is very simple now for those of us who have the knowledge of an array of facts before us, to see what Lincoln then saw, but we must remember when he spoke those words, he was the very storm center and chief actor in the social upheaval without the advantage of hindsight. Lincoln, however, was not completely in the dark insofar as Jesuit and Catholic intrigue was concerned apart from his friend Chiniquy. From the *U.S. War Department's Official Records of the Union and Confederate Armies in the War of the Rebellion* comes this telling article of correspondence just prior to the draft in which it was asserted that the followers of Archbishop John Hughes was ultimately responsible for the riots in New York:

HDQRS. THIRTEENTH DISTRICT OF NEW YORK,
Kingston, July 14, 1863.

Col. JAMES B. FRY

Provost-Marshal-General:

SIR: I desire to submit the following facts in relation to this district:

During the progress of the enrollment the enrolling officer was obstructed in the performance of his duties at various times in the village of Rondout, also in the west part of this town, **both localities largely settled by the Irish people. This resistance was mostly made by the Irish women.** But for this I should have arrested the parties engaged in this disturbance.

I called upon the Catholic priest, who assured me that all he could do to restore order should be done. After this better order prevailed. By careful management and stratagem we succeeded in making the enrollment. I had hoped that order would prevail.

I am creditably informed this morning that a large meeting was held at Rondout last evening, mostly made up of the Irish. At that meeting resolutions were adopted to resist the draft at all and any hazard, and today men are seen at various places in small groups making threats of resistance, &c. Rondout is one mile and a half from these headquarters.

I have consulted with General Samson, the only military officer in this district. He has no military at his command save one horse company, and that is wholly made up of Germans.

I submit these facts to you for your consideration. I desire that the business in this district should be done decently and in order. Again, we have no arms in this district and are wholly unprotected except my deputy and two special officers.

I am, sir, your obedient servant,

JOSHUA FIERO JR.,
Captain and Provost-Marshal

Lincoln was warned repeatedly, from many people, about the threat of assassination. I present here a letter from a friend in 1860, just prior to Lincoln's election:

From Oliver H. P. Parker to Abraham Lincoln,

September 1860

Mr. Lincoln, will you please read the accompanying document, which is not an application for office, but is on the subject of the preservation of his life and health, and future welfare. Although you may have had warnings of the same nature, the writer thinks perhaps there are certain facts therein contained that cannot be otherwise obtained,

No. 310 New Street Philadelphia, September 7th 1860.

Dear Sir

You will excuse the liberty I have taken, of addressing you without a personal acquaintance, or a formal introduction:—As you are the candidate of the party of which I have the pleasure of being a member. (You thereby becoming public property,) I do not feel as though I was committing a breach of etiquette, by addressing you on a subject that I think is of vital importance to yourself, and one that I hope you will give due consideration and act accordingly:—

If the Political signs of the times are not deceptive, you will be duly and constitutionally, Elected President of the United States; at our coming Election by a majority of your fellow citizens:—If Such shall be the case, it becomes necessary that you shall be duly inaugurated into office, and that your life and health shall be preserved, to carry out the doctrines, and principles on which you will be elected:—

Now Sir in my humble opinion it will require on your part, if elected the greatest vigilance, and precaution to preserve, your life and health, and it is to that end, that I write, to give you due warning of what I fear will be your end unless you are most watchful and vigilant on that subject:—

I have given the subject of the very sudden, and I may say, mysterious deaths of some of our free State Presidents, and the sudden Political somersets of the vice Presidents who by law succeeded them to the Presidency, much thought, and a very thorough private investigation, and I think a stronger case can be made out, in favor of the theory I am about to advance to you, by circumstantial evidences, and remarkable coincidences, than has suspended many a poor creature between Heaven and Earth by our Courts of justice:—

In 1840 a National convention of the old Whig Party met at Harrisburg Pennsylvania to nominate candidates for President and Vice President, and at that time the feelings of a large portion of the Whigs were for the nomination of Henry Clay, but the convention in its wisdom and for expediency concluded to give that great man Henry Clay the go by, and nominated Gen. Harrison, and I believe that if you will refer to the vote of that Convention, you will find that Gen. Harrison's vote was exclusively from the free states, and that the votes of every southern delegate in that convention was cast against Harrison (unanimously) and when the convention came to the nomination of a candidate for Vice President John Tyler, a hypocritical Virginia slave owner, who shed crocodile tears because Henry Clay was not nominated for President, was selected, not from any worth or merit, but to satisfy the slave interest of the convention:—The ticket was made and sent to the people for their rejection or approval, and as you well remember Tippecanoe and Tyler too, were put through by the people with a rush, and as every honest Whig supposed to the entire satisfaction to a large portion of the people of the United States, what was the result, Gen Harrison was installed into office on the 4th of March 1841, and lived just one month when he died suddenly, (and I may say mysteriously) which caused this country and I may say the nation to mourn for the loss of that good old man:—

It was well known that Gen. Harrison was a free State man, with strong feelings against the extension of our nation's curse negro slavery, and in favor of freedom, and free Territory, which was the cause of the Southern vote of the convention which nominated him, being cast solid against him:—

After Harrison's death his remains was placed in a sarcophagus to be conveyed to North Bend, its final resting place, and a committee of Congress was appointed to accompany the funeral cortège to North Bend:—The Chairman of that Committee was the Hon Thos. Ewing Senator from Ohio, and when they arrived at the place of destination the Sarcophagus was opened and to the Surprise of all, the head and chest of the corpse was very much swollen, and the face and breast was as black as though the blood had been drawn to the skin by bruises:—The matter was talked over by the Committee and I am informed it was declared by a Doctor who was present, that nothing but Poison would produce that result, and suggested an investigation, when Mr. Ewing, replied, close up the sarcophagus, and deposit it in its final resting place, for said he, if on investigation it should be found that Poison was the cause of his death, it would involve the country in a civil war.:—Thus his body was consigned to the grave without investigation, and the People left in ignorance as to the real cause of Harrisons Death, which, was by Poison beyond a possibility of doubt:—

By Law, that arch Traitor John Tyler assumed the responsibilities of the office, that the people had elected, Harrison to fill, and he being a southern Pro Slavery man, and a fit and willing tool of the slave oligarchy, went back to his first love, (viz Loco-focoism) and turned traitor to the party that had elected him, and you know well what his history was whilst he held the reins of government in his hands, and how well, and truly he carried out all of the dictations, of the Southern Slave party, and how he betrayed the Whig Party that had elected him, and how heartily he was, and is despised by the whole country north, up to the present time; He lived out his term of office and received the reward of his masters:—

In 1844 James K Polk of Tennessee a southern Proslavery Loco foco was elected President, and George M Dallas a northern Loco foco with southern views, (who betrayed his own state as Judas betrayed his Master) was elected vice President:—They being the right kind of materials, ready and willing to carry out all of the mandates of their Masters:—They lived out their terms of office, to the full and entire satisfaction of the two hundred and fifty thousand Slave owners of the South, and they received their rewards:—They were elected by a palpable fraud, viz. Polk Dallas and the tariff of 42, Polk is a better tariff man than Henry Clay. The tariff is safer in the hands of Polk and Dallas, than in the hands of Clay and Freelignhysen, all of which was a known, and willful fraud on the People, and our cold Hearted, unprincipled President James Buchanan, then traveled through Pennsylvania, making Tariff speeches and promulgating the fraud in almost every County:—

In 1848, Gen. Zachy. Taylor, that good honest southerner, was elected President, and Millard Fillmore, an anti-slavery man of New York State was elected Vice President:—Gen. Taylor was duly inaugurated into office, and entered, on his duties, as President, of the United States, and his Administrative policy, was much feared, and doubted by many of the Anti-Slavery extension men north, and as you know his policy was uncertain for some time after his inauguration. But he being a true National man, and strictly honest, and free from all sectional prejudices, soon dispelled all fears from the minds of those who had doubted him before, and as you are better acquainted with his political history than I am, I will only illustrate my position by quoting sufficient for that purpose;—He was decidedly opposed to the further extension of slavery into territory north of 36.30 and desired, and was using the whole force, and power of his administration to bring New Mexico into the Union as a free state;—He also believed that the Missouri compromise was Strictly constitutional, and one of the most Sacred compromises of the Slave question, and I am credibly informed that five days before his sudden death, he had high and angry words with some of his prominent Southern friends, on the subject of extending Slavery into New Mexico, and that he said to them, he was the President of the Whole United States, and that he had found certain States and territories free, and he would never with his consent, agree to force or extend that damnable curse into any territory that is now free, or north of 36.30, and would use all of his power against it; consequently he did not Suit the Slave oligarchy, and on the 9th of July, one year four months and five days after his inauguration he died suddenly, as did Harrison, and with the same apparent disease, which caused the Nation to mourn again for the loss of that good old chieftain President:—His death was attributed to his eating a cherry pie the day before his death:—I have no doubt but the pie was the cause of his death, but in the pie was poison—for I cannot believe that an old Soldier who had been used to the hardships of a camp life for thirty years could be killed by eating a simple cherry pie; if there had been no poison in it, but my opinion is that the Borgia's were about:—

By law the New York anti-Slavery man Millard Fillmore succeeded Gen. Taylor as President, and it was strange to see what a perfect somerset he turned, how soon he became what he chose to term a National Man, and how soon he lost all of his long cherished Anti-Slavery notions, and how soon he became a pet of the slave Power at Washington, and that his former York State notions did not suit in a southern atmosphere, and he had then discovered that he suddenly became very National in his views; How willing he was to advocate and sign the fugitive slave law, as a finality on the nigger question, and then what a favorite he became with the whole South:—He lived out his term of office, and received his reward, and after he retired from office, before going home to Buffalo, he made a tour through almost the entire South, and you remember how he was feasted, toasted, and eulogised, by the Slave owners from Maryland to Louisiana, and cheered on his road throughout the entire south, and as soon as he struck free territory, how he made a Straight line for home, not stopping to receive the congratulations of his free state friends:—There is much more that might be said in relation to Mr. Fillmore, and the Slave propagandists, but I have said enough:—The original contract between the high contracting Parties, I suppose has been strictly carried out:—

In 1852, Franklin Pearce, a weak kneed, New Hampshire Loco foco, was elected President, and he being rather of a fainting disposition, and of a feminine tendency, and very unsteady in his nerves, and easily flattered, which made him a fit subject for the Slave power to operate upon, and well he done their biddings. The result was the repeal of the Missouri compromise. (Which measure was headed by that Arch Demagogue, Stephen A Douglass.).., The civil war in Kansas with all of the enormities connected therewith;—The sacrilegious outrages of the border ruffians, in spreading broadcast over the territory death and devastation;—The violation of the ballot boxes:—The Passage of laws that would disgrace the heathen, are all evidences of the unholy dictations he received from his masters, and in short he went over to them body, soul, and breeches, and he lived out his term of office, and done his biddings nobly, and received his reward:—

In 1856 James Buchanan a cold Hearted, Pennsylvania Locofoco was elected President, and shortly after it was known that he was elected a delegation of Southern Slave owners, with Governor Wise of Virginia at their head made him, a visit at Wheatland and after the interview between the President elect, and the slave oligarchy, it is generally reported, and believed that Mr. Buchanan was rather stubborn, and would not work right in the traces, as to the policy of his coming administration, and the Slave power went home somewhat discouraged with the coming President, and they were in great consternation for a time and the southern papers, many of them actually threatened that the southern electors should vote for some other candidate, or person for President instead of Buchanan, for he was not right on the southern questions;—But after further consideration the electors did vote for Buck, and he was elected:—

In due time Mr. Buchanan engaged rooms at the National Hotel in Washington City, and that fact being published all over the country which caused a perfect rush of office seekers and politicians, to the National when Mr. Buchanan arrived, and during his stay at the National there was near fifteen hundred guests:—And over five hundred of that number were poisoned, and about fifty of them died;—and what is most strange in the matter, there were but three (I believe) of the guests, who belonged to the South who were afflicted, and they very slightly;—when it is known that a large majority of the guests were southerners;—The first theory started, was that poisoned rats had got into the water, but that theory soon exploded, and then another idea was concocted, viz that the cause was the poisonous gases that came from the Sewers that were connected with the Sinks of the Hotel, but that too soon exploded, likewise;—And finally a committee of scientific Gentlemen were appointed to give the matter a thorough investigation and if possible determine what was the cause of the dreadful destruction of life and health, and after a thorough and careful investigation it was found to be Pulverized Glass mixed with very fine pulverized Sugar, but on consultation, it was determined not to make the real cause public, because it would be dangerous on account of it being so easy for servants by that means to poison the whole community:—Now you see how cunningly the whole thing was managed, the poisoned rat story answered for a time, but was soon abandoned, next the Sewer dodge was taken up and answered for a short period, to divert the attention of the anxious public ~~for a short time~~ (~~longer,~~ that too had to be abandoned also) and when the real cause was ascertained, it was thought best not to make it public on account of the servants;—Thus you will see how nicely the slave power manages to keep the public ignorant of their black deeds;—Mr. Buchanan was warned of his danger by several letters without signatures, but he gave them no notice, and at the time it occurred it was really a fearful thing to think about, but since the southern policy has been fully developed, the whole thing becomes perfectly clear, and plain, and not mysterious as it, at one time appeared, we hear southerners swearing vehemently almost daily, that if Lincoln is elected he shall never take his seat, &c. and I do not know how they are to prevent it unless it is by making poisoning presidents a part of their nigger doctrine;—

Mr. Breckenridge, the Vice President being a true southern Pro-slavery man, would have been a very acceptable swap for Mr. Buchanan, at that time, he being a man in whom they could have full confidence and would be entirely satisfactory to the slave power;—Mr. Buchanan was however permitted to live, but he would not be now living, if he had not sold himself to the slave oligarchy Body and Soul, and gone over to them more thoroughly than any of his predecessors:—The Borgia's of Washington were after him, as they will be after every President, who does not consent to the Pro-slavery side of the question as soon (or before) he gets into office, and I am satisfied that the lives of our Presidents, depends, on their views, and opinions of a certain domestic institution which our beloved country unfortunately is cursed with viz Negro-Slavery:—

Now I will ask you in all sincerity can these things be accidental;—do not the coincidences and facts combined, show strong indications of foul play, and are not the coincidences very remarkable:—Pro-Slavery Presidents, live out their terms of offices and those having different views are doomed to short existences in office, and their deaths are sudden and mysterious:—Sir our beloved country is under a more despotic rule than almost any other country known, and that too under the name of Democracy without a single trace or landmark of true democracy being left, for such old Federalists as ten cent Jimmy to swear by:—And the Borgia's of Washington are ready to do the biddings of their masters faithfully whenever it shall be deemed expedient to get a President or high official out of the way of the Slave Despots:—

I being strongly impressed with the belief that Free State Presidents were foully dealt with, took occasion to give that matter my particular attention and in my private investigations of the attempt to poison Mr. Buchanan, I happened to get hold of the Head waiter in the Ladies dining room at the time the occurrence took place;—He having once been head waiter for me was very friendly, and much attached to me:—I said to him John, how is it about the attempt to Poison old Buck you was there at the time and I would take your opinions about it sooner than I would those who held higher rank in society than you do, this somewhat flattered his vanity, and after a little hesitation, he said well it was not Poisoned Rats for Devil the poisoned rat was there ever in the house as long as I was there;—nor was it the Poison arising from the sewers for if it had of been that, it would have afflicted all alike:—Well, said I, John what do you think then was the cause of the poison being in the House, after some little delay in answering, he said to be candid with you, my opinion is that it was in some very fine pulverized sugar that the Steward of the Hotel bought a few days before Mr. Buchanan arrived, for said he, we had no occasion for that sugar we had a large quantity of all kinds of sugar in the store room when that was bought;—plenty of crushed, sand, St Domingo and brown sugars, plenty of all kinds necessary for a Hotel, and the Steward had no occasion whatever to buy the 4 or 5 barrels of that very fine pulverized sugar said he I never saw such fine pulverized sugar before:—I then said to him John if the Poison was in that Sugar how did it happen that so many of the Northern people were Poisoned and only about three of the Southerners when you know that a large majority of the guests were from the South;—Och you an old Hotel keeper and don't see how that could happen, why you know that for Tea nearly every person from the North drinks tea, and those from the south Coffee, and we all had our orders, that when they called for tea to hand them that fine pulverized Sugar and when they called for Coffee to hand the crushed or St Domingo Sugar and said he that is the way that happened and he then remarked you did not hear of any of the family or the servants being poisoned:—I then said who was the Steward, well said he his name is --- --- and he is an Irishman:—I then asked if he was a Roman Catholic, he said yes sir the same as I am, and I will tell you no lie about it:—I then asked him what had become of the Steward he said he could not tell where he went he left Washington and I can't tell where he went to;—I then asked him do you suppose he was paid for his services in that black deed;—well said he my opinion is that any person who is base enough to do the deed that he would be rascal enough to not do it without being well paid for such wickedness said he I am sure of that:—

This was before the Committee of Scientific Gentlemen were appointed to investigate and determine the real cause, and after the cause was ascertained it proved to be in this fine pulverized Sugar just as John had told me he believed it was and the Poison was fine pulverized glass mixed with fine Pulverized Sugar:—And there is no doubt but the compound of Sugar and glass was specially prepared by someone for the occasion, and placed in a position where the Steward was directed to go and get it, and if it could be traced out you would find that the whole thing was done by the directions of the Slave power, thinking to get old Buck out of the way and to make room for Brackenridge their friend to take his place:—

Now Sir don't you think the proofs are strong and the remarkable coincidences are unexplainable:—And it certainly behooves you to be cautious and pay heed to the warnings before you, and I will suggest cooks with you from your home those whom you know to be honest true and faithful, and cannot be bribed or bought, for as certain as your name is Abraham Lincoln unless you are cautious your Reign will be short, and you and Mr. Hamlin will both be put out of the way to make room for a creature of the Senate who will do the biddings of the Slave Oligarchy and unless you do as many of your predecessors have done, go over to the Slave Power body and soul you will be ~~shipped~~ slipped out of existence unless you are as watchful, as sure as you now live:—

You are the candidate of the great reform party, and we who are working for your election hope to see you live and carry out those great national reforms, and we hope you will stand firm to your principles, and give us a good old Henry Clay Tariff for protection to American industry and Manufactories, which we hope to get under your Administration, together with all other reforms laid down in the Chicago Platform, and if elected we do not want to see the head cut off of our Party as has been the case with the two last Whig Presidents but we want you to live;—Therefore your salvation is caution, and vigilance;—In the selection of your servants be careful not to have any Roman Catholics or Papists about you have none but American born, black and white and have nothing but Protestants, about you, and then I will feel as though you will be comparatively safe;—We of Penna. desire to see you live out your term of office, and to see the Principles on which you will be elected faithfully carried out, and to see a quiet and just end to this vexatious and interminable Nigger agitation, and the Slave extension question forever settled, and the country once more in Peace Prosperity and quietness:—And we desire further to see you faithfully carry out all of the compromises of our (Mag-na- char-ta) the Constitution, to so administer the affairs of Government that justice will be done to all, and by so doing our Southern Brethren will learn by you that justice can be done to all, North, South, East and West even if their President is as they in their perfidy choose to call him, a d--d Black Republican.

Very Respectfully Yours

Oliver H. P. Parker

Late Proprietor of the Franklin House of this City

Mr. Lincoln, a man who was well grounded in the Bible, had a prophetic sense almost uncanny, which alone made him superior to any of his contemporaries. More than once he told his close friends that he had a strong premonition that he would not outlast the Rebellion, that his work would be finished with it. Again I quote from Chiniquy's book

> "You are not the first to warn me against the dangers of assassination. My ambassadors in Italy, France and England, as well as Professor Morse, have many times warned me against the plots of the murderers, which they have detected in those different countries. But I see no other safeguard against those murderers but to be always ready to die, as Christ advises it. As we must all die sooner or later, it makes very little difference to me whether I die from a dagger plunged through my heart or from an inflammation of the lungs. Let me tell you that I have lately read a passage in the Old Testament, which had made a profound, and, I hope, a salutary impression on me. Here is that passage. 'Ye shall not fear them: for the Lord your God He shall fight for you. And I besought the Lord at that time, saying, O Lord God, Thou hast begun to show thy servant Thy greatness and Thy mighty hand; for what God is there, in heaven or in earth, that can do according to Thy words, and according to Thy might! I pray Thee, let me go over, and see the good land that is beyond Jordan, that goodly mountain, and Lebanon. But the Lord was wroth with me for your sakes, and would not hear me: and the Lord said unto me, Let it suffice thee: speak no more unto me of this matter. Get thee up into the top of Pisgah, and lift up thine eyes westward, and northward, and southward, and eastward, and behold it with thine eyes: for thou shalt not go over this Jordan.'
>
> "Charles, let me tell you that I have read these strange and beautiful verses several times these last few weeks. The more I read them, the more it seems to me that God has written them for me as well as Moses. Has He not taken me from my poor log cabin by the hand, as He did with Moses in the reeds of the Nile, to put me at the head of the greatest and the most blessed of modern nations, just as He put that prophet at the head of the most blessed nations of ancient times? Has not Jehovah granted me a privilege which was not granted to any living man, when I broke the fetters of four millions of men and made them free? Has not our God given me the most

glorious victories over our enemies? Are not the armies of the Confederacy so reduced to a handful of men when compared to what they were two years ago, that the day is fast approaching when they will have to surrender?

"Now I see the end of this terrible conflict, with the same joy of Moses at the end of his forty years in the wilderness. I pray my God to grant me to see the days of peace, and untold prosperity, which will follow this cruel war, as Moses asked God to see the other side of Jordan and enter the Promised Land. But do you know that I hear in my soul, as the voice of God, giving me the rebuke which was given to Moses?

"Yes! Every time that my soul goes to God to ask the favor of seeing the other side of Jordan, and eating the fruits of that peace, after which I am longing with such an unspeakable desire, do you know that there is a still, but solemn voice, which tells me that I will see those things, only from a long distance, and that I will be among the dead, when the nation which God granted me to lead through those awful trials, will cross the Jordan, and dwell in that Land of Promise, where peace, industry, happiness and liberty will make everyone happy; and why so? Because He has already given me favors, which He never gave, I dare say, to any man, in these latter days.

"Why did God Almighty refuse to Moses the favor of crossing the Jordan, and entering the Promised Land? It was on account of this own nation's sin! That law of divine retribution and justice, by which one must suffer for another is surely a terrible mystery. But it is a fact, which no man who has any intelligence and knowledge can deny. Moses, who knew that law, though he probably did not understand it better than we do, calmly says to his people, 'God was wroth with me for your sakes.' The judgments of Jehovah are true and righteous altogether.

"But though we do not understand that mysterious and terrible law, we find it written in letters of tears and blood wherever we go. We do not find a single page of history, without finding undeniable traces of its existence.

"So many plots have been made against my life, that it is a real miracle that they have all failed, when we consider that the great majority of them were in the hands of the skillful murderers, evidently trained by the Jesuits.

But can we expect that God will make a perpetual miracle to save my life? I believe not. The Jesuits are so expert in those deeds of blood, that Henry IV said that it was impossible to escape them, and he became their victim, though he did all that could be done to protect himself. My escape from their hands, since the letter of the Pope to Jeff Davis has sharpened a million daggers to pierce my breast, would be more than a miracle.

"But just as Jehovah heard no murmur from the lips of Moses when He told him that he had to die, before crossing the Jordan, for the sins of his people; so I hope and pray that He will hear no murmur from me when I fall for my nation's sake." (7)

Endnotes

1 The Suppressed Truth about the Assassination of Abraham Lincoln, Burke McCarty, (by permission Merrimac, Mass.: Destiny Publishers, 1973; originally published 1923) p.57

2 Ibid. pp.57-63
3 Ibid. p.62
4 Fifty Years in the Church of Rome, Charles Chiniquy, (by permission Chick publications, Chino, Ca.) p.301
5 The Suppressed Truth About the Assassination of Abraham Lincoln, Burke McCarty, p.65 by permission
6 Fifty Years in the Church of Rome pp.296-7; 305-6 by permission
7 Ibid. pp.301-3

Chapter 7

Catholic stance on slavery; its effect on Jefferson Davis; Davis writes to Pope Pius IX; correspondence between Davis and the Vatican; Britain's stance; Lincoln gives Napoleon an ultimatum; plots by Confederates based in Canada

Disruption has always been the first motive of the Jesuits, and black slavery was the rock upon which they planned to rend the United States Government. There was no other principle, no ethics involved, except the fundamental principles of the divine right rule of the popes of Rome.

From the earliest times the Roman Church advocated human slavery. In the Middle Ages, when feudal slavery flourished, the church fattened on the exploitation of the serfs who were bought and sold with the land. These serfs were supposed to have no souls, and were in precisely the same category as cattle. The great monasteries and nunneries were among the largest owners of serfs. For instance, had Joan D'Arc lived four hundred years earlier, she and her family would have been among the serfs attached to the Monastery of San Ramey. In short, serfdom was the basis of the wealth of the papacy.

It is true that in rare cases the church lifted out of serfdom, a boy in whom it recognized some peculiar native talent or personal trait which might be cultivated and turned to its own advantage, but the act was simply the removal from the envelopment of serfdom to that of ecclesiastical slavery for further and more useful exploitation by more exacting task masters, for the Roman Church had always enslaved the minds of its members. The Jesuit Oath exacts the obedience of "cadavers."

The following excerpt from the *Augusta Chronicle* 2006 under the title "*Church & State*" demonstrates that they do not really hold much shame about the fact, rather there seems to be an attempt to justify it, even to this day:

> "...Patrick Lynch, another Irishman who became bishop, was raised in Charleston, the son of a slave owner. *As bishop, he owned 100 slaves himself. Although he believed it was wrong to trade, abuse or neglect slaves, he defended slavery as a part of the culture and economy.* When South Carolina broke with the Union, he pledged his allegiance to his state and then to the Confederacy.
>
> The Confederacy sent him to the Vatican as its representative, but the Vatican did not recognize him. Instead, it gave him a new set of vestments and told him to go home. [In other words, he was promoted and told that the job had been filled by someone less obvious. – Ed.]
>
> After the South lost the war, he was barred from entering the United States. It took months to get a pardon from President Andrew Johnson to allow his re-entry."

In the "*Doctrine of the Jesuits*" by Gury, translated into French by a brilliant educator and statesman, Paul Bert in 1879, we find the position of the church and the Jesuits on the issue of black slavery quoted as follows:

> "Slavery does not constitute a crime before any law, divine or human. What reasons can we have for undermining the foundations of slavery with the same zeal that ought always to animate us into overcoming evil? When one thinks of the state of degradation in which the hordes of Africa live, the slave trade may be considered a providential act, and we almost repudiate the philanthropy which sees in man one thing, material liberty." (1)

This quote was the virus to which Lincoln referred and with which the youths of the best families of the Southern Confederacy were inoculated, and which made the leaders of the ultra pro-slavery forces an easy prey to the Roman hierarchy and its priesthood in the great conspiracy of destruction which Lincoln saw.

It was the virus which was let into the veins of Mary E. Surratt and was passed on by her to her son, the arch-conspirator, John H. Surratt; it was the opiate which silenced the voice of conscience and kindness of the heart of John Wilkes Booth, and nerved his hand to send the bullet into the great brain of Abraham Lincoln; it was the deadly drug which made Lewis Payne, the unfortunate, "Davy" Herold, the shiftless Edward Spangler, and the non-Catholic tools, wax in the hands of the Leopoldines and the Jesuits in the conspiracy to ruin Popular Government.

The Jesuit virus that "Slavery does not constitute a crime before any law, divine or human," was the drug that set the blood of the slave owners on fire and justified their "cause." It was what distorted their vision, controlled their ethics and appealed so strongly to their economic interests. It was the one big urge underlying the whole progress of the secessionists.

In the book "*A Memoir*" by Jefferson Davis, the leader of the Southern Confederacy, published by his wife after his death, we find this remark:

> "Mr. Davis's early education had always inclined in the Roman Catholics, friends who could not be alienated from the oppressed." In the second chapter Davis is quoted as follows:
>
> "The Kentucky Catholic school called St. Thomas College, when I was there was connected with the church. The priests were Dominicans. They held large property; productive fields, slaves, flour mills, flocks and herds. As an association they were rich. Individually, they were vowed to poverty and self-abnegation. They were diligent, in the care, both spiritual and material, of their parishioner's wants. When I entered the school, a large majority of the boys belonged to the Roman Catholic Church. After a short time I was the only Protestant boy remaining, and also the smallest boy in the school. From whatever reason, the priests were particularly kind to me. Father Wallace, afterwards bishop of Nashville, treated me with the fondness of a near relative." (2)

It is very obvious from the above that the "kindness" shown to Jefferson Davis as a child clung to him and influenced his whole life. It bore fruit, and his friendliness to the Catholic Church was well repaid by that institution.

When Mr. Davis had been arrested after the close of the Civil War and was to be tried for treason, it was the distinguished Catholic attorney, Charles O'Connor, of New York City, who offered his services, which were accepted in Mr. Davis's defense.

Mary Surratt

During the year of 1863, especially after the Battle of Gettysburg, which had virtually driven the wooden stake through the heart of the Southern Rebellion, a flurry of correspondence between Davis and Pope Pius IX took place for the purpose of swaying the cause of the Confederacy toward the stated goal of the Treaty of Verona.

On September 4th 1863 the following letter to a priest of Rome began the push to solicit Vatican help in the Confederate cause:

DEPARTMENT OF STATE,
Richmond, September 4, 1863.

SIR:

The Secretary of War having relieved you temporarily from service in the army and placed you at the disposal of this Department for the purpose mentioned in our conferences, I now proceed to give you the instructions by which you are to be guided. With this view I copy the following passages of the instructions heretofore given to Lieutenant Capston, who was sent out by this Department in July last on a similar mission to that now confided to you.

The duty which it is proposed to entrust to you is that of a private and confidential agent of this Government for the purpose of proceeding to Ireland and there using all legitimate means to enlighten the population as to the true nature and character of the contest now waged on this continent, with the view of defeating the attempts made by the agents of the United States to obtain in Ireland recruits for their armies. It is understood that under the guise of assisting needy persons to emigrate, a regular organization has been formed of agents in Ireland, who leave untried no method of deceiving the laboring population into emigrating, for the ostensible purpose of seeking employment in the United States, but really for recruiting the Federal armies.

The means to be used by you can scarcely be suggested from this side, but they are to be confined to such as are strictly legitimate, honorable, and proper. We rely on truth and justice alone. Throw yourself as much as possible into close communication with the people where the agents of our enemies are at work. Inform them by every means you can devise of the true purposes of those who seek to induce them to emigrate. Explain to them the nature of the warfare which is carried on here. Picture to them the fate of their unhappy countrymen who have already fallen victims to the arts of the Federals. Relate to them the story of Meagher's brigade, its formation, and its fate. Explain to them that they will be called on to meet Irishmen in battle, and thus to imbrue their hands in the blood of their own friends and perhaps kinsmen in a quarrel which does not concern them and in which all the feelings of a common humanity should induce them to refuse taking part against us. Contrast the policy of the Federal and Confederate States in former times in their treatment of foreigners in order to satisfy Irishmen where true sympathy in their favor was found in periods of trial. At the North the Know Nothing Party, based on hatred to foreigners and especially to Catholics, was triumphant in its career. In the South it was crushed Virginia taking the lead in trampling it under foot. In this war such has been the hatred of the New England Puritans to Irishmen and Catholics that in several instances the chapels and places of worship of the Irish Catholics have been burnt or shamefully desecrated by the regiments of volunteers from New England. These facts have been published in Northern papers. Take the New York Freeman's journal and you will see shocking details, not coming from Confederate sources but from the officers of the United States themselves. Lay all these matters fully before the people, who are now called on to join these ferocious persecutors in the destruction of this nation where all religions and all nationalities meet equal justice and protection both from the people and the laws.

These views may be urged by any proper means you can devise; through the press; by mixing with the people themselves; and by disseminating the facts amongst persons who have influence with the people.

The laws of England must be strictly respected and obeyed by you. While prudence dictates that you should not reveal your agency nor the purpose for which you go abroad, it is not desired nor expected that you use any dishonest disguise or false pretenses. Your mission is, although secret, honorable, and the means employed must be such as this Government may fearfully [fearlessly] avow and openly justify if your conduct should ever be called into question. On this point there must be no room whatever for doubt or cavil.

If, in order fully to carry out the objects of the Government as above expressed, you should deem it advisable to go to Rome for the purpose of obtaining such sanction from the sovereign pontiff as will strengthen your hands and give efficiency to your action, you are at liberty to do so, as well as to invite to your assistance any Catholic prelate from the Northern States known to you to share your convictions of

the justice of our cause and of the duty of laboring for its success.

You will, while engaged in the service of this Department, be provided with funds at the rate of £20 sterling per month for your personal expenses. Your passage to and from Europe will be provided at the expense of the Department, and you will receive herewith a letter of introduction to our private agent in London in which, as you perceive, he is instructed to provide at his discretion any small sums that you may need for the disbursement of expenses connected with your mission, such as costs of printing, extra traveling expenses, and the like. He will also provide the remuneration for your associate from the North, if you can obtain one entirely trustworthy and you find it advisable to secure his aid.

The Department will expect to hear from you on the subject of your duties and to receive a report from you at least once a month, and you can address your communications through the agent above referred to, and by whom they will be forwarded.

The Department expects much from your zeal, activity, and discretion, and is fully confident that you will justify its anticipations of the good to be effected by your mission.

You will receive herewith the sum of $1,212.50 in gold, to be applied to the expenses of your voyage and to your salary. You will please send an account to the Department with proper vouchers of the amount spent by you for the voyage to London, and the remaining sum will be retained in payment of your salary till exhausted.

I am, very respectfully, etc.,

J. P. BENJAMIN,
Secretary of State

Rev. Father JOHN BANNON,
Richmond

On September 25, 1863, Davis addressed the following letter to Pius IX through his man in Rome, J.P. Benjamin, Secretary of State, C.S.A.:

Richmond, Va., Sept. 25, 1863

Very Venerable Sovereign Pontiff:

The letters which you have written to the clergy of New Orleans and New York have been committed to me, and I have read with emotion the deep grief therein expressed for the ruin and devastation caused by the war, which is now being waged against the States and the people who have selected me as their president, and your orders to your clergy to exhort the people to peace and charity. I am deeply sensible of the Christian charity which has impelled you to this reiterated appeal to the clergy. It is for this reason I feel it my duty to express personally and in the name of the Confederate States of America our gratitude for such sentiments of Christian good feeling and love, and to assure Your Holiness, that the people threatened even on their own hearts, with the most cruel oppression and terrible carnage is desirous as it always has been, to see the end of this impious war; that we have ever addressed prayers to heaven for that cause which Your Holiness now desires; that we desire none of our enemies' possessions, that we merely fight to resist the devastation of our country and the shedding of our best blood, and to force them to let us live in peace under the protection of our own institutions and under our own laws, which not only insure to everyone the enjoyment of his temporal rights but also the free exercise of his religion.

I pray your Holiness to accept on the part of myself and the people of the Confederate States our sincere thanks for the efforts in favor of peace.

May the Lord preserve the days of Your Holiness and keep you under His divine protection.

Jefferson Davis (3)

The following correspondence, which led up to the Pope's letter to Davis will now be presented in order to show the extent to which the Papacy was involved in the support of the Confederacy and the destruction of the United States. It comes from the Official Records of the Union and Confederate Navies in the War of the Rebellion, Series II, Volume 3 located in the National Archives of the United States in Washington, D.C.

Judah P. Benjamin

No.66.]

Rome, November, 1863

Sir: As I expected at the date of my no. 65, I reached here on the 9th instant, late in the afternoon.

On the 11th, at half past 1p.m., I sought and promptly obtained an interview with his Eminence, the Cardinal Secretary of State, Antonelli. I at once explained to him the object of my mission to Rome and he instantly assured me that he would obtain for me an audience of the sovereign Pontiff. His Eminence then remarked that he would not withhold from me an expression of his unbounded admiration of the wonderful powers which we had exhibited in the field of resistance to a war which had been prosecuted with an energy, aided by the employment of all the recent improvements in the instruments for the destruction of life and property, unparalleled, perhaps, in the world's history.

He asked me several questions with respect to President Davis, at the end of which he observed that he certainly had created for himself a name that would rank with those of the most illustrious statesmen of modern times. He manifested an earnest desire for the definitive termination of hostilities, and observed that there was nothing the government of the Holy See could do with propriety to occasion such a result that it was not prepared to do. I seized the utterance of this assurance to inform him that but for the European recruits received by the North, numbering annually something like 100,000, the Lincoln Administration; in all likelihood, would have been compelled some time before this to have retired from the contest, that nearly all those recruits were from Ireland, and that Christianity had cause to weep at such a fiendish destruction of life as occurred from the beguiling of those people from their homes to take up arms against citizens who had never harmed or wronged them in the slightest degree. He appeared to be touched by my statement, and intimated that an evil so disgraceful to humanity was not beyond the reach of a salutary remedy.

His Eminence, after a short pause, took a rapid survey of the affairs of the nations of the earth, and drew a rather somber picture of the future, particularly of Europe. He did not attempt to conceal his dislike of England, his want of sempathy with Russia, his distrust of any benefits which might be expected from the congress proposed by France. "If old guaranties," said he, emphatically, "are of no value, new ones will be too feeble to resist expediency when sustained by might."

This is but a short and otherwise imperfect outline of one of the most interesting official interviews I ever enjoyed, an interview which was of lengthened duration and marked from beginning to end with extreme cordiality and courtesy by the distinguished functionary by whom it was accorded. I will add, lest I may not have been sufficiently explicit on that point, that it took place in his office in the Vatican, where he receives all the foreign ministers.

I have the honor to be, sir, very respectfully, your obedient servant,

A. DUDLEY MANN,
Hon, J.P.BENJAMIN,
Secretary of State, C.S.A., Richmond, Va.

No.67]

Rome, November 14, 1863

Sir: At 3 o'clock on the afternoon of yesterday I received a formal notification that his Holiness would favor me with an audience, embracing my private secretary, Mr. W. Grayson Mann, today at 12 o'clock.

I accordingly proceeded to the Vatican sufficiently early to enable me to reach there fifteen minutes in advance of the designated hour. In five minutes afterwards - ten minutes prior to the appointed time - a message came from the Sovereign Pontiff that he was ready to receive me, and I was accordingly conducted into his presence.

His Holiness stated, after I had taken my stand near to his side, that he had been so afflicted by the horrors of the war in America that many months ago he had written to the Archbishops of New Orleans and New York to use all the influence that they could properly employ for terminating with as little delay as possible the deplorable state of hostilities; that from the former he had received no answer, but that he had heard from the latter and that his communication was not such as to inspire hopes that his ardent wishes would be speedily gratified.

I then remarked that it is to a sense of profound gratitude of the Executive of the Confederate States and of my countrymen, for the earnest manifestations which your Holiness made in the appeal referred to, that I am indebted for the distinguished honor for which I now enjoy. President Davis has appointed me special envoy to convey in person to your Holiness this letter, which I trust, you will receive in a similar spirit to that which animated its author."

Looking for a moment at the address and afterwards at the seal of the letter, his Holiness took his scissors and cut the envelope. Upon opening it he observed: "I see it is in English, a language which I do not understand." I remarked: "If it will be agreeable to your Holiness, my Secretary will translate its contents to you." He replied: "I shall be pleased if he will do so." The translation was rendered in a slow, solemn, and emphatic pronunciation. During its progress, I did not cease for an instant to carefully survey the features of the Sovereign Pontiff. A sweeter expression of pious affection, of tender benignity, never adorned the face of mortal man. No picture can adequately represent him when exclusively absorbed in Christian contemplation. Every sentence of the letter seemed to sensibly affect him. At the conclusion of each, he would lay his hand down upon the desk and bow his head approvingly. When the passage was reached wherein the President states, in such sublime and affecting language, "We have offered up at the footstool of our Father who is in Heaven prayers inspired by the same feelings which animate your Holiness," his deep sunken orbs visibly moistened were upturned toward that throne upon which ever sits the Prince of Peace, indicating that his heart was pleading for our deliverance from that causeless and merciless war which is prosecuted against us. The soul of infidelity - if, indeed, infidelity have a soul - would have melted in view of so sacred a spectacle.

The emotion occasioned by the translation was succeeded by a silence of some time. At length his Holiness asked whether President Davis was a Catholic. I answered in the negative. He then asked if I was one. I assured him I was not.

His Holiness now stated, to use his own language, that "Lincoln & Co." had endeavored to create an impression abroad that they were fighting for the abolition of slavery, and that it might perhaps be judicious in us to consent to gradual emancipation. I replied that the subject of slavery was one over which the Government of the Confederate States, like that of the old United States, had no control whatever, that all ameliorations with regard to the institution must proceed from the States themselves, which were as sovereign in their character in this regard as were France, Austria, or any other continental power; that true philanthropy shuddered at the thought of the liberation of the slave in the manner attempted by, "Lincoln & Co."; that such a procedure would be practically to convert the well cared for civilized negro into a semi-barbarian; that such of our slaves had been captured or decoyed off by our enemy were in an incomparably worse condition than while they were in the service of their masters; that they wished to return to their old homes, the love of which was the strongest of their affections; that, if indeed, African slavery were an evil, there was a power which, in its own good time, would doubtless remove that evil in a more gentle manner than that of causing the earth to be deluged with blood for its sudden overthrow.

His Holiness received these remarks with an approving expression. He then said that I had reason to be proud of the self - sacrificing devotion of my countrymen from the beginning to the cause for which they were contending. "The most ample reason," I replied, "and yet, scarcely so much as of my countrywomen, whose patriotism, whose sorrows and privations, whose transformation in many instances from luxury to penury, were unparalleled and could not be adequately described by any living language. There they had been from the beginning - there they were still more resolute, if possible, than ever, emulating in devotion, earthly though it was in its character, those holy female spirits who were last at the cross.

His Holiness received this statement with evident satisfaction, and then said: "I would like to do anything that can be effectively done, or that even promises good results, to aid in putting an end to this most terrible war, which is harming the good of all the earth, if I knew how to proceed."

I availed myself of this declaration to inform his Holiness that it was not the armies of Northern birth which the South was encountering in hostile array, but that it was the armies of European creation, occasioned by the Irish and Germans, chiefly by the former, who were influenced to emigrate (by circulars from Lincoln & Co." to their numerous agents abroad) ostensibly for the purpose of securing high wages but in reality to fill up the constantly depleted ranks of our enemy; that those poor unfortunates were tempted by high bounties (amounting to $500, $600, and $700) to enlist and take up arms against us; that once in the service they were invariably placed in the most exposed points of danger in the battlefield; that in consequence thereof an instance had occurred in which an entire brigade had been left dead or wounded upon the ground; that but for the foreign recruits the North would have most likely broken down months ago in the absurd attempt to overpower the South.

His Holiness expressed his utter astonishment, repeatedly throwing up his hands, at the employment of such means against us, and the cruelty attendant upon such unscrupulous operations.

"But, your Holiness," I said. "Lincoln & Co. are even more wicked, if possible, in their ways than in decoying innocent Irishmen from homes to be murdered in cold blood. Their champions, and would your Holiness believe it unless it were authoritatively communicated to you, their pulpit champions have boldly asserted as a sentiment: "Greek fire for the families and cities of the rebels and hell fire for their chiefs."

His Holiness was startled at this information, and immediately observed:

"Certainly no Catholic could reiterate so monstrous a sentiment." I replied: "Assuredly not. It finds a place exclusively in the hearts of the fiendish, vagrant, pulpit buffoons whose number is legion and who impiously undertake to teach the doctrines of Christ for ulterior sinister purposes."

His Holiness now observed: "I will write a letter to President Davis, and of such a character that it may be published for general perusal." I expressed my heartfelt gratification for the assertion of this purpose. He then remarked, half inquiringly: "You will remain here for several months?" I, of course, could not do otherwise than to answer in the affirmative. Turning to my secretary, he asked several questions personal to himself and bestowed upon him a handsome compliment. He then extended his hand as a signal for the end of the audience and I retired.

Thus terminated one among the most remarkable conferences that ever a foreign representative had with a potentate of the earth. And such a potentate! A potentate who wields the consciences of 175,000,000 of the civilized race, and who is adored by that immense number as the vice regent of Almighty God in this sublunary sphere.

How strikingly majestic the conduct of the government of the Pontifical State in its bearing toward me when contrasted with the sneaking subterfuges to which some of the governments of western Europe have had recourse in order to evade intercourse with our commissioners. Here I was openly received by appointment at court in accordance with established usages and customs and treated from beginning to end with a consideration which might be envied by the envoy of the oldest member of the family of nations. The audience was of forty minutes duration, an unusually long one.

I have written this dispatch very hurriedly and fear that it will barely be in time for the monthly steamer which goes off from Liverpool with the mails from the Bahama Islands next Saturday.

I have the honor to be, sir, very respectfully, your obedient servant.

A. DUDLEY MANN.

Hon. J.P. BENJAMIN,
Secretary of State, C.S.A., Richmond, Va.

No. 68]

Rome, November 21, 1863

Sir: I confidently trust that my Nos. 66 and 67, giving detailed accounts of my audience with the Sovereign Pontiff and of my interview with the Cardinal Secretary of State, will have been in your possession some days previous to the arrival of this. Lest, however, they may have been delayed on their way to their destination, I will state that my reception at the Vatican was cordial in the broadest sense of the word, and that my mission has been successful as the President could have possibly desired it to be.

On the 19th I had a second interview with Cardinal Antonelli. I intended it to be of short duration, but he became so much interested in the communications which I made to him that he prolonged it for nearly an hour. He took the occasion to inform me, at the commencement that the acting representative of the United States had obtained an interview of him the day before to remonstrate against the facilities afforded by the government of the Holy See to "Rebels" for entering and abiding in Rome; and that he, the cardinal, promptly replied that he intended to take such "Rebels" under his special protection, because it would be making exactions upon elevated humanity which it was incapable of conscientiously complying with, to expect them to take an oath of allegiance to a country which they bitterly detested. I may add, in this connection, that such passports as you may issue will receive the visa of the nuncio at Paris or Brussels, and that there is now nowhere that the nationality of a citizen of the Confederate States is not as much respected as that of the United States except in the dark hole of the North of Europe.

We have been virtually, if not practically, recognized here. While I was in the foreign office the day before yesterday, foreign ministers were kept waiting for a considerable length of time in the antechamber in order that my interview might not be disturbed. Frequently the cardinal would take my hand in his and exclaim: "Mon cher your government has accomplished prodigies, alike in the cabinet and in the field."

Antonelli is emphatically the State. He is perhaps the very best informed statesman of his time. His channels for obtaining intelligence from every quarter of the earth are more multifarious and reliable than even those of the French. [Note: the confessional box has been described as the greatest intelligence tool ever devised-Ed.] His worst enemies accord him abilities of the very highest order. They say that he is utterly unscrupulous as to the means which he employs, but that no other man could have saved the temporal power of the Pope. He is bold, courageous, resolute, and is a great admirer of President Davis, because he is distinguished by those qualities, qualities which, if supported by good judgment, will, in his opinion, ever win the object to which they are devoted.

Of course I can form no conjecture when the letter of his Holiness to the President will be ready for delivery. Weeks, perhaps months, may elapse first. With my explanations to him upon the subject of slavery, I indulge the hope that he will not allude, hurtfully to us, to the subject. As soon as I receive it I will endeavor to prevail with him to have the correspondence published in the official Journal here, or to give me permission to bring it out in the Paris Moniteur. Its information would be powerful upon all the Catholic governments in both hemispheres, and I would return to Brussels and make an appeal to King Leopold to exert himself with Great Britain, Prussia, etc., in our behalf. Thus I am exceedingly hopeful that before spring our independence will be generally acknowledged. Russia alone will most probably stand aloof until we are recognized by the North, as she has now; at least ostensibly, identify her fortunes with that distracted and demon-like division of the old Union.

So far my mission has not found its way into the newspapers. I wish to keep it secret in order that the publication of the letters may, from the unexpectedness, cause a salutary sensation everywhere when it occurs.

LETTER FROM POPE PIUS IX TO JEFFERSON DAVIS.

To the Illustrious and Honorable Jefferson Davis, President of the Confederate States of America:

Illustrious and Honorable Sir—Greeting: We recently received, with all the kindness due to him, the envoy sent by your Excellency to convey to Us your letter dated the 23d of the month of September of the present year. It was certainly a cause of no ordinary rejoicing to Us to be informed by this gentleman, and by the letter of your Excellency of the lively satisfaction you experienced and of the deep sense of gratitude you entertained toward Us, Illustrious and honorable Sir when you first perused Our letters addressed to those Venerable Brothers, John, Archbishop of New York, and John, Archbishop of New Orleans, on the 18th of October of last year, in which We again and again strongly urged and exhorted those Venerable Brothers, on account of their great piety and episcopal solicitude, to make it the object of their constant efforts and of their earnest study, acting thus in Our name to put an end to that fatal civil war prevailing in that country, and to re-establish among the American people peace and concord, as well as feelings of mutual charity and love. It was peculiarly gratifying to Us to hear that you, illustrious and honorable Sir, as well as the people whom you govern, are animated by the same desire for peace and tranquility which We so earnestly inculcated in the letters referred to addressed to said Venerable Brothers. Would to God that the other inhabitants of those regions (the Northern people) and their rulers, seriously reflecting upon the fearful nature of intestine warfare, might in a dispassionate mood hearken to and adopt the counsels of peace! We on Our part shall not cease offering up Our most fervent prayers to Almighty God, begging and supplicating Him in His goodness to pour out upon all the people of America a spirit of Christian charity and peace, and to rescue them from the multitudes of evil now afflicting them. We also pray the same all-clement Lord of Mercies to shine upon your Excellency the light of His divine grace, and to unite you and Ourselves in bonds of perfect love.

Given at Rome at St. Peter's, the 3d day of December, 1863, in the Eighteenth year of Our Pontificate. PIUS, P. P. IX.

I have reason to believe that what I have said in high places in relation to Irish emigration to New York were words in season.

I have the honor to be sir, very respectfully, your obedient servant,

A. DUDLEY MANN,

Hon. J.P. BENJAMIN
Secretary of State, C.S.A., Richmond, Va.

ALBERGO D'INGHILTERRA,
Rome, November 21, 1863.

MY DEAR SIR:

Immediately on my arrival here I sought the residence of the Right Rev. Bishop Lynch and learned that he had left Rome, to be absent several weeks, in consequence of which the duty devolved upon me of delivering your dispatch to the Roman Government. I lost no time in addressing a note to Cardinal Antonelli (a copy of which I hand you), and he promptly returned an answer to my messenger saying it would give him pleasure to receive me the next day (Saturday) at 2 o'clock.

Accordingly I waited on the cardinal at the appointed hour and he gave me a most cordial greeting, shaking my hand warmly, and, leading me to a seat near his desk, he at once entered upon the discussion of the affairs of the Confederate States. He made no secret of his sympathy with our cause and had not the slightest hesitation in saying he desired our success. He displayed entire familiarity with the state of things both at the North and South, and especially with the necessity of receiving Northern accounts with due modification. He adverted to the case of the *Florida* and pronounced it an inexcusable outrage, and added that he had received a letter from Brazil which stated prompt redress would be demanded; and, further, that it was an offense which no European Government could quietly submit to without protest.

I can not detail everything that dropped from his Eminence during my interview, which lasted over half an hour, but I was more than gratified with the great interest he manifested in the cause dear to our hearts.

At the first opening in the conversation I formally presented the joint letter of the Commissioners (with the enclosed documents), which he read in my presence and then remarked that it should have his more deliberate examination and would then be laid before the Holy Father. I rose to leave when he said he would be glad to present me to the Holy Father and would send me word when the interview could be had. Of course I was only too happy to have so favorable an opportunity of doing my utmost to follow up the manifesto of our Government by whatever eloquence I can command, and as I am to have the services of Monsignor Talbot as my interpreter, I hope to do some little good. Monsignor Talbot is an English ecclesiastic and attached to the household of the Holy Father.

After thanking his Eminence cordially for his kind reception I took my leave, he again shaking me by the hand and leading me across several apartments to the last door.

I am thus minute that I may show you exactly how our cause stands with this court and how I have been able to carry out your wishes in the absence of our regular representative.

Very truly,

J. T. SOUTTER.

His Eminence Monseigneur Cardinal ANTONELLI,
Secretary of State and Minister of Foreign Affairs of the Roman States.

No. 69]
Rome, December 9, 1863

Sir: The Cardinal Secretary of State, Antonelli, officially transmitted to me yesterday the answer of the Pope to the President. In the very direction of this communication there is a positive recognition of our government.

It is addressed "to the Illustrious and Honorable Jefferson Davis, President of the Confederate States of America."

Thus we are acknowledged, by as high an authority as this world contains, to be an independent power of the earth.

I congratulate you, I congratulate the President, I congratulate his cabinet; in short, I congratulate all my true-hearted countrymen and countrywomen, upon this benign escent [sic]. The hand of the Lord has been in it, and eternal glory and praise be to His holy and righteous name.

The document is in the Latin language, as are all documents prepared by the Pope. I cannot incur the risk of its capture at sea, and, therefore, I shall retain it until I can convey it, with entire certainty, to the President. It will adorn the archives of our country in all coming time.

I expect to receive a copy of it in time for transmission by the steamer which carries this (via New York) at Nassau.

I shall leave here by the 15th instant, and will proceed to Paris and from thence to Brussels and London.

The example of the Sovereign Pontiff, if I am not much mistaken, will exercise a salutary influence upon both the Catholic and Protestant governments of Western Europe. Humanity will be aroused everywhere to the importance of its early emulation.

I have studiously endeavored to prevent the appearance of any telegraphic or other communications in the newspapers in relation to my mission. The nature of it, however, is generally known in official circles here, and it has been mentioned in one or more journals. The letters, in my opinion, ought to be officially published in Richmond, under a call for their correspondence by the one or the other branch of Congress. In the mean time I shall communicate to the European press, probably through the London Times, the substance of those letters.

I regard such a procedure as of primary importance in view of the interests of peace, and I am quite sure that the holy father would rejoice at seeing those interests benefited in this or any other effective manner.

I have the honor to be, sir, very respectively, your obedient servant,

A. DUDLEY MANN

Hon. J.P. BENJAMIN,
Secretary of State, C.S.A., Richmond, Va.

PARIS, *December 28, 1863.*

[No. 71]

SIR: Upon quitting Rome I went direct to Naples, an agreeable railroad run of nine hours' duration.

I was anxious to see the operations of a liberal system of government upon the recognized "Queen City" of southern Europe. It had been often said that no political influences could relieve her from the enervating effects of a tropical climate; that it was not so much tyrannous rule as a scorching sun that impaired her energies; but to my astonishment, I found her among the most demonstrative commercial cities which I have visited upon the Continent. In all the pursuits in which she is engaged there seems to be an industrious activity which would contrast not unfavorably with that of New Orleans in her most prosperous days. Numbering already some 500,000 inhabitants her course seems to be rapidly onward and upward. I was assured, from various reliable sources, that she had entered upon an utterly new existence since she cast off the iron yoke of King Bomba; that she was eminently prosperous; that the idle did not infest her streets as formerly; and that labor was adequately rewarded for its toils.

After a sojourn of four days I embarked for Leghorn, and from thence traveled leisurely—stopping at Pisa, Florence, and Bologna several days—to Turin, where I remained only eighteen hours. The King was absent. Had he been at home I should have been inclined to ask an audience of him, as a citizen of the Confederate States.

Throughout Italy, as far as I was enabled to ascertain from my bankers and numerous other intelli-

gent individuals, enlightened public sentiment is beginning steadily to array itself against "Lincoln and Company," and to manifest an earnest desire for the establishment of peace. There is no longer a charm in the name of Garibaldi. even for the masses. He is generally esteemed as patriotic, pure and heroic. but deplorably deficient in that most essential quality to the creation of true greatness—common sense. **The impious comparison which he made of Abraham Lincoln to Jesus Christ has damaged largely his reputation in all Catholic circles while it has popularized our cause.**

From Turin I crossed over Mont Cenis and hastened to this metropolis, where I arrived at 8 o'clock the day after Christmas. At 11 I visited Mr. Slidell, who immediately dispatched his servant to inform Mr. Mason that I was with him. In a few minutes Mr. Mason came in. I then communicated to them in detail the incidents of my mission to Rome, and placed before them copies of the correspondence between the President and the Pope. **After its careful perusal, they united in opinion that its early publication on this side of the Atlantic was of almost paramount importance to the influencing of valuable public opinion, in both hemispheres, in our favor.** I hesitated as to the propriety of such a procedure with respect to the letter of the Pope, before the reception of its contents by the President, notwithstanding his Holiness prepared it for universal dissemination. I preferred to give, instead, it's supposed substances with **the direction, which in itself was positive recognition.** But I was met by the remark that the nature of the document for practical effect, would be vastly impaired before it could appear to the public eye at Richmond under the authorization of the President. I then placed in the hands of Mr. Slidell a copy of the correspondence, which was subsequently recopied by Mr. Eustis. Mr. Slidell was to go today to the foreign office to secure its insertion in the Moniteur.

I leave here at 5 o'clock this afternoon for Brussels. After a sojourn there of a few days, where a heavy correspondence of two months' accumulation awaits me, I shall go over to London to make the result of my visit to Rome as advantageously known as possible. Mr. Mason and Mr. Slidell cordially approved of this intention. Indeed, I was earnestly urged by them not to relinquish my purpose.

I have the honor to be, sir, very respectfully, your obedient servant,

A. DUDLEY MANN

Hon. J. P. BENJAMIN,
Secretary of State, C. S. A., Richmond, Va.

[Translation of Cardinal Antonelli's dispatch]

ROME, *December 2, 1863.*

HONORABLE GENTLEMEN: Your colleague, Mr. Soutter, has handed me your letter of 11th November, with which, in conformity with the instructions of your Government, **you have sent me a copy of the manifesto issued by the Congress of the Confederate States and approved by the most honorable President, in order that the attention of the government of the Holy See, to whom, as well as to the other Governments, you have addressed yourselves, might be called to it. The sentiments expressed in the manifesto tending, as they do, to the cessation of the most bloody war which still rages in your countries and the putting an end to the disasters which accompany it by proceeding to negotiations for peace**, being entirely in accordance with the disposition and character of the august head of the Catholic Church, I did not hesitate a moment in bringing it to the notice of the Holy Father.

His Holiness, who has been deeply afflicted by the accounts of the frightful carnage of this obstinate struggle, has heard with satisfaction the expression of the same sentiments; being the vicar on earth of that God who is the author of peace, he yearns to see these wraths appeased and peace restored. In proof of this he wrote to the archbishops of New York and New Orleans as far back as 18th October, 1862. inviting them to exert themselves in bringing about this holy object. You may then, honorable gentlemen, feel well assured that whenever a favorable occasion shall present itself, his holiness will not fail to avail himself of it to hasten so desirable a result and that all nations may be united in the bonds of charity.

In acquainting you with this benignant disposition of the Holy Father, I am pleased to declare myself with sentiments of the most distinguished esteem.

Truly, your servant,

G. CAR. ANTONELLI.
[DELLA S. S. L'I'MO.]

Messrs. A. DUDLEY MANN, J. M. MASON, JOHN SLIDELL
Commissioners of the Confederate States of America, Paris

DEPARTMENT OF STATE,
Richmond, January 28, 1864.

SIR: I have the honor to acknowledge receipt of your several dispatches. Nos. 50, 50 bis, and 51, dated, respectively, on the 3d, 6th, and 15th ultimo, and received, together on the 16th instant.

Your No. 50 bis. in relation to Mr. de Leon, bears nearly the same date as my dispatch to you on the same subject and requires no special remark. While appreciating the motives which induced your forbearance from complaint, I can not but think that the Department ought to have been apprised earlier of the facts related in your dispatch, especially as to his opening, without the slightest warrant of authority, the sealed dispatches addressed to you, and committed to his care. This fault was of so very grave a nature that it alone would probably have sufficed to put an end to Mr. de Leon's agency, and we should thus have been spared the annoyance of the scandal created by the interception and publication of the objectionable correspondence which caused his removal. Your No. 50 bis has been considered official and placed in the regular files, notwithstanding the doubt intimated in its concluding passages, because the subject had already taken its proper place in the official correspondence of the Department.

Reverting to more agreeable duties, I observe with a satisfaction, which has been shared by the President, the continued manifestations by a high personage of favorable dispositions toward the Confederacy, as evinced not only in the matter of the *Rappahannock* but in the communication of the dispatch as related in your No. 51, and which was fully understood by reference to your No. 32. I trust that intelligence equally favorable will soon be received on the whole subject connected with the postscript of my No. 27.

I take it for granted that you have seen the correspondence between the President and the Pope, but enclose it, as published here, with the translation made in the Department of the Pope's letters. The effect on our people has been good, and we hope that some benefit will be experienced from this correspondence in the influence excited on Roman Catholics in the North.

The President thinks you are mistaken in your estimate of the person who wrote you the note from Trieste of 7th November last, as copied into your No. 50. At all events, from the beginning of the war that person has been constantly writing to the President with expressions of warm sympathy for our cause, and has in various ways manifested in it an interest which the President would be loath to suspect as simulated or assumed for treacherous purposes. If you can give any of the grounds which have excited your suspicions, they might be sent in cipher, for it is of course important that the President should not entertain a mistaken impression on this point.

On the whole subject embraced in the Trieste letter, and in your Nos. 50 and 51, my last dispatch No. 27 will have given you the fullest information of the views and policy of this Government and of the measures adopted to carry them into effect. We await with interest the result of the deliberation of the archduke on the subject of accepting the throne of Mexico. The announcement of the French Government to the Corps Legislatif that the "sole reservation" was in relation to the popular vote of the

Mexicans justified us in considering the matter as settled, and we were not prepared for the information to the contrary contained in your dispatches. Recent Northern papers bring news to the 2d January (more than two weeks later than your No. 51), announcing that the French journals deny that the archduke has imposed conditions on his acceptance, and thus give color to the inference that his hesitation is at an end. I need hardly add that our interests are so deeply affected in this whole subject that we await with solicitude the official news that is to banish all doubt as to the future government of Mexico.

You will perceive by what was stated in my No. 27 that your note to the Emperor of 4th December was in entire accordance with the views entertained here, and that there was even identity in the observation made, that each musket intercepted was equivalent to abstracting a soldier from our ranks. We still remain without news of the French occupation of Matamoras, although daily hoping to receive it. The delay of the French commanders in a movement so important confirms my impression that they are anxious to avoid a possible conflict with our enemies, rather than to conduct their operations in the most effective manner.

The correspondence with Messrs. Fraser, Trenholm & Co. relative to the captured silver has been copied and sent to the Secretary of the Navy.

I am, respectfully, your obedient servant,

J. P. BENJAMIN,
Secretary of State

Hon. JOHN SLIDELL,
Paris, France.

Here is the Pope's reply:

Illustrious and Honorable President,
Salutation.

We have just received with all suitable welcome the persons sent by you to place in our hands your letter dated the 25th of September last. Not slight was the pleasure we experienced when we learned from those persons and the letter, with what feelings of joy and gratitude, illustrious and honorable President, as soon as you were informed of our letters to our venerable brother, John, Archbishop of New York and John, Archbishop of New Orleans, dated the 18th of October of last year, and in which we have with all our strength exerted and exhorted those venerable brothers that in their Episcopal piety and solicitude they should endeavor with the most ardent zeal and in our name, to bring about the end of that fatal Civil War which has broken out in those countries in order that the American people may obtain peace and concord and dwell charitably together.

It is particularly agreeable to us to see that you, illustrious and honorable President, and your people, were animated with the same desires of peace and tranquility which we have in our letters inculcated upon our venerable brothers. May it please God at the same time to make other people of America and their rulers reflecting seriously how terrible is civil war and what calamities it engenders, listen to the inspirations of a calmer spirit and adopt resolutely the part of peace.

As for us, we shall not cease to offer up the most fervent prayers to God Almighty that He may pour out upon all the people of America the spirit of peace and charity, and that He will stop the great evils which afflict them. We at the same time beseech the God of Pity to shed abroad upon you, the light of His Grace and attach you to us by a perfect friendship.

Given at Rome, at St. Peters the 3rd day of December, 1863 of our

Pontificate Eighteen

Pius IX

The reader will note the recognition by the Pope of a divided country and also the recognition of Davis as the President. It was on the publication of this letter that the large desertions of Roman Catholics from the ranks of the North began.

Upon the publication of this letter, the emotional Charles Chiniquy thought it his duty to go to Washington and tell Lincoln the full implication of its contents. He said:

> "My dear president, it is just that letter which brought me to your presence again. That letter is a poisoned arrow thrown by the pope at you personally; it is your death warrant. Before the letter every Catholic could see that their Church as a whole was against this free republic. However, a good number of liberty loving Irish, German and French Catholics, following more the instincts of their noble nature than the degrading principles of their Church, enrolled themselves under the banners of liberty, and they have fought like heroes. To detach these men from the rank and file of the Northern armies, and force them to help the cause of the rebellion, became the object of the Jesuits.
>
> "Secret pressing letters were addressed from Rome to the Bishops, ordering them to weaken your armies by detaching those men from you. The Bishops refused; for they would be exposing themselves as traitors and be shot. But they advised the pope to acknowledge, at once, the legitimacy of the Southern republic, and to take Jeff Davis under his supreme protection, by a letter, which would be read everywhere.
>
> "That letter tells every Roman Catholic that you are a blood-thirsty tyrant fighting against a government which the infallible and holy pope of Rome recognizes as legitimate. The pope, by this letter, tells his blind slaves that you are outraging the God of heaven and earth, by continuing such a bloody conflict.
>
> "By this letter of the pope to Jeff Davis you are not only an apostate, as you were thought before, whom every man had the right to kill, according to the canonical laws of Rome; but you are more vile, criminal and cruel than the horse thief, the public bandit, and the lawless brigand robber and murderer.
>
> "And, my dear president, this is not a fancy imagination on my part, it is the unanimous explanation given me by a great number of the priests of Rome, with whom I have had the occasion to speak on that subject. In the name of God, and in the name of our dear country, which is so much in need of your services, I plead that you may pay more attention to protect your precious life, and not continue to expose yourself as you have done till now." (4)

Lincoln then insightfully replied:

"You confirm my views of the letter of the Pope. Professor Morse is of the same mind. It is indeed the most perfidious act which could occur under present circumstances. You are perfectly correct when you say it was to detach the Roman Catholics who had enrolled themselves in our armies. Since the publication of that letter, a great number of them have deserted their banners and turned traitor. One of the few who have not is Sheridan, worth a whole army by his ability, his patriotism and his heroic courage. It is true also, that Meade has remained with us, and gained the bloody battle of Gettysburg. But how could he lose it, when he was surrounded by such heroes as Howard, Reynolds, Buford, Wadsworth, Cutler, Slocum, Sickles, Hancock and Barnes. But it is evident that his Romanism superseded his patriotism after the battle. He let the army of Lee escape when he could have easily cut off his retreat and forced him to surrender after losing nearly half of his soldiers the last three days' carnage.

"When Meade was to order the pursuit after the battle, a stranger came in haste to the headquarters, and that stranger was a distinguished Jesuit. After ten minutes' conversation with him, Meade made such arrangements for the pursuit of the enemy that Lee escaped almost untouched with the loss of only two guns!

"You are right that this letter of the Pope has entirely changed the nature and the ground of the war. Before they read it, the Roman Catholics could see that I was fighting against Jeff Davis and his Southern Confederacy. But now, they must believe that it is against Christ and His holy vicar, the Pope, that I am raising my sacrilegious hands; and we have the daily proofs that their indignation, their hatred, their malice, against me are a hundredfold intensified. New projects of assassination are detected almost every day, accompanied with such savage circumstances that they bring to my memory the massacre of St. Bartholomew and the Gunpowder Plot. Our investigation indicates that they come from the same masters in the art of murder, the Jesuits.

"The New York riots were evidently a Romish plot from beginning to end. We have the proofs in hand that they were the work of Bishop Hughes and his emissaries. No doubt can remain about the bloody attempts of Rome to destroy New York, when we know the easy way it was stopped. I wrote to Bishop Hughes, telling him that the whole country would hold him responsible for it if he would not stop it at once. He then gathered the rioters to his palace, called them his 'dear friends', invited them to go back home peacefully, and all was finished! So Jupiter of old used to raise a storm and stop it with a nod of his head!

"From the beginning of our civil war, there has been, not a secret, but a public alliance, between the Pope of Rome and Jeff Davis. The Pope and his Jesuits have advised, supported, and directed Jeff Davis on the land, from the first gun fired at Fort Sumter by the Catholic Beauregard, they are helping him on the sea by guiding and supporting the Catholic Semmes on the ocean.

"In my interview with Bishop Hughes, I told him 'that every stranger who had sworn allegiance to our government by becoming United States citizens, like himself, was liable to be shot or hung as a traitor and a spy'. After I had put this flea in the ears of the Bishop, I requested him to go and report my words to the Pope. My hope was that he would advise them, for their own interest, to become loyal and true to their allegiance and help us through the remaining part of the war. But the result has been the very contrary. The Pope has thrown away the mask, and shown himself the public partisan and the protector of the rebellion, by taking Jeff Davis by the hand, and impudently recognizing the Southern States as a legitimate government. Now I have the proof in hand that the very Bishop Hughes, whom I had sent to Rome to induce the Pope to urge the Roman Catholics of the North at least, to be true to their allegiance, and whom I thanked publicly, when, under the impression that he had acted honestly, according to the promise he had given me, is the very man who advised the Pope to recognize the legitimacy of the Southern republic, and put the whole weight of his tiara in the balance against us in favor of our enemies! Such is the perfidy of the Jesuits.

"Till lately, I was in favor of the unlimited liberty of conscience as our constitution gives it to the Roman Catholics. But now, it seems to me that, sooner or later, the people will be forced to put a restriction to that clause towards the papists. Is it not an act of folly to give absolute liberty of conscience to a set of men who are publicly sworn to cut our throats the very day they have the opportunity? Is it right to give the privilege of citizenship to men who are sworn and public enemies of our Constitution, our laws, our liberties, and our lives?

"The very moment that popery assumed the right of life and death on a citizen of France, Spain, Germany, England or the United States, it assumed to be the power, the government of France, Spain, Germany, England and the United States. Those States then committed a suicidal act by allowing popery to put a foot on their territory with the privilege of citizenship. The power to life and death is the supreme power and two supreme powers cannot exist on the same territory without anarchy, riots, bloodshed, and civil wars without end. When popery will give up the power of life and death which it proclaims as its own divine power in all its theological books and canon laws, then, and then alone, it can be tolerated and can receive the privileges of citizenship in a free country.

"Is it not an absurdity to give a man a thing which he has sworn to hate, curse and destroy? And does not the Catholic Church of Rome hate, curse and destroy liberty of conscience whenever she can do it safely? I am for liberty of conscience in its highest, noblest, broadest sense. But I cannot give liberty of conscience to the Pope and his followers so long as they tell me in all their councils, theologians and canon laws, that their liberty of conscience orders them to burn my wife, strangle my children, and cut my throat when they find the opportunity! This does not seem to be understood by the people today. But sooner or later, the light of common sense will make it clear to everyone that no liberty of conscience can be granted to men who are sworn to obey a pope, who pretends to have the right to put to death those who differ from him in religion. (Fifty Years in the Church of Rome)

On the whole, surely no one can deny that Rome's fatal virus worked in the veins of this Ultra-Pro-Slavery leader in the Rebellion, and that Lincoln was right when he recognized the "anti-social and anti-Christian views" of the foe with which he struggled. The fact that Jefferson Davis was not a professed Roman Catholic did not in the slightest curtail his usefulness as a Leopoldine.

A sense of justice and gratitude should compel every loyal American to remember the decisive and correct attitude of the British government at the psychological moment of their Civil War. It stands in sharp contrast with the meddlesome letter of the Pope. On page 476 of the "*Memoirs*" completed by Mrs. Davis, it quotes in full the ultimatum of England, which was received by Davis at Richmond through the British Consul, which says in part:

> "After consulting with the law officers of the Crown, Her Majesty's government have come to the decision that the agents of the authorities of the so-called Confederate States have been engaged in building vessels which would be at least partially equipped for war purposes on leaving the ports of this country; that these war vessels would undoubtedly be used against the United States, a country with which this government is at peace; that this would be a violation of the neutrality laws of the realm; and that the Government of the United States would have just grounds for serious complaint against Her Majesty's Government, should they permit such an infraction of the friendly relations subsisting between the two countries. No matter what might be the difficulty of proving in a court of law that the parties procuring the building of these vessels are agents of the so-called Confederate States, it is universally understood throughout the world that they are so, and Her Majesty's Government are satisfied that Mr. Davis would not deny that they are so. Under these circumstances, Her Majesty's Government protests and remonstrates against any further efforts being made on the part of the so-called Confederate States, or the authorities or agents thereof to build or cause to be built, to purchase or cause to be purchased, any such vessels as those styled as "Rams," or any other vessels to be used for war purposes against the United States, or against any country with which the United Kingdom is at peace or on terms of amity; and Her Majesty's Government further protests against all acts in violation of the neutrality laws of the realms.
>
> I have the honour to be your Lordship's obedient servant,
>
> (signed) Russell" (4)

Those are the words with the "bark on". No recognition of "Your Illustrious and Honorable President." Only the recognition of a United States and preservation of the Union for which Lincoln was contending and gave his life.

Roman Catholic Mass near Washington D.C. 1862

On July 26, 1862 in a letter to Reverdy Johnson, who, incidentally was the attorney for Mary E. Surratt, Mr. Lincoln said:

> "I am a patient man, always willing to forgive on the Christian terms of repentance, and also to give ample time for repentance. Still, I must save the government if possible. What I cannot do, of course I will not do; but it may as well be understood, once for all, that I do not surrender this game leaving any available card unplayed." (5)

This was the same expression of sentiment which had caused the death of William Henry Harrison, the ninth President and Zachary Taylor, the twelfth President, the preservation of the Union and the fact that

Lincoln did it, was the grounds for his physical death, by these wreckers.

Nor did Lincoln stop pouring out his patriotic soul all during these trying four years. On August 15, 1863, he gave his opinion upon the Draft as follows:

> "Shall we shrink from the necessary means to maintain our free government, which our grandfathers employed to establish, and our fathers have already employed once to maintain it? Are we degenerate? Has the manhood of our race run out? (Complete Works, Nicolay & Hay, Vol. II, pg. 391)

The President spent the first months of his administration feeling his way, so to speak. Delving into the conditions in the various departments, finding traitors and carefully replacing them with those who he knew to be true. The lesson he was learning would have staggered a man of less courage than Lincoln - the steadfast, unyielding patriot, when any principle of right was in the balance.

It was the sifting time for Lincoln. In his letter to Corning, June 1863 he wrote:

> "The man who stands by and says nothing when the peril of his country's government is discussed, cannot be misunderstood. If not hindered, he is sure to help the enemy; much more, if he talks ambiguously - talks for his country 'with buts and ifs and ands.'" (Barrett, pg. 632)

In addressing the members of the general assembly Presbyterian Church, President Lincoln said:

> "As a pilot, I have used my best exertions to keep afloat our ship of state; and shall be glad to resign my trust at the appointed time to another pilot more skillful and successful than I may prove. In every case and at all hazards the government must be perpetuated." (Complete Works, Nicolay & Hay, Vol. II, Pg. 342)

Thus almost daily was Lincoln telling his American creed, adding fuel to the fires of hatred which were burning in the hearts of his country's enemies. Spurred on like demons, they rounded up their hellhounds in and about Washington for the final perfidious act.

It finally became manifest to President Lincoln that the presence of the foreign troops in Mexico was a menace to the safety of the United States, and through their Consul at Paris, his government served notice upon Napoleon, that Jesuit tool of Pius IX, that his troops must be removed from Mexico within the time dictated by him.

Jesuit trained and educated General Beauregard

That there could be no misunderstanding concerning the attitude of the Lincoln administration toward the Republic of Mexico, was made plainly evident by the "note" sent through Secretary of State Seward to their Consul at Paris to be delivered to Napoleon III which reads:

> "The United States government does not desire to suppress the fact that their sympathies are with Mexico, that is to say with the Republic of Mexico nor does the United States government in any sense, for any purpose, disapprove of the Republican government, now in force in Mexico, or distrust the administration. Neither was there any disposition apparently to deny the Liberals of Mexico financial assistance." (6)

Maximilian's Imperial Mexican Flag

When President Lincoln submitted to the Senate a Treaty granting a loan of 11 million dollars to the Republic of Mexico, although he made no recommendations upon the subject, it was a sufficient hint which expressed his sympathy.

The demand that the French troops be removed from Mexico was complied with to the letter, owing to complications in the situation in which France at the time was involved in Europe she feared war with the United States.

As can be imagined, this was a terrible blow to the conspirators in Europe, Canada and Mexico, not to speak of their tools in the United States itself.

Insofar as the Canadian connection was concerned, a plot was conceived by the divine-righters of Europe, which was to become the forerunner to the modern use of bio-terrorism. The targets eerily foreshadow the anthrax events subsequent to the events of Sept.11, 2001. It was recorded for posterity by Brig. General Thomas M. Harris, a member of the military commission, which tried the conspirators of Lincoln's assassination, in his book, "*Assassination of Lincoln, a History of the Great Conspiracy,*" and has been buried for over one hundred years. This fascinating blow-by-blow account has been reproduced here.

> "During the progress of this trial for the extradition of the raiders, Thompson, Clay, Tucker, and Sanders necessarily held a kind of professional intercourse with the counsel representing the United States. Sanders, on one occasion, became full of self-importance, as also, probably, of whiskey, when his discretion forsook him, and he gave vent to the vaunting and boasting of a braggadocio. He said this raid was not the last that would occur, but...that many Yankee sons of bitches would be killed. He said they had their plans perfectly organized, and men ready to sack and burn Buffalo, Detroit, New York, Washington and other places, and any preparations that could be made by the government to prevent them, would not, though they might delay them for a time. Several other raids were planned, but were prevented by

preparations which the government was enabled to make by being informed of them in advance by persons engaged in its secret service, or by other friends in Canada, who, being in the confidence of the conspirators, became informed as to their plans.

"These plans involved a warfare against non-combatants; a war, as we shall see, of poisoning reservoirs, of burning towns and cities by wholesale; a war of the destruction of men, women and children; of burning hospitals, churches and private dwellings; a war for the destruction of life and property; in short, a war against humanity. The City of New York came in for a large share of their consideration. The destruction of the Croton dam was an enterprise that seemed very desirable to them. The poisoning of the reservoirs supplying the city with water was much discussed. This was one of the hobbies of the infamous Dr. Blackburn and a Mr. M. A. Pallen of Mississippi, who had been a surgeon in the rebel army. Amongst the poisons they had considered arsenic, strychnine, and prussic acid as available. Blackburn thought the project feasible. Thompson feared it would be impossible to collect so large a quantity of poisonous matter without exciting suspicion and leading to the detection of the parties engaged in it. Pallen and others thought it could be managed in Europe. Blackburn, Pallen, Thompson, Sanders, and Cleary fully and freely discussed this matter in June 1864.

"The moral question involved in the destruction of the American commercial metropolis, men, women and children, did not enter into their thoughts; it was, in fact, a scheme dear to their hearts; the difficulties attending its accomplishment were the only things that gave them any trouble.

"This is that same Dr. Blackburn who, with the approbation of Thompson and his gang, made an effort in the summer of 1864 to spread pestilence in Washington City, and other cities occupied by federal troops, as far south as could be reached, by means of clothing infested with yellow fever, typhoid and with small pox.

"Conover testified to this positively as one of their many wicked schemes to spread consternation over the North, and so demoralize the people that they would be willing to make peace on any terms.

“As this last scheme is so monstrous in character that it can only be believed on the fullest proof, I give the testimony of Godfrey Joseph Hyams before the commission, in full:

“I am a native of London, England, but I have lived south nine or ten years. During the past year I have resided in Toronto, Canada. About the middle of December, 1863, I made the acquaintance of Dr. Blackburn. I was introduced to him by the Reverend (R.C.) Stewart Robinson at the Queen’s Hotel in Toronto. I knew him by sight previously, but before that had no conversation with him. I knew that he was a Confederate and was working for the rebellion. Dr. Blackburn was then about to take south some men who had escaped from the federal service, and I asked to go with him. He asked me if I wanted to go south and serve the Confederacy. I said I did. He then told me to come upstairs, and after we had entered his room he pledged his word as a Freemason, and offered his hand in friendship, that he would never deceive me. He said he wanted to confide to me an expedition. I told him I would not care if I did. He said I would make an independent fortune by it, at least one hundred thousand dollars, and get more honor and glory to my name than General Lee, and be of more assistance to the Confederate government than if I was to take one hundred thousand soldiers to reinforce General Lee. I pledged my word that I would go if I could do any good. He then told me he wanted me to take a certain quantity of clothing, consisting of shirts, coats, and underclothing, into the States, and dispose of them by auction. I was to take them to Washington City, to Norfolk, and as far south as I could possibly go, where the federal government held possession and had the most troops, and to sell them on a hot day or of a night; that it did not matter what money I got for them, I had just to dispose of them in the best market where there were the most troops, and where they would be most effective, and then come away. He told me I should have one hundred thousand dollars for my services, sixty thousand of it directly after I returned to Toronto; but he said that would not be a circumstance to what I should get. He said I might make ten times one hundred thousand dollars. I was to stay in Toronto, and go on with my legitimate business until I heard from him. He told me to keep quiet, and if I moved anywhere I was to inform Reverend Stewart Robinson where I went to, and he would telegraph for me, or write to me through him.

"Sometime in the month of May, 1864, I went to my work and worked on until the 8th day of June, 1864; it was on a Saturday night; I had been out to take a pair of boots home to a customer of mine; when I returned home my wife had a letter for me from Dr. Blackburn, which Reverend Stewart Robinson had left in passing there. I read the letter, and went out to see Reverend Robinson. I asked him what I was to do about it. He said he did not know anything about it; that he did not want to furnish any means to commit an overt act against the United States government. He advised me to borrow from Mr. Preston, who keeps a tobacco manufactory in Toronto, enough money to take me to Montreal, and there get money from Mr. Slaughter, according to the directions contained in Dr. Blackburn's letter. This letter instructed me to proceed from Montreal to Halifax to meet Dr. Blackburn; it was dated Havana, May 10th, 1864.

"I went to Halifax to a gentleman by the name of Alexander H. Keith, Jr., a local brewer, and remained under his care until Dr. Blackburn arrived in the steamer 'Alpha,' on the 12th of July, 1864. When Dr. Blackburn arrived he sent to the Farmer's Hotel, where I was staying, for me. I went to see him, and he told me that the goods were on board the steamer 'Alpha,' and that the second officer, told me to get an express wagon and take it down to Cunard's steamboat wharf. I did so, and there got eight trunks and a valise. I was directed to take them to my hotel, and put them in a private room. I put them in Mr. Doran's private sitting-room. I then went around to Dr. Blackburn, and told him I had the goods off the steamer. He told me that the five trunks tied up with ropes were the ones for me to take, and asked me if I would take the valise to the States and send it by express with an accompanying letter, as a donation to President Lincoln. I objected to taking it, and refused to do so. I then took three of the trunks and the valise around to the hotel. He was then staying at the Halifax Hotel. The trunks had Spanish marks upon them, and he told me to scrape them off, and that Mr. Hill would go with me the next morning and make arrangements with some captain of a vessel to take them. There were two vessels there running to Boston, and I was to make an arrangement with either of them to smuggle the trunks through to Boston. The next morning I went down with Mr. Hill to the vessels. Mr. Hill had a private conversation with Captain McGregor, the captain of the first vessel, to whom we applied to take the goods, and he refused.

"We then went to see Captain O'Brien of the bark 'Halifax.' Hill told him that I had some presents in my trunks, consisting of silks, satin dresses, etc., that I wanted to take to my friends. The captain and Mr. Hill had a private conversation, and when the Captain came out he consented to take them. I was to give him a twenty dollar gold piece for smuggling them in. I put them on board the vessel that day and he stowed them away. The vessel lay five days at Boston before he could get a chance to get them off, but finally he succeeded in getting them off, and expressed them to Philadelphia, where I received them and brought them to Baltimore. I then took out the goods, which were very much rumpled, and smoothed them out and arranged them, bought some new trunks, and repacked them and brought them to Washington. Dr. Blackburn, by way of caution, asked me before leaving if I had had the yellow fever, and on my saying 'no,' he said, 'You must have a preventive against taking it. You must get some camphor and chew it, and get some strong cigars, the strongest you can get; and be sure to keep gloves on your hands when handling the things.' He gave me some cigars that he said he had bought in Havana, which he said were strong enough for anything. When I arrived in Washington, I turned over five of the trunks to Messrs. W. L. Wall & Company, commission merchants in this city, and four to a man by the name of Myers, from Boston, a sutler for Siegel's or Weitzel's division. He said he had some goods which he was going to take to New Berne, N.C., and I told him that I had a lot of goods that I wanted to sell, and, to make the best market I could for them, I would turn them over to him on commission. I also told him I would shortly have more, and mentioned that I had disposed of some to Wall & Company, of this city. Dr. Blackburn told me, when I was making arrangements, that I should let the parties to whom I disposed of my goods know that I would have a big lot to sell, as it was in contemplation to get together about a million dollars' worth of goods and dispose of them in that way. Dr. Blackburn stated that his object in having these goods disposed of in different cities was to destroy the armies, or anybody else that they came in contact with. All these goods, he told me, had been carefully infected in Bermuda with yellow fever, small pox, typhoid, and other contagious diseases.

"The goods in the valise, which were intended for President Lincoln, I understood him to say had been infected with yellow fever and small pox. This valise I declined taking charge of and turned it over to him in Halifax, and I afterwards heard that it had been sent to the President. On the five trunks that I turned over to Wall & Company I got an advance of one hundred dollars. Among these five trunks there was one that was always spoken of by Blackburn to me as the 'Big Number 2,' which he said I must be sure to have sold in Washington. On disposing of the trunks I immediately left Washington, and went straight through until I got to Hamilton, Canada. In the waiting-room there I met Mr. Holcomb and Clement C. Clay. They both rose, shook hands with me, and congratulated me upon my safe return, and upon my making a fortune. They told me I should be a gentleman for the future, instead of a working man and a mechanic. They seemed perfectly to understand the business in which I had been engaged.

"Mr. Holcomb told me that Dr. Blackburn was at the Donegan Hotel, in Montreal, and that I had better telegraph to him stating that I had returned. As Dr. Blackburn had requested me to telegraph to him as soon as I got into Canada, I did so, and the next night, between eleven and twelve o'clock, Dr. Blackburn came up and knocked at the door of my house. I was in bed at the time. I looked out of the window, and saw Dr. Blackburn there. Said he, 'Come down, Hyams, and open the door; you are like all damned rascals who have been doing something wrong - you're afraid that the devil is after you.' He was in company with Bennett H. Young. I came down and let him in. He asked me how I had disposed of the goods and I told him. 'Well,' said he, 'that is all right as long as "Big Number 2" went into Washington; it will kill them at sixty yards distance.' I then told the doctor that everything had gone wrong at my home in my absence; that I needed some funds; that my family needed money. He said he would go to Colonel Jacob Thompson and make arrangements for me to draw upon him for any amount of money that I required. He then said that the British authorities had solicited his services in attending the yellow fever that was then raging in Bermuda; that he was going on there; and that as soon as he came back he would see me. I went up to Jacob Thompson the next morning, and told him what Dr. Blackburn had said. He said, 'Yes'; Dr, Blackburn had been there and had made arrangements for me to draw one hundred dollars whenever it was shown that I had made disposition of the goods according to his directions. I told him I needed money; that I had been so long away from home that everything I had was gone, and I wanted money to pay my rent, etc. He said, 'I will give you fifty dollars now, but it is against Dr. Blackburn's request; when you show me that you have sold the goods, I will give you the balance.' He asked me to give him a receipt, which I did: 'Received of Jacob Thompson the sum of fifty dollars on account of Dr. Blackburn.' That was about the 11th or 12th of August last. The next day I wrote to Messrs. Wall & Company, of Washington, desiring them to send me an account of the sales, and the balance due me. When I received their answer, I took it to Colonel Thompson. He then said he was perfectly satisfied I had done my part, and gave me a check for fifty dollars on the Ontario Bank. I gave him a receipt: 'Received of Jacob Thompson one hundred dollars in full on account of Dr. Luke P. Blackburn.' I told Thompson of the large sum which Dr. Blackburn had promised me for my services and that he and Mr. Holcomb had both told me that the Confederate government had appropriated two million dollars for the purpose of carrying it out; but he would not pay me any more.

"When Dr. Blackburn returned from Bermuda, I wrote to him at Montreal, and told him I wanted some money, and that he ought to send me some; but he made no reply to my letter. I was then sent down to Montreal with a commission for Bennett H. Young, to be used in his defense in the St. Albans raid case. I there met Dr. Blackburn. He said I had written some hard letters to him, abusing him, and that he had no money to give me. He then got into his carriage at the door and rode off to some races, I think, and never gave me any more satisfaction. As I wanted money before leaving for the States, I went to the Clifton House, Niagara. Dr. Blackburn told me he had no money with him then, but that he would go to Mr. Holcomb and get some, as he had Confederate funds with him. Blackburn said that when I returned he would get the money for the expedition from either Holcomb or Thompson, it did not matter which. From this, and from Holcomb and Clay both shaking hands with me and congratulating me at Hamilton upon my safe return, I thought, of course, they knew all about it. I do not know that Reverend Stewart Robinson knew all of the business in which I was engaged, but he took good care of me while I was in Toronto, in the fall, and until Dr. Blackburn wrote for me in the spring; and when he gave me Dr. Blackburn's letter, he told me to borrow the money from Mr. Preston to take me to Montreal, as he said he did not want to commit an overt act against the Government of the United States himself.

"Mr. Preston lent me ten dollars to go to Montreal. On arriving at that place, according to the directions of Dr. Blackburn's letter, I went to Mr. Slaughter to get the means to take me to Halifax. Mr. Slaughter was short of funds, and had only twenty dollars that he could give me. He said that I had better go to Mr. Holcomb, who was staying at the Donegan Hotel, and he would give me the balance. I went up to the Hotel and sent up my name, and he sent for me to come up. I told him I wanted some money to take me to Halifax; he asked me how much I wanted; I told him as much as would make up forty dollars; he said, 'You had better take fifty dollars,' but as I did not want that much I took enough to make forty dollars. When I came to Washington to dispose of my goods, which was on the 5th of August, 1864, I put up at the National Hotel, registered my name as J. W. Harris, under which name I did business with Wall & Company."

This is a straightforward account of the efforts and the means used to spread disease and death amongst citizens and soldiers alike, in the capital of the nation, and in other cities. Mr. Hyams, who, to gratify his desire for revenge on the originators of the plan, and who was just as guilty, came before the commission to reveal the whole history of the plot. No one who reads his story would doubt that he was lacking a conscience and who, hoping to obtain a rather large sum of money, was willing to make himself an instrument in the wholesale and indiscriminate destruction of human life. He was evidently a man well qualified for the task; in the first place he was destitute of conscience, and a man of a high degree of intelligence and a solid knowledge of affairs. He was selected by the Reverend Stewart Robinson and backed by Dr. Blackburn. He was totally deceived by all the parties involved including the Reverend Robinson and vowed revenge after being put off and then given the pitiful sum of one hundred dollars.

These men had also planned to poison the water supply of New York City to the extent of fatality to its entire population, men, women, and children - old age and helpless infancy doomed to death by the scope of their plans. Hyam's story bears on its face the marks of a truthful narrative of the facts, just as they occurred, and it does not follow that because a man is a confessed scoundrel he is incapable of telling the truth. Hyam's testimony was fully confirmed by the testimony of Wall & Company and by the register of the National Hotel of that date."

For some reason the infection was a failure in Washington City; but not so with the goods sent by Myers to New Berne, North Carolina. History mentions that in the latter part of the summer of 1864, an epidemic of yellow fever that killed thousands of people, both civilians and soldiers. There is no doubt that this epidemic was due to the infection carried in the clothing that Myers received from Hyams; and that in the great day of final account these men will find themselves arraigned as the murderers of all those who fell as the victims of their plot, before a tribunal that is infinitely perfect in its knowledge and just in its decisions.

On November 25, 1864 an attempt was made to destroy by fire the city of New York. This plan too, was conceived by the rebels based in Canada, and the plot was revealed by Robert C. Kennedy just before his execution by the commission of which Thomas Harris sat as a member. The account is as follows:

"After my escape from Johnson's Island I went to Canada, where I met a number of Confederates. They asked me if I was willing to go on an expedition. I replied: 'Yes, if it is in the service of my country.' They said: 'It is all right,' but gave me no intimation of its nature, nor did I ask for any. I was then sent to New York, where I stayed for some time. There were eight men in our party, of whom two fled to Canada. After we had been in New York three weeks we were told that the object of our expedition was to retaliate on the North for the atrocities in the Shenandoah Valley. It was designed to set fire to the city on the night of the Presidential election; but the phosphorous was not yet ready, and it was put off until the 25th of November. I was stopping at the Belmont House, but moved into Prince Street. I set fire to four places - in Barnum's Museum, Lovejoy's Hotel, Tammany Hotel, and the New England House. The others merely started fires in the house where each one was lodging, and then ran off. Had they all done as I did, we would have had thirty-two fires and played a huge joke on the fire department. I know that I am to be hung for setting fire to Barnum's Museum, but that was only a joke. I had no idea of doing it. I had been drinking and went in there with a friend, and just to scare the people, I emptied a bottle of phosphorous on the floor. We knew it would not set fire to the wood, for we had tried it before, and at one time had concluded to give the thing up. After setting fire to my four places, I walked the streets all night, and went to the Exchange Hotel early in the morning. We all met there that morning and the next night. My friend and I had rooms there, but we sat in the office nearly all the time reading the papers, while we were watched by the detectives, of whom the hotel was full. I expected to die then, and if I had it would have been all right; but now it seems rather hard. I escaped to Canada and was glad enough when I crossed the bridge in safety. I desired, however, to return to my command, and started with my friend for the Confederacy via Detroit. Just before entering the city he received an intimation that the detectives were on the lookout for us, and giving me the signal he jumped from the cars. I did not notice the signal, but kept on and was arrested in the depot. We wanted to let the people of the North understand that there were two sides to this war, and that they could not be rolling in wealth and comfort while we at the South were bearing all the hardships and privations. In retaliation for Sheridan's atrocities in the Shenandoah Valley, we desired to destroy property; not the lives of women and children, although that would, of course, followed in its train."

Although this attempt failed miserably, it demonstrates that the capacity to kill innocents was inconsequential in a moral sense. Harris states,

"...While honestly confessing his own part in it, he is very careful not to compromise anybody else. But we are not left without information as to who were the employers of him and his gang; and here again Thompson and his fellow agents of the rebel government in Canada as well as the Reverend Stewart Robinson, are made to appear to be its originators, and must be held responsible." (7)

The annals of no age of the world, or of the most rude and savage people of the earth, save the Nazi era, afford examples more atrocious than those planned and executed, or attempted to be executed, by these agents of Jefferson Davis in Canada, and by other agents whose deeds were sanctioned and paid for by the Jesuits and Jeff Davis and his Secretary of State Benjamin.

Back on the Mexican front events were shaping up in favor of the new Republic. The Empress Carolotte within a few months after their arrival in Mexico City, was sent to Rome by Maximilian to explain in person that the strength of Popular Government there had been severely underestimated; that it was impossible to restore the Church property and the rights of the clergy. The important part of her mission, however, was to ask for more troops.

Her reception at the Vatican was simply withering; the Pope was so chagrined and angry at the failure of his designs and so severe in his reproach that the sensitive princess was carried out bodily in an unconscious state, upon which she recovered a mental wreck. She was incarcerated in the Castle of Bouchet near Brussels, Belgium, where she was placed under constant surveillance, and was unaware that on June 19, 1867, Maximilian, her husband, was shot at sunrise at Queretaro, Mexico, by the Revolutionists.

A victory for the North was not indicated until the very last days of the War. The Leopoldines left no stone unturned to defeat Lincoln's re-nomination. They fully realized that if they did not, it meant their doom. When the news of his re-election was flashed over the wires, they did not give up. They redoubled their efforts. They saw more clearly than ever before that Abraham Lincoln was their sworn enemy. They knew only too well that he would be the stumbling block to their future plans, for they felt that in Lincoln they would always encounter a powerful champion for the preservation of the Union and all its institutions. They feared with a deadly fear the influence of his able pen and voice. They knew that to permit this calm, thorough, clear-visioned man who had such a complete estimate of their perfidious designs to serve at the helm during the reconstruction period would mean their ultimate rout in the political affairs of the United States.

Other Official correspondence is shown here which serves to add to the bulk of evidence of Vatican and Jesuit treachery in the War of the Rebellion, the first from 'Stonewall' Jackson...

HEADQUARTERS VALLEY DISTRICT
Romney, Va., January 17, 1862.

General JOSEPH E. JOHNSTON
Commanding Department of Northern Virginia:

GENERAL: Your letter of the 16th is at hand, and I hasten to reply that I have not enough troops for the proper defense of this district, as from the most reliable information that I have recently received the enemy's force in and about Cumberland is near 12,000—in Hancock 2,000, in Hagerstown 2,000, and in Fredericktown 8,000. Of the force in Williamsport I am not so well informed, but there is reason to believe that it is larger than in Hancock.

General Loring's command has not all arrived here from Morgan, but so soon as it does I hope to be able to leave him with his command to occupy the valley of the South Branch, while Garnett's brigade will return to Winchester and near Centreville, should you so direct; but in my opinion it should not go farther than Winchester, if the enemy are to be kept out of this district. Since leaving Winchester General Loring's command has become very much demoralized.

I have taken special pains to obtain information respecting General Banks, but I have not been informed of his having gone east. **I will see what can be effected through the Catholic priests in Martinsburg.**

I am establishing lines of couriers through this district. From Winchester I can send dispatches to Leesburg in three hours. I have thought that if you had a line of couriers between Leesburg and Manassas no additional one for carrying dispatches between Manassas and Winchester would be necessary; but should you desire an additional line, please indicate the route and I will have it established immediately.

I am, general, very respectfully, your obedient servant,

T. J. JACKSON,
Major-General, Commanding.

From John E. Tallon to Abraham Lincoln,

December 26, 1863

Donaldsonville

—La—

Dec 26. 1863

Honorable Sir,

I presume to write to you because I have always found it best to write to the "Fountain Head"

1st The Coloured Population on the Government plantations are in a most deplorable condition—they have no blankets—no clothing—half starved—not a single blanket has come this year—They are truly miserable—As I am the Government Physician for those poor creatures, I make this communication to you "in confidence and confide in your honor because if it known or discovered that I wrote the above, I would immediately lose my situation—I most respectfully recommend old Dr. E. C. Hyde 219 Tchoupitoulas Street New Orleans—as a most proper man to inspect the Government Plantations and to report to the Government—Dr. Hyde is well off in the world—is most zealous for the coloured population—and loyal to the Republican Administration in the highest degree—I beseech Your Excellency to enquire into those matters and when you find that old Dr. Hyde is the man I represent him to be, to appoint him with full power to remedy abuses—

[Note 1 According to General Orders No. 331, issued on October 9, 1863, property abandoned by rebels was placed under the control of the Treasury Department. A War Department circular issued on October 27, 1863 gave Treasury agents the authority to lease abandoned property to former slaves. Lincoln was not satisfied with the Treasury Department's administration of the government plantations and in February 1864 he gave the responsibility to Lorenzo Thomas. See *Official Records*, Series III, Volume 3, 872, 939 - 40 and *Collected Works*, VII, 212.]

2nd Captain Rudgers the Provost Marshall at Napoleonville has been removed out of Napoleonville at the instigations of the Masters there upon various charges—on last Thursday when riding up from General Martin's Plantation where I went to visit the sick coloured people, I learned at Napoleonville the true state of the Case—Captain Rudgers was accused of "giving the "niggers" too much liberty"—that a nigger's oath is "now as good as a white man's since this Provost Marshall" arrived—that he "raises hell among the niggers"—that he is ultra—and that he reproves the Planters in defense of the coloured people &c—that he is "no favorite with citizens of Napoleonville because of giving so much liberty to the niggers"—To speak truly, he is hated because he is a benevolent, and a true hearted man—I do most respectfully entreat of your Excellency to have him again restored to Napoleonville and to cause Mr. Foley—Madame Ratcliffe and other Rebel notabilities of Napoleonville, to take your new oath (2)

[Note 2 "New oath" is a reference to the loyalty oath in Lincoln's December 8, 1863 Proclamation of Amnesty and Reconstruction.]

3rd There is a class of persons at New Orleans &c called "British Subjects" who profess Neutrality with their tongues but in heart and in acts—and in every way favor the Rebels—Put a clause in the alien oath against Slavery, if they refuse to take it, let them be sent over the lines—

4th I most respectfully ask Your Excellency—to cause enquiry into the antecedents of persons holding Government situations at New Orleans—&c if they ever held appointments from the Rebels—or were well known rebels previous to obtaining those situations, let them be dismissed

5th **The Roman Catholic Clergy of Louisiana generally, I believe are Rebels at heart**,—and possess great influence in giving advice—I beseech and entreat your Excellency to oblige all of them to take the New oath and to have them sworn before the coming elections take place—Remember to do so, it is for the Cause of God and liberty; if any clergyman refuse, he is allied with Satan—and ought to be sent to Ship Island with a ball and chain—

I again beseech and entreat Your Excellency not to forget the cause of the poor colored people on the Government Plantations—and also to ~~inquire~~ appoint Dr. E. C. Hyde 219. Tchoupitoulas St. New Orleans—to go round on all the Government plantations and to report the real state of things to the Government—let him have power to remedy abuses—oblige him to go in person and allow no deputy in his stead—

Trusting Your Excellency will forgive this great liberty I remain from my heart your most respectful and most devoted adherent as well as of the venerated "Republican Party" to whom may God grant a perpetual election—as well as success in their most noble cause

John. E. Tallon M. D

A. A. Surgeon in the U. S. Army and Government Physician for the sick ~~coloured pop~~ contrabands! at Donaldsonville and vicinity—

RICHMOND HOUSE
Richmond, January 6, 1864.

His Excellency JEFFERSON DAVIS
President Confederate States of America:

DEAR SIR: I beg leave to call your attention to a weak point in the enemy's lines to which your mind may not have been directed. I allude to the Irish element in the Northern population. A resident of twenty years in Philadelphia, seventeen of which I was a wholesale bookseller, publisher, &c., and having quite a number of that class in my employment in binding, printing-office, and store, coupled with the fact that my parents were natives of Ireland, naturally created in my mind a sympathy for them, more especially as they were, about the time of my going to Philadelphia, objects of bitter and most intense persecution by an ignorant band of bigots. The interest I felt and manifested for them soon gave me quite an extensive acquaintance among them. I merely mention this fact to show you that my estimate of their character and knowledge of their views upon our question is not based upon superficial information. As soon as civil war seemed inevitable I began the tedious task of selling out and collecting, in order that I might hasten to this my native place. The regular routine of business broken up, I had much leisure time, which I used to the best advantage for the furtherance of our cause. Partly from the calls of business, together with a desire to see and converse with the Irish operatives in the coal mines of Pennsylvania, I visited during the summer of 1861 the counties of Lehigh, Carbon, Schuylkill, Berks, &c. I asserted that the native American and Know-Nothing were identical with the Black Republican party. I reminded them that the former had burned their churches in 1844; the Know-Nothing party had proscribed every man who had a Mc or an 0 to his name during the winter of 1857 and 1858, driving many thousands of families into starvation during the continuance of that short but certainly most severe financial storm which raged throughout the North at that period. Failing to accomplish their full purpose at each of these times by reason of the steady opposition of the South, and especially Virginia, where Know-Nothingism met its death, they changed their name and tactics, and by a loud outcry for the negro, for whom they had no real sympathy, but used him as a weapon against both the Irish and the South—their chief aim and object being to free the negro as far as they could, bring him North, put him in competition with the white labor, believing that they would work cheaper than the Irish, and, above all, they would not be permitted to vote. The effect of these short conversations, I can assure you, were most happy, and what added point to my argument was that many of these men had been driven from places of public employment during the winter of 1857 and 1858 by the Know-Nothing party, which was then in power in the select and common councils of Philadelphia. After the first battle of Manassas, T. F. Meagher came to Philadelphia to drum up recruits for his Irish Brigade. He made a capital speech; I feared a telling one. I worked night and day to neutralize his speech. His treatment of the Irish girl who aided him in making his escape from Australia, and his subsequent marriage with a Yankee girl, was an admirable argument against him, which I failed not to use on every occasion. The result was he obtained but few recruits in Philadelphia—not more than a corporal's guard. **I mention these circumstances to show you that the great body of Irish at the North feel a deep interest in our success, more especially in Pennsylvania, where they have been subjected to bitter persecution. Although I am an elder in the Presbyterian Church, yet I had conversations with quite a number of Roman Catholic priests at the North, all of whom, with one exception, expressed the utmost confidence and sympathy in our success.** Private letters which I received from James A. McMaster, editor of the Freeman's Journal, allude to the efforts which the North were making most cunningly to identify the South with these objectionable parties; a fact that I had noticed such artists, with those who had any knowledge of the subject, would awake only a feeling of indignation and contempt; but we know there are many Irish (those but recently arrived) who would believe the statement; and I have no doubt that the burning of the convent at Charlestown, Mass., by a mob has ere this been located at Charleston, S. C.

I owe you an apology for thus troubling you with this communication, but I do it from the best motives for our good. The views generally met the cordial approval of Hon. James A. Bayard, of Delaware, and Hon. Charles Brown, of Philadelphia, with the latter of whom I had frequent interviews before I left, March, 1862. In your judgment you may see some plan by which this party might be strengthened and encouraged by some complimentary allusion to the Irish in our Confederacy.

Begging pardon for the liberty I take, I remain, dear sir, yours, very respectfully,

S. C. HAYES
C.S. Register's Office.

After writing the above my attention was attracted by a letter from Mr. Smith O'Brien in the Sentinel, which I concluded to read before I sent this, thinking possibly that the same suggestions I make might meet your eye in a more agreeable form. I see nothing, however, in the letter or the editorial but additional evidence to my mind that we ought now to have the very best writers in the Confederacy engaged either as editors or regular contributors to the press. I have seen the evil effects flowing from the editorial attacks upon Mr. Benjamin in the Richmond papers. Mr. Chase, I have no doubt, had much cause to thank the Richmond editors for applying the name Jew as a term of contemptuous reproach to our Secretary of State, for large subscription to his 7.30 stock was made immediately by this very class at the North, some of whom remarked to me in the streets of Philadelphia, "Puritanism is worse at the South than in New England." Hon. James A. Bayard, of Delaware, in a conversation I had with him in February, 1862, remarked that if President Davis could obtain the cordial support of all the papers of the South, which he richly deserved, the war would close in six months, but that the silly attacks in the Richmond press tended to prolong the struggle, as it gave point to the abolitionists, who claim that there is a large Union element at the South. I feel very great hesitation in sending this to you, but I think it can certainly do no harm, except it be adding additional trouble to you in reading it.

Yours, very respectfully,

S. C. HAYES
C.S. Register's Office.

[First endorsement]

General Bragg for consideration.

J. D.

[Second endorsement]

HDQRS. ARMIES OF THE CONFEDERATE STATES,
August 22, 1864.

Respectfully returned to His Excellency the President.

This paper contains suggestions which I deem valuable and practicable. The employment of some judicious person to operate on this class of people through our own press and that of the North would no doubt be attended with good results. In this connection I suggest the printing in English, German, and French a large number of the recent general orders inviting foreigners in the Federal ranks to come to us and offering them protection. With care many of these papers could be introduced into the enemy's lines.

BRAXTON BRAGG.

[Third endorsement]

AUGUST 24, 1864.

Secretary of War for consideration and conference.

WHEELING VA., *June 1, 1863.*

Lieut. Col. W. H. CHESEBROUGH, *Assistant Adjutant-General,*

SIR: On the 21st ultimo I had the honor to submit the case of Rev. Daniel O'Connor, late Catholic priest at Weston, Va., sent here as a prisoner by order of Brigadier-General Roberts. Mr. O'Connor has solicited today an early decision regarding himself. As **he does not hesitate to follow in the footsteps of his bishop and declares his sympathy with the rebels while claiming that he is not an American citizen,** I respectfully suggest that he be ordered to leave this State, and if possible that he be directed to leave the United States. He has relatives in Canada.

Very respectfully,

JOS. DARR, JR.,
Major and Military Commander.

HEADQUARTERS SHELBY'S DIVISION
Camp No. 15, October 6, 1864.

Lieut. Col. L. A. MACLEAN,
Assistant Adjutant-General, Army of Missouri:

COLONEL: I arrived at this place (Westphalia) yesterday afternoon and found no enemy. Colonel Shanks got in last night from Osage bridge. He captured the guard of 80-odd men and burned the bridge and depot and other U. S. property. I learn that the river can be forded at two or three different places near here, at which there are guards of some strength. I shall move on to Prince's Ford this morning and ascertain their strength, and from there on to Jefferson City unless I receive further orders. Dispatch me as to what I shall do. Colonel Shanks brought in the arms and equipments of the captured guard. **I find that this settlement is Catholic and composed of Southern sympathizers.** I have done all in my power to protect them, and will leave one company here as a guard until your advance guard arrives.

Very respectfully, your obedient servant,

JO. O. SHELBY
Brigadier-General, Commanding.

P.S.—I leave about 100 prisoners here for Colonel Shaler to parole.

JO. O. SHELBY
Brigadier-General.

ADJUTANT AND INSPECTOR GENERAL'S OFFICE
Richmond, Va., January 10, 1865.

Edwin Stanton Secretary of War, Radical Red Republican

Maj. Gen. D. H. MAURY,
Comdg. Dept. of Alabama, Mississippi, and East Louisiana:

GENERAL: The letter of Maj. M. O. Tracy, Thirteenth Louisiana Regiment, relating to the subject of recruiting prisoners of war, has been forwarded to this Department with your endorsement asking instructions in such cases.

The Secretary of War directs me to say that the Department considers it desirable in general that prisoners of war, if received as recruits, should not be placed in new organizations nor collected in large numbers in those now existing, but should be distributed as much as possible among companies, regiments, and brigades of undoubted fidelity.

In one case in which a new battalion was formed from such material a conspiracy was discovered; and although it was promptly crushed, yet it was found expedient to disband the battalion.

Nevertheless, the experiment is now in course of trial by other officers, who believe that **by recruiting chiefly among Catholic Irish and other foreigners and obtaining the influence of the Catholic priesthood they may secure faithful soldiers.**

As to the material to be received as recruits, it is recommended that Catholic Irish be preferred, and next to them other foreigners.

Men born in the United States should not be received unless known to have sincere and positive predilections for the South. Natives of the Southern States may be received more freely.

After giving these general instructions the Honorable Secretary sums up his views in the following words:

That if separate organizations be ventured at all, they be only small battalions; that in recruiting largely for a brigade or any much reduced organization, every possible precaution should be taken in selection, and that some previous trial of these men should be made where they would be surrounded by our men before they are fully relied on in positions of trust and importance.

Very respectfully, general, your obedient servant,

JNO. BLAIR HOGE,
Major and Assistant Adjutant-General.

WAR DEPARTMENT
Washington, September 19, 1863.

Governor MORTON,
Indianapolis:

You are authorized to release **the 200 Catholic Confederates** mentioned in your telegraph, and the colonel of the Thirty-fifth Indiana is authorized to enlist and muster them into his regiment, but without premium, advance pay, or bounty.

The commandant of Camp Morton on presentation of this telegram and your request will discharge them, making out a muster roll or descriptive list and returning it to the Commissary-General of Prisoners.

EDWIN M. STANTON
Secretary of War.

Endnotes

1 Sourced from the U.S. National Archives

2 Ibid

3 Ibid.

4 Fifty Years in the Church of Rome, Charles Chiniquy, (by permission Chick Publications, Chino, Ca.) originally published 1883, pp.297-301

5 U.S. National Archives

6 Ibid.

7 Assassination of Lincoln, a History of the Great Conspiracy, Brig. Ben. U.S.V. and Major General by Brevet, Thomas M. Harris, (Boston, Mass. American Citizen Company, Chapter X) pp.123- 133

SATAN TEMPTING BOOTH TO THE MURDER OF THE PRESIDENT

By the President of the United States of America
A Proclamation

A Day of National Fasting and Prayer

Whereas the Senate of the United States, devoutly recognizing the supreme authority and just government of Almighty God in all the affairs of men and of nations, has by a resolution requested the President to designate and set apart a day for national prayer and humiliation; and

Whereas it is the duty of nations as well as of men to own their dependence upon the overruling power of God, to confess their sins and transgressions in humble sorrow, yet with assured hope that genuine repentance will lead to mercy and pardon, and to recognize the sublime truth, announced in the Holy Scriptures and proven by all history, that those nations only are blessed whose God is the Lord;

And, insomuch as we know that by His divine law nations, like individuals, are subjected to punishments and chastisements in this world, may we not justly fear that the awful calamity of civil war which now desolates the land may be but a punishment inflicted upon us for our presumptuous sins, to the needful end of our national reformation as a whole people? We have been the recipients of the choicest bounties of Heaven; we have been preserved these many years in peace and prosperity; we have grown in numbers, wealth, and power as no other nation has ever grown. But we have forgotten God. We have forgotten the gracious hand which preserved us in peace and multiplied and enriched and strengthened us, and we have vainly imagined, in the deceitfulness of our hearts, that all these blessings were produced by some superior wisdom and virtue of our own. Intoxicated with unbroken success, we have become too self-sufficient to feel the necessity of redeeming and preserving grace, too proud to pray to the God that made us.

It behooves us, then, to humble ourselves before the offended Power, to confess our national sins, and to pray for clemency and forgiveness.

Now, therefore, in compliance with the request, and fully concurring in the views of the Senate, I do by this my proclamation designate and set apart Thursday, the 30th day of April, 1863, as a day of national humiliation, fasting, and prayer. And I do hereby request all the people to abstain on that day from their ordinary secular pursuits, and to unite at their several places of public worship and their respective homes in keeping the day holy to the Lord and devoted to the humble discharge of the religious duties proper to that solemn occasion.

All this being done in sincerity and truth, let us then rest humbly in the hope authorized by the divine teachings that the united cry of the nation will be heard on high and answered with blessings no less than the pardon of our national sins and the restoration of our now divided and suffering country to its former happy condition of unity and peace. In witness whereof I have hereunto set my hand and caused the seal of the United States to be affixed.

Done at the city of Washington, this 30th day of March, A. D. 1863, and of the Independence of the United States the eighty-seventh.

ABRAHAM LINCOLN.
By the President:
WILLIAM H. SEWARD, Secretary of State

*90 days after this was signed God answered back with the twin victories of Vicksburg and Gettysburg.

Chapter 8

John Wilkes Booth is introduced; Booth's career- a character study; Booth joins the Knights of the Golden Circle; the KGC oath; testimony of Rear Admiral George Baird about Booth; the hit squad; a study of John H. Surratt; Lincoln asks Charles Chiniquy a question- Chiniquy's reply; a letter to Lincoln from a concerned citizen; a quote from Edwin A. Sherman

One Sunday morning, during November 1864, as the congregation of the little Roman Catholic Church of St. Mary's, Charles County, Maryland, was filing out after high mass and stood about in groups on the lawn talking in subdued voices about the news from the "front" which was not far distant, a handsome young man with dark, glowing eyes, jet black curly hair, a swinging gait and the grooming of a city man of culture, sauntered out from the church and stood scanning the crowd; he finally made his way to a group, the centre of which was a Dr. Queen, a leading physician of that locality, and member of one of the prominent families.

The stranger presented a card and the physician on glancing at it extended his hand and gave the gentleman a most cordial welcome. The contents of the card admitted him to the confidence and homes of these Roman devotees, every one of whom was a strong secessionist. The doctor introduced the stranger, who was none other than John Wilkes Booth, son of the distinguished actor, Junius Brutus Booth.

John Wilkes Booth was the most eminent young tragedian at the time in the country, by far the most talented of the Booth brothers. He had accumulated by his profession some $25,000, which was quite a fortune in those days for a young man in his twenties to accumulate.

Booth was what is known as a "traveling star," having with great success played most of the big cities in the United States and Canada. He was exceptionally popular with the members of his craft and up until he was caught in the Jesuit web, his entire thought and ambition was devoted to his art.

John Booth had chosen to work under the name of Wilkes until he gained recognition independent of the family name, desiring to win on his own merits his theatrical laurels. This in itself demonstrated a principle somewhat out of the ordinary. After a pronounced success under the name of John Wilkes, he allowed himself to be starred under his own name. He assumed no airs, nor was he given to egotism as members of this profession of lesser distinction and talent are prone to be. There is no better way of estimating a man or woman's disposition more certainly than from the opinion of those with whom he comes in daily contact in his vocation. I give the tribute paid to John Booth before he fell under the spell of the Jesuit psyche, at least before it had taken a fatal hold of him. The witness is none other than that queen of tragedy of the late Eighteen hundred's, Clara Morris. She is quoted thus:

> "In glancing back over two crowded and busy seasons, one figure stands out in clearness and beauty. In this case so far as my personal knowledge does, there is nothing derogatory to dignity and manhood in being called 'beautiful' for he was that bud of splendid promise blasted to the core before its triumphant blooming, known to the world as a madman and assassin, but to the profession as 'that unhappy boy, John Wilkes Booth.'
> He was so young, so bright, so kind.
>
> "I could not have known him well? Of course, too, there are two or three different people in every man's skin. Yet when we remember that stars are not in the habit of showing their brightest, best side at rehearsals, we cannot help feeling both respect and liking for the one who does.

“There are not many men who can receive a gash over the eye at a scene at night without at least a momentary outburst of temper, but when the combat between Richard and Richmond was being rehearsed, John Wilkes Booth had again and again, urged McCullom - that six foot tall and handsome man who used to entrust me with the care of his watch during such encounters, 'Come on hard, come on hot, old fellow! Harder, faster!" That he would take the chances of a blow if only they could make a hot fight of it. Mr. McCullom, who was a cold man at night, became nervous in his efforts to act like a fiery one. He forgot that he had struck the full number of hard blows and when Booth was expecting a thrust, McCullom wielding his sword with both hands brought it down with an awful force fair across Booth's forehead. A cry of horror arose, for in one moment his face was marked in blood, one eyebrow was cut through. Then came simultaneously one deep groan from Richard (Booth) and an exclamation of 'Oh good God, good God!' from Richmond (McCullom) who stood trembling like a leaf and staring at his work. Booth, flinging the blood from his eyes with his left hand, said as gently as a man could speak:

'That is all right, old man. Never mind me, only come on hard, and save the fight,' which he resumed at once.

And although he was perceptibly weakened, it required a sharp order from Mr. Ellsler to ring the first curtain bell to force him to bring the fight to a close a single blow shorter than usual. There was a running to and fro with ice and vinegar, raw steak and raw oysters, and when the doctor placed a few stitches where they were most required, Booth laughingly declared that there were provisions enough to start a restaurant.

“McCullom came to try to apologize, to explain, but Booth would have none of it. He held out his hand saying, 'Why, old fellow, you look as if you lost the blood. Don't worry - now, if my eye had gone, that would have been bad.' So, with light words he turned to set the unfortunate man at ease, and though he must have suffered much mortification and pain from the eye, he never made a sign showing it.

“John Wilkes Booth, like his next elder brother, was rather lacking in height, but his head and throat and the manner of their rising from his shoulders were truly beautiful. His coloring was unusual, the ivory pallor of his skin, the inky blackness of dusky curly hair, the heavy lids of his glowing eyes, were all oriental, and they gave a touch of mystery to his face when it fell into gravity, but there was generally a flash of white teeth behind his black silky mustache.

“Now it is scarcely exaggerating to say that the fair sex was in love with John Wilkes Booth, or John Booth as he was called, the name Wilkes apparently being unknown to his family and close friends. I played with John Wilkes to my great joy, playing "Player Queen" in the "Marble Heart." I was one of the group of three statues in the first act, then a girl in my teens.

“With all my admiration for the person and genius of John Wilkes Booth, his crime I cannot condone. The killing of that homely, tender-hearted father Abraham Lincoln, a rare combination of courage, justice, and humanity, whose death at the hands of an actor will be a grief of horror and shame to the profession forever. And I cannot believe that John Wilkes Booth was the leader of a band of bloody conspirators.

“Who shall draw the line and say, 'Here genius ends and madness begins?' There was that touch of strangeness, in Edwin it was a profound melancholy; in John it was an exaggeration of spirit, almost a madness. There was the natural vanity of the actor too who craves a dramatic selection in real life. There was also his passionate love and sympathy for the South, which was easier to play upon than a pipe.

“Undoubtedly he conspired to kidnap the President; that would appeal to him. But after that I truly believe he was a **tool;** certainly he was no leader. Those who led him knew his courage, his belief in fate, his loyalty to his friends, and because they knew these things **he drew the lot as it was meant he should from the first.** Then, half mad, he accepted the part fate cast him for and committed the murderous crime.

"God moves in a mysterious way
And His wonders to perform."

'And God shutteth not up his mercies forever in displeasure.'

> "We can only shiver and turn our thoughts away from the bright light that went out in such utter darkness; poor, guilty, unhappy, John Wilkes Booth." (1)

John Wilkes was the only member of the Booth family whose sympathy was with the Confederacy. According to the "*Great Conspiracy*" a book published in 1866 by Barclay Co., in Philadelphia, Pa., John Wilkes Booth had been initiated into the Knights of the Golden Circle in Baltimore in the fall of 1860, "in a residence opposite the Cathedral."

The writer of that book was the authority for the following oath of the Knights of the Golden Circle, a society named after a highly lucrative slave trade area of the Caribbean in which the large slave proceeds helped to finance the Confederate cause. Counted among its members was the name of Jesse James, the infamous outlaw. Both James and John Wilkes Booth took this oath:

> "I... do swear by the blood of Jesus Christ, by the wounds of the most Sacred Body; by the Dolors of His immaculate Mother, and in the name of the Holy and Undivided Trinity, that I will solemnly keep all secrets of the Golden Circle; that I will faithfully perform whatever I may be commanded, and that I shall always hold myself in readiness to obey the mandates of the said Circle, whether at bed, or board, at the festive circle, or at the grave, and if I shall hesitate or divulge the secret may I incur the severest of penalties to which flesh is heir.
>
> "May I be cursed in all the relation of my life, in mind, body, and state, and may the pangs of hell be my eternal portion.
>
> "I feel honored fellow knights and companions of the Golden Circle that you have deigned to admit me. No efforts shall be wanting on my part to advance the interests of the organization...
>
> "A distinguished Latin Author has justly remarked, that it is sweet and profitable to die for one's country. I have but one life and am ready to give it should it be necessary........."

The President rises and says:

> "Sir Knight you have just taken a most solemn adjuration and believe me that you are known to all members in every part of the country. The Order is extensive and though the government is zealous and would freely spend thousands to unveil our designs, all efforts have hitherto been fruitless. No traitor has yet appeared among us, and inevitable ruin awaits the individual who would play the part of a Benedict Arnold. No public steps would be taken. He would disappear and leave it to you to judge his fate. "Dead men tell no tales." Ponder well on these things, and remember you cannot escape us.
>
> "Members give the hand of fellowship to our new Knight." (*The Great Conspiracy* published by Barclay 1865) (2)

The password to this organization was "Rome. Beware of the Negroes."

Papal Allocution – Snuffing Out Civilisation

That the author of the book, "*The Great Conspiracy*," was thoroughly informed upon the details which could scarcely have come from anything short of actual membership in the organization is plainly evident. He also seems to have had knowledge of the assassinations of Presidents Harrison and Taylor. The incident recorded below occurred just after the re-election of President Lincoln. Booth, sitting in a hotel lobby one day, appeared very dejected; he was aroused by the following remark, which evidently was part of the secret phraseology of the Knights of the Golden Circle:

> "It would be a queer thing were Lincoln to die and Andy Johnson be President after all."
>
> "What makes you think so?"
>
> "Why, you know that Harrison and Taylor and that Fillmore and Tyler were Presidents. Lincoln may take it into his head to follow their example. Perhaps neither Lincoln nor Johnson will serve their terms out."
>
> "Do you mean that the President and the Vice President both will die? Such a thing has never happened before in the United States."
>
> "But it may occur nevertheless..................Lincoln and Johnson are both mortals...I feel certain that ere another month Lincoln will die...Yes, he may die of some disease."
>
> "You said I believe, sir, that the President might die of some disease?"
>
> "Yes, sir, of such diseases as commonly prevail in Rome."
>
> "What diseases are they?" asked Booth.
>
> "All to which flesh is heir, the malaria from the Pontine marshes carries off hundreds; the plague of its day almost decimated the capitol of the Caesars...but I tell you again that the President will die of a disease from Rome."
>
> Booth: "Sir, as you are well versed in history perhaps you can answer me one question, which one of all the sovereigns of all Italy had the most fickle wife?"

> "I am an indifferent guesser of conundrums, but I suppose the Doge."
>
> **Ques.** "Which Doge, he of Venice or Genoa?"
>
> **Ans.** "He of Venice, because he wedded the sea with a golden circlet. You remember Byron's beautiful lines?" (3)

After this "test" Booth was invited to the gentleman's room where they conferred privately.

The same authority states that John Wilkes Booth was initiated in this Order as early as 1860. The following letter is quoted from Booth to a brother Sir Knight:

> "Dear Sir: The K.G.C. had a meeting; I was initiated. 'The die is cast and I have crossed the Rubicon' and can never return. They tell me that Lincoln, the damn chicken-hearted nigger lover, will perhaps be inaugurated, but I most heartily wish, 'That never shall sun that morrow see.' I am devoted to the South, mind, and body, so that she gains her independence, I don't care what becomes of me. If I am sacrificed, I know that my country will grant me immortality; if I escape, so much the better, I can serve her in other ways. One thing is very clear to my mind, the South must take some decisive step. She must throw a bombshell into the enemy's hand that shall spread terror and consternation wherever it goes. You know what I mean, so don't be surprised.
>
> Sincerely yours, John Wilkes Booth." (*The Great Conspiracy* Pg. 26) (4)

This authority also gave a letter signed "Veritas" (truth) to Booth, which one would be strongly inclined to believe may have been written by a priest judging by the style and Latin quotations-possibly his ecclesiastical sponsor. It reads:

> "My dear Booth: Since you left us, the Circle held another meeting. The members are all exceedingly dissatisfied and if something be not speedily done, the Southern cause is lost forever. Important dispatches

have been received from Canada. They spoke out almost too plainly to be sent by mail, but as there was no signature and addressed to a feigned name, I do not suppose there was any danger. There is to be a ball or party at the White House and the APE, I suppose, will be there in all his glory retailing his filthy anecdotes and pointless jests till they fall on the ear, usque ad nauseum. Did you see what is the determination of the Lincoln Cabinet about confiscation? There is a clerk by the name of Charles Morton, who is employed in one of the government offices. He is gentlemanly but vain and exceedingly soft. I am told he drinks. Anyhow, make his acquaintance and see what can be got out of him. Handle him tenderly and you will be sure to catch your fish. Should you want any more money you will know where to send for it. An idea has struck me; you know in the correspondence between Sir Henry Clinton Arnold and Andre the whole matter was treated in a mercantile way. We, for the sake of safety and to make assurance doubly sure, must do the same. I will not detain you any longer, but give you an opportunity to read about our friends in Canada. Whatever be the results, rely on me. Sincerely your friend, Veritas." (5)

John Harrison Surratt – Jesuit trained Arch conspirator

The statements made by his professional friend, John McCullough, of a visit he paid Booth at the National Hotel, showed the deadly influence when he said:

> "At another time I came over suddenly from New York, and being in the habit of going right into Booth's room without knocking, I turned the knob and pushed right in. At the first wink I saw Booth sitting behind a table on which was a map, knife and a pistol. He had gauntlets on his hands and spurs on his boots and a military hat of a slouch character on his head. As the door opened he seized the knife and came for me. Said I, 'John, what in the name of sense is the matter with you - are you crazy?'
>
> "He heard my voice and arrested himself, and placed his hands before his eyes like a man dissipating a dream, and then said, 'Why, Johnny, how are you?' When I heard that it was he who killed Lincoln, I thought that he had been at the time I describe ready to carry out his purpose." (6)

A man by the name of Rear Admiral George W. Baird, U.S.N. retired had a brief acquaintance with Booth prior to his identification by the same after Lincoln's assassination. He records from his diary the following:

> "My acquaintance with John Wilkes Booth was not at all intimate. I met him in New Orleans in the winter of '63 and '64, when he was playing in the theatre there in 'Marble Hearts' and he was splendid in his part. My acquaintance was what may be called a bar-room acquaintance.
>
> I was introduced to him by a young officer of my ship the "Pensacola" whose name was Fitch and who afterwards married the eldest daughter of General Sherman. Booth seemed to be a congenial fellow with a sense of humor and I thought was very temperate in his habits, not like his father in that respect. The War was at its height and was freely discussed, but Booth did not seem to be too much interested in it. He was from Maryland, whose population was divided, though men as a rule believed it proper to side with their state. My ship

went north in the spring of 1864 and I was assigned to my duty in the navy department.

In 1850 when I was seven years of age, I went to school in Washington to two reverend gentlemen Cox and Marlot, who taught in the lower story of the Masonic Hall, Virginia Avenue and Fourth Street East. The boy who sat by me about my own age was David Herold, a little round headed, round eyed, round bodied boy, whose general rotundity was completed by a voice that rolled his R's. I envied David his disposition in that he got along with the big boys so well. When a big boy imposed on David, he would escape with a funny remark which was called witty, which generally got a laugh, and David was called popular. When a big boy impressed on me, I hated him; I hate him yet. David's father, Mr. George Herold, and my father were members of Christ Church Episcopal. My people were members of the Baptist Church. When I left that school about a year later, I lost sight of David. I heard he became a drug clerk.

On the night of the 14th of April, 1865 I went to call on a young lady and about 10:30 her brother came in and said Abe Lincoln is dead. He had been to the theatre to see Laura Keene in "Our American Cousin" and during the play a man had got into the box where the President was, and had shot the President, jumped out of the box on to the stage, and escaped from the back of the stage. I left at once; saw policemen at the corner whom I interrogated and they confirmed the story. I inquired as to the appearance of the assassin and was not only given a description that fitted but said he resembled me, and I thought that I had better hurry to my boarding house. On arriving at my boarding house Dr. Ludlam and Mr. Fitch inquired if I had heard the news and suggested that we go down town and get the latest "bricks" but nothing could induce me to appear on the streets again that night. The people were wild with excitement. I never heard such threats of vengeance.

Before 10:00 o'clock the next morning almost every house was draped in mourning. People had exhausted the stores here and wired Baltimore for black crepe and cambric. Dan Ballauf, the model maker, was standing leaning on the lower box in the theatre and saw it all. He denied the report that Booth had uttered the words "sic semper tyrannis," but the newspapers had printed it. The newspapers had the story very early, that John Wilkes Booth was the assassin and David Herold was the accomplice.

Though never intimate with John Wilkes Booth, I admired him, his voice, power of declaiming. I took drinks with him at the Franklin House, Custom House Street, a place frequented by army and navy officers. He seemed to me to have no interest in the war. It was hard to understand. I had not seen him but once in Washington and that about three weeks before the murder of the President. It was on a Sunday when he was coming out of Saint Aloysius Catholic Church Vesper Service - great crowds of various creeds used to go to that vespers where the music was good. I think Mme. Kretzmayer was the attractive soprano.

A large reward was offered for Booth's arrest and conviction. The War had practically ended and our troops were at liberty to travel in any state without molestation. I was detailed to make a series of experiments in the Navy Yard, and after Booth's body was brought to the Navy Yard and lay on board the "Montauk" this happened:

I was called on board the Montauk by Lieut. W. W. Crowninshield, to identify the body of John Wilkes Booth, which I did. I noticed a piece of cord about the size of a cod line on his (Booth's) neck and invited Crowninshield's attention to it, who pulled it out and on it was a small Roman Catholic medal. Surgeon General Barnes arrived at that moment and probed the wound in Booth's neck.

I got a horse and buggy and drove down to Surrattville the following day. The house they said belonged to Mrs. Surratt and had been leased to John M. Lloyd whom I knew. He was a policeman at Washington during all of Buchannan's administration and bore an excellent reputation. I inquired of some boys whom I found very communicative. One boy said that Mr. Jenkins, brother of Mrs. Surratt, and Mr. Griffith and Mr. Wylie (or Wyville) and Mr. Lloyd were all out that night listening for the horses coming, that when the two men came, fresh horses were brought out of the stable, saddles transferred from the tired horses to the fresh, and the men rode on. On May 22, 1865, I went to Baltimore on duty in connection with the "Pensacola."

The "*Washington Star*" of May 12, 1865 gives Lloyd's testimony as follows:

"Some time ago two carbines and some pistols were left at my house. The Friday before the assassination Mrs. Surratt came to my house and told me to have the carbines and pistols ready as two men would call for them. On the night of the assassination Booth and Herold rode up to the house; Herold dismounted, went in, and took a carbine and the pistols. Booth would not take his carbine on account of his lame ankle."

The "*Washington Star*" of the 15th said:

"Lloyd testified that it was John Surratt who brought the carbines. A watchman saw Mrs. Surratt, Booth, John Surratt, and Dr. Mudd together on Seventh Street, and that Booth was a frequent visitor at the house of Mrs. Surratt, and their interviews were always apart."

...I was retired from active duty by law in 1905 but continued on duty until 1906. The next year I passed some days at Poland Springs, Maine. Among other Washingtonians was Mr. Crosby Noyes, principal editor of the "Washington Star," who told me he was the reporter for the "Star" at the trial of the conspirators, and he was satisfied that Mrs. Surratt and all the rest of them were guilty.

I was at sea when John Surratt was tried. My information on that trial was that printed in the "Washington Star." Surratt was poor, but Mr. R.T. Merrick, a Roman Catholic lawyer, was his principal counsel and it was commonly reported that he paid the entire expense of the trial. His associate counsel was Mr. Joseph Bradley, a famous criminal lawyer, who rarely, if ever, lost a case, and to whom the bad cases usually came.

Quoting from the "*Evening Star*" of September 23, 1868:

"Judge Wylie on the bench, Messrs. Merrick and Bradley argued on a demur to the plea of the amnesty proclamation which had been issued by the government in favor of the Confederates who had been in arms against the government. Their purpose was to make it apply to the case of John Surratt who had been tried for conspiracy to murder the President, and in whose case a year ago the jury had been hung.

"Merrick said the court was not technically a Court of the United States, wherein the judge held that the Court held that the Circuit Court of the District of Columbia was not on the same footing as the United States District Courts, though the judges of such Courts were vested with the same power.

"He would submit in view of the double character of the Court that to except a person of some felony he must be indicted for felony in some Circuit Court of the United States. He referred to the Bankrupt Act.

"Mr. Bradley referred the Court to several authorities. The Court suffered counsel to amend the plea."

From the "*Evening Star*" of September 24, 1868, Page 4, Column 2, viz:

"A NEW MOVE BY THE DEFENSE, STATUTE OF LIMITATION, DISCHARGE OF THE PRISONER.

"Mr. Merrick stated that he had presented a new plea. He claimed the indictment defective in that it did not aver that Surratt had not fled from Justice." The paper stated that he walked out of the court unmolested.

I saw the medal when it was taken off Booth's neck and I saw it afterwards in the War Department. It was kept in a safe of the Judge Advocate General. It was in a little tin box which also contained a newspaper scrap referring to it with the bullet from Booth's neck, and I think the derringer also.

When I became superintendent of the S.W. and Navy Department in 1895, I asked the messenger at the Judge Advocate General's door if the relics were still on exhibit as I wanted to show them to some friends, and he said that they were all there but the medal, that the Secretary of War, (Mr. Lamont) had sent for them and they remained on his desk four months, and when returned the medal was missing.

John M. Lloyd, the Washington policeman in 1857-59-60 bore a good reputation. I think the claim that he was intemperate or a sot as Mr. Brophy called him was all propaganda. A policeman knows how to testify and he knows the penalty. I was reluctant to believe Lloyd a conspirator until the boys at Surrattville told me of the story of Lloyd, Jenkins, Wylie, et al listening for the coming of Booth that night, and his testimony confirmed it. One of the propaganda writers says that Lloyd had to be awakened from a drunken stupor that night when Booth arrived, when the boys, who had no purpose to serve, told me that Lloyd was wide awake on the road listening for horses. They said that when the horses were plainly heard, that Lloyd, et al, went into the stable and brought out fresh horses as if in a hurry. Lloyd and his wife (whom I also knew) were Roman Catholics, and I believe members of St. Dominic's Congregation. The testimony shows Lloyd drunk but once; it was when he met Mrs. Surratt in Uniontown, now called Anacostia, and that was on the eve of the frightful tragedy and he might have needed "Dutch courage." My impression was that the effort to damage Lloyd's character was for the sole purpose of impeaching his testimony. I always thought he found himself in serious trouble and told the truth to save his neck." (7)

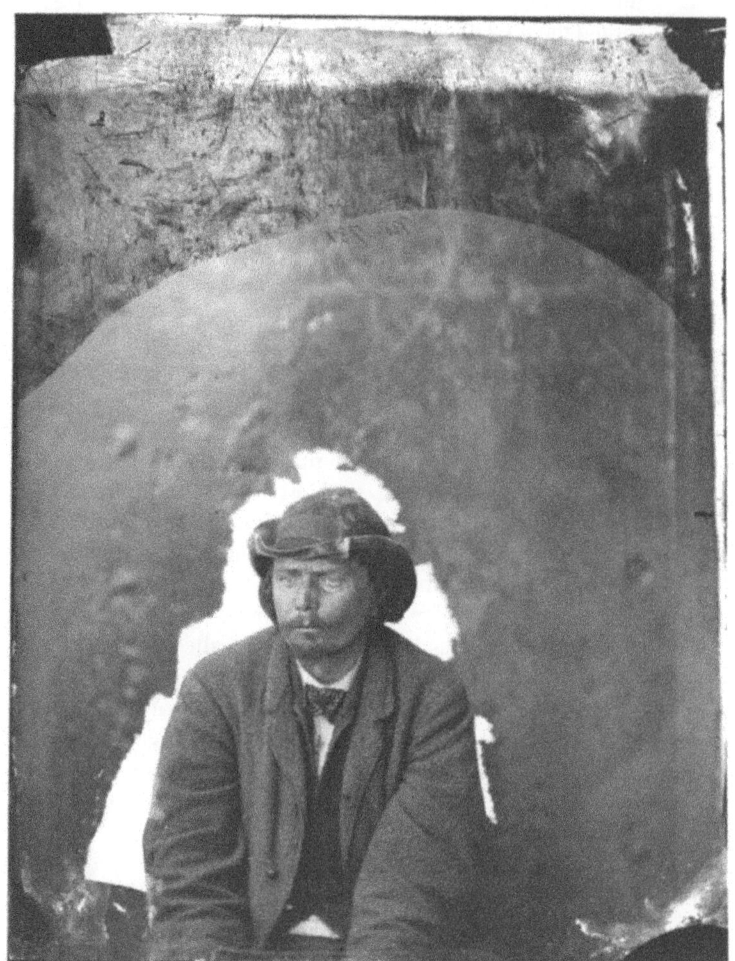

George Atzerodt - Lincoln conspirator

After an intensified pursuit of thirteen days south of Washington from along the Bryantown Road, John Wilkes Booth and David Herold were tracked to the Garrett tobacco plantation near Port Royal, Virginia by government troops under Colonel Conger. A squad commanded by Lt. Baker surrounded the tobacco barn on the Garrett farm and ordered Booth to surrender, which he refused to do. "Davy" Herold, however, asked to surrender and was allowed to come out. He was handcuffed and placed under the charge of a squad of cavalrymen. The barn was finally torched by Col. Conger.

Booth, who could now be plainly seen by the light of the flames, was peering out, when a bullet from the revolver of Sgt. Boston Corbett hit Booth in the back of the head and Booth crumpled up on the barn floor. He was dragged out by the soldiers and lay on the grass, apparently dead, but was revived by a splash of cold water in the face. The bullet had entered at almost the exact same spot in which his own bullet had pierced the head of President Lincoln. He was carried and laid upon the porch in front of the Garrett house where he suffered several hours of the most intense agony. Noting his lips moving, an officer stooped down and heard him whisper: "Tell my mother - tell my mother - I died for my country - and I did what I thought best."

Indicating a desire that his paralyzed arms be held up, which was done, contemplating them, he murmured, "useless, useless." These were his last words.

The body was taken by wagon to the river and placed on board the Gunboat Montauk and brought to Washington, and Admiral Baird was one of the men who made positive identification.

From Adm. Baird's notes one would assume that as late as the winter of '64, only a few months prior to Booth's coming to Washington, he was indifferent on the subject of the war. The fact that he was in New Orleans where he would have been very safe in expressing his opinion in favor of the South would seem to indicate he had no great feeling on the subject.

There seems to be no doubt but that Clara Morris was perfectly correct in her statement that John Wilkes Booth was the victim chosen from the beginning and that he “Drew the lot” after his New Orleans engagement where Adm. Baird had seen him. From the time he registered at the National Hotel in November 1864, it is plainly evident that he became obsessed with the idea, and the working of the virus is traceable in his every act from that time on. He lost all interest in his profession - a thing in itself most remarkable, for which we can only account in the one way.

In the chaotic hours following the attacks on Lincoln and the Seward's, senior Detective Lee had been hand-picked to guard Vice President Johnson's nearby room in the Kirkwood House Hotel. Both Booth and conspirator George Atzerodt had been in and out of the hotel that day. Lee's charge, Vice President Johnson, was the next assassination target.

Shortly before 10 o'clock that evening of April 14th, 1865, a rumpled looking man tied his mare to the weathered railing in front of the Kirkwood Hotel and shuffled into the dimly lit barroom. Ordering a whiskey, he stared blankly into the dark corners of the empty room.

Only the sizzle of the gas jets could be heard. George Atzerodt had come to this special place on this particular evening at the demand of Booth. It was only hours before that Booth had ordered Atzerodt to kill the Vice President and thereby wreak havoc on the government. As Atzerodt fingered his whiskey, Johnson lay sleeping only steps away in one of the Kirkwood's rooms.

Whatever Atzerodt thought of Johnson or Lincoln or the war, murder was not among his capabilities. Atzerodt began to nod off while the city was buzzing with activity. Secretary of War Edwin Stanton was busy collecting testimony on the night's events.

Major James Obeirne, head of the District Board of Enrollment, was busy directing his men in an effort to make sense of the confusion that was unfolding. Finally, a bit after midnight, Obeirne sent his top Detective John Lee to the Kirkwood to guard Johnson.

According to Lee's testimony at the conspiracy trial, 'a person employed in the House, whom I knew, told me there had been a suspicious looking man who had taken a room the day previous.' On examining the hotel register, Lee was shown the name 'G.A. Atzerodt' and immediately told the desk clerk to take him to the room. Finding the door locked and being told that Atzerodt had the only key, Lee forced the door. The contents proved to be of enormous importance. Included in the room were a revolver, capped and loaded, a map of Virginia and a black coat in the pocket of which was found a bank book showing a credit of $445 to Mr. John Wilkes Booth.

Lee's major find were the first proofs of a conspiracy, and of Booth's identity. A letter from the bartender of the Kirkwood, Michael Henry, who first informed Lee of Atzerodt's suspicious presence, is quoted in full:

> July 20th, 1865
> Major Jas. R. Obeirne
> Provost Marshall of the District of Columbia
>
> Dear Sir:
> Having on or about the 14th of April given information to the Detectives then on duty guarding Mr. Johnson's room, of one suspicious character in room 126 of the hotel, which on being searched proved to be Atzerodt's and from the things found in the room he was caught. I would like you to give this due consideration and if it's worth anything I hope to receive it. This statement I can prove by two or three Detectives now in the service of the Government.
>
> Yours Most Respectfully,
> Michael Henry Bartender

Henry's letter was submitted to Obeirne in an attempt to gain him a share of the reward money. He did not receive a cent.

I now turn my attention to that arch-conspirator, John H. Surratt. John Harrison Surratt was the nineteen year old son of Mrs. Mary E. Surratt, and was chosen by the Jesuits as the arch conspirator in the assassination of Abraham Lincoln. He had studied three years in preparation for the Roman Priesthood at the Sulpician Fathers monastery, at Charles County, Maryland, prior to the breaking out of the Civil War.

The Sulpician Fathers is a branch of the Jesuit Order. At this Sulpician monastery Surratt was introduced to another theological student, Louis J. Weichmann of Philadelphia with whom he formed a close friendship, when in 1862 young Surratt was called to his home in Surrattville, a crossroads village 13 miles south of Washington, by the death of his father. The elder Surratt had been a railroad contractor, and had accumulated some money, which was partly invested in slaves and a plantation and tavern at Surrattville where he served as postmaster at the time of his demise.

The family consisted of Isaac, the eldest son, a civil engineer, who enlisted in the Southern Cause at the very beginning of the war and who the last heard of him had joined Maximilian's forces in Mexico; Anna, the only daughter, a girl in her early twenties, and John H., the youngest.

The Surratt's were all ardent secessionists and fanatical Roman Catholics. Mrs. Surratt was, early in life, converted to Romanism from the Protestant faith. Her children were Romanists from birth.

That John Harrison Surratt, was cool, clever, calculating and crafty, far in advance of his years, is shown by the fact that at the very beginning of the Rebellion he was selected to do important work in the Southern secret service, bearing the most important dispatches from Jefferson Davis at Richmond to his agents at Washington and to the members of his 'kitchen cabinet' in Montreal, Canada.

Jesuit priest Bernard F. Wiget –
Confessor and confidante to the Surratt's
Mastermind behind the Lincoln assassination

On his return home from the monastery near Baltimore, John Surratt was sworn in as postmaster in his father's place at Surrattville. His Jesuit training enabled him to lift his hand and swear undivided allegiance to the United States. So much for a Jesuit's oath. To get a complete estimate of John Surratt's part in the conspiracy to murder President Lincoln and other heads of the administration we must fully consider the preliminary training he received.

This boy, (for we must remember that he was but in his teens, at his entrance into this plot) was never free from the espionage and evil influence of the Romish church from his baptism in infancy to the day of his death at the age of seventy-two years. When he was but twelve years old he was placed in Gonzaga College, Washington, D.C., a Catholic prepatory school, under the tutelage of Priest Wiget, who was the confessor for years of both himself and his mother.

After leaving Gonzaga College he spent two years at Georgetown in the Jesuit College before leaving for the Sulpician Fathers monastery. I am calling the attention of the reader to this fact when you come to pass judgment on this young man, that you may place the blame for his conduct where it belongs - on the Jesuit psychology inculcated by the priests of the Roman Church.

That he was a leader and a dependable one, in this conspiracy of wholesale assassination, is shown by the fact that the object of John Wilkes Booth's first visit to St. Mary's Catholic Church in Howard County, Maryland, was to learn the whereabouts in Washington of John Surratt.

Young Surratt, had then, never the slightest chance or desire to escape from the deadly virus. This virus stultified every personal ambition, even the strongest instinct in the human mind - self-preservation is thrust aside when the victim hears the call of duty to "the holy mother church". Then, mother love, father love, brother love - all must yield to this cursed thing. This complete and absolute mental control which Rome exerted over its dupes whom it permitted to have no more will of their own, nor resistance, than that of a cadaver. 'Perinda ac cadaver' (as a corpse) to be moved here, or there, at the will of the manipulator. The mother, Mary E. Surratt, the intimate associate of priests, her soul deadened by the fatal virus of the Jesuit training, had passed on to her son the terrible inheritance which made him wax in the black hands of the Vatican intriguers, to mold as they would.

During Surratt's theological training he had studied St. Thomas Aquinas, who justifies the assassination of heretics, or anyone who apostatizes from the Romish church. It was a significant and eloquent fact that the Jesuits released from time to time during the war the report that President Lincoln had been, in his infancy, baptized by a Catholic priest. On one of his visits to the White House of the Rev. Charles Chiniquy to warn President Lincoln of his danger in assassination, Mr. Lincoln is quoted by Chiniquy in his book, *'Fifty years in the Church of Rome'* as follows:

> "Father Chiniquy, I want your views about a thing which is exceedingly puzzling to me and you are the only one to whom I would like to speak on the subject. A great number of Democratic papers have been sent me lately, evidently written by Roman Catholics, publishing that I was born a Roman Catholic and baptized by a priest. They call me a renegade and apostate on account of that, and they heap mountains of abuses on my head. But the persistency of the Romish press to present this falsehood to their readers as gospel truth, must have a meaning. Please tell me, as briefly as possible, what you think about it."
>
> "My dear president," I answered, "it was just this strange story which brought me here yesterday. I wept as a child when I read it for the first time. For I believe that it is your sentence of death and I have it from the lips of a converted priest, that they have invented this falsehood to excite the fanaticism of the Roman Catholic murderers, whom they hope to find, sooner or later, to strike you down. They want to brand your face with the ignominious mark of apostasy. In the Church of Rome an apostate is an outcast who has no place in society and no right to live."
>
> "The Catholic hierarchy of the United States is on the side of the rebels as incontrovertible evidence that

Rome wants to destroy this republic. You are, by your personal virtues, your popularity, your love for liberty, your position, the greatest obstacle to their diabolical schemes. Their hatred is concentrated upon you. My blood chills when I contemplate the day when Rome will add to all her other iniquities the murder of Abraham Lincoln."

Lincoln then responded:

"I will repeat to you what I said at Urbana: 'Man must not care where and when he will die, provided he dies at the post of honor and duty.' But I may add today, that I have the presentiment that God will call me to Him through the hand of an assassin. Let his will, and not mine be done. I will be forever grateful for the warning words you have addressed to me about the dangers ahead to my life, from Rome. I know that they are not imaginary dangers. If I were fighting against a Protestant South, as a nation, there would be no danger of assassination. The nations who read the Bible fight bravely on the battlefields, but they do not assassinate their enemies. The pope and the Jesuits, with their infernal Inquisition, are the only organized powers in the world which have recourse to the dagger of the assassin to murder those whom they cannot convince with their arguments or conquer with the sword.... This civil war seems to be nothing but a political affair to those who do not see, as I do, the secret springs of that terrible drama. But it is more a religious than a civil war...I understand, now, why the patriots of France, who determined to see the colors of liberty floating over their great and beautiful country, were forced to hang or shoot almost all the priests and the monks as the irreconcilable enemies of liberty...Their extermination in France was one of those terrible necessities which no human wisdom could avoid..." (8)

The following letter to President Lincoln, supplied by the Library of Congress, sheds further light on the concerns of the American public, who were not ignorant of what was taking place in the war where the religious element was concerned.

Grove P.O. Walworth Co.
Wisconsin Feb. 7th 1865

The President

Dear Sir,

For your office first; I honor you! And much more so, for the plain Christian course you have pursued in your administration. Were it not for a humble trust in a Divine overruling power; I should feel greatly alarmed for the safety of my country – just at this present crisis.

Do you Sir, not foresee some danger from Catholicism spread as its numbers are, all over the Union. They follow and obey their priests, implicitly and they again their heads, so that one man can cause the uprising of this entire body of secret sworn hordes, sworn to destroy the Heretic and think they are doing God service!

About ten years ago, when we resided in New Hampshire, a Mr. White while traveling, in passing through Whitewater, heard something said of a beautiful new Catholic Church, being a Master Builder, expressed a wish to see it and was told that he was not allowed, but while walking past, he fixed his eye upon it, and continued approaching – being fully absorbed in the building. When suddenly he found himself looking down into the basement. A priest stood there beside an open box of cutlasses and knives and he stood in astonishment, watching their movements.

When he suddenly received a blow that nearly prostrated him! Turning, he beheld a powerful Irishman and being himself a powerful man, he leveled him with one blow. When suddenly thinking; leapt back to the window to see what effect the outcry of the man had on those within. The weapons, box and all had disappeared, but the men!

One of our good Brothers in the Church mentioned these particulars to a man that he had many times befriended, an Irish Catholic. He was silent for a time, but on being urged, at length said – "Well, the Catholics would have risen and massacred the Protestants, ere this, the time was appointed, but this trouble about the Know Nothings has prevented it and put it back for a little – but it will come, and much sooner than you think, and where will you be; I will be off on one side."

From this, and other circumstances – I have no doubt in my mind but that every Catholic Church contains a sufficient amount of arms for its members and if this is the case it is a fearful state of things, for here in the North we have no arms.

We have a daughter married to a young lawyer, the son of a lawyer residing in St. John's, New Brunswick who in her last letter stated that there was much talk there about a report, that the Catholics were intending to rise and murder all Protestants on the Tenth of March next, but the truth of it they are not saying! It is possible that the 4th of March may be the time specified with regard to the United States. And if this is permitted to reach your hand, in safety, you may have time to guard not only your own well-being but that of Washington.

It is possible that the meetings of these Fenian Brethren are all connected with this plot and Maximilian being placed where he is, looks ominous, and this pouring out of Emigrants from Ireland by the thousands in the dead of winter [Note: as a result of the Jesuit planned and executed potato famine–Ed.] is no doubt the work of the Pope. Our people are asleep to this matter. <u>*Hence our danger*</u>.

I know by experience, Honored Sir, we have every cause to trust <u>Him!</u> Who's eye, never sleeps, nor slumbers. When the first Iron Clad Reb ram made its appearance, doing such havoc in our little fleet, it then seemed to me, that unless the Lord interposed for us, that our cause was lost. I was enabled to ask, nothing doubting and praised be His name, how quickly He came to our rescue. This encouraged me to ask in another almost similar case and with equal success – bless the lord, and I was emboldened to go to the Lord with the cause upon the High Seas, of that daring Pirate Semmes, in this instance, the answer did not come too quickly – but when it did come how my soul overflowed with joy and gratitude.

Finding he had made his escape I then was enabled to ask that he might not again molest us as a Pirate. Thus far the good Lord has heard and answered – and I have no doubt will continue to do so – help me to render him suitable praise – for myself I am truly thankful to be able to say I have no fears of death. Yet for others I fear much. I know the Lord is able to put to flight the armies of the Alien, and if they are plotting a midnight assassin on so stupendous a scale – my trust is that He will lay His hand on all the leaders. It has been on my mind to write you what is in my heart with regard to this subject – for some days. It is now done and I am thankful. May His blessing accompany it – and bring good out of it in some way. May our civil and religious rights be preserved to us and our children is the fervent prayer of

Your humble servant
Mrs. Louise Harrison

To the President

P.S. Feb. 16 The rumor of those two Rebel Rams being lent out by France is truly appalling in connection with the above and if it should prove true, unless the Lord interpose for us, ours is a hopeless cause. I enclose this under cover to Senator Dolittle – thinking that it may go more safely – though he knows nothing of its contents. If this reaches you privately, as a token thereof please enclose me a photograph immediately of yourself or a paper if that takes too much time. The former would be preferred. L. H.

About November 1, 1863, Mrs. Surratt and her family moved to their residence at 541 H. St. Washington, D.C., where she opened a select boarding house. Select to the extent that there were no 'heretics' among her boarders. The first to come was Louis J. Weichmann, who had been for three years a classmate of John Surratt's at the Sulpician Fathers monastery where Weichmann also was preparing for the Roman priesthood.

Davy Herold – Lincoln Conspirator

A few days before Christmas, 1864, young Weichmann invited Surratt to go with him over to Pennsylvania Avenue to select some Christmas gifts for his sisters in Philadelphia. As they were nearing the Avenue on 7 Street, Weichmann said, "John, someone is calling you," and Surratt, turning, saw Dr. Mudd of Bryantown and a younger man with him, whom he introduced as John Wilkes Booth. After the introductions were over Booth invited the party up to his room at the National Hotel, where he ordered wine and cigars for the group. From this meeting on John Booth was a constant visitor to the Surratt home on H Street, which was the rendezvous of the conspirators up to the very day of the assassination. It was also the mecca of various Roman Catholic priests, among whom were the Reverends Walters and Wiget of St. Patrick's Church, 10th and G Streets, of which the Surratt's were members.

From their first meeting Booth and Surratt busied themselves selecting their associates. David Herold was the choice of John Surratt who had known him from his college days at Georgetown University. The testimony of Louis J. Weichmann, a college friend of Surratt and the State's premier witness at the trials of the conspirators shows that Surratt had introduced him to David Herold as one of the members of the Washington Marine Band which had serenaded the Surratt tavern at midnight on one occasion when Weichmann was spending the weekend there. This was a year before Booth's appearance in Washington. There is no doubt but that all the conspirators were members of the Knights of the Golden Circle; there is also no doubt that while some of them were nominal Protestants they were wholly papalized and therefore not Protestants at all in the true sense of the name. All through the testimony we see that Booth and Atzerodt were at "mass."

It is morally certain that Booth himself had been secretly taken into the Roman Church when he was given the "Agnes Dei" medal, which was taken from his neck. "Agnes Dei" means Lamb of God; it indicates sacrifice - the shedding of blood. There is all likelihood that it was made in Rome, probably sent direct from the Pope as was Pius IXth's letter to Jeff Davis, a distinction that would tend to flatter the vanity of John Wilkes Booth.

Michael O' Laughlin – Lincoln conspirator

Michael O'Laughlin, another conspirator, was from Baltimore and was a Roman Catholic Irishman. Sam Arnold, it appears, had attended the same school with John Wilkes Booth in their childhood and was a nominal Protestant. George Atzerodt was the "rough" man, that is the uncultured and uneducated one, who was an Austrian Catholic, but not over religious. He attended Mass with Louis Weichmann at the Piscataway Church and St. Patrick's church in Washington. Louis Payne, the man delegated to murder Secretary of State Seward, and almost accomplished the deed, really demonstrated more strength of character and less cowardice than any of the other conspirators. As far as is known he was the son of a Protestant minister. He refused to tell anything about himself, but when he went to his death he was courageous to a degree that astonished the newspaper correspondents. Edward Spangler, another conspirator, was a roustabout employee at Ford's Theatre, and was considered a drunk. He had great admiration for John Booth and was a fervent Southern supporter who had a strong dislike for Abraham Lincoln, which he often expressed.

With the breaking out of the Civil War Louis Weichmann's college studies were interrupted and he came to Washington where he obtained a position as Professor at Gonzaga College.

During the spring vacation of '63, Weichmann proposed that he and Surratt pay a visit to their Alma Mater near Baltimore. They were received with warm cordiality by both professors and students who were eager to learn the progress of the war. During this visit, according to documentary evidence to be introduced later on, both men freely expressed their pro-Southern views. This was the beginning of an acquaintance which was to end very disastrously for Surratt.

Before closing this chapter in reference to the religion of John Wilkes Booth I would mention that his family were members of the Episcopal church in Baltimore.

Union Army Col. Edwin A. Sherman, who had exchanged information with Charles Chiniquy and author of the book, "*The Engineer Corps of Hell*," had this to say on page 213:

> "It has been told to us, coming from what we believe to be true authority, that Booth, about three weeks before he committed the crime, was admitted to the Roman

Catholic church, and privately received the sacraments from no less a personage than Archbishop Spaulding himself, which he did to silence any conscientious scruples that he might have in taking Abraham Lincoln's life, and that he might have the whole influence and sympathy of persons in that faith in protecting and concealing himself when the act was done, to aid him in it. He certainly had that aid and influence in planning and accomplishing his hellish work and in making his escape, and it could not have been more cheerfully and faithfully rendered that it was, even if he had been a Jesuit priest himself. We believe the statement to be true; and it was but a short time after that Archbishop Spaulding received a donation of funds for the specific purpose which was to uniform and equip a military body in the same manner and style as the Papal Guard at Rome.

"The uniforms, muskets, cartridge boxes and belts all bearing the Papal coat of arms and consecrated by the Pope himself, were sent to Archbishop Spaulding at Baltimore; and when he died he was buried with military honors and his remains escorted by the same military bodyguard. The entire diocese of Archbishop Spaulding was rebel to the core and fierce in its hatred of Lincoln." (9)

In the book, *Washington in the Lap of Rome*, by Justin Fulton D.D. published 1888 p. 39-41 we find the actual ceremony that Booth, Surratt and probably Payne/Powell participated in prior to their deeds of April 15, 1865 –

"The following is the Jesuit's manner of consecrating both the persons and weapons employed for the murdering of kings and princes by them accounted heretics.

The person…is immediately conducted into their *sanctum sanctorum,* designed for prayer and meditation. There the dagger (or other weapon) is produced, carefully wrapped up in a linen safeguard, enclosed in an iron sheath, engraven with several enigmatical characters, and accompanied with an *Agnes Dei*; certainly, a most monstrous confutation so unadvisedly to intertwine the height of murderous villainy and the most sacred emblem of meekness together. The dagger, unsheathed, is hypocritically bedewed with holy water, and the handle, adorned with a certain number of coral beads, put into his hand, thereby assuring the credulous fool that as many effectual stabs as he gives the assassinated prince, so many souls should he redeem out of purgatory on his own account. Then they deliver the dagger into the homicide's hands, with a solemn recommendation, in these words:

"Elected son of God, receive the sword of Jephthah; the sword of Samson, which was the jawbone of an ass; the sword of David, wherewith he smote off the head of Goliath; the sword of Gideon; the sword of Judith; The sword of the Maccabees; the sword of Pope Julius II, wherewith he cut off the lives of several princes, his enemies, filling the whole cities with slaughter and blood. Go forth prudently, courageously, and the lord strengthen thine arm"

Which being pronounced, they all fall upon their knees, and the Superior of the Jesuits pronounces the following exorcism;

"Attend, O ye Cherubim, descend and be present, O Seraphim. You thrones, you powers, you holy angels, come down and fill this blessed vessel – the parricide-with eternal glory; and daily offer to him (for it is but a small reward) the crown of the blessed Virgin Mary, and all of the holy patriarchs and martyrs. He is no more concerned among us; he is now of your celestial fraternity. And thou, O God, most terrible and inaccessible, who yet has revealed to this instrument of thine, in thy dedicated place of our prayer and meditation, that such a prince is to be cut off as a tyrant and a heretic, and his dominions to be translated to another line, confirm and strengthen, we beseech thee, this instrument of thine, whom we have consecrated and dedicated to that sacred office, that he may be able to accomplish thy will. Grant him the habergeon of thy divine omnipotentency, that he may be enabled to escape the hands of his pursuers. Give him wings, that he may avoid the designs of all that lie in wait for his destruction. Infuse into his soul the beams of thy consolation, to uphold and sustain the weak palace of his body; that contemning all fears, he may be able to show a cheerful and lively countenance in the midst of present torments or prolonged imprisonments; and that he may sing and rejoice with a more ordinary exultation, whatever death he undergoes."

This exorcism being finished, the parricide is then brought to the altar, over which, at that time, hangs a picture of James Clement, a Dominican friar, with the fingers of several angels protecting him and conducting him to heaven. Clement was responsible for the murder of King Henry III, King of France. The parricide is then given a celestial coronet with a recital of these words:

"Lord, look down and behold this arm of thine, the executioner of thy justice; let all thy saints arise and give place to him"."

Cardinal Antonelli –
Prime suspect in issuing the order to assassinate Lincoln

Endnotes

1 The Suppressed Truth about the Assassination of Abraham Lincoln, Burke McCarty, (by permission Merrimac, Mass. Destiny Publishers, 1973; originally published 1923) pp.85-90
2 Ibid. pp.90-91
3 Ibid. pp.91-92
4 Ibid. p.92
5 Ibid. P.93
6 Ibid. p.94
7 Ibid. pp. 95-102
8 Fifty Years in the Church of Rome, Charles Chiniquy, (by permission Chick Publications, Chino. Ca. originally published 1883) pp.293-295
9 The Engineer Corps of Hell, or Rome's Sappers and Miners, Edwin A. Sherman, Oakland, Ca., compiler; private subscription

Chapter 9

The day of infamy; Lincoln is killed; Secretary of State Seward survives the attempt on his life; Booth escapes; the role of Surratt and the church; the argument of Judge John A. Bingham; the role of Doctor Mudd

And now we come to the darkest day in the history of the United States, April 14, 1865. The Surrender of Lee, April 3, 1865, to the "Little Smoking General" Grant, came like a thunderbolt out of a clear sky, and was a terrific blow to the hopes of the South, as well as unexpected victory to the North. The people were wild with excitement and joy.

The figure of Abraham Lincoln will ever stand out on the pages of history, not only in the minds of the people in his own country, but in those of the peoples of the world, as the savior of the New Concept of Popular Government.

Lincoln breathed a sigh of relief when he arose this bright balmy April morning and gazed at nature's spring garb. During breakfast with his family he had suggested to his good wife Mary that they two alone should take a long drive in the country which called so strongly to this heavy laden man. Accordingly, after a few preliminary office duties were gotten out of the way, the President returned to the White House, and he and Mrs. Lincoln got into their carriage and drove out through the city over the Potomac River bridge into the country. The fruit trees were white with blossoms, the roadsides green, and the birds flitting in and out through the hedges seemed to surpass themselves with their songs.

President Lincoln began to talk of their future. He confessed to her that he would welcome the day when his administration would be over, and they could return to private life, never to leave it again.

> "I have managed, my dear, by strict economy, to save a little nest egg out of my salary, so we will go back to Springfield to live, and I hope not to have to work quite so hard. We can visit with our friends and neighbors and enjoy life a bit."(1)

He then unfolded to her his plans to take up his law practice again and the threads of life where he had left them when he came to Washington, a little over four years ago. After driving several hours, and being rested by the quiet of the country and sweet breath of spring, this simple-hearted and plain man and his wife returned to the White House.

The day began for John Wilkes Booth with his usual trip to Graves Theatre where he received his mail. This morning he had several letters, and after chatting pleasantly with the members of the cast present for rehearsal, as was his custom, he sauntered away toward the Kirkwood House, where the Vice President was stopping. He sent up the following card to Mr. Johnson, which will always remain a mystery:

> "For Mr. Andrew Johnson:
> Don't wish to disturb you; are you at home?
> John Wilkes Booth" (2)

After his call at the Kirkwood House, he went to the livery barn of J. Pumphreys on C Street, back of the National Hotel. Here he engaged a horse to be ready that afternoon at four thirty. He had been in the habit lately of hiring his horses here after he had sold his own a few weeks previous. On this occasion he asked for a particular sorrel horse, which he preferred, but was told it was out at the time, so he accepted instead a small bay mare.

Booth was an expert horseman and fencer, and spent most of his time on horseback riding and the latter hobby, when he found a man who was skillful enough to interest him. After his arrangement for the horse was completed, he spent a large part of the day conferring with the other conspirators, who were in the city, Mrs. Surratt, John Surratt, O'Laughlin, Herold, Spangler and Atzerodt.

The evening of this same day, April 14, 1865, on which Mr. Lincoln and his wife went for their last drive in the country, the managers of Ford's Theatre featured the fact in the local press that the President and General U.S. Grant would attend the performance of "Our American Cousin" at the theatre in the evening. This would have been the first public appearance of General Grant since the surrender of Lee, and the word that the people would have an opportunity to greet their hero that night at Ford's Theatre caused a rush on the box office, and the performance opened with a sellout.

The Presidential party did not show up until nine thirty. When the tall, gaunt figure of the tired-eyed President made its appearance in the flag-draped box the house went wild with delight, and the orchestra struck up "Hail to the Chief"; the house arose as one body. For several minutes the cheering continued and the President bowed and bowed his acknowledgments.

The absence of General Grant was soon noticed, but this did not dampen the welcome for the great man, who had sent out, but a few days previous, the most wonderful and extraordinary message to a conquered enemy the world had ever heard, namely, for them to return to their homes, and help in the reconstruction of the Republic. No punishment, no criticisms, no bitterness, but simply to return to their homes and set about rebuilding what they had tried to destroy, in a spirit of "With charity for all and malice toward none."

The President and Mrs. Lincoln, upon receiving the regrets of General Grant and wife, who had been called to the bedside of their daughter, Miss Nellie, who was ill at a private boarding school in New Jersey, had invited Major Rathbone and his fiancé, Miss Harris, daughter of Senator Harris, to accompany them. The party seated themselves after the long ovation given the President, and turned their attention to the comedy of which Mr. Lincoln was very fond.

Miss Laura Keene was playing the star lead that evening, assisted by a cast of prominent actors, and the play went with a zest, the audience receiving it with a gale of laughter as one funny scene after another passed. The President chuckled quietly in his own quizzical manner. While this scene was taking place inside, a most unusual play was transpiring on the outside.

Sgt. Dye, a member of the government service, was sitting in front of the restaurant next door to the entrance of the theatre on 10th Street, talking with some of the other men who were enjoying the warm evening and their cigars, when a tall young man well dressed, stepped to the front of the theatre on the sidewalk, and called the time. This did not attract any particular attention until he had repeated it at an interval of every fifteen minutes for the third time, at ten fifteen. He disappeared and Sgt. Dye's curiosity was aroused by his strange conduct. He got up and started to walk in the direction the young stranger had taken, when wild cries and confusion within the theatre reached the street.

"The President is shot," "The President is killed," finally was heard. The entrance doors burst open, and men, insane with fright, bolted out giving the call to those on the street, then rushed back in.

At a moment before the last call of the time in front of the theatre, John Wilkes Booth stepped out of the bar attached to the theatre on 10th Street, where he had called for several brandies, walked rapidly into the front lobby, passed the doorman at the centre aisle with a genial nod, calling him by name, which was answered in the spirit which John Booth's greetings generally were. He passed over to the side aisle and started down when his passage was barred by the arm of the head usher, who was talking with some of his friends in the aisle. Booth put his arm around the shoulder of the man and peering into his face said melodiously, “Why, you don't want to keep me out, do you old boy?” The usher, swinging around said, "No, indeed, Mr. Booth. Allow me to present you to my friends." Booth acknowledged the introduction graciously and turning, sauntered down the aisle toward the box occupied by the Presidential party.

He passed the man on guard, who for the moment left the door of the box and was watching the play from a nearby seat. Booth entered the box, stealthily placing the board in the socket on the inside, which had been made ready that day, by Spangler, the stage carpenter.

Booth's entrance was so quiet that it attracted no attention whatever from any of the party, all of whom had their eyes fixed upon the stage where the only two people were Laura Keene and Harry Hawks as Asa Trenchard. The lines and situation were exceedingly funny and the house was enjoying the comedy.

Booth, after securing the door from any interference from the outside, crept close to the back of the President's chair, whipped out his derringer with his right hand and a dagger with his left, placing the revolver just above the back of the chair. There was a muffled report, a whiff of smoke, and the President's head dropped upon his breast. The intruder darted toward the railing in front of the box, but before he reached it, Major Rathbone, horror-stricken, but not really knowing just what had happened, bounded to his feet. He reached out to grab the assassin, who dropping his revolver, slashed viciously at him, warding him off by an ugly stab which cut his sleeve from shoulder to wrist from which the blood spurted. Booth then sprang over the balustrade of the box onto the stage twelve feet below, but his spur caught in the large American flag which had been draped around the Stuart's Washington portrait on the front of the box, and he fell to the stage, breaking a small bone in his leg. He bounded to his feet instantly and darted away from the stage past the petrified actors, out through the rear door, where he mounted his horse which he had gotten from the candy butcher, called "Peanuts John" to hold for him just before he entered the front door a few minutes previous.

Joseph P. Stewart, a man from the audience, who had taken in the situation before others in the audience had recovered from their horror, scrambled to the stage yelling, “Stop that man” and rushed after the assassin, but just as Booth darted through the alley door someone in the dark slammed it shut before he could get it opened, the man mounted his horse and dashed madly away in the darkness.

Spangler, the stage carpenter, the testimony developed, was the man who had slammed the door. He had been heard to promise his assistance to Booth earlier in the evening when he had dismounted from his horse. For this and disloyal statements about the President which he had been heard to make, he received a sentence of six years at the Dry Tortugas prison.

The gaunt body of the dying President was tenderly carried out of the theatre on the door of the box, which had been hastily removed and pressed into service as a stretcher, across the street to a three story brick house of a man by the name of Peterson, who rented his rooms furnished to the business men employed at the stores and nearby theatres.

The stretcher-bearers carried him to the bedroom in the rear of the hall on the first floor and into a room occupied by a returned soldier by the name of William Clark. The bed was a single bed and the body of the President had to be laid diagonally across on account of his great height.

The pitiful scene here can barely be portrayed by words. The hysterical sobs of Mrs. Lincoln wailing, "Oh, why did they take him, why did they not take me?" was heartbreaking.

Capt. Robert Lincoln, who had just returned from the front a few days before, was immediately summoned from the White House, where he was entertaining a college friend, to the bedside of his dying father. He spent the time alternately trying to comfort his mother in the front parlor and watching at the bedside of his father.

Soon the members of Mr. Lincoln's cabinet had gathered in the sick room and Dr. Gurley, Protestant minister, and Surgeon General Barnes, came as soon as possible from the bedside of the Secretary of State Seward, the Surgeon having been called there after Lewis Payne had stabbed Mr. Seward. Mr. Seward was now hovering between life and death. General Stanton, the cold, severe, dignified man, who had never been known to show any emotion, dropped to his knees at the foot of the bed on which the President lay, buried his face in the covering and wept like a child. Senator Charles Sumner, who, perhaps, loved Lincoln with the deepest and most ardent love of them all, never stirred from his place at the bed, holding his hand, and aiding the physicians, and watching with bated breath for the slightest sign of returning consciousness. But the wounded man never for one instant recovered, and died without knowing what had occurred. From the moment the physicians first reached him and found the wound, they knew it was mortal.

The President died a few minutes after seven a.m. the next morning. Secretary Stanton as he watched the life of the great man flow out, turned to those in the room and said, "And now, he belongs to the ages."

The letters of condolences that came from every quarter of the civilized world let no doubt be known that Lincoln was regarded highly, not just in his own country, but the world. The letters, and there are thousands, are all collected and placed in order of national origin. The following extracts, from the nation of Italy are taken from the files of the U.S. State Department, who first made them public in 1867 and are a very brief example…

> From: Democratic Association of Florence to the free people of the United States of America. (Translation)
> May 8, 1865
>
> The furies of despotism and of servitude, deceived in their infamous hopes, incapable of sustaining any longer their combat against liberty, before falling into the abyss which threatened them, strengthened the arm of a murderer, and as they opened the fratricidal war with the gibbet of the martyr of the cause of abolition, John Brown, so they ended it, worthy of themselves, in the most ferocious and stupid of all crimes, the murder of a great citizen.
>
> Now liberty, in stigmatizing the cause of her enemies, will have only to show to the world this gibbet and this murderer, and the people looking upon them cannot do otherwise than recollect that despots have had a share in this; that in some courts of Europe Mason, Slidell, and the ferocious pirates of the Alabama found protection, encouragement, and applause, and finally the wicked instigator of the civil war, Jefferson Davis, obtained consolation, praises, and hope even in the paternal benediction of the Pope. [...] pp. 583-84
>
> From: Fraternity of the artisans of Italy to the people of the United States. (Translation)
> April 27, 1865
>
> ... the fraternal love which unites to you, free citizens, every heart which beats for and desires the complete triumph of the rights of

humanity. But, alas! The hand of an infamous assassin (the agent, doubtless, of a mysterious and iniquitous plot prepared against the national liberty) has taken away the precious life of your Chief Magistrate ...pp. 584-85

From: American meeting in Florence on account of the death of Abraham Lincoln. Florence, Italy, May 2, 1865

That while we see in the assassination of President Lincoln an act of barbarity unparalleled in the annals of crime, yet we are constrained to regard and denounce it as naturally and logically related to the grand conspiracy which has aimed at the overthrow of our republican institutions. [...] pp. 586-87

From: The Mechanics' Society and the Society of Progress of Forli to the American people. (Translation)
Forli, May 1, 1865

... The real design of his assassination is a secret still hidden in the mysteries of a deep policy, and we have not the divining power to find it out; ...

Lincoln's is a great name, that will ever be remembered as the name of the champion of all democratic virtues. He has unmasked monarchy by giving true liberty and independence to a weary world. His martyrdom will be a baptism more powerful than that required by the Roman church; it is sacrament of blood—the other is of water. Lincoln and progress are synonymous; ... pp.587-88

From: The Union of Operatives, Genoa, May 4, 1865 (Translation)

[...]

We feel certain that your great republic, which in a few years has displayed so many miracles of valor, constancy and sacrifice, as to fill the world with surprise, purified from the foul stain of slavery, regenerated in blood, and blessed by all humanity, will be more glorious and powerful than before the war, furnish a model for European nations, and lift up the beacon of hope for oppressed people.

Faithful to the Monroe doctrine, you will not, we are sure, tolerate the planting of a foreign monarchy on the borders of your own land, which is the sacred asylum of liberty.

We beg you to convey to your government and fellow-citizens these sentiments of admiration and affection which we cherish for your country and her cause.

Note: The Union of Operatives has unanimously voted this address, and further resolved to drape its flag in mourning for one year. pp. 589-90

From: Workingmen's Benevolent Society of Naples, May 4, 1865 (Translation)

[...]

... We are glad that so much glory falls to the lot of a people who jealously guarded the light-house of liberty, a divinity banished from the Old World to find refuge in the New, whose once vast solicitudes are now filled with inhabitants. Our eyes have long been turned to that beacon, and are bent on it now hoping to see that torrent of light shed its blessings upon this old and corrupt hemisphere. [...] pp. 596-97

From: The studious youths of Naples. (Translation)

Americans of the Union: Despotism, priestly and political, diplomatic hypocrisy, and a tradition of blood have fettered the Italian emancipation with so many snares that we, overwhelmed with grief and disgusted with this depraved Old World, turn with confiding looks to the New one, and our souls rejoice at the grand spectacle you show us. Oh, Americans! you who have conquered your own independence by your virtue only—in the sacredness of the laws constitutes only one a free family, without kings or myrmidons, without priests or deceitful idols. p. 597-98

From: Italian Electoral Association—General Garibaldi, Honorary President. Naples, May 2, 1865 (Translation)

... This event has moved the world more than it has ever done before, or will ever do at the death of a pope or reigning emperor, by will of God, because the man whose loss we deplore was not raised in virtue of chimerical rights, but by the free vote of the people. [...] p. 599

From: Union of Operatives at San Pier d'Arena Genoa, May 7, 1865 (Translation)

[...]

Happy, O American people, are you who secured your liberties with your own blood, and have had the courage to maintain them at the same great sacrifice. Firm as a rock in the sea, you may defy those of your enemies who still govern in the name of divine right in every corner of the world, and especially in our Europe, where they are stronger than elsewhere, and fear that the blessing of liberty enjoyed in your country may stimulate the people to imitate your examples and overturn those rotten edifices which are called thrones.

To us, who enjoy a shadow of liberty, there remains no other path to the blessings which you possess than to take you for guide, and move after you towards a true democracy. [...] pp. 606-7

From: Italian Union Committee of Sienna (Translation)

May 18, 1865

[...]

The free fatherland of Washington and of Benjamin Franklin, a hospitable soil to all who emigrate from the despotisms of ancient Europe, mourns, in the murder of its new liberator, an event the equal of which does not exist. [...] p. 608

From: The Italian Society of United Mechanics of Turin (Translation)
30 April, 1865

May free America find a successor worthy of Abraham Lincoln, and may the Monroe doctrine prevail for the good of the country. [...] p. 616

At the same time that Booth assassinated the President, Lewis Payne, who some months before joined the Conspiracy, rode up to the front of the residence of the Secretary of State, William Seward, and tied his horse to the hitching post. Mr. Seward had been ill for three weeks and was suffering a broken jaw, the result of the running away of his team of horses, and was under the constant care of male nurses.

Payne rang the bell and the door was answered by the black butler. He told the butler that he had been sent with some medicine, which he must take to the sick room. The butler refused to allow him to enter, saying that he had orders to allow no one to go to Mr. Seward's room. The stranger, after a short struggle, knocked him down, and went bounding up the stairs. He rushed into the sick chamber, after felling each of the two sons of the Secretary, one of whom had his skull smashed in and later died. He then sprang upon the sick man and seriously stabbed him in the chest three times. By a superhuman effort the Secretary struggled out of bed with his assailant who left him in a heap on the floor, bleeding from the wounds he had inflicted. After his assault on Secretary Seward, Payne rushed down the stairs, yelling at the top of his lungs, "I am mad, I am mad." He most likely was. He was entirely under the control of the hypnotic influences of the people in whose power he had allowed himself to be.

Payne/Powell – Lincoln conspirator

Payne/Powell – Lincoln conspirator

It was part of the plan that Michael O'Laughlin one of the conspirators from Baltimore, was to have murdered General Grant that night. But owing to the change of the General's plans, this was not possible.

To Atzerodt, it fell to assassinate Vice President Johnson, but he became frightened and spent the day riding the other direction into the country on a horse from the livery barn in Washington, where he was found several days later with relatives of his below Washington. He made a written confession before he was executed which confirmed the presence of Surratt in Washington that fatal day, a fact which nine reputable witnesses had sworn to.

Booth familiarized himself with every road leading out of Washington to the south, and had studied and planned his escape with careful attention. It is not likely that he would ever have been caught, had he not broken the bone in his left leg in his jump. This was the providential handicap which hampered not only himself and Herold, but those of his friends who were ready to assist him. There is not the least doubt but that every mile of that wild ride had been planned in advance - weeks in advance. The intense agony which Booth suffered every moment from the time he first met with the accident when jumping from the box doomed his chances of escape.

The little bay mare dashed madly along under the cruel urge of his spurs as he sped over the Potomac bridge which led to the Bryantown road. He passed the soldier at the bridge, after having told him his name, and was swallowed up in the blackness of the night. The moon was veiled behind a huge bank of clouds. Presently the guard at the bridge heard the clatter of another horse's hoofs approaching and the horse and rider soon came into sight on the bridge. The guard stopped him and asked him to give an account of himself before allowing him to continue. This was Herold and in explanation he gave a false name saying that he had been in bad company which delayed him from returning home before sundown. He was permitted to pass. He cut his spurs into his horse and sped along, finally catching up to Booth, before they reached Surrattville, where they were expected by the tenant Lloyd who had been visited by Mrs. Surratt that afternoon and who instructed him (Lloyd) to "Have those shooting irons" and other things ready, that they would be needed that night.

Herold drew up to the tavern, sprang from his horse and dashed madly into the barroom saying, "Lloyd, for God's sake, make haste and get those things."

Lloyd testified at the trials that he gave the carbines which had been left six weeks before with him to be called for later on; that Mrs. Surratt had been driven down from Washington on Friday the 14th to his house by Weichmann; that he met them on the road on his way to Washington; that he got out of his buggy and went over to the side of their buggy and after a few moments of conversation she told him to "Have those shooting irons ready; that they would be called for soon." Weichmann also testified that he overheard this order by Mrs. Surratt.

Mrs. Surratt brought with her on this trip, the day of the assassination, a package containing Booth's binoculars, to be handed out when called for. Herold took a bottle of whiskey out to Booth, who, owing to his suffering, did not come in. They only took one of the revolvers, so Lloyd testified. Herold turned as he was about to drive off and said, "I'm pretty sure that we have assassinated the President and Secretary Seward."

The two riders put their spurs into their horses and set off down the road to the little village of T.B. at full speed. The next stop was made at the residence of Dr. Samuel A. Mudd, where they arrived at four o'clock on the Saturday morning. This conspirator housed them and set the bone in Booth's leg. He bound it up in splints improvised from pieces of a cigar box, after which Booth was helped upstairs to bed where he remained until the afternoon of the same day.

O'Laughlin had come to Washington on Thursday, the day before the assassination, with three of his co-religionists who prepared to make a perfectly good bullet-proof alibi for their friend O'Laughlin, which was the rule with Roman Catholic criminals. They were so solicitous in this intent that they over-reached themselves and ruined it.

The great grievance of the Catholic Church is that Mary E. Surratt was brought before a Military tribunal, instead of a civil court. The real basis for this complaint, was however, that there could be no political influence brought to bear on a Military court, which the hanging of four conspirators and life sentences of three others bears out. Since there is no better way to fully explain the situation than that used in the closing argument of the Judge Advocate, John A. Bingham, I will rely on excerpts from that document to give the facts.

ARGUMENT OF JOHN A. BINGHAM, Special Judge Advocate

IN REPLY TO THE SEVERAL ARGUMENTS IN DEFENSE OF MARY E. SURRATT AND OTHERS, CHARGED WITH CONSPIRACY AND THE MURDER OF ABRAHAM LINCOLN, LATE PRESIDENT OF THE UNITED STATES

May it please the Court: The conspiracy here charged and specified and the acts alleged to have been committed in pursuance thereof, and with the intent laid, constitute a crime, the atrocity of which has sent a shudder through the civilized world. All that was agreed upon and attempted by the alleged inciters and instigators of this crime constitutes a combination of atrocities with scarcely a parallel in the annals of the human race. Whether the prisoners at your bar are guilty of the conspiracy and the acts alleged to have been done...as set forth in the charge and specification, is a question, the determination of which rests solely with this honorable court, and in passing upon which, this court are the sole judges of the law and the fact.

In presenting my views upon the questions of law raised by the several counsel for the defense, and also on the testimony adduced for and against the accused, I desire to be just to them, just to you, just to my country, and just to my own convictions. The issue joined involves the highest interests of the accused, and, in my judgment, the highest interests of the whole people of the United States.... A wrongful and illegal conviction, or a wrongful and illegal acquittal upon this dread issue, would impair somewhat the security of every man's life, and shake the stability of the Republic.

The crime charged and specified upon your record is not simply the crime of murdering a human being, but it is a crime of killing and murdering on the 14th of April, A.D. 1865, within the Military Department of Washington and the entrenched lines thereof, Abraham Lincoln, then President of the United States, and Commander in Chief of the Army and Navy there; and then and there assaulting with intent to kill and murder, Wm. H. Seward, then Secretary of State of the United States; and then and there lying in wait to kill and murder Andrew Johnson, the Vice President of the United States; and Ulysses S.

Grant, then Lieutenant General and in Command of the Army of the United States, in pursuance of a treasonable conspiracy entered into by the accused with one John Wilkes Booth, and John H. Surratt, upon the instigation of Jefferson Davis, Jacob Thompson, Clement C. Clay, George N. Sanders and others, with intent thereby to aid the existing Rebellion and subvert the Constitution and laws of the United States.

The Government in preferring this charge, does not indict the whole people of any State or section, but only the alleged parties to this unnatural and atrocious crime. The President of the United States in the discharge of his duty as Commander in Chief of the Army and by virtue of the power invested in him by the Constitution and laws of the United States, has constituted you a military court, to hear and determine the issue joined against the accused, and has constituted you a court for no other purpose whatever. To this charge and specification the defendants have pleaded first, that this court has no jurisdiction in the premises; and, secondly, not guilty."

After a careful covering of every point raised by the defense, embellished with numerous citations of legal authorities and court decisions as to both of the points raised by the defense, the Judge Advocate continued:

"It only remains for me to sum up the evidence and present my views of the law arising upon the facts in the case on trial. The questions of fact involved in the issue are:

First, did the accused, or any two of them, confederate and conspire together as charged? - and

Second, did the accused, or any of them, in pursuance of such conspiracy, with the intent alleged, commit either or all of the several acts specified?

If the conspiracy be established, as laid, it results that whatever was said or done by either of the parties in the furtherance or execution of the common design is the declaration or act of all the other parties of the conspiracy; and this whether the other parties, at the time such words were uttered, or such acts done by their confederates, were present or absent - here, within the entrenched

> lines of your Capitol, or crouching behind the entrenched lines of Richmond, or awaiting the results of their murderous plot against their country, in Canada...The same rule obtains in cases of treason. A conspiracy is rarely if ever proved by positive testimony. When a crime of high magnitude is about to be perpetrated by a combination of individuals, they do not act openly, but covertly and secretly. The purpose formed is known only to those who enter into it...Unless one of the original conspirators betray his companions and give evidence against them, their guilt can be proved only by circumstantial evidence."

During the course of Judge Advocate Bingham's address the influence of the Jesuit theology was brought up in his reference to Jacob Thompson, one of the conspirators referred to, who was a leader in the group of Confederates of Montreal, when he said:

> "In speaking of this assassination of the President and others, Jacob Thompson said that it was only removing them from office, that ***the killing of a tyrant was no murder***." (3)

Emanuel Sa, a Jesuit authority, said, "The tyrant is illegitimate; and any man whatever of the people has a right to kill him. (Umiquis - que de populo potest ocidere.)

Potomac River Bridge

Note this bit of evidence referred to by the distinguished Bingham:

"Dr. Merritt testified further that after this meeting in Montreal he had a conversation with Clement C. Clay in Toronto about the letter from Jefferson Davis which Sanders had exhibited and in which conversation Clay gave the witness to understand that he knew the nature of the letter perfectly and remarked that he thought, "The end would justify the means." The witness also testified to the presence of Booth with Sanders in Montreal last fall and of Surratt in Toronto in February last."

The above is certainly proof of Jesuit influence. Continuing below the record shows:

"John Wilkes Booth having entered into this conspiracy in Canada, as has been shown, as early as October, he is next found in the City of New York on the 11th day, as I claim of November, in disguise, in conversation with another, the conversation disclosing to the witness, Mrs. Hudspeth, that they had some matter of personal in-

> terest between them; that upon one of them the lot had fallen to go to Washington...upon the other to go to Newbern. This witness upon being shown the photograph of Booth swears that "the face is the same" that of one of the men, who, she says, was a young man of education and culture, as appeared by his conversation, and who had a scar like a bite near the jawbone. It is a fact proved here by the Surgeon General that Booth had such a scar on the side of his neck."

It was this witness that found the letter on the floor of the railway car which Booth dropped and which was transmitted from her to the War Department on November 17, 1864. The letter was delivered to President Lincoln, who after having read it wrote the word "Assassination" across it, and filed it in his office where it was found after his death and was placed in evidence as a court exhibit. The letter read as follows:

> "Dear Louis:
>
> The time has come at last that we have all so wished for, and upon you everything depends. As it was decided, before you left, we were to cast lots, we accordingly did so, and you are to be the Charlotte Corday of the Nineteenth Century. When you remember the fearful solemn vow that was taken by us, you will feel there is no drawback. Abe must die, and now. You can choose your weapons, the cup, the knife, the bullet. The cup failed us once and might again. Johnson who will give this has been like an enraged demon since the meeting, because it has not fallen to him to rid the world of a monster...You know where to find your friends. Your disguises are so perfect and complete that without one knew your face no police telegraphic dispatch would catch you. The English gentleman, Harcourt, must not act hastily. Remember, he has ten days. Strike for your home; strike for your country; bide your time, but strike sure. Get introduced; congratulate him; listen to his stories (not many more will the brute tell to earthly friends;) do anything but fail, and meet us at the appointed place within the fortnight. You will probably hear from me in Washington. Sanders is doing us no good in Canada.
>
> Chas. Selby" (4)

I quote again from Judge Bingham:

"Although this letter would imply that the assassination spoken of was to take place speedily, yet the party was to bide his time...The letter declares that Abraham Lincoln must die and now, meaning as soon as the agents can be employed and the work done. To that end you will bide your time."

"Even Booth's co-conspirator, Payne, now on his trial...says Booth had just been to Canada, "Was filled with a mighty scheme and was lying in wait for agents." Booth asked the co-operation of the prisoner and said, 'I will give you as much money as you want; but you must swear to stick to me. It is in the oil business.' This you are told by the accused was early in March last...In the latter part of November, 1864, Booth visits Charles County, Maryland, and is in company with one of the prisoners, Dr. Samuel A. Mudd, with whom he lodged overnight, and through whom he procures of Gardner one of the several horses which were at his disposal and used by him and his co-conspirator in Washington on the night of the assassination."

"Some time during December last it is in the testimony that the prisoner Mudd introduced Booth to John H. Surratt and the witness Weichmann; that Booth invited them to the National Hotel; that when there in the room to which Booth took them, Mudd went out into the passage, called Booth out and had a private conversation with him, leaving the witness and Surratt in the room. Upon their return to the room. Booth went out with Surratt and upon their coming in all three - Booth, Surratt and Samuel A. Mudd went out together and had a conversation in the passage, leaving Weichmann alone. Up to the time of this interview it seems that neither the witnesses or Surratt had any knowledge of Booth as they were then introduced to him by Dr. Mudd. Whether Surratt had previously known Booth it is not important to inquire. Mudd deemed it necessary, perhaps a wise precaution, to introduce Surratt to Booth; he also deemed it necessary to have a private conversation with Booth shortly afterwards. Had this conversation, no part of which was heard by Weichmann, been perfectly innocent, it is not to be presumed that Dr. Mudd, who was an entire stranger to the witness, would have deemed it necessary to hold the conversation secretly, nor to have volunteered to tell the witness, or rather pretend to tell him what the conversation was...And if it was necessary to withdraw and talk by themselves secretly, about the sale of a farm, why should they disclose the fact to the very man from whom they had concealed it?"

Sam Arnold – Lincoln conspirator

As a matter of fact the above conversation about the purchase of Mudd's farm by Booth was merely a ruse to deceive Weichmann. The entire conversation was talking over the shortest and safest route for flight from the Capitol by which to reach their friends south of Washington.

A number of Dr. Mudd's slaves testified that he was absent from his home at this time which corroborated Weichmann's testimony. I quote again from the summary of the evidence at the trials by Judge Advocate Bingham referring to O'laughlin as follows:

> "Michael O'Laughlin had come to Washington on the 13th of April, 1865, the day preceding the assassination, had sought out his victim, General Grant, at the house of the Secretary of War, that he might be able with certainty to identify him, and that at the very hour when these preparations were going on, was lying in wait at Rullman's on the Avenue, keeping watch, and declaring as he did, at about ten o'clock P.M. when told that the fatal blow had been struck by Booth, "I don't believe Booth did it." During the day and night before he had been visiting Booth, and doubtless encouraging him, and at that very hour was in position, at a convenient distance to aid and protect him in his flight, as well as to execute his own part of this conspiracy, by inflicting death on General Grant who happily, was not at the theatre, nor in the city, having left the city that day."

> "Who doubts that Booth ascertained in the course of the day that General Grant would not be present at the theatre? O'Laughlin, who was to murder General Grant, instead of entering the box with Booth, was detailed to lie in wait, and watch and support him."

> "His declarations of his reasons for his changing his lodgings here and in Baltimore, so ably, and so ingeniously presented in the arguments of his learned counsel (Mr. Cox), avail nothing before the blasting fact, that he did change his lodgings and declared: 'He knew nothing of the affair whatever.'"

> "O'Laughlin who said he was in the 'oil business' which Booth, Surratt, Payne and Arnold, have all declared meant this conspiracy, says he "knew nothing of the affair." O'Laughlin, to whom Booth sent the dispatches of the 13th and 27th of March, - O'Laughlin who is named in Arnold's letter as one of the conspirators, and who searched for General Grant on Thursday night, laid in wait for him on Friday, was defeated by that Providence "which shapes our ends," and laid in wait to aid Booth and Payne, declares, he "knows nothing about the

matter." Such a denial is as false and inexcusable as Peter's denial of our Lord."

While these preparations were going on, Mudd was awaiting the execution of the plot, ready to faithfully perform his part in securing the safe escape of the murderers. Arnold was at his post at Fortress Monroe, awaiting the meeting referred to in his letter of March 27, wherein he said they were not to 'Meet for a month or so,' which month had more than expired on the day of the murder, for his letter and testimony disclose that this month of suspensions began to run from about the first week in March. He stood ready with the arms with which Booth had furnished him, to aid the escape of the murderers by that route, and secure their communication with their employers. He had given the assurance in that letter to Booth that although the Government "suspicioned" them, and the undertaking was becoming "complicated" yet a time "more propitious would arrive," for the consummation of this conspiracy in which he "was one" with Booth and when he "would be better prepared to again be with him."

It was upon the above evidence for which O'Laughlin and Arnold were convicted and sentenced to the Dry Tortugas.

Judge John A, Bingham

And now I will quote from the same document the summing up of the evidence against Mary E. Surratt, for as a matter of facts tersely stated nothing could surpass that of the Judge Advocate, John A. Bingham.

> "That Mary E. Surratt is as guilty as her son, as having thus conspired and combined and confederated, to do this murder, in aid of this rebellion, is clear. First, her house was the headquarters of Booth, John Surratt, Atzerodt, Payne and Herold; she is inquired for by Payne, and she is visited by Booth, and holds private conversations with him. His picture, together with the chief conspirator, Jefferson Davis, is found in her house. She sends to Booth for a carriage to take her on the 11th of April to Surrattville, for the purpose of perfecting the arrangement deemed necessary to the successful execution of the conspiracy, and especially to facilitate and protect the conspirators in their escape from justice. On that occasion, Booth, having disposed of his carriage, gives to the agent she employed (Weichmann) ten dollars with which to hire a conveyance for that purpose. And yet the pretense is made that Mrs. Surratt went on the 11th of April to Surrattville on exclusively her own private and lawful business. Can anyone tell. if that be so, how it comes that she should apply to Booth for a conveyance? And how it comes that he, of his own accord, having no conveyance to furnish her, should send her ten dollars with which to procure it?"
>
> "There is not the slightest indication that Booth was under the slightest obligation to her, or that she had any claim upon him, either for a conveyance, or for the means with which to procure one except that he was bound to contribute, being the agent of the conspirators in Canada and Richmond, whatever money might be necessary to the consummation of this infernal plot. On that day, the 11th of April, John H. Surratt had not returned from Canada with the funds furnished him by Thompson."
>
> "Upon that journey of the 11th, the accused, Mary E. Surratt, met with the witness, John M. Lloyd at Uniontown (her tenant at Surrattville). She called him; he got out of his carriage and came to her; she whispered to him in so low a tone that her attendant could not hear her words, though Lloyd to whom they were spoken, did distinctly hear them, and testifies that she told him he should

have those "shooting irons" ready, meaning the carbines, which her son, and Herold and Atzerodt had deposited with him, and added the reason, "for they would soon be called for." On the day of the assassination, she again sent for Booth, had an interview with him in her own house, and immediately again went to Surrattville, and then, about six o'clock in the afternoon, she delivered to Lloyd a field glass and told him to "Have two bottles of whiskey and the carbines ready, as they would be called for that night." Having thus perfected the arrangement, she returned to Washington to her own house at about half past eight o'clock, to await the final result. How could this woman anticipate on Friday afternoon at six o'clock, that these arms would be called for, and would be needed that night, unless she was in the conspiracy and knew the blow was to be struck, and the flight of the assassins attempted and by that route?"

"Was not the private conversation with Booth held with her in her parlor on the afternoon of the 14th of April, just before she left on this business in relation to the orders she should give to have the shooting arms ready?"

"An endeavor is made to impeach Lloyd. But the Court will observe that no witness has been called who contradicts Lloyd's statement in any material matter; neither has his general character for truth been assailed. How, then, is he impeached? Is it claimed that his testimony shows that he was a party to the conspiracy? Then, it is conceded by those who set up any such a pretense that there was a conspiracy. A conspiracy between whom? There can be no conspiracy without the co-operation, or agreement, between two or more persons. Who were the other parties to it? Was it Mary E. Surratt? Was it John H. Surratt? Was it George Atzerodt. David Herold? Those are the only persons so far as his own testimony, or the testimony of any other witnesses discloses, with whom he had any communication whatever on any subject immediately or remotely touching this conspiracy before the assassination. His receipt and concealment of the arms, are unexplained evidence that he was in the conspiracy."

"The explanation is, that he depended on Mary E. Surratt; was her tenant, and his declaration, given in evidence by the accused, himself, is that: 'She had ruined him and brought this trouble upon him.' But because he was weak enough, or wicked enough, to become the guilty depository of these arms, and to deliver them on the order of Mary E. Surratt, to the assassins, it does not follow, that he concealed the fact that the arms had been left and called for. He so testifies himself, but he gives the reason, that he did it only from apprehension of danger to his life. If he were in the conspiracy, his general credit being unchallenged, his testimony being uncontradicted in any material matter, he is to be believed, and cannot be disbelieved if his testimony is substantially corroborated by other reliable witnesses."

Samuel Mudd

"Is he not corroborated touching the deposit of arms by the fact that the arms are produced in court, one of which was found upon the person of Booth at the time he was overtaken and slain, and which is identified as the same which had been left with Lloyd, by Herold, Surratt and Atzerodt? Is he not corroborated in the fact of the first interview with Mrs. Surratt by the joint testimony of Mrs. Offut (his sister-in-law), and Louis J. Weichmann, each of whom testified, (and they are contradicted by no one) that, on Tuesday, the 11th of April, at Uniontown, Mrs. Surratt called Mr. Lloyd to come to her, which he did, and she held a secret conversation with him? Is he not corroborated as to the last conversation on the 14th of April by the testimony of Mrs. Offut, who swears that upon that evening, April 14th, she saw the prisoner, Mary

E. Surratt, at Lloyd's house, approach and hold a conversation with him? Is he not corroborated in the fact, to which he swears that Mrs. Surratt delivered to him at that time, the field glasses wrapped in paper, by the sworn statement of Weichmann, that Mrs. Surratt took with her on that occasion two packages, both of which were wrapped in paper, and one of which he describes as a small package, about six inches in diameter? The attempt was made, by calling Mrs. Offut, to prove that no such package was delivered, but it failed; she merely states, that Mrs. Surratt delivered a package wrapped in paper to her, after her arrival there, and before Lloyd came in, which was laid down in the room. But whether it is the package about which Lloyd testifies, or the other package, of the two about which Weichmann testifies, as having been carried there that day by Mrs. Surratt, does not appear. Neither does this witness pretend to say that Mrs. Surratt, after she had delivered it to her, and the witness had laid it down in the room, did not again take it up, if it were the same, and put it into the hands of Lloyd. She only knows that she did not see it done; but she did see Lloyd with a package like the one she received in the room before Mrs. Surratt left. How it came in his possession she is not able to state; nor that the package was that Mrs. Surratt first handed her; nor which of the packages she afterwards saw in the hands of Lloyd."

"But there is one other fact in this case that puts forever at rest the question of the guilty participation of the prisoner, Mrs. Surratt, in this conspiracy and murder; and that is, that Payne who had lodged four days in her house - who, during all of that time had sat at her table, and who had often conversed with her - when the guilt of his great crime was upon him, and he knew not where else he could go safely, to find a co-conspirator, and that he could trust none, that was not like himself, guilty, with even the knowledge of his presence, under the cover of darkness, after wandering for three days and nights, skulking before the pursuing officers, at the hour of midnight found his way to the door of Mrs. Surratt, rang the bell, was admitted, and upon being asked, 'Whom do you want to see?' Replied, 'Mrs. Surratt.' He was then asked by the officer Morgan, what he came at that time of night for, to which he replied, 'To dig a gutter in the morning,' that Mrs. Surratt had sent for him. Afterwards he said that Mrs. Surratt knew he was a poor man and came to him. Being asked where he last worked, he replied: 'Some-

> times on I street; and where he boarded, he replied, that he had no boarding house but was a poor man who got his living with the pick, which he bore upon his shoulder, having stolen it from the entrenchments of the Capital. Upon being pressed why he came there at that time of night to go to work, he answered that he simply called to see what time he should go to work in the morning. Upon being told by the officer who fortunately preceded him to this house, that he would have to go to the Provost-Marshal's office, he moved and did not answer, whereupon Mrs. Surratt was asked to step into the hall and state whether she knew this man. Raising her right hand, she exclaimed: 'Before God, sir, I have not seen that man before; I have not hired him; I do not know anything about him.' The hall was brilliantly lighted."
>
> "If not one word had been said, the mere act of Payne in flying to her house for shelter, would have borne witness against her, strong as proofs from Holy Writ. But, when she denies, after hearing his declarations that she had sent for him, or that she had never seen him, and knew nothing of him, when, in point of fact, she had seen him four consecutive days, in her own house (that same house) in the same clothing which he wore, who can resist for a moment, the conclusion that these parties, were alike, guilty?"

And this is the woman whom the Roman hierarchy in the United States wanted to make a martyr of.

Contemplate the female Jesuit, without being asked to swear to her denial, volunteered to lift her hand and in the name of her God, perjure herself in the presence of those witnesses. Do you doubt that she was a lay Jesuit? Let me quote the "Doctrine of the Jesuits" on this point:

Under "Of Lying and False Swearing" in JUDICIO TEOLOGICA, Basnedi, Jesuit authority, page 278, we find:

> “If you believe in an inconvertible manner, that you are commanded to lie, then lie."

I also present this quote from the Jesuit Father Stoz in "Of the Tribunal of the Penitent:"

> "When a crime is secret, the culpability of the crime may be denied; it being understood publicly."

Mary E. Surratt knew the command of her church at that moment, and in order to save it from scandal and culpability in this great crime, as well as her own life and safety, she was dispensed to lie, and so without any hesitancy she raised her right hand and swore to this lie.

Continuing, Judge Bingham said:

> "Mrs. Surratt had arrived at home from the completion of her part in the plot, about half past eight in the evening. A few minutes afterwards she was called to the parlor, and there had a private interview with someone unseen, but whose retreating footsteps were heard by the witness, Weichmann. This was doubtless the secret, and last visit of John H. Surratt to his mother, who had instigated and encouraged him to strike this traitorous and murderous blow at his country.
>
> "Booth proceeded to the theatre about nine o'clock in the evening, at the same time that Atzerodt and Payne and Herold were riding the streets, while Surratt, having parted with his mother at the brief interview in her parlor, from which his retreating steps were heard, was walking the Avenue (Pennsylvania) booted and spurred, and doubtless consulting with O'laughlin. When Booth reached the rear of the theatre, he called Spangler to him and received from Spangler his pledge to help him all he could, when, with Booth, he entered the theatre by the stage door, doubtless to see the way was clear from the box to the rear door of the theatre, and to look upon their victim, whose erect position they could study from the stage. After this view Booth passes to the street in front of the theatre, where on the pavement, with other conspirators, yet unknown, among them one described as a low-browed villain, he awaits the appointed moment.... Presently, as the hour of ten o'clock approached, one of his guilty associates calls the time; they wait; again, as the appointed time draws nigh, he calls the time; and fi-

nally when the fatal moment arrives, he repeats in a louder tone 'Ten minutes past ten o'clock, ten minutes past ten o'clock'...The hour has come when the red right hand of these murderous conspirators should strike, and the dreadful deed of assassination be done."

"Booth at the appointed moment entered the theatre, ascended to the dress circle, passed to the right, paused a moment looking down, doubtless to see if Spangler was at his post, and approached the outer door of the closed passage leading to the box, occupied by the President, pressed it open, passed in, and closed the passage door behind him. Spangler's bar was in its place and was readily adjusted by Booth in the mortise, and pressed against the inner side of the door, so that he was secure from interruption from without. He passed on to the next door, immediately behind the President, and stopping, looks through the aperture in the door into the President's box, and deliberately observes the precise position of his victim seated in the chair, which had been prepared by the conspirators, as the altar for sacrifice, looking calmly and quietly down upon the glad and grateful people, whom by his fidelity he had saved from the peril which had threatened the destruction of their government, and all they held dear, this side of the grave, and whom he had come, upon invitation, to greet with his presence, with the words still lingering upon his lips, which he had uttered with uncovered head and uplifted hand, before God, and his country, when on the fourth of last March, he took again the oath to preserve, protect and defend the Constitution, declaring that he entered upon the duties of his great office 'With malice toward none and charity for all.'"

"In a moment more, strengthened by the knowledge that his conspirators were all at their posts, seven at least of them present in the city, two of them, Mudd and Arnold, at their appointed places, watching for his coming, this hired assassin moves stealthily through the door, the fastening of which had been removed to facilitate his entrance, fires upon his victim, and the martyred spirit of Abraham Lincoln ascends to God."

Judge Bingham then picked up the thread of evidence by which Booth and Herold were left at the home of Dr. Mudd:

"...They arrived early in the morning before day, and no man knows at what hour they left. Herold rode towards Bryantown with Mudd, about three o'clock that afternoon, in the vicinity of which place he parted with him, remaining in the swamp, and was afterwards seen returning the same afternoon in the direction of Mudd's house, a little before sundown, about which time Mudd returned from Bryantown towards his home.

This village, at the time Mudd was in it, was thronged with soldiers in pursuit of the murderers of the President, and although great care had been taken by the defense to deny that anyone said in the presence of Dr. Mudd, either there or elsewhere on that day, who had committed this crime, yet it is in evidence by two witnesses, whose truthfulness no man questions, that upon Mudd's return to his own house that afternoon, he stated that Booth was the murderer of the President...but took care to make the further remark that Booth had brothers, and that he did not know which of them had done the act."

"When did Dr. Mudd learn that Booth had brothers? And what is still more pertinent to this inquiry, from whom did he learn that either, John Wilkes Booth or any of his brothers, had murdered the President?"

"It is clear that Booth remained in Mudd's house until some time in the afternoon of Saturday; that Herold left the house alone, as one witness states, being seen to pass the window; that he alone of these two assassins was in the company of Dr. Mudd on his way to Bryantown. It does not appear that Herold returned to Mudd's house. It is a confession of Dr. Mudd himself, proven by one of the witnesses that Booth left his house on crutches and went in the direction of the swamp. How long did he remain there, and what became of the horses that Booth and Herold rode to his house and which were put in his stable, are facts nowhere disclosed by the evidence. The owners testify that they have never seen the horses since."

As a matter of fact, it afterward developed, Herold, while he and Booth skulked in the timbers near the place of Thomas Jones, not very far away from the road on which they could see the soldiers and searchers riding up and down, feared the horses might, by neighing, attract the attention of the riders and be betrayed, so he led the horses a safe distance away and shot them.

In Brig. Gen. Harris's book on the conspiracy, he describes Dr. Mudd as follows:

> "Mudd's expression of countenance was that of a hypocrite. He had the bump of secretiveness largely developed, and it would have taken months of favorable acquaintanceship to have removed the unfavorable impression made by the first scanning of the man. He had the appearance of a natural born liar and deceiver. Mudd was a physician living on a farm. He had a considerable number of slaves at the breaking out of the Rebellion, most of whom had left him during the previous winter. His father, also living in the neighborhood, was a large land and slave holder, and Mudd's disloyalty was, no doubt, of the rabid type. His home was a place for returned Rebel soldiers and recruiting parties, and he had a place of concealment in the pines near his house, where they were sheltered and cared for, the doctor sending their food to them by his slaves; and if at any time any of these parties ventured to his house to take their meals, a slave was always placed on guard to give notice of the approach of anyone." (5)

Mudd not only entertained Booth a weekend in November, but he was known to have made several trips to Washington that winter, and each time was in conference with both Booth and Surratt. There is no doubt that Booth's Knight of the Golden Circle signals and signs did not give him entrance to the Romanists in the community south of Washington, in which St. Mary's Catholic Church was the center, and to which he and Herold fled after the deed committed in Ford's Theatre.

The next damaging evidence against Dr. Mudd was when the officers visited his house on the trail of the two fugitives and he emphatically denied that he had any strange visitors. It was not until the third visit, when the officers, fortified by definite facts informed him that they would have to search the house that he admitted the presence of the two men, one wounded, who had been there the Saturday after the assassination. Mrs. Mudd disappeared and in a few minutes came in bringing the bootleg, which Mudd had cut from Booth's boot when he bandaged his leg. On the bootleg were the initials "J.W.B." written in India ink inside. Even then neither Mudd nor his wife told an accurate story.

Both denied that they had any idea it was Booth, notwithstanding the fact that they were well acquainted with him, and notwithstanding that this was a personality with a voice and manner that once known could never be forgotten.

When Mudd was being taken to the Dry Tortugas after his conviction, he admitted to the officers who had him in charge, that he recognized Booth and Herold the morning after the murder when he came to have his leg dressed.

Mudd only served three years' imprisonment and was freed with Spangler, as was Arnold. O'laughlin died of Yellow Fever in an epidemic in the prison, and Dr. Mudd rendered his professional services so efficiently, that it was on this ground he was discharged by President Johnson, who had promised he would do so before retiring from office. The liberation of these assassins of President Lincoln by his successor caused much sharp comment and criticism from Lincoln's friends.

Of an interesting note, in the book written by the daughter of Dr. Mudd, she proudly boasts of the fact that her mother is a graduate of the Visitation Convent at Georgetown and that on graduation her diploma was presented to her class by "Cardinal Bodini, who was the first papal Legate to the United States."(6)

The lady did not state, perhaps she did not know, that Cardinal Bodini, prior to his elevation as papal Legate was known all over Italy as the "Butcher of Bologna," because of the multitude of Italian patriots he ordered put to death and that he gave the order that the Revolutionary priest, Ugo Bassi, who was a follower of Garibaldi, should be tortured three hours before his execution. She neglects also to state that this was the same Cardinal Bodini, who was forced to leave the United States.

Spangler, broken in health, returned with Dr. Mudd and made his home with him until his death in 1875. He is buried in the cemetery, two miles from the Mudd residence, near St. Peter's church. Dr. Mudd lies buried in the little country graveyard connected with St. Mary's church where he first met Booth in November 1864.

The body of John Wilkes Booth was given to his brother, Edwin, who had it removed from the old penitentiary in the Arsenal grounds, where it had been since the burial of the other four conspirators, by a Baltimore undertaker, assisted by a local Washington funeral director, Harvey & Marr, to Baltimore, and buried in the Booth family plot at Greenmount cemetery.

Michael O'Laughlin's mother was given the body of her son, which was shipped from the prison burial ground and placed in the Catholic cemetery in Baltimore.

Endnotes

1 The Suppressed Truth About the Assassination of Abraham Lincoln, Burke McCarty, p.114 by permission (Destiny Publishers, Merrimac, Mass.)
2 A True History of the Assassination of Abraham Lincoln and the Conspiracy of 1865, Louis Weichmann, Random House Publishing, New York, 1975, p.139
3 Sourced from the World Wide Web (internet) Bank of Wisdom, box 926, Louisville, Ky. 40201
4 A True History of the Assassination of Abraham Lincoln and the Conspiracy of 1865, Louis Weichmann, p.64
5 Assassination of Lincoln, a History of the Great Conspiracy, Thomas M. Harris, p.845
6 The Suppressed Truth about the Assassination of Abraham Lincoln, Burke McCarty, p.150 by permission

Chapter 10

John H. Surratt-arch conspirator; how the Catholic Church was involved; Surratt escapes to Canada; he joins the Papal army; the hunt for Surratt; his capture

Now, we will take up the trail of the arch-conspirator and assassin, John Harrison Surratt, the man who called the time in front of Ford's Theatre the night of the murder of President Lincoln, and track him, step by step, to the very shadow of the Vatican, whose protection he sought and received, until a formal demand was made by the United States government for his return for trial for the murder of Abraham Lincoln.

SURRAT.

BOOTH.

HAROLD.

War Department, Washington, April 20, 1865,

$100,000 REWARD!

THE MURDERER

Of our late beloved President, Abraham Lincoln,

IS STILL AT LARGE.

$50,000 REWARD

Will be paid by this Department for his apprehension, in addition to any reward offered by Municipal Authorities or State Executives.

$25,000 REWARD

Will be paid for the apprehension of JOHN H. SURRATT, one of Booth's Accomplices.

$25,000 REWARD

Will be paid for the apprehension of David C. Harold, another of Booth's accomplices.

LIBERAL REWARDS will be paid for any information that shall conduce to the arrest of either of the above-named criminals, or their accomplices.

All persons harboring or secreting the said persons, or either of them, or aiding or assisting their concealment or escape, will be treated as accomplices in the murder of the President and the attempted assassination of the Secretary of State, and shall be subject to trial before a Military Commission and the punishment of DEATH.

Let the stain of innocent blood be removed from the land by the arrest and punishment of the murderers.

All good citizens are exhorted to aid public justice on this occasion. Every man should consider his own conscience charged with this solemn duty, and rest neither night nor day until it be accomplished.

EDWIN M. STANTON, Secretary of War.

DESCRIPTIONS.—BOOTH is Five Feet 7 or 8 inches high, slender build, high forehead, black hair, black eyes, and wears a heavy black moustache.

JOHN H. SURRAT is about 5 feet, 9 inches. Hair rather thin and dark; eyes rather light; no beard. Would weigh 145 or 150 pounds. Complexion rather pale and clear, with color in his cheeks. Wore light clothes of fine quality. Shoulders square; cheek bones rather prominent; chin narrow; ears projecting at the top; forehead rather low and square, but broad. Parts his hair on the right side; neck rather long. His lips are firmly set. A slim man.

DAVID C. HAROLD is five feet six inches high, hair dark, eyes dark, eyebrows rather heavy, full face, nose short, hand short and fleshy, feet small, instep high, round bodied, naturally quick and active, slightly closes his eyes when looking at a person.

NOTICE.—In addition to the above, State and other authorities have offered rewards amounting to almost one hundred thousand dollars, making an aggregate of about TWO HUNDRED THOUSAND DOLLARS.

John H. Surratt in Papal Zouave uniform

In order to explain exactly how the Roman Church is implicated in this great treason plot, I ask your patience and careful reading of this subject which has lain for over a century buried in the oblivion where the Jesuits have placed it and from which we have resurrected it and pieced it together, in what I hope may prove a readable shape, to be understood and the information passed on.

It is safe to say that the escape of this tool of the Roman priesthood was one of the most spectacular in all history. It began the very night after the tragic scene in Ford's Theatre.

It will probably never be known positively by what means Surratt made good his escape from Washington that night, or early the next morning, for he died without having revealed it. But this is certain; he succeeded in making his escape safely to Montreal, Quebec, Canada, and was lodged securely in the house of the parents of the Roman Catholic priest, La Pierre, who was waiting and ready to receive him, close by the papal palace of the Archbishop to whom he was secretary.

Then began in the United States what was one of the most extraordinary manhunts for Surratt that ever occurred, before or since, in the history of this country. The rewards by the government amounted to twenty five thousand dollars, and every detective in the government secret service, every detective in the private sector, and every amateur sleuth engaged in this drive to recover this nineteen year old boy, leader of the gang of laymen who were instigated, aided, urged, and abetted by the priests of the church of Rome, to complete the destruction of the United States, which had recently been recovered from the horrible cataclysm which the foreign enemies had precipitated four years previous.

The government secret service, under the direction of the War Department, sent out the following letter:

> "Headquarters Department of Washington,
> Washington, D.C., April 16, 1865
>
> Special orders, No. 68.
>
> Special officers, James A. McDevitt, George Holohan, and Louis J. Weichmann, are hereby ordered to New York on important government business, and after executing their private orders, to return to this city and report

at these headquarters. The Quartermaster's Department will furnish the necessary transportation.

By command of Major-General Augur T. Ingraham, Colonel and Provost-Marshall-General. Defenses North of Potomac." (1)

These officers after leaving Washington, arrived in Montreal on April 20th, and registered at the St. James Hotel. They searched the registers of the hotels in that city, and found that Surratt had arrived at the St. Lawrence Hall Hotel on April 6th, and checked out on the 12th of that month; that he had returned on the 18th and left a few hours later. They learned on further investigation that he had stayed at the home of a man by the name of Porterfield, a Secessionist from Tennessee, who was one of the agents for the Confederacy in that city, and that Surratt had left that house with another man dressed exactly like himself, each taking a carriage and being driven in different directions. At this point the trail ended until the government learned of his sailing on the "Peruvian", an English steamer, plying between Quebec City and Liverpool, according to the Congressional record of that year.

The Secretary of State received the following coded telegram from the U. S. Consul in Montreal, J. F. Potter:

"No.236
Mr. Potter to Mr. Seward

U. S. Consul, B. N. A. F.

Montreal, Oct. 27, 1865

Sir: Have just had a personal interview with Dr. L. J. McMillan. He informs me that just before the steamer Peruvian sailed, a person with whom he was acquainted, asked him if he was willing that a gentleman who had been somewhat compromised by the recent troubles in the United States, should pass as his friend on board on the passage out. The Doctor refused to acknowledge the person as his friend, until he should know who he was.

Subsequently, the same person, accompanied by a party, Priest La Pierre, came on board before the ship left port, whom he introduced to the surgeon as Mr. McCarthy made himself known to the Doctor as John H. Surratt, and related to him many of the particulars of the conspiracy. He said he had been secreted in Montreal most of the time, with the exception of a few weeks, when he was with a Catholic priest down the river. He also stated that Porterfield of this city, formerly of Tennessee, assisted in secreting him. The Doctor also informed same that Surratt had dyed his hair, eyebrows and mustache, black-stained his face, and wore glasses. He landed in Londonderry, Ireland, fearing he might be watched and detected in Liverpool.

Priest LaPierre

He told him he was obliged to remain until he could receive money from Montreal. He requested the Doctor to see his friend in this city, and bring him funds. After the return of the Peruvian, the Doctor was transferred to the 'Nova Scotian'. When I saw him he had just had an interview with his friend who had introduced him to Surratt, as McCarthy, who told him he was expecting funds from Washington, D.C., but that they had not come yet.

The Doctor says that Surratt manifests no signs of penitence, but justifies his action, and was bold and defiant, when he speaks of the assassination of Abraham Lincoln. To illustrate this: He told me that Surratt remarked repeatedly, that he only desired to live two years longer, in which time he would serve President Johnson as Booth served Lincoln. The Doctor said he felt it his duty to give me this information for he regarded Surratt a desperate wretch, and an enemy to society, who should be apprehended and brought to justice."

Signed John F. Potter." (2)

With this important information, the United States Consul received no reply from the War Department, as he expected and the next day he followed it with a telegram, also in code, printed below:

"No.236 Mr. Potter to Mr. Seward

U. S. Consul General,
Montreal, Can., Oct. 25, 1865

Sir: I sent you a telegram in cipher with information to the Department that John H. Surratt left Three Rivers, in September, for Liverpool, where he is now, awaiting the arrival of the Nova Scotian, which sails on Saturday, next, by which he expects to receive money from parties in this city by hand of Ship Surgeon - I have information from Dr. McMillan, Surratt intends to go to Rome. He was secreted at Three Rivers by a Catholic priest, with whom he lived. I have requested instruction in my telegram, but hearing nothing yet, I scarcely know what course to take.

If an officer could proceed to England on this ship, no doubt, Surratt's arrest might be effected, and this, the last of the conspirators against the lives of the President and Secretary of State be brought to justice. If I hear nothing from Washington tomorrow, I shall go to Quebec to see further on the subject.

Respectfully, John F. Potter" (3)

And now a most peculiar phase of the remarkable case presents itself to us. The U.S. War Department with the full knowledge of the exact whereabouts of the arch-criminal, who not only assisted, but led in, and actually directed the murder of the President of the United States and Secretary of State, William H. Seward, refused to make the least attempt to arrest the said John H. Surratt, which the following cable to the U. S. Consul in Liverpool shows:

"Mr. Hunter to Mr. Wilding

Dept. of State; Oct. 13, 1865

Sir: Your dispatches 541-543 inclusive have been received. In reply to your No. 538, I have to inform you, that upon consultation with the Secretary of War and Judge Advocate General, it is thought advisable that no action be taken in regard to the arrest of the supposed John H. Surratt, at present.

W. H. Hunter,
Acting Secretary"
(4)

Then in only a few weeks from that date, the following order was sent to the War Department from Andrew Johnson, President of the United States, and successor to Abraham Lincoln:

General Order No. 164
War Department,
Adj. General's Office,
Washington, Nov. 24, 1865

All persons claiming reward for the apprehension of John Wilkes Booth, Lewis Payne, G. A. Atzerodt, David E. Herold, and Jefferson Davis, or either of them, are notified to file their claims and their proofs with the Adj. General for final adjudication by the special commission appointed, to award and determine upon the validity of such claims before the first day of January next, after which no claims will be received.

The reward for the arrest of Jacob Thompson, Beverly Tucker, George W. Sanders, Wm. G. Cleary, and John H. Surratt, are hereby revoked.

By Order of the President of the United States
E. D. Townsend
Ass't. Adj. General" (5)

Naturally, with the revoking of the reward for the arrest of Surratt, his chances for his safety from expiating his crime were multiplied many fold.

On September 30, 1865, the U. S. Consulate at Liverpool, sent the following cable in code to the Secretary of State at Washington:

Mr. Wilding to Mr. Seward
No. 539
U. S. Consulate, Liverpool,
Sept. 30, 1865

Sir: Since my dispatch No. 538, the supposed Surratt has arrived in Liverpool and is now staying at the Oratory of the Roman Catholic Church of the Holy Cross. His appearance indicates him to be about 21 years of age, rather tall and tolerably good-looking. According to the reports Mrs. Surratt was a very devout Roman Catholic, and I know clergymen of that persuasion on their way to and from America, have frequently lodged, while in Liverpool, at that same Oratory, so that the fact of this young man going there, somewhat favors the belief, that he is the real Surratt. I cannot, of course, do anything further in the matter without Mr. Adams' instructions, and a warrant. If it be Surratt, such a wretch ought not to escape.

Yours, respectfully,
Your obedient servant, H. Wilding" (6)

The Oratory of the Holy Cross was the Roman Catholic Clearing House through which the ecclesiastical agents passed between the United States and the Vatican, during their activities throughout the Civil War.

And now, with the official correspondence to show us Surratt's moves I would like to fill up the open spaces.

When Surratt left the home of Porterfield, he was taken under the wings of the French priests from under which he never departed until they had seen the ship surgeon on the Peruvian and arranged for his safe passage as we have seen. The facts brought out at the two trials of Surratt, after he had finally been returned to the United States, showed that the fugitive had gone to the little village of St. Liboire, some sixty miles outside of Montreal, skirting the pine woods, and an ideal place for the purpose. The parish priest's name was Boucher. Here he secreted Surratt for several weeks, when the hunt got too hot in Montreal which was being combed thoroughly for him.

St. Liboire was out of the way of the general traffic, and the inhabitants, French Catholics, who worked for the most part in lumber camps, and were by their location, as well as their lack of education, cut off from the rest of the world and its doings, as if they were people from another planet. They were subservient to their priest, so much so, that they would no more have thought of criticizing his acts, than they would of God Himself. Consequently, when a strange young man appeared at the parish house nothing was thought of it, or if, perchance, someone with just a drop of rebellious blood in him, might have asked himself, "Is this another mouth to feed?" he would whisper it so softly that even his guardian angel could not hear it, and would quickly "bless" himself, for daring to criticize or find fault with what his "Bon Pere" should take it into his head to do.

After several weeks of this life in the Canadian village, Surratt became restless and anxious to hear from the States, for we must remember that all his mail and the newspapers were censored by his priestly guardians, as he afterwards told in his Rockville lecture. Each time the "Holy Mother Church" would step in and allay his anxiety and he received almost weekly visits from that other "Valued and trusted friend," Priest LaPierre of Montreal. Once when he insisted, Priest LaPierre took him back to Montreal, himself, in citizen's clothes, and Surratt disguised as a hunter.

You will note the solicitude of these French priests concerning this American youth who had a price of twenty-five thousand dollars on his head, "dead or alive." It was an elegant fact, not only of their own personal guilt, but the guilt of their church, that they never thought of surrendering him and receiving their reward considering their love of money.

Do you think for one moment that these priests in Canada, or the priests in Washington, would have dared to have become parties in this conspiracy, thereby involving their church, without the full knowledge of the Roman hierarchy? Priests receive all their orders from the Pope through their Bishops.

Would this obscure, native-born American boy have been so carefully protected and cared for as he was by these priests, without the command of the Vatican?

You must remember that the United States government had broadcast the warning that anyone who would be found "aiding, abetting, protecting, comforting," or in any way assisting any of the conspirators, would be held as co-partners in the crime with them, and dealt with accordingly.

There is not a record that I have been able to find, wherein there is one word of criticism, one word of disapproval, one word of official regret, or otherwise, on the part of the Roman Catholic Hierarchy for the participation of the Romanists connected with this conspiracy, which consummated in the murder of Abraham Lincoln.

One would think that in the year 2000, when the Vatican would have everyone believe that she wished to have the world forgive her "sins," which appear to have amassed clear up to heaven, at least the mention would have been made in this regard, especially now when the Catholic Church and the United States Government seem to be working hand in hand to combat “terrorism" worldwide. A “terrorism” rooted incidentally and so far as both are concerned, in Islam, an arch-rival of Rome.

Jacob Thompson

There is not in the large collection of official condolences received by the United States Government upon the death of Abraham Lincoln, coming from every civilized country in the world, one word from the Pope of Rome. And this in view of the fact that the Pope was King of the Papal States and had more subjects in the United States than any other ruler in Europe.

Pius IX by his silence at this time, made a confession of his guilt in letters of fire – unquenchable fire - which brands him and his Jesuits with the brand of Cain in the hearts and minds of the American People, when they shall have been given a full knowledge of their (the Jesuits) responsibility in the conspiracy of destruction of this popular government on that Good Friday night in Ford's Theatre, April 14, 1865.

Who, among the government detectives from the United States, would have thought to search the houses of the priests for their fugitive? How much chance would they have had to secure a search warrant for such a search in French Canada if they had?

The Roman Catholic system operated in safety through its institutions in the United States and Canada, and it was only in Catholic Mexico where the people who had been burdened by the Papal yoke, had been progressive enough to make laws and operate them that a search warrant could be obtained with which the habitations of the Pope of Rome in their country could be reached.

In Mexico, a Roman Catholic priest or nun did not have the right of the vote. They could not enjoy any of the rights or privileges of citizenship. And yet the supposedly intelligent Americans, not only permitted them to vote, but to become the dominant force in the politics of every large city in the United States.

All the powerful machinery of the Hierarchy of the Roman Catholic Church was set in motion from the moment after the murder of Mr. Lincoln to shield Surratt and defeat justice for his crime, and we have public documents with which to brand these ecclesiastical plotters. Notwithstanding the fact that the U.S. War Department knew exactly every step taken by the young fugitive, from the day he sailed for Europe, no effort was made to arrest him. The startling knowledge, however, came to the attention of certain members of Congress, and the matter was brought up in that body, and a committee appointed to investigate the same. I herewith give the report of this committee in full:

OFFICIAL REPORT ON JOHN H. SURRATT ISSUED BY SECRETARY OF STATE FOR CONGRESSIONAL RECORD

39th Congress, House of Representatives.
Report 33, 2nd Session, March 2, 1867

REPORT OF JUDICIARY COMMITTEE

That John H. Surratt, sailed from Canada about September fifteenth, 1865, for Liverpool; that information was received by Secretary of State, Wm. H. Seward, from Mr. Wilding, Vice-Consul at Liverpool, by communication, dated September 27, 1865; that Surratt was at that time in Liverpool, or expected in a day or two.

By dispatch, from Wilding September 30, 1865, the supposed Surratt had arrived and was staying at the Oratory of the Roman Catholic church of the Holy Cross, and that he, Wilding, could do nothing in the matter without instructions from our Minister in England, Mr. Adams, and a warrant.

The Secretary of State, received a dispatch from Mr. Potter, our Consul General at Montreal, Canada, October 25, 1865, informing him that Surratt left Canada for Liverpool, the September previous, and was there waiting the arrival of a steamer by which he expected money, which steamer had not yet left Canada, and that he was intending to go to Rome.

Upon November 11, 1865, Mr. Potter received a dispatch from the Department of State, that the information in his dispatch had been properly availed of, and that on the 13th day of November, the Secretary of State, requested the Attorney General of the United States, to procure indictment against Surratt, as soon as convenient, with a view to demand his surrender.

Our Minister, Mr. Rufus King, at Rome, commenced as early as April 23, 1866, stated in his dispatch, that information of Surratt, under the name of "Watson" had enlisted in the Papal Zouaves, then stationed at Sezzes.

In a dispatch, August 8, 1865, said he repeated information communicated to him, to Cardinal Antonelli, in regard to Surratt; that his Eminence, was greatly interested by it, and intimated that if the American government desired the surrender if the criminal, there would probably be no difficulty in the way.

REPORT OF THE COMMITTEE

1st. That the Executive did not send any detective or agent to Liverpool to identify Surratt, or trace his movements, notwithstanding there was ample opportunity, for doing so, as appears in the communication from Potter.

2nd. That the Executive did not cause notice to be given to our Minister at Rome; that Surratt intended going there, when the government had every reason to believe, such was his intention.

3rd. That on November 24th, 1865, an order was issued from the War Department, revoking the reward offered for the arrest of John H. Surratt.

4th. That from the reception of the communications of Mr. King, August 8th, 1866, to October 16th, 1866, no steps were taken, either to identify or procure the arrest of Surratt, then known to be in the Military service of the Pope.

The testimony of the Secretary of State, Secretary of War, and others which is herewith submitted, tending to justify acts of the government in the premises, does not, in the opinion of your committee, excuse the great delay in arresting a person charged with complicity in the assassination of the late President Abraham Lincoln.

They are constrained from testimony to report that, in their opinion, due diligence in the arrest of John H. Surratt, was not exercised by the Executive Department of the government.

Respectfully submitted,

F.E.Woodbridge, for Committee." (7)

So ends the report of that splendid, fearless group of men, chosen by the House of Representatives to look into the matter.

It seems almost incredible that the memory of Abraham Lincoln could have been so soon forgotten. That the virus of which he had such a clear knowledge should have been making its deadly inroads in the veins of his successor and the Secretary of State, William H. Seward, whose life hung in the balance for days, caused by the hand of one of the assassins under the personal direction of this same Surratt.

I now call attention to the communication from the United States Consul at Rome, at the time, General Rufus King:

No. 33

Regarding Sainte-Marie Ames
(Gen. Rufus King to Mr. Seward)

2nd Session

Legation U. S., Rome

April 23, 1866

Sir:

On Saturday last, the 21st, Henry de Sainte-Marie, called upon me for the purpose, as he said, of communicating the information that John H. Surratt, who is charged with complicity in the murder of President Lincoln, but made his escape at the time, from the United States, had recently enlisted in the Papal Zouaves, under the name of "John Watson," and is now stationed with his company at Sezze.

My informant said that he had known Surratt in America; that he recognized him as soon as he saw him at

Sezzes; that he called him by his proper name, and that Surratt acknowledged that he participated in the plot against Lincoln's life...He further said that Surratt seemed to be well supplied with money, and appealed to him, Sainte-Marie, not to reveal his secret. Sainte-Marie, expressed an earnest desire, that if any steps were taken toward reclaiming Surratt as a criminal, that he (Sainte-Marie) should not be known in the matter.

He spoke positively, in answer to my questions as to his acquaintance with Surratt, and he certainly thinks this was the man, and there seemed such an entire absence of motive, for any false statements on the subject, that I could not very well doubt the truth of what he said.

I deemed it my duty, therefore, to present the circumstances to the Department, and ask instructions.

Respectfully,

RUFUS KING" (8)

An affidavit from an Irish Catholic, Edward O'Connor, a book dealer there, gave this illumination upon Surratt's movement:

"About twelve months ago, Mr. Surratt came to Rome under the name of "Watson." In Canada he procured letters from several priests to friends in England. Having left England for Rome, he got letters for some people here, among others for the Reverend Dr. Neane, Rector of the English College. Being detained some days in Cevita Vecchia, and having no money to pay his expenses, he wrote the Reverend Dr. Neane, from whom he received fifty francs. On his arrival here, he went to the English College, where he lived for some time; after that he entered the Papal service.

Rome, November 25, 1866." (8)

O'Connor also turned over a letter received by him from Surratt. This letter is included in the official papers in the archives of the United States and reads as follows:

"Edw. O'Connor, Esq.,
Rome, Italy

Dear Sir:

Will you be so kind as to send me a French and English grammar, the best method you have. I think Ollendorf's is the most in use. When I come to Rome I will settle with you. Shall be in, in the course of two or three weeks. If you should have time to reply to me, please give me all the news you can. By so doing, you will greatly oblige,

Your friend,
John Watson, Co. 3" (9)

Surratt's handwriting was identified in this letter. It is perceptible that O'Connor knew the nature of the "news" wanted by his friend Watson. The statement of O'Connor shows that Surratt had evidently related to him about his letters of reference, and his pecuniary embarrassment would indicate some confidence in that gentleman.

It is telling that a Roman priest, in the City of Rome, would advance a sum of money to a foreign youth, as the Reverend Dr. Neane did. This, in itself, without any of the other tremendous facts showing the aid that this young traitor received from the priests in Washington, Canada, England and Italy, was sufficient to have brought them to justice by hanging them on the same scaffold with their dupes.

I now produce another communication in this government correspondence, which speaks for itself:

"No. 43
Mr. Seward to Mr. King
(Extracts - Confidential)

Department of State,
Washington, October 16, 1866

Sir:

Mr. King's private letter written from Hamburg has just been received. It is accompanied by a letter from Sainte Marie of the 12th of September, to Mr. Hooker. I think it expedient that you do the following things:

1st. Employ a confidential person to visit Velletri, and ascertain by comparison with the photo sent whether the person indicated by Sainte Marie, is really John Surratt.

2nd. Pay Sainte Marie to get his release in consideration of the information he has already communicated on the subject.

3rd. Seek an interview with Cardinal Antonelli and referring to an intimation made by him to Mr. King's letter No. 62...Ask the Cardinal whether his Holiness would now be willing in an absence of an extradition treaty, to deliver John H. Surratt upon an authentic indictment, and at the request of the Department, for complicity in the assassination of the late President Lincoln, or whether, in the event of this request being declined, his Holiness would enter into an extradition treaty with us, which would enable us to reach the surrender of Surratt.

4th. Ask as a favor of this government, that neither Sainte Marie nor Surratt be discharged from the papal army, until we have had time to communicate concerning them, after receiving a prompt reply from you to this communication.

Sainte Marie should be told confidentially, that the subject of his communication to Mr. Hooker is under consideration here.

Yours respectfully, W. H. Seward" (10)

The following from General King gives further light:

"No.59

Mr. King to Mr. Seward

Legation U. S., Rome,

July 14, 1866

Dear Sir:

Henri de Sainte Marie's deposition. In compliance with instructions heretofore received, I have obtained and herewith transmit, an additional statement, sworn and subscribed to, by Sainte Marie, touching John H. Surratt's acknowledged complicity in the assassination of the late President Lincoln.

Sainte Marie again expressed to me his great desire to return to America and give his evidence in person. He thinks his life would be in danger here, if it would be known...that he betrayed Surratt's secret.

I have the honor to be with great respect,

Rufus King" (11)

The REAL Lincoln assassins

Again we hear from General King after a visit to Cardinal Antonelli. That cunning old fox saw that to attempt to refuse to surrender their protégé would have been a dangerous move. There was, for instance, more than a billion dollars' worth of church property in the United States, and the temper of the great masses of red-blooded Americans was not to be trifled with. There were thousands of priests and nuns as well, and a refusal, or further protection to this young monster might precipitate such a revulsion of feeling, if the inner facts were to become known, as to jeopardize not only the property, but start a religious war, to which there was no question as to the outcome.

I deem this a proper place to quote again from the book, "*The Roman Question*," the description of Antonelli's appearance:

> "In this year of grace, 1859, he is fifty-three years of age. He presents the appearance of a well preserved man; his frame is slight but robust; his constitution that of a mountaineer. The breadth of his forehead, the brilliancy of his eyes, his beak-like nose, and all the upper part of his face, inspire a certain awe. His countenance, of almost Moorish hue, is at times lit up by flashes of intellect. But his heavy jaw, his long fang-like teeth, and his thick lips express the grossest appetites. He gives you the idea of a minister grafted on a savage. When he assists the Pope in the ceremonies of Holy Week, he is magnificently disdainful and impertinent. He turns from time to time in the direction of the diplomatic tribune, and looks without a smile at the poor ambassadors, whom he cajoles from morning to night. You admire the actor who bullies his public. But when at an evening party he engages in close conversation with a handsome woman, the play of his countenance shows the direction of his thoughts, and those of the imaginative observer are imperceptibly carried to a roadside in a lonely forest, in which the principal objects are prostrate postilions, an overturned carriage, trembling females, and a select party of the inhabitants of Sonnino!

He lives in the Vatican, immediately over the Pope. The Romans ask punningly, which is the uppermost, the Pope or Antonelli? All classes of society hate him equally. He is the only living man concerning whom an entire people is agreed. He wishes to restore the absolute power of the Pope, in order that he may dispose of it at his ease. He returns to Rome and for ten years continues to reign over a timid old man and an enslaved people, opposing a passive resistance to all the counsels of diplomacy, and all the demands of Europe." (12)

** ** ** ** ** **

"No. 62
Mr. King to Mr. Seward,
Legation U. S. Rome,

August. 8, 1866
Sir:

I availed myself of the opportunity to repeat to the Cardinal the information communicated by Henri Sainte Marie in regard to Surratt. His Eminence was greatly interested and intimated that if the American government desired the surrender of the criminal, there would probably be no difficulty in the way.

He added, that there was indeed no extradition treaty between the two countries, and that to surrender a criminal, where capital punishment was likely to ensue, was not exactly in accordance with the spirit of the papal government, but, that in so grave and so exceptional a case, and with the understanding that the United States under parallel conditions would do as they desired to be done by, and that he thought that the request of the United States department for Surratt's surrender would be granted." (13)

Rufus King

Antonelli had just inserted the entering wedge whereby Surratt's surrender was on a condition that would save his neck, i.e. the issue of capital punishment. One has to ask, since when did the "spirit" of the papal government become so compassionate? The massacre of St. Bartholomew, the burning at the stake of Bruno, Savonarola, John Huss, Joan D'Arc and many others has spoken volumes down through the ages, but with this young criminal who was perinde ac cadaver (as a corpse) in the hands of Pius IX and his Jesuits, how very solicitous they were, going just as far as they dared, to save him.

What cowardly and reprehensible conduct the men at the head of the United States government were guilty of in the case of Henri Sainte Marie, who took his life in his hands when he informed General King of John Surratt's identity. They procrastinated for months and kept him sweating while he awaited some action, and then it took a Congressional investigation and a stinging rebuke and order from Congress before the proper steps were taken to bring Surratt to justice.

I now present the sequel of the communications from Mr. King from Hamburg.

"Hamburg, September 23, 1866

My dear Governor:

I enclose a letter forwarded from Rome a few days since, in which Sainte Marie related his griefs to Mr. Hooker. He thinks, of course, that too little notice has been taken to his statements about Surratt, but would be satisfied, I have no doubt, if his discharge from the Pontifical Zouaves were procured, and the means furnished him to pay his passage home to Canada, where his old mother is still living. His discharge, I could obtain without difficulty, if desirable.

Faithfully yours,
Rufus King" (14)

The telegraph lines and mail service in the pontifical states were, of course, entirely in the hands of the prelates of the Pope, and under the strictest censorship.

It goes without saying that no state papers passed through the mails in the pontifical states from the U. S. consuls to their government, that were not read by the priestly spies and reported to "His Eminence," copied and filed away for future reference, if they so desired. The following letter gives us an interesting highlight on the Jesuit system and the credulity of a Protestant American's psychology.

"Legation U. S. Rome, July 14, 1866

My dear Governor:

As you will learn from the accompanying dispatch, the missing documents from the State Department arrived all right today. I cannot imagine how, or where they have been delayed.

I will act forthwith upon the instructions in regard to Sainte Marie. He is willing and anxious to return to the United States, and can get his release from the Pope's army, by paying fifty dollars, or so. I should judge his parole evidence would be much more desirable than any certified statement. He would expect to have his expenses paid and some compensation for his time.

Faithfully yours, Rufus King" (15)

The reader will recall that Sainte Marie was cut off from any reward, which the government had offered by a revocation which President Johnson ordered. Congress, however, voted Sainte Marie, a gift of ten thousand dollars for his services.

President Johnson was a drunkard. He came from a disloyal State. His revocation of a reward for the arrest of John H. Surratt is conclusive proof, to say the least, that he was playing politics, which under the gravity of the situation would make his conduct criminal. Andrew Johnson, the drunkard, had nothing in common with Abraham Lincoln. Lincoln's pure, sober, honorable life was a rebuke to such a man as Johnson. At the first opportunity, the latter dared to take advantage of, to show his dislike, which amounted to absolute disrespect to the memory of Lincoln. It was President Johnson that paralyzed the arm of the Department of State in regard to Surratt's arrest. The whole official inertness amounting to treason it would seem, should be laid at Johnson's door.

That the spirit of the Roman Catholic Church at the time may be truly demonstrated in the pontifical army, a perusal of the following document will be enlightening:

"No.72
Mr. King to Mr. Seward,

Legation U. S. Rome,

December 17, 1866

Sir:

I hasten to acknowledge receipt of the dispatches Nos. 44-45-46-47, of the State Department...relative to the affair of John H. Surratt...It will give me pleasure to convey to Cardinal Antonelli, the assurance of the President's sincere satisfaction with the prompt and friendly actions of the papal court...Sainte Marie, who first informed me of Surratt being in the corps of Zouaves, has been discharged from the papal service, at my request.

Threats had been made against him by some of his comrades, and thinking that his life might not be altogether safe, and that he might be wanted at Alexandria as a witness to identify Surratt, I put him in charge of Captain Jeffers, and he sailed on the Swatara on Friday last. His great desire seems to be to return to America, and aid in bringing Surratt to justice. I have seen, as yet, no reason to doubt his good faith, or question the truth of his statements.

Rufus King" (16)

Surratt, one of the murderers of the great Lincoln, was the hero and Sainte Marie, the traitor. The difference in sentiment of the papal troops and the people of Italy, the Revolutionists, who were struggling for a free and united Italy under Garibaldi, and Victor Emmanuel, can be appreciated if the reader will peruse the letters of condolence which were received by the United States government after they learned of the assassination of Mr. Lincoln. Every workingman's organization of Italy sent the most beautiful messages, and their intimate knowledge of the life of Lincoln was astonishing. The bold frankness in many of them in placing the blame on the Jesuits was truly revealing. I know nothing that will give the reader the mental attitude of the difference of sentiment, and show up the venom of the Pope's silence on President Lincoln's murder, than a perusal of these messages. I do not give them here, but invite the reader to visit Washington D.C. and read them for him/herself.

After an extended diplomatic dickering, which covered several months after its initiation; the Secretary of State, Cardinal Antonelli, gave the order for Surratt's arrest. The official papers are quite interesting and educational. I give them in full. They are all official translations of the originals, in Italian. The Lt. Colonel in charge at the time was an Austrian, whom the patriotic Italians greatly hated.

"Enclosure 'C' (Translation)
Kausler to Lieut. Col. Allet

November 5, 1866

Colonel: Cause the Zouave Watson to be arrested and to be conveyed under safe military escort to the military prison at Rome. It is of much importance that this order be scrupulously fulfilled.

The General Pro-Minister, Kausler
Lieut.Col.Allet,Com.
Battalion of Zouaves, Velletri"

No. 463

General: I have the honor to inform you that the Zouave Watson (John) has been arrested at Veroli, and will be conducted tomorrow under a good escort to Rome.

I have the honor to be General, your most humble subordinate,

Lieut. Col. Allet,
Pontifical Zouave Commander of Battalion" (17)

And now comes the surprise, by way of:

"(Enclosure 'E' Translation)

Presented at Velletri, November 8, 1866, 8:35 A. M.
Arrived at Rome, November 8, 1866, 8:50 A. M.

His Excellency, Minister of Arma, Rome

I received the following telegram, dated 4:30 A. M. from Zambilly: At the moment he left the prison and while surrounded by six men as a guard, Watson threw himself into a ravine, about a hundred feet, perpendicular in depth, which defends the prison. Fifty Zouaves in pursuit of him.

Zambilly.

I will transmit your Excellency the intelligence I may receive by telegram.

Allet, Lieut. Col."

It was now up to the Austrian commander to flim-flam the American Consuls and State Department by giving this soap opera the semblance of genuineness to cover the investigation, which was sure to follow.

> "Kausler to Cardinal Antonelli.
> Ministry of Arms, Cabinet of the Pro-Minister,
>
> November 8, 1866
>
> Most Reverend Eminence:
>
> I have the honor to transmit to your most reverend Eminence, the accompanying documents on the arrest and escape of the Zouave Watson, of the 3rd. Co.; and I shall not fail to communicate such further information as I may receive, as the result of the pursuit of this individual.
>
> Bowing to kiss the sacred purple, I am proud to subscribe myself with profound devotion, your most Reverend Eminence's most humble and obedient servant.
>
> His most Reverend Eminence Kausler
> The Cardinal Antonelli, Secretary of State"
>
> (18)

Wasn't this a most interesting scenario? The fact that his ecclesiastical protectors gave Surratt warning will now be explored.

> "Lieut. Col. Allet to Kausler
>
> My General:
>
> Following out your Excellency's orders, I sent this morning to Veroli, Lieut. De Farnel, to make an examination of the escape of Zouave Watson. I have learned some other details of this unfortunate business. Watson, at the moment he was arrested, must have been on his guard, having obtained knowledge of a letter addressed...which concerned him probably. This letter was sent by mistake to a trumpeter named...was opened by him and shown to Watson, because it was written in Eng-

lish. I have sent it to your Eminence, with a report from Captain Zambilly.

I am assured that the escape of Watson savors of a prodigy. He leaped from a height of 23 feet on a narrow rock, beyond which is a precipice. The filth from the barracks accumulated on the rocks, and in this manner the fall of Watson was broken. Had he leaped a little further he would have fallen in an abyss.

I am, etc. etc." (19)

I now present a description of the arrest of Surratt given in the report from Lieut. Col. Allet.

"...Then, the prisoner was awakened, who arose and put on his gaiters and took his coffee with the calmness and phlegm quite English. The gate of the prison opens on a platform which overlooks the country, situated at least thirty feet below the windows of the prison.

Beside the gate of the prison are the priories of the Barracks. Watson asked permission to halt there. Corp. Warrin who had six men with him as guards, allowed him to stop, very naturally, not doubting, neither he, nor the Zouaves, present, that the prisoner was going to try to escape at a place which seemed quite impossible to us, is quite clear. In fact, Watson who seemed quiet, seized the balustrade, made a leap, and cast himself into the void, falling on the uneven rocks where he might have broken his bones a thousand times, and gained the depth of the valley below.

Patrols were immediately organized, but in vain! We saw a peasant who told us he had seen an unarmed Zouave going towards Commari which is the way to Piedmont...Lieut. Mosley and I have been to examine the localities and we asked ourselves how one could make such a leap without breaking arms and legs?

DeZambilly, Com. of Detachment"

That Surratt was given his warning by some emissary of the Pope's government is beyond doubt. Would one think for a moment if Surratt's crime, for instance, had been the murder of a priest, he would have escaped?

The United States government, through General King, demanded a report of the affair, and his request was complied with by Cardinal Antonelli and the above translations were made and sent to Washington where they are now with the data pertaining to the affairs of Surratt. Mr. King sent the following letter to Mr. Marsh, the U. S. Consul at Florence, Italy, by courier:

> "Mr. King to Mr. Marsh
> (Enclosure 'A' Confidential)
>
> Dear Sir:
>
> I send to you under very peculiar circumstances and as a bearer of these dispatches, my friend, Mr. Robert McPherson. He will tell you the story which the accompanying dispatches will help to illustrate.
>
> Rufus King
>
> On November 13th" (20)

The dispatches referred to above are the ones given here, pertaining to the arrest and "escape" of Surratt. We see now the pontifical government maneuvered to permit Surratt to be taken on condition that he be not condemned to death; we see by some friendly advance information he was prepared for his arrest and took it with perfect calmness and nonchalance, notwithstanding the fact he was aroused from his sleep and that "he put on his gaiter and took his coffee, with a calmness that was quite English." We see that his arrest was a farce and that he was permitted to "escape." We see Antonelli assuring the U. S. Consul that he had undoubtedly "made good his escape" and was in Italian territory.

After the order of Cardinal Antonelli for the arrest of Surratt from the Papal Guard had been given the official wires of the United States were busy. The following orders were telegraphed to the officers of the United States Fleet in the Mediterranean.

"Rome, November 16, 1866, 11:50 A.M.

His Excellency, Mr. Harvey American Minister, Lisbon

Inform Adm. Goldsborough that very important matters renders the immediate presence of one of our ships-of-war necessary at Vecchia

Rufus King"

Mr. Harvey's reply was:

"As Rear Admiral Goldsborough is not now in port, I sent immediately for Commodore Steedman, who arrived here some days ago, and who is now the superior officer present, in order to consult as to the proper measures to be adopted.

The U. S. Steamer Swatara, left here yesterday for Tangier, Gibraltar, and other ports in the Mediterranean, and if the Rear Admiral who is believed to have left Cherbourg for Lisbon, within the last few days, does not appear as soon as expected, Commodore Steedman will intercept and order the Swatara by telegram to proceed to Civiti Vecchia.

Harvey" (21)

On November 17, 1866, a telegram from Minister Harvey announced that the Swatara had been ordered to Civiti Vecchia, which arrived in due time, but Surratt had made his escape on a steamer which left Naples for Egypt and Henri de Sainte Marie was placed on board the Swatara, and held awaiting word from the U. S. Consul at Alexandria. The vessel upon which Surratt sailed put in at Malta. The American Minister there who had been notified to be on the alert for Surratt, found that he was on board and cabled the U. S. Consul at Rome. This message was sent on to the U. S. Minister at Alexandria, Egypt, so that when the ship arrived at that port, it found Mr. Hale, the U. S. Consul General, waiting for him. I will let the official wire to the United States War Department describe his arrival.

"(Extract)

> It was easy to distinguish him, (Surratt) from among the seventy-eight third-class passengers by his Zouave uniform and scarcely less easy, by his almost unmistakable American type of countenance. I said at once to him, "You are the man I want; you are an American?" He said 'Yes sir.' I said, 'You doubtless know why I want you? What is your name?' He said, promptly, 'Walters.' I said, 'I believe your name is Surratt.' and in arresting him I mentioned my official position as United States Consul-General.
>
> The Director of Quarantine speedily arranged sufficient escort of soldiers, by whom the prisoner was conducted to a safe place within the Quarantine walls. Although the walk occupied several minutes, the prisoner close at my side, made no remark whatever, displaying neither surprise nor irritation.
>
> Arrived at the place prepared, I gave him the usual magisterial caution, that he was not obliged to say anything, and that anything he did say would be taken down in writing. He said, 'I have nothing to say. I want nothing but what is right.' He declared he had neither transportation nor luggage, nor money, except six francs. His companions confirmed his statement. They said he came to Naples, a deserter from the Papal army at Rome. I find he has no papers, no clothes but those he is wearing. The appearance of the prisoner answers very well the description given by witness. Weichmann on page 116 of Pitman's Report, sent me by the government Hale" (22)

Here, again, we see Surratt, under the most trying circumstances under which an innocent man would have broken, taking his arrest with amazing coolness, the same, in fact, which he displayed previously, when he was taken at Velletri, although, so far as is known, that was the first time that he had ever been arrested. He was beyond doubt, fortified by the assurance that he was under the protection of the Vatican, and he had, like all Jesuits, a clear understanding of all that fact guaranteed. He was clever enough to realize that with his inner knowledge of this whole sordid transaction, his "Holy" Church would be compelled to continue its protection as their interests were inseparable. His confidence must have been further intensified by the fact that he would not have to face a military tribunal, as had his mother, and the rest of his co-conspirators, who were executed, and that the political influence of the Jesuit machine already had reached the presidential chair, so recently occupied by his victim, Abraham Lincoln.

General Garibaldi

Taking stock of the above facts, the young monster had good and sufficient reason to be philosophical about his present condition. He was probably rather relieved when he found himself a manacled prisoner, with his face turned homeward to the country of his nativity, to the country he had so miserably betrayed. He knew many staunch friends awaited him, friends, who, like himself, hated the government.

Before going further we present another official communication of this matter, which throws added light upon the situation in Italy when the Pope was King.

"Mr. Marsh to Mr. Seward

Legation of U. S. Florence, Italy, Nov. 18, 1866

Sir: On my arrival from Venice on Tuesday morning, I found the papers, copies and translation, of which marked respectively, A B C D and E, are hereto annexed. Mr. McPherson introduced by a letter, marked A, had gone to Leghorn, and I had no other information on the subject of his mission, than such as the papers referred to above have furnished.

I lost no time in seeing the Secretary of the Minister of Foreign Affairs. I stated to him such facts as I was possessed of, and enquired whether he thought his government would surrender Surratt to the United States for trial, if he should be found in Italian territory. He replied, he thought the accused man would be surrendered on proper demand and proof, but probably, only on stipulation on our part, that the punishment of death, should not be inflicted on him.

Having no instruction on the subject, and knowing nothing of those Mr. K received, and at that time having no reason to suppose that Surratt had escaped into the territory of the King, I did not pursue the discussion further...I doubt whether in case of surrender of Surratt, a formal stipulation to exempt him from punishment by death, will be insisted upon.

In the famous LaGala escape, Mr. Viscount Venosto, then, as now, Minister of Foreign Affairs, refused to enter into such a stipulation, on the extradition of the offenders, but nevertheless, the government yielded to the intercession of the Emperor of France, and the sentences of those atrocious criminals, though convicted of numerous murders, robberies and even cannibalism, were commuted, and I suppose the government of Italy, would strongly oppose capital punishment and recommend Surratt to mercy, if he surrendered to us.

The public sentiment of all classes in Italy, is decidedly averse to the infliction of capital punishment, and I shall not go too far, if I add, to any severe or adequate punishment for grave offences.

Marsh" (23)

There was a psychological reason for the innate enmity in the hearts of Romanists for severe punishment. It is traceable to the long dark centuries of unjust, atrocious cruelties of the misrule, which the Italians endured, under the reigns of the popes of Rome. Suppression of any peoples, if they are continued for ages, will react and have a strong tendency to make government of any sort resented and distasteful to them.

Surratt did not overestimate the protection of his church, for from the moment he landed back in the United States, he was greeted and sustained by the priests of that church. When his trial began in Washington on June 10, 1867, the presence of Roman priests and the students from the Jesuit Monastery at Georgetown and the Sulpician Monastery where he had studied three years for the priesthood, were the most noticeable features of the sessions. Although he declared himself bankrupt, he was furnished with the services of the best lawyers. When it became necessary to furnish bail for his final release, it was immediately presented by an Irish woman he did not even know, to the amount of thirty thousand dollars. According to press reports this stood there until his death in 1916. That is some friendship, is it not?

To close this chapter I would now like to present the affidavit of Henri de Sainte Marie:

Aims Report, House of Representatives,
39th Session Congress,
Page 15, Ex. document No. 9 Rome,
July 10, 1866

"I, Henri de Ste. Marie, a native of Canada, British America, age 33, do swear and declare under oath, that about six months previous to the assassination of Abraham Lincoln, I was living in Maryland, at a small village called Ellangowan, or Little Texas, about 25 or 30 miles from Baltimore, where I was engaged as a teacher for a period of about 5 months. I there and then got acquainted with Louis J. Weichmann and John H. Surratt, who came to that locality to pay a visit to the parish priest. At that first interview a great deal was said about the war and slavery, the sentiment expressed by the two individuals being more than strongly secessionist. In the course of the conversation I remember Surratt to have said that President Lincoln would certainly pay for the men that were slain during the war. About a month afterward I removed to Washington at the instigation of Weichmann and got a situation as tutor at Gonzaga College where he was himself engaged. Surratt visited us weekly, and once he offered to send me South, but I declined.

I did not remain more than a month at Washington, not being able to agree with Weichmann and enlisted in the army of the North as stated in my first statement in writing to General King.

I have met Surratt here in Italy at a small town called Velletri. He is now known under the name of 'John Watson.' I recognized him before he made himself known to me and told him privately, "You are John Surratt, the person I have known in Maryland." He acknowledged he was and begged me to keep the thing secret. After some conversation we spoke of the unfortunate affair, of the assassination of President Lincoln, and these were his words: 'Damn the Yankees, they have killed my mother; but I have done them as much harm as I could, We have killed Lincoln the nigger's friend.' He then said, speaking of his mother, 'Had it not been for me and that coward Weichmann, my mother would be living yet. It was fear made him speak. Had he kept his tongue, there was no danger for him; but if I ever return to America or meet him elsewhere I shall kill him.'

He then said he was in the secret service of the South. and Weichmann, who was in some department there, used to steal copies of the dispatches and forward them to him and thence to Richmond. Speaking of the murder he said, they had acted under the orders of men who were not yet known, some of whom are still in New York and others in London. I am aware that money is sent to him yet - from London.

'When I left Canada,' he said, 'I had but a little money, but I had a letter from a party in London. I was in disguise, with dyed hair and a false beard; that party sent me to a hotel, where he told me to remain until I heard from him. After a few weeks he came to me and proposed to me to go to Spain, but I declined, and he asked me to go to Paris. He gave me seventy pounds with a letter of introduction to a party there who sent me here to Rome where I joined the Zouaves.'

He says he can get money in Rome any time. I believe he is protected by the clergy and that the murder is the result of a ***deep laid plot***, not only against the life of President Lincoln but ***against the existence of the republic, as we are aware that priesthood and royalty are and always have been opposed to liberty."***[emphasis added]

"That such men as Surratt, Booth, Weichmann and others of their own accord planned and executed the infernal plot which resulted in the death of President Lincoln is impossible. There are others behind the curtain who have pulled the strings to make these scoundrels act....

"He says he does not regret what has taken place and he will visit New York in a year or two, as there is a heavy shipping firm there that had much to do with the

South, and he is surprised that they have not been suspected.

This is the exact truth of what I know about Surratt. More I could not learn, being afraid to awaken his suspicion and further I do not say."

Sworn and subscribed before me at the American Legation in Rome, this tenth day of July, 1866, as witness my hand and seal.

Signed: Henri de Ste. Marie
Rufus King, Minister Resident." (24)

Pope Pius IX – King of the Papal States and despot

ENDNOTES

1 A True History of the Assassination of Abraham Lincoln and of the Conspiracy of 1865, Louis J. Weichmann, (New York, Random House Publishing, 1975) p.220

2 Sourced from University of Missouri Kansas City, law dept.; U.S. National Archives; Library of Congress among hundreds of sites

3 Ibid.
4 Ibid.
5 Ibid.
6 Ibid.
7 Ibid.
8 Ibid.
9 Ibid.
10 Ibid.
11 Ibid.
12 Ibid.
13 Ibid.
14 Ibid.
15 Ibid.
16 Ibid.
17 Ibid.
18 Ibid.
19 Ibid.
20 Ibid.
21 Ibid.
22 Ibid.
23 Ibid.
24 Ibid.

Chapter 11

The trial of John H. Surratt

From the very moment the Swatara, the specially chartered warship, reached the United States with John H. Surratt, bound hand and foot on board, all the wheels of the Roman Catholic political machine were set in motion for his certain release. The intense excitement which had enveloped the trials of the conspirators two years previous had naturally subsided perceptibly, this, of course, being an advantage to the prisoner, and the smallest details were looked after by the array of high priced lawyers who fought the two legal battles for this penniless assassin.

His attorneys, Messrs. Merrick, Bradley and Bradley were Catholic. They left no stone unturned in the building of his defense, although his alibi, so carefully planned and presented, was soon shattered by a number of reputable witnesses who could not be shaken by the unprofessional tactics which these lawyers resorted to.

The first step in the proceedings was a motion filed by the States' lawyers from which I quote in part

IN THE SUPREME COURT OF THE DISTRICT OF COLUMBIA, UNITED STATES AGAINST JOHN H. SURRATT, INDICTMENT: MURDER

"And now, at this day, to-wit, on the 10th day of June, A. D., 1867 come the United States and the said John H. Surratt, by their respective attorneys and the jurors of the jury, impaneled and summoned also to come; and hereupon the said United States by their attorney challenge the array of the said panel, because he saith,

> that the said jurors comprising the said panel, were not drawn according to the law, and that the names from which said jurors were drawn, were not selected according to law, wherefore, he prays judgment, and that the said panel may be quashed.
>
> This motion, if your Honor please, is sustained by an affidavit which I hold in my hand, and which, with the permission of your Honor, I will now proceed to read. We think after this affidavit shall have been read it will not be found necessary to introduce any oral testimony." (1)

The reader will note that the two charges made were that the names were not drawn according to law; and that they were not selected according to law.

The law required that the registrar of the City of Washington should make out a list of four hundred names on or before the first day of February; the City Clerk of Georgetown was to make out a list of eighty names to be selected; and the Clerk of the Levy Court of the County of Washington was to make out a list of forty names to be selected; and that such lists should be preserved, and any names that had not been drawn for service during the year, might be transferred to the lists made up for the subsequent year. After this had been done the officers should meet and jointly select their respective lists of the number specified; the names being written by each officer on a separate paper, folded or rolled up, so that no one could see the name, and then deposited in a box provided for that purpose. The box was then to be thoroughly shaken and officially sealed, and then by these three officers, given into the custody of the clerk of the County Court of Washington City for safe keeping.

These same officers were to meet in the City Hall, Washington City at least ten days before the commencement of each term of the Circuit Court, or Criminal Court, and there the Clerk of the Circuit Court was to publicly, and in their presence, break the seal of the box and proceed to draw out the number of names required. If it were a Grand Jury Court, the first twenty-three names drawn, were to constitute the grand jury, for the term. This having been done, the box was to be sealed and returned to the clerk for safe keeping.

The clerk of the Circuit Court at that time was a Samuel E. Douglas, registrar of the City of Washington. His examination showed that no such lists had been made out as required; that no joint action had been had by these three officials, but that each one had written his own required list, and deposited it in the box independently of the others.

It was also brought to the attention of the Court that these officers had not sealed the box as required, but had it delivered to the clerk to be sealed by him. It was also shown that the names had been drawn, not by the clerk of the Circuit Court, but by the clerk of the City of Georgetown.

There was nothing to prevent the Georgetown clerk from carrying any of the names of the jurors whom he might have seen fit, and who might have been "fixed," in his hand, and when he put his hand in the box, which was a perfectly illegal act, to have withdrawn the very names he held in his hand.

The entire procedure was so infamously bold and irregular that the Court said: "My order is that the marshal summon twenty-six talesmen." This occupied several days. After the jury had been selected, Surratt's attorneys filed the following to be made the basis of carrying the case up on a writ of error:

"IN THE SUPREME COURT OF THE DISTRICT OF COLUMBIA, THE UNITED STATES VS JOHN H. SURRATT, IN THE CRIMINAL COURT MARCH TERM, 1867

And the said Marshal of the District of Columbia, in obedience to the order of the Court, made in this case on the 12th of June, this day makes return that he hath summoned, and now hath in court here, twenty-six jurors, talesmen, as a panel, from which to form a jury to try the said cause, and the names of the twenty-six jurors, so returned being called by the clerk of said court, and they were called, the said John H. Surratt, by his attorneys, doth challenge the array of the said panel, because, he saith, it doth plainly appear by the records and the proceedings of the court in this cause, that no jurors have ever been summoned according to law, to serve during the present term of this court, and no names of jurors, duly and lawfully summoned, have been placed in the box, provided for in the fourth section of the Act of Congress, entitled: 'An act providing for the selection of jurors to serve in the several courts of the district approved, sixteenth day of June, 1862, on or before the first day of February, 1867, to serve for the ensuing year; wherefore, he prays judgment, that the panel now returned by the said Marshal, and now in the court here, be quashed.

Merrick, Bradley & Bradley,

Attorneys for Surratt" (2)

It is a notable fact that there were sixteen Romanists out of the twenty-six in the first panel drawn in that irregular manner.

The answer filed in the motion of Surratt's attorneys was the first step in this bitterly contested case and while the prisoner was, according to his own statement, absolutely penniless, he was represented by an expensive array of legal talent and where the money came from reimbursing them remains a mystery to this day.

Georgetown- Jesuitized Georgetown - was constantly in evidence at the trial. The priests from the Jesuit college were there, and the students who were just dismissed for their vacations, were on hand and would always make it a particular point to greet Surratt who had been a student of that institution for two years, most cordially, and he was scarcely ever without a priest at his side. It is small wonder that the priests of Rome gave every assistance to the prisoner at the bar. Their interests were inseparable. The interest of the Roman church in the United States was deeply involved and no one appreciated this more than Surratt. He was confident and defiant all through the weeks, of what would have been to most young men an unendurable ordeal, stimulated by the knowledge that all of the powerful machinery of his church was being used in his defense and that his liberty was guaranteed.

President Johnson

John Surratt was a bold, cold-blooded, unscrupulous, unrepentant criminal, who had been steeped in the immoral teachings of the doctrines of the Jesuits from his earliest childhood when his misguided mother had placed him under the guidance of priest Wiget at the Boy's Preparatory School at Gonzaga College, a fact which was testified to by that gentleman at Surratt's trial.

Surratt's lawyers presented the following petition at the beginning of the trial:

> "To the Honorable, the Justices of the Supreme Court of the District of Columbia, holding the Criminal Court in March Term, 1867.
>
> The petition of John H. Surratt shows that he has been put upon his trial in a capital case in this court; that he has exhausted all his means, and such further means as have been furnished him by the liberality of his friends, in preparing for his defense, and he is now unable to procure the attendance of his witnesses. He therefore prays your Honor for an order that process may issue to summon his witnesses, and to compel their attendance at the cost of the government of the United States, according to the statute in such cases made and provided." (3)

The petition was granted by the court.

From the very beginning, duplicity and innuendo were used, and unprofessional conduct of the most flagrant character was resorted to. The States' witnesses were badgered, abused and bulldozed, so much so that the Judge had to intervene more than once. Especially was this the fact in the case of Dr. McMillen, the ship surgeon of the Peruvian, to whom priest LaPierre introduced Surratt under the name of "McCarthy."

The physician made a splendid witness and refused to be confused, but the attorney for the defendant was so abusive that the witness gave a very angry response in pure self-defense.

The papal venom showed itself all through the trials of Surratt in the never ceasing effort of his attorneys to stab the memory of Lincoln and through their contention that the Military Court which had convicted Surratt's mother, had been a usurpation of power by President Johnson, and the act of a tyrant. When one reads the records of those trials, one marvels that in so short a time after the passing out of that great man, these tools of the ecclesiastical murderers would dare to venture so far out in the open, with their treasonable utterances.

When court was called to order in the John H. Surratt trial, Judge Fisher, presiding, said,

> "Gentlemen, this is the day assigned for the trial of John H. Surratt, indicted for the murder of Abraham Lincoln, late president of the United States. Are you ready to proceed?"

Surratt's lawyer, Mr. Bradley, answered:

> "The prisoner is ready, sir, and has been from the first." (4)

This unnecessary falsehood was a beginning quite in keeping with the life and action of the prisoner, and his Jesuit attorney brazenly tried to implant in the minds of the jury the innocence of his client who had fled to Canada, then put the Atlantic ocean between him and his pursuers and when arrested at Velletri, Italy, dashed himself down an unscalable precipice to evade being returned to his native land. Nothing less than Roman effrontery could have proffered such an answer to that question, "Are you ready?"

The Roman Catholic religion was first dragged in by Surratt's own lawyer, R. T. Merrick, when they called attention to a telegraph dispatch to the *New York Herald*, in which the fact that the State had demanded a new jury impaneled because there were sixteen Romanists out of the twenty-six jurors called in the first panel.

The district attorney interrupted by showing that the news came from Washington and as afterwards proved that it was but one of many press dispatches, which were instigated by the defense to prejudice the public in Surratt's favor. If there were no other signs to indicate that the hand of Rome was the guiding one in the trials of Surratt, this alone would be sufficient to the esoteric.

Assistant District Attorney Nathaniel Wilson who made the opening address on June 18th made a most convincing presentation of the charges against the prisoner. It ran in part as follows:

> "May it please your Honor, and gentlemen of the jury, you are doubtless aware that it is customary in criminal cases, for the prosecution at the beginning of the trial, to inform the jury of the nature of the offense to be inquired into, and of the proof that will be offered in support of the charge of the indictment....
>
> "The Grand Jury of the District of Columbia has indicted the prisoner at the bar, John H. Surratt, as one of the murderers of Abraham Lincoln. It has become your duty to judge whether he is guilty or innocent of that charge - a duty, than which more solemn or momentous, was never committed to human intelligence. You are to turn back the leaves of history, to that red page, on which is recorded in letters of blood the awful incidents of that April night on which the assassins' work was done on the body of the chief Magistrate of the American Republic - a night, on which for the first time in our existence as a nation, a blow was struck with the fell purpose, not only to destroy a human life, but the life of the nation, the life of LIBERTY itself.
>
> "Though more than two years have passed since then, you scarcely need witnesses to describe to you the scene in Ford's Theatre, as it was visible in the last hour of the President's conscious life...Persons who were pre-

sent will tell you that about twenty minutes past ten o'clock, the 14th of April, 1865, on that night, John Wilkes Booth, armed with pistol and knife, passed rapidly from the front door of the theatre, ascended to the dress circle, and entered the President's box. By the discharge of a pistol he inflicted a death wound, then leaped upon the stage, and passing rapidly across it, disappeared into the darkness of the night.

"We shall prove to your entire satisfaction, by competent and credible witnesses, that at that time, the prisoner at the bar was present, aiding and abetting that murder; and that at ten minutes past ten o'clock that night, he was in front of that theatre in the company of Booth. You shall hear what he then said and did. You shall know that his cool and calculating malice was the director of the bullet that pierced the brain of the President, and the knife that fell upon the venerable Secretary of State. You shall know that the prisoner at the bar was the contriver of that villainy, and that from the presence of the prisoner, Booth, drunk with theatric passion and traitorous hate, rushed directly to the execution of their mutual will. We shall further prove to you, that their companionship upon that occasion was not an accidental or unexpected one, but that the butchery that ensued was the ripe result of a long premeditated plot, in which the prisoner was the chief conspirator.

"It will be proved to you that he is a traitor to the government that protected him; a spy in the employ of the enemies of his country in the years 1864-65; he passed repeatedly from Richmond to Washington from Washington to Canada, weaving the web of his nefarious scheme, plotting the overthrow of this government, the defeat of its armies, and the slaughter of his countrymen; and as showing the venom of his intent, as showing a mind insensible to every moral obligation and fatally bent on mischief - we shall prove his gleeful boasts, that during these journeys, he had shot down in cold blood, weak, unarmed soldiers, fleeing from rebel prisons.

"It will be proved to you that he made his home in this city, the rendezvous for the tools and agents in what he called his 'bloody work' and that his hand deposited at Surrattville, in a convenient place, the very weapons obtained by Booth while escaping, one of which fell, or was wrenched from Booth's death grip, at the moment of his capture.

"While in Montreal, Canada, where he had gone from Richmond on the 10th day of April, on the Monday before the assassination, Surratt received a summons from his co-conspirator, Booth, requiring his immediate presence in this city. In obedience to that preconcerted signal, he at once left Canada and arrived here on the 14th. By numerous, I had almost said a multitude of witnesses, we shall make the proof to be clear as the noonday sun...that he was here during the day of that fatal Friday, as well as present at the theatre that night...We shall show him to you on Pennsylvania Avenue, booted and spurred, awaiting the arrival of the fatal moment.

"We shall show him in conference with Herold in the evening; we shall show him purchasing a contrivance for disguise an hour or two before the murder. When the last blow had been struck, when he had done his utmost to bring anarchy and desolation upon his native land, he turned his back upon the abomination he had wrought, he turned his back upon his home and kindred and commenced a shuddering flight. We shall trace that flight, because in law, flight is the criminal's inarticulate confession, and because it happened in this case, as it always happens...that in some moment of fear or elation, or of fancied security, he too, to others, confessed his guilty deeds. He fled to Canada. We will prove to you the hour of his arrival there and the route he took...He found there safe concealment and remained there several months...In the following September, he took his flight...Still in the disguise and with painted face, painted hair, painted hand, he took ship to cross the Atlantic. In mid-ocean he revealed himself and related his exploits, and spoke freely of his connection with Booth in the conspiracy relating to the President. He rejoiced in the death of the President, he lifted his impious hands to heaven, and expressed a wish that he might live to return to America and serve Andrew Johnson as Abraham Lincoln had been served. He was hidden for a time in England, and found there sympathy and hospitality...From England he went to Rome and hid himself in the ranks of the papal army in the guise of a private soldier. Having placed almost the diameter of the globe between himself and the dead body of his victim, he might well fancy that pursuit was baffled...but he was discovered by an acquaintance of his boyhood. When denial would not avail, he admitted his identity and avowed his guilt in these memorable words: 'I have done the Yankees as much harm as I could. We have killed Lincoln, the niggers' friend!'

"The man to whom Surratt made this statement did as was his high duty to do - he made known his discovery to the American Minister...Having him arrested, he escaped from his guards by a leap down a precipice... He made his way to Naples and then took passage on a steamer that carried him across the Mediterranean Sea to Alexandria, Egypt...The inexorable lightening thrilled along the wires that stretch through the wasted waters which roll between the shores of Italy and Egypt and spake in his ear the word of terrible command; from Alexandria...manacled, he was made to turn his face towards the land he had polluted by the curse of murder. He is here at last to be tried for his crime." (5)

In his closing argument attorney Carrington for the Prosecution referring to Surratt's mother in connection with him said:

"Now, gentlemen of the jury, let us view the connection of Mrs. Surratt with this assassination. I feel the delicacy of the ground upon which I stand. I know the situation. I know that you dislike to consider this question which has been forced upon you. I do not want to do it. My duty is to prosecute the prisoner, but one of the counsel has said she was murdered, and another that she was butchered, and it becomes my duty to trace her connection with this crime, and then leave it to you, to say whether she was guilty...of the crime for which she suffered.

"First, I call your attention to the fact which we have already adverted; that her house, 541 H Street, was the rendezvous for these conspirators. Now, gentlemen, will you pause for a moment and let me ask you how you can reconcile that with innocence? You remember the law, that it is not how much a party did, but whether she had anything to do with it. Can you, I say, reconcile it with innocence that this woman's house should have been the rendezvous of Booth, Lewis Payne, Atzerodt,

Herold and John Surratt? Would you not know by intuition? Would you not know by their conversation? Would not your judgment and your hearts tell you who they were and what they contemplated?

"...Secondly, who furnished the arms with which this bloody deed was done?...According to the testimony of John M. Lloyd, this is shown. Do you believe him, or disbelieve him? My friend, Mr. Bradley...said he was a common drunkard; but, mark you, he was an attendant and friend of Mrs. Surratt."

(Mr. Bradley) 'Who says so?'

(District Attorney) "I will prove it. When I was examining that witness and proposed to ask him certain questions in reference to Mrs. Mary E. Surratt, he said,'Mr. Carrington,' for he knew me personally, 'I do not wish to talk about Mrs. Surratt, for she is not on trial.' I said, 'Go on, Mr. Lloyd'...I applied to the court and the court said it was his duty to answer. He saw her continually. He lived in her house; he drank her liquor. Why, this evidence shows that John H. Surratt, Herold and John M. Lloyd played cards and drank together. But, says the friend and companion (Lloyd) of the prisoner at the bar, (Surratt) unwilling to testify against her, when put on solemn oath... he says certain arms were furnished him by the prisoner at the bar who showed him where they could be safely concealed...he (Lloyd) protesting that it might get him into personal difficulty. The mother knew about the transaction, for on the 11th of April we have Lloyd's own testimony that she asked him where those shooting arms were, and said that they might be needed soon. I say, first her house is the rendezvous; secondly, she furnished arms or knows of their being furnished.

"On the night of the 14th of April, Booth and Herold are leaving Washington in flight for their lives. At Surrattville they call for whiskey from the agent (Lloyd) and friend of the prisoner and his mother. She gives them a home, gives them arms, gives them whiskey, not to nerve them, but to refresh them after the commission of their horrid crime.

"But Booth, in making his escape, needs something more than whiskey and arms...He needs a field glass, and has it delivered for him by his friend and agent, Mrs. Surratt. With the defense, no witness told the truth whose testimony went to convict their client, whilst the stories of the most infamous men, self-confessed scoundrels and accomplices, after the fact, if not before the fact, such as Fathers Boucher and Cameron, must be taken as gospel truth!

There were some eight or nine reputable witnesses who testified to having seen John Surratt in Washington on the day of the murder. Sgt. Dye positively identified him as the young man who called the time before Ford's Theatre on the evening of the murder. A black cook who had been engaged by Mrs. Surratt during John's absence testified that Mrs. Surratt had ordered her on the day of the assassination to bring a pot of tea and some toast into the dining room for John. While serving it to him, Mrs. Surratt said, "This is my son John; don't you think he looks more like his sister Anna?" (6)

TESTIMONY OF SHIP SURGEON DR. L. J. McMILLEN, THE PERUVIAN

Washington D. C., Tuesday, June 1867

Question. Did you know John H. Surratt? If so state where and under what circumstances.

Answer. I became acquainted with John H. Surratt in the month of September, 1865. I did not know him under the name of Surratt. He was introduced to me under the name of "McCarthy" by a gentleman in Montreal who kept him in secrecy after the assassination of Mr. Lincoln. I was then ship surgeon of the steamship Peruvian plying between Quebec and Liverpool. He came on board on September 11, 1865. I never suspected who he was until after we left. One day he inquired of me, "Who is that gentleman?" pointing to a passenger. He said he believed he was an American detective and that he was after himself. "But," said he, "if he is (he put his hand in his pocket and drew out a revolver) that will settle him." Then I began to suspect - not that he was Surratt but that he had been connected with the Rebellion here in some way. After that he would be with me continually every day, because I was the only person on board he knew, having been introduced to him by my friend, and he seemed not to care for being in the company of any one else. He used to come to me when I was alone and ask me to walk with him on deck; and he would always talk about what happened here during the war. He told me that he had been from the beginning in the Confederate States' service, carrying dispatches between here and Richmond, and also as far as Montreal; that he and Booth at first had planned the abduction of President Lincoln; that, however, they could not succeed in that way and they thought it necessary to change their plan. After this, before the assassination, Surratt was in Montreal when he received a letter from Booth ordering him immediately to Washington; that it was necessary to act and act promptly and he was to leave Montreal immediately for Washington. He did not tell me he came here, but he told me he came as far as Elmira, N.Y., and from that place telegraphed to New York to find out whether Booth had already left for Washington and was answered that he had. He did not tell me that he had gone any farther than Elmira. The next place that he spoke to me was St. Albans, Vermont, where he said he arrived early one morning about breakfast time and went to a hotel there for breakfast. When he was sitting at the table he heard several talking about the assassination and he inquired, "What was up?" They asked if he did not know President Lincoln had been assassinated. He said, "I do not believe it, because the story is too good to be true," On that a gentleman pulled out a newspaper and handed it to him. He opened it and saw his own name as one of the assassins. He said this unnerved him so much that the paper fell out of his hands and he immediately left the room. As he was going out through the house he heard another party say, that Surratt must have been or was at the time in St. Albans, because such a person (mentioning that person's name) had found a handkerchief on the street with Surratt's name on it. He told me he actually looked in his pocket and found that he had lost his handkerchief. From that place he went to Canada and was concealed there from April to September.

There were a great many things he told me that I had forgotten, or at least are not fresh in my memory. At the time I paid particular attention to what he said, and when I first made a deposition in Liverpool, everything was fresh in my memory...

The first time I was sure he was Surratt was on the day he was talking about his mother having been hung. He did not call her Mrs. Surratt or by any other name, but just spoke about his mother having been hung; of course I knew well enough that there was only one woman that had been hung in connection with the assassination so I was pretty certain he was her son. He also asked me who I did believe he was. I was not sure who were the parties that escaped...so I answered that I believed he was either Surratt or Payne. He gave me no reply but only laughed.

But the last day he was on board he called me aside and began to talk of the assassination. It was in the evening and we were alone together and he took out his revolver which was always in his pocket, pointed it at the heavens and said, "I hope and wish to live just a few years more - two will do me - and then I shall go back to the United States and I shall serve Andy Johnson as Abraham Lincoln has been served." I asked him why? "Because he has been the cause of my mother being hung." I then said, "Now who are you?" I was pretty sure then who he was but still he had not given me his name himself. He looked around to see whether any one was near us and said," I am Surratt."

I made this affidavit September 25th in Liverpool. Next day would be Wednesday the 26th. I told Mr. Wilding, United States Consul, he would be in Liverpool in a day or two. On Wednesday the 26th, Surratt came to my boarding house but I was absent...

He returned in the evening and wanted me to go with him to a place he had been recommended to go, but he could not find the place, so I went with him. Mr. Wilding, think had sent a detective to watch us for I saw a man follow us from the time we left my house until I left Surratt and he went to that house to which he had been recommended. (Oratory of the Holy Cross Church). He promised to see me next day but didn't. I got a short note stating he intended to go to London but when he got to the station there were several Americans there and he was afraid of being recognized, and did not go any farther.

In a few days again I saw him and he gave me a letter to bring back to the party who had taken care of him in Montreal. He expected some money because when he got to Liverpool he had very little money...He told me he expected a remittance from Washington but it would come through his friend in Montreal, and that I would very likely be charged with it when I returned." (7)

Testimony of F. L. Smoot, June 2nd

(Conversation with Mr. Joseph T. Nott occurred in the bar room of the Surratt Tavern, at Surrattville on April 15th)

Mr. Nott said: "He reckoned John was in New York by this time." I asked him why he thought so and he said, "My God! John knows all about this murder. Do you suppose he is going to stay in Washington and let them catch him?" I pretended to be much surprised and said, "Is that so?" He replied, "It is by God! I could have told you this thing was coming to pass six months ago." Then, putting his hand on my shoulder, "Keep that in your own skin, my boy. Don't mention it; if you do it will ruin me forever." (8)

Joseph T. Nott was Lloyd's bartender at the Surratt Tavern.

Lincoln's flag at Fords theatre

General Harris in his book "*Assassination of Lincoln a History of the Great Conspiracy*" on page 280 says:

> "Mr. Merrick then went on to meet the argument that Surratt had confessed his guilt by flight, by declaring that the mad passions of the hour and tyrannical usurpations of the government in its methods of dealing with those charged with this crime, by sending them before a military commission instead of a civil court for trial, justified him in his flight. He (Merrick) then went on to vindicate the Catholic Church which he claimed had been assailed in this matter. The only reference to the Catholic Church in connection with this trial had been made in the public press. The prosecution had carefully abstained from any assault on that church, and had tried to exclude religious prejudices from the minds of the jurors. Mr. Merrick, however, seized the occasion to pass a eulogium on that church, in which he showed as much disregard for facts of history, as he did for the proven facts in this case. Perhaps, he felt this vindication to be called for from the fact, that most of the conspirators were Catholics in religion, and the further fact that the friends who waited and watched for the return of his

client, to Montreal, after the assassination, and who on his return, spirited him away (priests La Pierre and Boucher) and kept him secreted five months, and then helped him off to Italy, where he was found in the ranks of the Pope's army, and who voluntarily came before the court on this trial to testify, and to procure testimony in his behalf, were priests from that church."

Continuing, General Harris comments:

"In his eulogium on that church he forgot to mention the fact that the pope, during the progress of the war, acknowledged the Southern Confederacy, and wrote a sympathizing letter to Jefferson Davis, in which he called him his dear son, and by implication denounced President Lincoln as a tyrant.

"He could have scarcely forgotten that the pope of Rome had sought to take advantage of the arduous struggle in which our government was engaged for the preservation of its life, to establish a Catholic empire in Mexico, and had sent Maximilian, a Catholic prince, to reign over, at the time, unhappy people, under the protection of the arms of France, lent to the furtherance of his un-holy purpose, by the last loyal son of the church, that ever occupied a throne in Europe.

"Perhaps, he did not realize that it was God who frustrated the last grasp of the drowning man at a straw that eluded his grasp, by preparing for his holiness, the pope, and for Louis Napoleon, just at that moment, the Franco-Prussian War, which resulted in the final loss of the temporal power to the pope, and with it, his grip on the world and his empire and crown, to the last servile supporter of his temporal pretensions - Napoleon IIIrd!

"To claim for that church, as Mr. Merrick did, friendship to civil liberty, respect for the rights of conscience and of private judgment, and love for our republican institutions, is to ignore or set at naught, all the dogmas of that church on the above questions and all the claims of the papacy. Mr. Merrick manifestly thought that the attitude of the Catholic clergy toward the assassination of the President could be hidden from public view, by his fulsome eulogy.

"The appeals made by the eminent counsel for the prisoner, to the political and religious prejudices of jurors, was ably seconded, all through the trial by the Jesuit priesthood of Washington City and the vicinity. It will be recalled by scores of people who attended the trial that not a day passed, but that some of these were in the courtroom as the most interested spectators. That they were not idle spectators, may be inferred from the fact, that whenever it seemed necessary to the prisoner's counsel to find witnesses to contradict any testimony, that was particularly damaging to their cause, they were always promptly found, and were almost uniformly Catholics in religion, as shown by their own testimony upon cross-examination.

"It was a remarkable fact also, that these witnesses were scarcely ever able to come from under the fire of Judge Pierrepont's searching cross-examination, uncrippled, and also, that when they took the risk of bringing two witnesses in rebuttal of the same testimony, their witnesses uniformly killed each other off, before they got through the ordeal. That tests the truthfulness of witnesses - cross-examination.

"Other outside influences were brought to bear on the jurors, such as these: Father J. B. Menu, from St. Charles College, (Sulpician Monastery) spent the day in the courtroom, sitting beside the prisoner all day, thus saying to the jury: 'You see which side I am on.' A great many of the students from the same college also visited the trial, it being vacation, and they uniformly took great pains to show their sympathy with the prisoner by shaking hands with him.

"The press also was prostituted almost daily by publishing cunningly devised paragraphs impugning the motives of the government in the prosecution and management of the case. Thus were the prejudices of the jurors appealed to and efforts also made to pervert public opinion." (8)

The above from General Harris who was present at the trials of Surratt, and who was also one of the Military Commission which tried and convicted Mrs. Surratt and the other three conspirators, recommending the death penalty, and sentences to the Dry Tortugas to four others, gives the reader a concise picture which correctly photographs the "fine Italian hand" which directed Surratt's attorneys in their line of action.

The courtroom of the Lincoln assassination trial

And now permit me to quote from the closing address of Judge Pierrepont, which is a masterpiece from a legal standpoint and a classic in pure English, superb in its logic and impregnable in its truth:

> "May it please your honor and gentlemen of the jury, I have not in the progress of this long and tedious case, had the opportunity as yet of addressing to you one word. My time has now arrived. Yea, all that a man hath, will he give for his life! When the book of Job was written, this was true, and it is just as true today. A man, in order to save his life, will give his property, will give his liberty, will sacrifice his good name, and will desert his father, his mother, his sister. He will lift up his hand before Almighty God, and swear that he is innocent of the crime with which he is charged.
>
> "He will bring in perjury upon his soul, giving all that he hath in the world, and be ready to take the chances and jump the life to come and so far as counsel place themselves in the situation of their client, and just

to the degree that they absorb his feelings, his terror and his purposes, just so far will counsel do the same.

"I am well aware, gentlemen, of the difficulties under which I labor in addressing you. The other counsel have all told you, that they know you, and that you know them. They know you in social life, and they know you in political affairs. They know your sympathies, your habits, your modes of thought, your prejudices, even. They know how to address you, and how to awaken your sympathies, whilst I come before you a total stranger. There is not a face in those seats that I have ever beheld until this trial commenced, and yet, I have a kind feeling pervading me, that we are not strangers.

“I feel as though we had a common origin, a common country, and a common religion, and that on many grounds we must have a common sympathy. I feel as though, if hereafter, I should meet you in my native city, or a foreign land, I should meet you not as strangers, but as friends. It was not a pleasant thing for me to come into this case. They had, perhaps, the right to ask, and so asking, I give you the answer. I was called into it, at a time ill-suited in every respect. I had just taken my seat in the convention called for the purpose of forming a new constitution for my State, and I was a member of the judiciary committee. The convention is now sitting, and I am absent, where I ought to be present. I feel, however, that I had no right to shirk this duty.

"The counsel asked whether I represented the Attorney General in this case...and so asking, I will give my answer. There is no mystery about the matter. The District Attorney feeling the magnitude of this case, felt that he ought to apply to the Attorney General for assistance in the prosecution of it, and he accordingly made the application. I have known the Attorney General for more than twenty years. Our relations have been most friendly, both in social and professional point of view. The Attorney General conferred with the Secretary of State, who is, as you know, from my own State, and they determined to ask me to assist in the prosecution of this cause...This is the way I happened to be engaged in this case...

"When the President of the United States was assassinated, I was one of the committee sent on by the citizens of New York, to attend his funeral. When standing, as I did stand, in the East room by the side of that coffin, if some citizen sympathizing with the enemies of my country had, because my tears were falling in sorrow over the murder of the President, there insulted me, and I had at that time repelled the insult with insult, I think my fellow citizens would have said to me, that my act was deserving of condemnation; that I had no right in that solemn, holy hour, to let my petty passions or my personal resentments disturb the sanctity of the scene. To my mind, the sanctity of this trial is far above that funeral occasion, solemn and holy as it was, and I should forever deem myself disgraced, if I should ever allow any passion of mine, or personal resentment of any kind, to bring me here into any petty quarrel over the murder of the President of the United States. I have tried to refrain from anything like that, and God helping me, I shall so endeavor to the end.

"To me, gentlemen, this prisoner at the bar is a pure abstraction. I have no feeling toward him whatever. I never saw him until I saw him in this room, and then it was under circumstances calculated to awaken only my sympathy...To me he is a stranger. Toward him I have no hostility, and I shall not utter one word of vituperation against him. I came to try one of the assassins of the President of the United States, indicted before you...so far as I am concerned, gentlemen, I believe that what you wish to know in this case is the truth...My duty is to aid you in coming to a just conclusion. I believe that it is your honest desire to find out whether the accused was engaged in this plot to overthrow the government, and assassinate the President of the United States. When this evidence is reviewed, and when it is honestly and fairly presented, when passions are laid aside, and when other people who have nothing whatever to do with the trial are kept out of this case, you will discover that in the whole history of jurisprudence, no murder was ever proved with the demonstration with which this has been proven before you. The facts, the proofs, the circumstances, all tend to one point, and all prove the case, not only beyond a reasonable doubt, but beyond any doubt.

"This has been, as I have already stated, a very protracted case. The evidence is scattered. It has come in, link by link, and as we could not have witnesses here in their order when you might have seen it in its logical bearings, we were obliged to take it as it came. I shall not attempt, gentlemen, to convince you by bold assertions of my own. I fancy I could make them as loudly and as confidently as the counsel for the other side, but I am not here for that purpose. The counsel are not witnesses in the case. We have come here for the purpose of ascertaining whether, under the law, and on the evidence presented, this man arraigned before you, is guilty as charged...My business is to prove to you from the evidence that this prisoner is guilty. If I do that, I shall ask your verdict. If I do not do that, I shall neither expect nor hope for it.

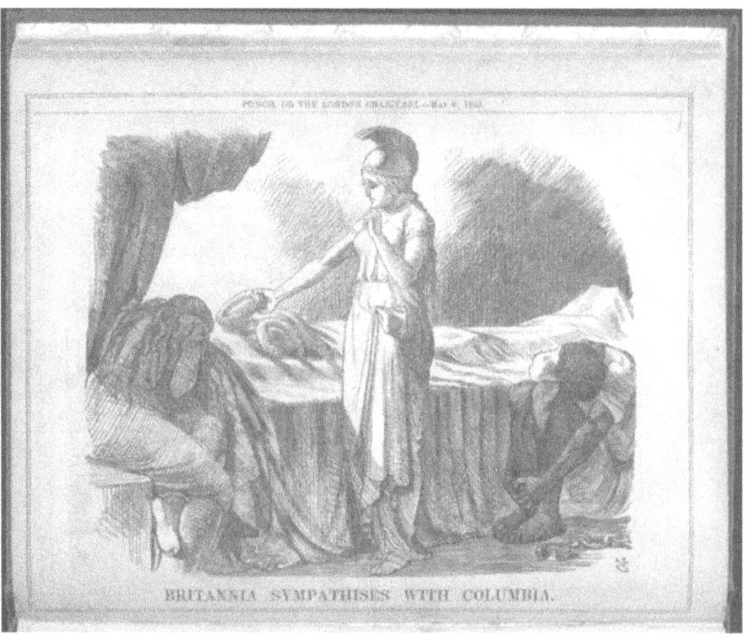

BRITANNIA SYMPATHISES WITH COLUMBIA.

"I listened to the two counsels who have addressed you for several days without one word of interruption. I listened to them respectfully and attentively. I know their earnestness, and I know the poetry that was brought into the case, and the feeling and the passion, that was attempted to be excited in your breasts, by bringing before you the ghost trailing her calico dress and making it rustle against these chairs. I have none of these powers which the gentlemen seem to possess, nor shall I attempt to invoke them. I have come to you for the purpose of proving that this party accused here, was engaged in this conspiracy to overthrow this government, which conspiracy resulted in the death of Abraham Lincoln, by a shot from a pistol in the hand of John Wilkes Booth. That is all there is to be proven in this case.

"I have not come here for the purpose of proving that Mrs. Surratt was guilty, or that she was innocent, and I do not understand why that subject was lugged into this case in the mode that it has been; nor do I understand why the counsel denounced the Military Commission which tried her, and thus indirectly censured in the severest manner, the President of the United States. The counsel certainly knew, when they were talking about that tribunal, and when they were thus denouncing it, that President Johnson, the President of the United States, ordered it with his own hand; that President Johnson, the President of the United States, signed the warrant that directed the execution; that President Johnson, President of the United States, when that record was presented to him, laid it before his Cabinet, and that every single member voted to confirm the sentence, and that the President with his own hand wrote his confirmation of it, and with his own hand signed the warrant. I hold in my hand the original record, and no other man, as it appears from that paper ordered it. No other one has touched this paper; and when it was suggested by some of the members of the Commission, that in consequence of the age, and the sex, of Mrs. Surratt, it might possibly be well to change her sentence to imprisonment for life, he signed the warrant for her death with the paper right before his eyes - and there it is (handing it to Mr. Merrick). My friend can read it for himself.

"My friends on the other side have undertaken to arraign the government of the United States against the prisoner. They have talked very loudly and eloquently, about this great government of twenty-five or thirty millions of people, being engaged in trying to bring to conviction, one poor young man, and have treated it as though it was a hostile act, as though two parties were litigants before you, the one trying to beat the other.

"Is it possible that it has come to this, that, in the City of Washington, where the President has been murdered, that when under the form of law, and before a court and jury of twelve men, an investigation is made, to ascertain whether the prisoner is guilty of this great crime, that the government is to be charged as seeking his blood, and its officers as lapping their tongues in the blood of the innocent? I quote the language exactly. It is a shocking thing to hear. What is the purpose of a government? What is the business of a government?

"According to the gentlemen's notion, when a murder is committed the government should not do anything towards ascertaining who perpetrated the murder, and if the government did undertake to investigate the matter and endeavor to find out whether the man charged with the crime is guilty, or not...the government and all connected with it, must be expected to be assailed as 'bloodhounds of the law,' and as seeking to 'lap their tongues in the blood of the innocent.' Is that the business of the government, and is it the business of the counsel, under any circumstances, thus to charge the government? What is government for? It is instituted for your protection and my protection, for the protection of us all. What could we do without it? Tell me, my learned and eloquent counsel on the other side, what would you do without government? What would you do in this city?" (9)

Thus Judge Pierrepont gave a direct and explicit analysis of anarchy as it was directed by the enemies of the United States in order to ruin forever Popular Government.

Judge Pierrepont

There were eighty-five witnesses and ninety-six in rebuttal, called by the government and Surratt called ninety-eight witnesses in chief and twenty-three in rebuttal.

The hearing began on June 17, 1867, and closed July 26, 1867. The arguments of the attorneys covered twelve days. The case went to the jury August 7. The jury brought in a report that they stood about even for conviction and acquittal, with no prospect of reaching an agreement. Surratt was remanded to jail.

His attorneys asked that he be released on bail, which was denied by the court. The following September the case was nolle prosequi. He was then indicted on the charge of engaging in rebellion. He was granted bail in the amount of $20,000.

A second indictment was found against him, but the district attorney entered a nolle prosequi on this. The prisoner was finally released and permitted to go free on a technicality - an omission of three words in the indictment, these being: "was a fugitive." All of this despite the fact that at both of his trials his guilt was proven beyond a shadow of a doubt.

Endnotes

1 Sourced from the U.S National Archives

2 Ibid.	6 Ibid
3 Ibid.	7 Ibid.
4 Ibid.	8 Ibid.
5 Ibid.	9 Ibid.

During Reconstruction the Catholic Bishops, being directed by the pope, agitated to have the Bible removed from the public schools. At that time this was the main textbook used for the teaching of moral and civil values and law. 'Boss' Tweed of New York's Tammany Hall gave his assistance in pushing the Bishop's goals. At the same time, the bishops demanded access to public taxes to fund their own schools. This was about the same time that the pope declared himself to be infallible. The following illustrations by Thomas Nast show the controversy.

"DON'T BELIEVE IN THAT."

WHAT THE IRISH ROMAN CATHOLIC CHILDREN WILL BE TOLD TO DO NEXT.
"Kick it out *Peaceably!*"

140 HARPER'S WEEKLY. [FEBRUARY 26, 1870.

"UNION IS STRENGTH."

DISTRIBUTION OF THE SECTARIAN FUND.

SECTARIAN BITTERNESS.

Th. Nast.

OUR COMMON SCHOOLS AS THEY ARE AND AS THEY MAY BE.

FACT AND FICTION.
AS HEAD OF THE ROMAN CATHOLIC CHURCH. | AS INFALLIBLE HEAD OF THE WORLD.

"I AM NOW INFALLIBLE"

OUR FOREIGN RULER (?)
F.K. "I will do your bidding, as you are infallible."

Chapter 12

The Rothschild's and the attempt to create a central bank

"We will hold the keys to the public Treasury..." Conference of Catholic Bishops, Buffalo, N.Y. 1852

Because Pope Clement XIV and the Catholic emperors across Europe were busy abolishing the Jesuits, they were not able to cooperate with each other well enough to stop the Protestant American experiment.

The Jesuits were greatly troubled because of their expulsions around the world, and they were forced to go underground. They used their agent, Adam Weishaupt, to create the Illuminati and used the Jesuit House of Rothschild to finance it. It was not just here, however, where Rothschild wealth was very helpful. America was becoming a giant of financial affluence and prosperity. Already, the Rothschild's were involved in extensive trading in the Americas. On top of their financial and mercantile empires, the Rothschild's were using their wealth to gain political and religious dominance in order to further the ends of the Jesuits in destroying Protestantism worldwide.

According to the ***Encyclopedia Judaica*** the Rothschild's are given the title, "*Guardians of the Vatican Treasury*". F. Tupper Saussy states in his, "*Rulers of Evil*",

> "The appointment of Rothschild gave the black papacy absolute financial privacy and secrecy. Who would ever search a family of orthodox Jews for the key to the wealth of the Roman Catholic Church?" F. Tupper Saussy, *Rulers of Evil,* Harper-Collins, p.160-161

The Jesuits used all their resources in their attempt to destroy America. They used the powerful financial empire of the Rothschild's to obtain control through money. Biographer Frederick Morton concluded that through the effective use of money the Rothschild's had successfully,

> "conquered the world more thoroughly, more cunningly, and much more lastingly than all the Caesars before or all the Hitler's after them." Frederick Morton, *The Rothschild's: A Family portrait*, Atheneum p.14

The Rothschild's believed that if they could control a nation's money, then they could control that country. This is clearly pointed out in the following statement from biographer Derek Wilson.

> "The banking community had always constituted a 'fifth estate' whose members were able, by their control of royal purse strings, to affect important events. But the house of Rothschild was immensely more powerful than any financial empire that had ever preceded it. It commanded vast wealth. It was international. It was independent. Royal governments were nervous of it because they could not control it. Popular governments hated it because it was not answerable to the people..." Derek Wilson, *Rothschild: The Wealth and Power of a Dynasty*, Charles Scribner's Sons, pp.78, 98, 99

Using the vast wealth of the Rothschild's, the Jesuits equipped armies to destroy countries that would not do what they dictated. They could buy politicians and through them change the very laws of a nation. This is exactly what they did in the United States and what they continue to do. The Jesuits have been using the Rothschild wealth to control major events behind the scenes world-wide for the last two centuries. This was true when they initially began, but today they control the central banks in each country including the Federal Reserve Bank to supply them with funds. To illustrate how the Jesuits and the Rothschild's have used countries and events to gain domination over nations and financial markets, we must look at the battle of Waterloo between France and England on June 19, 1815.

> "There were vast fortunes to be made, and lost, on the outcome of the Battle of Waterloo. The Stock Exchange in London was at fever pitch as traders awaited news of the outcome of this battle of the giants. If Britain lost, English consuls would plummet to unprecedented depths. If Britain was victorious, the value of the consul would leap to new dizzying heights.
>
> As the two huge armies closed in for the battle to the death, Nathan Rothschild had his agents working feverishly on both sides of the line to gather the most accurate possible information as the battle proceeded. Additional Rothschild agents were on hand to carry the intelligence bulletins to a Rothschild command post strategically located nearby.
>
> Late in the afternoon of June 16, 18815, a Rothschild representative jumped on board a specially chartered boat and headed out into the channel in a hurried dash for the English coast. In his possession was a top secret report from Rothschild's secret service agents on the progress of the crucial battle. This intelligence data would prove indispensable to Nathan in making some vital decisions.
>
> The special agent was met at Folkstone the following morning at dawn by Nathan Rothschild himself. After quickly scanning the highlights of the report Rothschild was on his way again, speeding towards London and the Stock Exchange.
>
> Arriving at the Exchange amid frantic speculation on the outcome of the battle, Nathan took up his usual position beside the famous "Rothschild Pillar". Without a sign of emotion, without the slightest change of facial expression the stony-faced, flint-eyed chief of the House of Rothschild gave a predetermined signal to his agents who were stationed nearby.
>
> Rothschild agents immediately began to dump consuls on the market. As hundreds of thousands of dollars' worth of consuls poured onto the market their value started to slide. Then they began to plummet.

Baron Rothschild

Nathan continued to lean against 'his' pillar, emotionless, expressionless. He continued to sell, and sell and sell. Consuls kept on falling. Word began to sweep through the Stock Exchange: 'Rothschild knows'. 'Wellington has lost at Waterloo'.

The selling turned into a panic as people rushed to unload their 'worthless' consuls or paper money for gold and silver in the hope of retaining at least part of their wealth. Consuls continued their nosedive towards oblivion. After several hours of feverish trading the consul lay in ruins. It was selling for about five cents on the dollar.

> Nathan Rothschild, emotionless and expressionless as ever, still leaned against his pillar. He continued to give subtle signals. But these signals were different. They were so subtly different that only the highly trained Rothschild agents could detect the change. On the cue from their boss dozens of Rothschild agents made their way to the order desks around the Exchange and bought every single consul in sight for just a 'song'.
>
> A short time later the 'official' news arrived in the British capital. England was now the master of the European scene.
>
> Within seconds the consul skyrocketed to above its original value. As the significance of the British victory began to sink into the public consciousness, the value of the consuls rose ever higher.
>
> Napoleon had 'met his Waterloo.' Nathan had bought control of the British economy. Overnight his already vast fortune was multiplied twenty times over."
>
> Des Griffin, *Descent into Slavery*, Emissary Publications, pp.27, 28

By 1815, the Jesuits had complete control over England. If a leader refused to do as he was told, money would be used to kill, smear, destroy, blackmail, or simply drive the person from office. This method has been used today to control people like George W. Bush, B.H Obama/Soetoro and British Prime Minister Tony Blair.

As the new nation of the United States began to spread its wings it would need a sound financial base from which to operate. It needed a bank, all right, but the bank used America instead of America using the bank. Financial genius and opportunist, Robert Morris organized the first bank. He and his associates believed that the bank should be modeled after the Bank of England. While the first bank in North America was not as ruthless as the central banks of today, it performed many of the operations of a modern central bank. 'Secret' investors put up $400,000 to start this bank. This attempt failed after two short years.

The central banks being established by the Jesuits and the Rothschild's are in no way similar to the neighbourhood banks that many use to manage their money. A closer look at the central bank will show why it is so dangerous. I will use the Federal Reserve Bank as a prime example.

The Federal Reserve Bank is not owned by the United States government, as many believe. The FED is a private bank and is owned by some of the richest and most powerful people in the world, such as the Rockefeller family. The FED has nothing to do with the U.S. government other than the fact that the government allows it to operate. The FED has a total, government enforced monopoly in money. Before the FED each individual bank competed with other banks and the customers and consumers got the best deal. This is, sadly, no more.

Here, roughly, is how the FED operates. Suppose the United States government wants to borrow a billion dollars, for say, to finance a war or establish a new social program. The government issues a bond for this amount, much as a water company does when it wants to raise money for a new pipeline. The government delivers this bond for the billion dollars to the Federal Reserve Bank. The FED takes the bond and writes an order to the Department of Printing and Engraving to print the billion dollars' worth of paper debt notes. After about two weeks or so, when the debt notes are printed, the Department of Printing and Engraving ships the notes to the FED, which then writes a cheque for about two thousand dollars to pay for the printing of the billion dollars' worth of notes. The FED then takes the notes and lends them to the United States government, and the people of the country pay interest at an exorbitant rate each year on these notes, which came out of nothing. The owners of the FED put up nothing for these notes. The taxes collected to pay the interest on these billion new dollars was then sent to the Vatican accounts in London. Forty percent was kept by the Rothschild cartel and sixty percent is transferred to the Vatican. Recently this income stream from the U.S. has been handed over to the new owners...China.

We see, therefore, that when the U.S. government goes into debt one dollar, a dollar plus the interest goes into the pockets of the owners of the FED. This is the biggest, most colossal theft ever perpetrated in the history of mankind, and oh-so slick. This simple operational fact is generally kept from the public and is the main reason why the Jesuits want to keep the public at large in the dark.

The Constitution of the United States gives to Congress the power to coin money. If Congress coined its own money as the Constitution directs, it would not have to pay the hundreds of billions of dollars of interest a year to the foreign bankers for the National debt, for money that came out of nothing. Money coined by Congress would be debt free.

Thomas Jefferson

Thomas Jefferson clearly saw what a central bank would do to America. He declared,

> "A private central bank issuing the public currency is a greater menace to the liberties of the people than a standing army." *The Writings of Thomas Jefferson, Volume X*, G.P. Putnam & Sons, p.31

Jefferson realized that if a central bank was ever set up in America, the bankers would have virtually unlimited amounts of money to control how lawmakers voted, and to control the media and what they said. Within a short time, these bankers would essentially rewrite the Constitution and the Bill of Rights by the unconstitutional laws that they would pass. Thomas Jefferson was completely correct, for today we have enough laws, such as the U.S. Patriot Act, the National Defense Act and the Homeland Security Act, to literally convert the United States into a police state, when all the provisions of these acts are implemented.

Just like the old bank of North America, the new Bank of the United States had eighty percent of its initial funding capital provided by 'secret' investors, and the government put up only twenty percent. Whoever these 'secret' investors were, they had incredible power in America because they had control of the money in America. Many books from the period tell us exactly who these 'secret' investors were.

> "Under the surface, the Rothschild's long had a powerful influence in dictating American financial laws. The law records show that *they were the power in the old Bank of the United States*." [emphasis added] Gustavus Myers, *History of the Great American Fortunes*, Random House, p.556

> "Over the years since N.M. [Nathan Rothschild] the Manchester textile manufacturer, had bought cotton from the Southern states, Rothschild's had developed heavy American commitments. Nathan…had made loans to various states of the Union, had been, for a time, the official European banker for the U.S. government and was a pledged supporter of the Bank of the United States" Derek Wilson, *Rothschild: The Wealth and Power of a Dynasty*, Charles Scribner's Sons, p.178

The Rothschild's and the Jesuits have been using their enormous wealth to take over the United States through traitorous politicians for many, many years.

During the time of the Rothschild's in Victorian England, Benjamin Disraeli was the Prime Minister for several years. In 1844, he wrote a political novel titled, *Corningsby*. One of the key characters in the book was a very powerful merchant and banker named Sidonia. It is apparent from the events chronicled, that Sidonia is none other than Nathan Rothschild. In the book Disraeli states, "Europe did require money, and Sidonia [Nathan Rothschild] was ready to lend it to Europe. France wanted some; Austria more; Prussia a little; Russia a few millions. Sidonia could furnish them all.

It is not difficult to conceive that, after having pursued the career we have intimated for about ten years, Sidonia had become one of the most considerable personages in Europe. He had established a brother, or a near relative, in whom he could confide, in most of the principal capitals. He was lord and master of the money market of the world, and of course virtually lord and master of everything else. He literally held the revenues of Southern Italy in pawn; and monarchs and ministers of all countries courted his advice and were guided by his suggestions" Benjamin Disraeli, *Corningsby,* Alfred A. Knopf, p. 225

The Jesuits and the Rothschild's would settle for nothing less.

Alexander Hamilton

Secretary of the Treasury, Alexander Hamilton, submitted a proposal to Congress in 1790 for a central bank. Hamilton had been an aid of Robert Morris in the initial experience of central banking in North America. During the Constitutional Convention of 1787 Hamilton had been a strong supporter of sound currency. Within three years he completely shifted his opinion to that of a banking system that could generate money in the same manner as the FED. According to G. Edward Griffin's book, *The Creature from Jekyll Island*, American Opinion, p. 328 Hamilton's loyalty had been compromised and bought by offers of enormous wealth.

After the Hamilton Central Bank failed, the Jesuits were able to establish a third central bank using Nicholas Biddle as their agent in 1816. The charter for this bank ran until 1836. Biddle made an attempt to renew the charter of this third bank during the Presidential campaign of 1832. Biddle believed that Andrew Jackson would not dare to risk his second term in office by opposing him, so Biddle felt that this was the perfect time to renew the bank's charter. Andrew Jackson understood the dangers of the central bank and vetoed the bill to renew. Jackson's argument was simple,

> "Is there no danger to our liberty and independence in a bank that in its nature has so little to bind it to our country? Is there not cause to tremble for the purity of our elections in peace and for the independence of our country in war? Of the course which would be pursued by ***a bank almost wholly owned by the subjects of a foreign power, and managed by those interests, if not affections*** would run in the same direction there can be no doubt...Controlling our currency, receiving our public monies, and holding thousands of our citizens in dependence, it ***would be more formidable and dangerous than a naval and military power of the enemy***. [Emphasis added] Herman E. Kross, *Documentary History of Banking and Currency in the United States*, Chelsea House, pp. 26,27

Jackson feared that the foreigners, who wanted to dominate and control America, would use the central bank to destroy her. The Rothschild's and the Jesuits have been doing just that for many years. The following quote demonstrates how Nicholas Biddle manipulated the Congress.

> "Biddle had one powerful advantage over his adversary. For all practical purposes, Congress was in his pocket. Or, more accurately, the product of his generosity was in the pockets of Congressmen. Following the Rothschild Formula, Biddle had been careful to reward compliant politicians with success in the business world. Few of them would bite the hand that fed them. Even the great Senator, Daniel Webster, found himself kneeling at Biddle's throne. Edward G. Griffin, *The Creature from Jekyll Island*, American opinion, p.351

In the early 1830's the Biddle-Rothschild-Jesuit plan was working perfectly. They controlled the United States Congress by giving them money to become successful in the business world. As long as the Congressmen voted as they were directed, their businesses did well, disobedience would dry up their entire financial windfall and their business would fail.

> "Biddle was not without resources. In keeping with his belief that banking was the ultimate source of power, he had regularly advanced funds to members of Congress when delay on appropriations bills had held up their pay. Daniel Webster was, at various times, a director of the Bank and on retainer as its counsel. "I believe my retainer has not been renewed or refreshed as usual. If it be wished that my relation to the Bank be continued, it may be well to send to me the usual retainers." Numerous other men of distinction had been accommodated, including members of the press. - John Kenneth Galbraith, *Money: Whence it Came, Whence it Went*, Houghton Mifflin, p.80

Webster's record in Congress had previously been in behalf of sound money. When Biddle bought Webster with money and other enticements, he succumbed and became a supporter of the corrupt banking objectives of Biddle. Webster became one of the central banks most avid supporters. In the early 1830's Congress had many Jesuits seeking to secretly undermine the great principles of the Constitution.

When Andrew Jackson finally ousted Biddle and the central bank, he had to face other more pressing issues, such as Jesuit assassins.

> "With these accomplishments close on the heels of his victory over the Bank, the President had earned the undying hatred of monetary scientists, both in America and abroad. It is not surprising, therefore, that on January 30, 1835, an assassination attempt was made against him. Miraculously, both pistols of the assailant misfired, and Jackson was spared by a quirk of fate. It was the first such attempt to be made against the life of a President of the United States. The would-be assassin was Richard Lawrence who either was truly insane or who pretended to be insane to escape the harsh punishment. [or protect those who hired him- Ed.] At any rate, Lawrence was found not guilty due to insanity. Later, he boasted to friends that he had been in touch with powerful people in Europe who had promised to protect him from punishment should he be caught. – Griffin, *The Creature From Jekyll Island*, p. 357

The Rothschild's and the Jesuits needed to regroup. For the next 20 years, the name of the game was assassination. Then came the U.S. Civil War. According to German Chancellor, Otto Von Bismarck, all of this was carefully planned,

> "The division of the United States into federations of equal force was decided long before the Civil War by the high financial powers of Europe. These bankers were afraid that the United States, if they remained in one block and as one nation, would attain economic and financial independence, which would upset their financial domination over Europe and the world. Of course, in the 'inner circle' of finance, the voice of the Rothschild's prevailed. They saw an opportunity for prodigious booty if they could substitute two feeble democracies, burdened with debt to the financiers in place of a vigorous Republic sufficient unto herself. Therefore, they sent their emissaries into the field to exploit the question of slavery and

> to drive a wedge between the two parts of the Union. The rupture between the North and the South became inevitable; the masters of European finance employed all their forces to bring it about and to turn it to their advantage. - [Quoted by] Griffin, *the Creature From Jekyll Island*, p. 374

The Rothschild's, guided by the Jesuits used the Civil War to divide the United States into two contending countries. The end result would be political and Constitutional control, along with material wealth in America, and would facilitate America becoming enslaved to the Jesuits. In spite of the fact that the Civil War failed to accomplish the much hoped for goals, the Jesuits have achieved many of these goals anyway, as conditions in the U.S. plainly demonstrate today.

Abraham Lincoln understood fully the insidious hand of the Rothschild's and the Jesuits in the Civil War. He understood the massive destructive power of these people. Lincoln greatly feared for the survival of America and did everything in his power to defeat their purposes. He said,

> "The money power [Rothschild's and Jesuits] preys upon the nation in times of peace and conspires against it in times of adversity. It is more despotic than monarchy, more insolvent than autocracy, more selfish than bureaucracy. I see in the near future a crisis approaching that unnerves me and causes me to tremble for the safety of my country. Corporations have been enthroned, an era of corruption will follow, and the money power of the country will endeavor to prolong its reign by working upon the prejudices of the people, until the wealth is aggregated in a few hands, and the republic is destroyed. – *The Lincoln Encyclopedia: The Spoken and Written Words of A. Lincoln*, Macmillan, p. 40

The hanging of the 4 Lincoln conspirators

Abraham Lincoln saw that the Rothschild-Jesuit scheme was compromising the leaders of America. By utilizing their endless fountain of money, these evil men controlled several political leaders at the highest levels of the American government in the 1800's. Today American politicians are selling out their country to the Jesuits for the chance at immense wealth and influence. In a speech in 1837, Lincoln declared,

> "No foreign power or combination of foreign powers could by force take a drink from the Ohio or make a track on the Blue Ridge. At what point, then, is the approach of danger to be expected? If it ever reaches us, it must spring from among us, it cannot come from abroad. If destruction be our lot, we must ourselves be its author and finisher. As a nation of freedom, we must live through all time or die of suicide." – Joan Veon, *The United Nations Global Straightjacket*, Hearthstone Publishing, p. 64

After the Civil War the country was bleeding and in disarray. The United States was vulnerable to even more Jesuit mischief and they took great advantage of the opening under the Reconstruction phase of the country.

SITTING OF THE COURT-MARTIAL AT WASHINGTON. INTERIOR VIEW OF THE COURT CHAMBER.

Setting of the court-martial at Washington Interior view of the court chamber

Chapter 13

Wrapping up the Lincoln period

The aim of the Jesuits in the United States was to ultimately extricate the Roman Catholic Church from its responsibility in the murder of Lincoln by exonerating Mary E. Surratt and her son John by placing the entire blame on John Wilkes Booth - the "Protestant." In the process they have robbed the American people of the most dramatic and important chapter in their history. History has a tendency to repeat itself and if the people have no sense of their history they are beautifully set up like bowling pins to accept anything which is purported to be "truth."

The activity in this direction of these Leopoldines - the Knights of Columbus - was significant. Wide publicity was given through the official press of the Knights of Columbus, in the years following, of an offer of five thousand dollars to "anyone who can prove that John Wilkes Booth was a Roman Catholic."

The goal was to whitewash the Surratt's before the Catholic Church could clean its skirts. Shortly after the century turned the documentary evidence pertaining to this tragedy had been so carefully and completely removed from the public eye that they felt it safe to openly refer to the death of Lincoln. But for years his name never passed the lips of either priests or the press of Rome.

There is much to convince the fair-minded investigator that John Wilkes Booth had been a convert to the Roman Church. The evidence in both of the trials of the conspirators and John H. Surratt shows that Booth was frequently at Mass in various Roman Churches. The fact that he wore an "Agnes Dei" bronze medal at the time of his death which was taken from his neck by Surgeon Barnes as his body lay on the Montauk, which had become corroded from the moisture of his body showed long wear. Only three weeks prior to the murder as Rear Admiral Baird tell us, he met Booth coming out of a Vesper Service at a Roman Catholic Church in Washington. This alone of course would not be conclusive, but taken together with other evidence strengthens the conclusion, that he was not only a professed Romanist, but that he was a devout one.

The close associates of Booth from his arrival in Washington from Montreal the middle of November, 1864, until his flight after the murder, were fanatical Romanists. His first visit the next day after he registered at the National Hotel was to the little Roman Church at St. Mary's near Bryantown. He had attended Mass and presented his credentials to the Roman Catholics, Drs. Queen and Mudd; was entertained by them and enquired for the whereabouts of John Surratt on that occasion, whom he met shortly afterwards in Washington and became a constant, almost daily, visitor at the Surratt home on H Street which was the meeting place of the Roman priests of Washington and vicinity.

The complete confidence which existed between Booth and the Surratt's is sufficient evidence that these schemers were taking no chances on any "Heretic." The fact that every member of this household was a Romanist, and undoubtedly a member of the Knights of the Golden Circle further confirms this belief.

Add to this the fact that Booth himself had taken the Jesuitized oath of the Order of the Knights of the Golden Circle, given in full in this book, we have another link in the chain of circumstantial evidence. He was under the influence of the small group of Confederate leaders in Montreal, who in turn were the most abject tools and associates of the French priests in that city. Considering these and other things we will be justified in concluding that if John Wilkes Booth was not a professed Romanist, he might as well have been and most certainly was nothing else.

There is no professed Catholic assassin in all history who was a more effectual dupe of the priests of Rome and their lay agents than this once brilliant, care free, talented young man whose most distinguishing characteristic, barring his kindly courtesy, was his reverence for his mother.

Without wishing to excuse or condone the cruel, cowardly act which snatched Abraham Lincoln away at the moment when his great wisdom, kindliness, and broad charity would have guided the re-construction as no other could, but the aim is to call attention to the instigators, higher up - the priests of Rome who were accessories both before and after the fact, and who have always escaped without even censor or suspicion, leaving their tools to pay the price.

Booth was chosen for this bloody deed with keen discernment and fine discrimination by these ecclesiastical plotters against the United States government. That he was a young man without much depth of character is to be conceded, for they do not seek strong characters to execute these wicked and dangerous deeds. No doubt the Jesuits followed Booth for several months, studying him, finding his most vulnerable point, delving into his very soul, before they decided to cast on him the leading role. There were many advantages in his selection. His profession and the well-known loyalty of the Booth family to the Government, placed him almost above suspicion. His knowledge of changing his appearance, his expertness in the use of firearms, horsemanship, fencing, etc., his pronounced personal magnetism and easy graceful manner and his childlike vanity without egotism, all tended to, from their standpoint make him an ideal candidate of their subtle influence. One other point, Booth, even if he had no previous idea of the responsibility of knowledge of the oath he was to take when he entered the Golden

Circle, must have fully realized after, that had he failed to carry out instructions after he had drawn the straw, it meant his own certain death.

Geniuses are usually so absorbed in the line of work in which their gift inclines them, that they are often easy victims of unscrupulous minds, and the dramatic instinct in this unfortunate young man would tend to make him particularly susceptible to the weird pagan ceremonies and strange garb of the Roman Church and its psychology.

Fords Theatre

Booth, by several authors, is charged with entering this conspiracy of murder and destruction from a monetary object. The value of a dollar does not go hand in hand with talent or genius. If so, it is the exception to the rule and John Wilkes Booth was not an exception. Actors make their money easily and quickly and the rule is that they let it go just as easily. It is unjust to attribute Booth's part in this affair to a mercenary motive and it is more than likely that he used much of his own money during this operation.

That John H. Surratt on the contrary, was mercenary and that money held a high place in his estimation is plentifully evidenced. He talked about the large sums of money he expected to get and repeatedly boasted to Weichmann and displayed the large bills and twenty dollar gold pieces in his possession while carrying on the Secret Service work in his excursions between Richmond, Washington and Canada.

It was his habit to show his money and talk of it to his friends in a boastful way. The testimony of Ste. Marie shows that he was still given to this while a member of the Pope's Army.

The difference in the filial devotion and the lack of it is very pronounced between these two young men. Surratt's immediate flight to Canada the morning after the tragedy at Ford's Theatre, where he had directed and called the time, where he remained in safety under the care of the Roman priests LaPierre and Boucher, during his mother's arrest, trial, conviction and execution; his heartless desertion of his mother and only sister, is unparalled as the most concentrated selfishness and base ingratitude and the only charitable thing to be said, is that it was due greatly to his theological training - or it might have been owing to the espionage of his priestly "protectors."

The review of the Trial of John H. Surratt made by Brig. Gen. T. M. Harris who was a member of the Military Court which tried and convicted the four conspirators and sentenced four others to the Dry Tortugas, was written in response to the charges of Mrs. Surratt's confessor, the pastor of St. Patrick's Roman Church, Washington, D. C., who had dared to raise his voice in defense of this woman twenty-seven years after her execution. General Harris' book, the only one of its kind and one in which this writer has referred to, has so effectually and completely "nailed" the ecclesiastical liar, that it has been removed from most of the libraries throughout the United States on account of its contents. Because it has been out of print for more than a century and is not easily accessible to the reader I am incorporating the entire chapter on "Father Walter" below:

> "From the time of the trial of the conspirators by a military commission, and the execution of Mrs. Surratt by the order of President Johnson, Father Walter, a secular priest of Washington City, has made himself conspicuous by his efforts to pervert public opinion on the result of the trial of the conspirators by the Commission. Whilst rebel lawyers, editors and politicians have bodily assailed the lawfulness of the Commission and have denounced it as an unconstitutional tribunal, and have characterized the trial as a "star chamber" trial, as a contrivance for taking human life under a mockery of a judicial procedure, with no purpose of securing the ends of justice, Father Walter and other priests whose sympathies were with the Southern Confederacy have earnestly seconded their efforts by the invention and circulation of cunningly devised falsehoods.
>
> Father Walter has every now and then bobbed up with the assertion of Mrs. Surratt's entire innocence. Knowing that not one in a thousand of our people has ever read the testimony on which she was convicted, he feels that he can boldly assert, 'There was not enough evidence against her to hang a cat.' He has also become bold enough to state as facts what the evidence shows to be falsehoods. As an example of this: In an article in the '*Catholic Review*' he asserts in regard to Mrs. Surratt's trip to Surrattville on the afternoon of the day of the assassination that she had ordered her carriage for the trip, which was purely on private business, on the forenoon of that day, and before it was known that the President would go to the theatre." Why, if this was true was it not proven in her defense? There was no such testimony produced. The testimony on this point against her was that shortly after two o'clock on that afternoon she went upstairs to Weichmann's room, tapped on the door, and when it was opened she said to Mr. Weichmann, 'I have just received a letter from Mr. Calvert that makes it necessary for me to go to Surrattville today and see Mr. Nothey. Would you be so good as to get a conveyance and drive me down?' Upon Weichmann's consenting to

do so, she handed him a ten-dollar bill with which to procure a conveyance. Surely, there is no evidence here that a carriage had been ordered already, as Weichmann was left free to procure a conveyance where he might see fit.

Weichmann went down stairs, and as he opened the front door he met John Wilkes Booth, who was in the act, as it were, of pulling the front door bell. Booth entered the house.

When young Weichmann returned, after having procured the buggy, he went up to his own room after some necessary articles of clothing, and as he again descended the stairs and passed by the parlor doors he observed that Booth was in the parlor conversing with Mrs. Surratt. In a little while Booth came down to the front door steps and waved his hand in token of adieu to Weichmann, who was standing at the curb.

What has been considered to be a secret of great importance was buried this week in the grave of Father Walter, a venerable priest of the Roman catholic church who has ministered in Washington for forty years and gained much prominence as spiritual adviser and confessor of Mrs. Surratt. The good father always believed that woman to be innocent of any criminal connection with the assassination of Lincoln, and repeatedly defended her memory with great vigor from the pulpit and in the press, but there was one mystery with which she was associated that he never revealed. On the day before her execution he made repeated and urgent attempts to obtain interviews with President Johnson and Mr. Stanton, who was then secretary of war. He wrote notes and sent messages to both those gentlemen, telling them that he had information of the gravest importance to communicate to them and begged their attention for a few moments, but Father Walter had called at the white house and war department so many times to plead for mercy for Mrs. Surratt that the president and secretary both denied him admission, under the supposition that he desired simply to renew his appeals.

A day or two after the execution Secretary Stanton sent word that he was now ready to receive the information, but Father Walter replied that it was too late, and never went to the white house or war department again. He had been frequently approached upon the subject, but had always intimated that there were facts of the gravest importance connected with the assassination of Lincoln which had never been made public. He steadfastly declined to reveal them on the grounds that their disclosure could benefit no one.

When Mrs. Surratt came and was in the act of getting into the buggy, she remembered she had forgotten something, and said, “Wait a moment, until I go and get those things of Mr. Booth’s.” She returned from the parlor with a package which was done up in brown paper, the contents of which the witness did not see, but which was afterwards shown to have been the field glass which

Booth sent to Lloyd by Mrs. Surratt, with a message to have it, with the two carbines and two bottles of whiskey, where they would be handy, as they would be called for that night. Lloyd swore that this was the message delivered to him by Mrs. Surratt in the private interview she sought with him in his backyard on his return home that evening, and that in accordance with these instructions he delivered them to Booth and Herold about midnight that night.

Now, let us see about the private business on which she professed to be going, and on which she claimed at her trial that she went. The letter from Mr. Calvert was a demand for money that she owed him, and was written at Bladensburg on the 12th of April. On the afternoon of the fourteenth she presented herself to Weichmann and claimed that she had just received it. It would seem very strange that it took this letter two days to reach her a distance of only six miles. She claimed that she must go and see Mr. Nothey who owed her and get money from him to pay her debt to Mr. Calvert. Mr. Nothey lived five miles below Surrattsville, and as she claimed that she had just received Mr. Calvert's letter, it was impossible that she could have made any arrangement with Nothey to meet her at Surrattsville that day. She did not meet him there, neither did she go to his house to see him. When she arrived at Surrattsville she took Weichmann into the parlor at the hotel and asked to write a letter for her to Mr. Nothey, which he did at her dictation; and this she sent to Mr. Nothey by Mr. Bennett Gwinn, a neighbor of his who happened to be passing down.

Now, in view of all these facts, can anyone see how her private business was in any way subserved by her trip to Surrattsville on that afternoon? She could as easily have written to Mr. Nothey from Washington as from Surrattsville. A postage stamp, a sheet of paper and an envelope would have saved her six dollars, the cost of her trip, and would have served her business just as well. The truth is that this talk of going on private business of her own was all a fabrication, first to deceive Mr. Weichmann as to the object of her trip, and then to be used, should it become necessary, in her defense. We have already seen what her real business was.

Father Walter falsifies again in the article referred to saying that she did not see Lloyd on that afternoon, but delivered the things to his sister-in-law, Mrs. Offutt.

Both Lloyd and his sister-in-law testified to her interview with him in his backyard, and Lloyd testified as to what passed between them on that occasion.

It would seem that Father Walter is going on the theory that we have forgotten so far past the time, and that the testimony has been so far forgotten that he can foist upon the public any statement that he may please to fabricate. We would kindly remind the reverend Father that no ultimate gain can be derived from an effort to suppress the truth. Neither can it be obliterated by our prejudices. We may misconstrue facts, but we cannot wipe them out by a mere stroke of a pen; and a fact once made can never be recalled. But I am not yet done with this Father. He prefaces his article in the "Review" with the statement that he heard Mrs. Surratt's last confession and that whilst his priestly vows do not permit him to reveal the secrets of the confessional, yet from knowledge in his possession he is prepared to assert her entire innocence of this most atrocious crime. He means that we shall understand that were he at liberty to give her last confession to the world, he would say that she then and there asserted her entire innocence.

Will Father Walter deny that under the teachings of the Roman Catholic Church he had an absolute right, with her consent, to make her confession public on this point? Nay, more, could not Mrs. Surratt have compelled him to do so in vindication of her good name, and the honor of the church of which she was a member? And having this consent, was it not his most solemn duty to proclaim her confessed innocence in every public way through the press and even from the very steps of the gallows? Why was not that confession made public? Why was it not reduced to writing and signed with her own hand? Why has it not, in its entirety, been given to the world?

Why must the public wait twenty-seven years, and instead of having the full confession, be required to content itself, in so great a case, with a mere assertion from the reverend Father, based on his alleged knowledge? Aye, Just there's the rub!

That confession of Mrs. Surratt's would have proved very interesting reading, and might have let in a flood of light on some of the places that are now very dark; it would, indeed, have shown how far Mrs. Surratt was involved in the abduction and assassination plots and to what degree she was the willing or unwilling tool of her son, and of John Wilkes Booth. That confession would have shown the object of Booth's visit to her on the very day and eve of the murder. It would have explained what she had in her mind when she carried Booth's field glass into the country and told Lloyd to have the "shooting irons" and two bottles of whiskey ready on that fatal night of the fourteenth of April. And if she did not explain satisfactorily every item of testimony which bore so heavily against her, then her last confession was worth nothing.

Father Walter never had at any time Mrs. Surratt's consent to make her confession public, and he dare not do so now after twenty-seven years have elapsed since he shrove his unfortunate penitent.

Why did Father Walter not do this? He was interesting himself very much in her behalf in trying to get her a reprieve; why did he not use this as an argument with the President in her behalf, that in her final confession she asserted her innocence? Why did he wait until the sentence had been confirmed by the President and a full Cabinet without a dissenting voice, and then had been carried into execution, before he put into circulation the story of her confessed innocence? And why does he refer to his priestly vows as his excuse for this conduct, when he knows full well that having gained Mrs. Surratt's consent to make her confession public as an entirety, these vows imposed upon him no such restrictions? In vindication of the Commission and also the Court of Review - the President and his Cabinet - we submit that the evidence shows her to have been guilty, no matter what she might have said, in her final confession.

Perhaps she had been led to believe that President Lincoln was an execrable tyrant, and that his death was no more than that of the "meanest nigger in the army." Her remarks to her daughter the night her house was searched indicate the views she took of the subject. "Anna, come what will, I am resigned. I think that Booth was only an instrument in the hands of the Almighty to punish this wicked and licentious people."

To one who could have taken this view of the case, Booth's act could not have been regarded as a crime: and she who rendered him all the aid she could would feel no guilt. They were only co-operating with the Almighty in the execution of vengeance. On the trial of

John H. Surratt, Mr. Merrick brought Father Walter on the stand and asked him if he heard the last confession of Mrs. Surratt, to which the Father answered, "I did, I gave her communion on Friday and prepared her for death."

Mr. Merrick in his argument before the jury said: "I asked him 'Did she tell you as she was marching to the scaffold that she was an innocent woman?' I told him not to answer that question before I desired him to. He nodded his head, but did not answer that question, because he had no right, as the other side objected."

Now, what was the object of all this? Mr. Merrick brought the Father on to the stand and asked him a question that had not the slightest relevancy to any issue before that jury. He knew, of course, that the prosecution would object, and that the question could not be answered. It was a direct question and could have been answered by "She did," or "She did not." Why does not the Father answer at once? He had been cautioned not to do so until desired, and so he waits for the prosecution to object and stop him from answering the question. Mr. Merrick, however, in his argument, assumes that the Father stood ready to say that, "She solemnly declared her innocence to me in her last confession," and throws the responsibility on the other side for not getting the answer. The argument was this: "You see that Father Walter stood ready to testify to this fact, but the prosecution objected, and so he could not do it."

Now, what has become of the Father's priestly vows, behind which he has always been hiding? Or was all this a mere piece of acting, to give the counsel a point from which to denounce the government, the Commission, and all who were concerned in visiting justice upon the assassins?

We believe it to be true that the laws of his church do not forbid him to make public, with her consent or command, her last confession on this point, and that the Father in making the statements he does at this late day is simply practicing sleight of hand upon the public. It is a very strange circumstance, too, that whilst Payne, Arnold, O'Laughlin, Atzerodt, and even John H. Surratt, admitted their connection with one or the other of the conspiracy plots, Mrs. Surratt has not left one word or line after her to explain away the incriminating evidence brought against her. The reason is plain; she could not

> have explained anything without involving herself and her son and giving away the whole case.
>
> For twenty-six years Father Walter and his rebel coadjutors have kept a paragraph going the rounds of the papers, stating as a fact that all the members of the Commission, but one, are dead, and that they died miserable deaths which marked them as the subjects of heaven's vengeance and that some of them perished from the violence of their own hands, being crazed with remorse.
>
> The truth is that at this writing, April, 1892, all the members of the Commission are alive except General Hunter and General Ekin. General Hunter lived to over four score years and General Ekin to seventy-three. The present writer is nearly seventy-nine and is still able to vindicate the truth in the interest of a true history of his period. Is it not high time that the American people should be fully informed as to this most important episode in their history, in order that they may not be misled by men who were not the friends, but the enemies, of our government in its struggle for its preservation and perpetuation?"

The above statement of facts is sufficient to refute the lying priest Walter and block the lying Roman Church's mad efforts to subvert this damning evidence of its own participation in Lincoln's murder and the attempted destruction of the United States.

OTHER TESTIMONY OF THE SURRATT'S CATHOLIC FRIENDS

Testimony of Miss Anna Ward, for the Defense, June 3rd.

> I reside at the Catholic Female Seminary on Tenth Street, Washington. I have been acquainted with Mrs. Surratt six or eight years. I have not been very intimate with Mrs. Surratt. She always bore the character of a perfect lady and a Christian, as far as my acquaintance with her extends.
>
> I received two letters from John H. Surratt postmarked Montreal, Canada, for his mother. I received the second the day of the assassination. I answered his letters to me, and left them with his mother as I sup-

> posed that she would be glad to hear from him. I have not seen him since. (1)

This Miss Ward, by the way, was twice brought into the trial, sufficient participation, it might seem, to involve her in conspiracy. Mr. Weichmann testified that in March, 1865, Surratt invited him to accompany him to the Herndon Hotel to see about securing a room. When they arrived Surratt called for the housekeeper, a Mrs. May Murray, and asked her to have the room in readiness for the man, not mentioning his name, whom Miss Ward a few days previous, had spoken to her about. The housekeeper seemed not to remember until Surratt further reminded her that it was, "For a delicate gentleman" who was to have his meals served in his room. With this refreshing she remembered. Surratt then told her that the gentleman would occupy the room on the following Monday. Later on, Weichmann met Atzerodt coming along Seventh Street, who told him in answer to his question as to where he was going, that he was going to the Herndon House. Weichmann then said "Is that Payne that is at the Herndon House?" Atzerodt answered, "Yes."

Then Miss Ward, this Catholic school teacher, was the one who prior to the crime, had been delegated, to establish an alibi for John H. Surratt by calling at the Surratt house on the day of the assassination with a letter which she had purported to have received that day from John Surratt in Canada. She proffered this information to Louis Weichmann, who happened to be at home. Weichmann did not read the letter, which somehow disappeared and was never introduced into evidence.

It was a fact worth noting from the amount of evidence, that Mrs. Surratt, a woman impoverished by the war with no special social standing should have had the privilege of such intimate acquaintance with so great an array of priests. I present the verbatim testimony of these reverend gentlemen, the very ones who conspired to train the chosen:

REV. B. F. WIGET FOR DEFENSE, MAY 25th

I am president of Gonzaga College, F Street between Tenth and Eleventh. It is about ten or eleven years since I became acquainted with Mrs. Mary E. Surratt. I know her very well, and I have always heard everyone speak very highly of her character as a lady and as a Christian. During all this acquaintance nothing has come to my knowledge respecting her character that could be called un-Christian.

I have a personal knowledge of her character as a Christian, but not as to her character for loyalty. My visits were all short and political affairs were never discussed; I was not her pastor. I first became acquainted with Mrs. Surratt from having her two sons with me. I have seen her perhaps once in six weeks. I cannot say that I remember hearing her utter a disloyal sentiment, nor do I remember hearing anyone talk about her being notoriously disloyal before her arrest. (2)

REV. FRANCES E. BOYLE FOR THE DEFENSE, MAY 25th

I am a Catholic priest. My residence is St. Peter's Church. I made the acquaintance of Mrs. Mary E. Surratt eight or ten years ago. I have always heard her well spoken of as an estimable lady. I do not undertake to say what her reputation for loyalty is. (3)

REV. CHARLES H. STONESTREET, FOR THE DEFENSE, MAY 26th

I am a pastor of Aloysius Church in this city. I first became acquainted with Mary E. Surratt twenty years ago. I have only seen her occasionally since. At the time of my acquaintance there was no question of her loyalty. (4)

Here is a most interesting point, at the Jesuit University at Georgetown in the cloister of one of the buildings there are a number of paintings of Jesuit priests connected with the institution, among whom is one labeled, Rev. Chas. H. Stonestreet. The reverend testified that at the time of his acquaintance there was no question about the lady's loyalty. No kidding! The question of loyalty had not even arisen twenty years before the war! Evidently this is an example of "Mental Reservation" of a Jesuit priest. All of them could have said: "I never questioned her loyalty." Mental reservation - (to the Holy Mother Church)

REV. PETER LANIHAN, DEFENSE, MAY 26th

> I am a Catholic priest. I reside near Beantown, Charles County, Md. I have been acquainted with Mrs. Surratt, prisoner at the bar, for about thirteen years; intimately so, for about nine years. In my estimation she is a good Christian woman and highly honorable. I have never on any occasion heard her express disloyal sentiments. I have been very familiar with her, staying at her house. (5)

In "The Doctrine of the Jesuits" by Gury, in the Eighth Precept of the Decalogue, page 156, 442-1 it reads:

> Is it not permitted to make use of the purely and properly mental restriction?" 443-2 answers: "It is sometimes permitted to make use of the mental restriction largely; that is to say, improperly mental, and also of unequivocal words, when the meaning of the speaker can be understood...Besides, the good of society demands that there should be a means to lawfully hide a secret; now there is no other way than by equivocation or restriction...One is permitted to use this restriction even under oath... 444: A culprit interrogated judicially, or not lawfully, by the judge, may answer that he has done nothing, meaning: "About which you have the right to question me."

The canon law of the Roman Church does not concede the right of any civil authority to question or cross-examine a priest. Not only that, but the canon law of the Roman Church automatically excommunicates any Catholic layman who would bring a priest into civil court. Consequently none of these priests' testimony was worth the paper it was written on in the matter of truth, and they were at perfect liberty to swear to anything they chose, or to whatever would seem best for the interest of the prisoner and their church.

This has profound implications in 2002 when there is now a crisis within the Catholic Church regarding the widespread publicity of pedophile and sex obsessed priests on a global scale and the role of the judiciary in prosecuting these "fudge packers and whoremongers" who explain to the victim that they cannot refuse the "love of God," meaning themselves, and still hope to remain true Catholics. This fact is recorded in the book by Charles Chiniquy, "*The Priest, the Woman and the Confessional*," an expose of the natural conclusion of the Vow of Celibacy or marriage, which is vastly different from a vow of *chastity*. This teaching is, however, in direct contravention of what Paul said to Timothy in his first letter to him which reads in chapter 4, "However, the Spirit says definitely that in the later periods of time some will fall away from the faith, paying attention to misleading inspired utterances and teachings of demons, by the hypocrisy of men who speak lies, marked in their conscience as with a branding iron, *forbidding to marry...*"

Gury in a footnote quotes Bessius, a Jesuit authority, as follows:

> "If a judge interrogates on an action, which must have been committed without sin, at least a moral one, the witness and the culprit are not obliged to answer according to the judge's intention."

REV. N. D. YOUNG, DEFENSE, MAY 26th

I am a Catholic priest. I reside at the pastoral home of St. Dominick's church on the Island and Sixth Street, Washington City. I became acquainted with Mary E. Surratt eight or ten years ago. My acquaintance has not been very intimate. I have occasionally seen her and visited with her. I had to pass her house about once a month, and I generally called there - sometimes stayed an hour. I have heard her spoken of with great praise. She never uttered any disloyal sentiments to me. (6)

Certainly the above testimony makes the position of Mrs. Surratt and her church beyond question, but to say that any one of these priests did not know that she was DISLOYAL TO THE UNION and entertained a deep hatred for President Lincoln, to whom she, like many others, attributed the loss of her wealth, would be incredulous in the extreme.

EXTRACTS FROM THE TESTIMONY OF

LOUIS J. WEICHMANN

Mrs. Surratt and her family are Catholics. John H. Surratt is a Catholic and was a student of divinity at the same college as myself. I met the prisoner, David E. Herold at Mrs. Surratt's house on one occasion. I also met him when we visited the theatre when Booth played Pescara; I met him at Mrs. Surratt's in the country in the spring of 1863 when I first made his acquaintance.

I met him (Herold) in the summer of 1864 at the Piscataway (Roman Catholic) church. These are the only times to my recollection I ever met him...I generally accompanied Mrs. Surratt to church on Sunday.

Surratt never intimated to me nor to anyone else to my knowledge that there was a purpose to assassinate the President. He stated to me in the presence of his sister shortly after he made the acquaintance of Booth that he was going to Europe on a cotton speculation.

> That three thousand dollars had been advanced to him by an elderly gentleman whose name he did not mention, residing somewhere in the neighborhood, that he would go to Liverpool and remain there probably two weeks to transact his business; then he would go to Nassau and from Nassau to Matamoras, Mexico and find his brother Isaac...His character at St. Charles College, Maryland, was excellent. On leaving college he shed tears and the president approaching him told him not to weep, that his conduct had been excellent during the three years he had been there, and that he would always be remembered by those in charge of the institution...
>
> I had been a companion of John H. Surratt for seven years (in answer to a question) No, I did not consider that I forfeited my friendship to him in mentioning my suspicions to Capt. Gleason. He forfeited his friendship to me by placing me in the position in which I now stand, testifying against him. I think I was more of a friend to him than he was to me. He knew I had permitted the blockade runner at the house without informing upon him, because I was his friend, but I hesitated for three days; still when my suspicions of danger to the government were aroused, I preferred the government to John Surratt. My remark to Captain Gleason about the possibility of the capture of the President was merely a casual remark. He laughed at the idea that such a thing could happen in a city guarded as Washington was." (7)

Mr. Weichmann also testified that on the night of the arrest he answered the doorbell when the detective rang it for the purpose of demanding admittance so that they might search the house. He knocked on Mrs. Surratt's door and informed her who was at the door and why they had come. Her answer was: "For God's sake, let them come in; I have been expecting them." (See page 394, Trial of Surratt by T.M Harris. This is an addendum to his work, "Assassination of Lincoln, a History of the Great Conspiracy; also supplemental affidavit of L. J. Weichmann)

Other comments by Gen. T. M. Harris are as follows:

> " 'When they inquired for her son, she said, "He is not here; I have not seen him for two weeks." This was a sufficient answer, but her guilty conscience would not let her stop here, she had to add, "There are a great many mothers who do not know where their sons are." Let us ask ourselves at this point, how many mothers in Washington City at that hour of that eventful night were lying awake expecting their houses to be searched by detectives? Our inner consciousness will unerringly dictate the answer, "Not one who was innocent of the crime" It is only necessary to say further, in regard to this defense set up of an alibi that although there is no more common defense resorted to by criminals, because there is none more easy of establishment, there was never perhaps in all the history of jurisprudence a weaker and more unsuccessful effort made to establish it, than in this defense.
>
> Probably no witness had ever been subjected to the severe grilling which Louis Weichmann received during these trials, his testimony at John H. Surratt's trial being precisely the same, and he could not be shaken by the badgering which the defense's lawyers resorted to. A lifelong persecution followed in consequence."

A relative of Weichmann's who was with him during his last illness said:

> "No one will ever know the sadness of Lou's life nor dream of how he was persecuted for simply telling the truth. The day before he died he motioned for a pencil and paper and before a witness wrote: 'To all Lovers of Truth, I Louis J. Weichmann, being of sound mind and memory, do declare that everything that I testified to at the trials of Mary E. Surratt and John H. Surratt, was the truth, the whole truth and nothing but the truth, so help me God. Louis J. Weichmann.' He died the next day." (8)

The "persecution" was that they accused him of swearing away the life of an innocent woman who had been a friend to him. For many years Mr. Weichmann was under the protection of the government where he held a public position in Philadelphia. He was practically excommunicated from the church although he in later years attended. On the other hand John H. Surratt, conspirator and assassin, was protected and supported by the priests up until his death April 22, 1916. The ground of Mary E. Surratt's grave was consecrated by the Roman Church.

Before I end this section of the book I cannot help but to call attention to God's "Wondrous ways" of just retribution. Contemplate, if you will, the small lonely headstone, labeled merely; "Mrs. Surratt" on the outskirts of the Roman Catholic cemetery in Washington, the scene of her wicked work and within a gunshot the magnificent white marble Lincoln Memorial as it stands overlooking the Potomac river, erected to the memory of the great American whom she and her priestly sponsors had tried so enthusiastically to destroy because he was the living embodiment of the triumph of Popular Government and every act of his life was a stinging rebuke to the tyrannical, corrupt system of which Mary E. Surratt, her son and the other papal assassins were legitimate products.

Reverting to the Secret Treaty of Verona, we recall that the "high contracting parties," on, "being convinced that the system of representative government is...incompatible with monarchial principles...engage mutually in the most solemn manner, to use all their efforts to put an end to the system of representative government...and to prevent its being introduced in those countries where it is not yet known." also came against freedom of the press.

"Article 2. As it cannot be doubted that the liberty of the press is the most powerful means used by the pretended supporters of the rights of nations...the high contracting parties promise reciprocally to adopt all proper measures to suppress it."

This process of destruction had gone on steadily from the assassination of several presidents of the

United States, which began in 1841, and has continued at intervals ever since.

Endnotes

1 Sourced from the U.S. National Archives
2 Ibid.
3 Ibid.
4 Ibid.
5 Ibid.
6 Ibid.
7 Ibid.
8 The Suppressed Truth about the Assassination of Abraham Lincoln, Burke McCarty, p.234 by permission

Young Pope Benedict XVI – Nazi and later to become head of the Inquisition

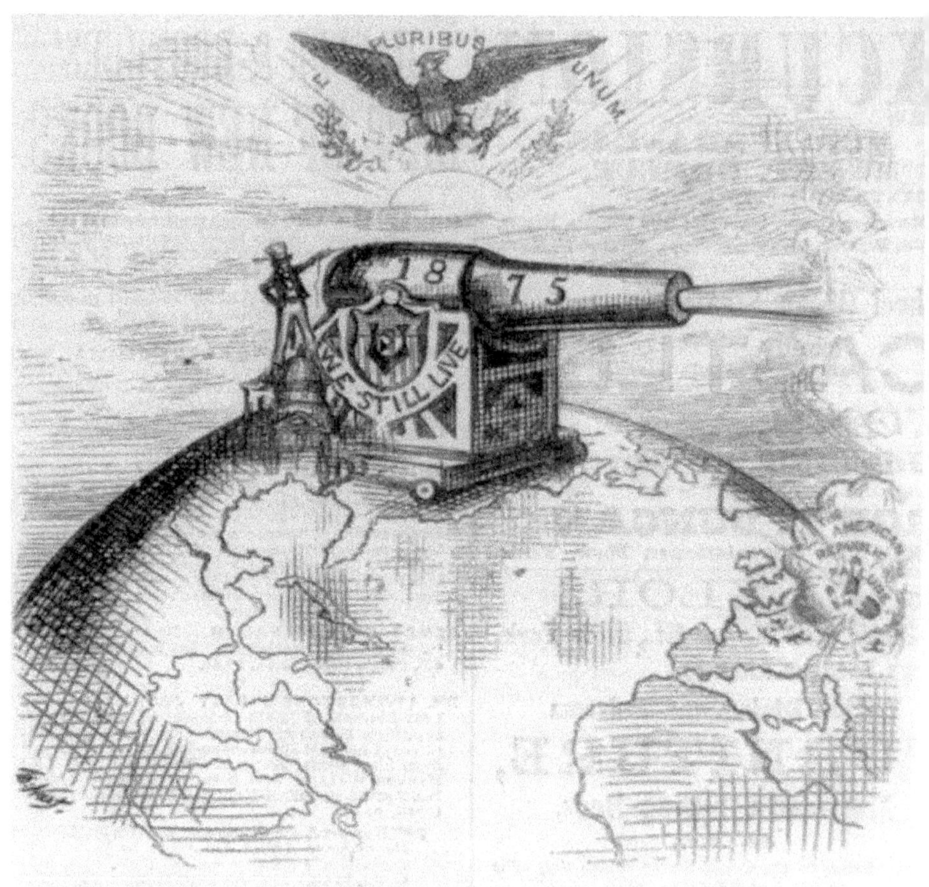

1775.—ANOTHER "SHOT HEARD ROUND THE WORLD."—1875.

EPILOGUE

Since the very first sitting of the U.S. government in 1789 the U.S. has been the sworn enemy of the Vatican led autocrats and globalists of Euope and the Americans have always stood as a bulwark against their global aspiations. But this is about to end. Why? Because of our collective national sins.

On Tuesday, April 19, 2005, 78 year old Cardinal Joseph Ratzinger of Germany, nicknamed the 'Panzer Kardinal', 'Cardinal NO' and 'God's Rottweiler', was crowned Pope Benedict XVI.

Ratzinger, whose Bavarian family were all closely tied to the Nazi Party, as were many *good* Catholics, was the Grand Inquisitor who ran the 'Office of the Holy Inquisition', now euphemistically called the 'Congregation for the Doctrine of the Faith' and is particularly intolerant toward free-thinking, freedom loving peoples everywhere. Ratzinger, in his younger days, was a keen member of the Hitler Youth under Pope Pius XII and was in charge of operating an anti-aircraft battery and later an anti-tank gun in the German Army in WWII. He claims he had no choice but to obey the Fatherland and join the army, but this is a false statement, which is evidenced by the thousands of Bible Students who put God's law first and refused to help the Nazi's. He said he defected to the Allied powers at the end of the war, but this too is in dispute.

Ratzinger is heavily political, controversial, militantly autocratic and polarizing. In the year 2000, while Pope John Paul II was busily apologizing for the past sixteen hundred years of sins against humanity, Ratzinger boldly stated with a straight face, "There is no salvation or truth outside of Rome…", thus claiming a non-negotiable monopoly on what defines "eternal values" and the right, like his Caesar predecessors, to kill anyone who disagrees, much to the consternation of 4/5 of the planet. Pope Francis has recently in 2014 re-iterated this.

Ratzinger, or Joey Ratz as some have been said to refer to him, was ordained by the Archbishop of Munich, Michael von Faulhaber – the most powerful Roman Senator in Bavaria. He is the man, who with his Jesuits at St. Michael's church, brought Hitler to power. Faulhaber's Canon was a Dominican named Patin. Patin was Himmler's cousin and an officer in the SS.

Pope Benedict XV was a war pope who oversaw the whole of WWI, which was waged almost exclusively among the nations of Christendom.

When Benito Mussolini became Italy's prime minister in 1926, he immediately began referring to his regime as the Holy Roman Empire.

It was a deeply revealing move. The Holy Roman Empire features prominently in the history of European civilization. The Oxford Dictionary defines it as the "empire set up in Western Europe following the coronation of Charlemagne as emperor in the year 800. It was created by the medieval papacy in an attempt to unite Christendom under one rule." Among historians, it is widely accepted that the Holy Roman Empire was the cyclical reincarnation of the Roman Empire—presided over in each case by the Roman Catholic Church.

Mussolini viewed his regime as the restoration of this ancient church-state combine that had repeatedly dominated the European continent. In 1929, he signed a pact with the Vatican making Roman Catholicism the only recognized religion in Fascist Italy. This agreement, known as the Lateran Treaty, delighted Pope Pius XI, who spoke of Mussolini as "a man sent by Providence." The treaty also pleased Cardinal Eugenio Pacelli, who would later become Pope Pius XII, the controversial pope during World War II.

The Lateran Treaty also got the attention of another rising authoritarian figure a little farther north, in Germany: Adolf Hitler.

Just days after Mussolini signed the Lateran Treaty in February 1929, Hitler wrote an article for the newspaper Völkischer Beobachter praising the agreement. Hitler held no political office at this time, but subsequent events reveal that he was already dreaming of the day when he would become a sort of German Mussolini, with the power to negotiate his own concordat with the Vatican.

Like Charlemagne and emperors of the Holy Roman Empire before him, Hitler knew he needed the support of the Vatican if he was to exercise full control over Germany—and eventually, Europe and the world.

Author Robert G. L. Waite, in his book *The Psychopathic God—Adolf Hitler*, comments on a telling statement of Hitler's: "'Above all, I have learned from the Jesuit order.' "Certainly the oath of direct obedience to the führer was strikingly reminiscent of the special oath that Jesuits swear to the pope. Moreover, Hitler spoke of his elite SS, who wore the sacred symbol and dressed in black, as his Society of Jesus. He also ordered SS officers to study the Spiritual Exercises of Ignatius of Loyola for training in the rigid discipline of the faith."

How many today realize just how much Adolf Hitler learned from the Vatican?

During the 1920s and 1930s, both Pius XI and Cardinal Pacelli were eager to give Hitler support in return for German protection against the spread of communism.

Like the popes of the Middle Ages, they looked to the Germanic tribes for protection.

Pacelli probably did more than anyone else outside of Germany to bring Hitler to power. First, he endorsed the Nationalist-Nazi-Catholic coalition that ushered Hitler into the German chancellorship. Second, he directed the German Catholic Center Party to vote for the Enabling Act that transformed Hitler into a dictator. Much of this history is recorded in the best-selling book *Hitler's Pope*, authored by John Cornwell. Cornwell was a devout Roman Catholic who was first inspired to write a book about Pius XII because he was upset by allegations that a Catholic pope actually aided and abetted the Third Reich. The Vatican granted him access to its archives so he could write a book defending Pius. Once inside the archives, however, Cornwell was led into a state of moral shock as he discovered the dark side of Eugenio Pacelli and his Vatican hierarchy.

When Pacelli moved from Bavaria to Rome in February 1930, he immediately began spending weeks at a time in the company of Monsignor Ludwig Kaas, leader of the German Catholic Center Party. During their time together, these two men drafted a Reich Concordat and discussed ways of bringing a government to power in Berlin that would look favorably on this concordat. Both Pius XI and Cardinal Pacelli encouraged Kaas and the Center Party leadership to explore the advantages of cooperation with Adolf Hitler and the National Socialist Party.

No one talks about this history today, but the Vatican was working to bring Hitler to power.

The Vatican's meddling eventually yielded results in January 1933, when Germany's governing coalition fell apart. It was Catholic Center Party deputy Franz von Papen who persuaded German President Paul von Hindenberg to grant Hitler the chancellorship of a Nationalist Nazi-Catholic coalition in which Papen was to be vice chancellor.

How many people remember this today? The Vatican played a central role in installing a government in Berlin that would be willing to sign an agreement binding the political destinies of Rome and Berlin!

Only a dictator, however, could grant Cardinal Pacelli the kind of concordat he was seeking. Thus, there could be no Reich Concordat unless the German Catholic Center Party and the German National People's Party lent their support to the Nazis in voting for the Enabling Act, which would grant Hitler dictatorial powers. This is why in the spring of 1933, Monsignor Kaas, in determined negotiations with both Hitler and Pacelli, pleaded with the parliamentarians of his party to vote "yes" to the act designed to confer the powers of the Reichstag to a single individual, Adolf Hitler. The Catholic parliamentarians responded to Kaas's plea, as did every other member of the Reichstag except those from the Social Democratic Party. On March 23, Hitler was granted the power to pass laws and make treaties without the future consent of the Reichstag—or anyone else in Germany. It is a fact largely ignored, or forgotton today that the Vatican was pivotal to Hitler gaining this powerful office in Germany.

As soon as he took office, Germany's dictator showed his gratitude to Pope Pius xi and Cardinal Pacelli by forming a treaty—the first of the Third Reich—with the Vatican!

German-Vatican Treaty

Cardinal Pacelli and German Vice Chancellor Franz von Papen signed the historic Reich Concordat on July 20, 1933—less than four months after Hitler was officially granted the powers of a dictator.

Notice what John Toland wrote in his book Adolf Hitler said concerning this concordat: "The church agreed to keep priest and religion out of politics while Hitler, among other things, granted complete freedom to confessional schools throughout the country, a notable victory for German Catholics. His Holiness welcomed Hitler's representative, Franz von Papen, most graciously and remarked how pleased he was that the German government now had at its head a man uncompromisingly opposed to communism and Russian nihilism in all its forms." Just as it had done so many times in the past, the Vatican gave moral and spiritual cover to a brutal dictator.

"The Vatican was so appreciative of being recognized as a full partner that it asked God to bless the Reich," Toland wrote. "On a more practical level, it ordered German bishops to swear allegiance to the National Socialist regime. The new oath concluded with these significant words: 'In the performance of my spiritual office and in my solicitude for the welfare and interest of the German Reich, I will endeavor to avoid all detrimental acts which might endanger it.'" Reading this history, one wonders how successful Hitler's Nazi Party would have been without the staunch support of the Catholic Church. Germany's ex-chancellor Heinrich Brüning, had no doubts who was primarily responsible for this nightmarish alliance. "Behind the agreement with Hitler stood not the pope, but the Vatican bureaucracy and its leader, Pacelli," Brüning said in 1935. "He visualized an authoritarian state and an authoritarian church directed by the Vatican bureaucracy, the two to conclude an eternal league with one another."

Read that powerful and condemning admission again.

And remember, Cardinal Pacelli—the man former Chancellor Brüning said was more responsible than any other in bringing Hitler to power—later became Pope Pius XII, the pope during the Second World War! Most Catholics today do not acknowledge Hitler's connection with Catholicism, but the truth is that Hitler and his cabal of leaders worked together with the Vatican hierarchy to resurrect the Holy Roman Empire.

In fact, without the Vatican's assistance, Hitler very likely would never have gained ultimate power over Germany!

During a cabinet meeting held six days before the signing of the Reich Concordat in 1933, Hitler expressed the opinion that the upcoming concordat had created an atmosphere of confidence that would be "especially significant in the urgent struggle against international Jewry."

Think about that statement. Hitler knew that an alliance with the Catholic Church would be advantageous to his "urgent struggle against international Jewry." Hitler obviously considered the Vatican an enemy of the Jews, and therefore an ally to his cause. Surely he had good reason to believe this.

There is no evidence Cardinal Pacelli even blinked an eye at Hitler's horrific ambitions. Rather, as John Cornwell brings out in Hitler's Pope, Pacelli had a habit of ignoring the plight of the Jews and turning a blind eye to other Nazi atrocities.

One example Cornwell uses to prove his point is particularly telling. It happened toward the end of the war. Pacelli—who was crowned Pope Pius xii in 1939—had been receiving information about Hitler's Final Solution (a strategy to eradicate the Jewish race) throughout 1942.

Jewish groups and Allied officials had repeatedly urged him to publicly condemn Nazi savagery. Under increasing pressure, Pius used a December 1942 radio address to refer to the many thousands who "sometimes only by reason of their nationality or race are marked down for death or gradual extinction." That was Pius xii's strongest objection to Hitler's genocidal rampage. He failed to even mention the führer by name. He made no mention of Nazis or Jews.

In October 1943, ten months after Pius's radio address, 365 of Hitler's SS troops entered Rome's old ghetto and started arresting Italian Jews. They rounded up 1,060 of them and transported them to a building called Collegio Militare—located less than half a mile from the Vatican.

German trucks carrying the prisoners even drove by St. Peter's Square so drivers could see the famous church.

According to Cornwell, Pope Pius was one of the first to be made aware of the Jewish arrests. The Jews were kept at the holding center for two days—right under the pope's nose—before boarding cattle cars to Auschwitz, where 80 percent of them were gassed within a week. The rest became slave laborers.

During the Jews' two-night confinement down street from the Vatican, the pope did nothing. The most powerful religious man in the world, commanding the allegiance of more than a half-billion Christians at that time, remained silent when a simple protest probably would likely have saved 1,045 lives. Only 15 of the 1,060 survived the war.

Television journalist Ed Bradley recounted these events during a 60 Minutes episode on March 19, 2000.

Bradley interviewed one of the Jewish survivors, who asked, "Didn't the pope know where they were taking us? Didn't he ask himself where those railroad tracks ended up? We were right under his window, but his voice wasn't lifted. Nobody came, not even to save a child."

Priest Peter Gumpel, Vatican representative, attempted to answer the victim's questions, saying the pope couldn't leave the Vatican because it was surrounded by German troops. He might have been arrested, Gumpel said. In quick reply, Bradley asked, "But wouldn't that be the kind of action that a true saint would have taken? Wouldn't that have been what Christ would have done?" Gumpel stuttered in his response, saying he did not know what Christ would have done.

But this matter goes far beyond just defending Pius XII in the face of harsh criticism. Gumpel is one of the Vatican's senior saint-makers, who happens to be in charge of Pope Pius XII's beatification process, the final hurdle to being named a saint. For 30 years he has been researching Pius's life to see if the man is worthy of sainthood. Put another way, his job is to find any evidence that would preclude Pius from beatification. He says he hasn't found any!

Near the end of his research, Gumpel told 60 Minutes he is "totally convinced that [Pius] did what he could [to help Jews during World War II], that he was a holy person and that he should be beatified." Asked if Cornwell's research in Hitler's Pope would have any bearing on the Vatican's final decision, Gumpel said it would "have no effect whatsoever because it's totally worthless from a historical point of view."

To cast aside Cornwell's book as totally worthless is remarkable, considering the depth of his research and the unprecedented access he had to the Vatican's own documents.

In July 1997, a United States Treasury document was published accusing the Vatican of hoarding Holocaust gold for the Croatian Nazi puppet regime during and after World War II. The Vatican dismissed the accusation as ridiculous. But then, when pressured by Jewish organizations to open its archives (which have been closed for 100 years) to dispel rumors of Nazi sympathies, the Vatican refused. Why? Could it be that it has something to hide?

In their book *Unholy Trinity*, Mark Aarons and John Loftus contend that the Vatican does have something to hide. Mark Aarons is an international award-winning investigative reporter and author of several books on intelligence-related issues. Based in Australia, he exposed war criminals in that country and prompted changes to Australian federal law. John Loftus, author of four intelligence-related history books, is the former chief prosecutor of the U.S. Justice Department's Nazi War Crimes Unit.

As such, he once held some of the highest security clearances in the world. These men provide substantial documentation for a version of events the Vatican would surely prefer buried.

During World War II, Germany devoted a lot of energy to conquering the Balkans. To do this, it brandished Roman Catholic Croatia as its chief weapon of destruction.

According to Aarons and Loftus, during the war, many Serbs were butchered by the Croats using medieval methods. "Eyes had been gouged out," they wrote, "limbs severed, intestines and other internal organs ripped from the bodies of the living. Some were slaughtered like beasts, their throats cut from ear to ear with special knives. Others died from blows to their heads with sledgehammers. Many more were simply burned alive."

Much more alarming, however, is that during this time when Croatian fascists were slaughtering Serbs, Croatian officials enjoyed a "special relationship" with the pope. Aarons and Loftus document how these atrocities were already underway when Pope Pius XII met with Ante Pavelic, Croatia's leader, in April 1941. The pope agreed to meet with Pavelic again in May 1943, by which time the Nazi atrocities against the Serbs were irrefutably known. (One Italian journalist interviewed Pavelic in his home and was shocked to find a large bowl of Serbian eyes the fascist leader had been collecting.) Yet, according to *Unholy Trinity*, "Pius himself promised to give Pavelic his personal blessing again. By this time, the Holy See possessed abundant evidence of the atrocities committed by his regime."

Any right-thinking person ought to ask why the highest officials in the Catholic Church, including the pope, would associate with and even protect Croatian fascists.

Is that the kind of history more "conservative" Vatican officials today want to conceal?

The Vatican's connection with this sordid history went beyond a simple blessing for murderous officials from the pope. As the war wound down and victory slipped from Germany's grip, the Vatican actually aided many of the worst criminals of the age—by smuggling them to safety.

Intelligence sources have confirmed that high-ranking ministers, civil servants, even Ante Pavelic himself, were able to disappear into thin air with help from the Vatican's "ratlines"—a postwar operation to protect Nazi leaders. At the time, the Vatican labeled these escapees "refugees."

But they were fascists who were helping Hitler's regime!

"For fugitive Nazis, all roads led to Rome," Aarons and Loftus wrote. "It is absurd to believe that 30,000 fugitive Nazis escaped to South America on the few U-Boats remaining at the end of the war, or that they all made their own travel arrangements," they wrote. "Draganovic's Ratline [the name given to the Vatican's smuggling operation] was truly professional, ensuring that many guilty war criminals reached safe havens. Often they did not end up in the remote jungles of South America, but settled instead in Britain, Canada, Australia and the United States. ..."The Vatican has consistently claimed that they were unaware of the identity of those who were undeserving of their humanitarian assistance. But some influential priests not only knew who the Nazis were, they actively sought them out and provided extra-special treatment."

One of the most ruthlessly efficient Nazi officials, Franz Stangl, commandant of the Treblinka extermination camp, came to Rome in 1948. He was looking for Roman Catholic Bishop Alois Hudal, rector of one of three seminaries for German priests in Rome. Hudal was well known throughout the Nazi underground. "Stangl described the power and influence of Hudal's extensive smuggling network for fugitive Nazis," Aarons and Loftus wrote.

Stangl later testified that Hudal had arranged "quarters in Rome where I was to stay till my papers came through. And he gave me a bit more money—I had almost nothing left." After several weeks, Hudal "called me in and gave me my new passport—a Red Cross Passport ...[he] got me an entrance visa to Syria and a job in a textile mill in Damascus, and he gave me a ticket for the ship.

So I went to Syria." ...Monsignor Karl Bayer, Rome director for Catholic relief organization Caritas, later admitted, "Perhaps Hudal did get batches of passports for these particular people." He said that any money Hudal gave Stangl would have come from Vatican funds: "The pope did provide money for this; in driblets sometimes, but it did come."

Simon Wiesenthal was the man responsible for Stangl's eventual recapture in Brazil in 1967. He is convinced that Bishop Hudal was also behind the smuggling of the most famous war criminal of World War II, "the architect of the Holocaust," Adolf Eichmann. Eichmann escaped from Europe after the war and remained hidden for 15 years before being captured. "Wiesenthal believes that Hudal equipped Eichmann with a new identity as a Croatian refugee called 'Richard Klement,' and sent him to Genoa," Aarons and Loftus wrote. "There Eichmann was apparently hidden in a monastery under Archbishop Siri's charitable control, before finally being smuggled to South America." All of Eichmann's traveling expenses to South America were paid by Caritas, a Catholic relief organization.

"Official Vatican historian Father Robert Graham admits that Hudal might have helped 'a handful, a mere handful of Nazi war criminals to escape,'" they wrote.

"When Eichmann was arrested it was alleged he passed through Rome and got some help from Bishop Hudal.

Hudal was asked about this and said, 'I don't know, I helped a lot of people and Eichmann may have been among them.' …

"If Eichmann was a case of unauthorized assistance, he was certainly not the only instance. Hudal seemed to make mistakes with frightening regularity. Wiesenthal recalls, 'During my search for Eichmann I found out that many [war criminals] were living in monasteries, equipped by Hudal with false documents,' showing they were refugees.

One point is certain: Many war criminals who escaped to South America have gratefully acknowledged that they owed their freedom to the Austrian-born bishop.

Bishop Hudal was known to be supportive of the Nazis. When he traveled to address German-speaking Catholics in the 1930s, he openly backed Adolf Hitler. In a speech in Rome he said the philosophies of the German Reich "accord both with Christian and national values."

He even published a treatise in 1936 called The Foundations of National Socialism, officially sanctioned by the church, praising the Nazis. "Apparently Hudal's high Nazi profile did not harm his Vatican career," Aarons and Loftus wrote. "[A]s Hudal's views grew more stridently and publicly pro-Nazi, nothing was done either to discipline or remove him from this powerful post. Instead the Vatican promoted him in une 1933 from priest to titular bishop, an extremely rare honor for a relatively lowly rector of a teaching college. ...

"Father Jacob Weinbacher ... has no doubt that 'Hudal was very close to [Pope] Pius XII ... they were friends.' ... Far from being just another anonymous cleric on the fringes of the Vatican, 'Hudal may well have been the sounding board for the pope in the German-speaking countries.'"

When it became clear that Germany would lose the war, Hudal determined to do all he could to undermine the Allied attempts to stamp out Nazism. "I felt duty bound after 1945 to devote my whole charitable work mainly to former National Socialists and fascists, especially to so-called 'war criminals,'" he said. Aarons and Loftus conclude: "Hudal's self-confessed activities are all the more controversial because he operated with the full authority of the Vatican."

Germany holds a cache of sealed files detailing this history and is fighting to keep it secret despite critics'objections. Nevertheless, what facts are available reveal that the Vatican was deeply involved with the Germans in World War II. There is simply no other explanation.

Roman Catholic Nazi rally 1938 – Church of Our Lady, Nuremburg. Hitler had just removed the Crown Jewels of Charlemagne's Holy Roman Empire from Vienna, Austria to have them blessed and dedicated in their new home of Nuremburg in Bavaria, Germany…the headquarters of the Military Company of Jesus.

Notice the Illuminati/Chaldean/Assyrian, 'Eye of Horus' pyramid design at the front of the building.

But most people continue to ignore the truth—to their own great peril.

The union of Church and State in any form, whether "Christian" or otherwise, is indeed a dangerous creature.

On the German Army belt buckles during both world wars we saw the inscription, Gott Mit Uns, (English translation) "God is on our side." All call for "holy wars" of one type or another.

On August 23, 2005 *Masonic Televangelist Pat Robertson* announced and promoted, much to the horror of honest and true Christians worldwide, what amounted to a Christian Fatwa, that being the necessity of assassinating Venezuelan President Hugo Chavez, thus throwing off the mask of Christian goodwill and benevolence and planting himself firmly in the camp of Jesuit controlled Pope Benedict in his modern crusade against Islam and everything not in accord with Vatican global policy. Completely forgetting the Commandment "You must not kill..." and the admonition by Jesus to love your enemies he exclaimed,

> "We have the ability to take him [Chavez] out, and I think the time has come that we exercise that ability. We don't need another $200-billion war to get rid of one, you know, strong-arm dictator. It's a whole lot easier to have some of the covert operatives do the job and then get it over with."

In the book "*The Secret History of the Jesuits*" by Edmund Paris, p.163, He quotes a communiqué of the Vatican via Madrid as follows:

> "Adolph Hitler, Son of the Catholic Church, died while defending Christianity. It is therefore understandable that words cannot be found to lament over his death, when so many were found to exalt his life. Over his mortal remains stands his victorious moral figure. With the palm of the martyr, God gives Hitler the laurels of victory." Paris stated, "This funeral oration of the Nazi chief, a challenge to the victorious allies, is voiced by the Holy See itself, under the cover of Franco's press."

Autocratically operated religions, when they wish to establish and exert control over a secular country, always attempt to operate through the auspices of another autocrat. If the leader of the country holds too much power in his office, he can effectively rule as a dictator, or the closest thing to it. The ones who can control the leader can then control the people of the nation.

Today [2005] there are over 600 clandestine prison camps in the United States, all fully operational and ready to receive prisoners. They are all staffed and even surrounded by full-time guards. But they are empty. These camps are to be operated by FEMA [Federal Emergency Management Agency] should Martial Law need to be implemented in the United States.

The *Rex 84 Program* was established on the premise that if a mass exodus of illegal aliens crossed the Mexican/U.S. border, they would be quickly rounded up and detained in detention centers by FEMA. Rex 84 allowed many military bases to be closed down and to be turned into prisons.

Operation Cable Splicer and ***Operation Garden Plot*** are the two sub programs that will be implemented once the ***Rex 84*** program is initiated for its proper purpose. ***Garden Plot*** is the program to control the population. ***Cable Splicer*** is the program for an orderly takeover of the state and local governments by the Federal government. FEMA is the executive arm of the coming police state and thus will head up all operations. The Presidential Executive Orders already listed on the Federal Register also are part of the legal framework for this operation.

The camps all have railroad facilities as well as roads leading to and from the detention facilities. Many also have an airport nearby. The majority of the camps can house a population of 20,000 prisoners. Currently, the largest of these facilities is just outside of Fairbanks, Alaska. The Alaskan facility is a massive mental health facility and can hold approximately two million people.

According to an anonymous friend living in Southern California, who wrote an article on his discoveries of such camps he says,

> "Over the last couple of months several of us have investigated three soon-to-be prison camps in the Southern California area. We had heard about these sites and wanted to see them for ourselves.
>
> The first one we observed was in Palmdale, California. It is not operating as a prison at the moment but is masquerading as part of a water facility. Now why would there be a facility of this nature out in the middle of nowhere with absolutely no prisoners? The fences that run for miles around this large facility all point inward, and there are large mounds of dirt and dry moat surrounding the central area so the inside area is not visible from the road. There are three large loading docks facing the entrance that can be observed from the road. What are these massive docks going to be used for?
>
> We observed white vans patrolling the area and one came out and greeted us with a friendly wave and

followed us until we had driven safely beyond the area. What would have happened had we decided to enter the open gate or ask questions?

This facility is across the street from the Palmdale Water Department. The area around the Water Department has fences pointing outward, to keep people out of the dangerous area so as not to drown. Yet, across the street, the fences all point inward. Why? To keep people in? What people? Who are going to be its occupants?

There are also signs posted every 50 feet stating: State of California Trespassing Loitering Forbidden By Law Section 555 California Penal Code.

The sign at the entrance says: Pearblossom Operations and Maintenance Subcenter Receiving Department, 34534 116th Street East. There is also a guard shack located at the entrance.

We didn't venture into this facility, but did circle around it to see if there was anything else visible from the road. We saw miles of fences with the tops pointed inward. There is a railroad track that runs next to the perimeter of this fenced area. The loading docks are large enough to hold railroad cars. The area could easily fit 100,000 people.

Another site is located in Brand Park in Glendale. There are newly constructed fences (all outfitted with new wiring that point inward). The fences surround a dry reservoir. There are also new buildings situated in the area. We questioned the idea that there were four armed military personnel walking the park. Since when does a public park need armed guards?

A third site visited was in the San Fernando Valley, adjacent to the Water District. Again, the area around the actual Water District had fences logically pointing out (to keep people out of the area). And the rest of the adjacent area which went on for several miles was ringed with fences and barbed wire facing inward (to keep people in?) Also, interesting was the fact that the addition to the tops of the fences were fairly new as not one sign of rust was on them. Within the grounds was a huge building that the guard said was a training range for policemen. There were newly constructed roads, new gray military looking buildings, and a landing strip. For what? Police cars were constantly patrolling the several mile perimeter of the area.

From the parking lot of the Odyssey Restaurant a better view could be taken of the area that was hidden from sight from the highway. There was an area that contained about 100 black boxes that looked like railroad cars. We had heard that loads of railroad cars have been manufactured in Oregon outfitted with shackles. From our position it was hard to determine if these were of that nature.

In searching the internet, I have discovered that there are about 600 of these prison sites around the country (and more literally popping up overnight as they work all night). They are manned but are sitting empty. We continuously hear that our current prisons are overcrowded, but what about these? What are they for? What is going to be the kick-off point to put these into full operation?"

On the *CBC* television news, April 15th, 2005, *Congressman Tom Tancredo R-Co* said,

"If we have another event like 9/11 we will pass stuff here that will make the Patriot Act look like a Sunday afternoon tea party..."

In the U.S. publication *The Christian Century,* on September 25, 1919, page 7, it read:

"The League of Nations [later to become the United Nations] idea is the extension to international relationships of the idea of the Kingdom of God as a world order of good will.... it is the thing all Christians pray for when they say, 'Thy Kingdom come.'"

Today there is a permanent seat in the United Nations which is reserved for the spiritual direction of this body and the Catholic Church by means of Vatican representation has made it known that she wishes to be that permanent head to the exclusion of all other faiths.

In an interview with the Jesuit General, Peter-Hans Kolvenbach, by the Spanish Catholic weekly magazine, *Alpha Y Omega* No. 369, September 25, 2003, Mr. Kolvenbach stated;

"As a result of the attack carried out on September 11th large-scale violence has become more painful, inhumane and unjust. This has triggered a distressing spiral of attacks and counter-attacks, which are bringing about considerable material losses, the weakening of human rights, and above all, indiscriminate deaths. Out of these physical and moral ruins, a ***new world order*** should emerge. [emphasis added] That is what we thought after experiencing the last world war, but the facts have belied the *hopes* we then had. That makes it difficult to *dream* of a ***new international order*** this time. However we must all *strive to define it* and *make it come true*. For us, Christians, the message of fraternity and solidarity to which the Lord summons us in the gospel is the primary incentive driving us to work for a more humane world – and hence, for a world that is more divine – one which goes beyond merely political structures. It is comforting that despite the reserve shown by certain important nations, ***the United Nations is recognized as an important political alternative."*** [emphasis added]

In other words the salvation of humanity rests in the obliteration of individual autonomous and independent nations, with their domestic laws, education and political bodies and the merging of these nations under the sole and supreme auspices of the U.N. Any who resist this human created, satanically inspired and therefore bound to fail globalization are, according to Roman canon law, worthy of death.

On January 27, 2013, CBS Sunday Morning aired a commentary by a constitutional law professor suggesting that for America to solve its many problems, it needs to abandon the Constitution.

"If we are to take back our own country, we have to start making decisions for ourselves, and stop deferring to an ancient and outdated document," said Louis Michael Seidman. This man teaches constitutional law at Georgetown University Law Center in Washington, D.C., and was speaking on one of the big three television networks.

In his most recent book, On Constitutional Disobedience, Seidman asked, "Why should we care about what the Constitution says? Should we feel obligated to obey it? How can we make decisions today based on a document created more than 200 years ago?"

This type of anti-Constitution reasoning is suddenly becoming quite popular. Do you know why? It is because of the Obama administration. It is taking actions just about every week that raise constitutional questions and that threaten to undermine America's foundational document.

ions are able to show the clearest possible evidence of being authorized so to collect.

Subscribers failing to get their papers regularly will confer a favor by notifying the publisher immediately, by postal card or otherwise.

THURSDAY, AUGUST 31 1893

ROMANISM AND THE REPUBLIC.

It seems to be necessary to expose the designs of Rome and to maintain the fight against the arrogant claims of the Papal system, since many of our public men will insist upon it that there is nothing to fear from this political machine. Even the President of the United States has seen fit to address a letter of congratulations to the Pope, and Mr. Cleveland goes so far as to say, "The pleasure attending this expression of my felicitations is much enhanced by the remembrance that His Holiness has always manifested a lively interest in the prosperity of the United States *and great admiration for our political institutions.*" The italics are ours. We are greatly surprised that a man of common sense, as the President appears to be, should intimate that he believes the Pope entertains a sincere admiration for our free institutions. The President shakes the faith of intelligent people in his good sense, and they do not wish to feel that the Chief Magistrate of the nation is indulging in hyperbole or hypocrisy, trying to tickle the fancy of the Pope.

But we get more puzzled over the matter when we read the closing paragraph of Grover's letter, in which he refers to "the kindnes with which His Holiness lately accepted a copy of the Constitution of the United States." If Mr. Leo has carefully read and studied that copy of our Constitution he certainly is a remarkable man if he can rise from its perusal with "a great admiration for our political institutions," for the Constitution of this Government is diametrically opposin to render obedience." Notice the arrogance in that sentence! Our Lord and Saviour never vested the least authority in the usurper at Rome, and we all know that the laws of the Republic continually set at naught the Pope's authority; but the wicked system of Romanism dare not resist the civil laws, knowing that it would be the most silly and unfortunate thing (for itself) to do. Rome is only waiting for an opportunity to enforce its claims. It is waiting the chance to put its energy in operation against civil governments and "heretics," as was done in the days of the Inquisition. Henry Charles Lea, in the *Forum*, February, 1890, said: "We can scarce hope that the time will not come when our Catholic fellow-citizens will be put to the strain of electing between the allegiance due to the State and that due to the Church."

The revised statutes of the United States declare: "The alien seeking citizenship must make oath to renounce forever all allegiance and fidelity to any foreign prince, potentate, state or sovereignty, in particular that to which he has been subject." Now, the Canon Law says: "No oaths are to be kept if they are against the interests of the Church of Rome." And again: "Oaths which are against the Church of Rome, are not to be called oaths, but perjuries." In a book used in Romish schools and colleges, prepared by a priest, F. X. Schouppe, and endorsed by Cardinal Manning, we read, "The civil laws are binding on the conscience only so long as they are conformable to the rights of the Catholic Church." This is a very elastic law, for no one can tell what Rome will not claim as her "rights." In fact, we all know that Rome claims to be supreme, and even Gladstone once held that the allegiance demanded by the Pope is inconsistent with good citizenship.

The Constitution of the United

cepted a copy of the Constitution of the United States." If Mr. Leo has carefully read and studied that copy of our Constitution he certainly is a remarkable man if he can rise from its perusal with "a great admiration for our political institutions," for the Constitution of this Government is diametrically opposed to the Canon Law of the Roman apostocy, and it rebukes the Pope's arrogant claims at every step.

We will endeavor briefly to point out the world-wide difference between Romanism and our popular form of government. In the second section of Article VI., of the Constitution it is declared: "This Constitution and the laws of the United States which shall be made in pursuance thereof . . . . . *shall be the supreme law of the land.*" The Canon Law of the Roman Church is essentially the constitution of that Church, binding upon Romanists everywhere. A part of this Canon Law is a bull published by Pope Benedict XIV., in which it is decreed that those who refuse to obey *any* "commands of the Court of Rome, if they be ecclesiastics, are *ipso facto* suspended from their orders and offices; and, if they are laymen, are smitten with excommunication."

The bull *Unam Sanctam* of

of the Catholic Church." This is a very elastic law, for no one can tell what Rome will not claim as her "rights." In fact, we all know that Rome claims to be supreme, and even Gladstone once held that the allegiance demanded by the Pope is inconsistent with good citizenship.

The Constitution of the United States guarantees liberty of conscience. The first amendment to that important document says: "Congress shall make no law respecting an establishment of religion or prohibiting the free exercise thereof." Pope Pius IX. in his Syllabus of Errors, declared it to be an error that, "Every man is free to embrace and profess the religion he shall believe true, guided by the light of reason." His predecessor, Gregory XVI., called liberty of conscience a *deliramentum*, that is, insanity. When, in 1855, Mexico adopted a constitution embodying the principles of religious toleration and subjected the clergy to the secular courts, Pius IX. on December 15th, 1856, annulled the constitution and forbade obedience to it. He did the same thing with Spain, July, 1855. Even a powerful empire like that of Austria fared no better when, in December, 1867, it decreed liberty of conscience and of the press, and in May, 1868, adopted a law of civil marriage; for

I find it intriguing that CBS broadcast this commentary right at the beginning of the second term of the most radically liberal president the United States has ever seen. This administration is very hostile to the Constitution, and the media agree. Can you imagine the media urging President Bush to bypass the Constitution to complete his agenda?

Last September, a panel of experts presented a list to the House Judiciary Committee of how President Obama is exceeding his constitutional constraints. Humanevents.com summarized the panel's findings this way:

"As president, Barack Obama has made a habit of bypassing or ignoring constitutional limitations on his power" (Sept. 12, 2012).

Here are some of the examples the panel gave: his abuse of executive power in connection with the Fast and Furious scandal; his decision to stop enforcing parts of America's immigration law; and his authorization of military action in Libya in 2011 without first consulting Congress. Some legislators are calling for legal action against the president for that last decision.

One of the panel's main points was how last year, the president sidestepped the Senate and made some unilateral "recess" appointments when the Senate was not even in recess. Recently a federal court ruled that this move was unconstitutional.

Sen. Mike Lee, a noted constitutional scholar in Congress, "told the committee that Obama's abuse of power by making recess appointments while the Senate was not actually in recess was a historic first" (ibid). *This has never happened before in U.S. history!*

This administration is pushing past the limits of executive power all the time. The New York Times wrote in April 2012,

"[I]ncreasingly in recent months, the administration has been seeking ways to act without Congress."

Even the president's allies in the media know this is happening. But very little is being done to stop it! How many people are even paying attention?

Do you realize how deadly dangerous this trend of lawlessness is? Very few people do. But it gives profound insight into the real nature of the threat facing America today.

Executive Orders

In his State of the Union address in February, President Obama said this: "I urge this Congress to pursue a bipartisan, market-based solution to climate change .... But if Congress won't act soon to protect future generations, I will. I will direct my cabinet to come up with executive actions we can take, now and in the future ...."

The president is taking these types of actions with greater and greater frequency. Here is what the Washington Post wrote just a couple of days before the president's address:

"President Obama is considering a series of new executive actions aimed at working around a recalcitrant Congress, including policies that could allow struggling homeowners to refinance their mortgages, provide new protections for gays and lesbians, make buildings more energy-efficient and toughen regulations for coal-fired power plants, according to people outside the White House involved in discussions on the issues. ...

"The moves underscore Obama's increasingly aggressive use of executive authority, including 23 administrative actions on gun violence last month and previous orders that delayed deportations of young illegal immigrants and will lower student loan payments.

"These and other potential actions suggest that Obama is likely to rely heavily on executive powers to set domestic policy in his second term" (February 10).

People's minds are getting conditioned to executive orders. That is all primarily intended to circumvent Congress and the Constitution. That is the aim.

President Obama's use of drones has come under criticism because it is also expanding his grip on power. First, he has launched five times more drone strikes than President Bush did, and in half the time. But critics are especially concerned that, according to a 16-page document the Department of Justice leaked to NBC, *<u>the administration believes it is above the law</u>*

and has power to kill any American citizens it considers a threat.

Here is what Judge Andrew Napolitano wrote in the Washington Times:

"Mr. Obama has argued that he can kill Americans whose deaths he believes will keep us all safer, without any due process whatsoever. No law authorizes that. His attorney general has argued that the president's careful consideration of each target and the narrow use of deadly force are an adequate and constitutional substitute for due process. No court has ever approved that."

Napolitano points out that this practice violates state and federal laws, executive orders prohibiting assassinations, language in the Declaration of Independence, and the Constitution.

Perhaps many or even most of the people being targeted in these attacks are threats to the United States. But I am deeply troubled by an administration so disdainful of the law that it is supposed to uphold!

This trend toward lawlessness is deadly! And I guarantee, based on biblical prophecy, that it is going to get far worse.

What is behind this push to undermine the law? This is the spiritual dimension we need to see.

The Greek Empire tried to establish the rule of law. It failed and its empire collapsed. The Roman Empire also tried to build a society based on law. It was unable to do so and the Roman Empire fell. Many other empires experienced the same failure.

The famous British historian Paul Johnson wrote an article titled "*No Law Without Order, No Freedom Without Law.*" It was printed in the Sunday Telegraph, Dec. 26, 1999. In it he wrote, "The rule of law, as distinct from the rule of a person, or class or people, and as opposed to the rule of force, is an abstract, sophisticated concept. It is mighty difficult to achieve. But until it is achieved, and established in the public mind with such vehemence that masses of individuals are prepared to die to uphold it, no other form of progress can be regarded as secure. The Greeks had tried to establish the rule of law but failed. The Romans had succeeded under their republic but Caesar and his successors had destroyed it. The essence of the rule of law is its impersonality, omnipotence and ubiquity. It is the same law for everyone, everywhere—kings, emperors, high priests, the state itself, are subject to it. If exceptions are made, the rule of law begins to collapse—that was the grand lesson of antiquity."

Yes, "that was the grand lesson" of history. But have we learned that lesson? Failure to do so means we pay the supreme sacrifice: loss of our republic.

The continual problem of man has been his failure to learn from history.

Are "masses of individuals ... prepared to die" to uphold America's rule of law? Mr. Johnson states that this is our only security!

In many cases our people are confused about what the law is. And many others want to change our laws, including our constitutional law.

Who is going to be willing to die for such confusion? Will such a deeply divided people sacrifice their lives for our republic and the rule of law?

Our generals in Britain and America know that we lack the will to win any hard-fought battle—even if it directly relates to our own freedom. For example, we had to be bombed into World War II. Even one of the most diabolical leaders in history, Adolf Hitler, could not rouse us to fight until we were bombed by Japan. And we are much more isolationist today.

We are not prepared to die to defend our security as we were in our past. This is the supreme sign that our will has been broken—and that our republic cannot stand.

Our forefathers were willing to die to establish the rule of law. Many Americans died in the Civil War to sustain our constitutional law.

How different they were from our people today!

Our Forefathers' Goal

Early immigrants who came to this land were often persecuted in the countries they left. They usually lacked religious freedom.

"[B]oth in Virginia and in New England to the north, the colonists were determined, God-fearing men," Mr. Johnson wrote, "often in search of a religious toleration denied them at home, who brought their families and were anxious to farm and establish permanent settlements. They put political and religious freedom before riches .... Thus took shape the economic dynamo that eventually became the United States—an experiment designed to establish the rule of God on Earth ..." (ibid).

What a goal. *They planned to establish the rule of God on Earth! That means they had the goal of each person keeping the Ten Commandments of God—the basis of all righteous law.*

How many Americans are willing to face that reality? Not many. Because then we would have to see that we often fight not to establish law, but to promote lawlessness!

Consider some statements from the Founding Fathers. In his first inaugural, President George Washington said,

"The foundations of our national policy will be laid in the pure and immutable principles of private morality."

And in his famous farewell address, he said,

"Of all the dispositions and habits which lead to political prosperity, religion and morality are indispensable supports."

Without religion and morality, Washington knew the American experiment was doomed to fail. John Adams backed him up: "Statesmen may plan and speculate for liberty, but it is religion and morality alone which can establish the principles upon which freedom can securely stand." Religion and morality are firmly rooted in divine law.

In 1954, Supreme Court Chief Justice Earl Warren wrote, "I believe the entire Bill of Rights came into being because of the knowledge our forefathers had of the Bible and their belief in it."

What political or religious leaders would make such statements as these men did? Even the politicians who established our republic were more spiritual than most of our religious leaders today!

The Constitution is the foundation of our republic. And the Ten Commandments were, in many ways, the foundation of the Constitution. Our forefathers believed that if we didn't keep God's Ten Commandments, our republic would collapse!

We can't afford to take the words of our founders lightly, if we want to see our nation stand.

It was much harder for our Founding Fathers to spill streams of blood winning our freedom, and to create and establish our constitutional law, than it is for us just to maintain it! So we ought to respect our Founding Fathers above ourselves. But we are too vain and arrogant to see how profoundly strong they were and how pathetically shallow and weak we are.

Noble Constitution

The Constitution was based to a great extent on God's law. That is why I believe it is the most noble document ever written by a government of this world.

What a rare document it is. Our forefathers had the awesome opportunity to establish the rule of God in the wealthiest country ever. So they established a Constitution to protect all of us from the extremes of human reason. Tyrants, unjust judges and biased leaders were controlled by this law.

Did our Founding Fathers know that the Bible interprets itself? To some extent, I believe they did. And they probably patterned the Constitution after the Bible, in that sense. The Constitution is a document that interprets itself probably better than any book or document other than the Bible.

We see indescribable confusion about the Bible today. Why? Because people won't let it interpret itself!

We received some foundational direction from Britain's Magna Carta. But Britain has no Constitution.

Our persecuted forefathers wanted their protection spelled out in detail. They had suffered intensely at the hands of tyrants. Such tribulation deepens a people's understanding about the value of freedom.

Will we have to experience indescribable tribulation before we can appreciate our freedom, which is given to us by the rule of law?

Modern secularists love to present Franklin as a nonreligious Deist who wanted to keep Christianity out of the public domain ... Like all the Founders, [he] did not want an official, state church like the nations of Europe. He did, however, want a society whose populace would be governed by Christian principles of virtue and morality.

In a letter dated July 2, 1756, Benjamin Franklin presented a proposal to George Whitefield, the most famous preacher of the Great Awakening, that they partner together to establish a Christian colony "in the Ohio," which was frontier country at the time.

In the letter, Franklin expressed confidence that God would give them success in such a project, "If we undertook it with a sincere regard to His honor." He wrote:

"I imagine we could do it effectually and without putting the nation at too much expense. What a glorious thing it would be, to settle in that fine country a large strong body of religious [Christian] and industrious people! What a security to the other colonies; and advantage to Britain, by increasing her people, territory, strength and commerce. Might it not greatly facilitate the introduction of pure religion among the heathen, if we could, by such a colony, show them a better sample of Christians...?" (Hyatt, The Faith and Vision of Benjamin Franklin, 40)

Friends to the Very End

Franklin had become friends with Whitefield 18 years prior to this when Whitefield visited Philadelphia and preached to massive outdoor crowds. Franklin attended the meetings and was attracted to this young, fiery revivalist who was nine years his junior. It proved to be the beginning of a close, life-long friendship.

Franklin and Whitefield became business partners with Franklin printing and distributing Whitefield's journals and sermons and advising him in business matters. Whitefield stayed in Franklin's home on at least one of his visits to Philadelphia and Franklin wrote to his brother in Boston, "Whitefield is a good man and I love him."

For the next 30 years, they carried on a lively and open correspondence. Whitefield often spoke about faith in Christ and admonished Franklin to make sure he was prepared for the next world. When Whitefield passed away in Newburyport, Connecticut, on Sept. 30, 1770, Franklin was in London. Obviously feeling a deep sense of loss, he wrote,

"I knew him intimately upwards of thirty years; his integrity, disinterestedness, and indefatigable zeal in prosecuting every good work, I have never seen equaled, I shall never see exceeded" (Hyatt, The Faith and Vision of Benjamin Franklin, 44).

Franklin's Missionary Vision

As a result of this friendship, Franklin moved away from his Deistic leanings and back toward his Puritan roots. The depth of Franklin's love and respect for Whitefield is demonstrated by the fact that he wanted Whitefield to be his partner in establishing a new colony on the Ohio frontier. Notice that Franklin wanted to populate it with a "religious" and industrious people. When Franklin, or any of the Founders, speak of a "religious" people they are referring to Christians.

Note also the missionary motive Franklin presented to Whitefield. He not only wanted to populate the colony with Christian people, he wanted the colony to be a base for introducing the Native Americans of that region to what he called "pure religion."

Since he is writing to Whitefield, there can be no doubt that "pure religion" in Franklin's mind was the evangelical revivalism that Whitefield preached in Philadelphia and throughout the Colonies.

Although time and circumstances did not allow them the opportunity to launch this project, I suggest that Franklin's vision for a Christian society never died but was fulfilled in the founding of the United States of America, of which he was one of the most important Founding Fathers.

Franklin's Commitment to Christian Values

Franklin was no fiery evangelist like Whitefield, but he became convinced that only Christianity provided the moral system for a stable and prosperous society. He knew that Christians were far from perfect, but at least they acknowledged a virtuous, moral standard toward which to strive and to which they could be called to adhere.

Franklin's belief in Christianity as a necessary moral force in society is why he rejected a manuscript from the well-known Deist, Thomas Paine, in which Paine attacked orthodox Christianity. Franklin, in very strong language, urged Paine not to print the book or even allow anyone else to see it. He wrote:

"I would advise you, therefore ... to burn this piece before it is seen by any other person; whereby you will save yourself a great deal of mortification by the enemies it may raise against you, and perhaps a good deal of regret and repentance. If men are so wicked with religion [Christianity], what would they be if without it" (Hyatt, The Faith and Vision of Benjamin Franklin, 49).

Franklin Calls the Constitutional Convention to Prayer

Whitfield's influence on Franklin can be seen at the Constitutional Convention 17 years after Whitefield's death. When the Convention reached an impasse and was in danger of disbanding without completing its work, it was Franklin, now 81 years of age, who arose and called the convention to prayer.

In his appeal, Franklin quoted from both the Psalms and the Gospels and reminded the attendees how God had answered their prayers during the war. Addressing the convention president, George Washington, Franklin said,

"How has it happened, sir, that we have not hitherto once thought of humbly appealing to the Father of lights to illuminate our understandings? In the beginning of the contest with Great Britain, when we were sensible to danger, we had daily prayers in this room for Divine protection. Our prayers, sir, were heard and they were graciously answered. I have lived, sir, a long time and the longer I live, the more convincing proofs I see of this truth—that God governs in the affairs of men. And if a sparrow cannot fall to the ground without His notice, is it probable that an empire can rise without His aid? We have been assured, sir, in the sacred writings that except the Lord build the house, they labor in vain that build it. I firmly believe this. I therefore beg leave to move that, henceforth, prayers imploring the assistance of Heaven and its blessing on our deliberation be held in this assembly every morning before we proceed to business" (Hyatt, The Faith and Vision of Benjamin Franklin, 62-63).

Although his proposal was not "formally" adopted, there was much response on a personal level because of the respect with which he was held. According to those present, "an atmosphere of reconciliation seemed to settle over the convention hall." Petty grievances and local interests were laid aside, and the delegates went on to complete their task of formulating the U.S. Constitution and Bill of Rights. I think Whitefield must have smiled down from Heaven on his old friend!

Yes, Franklin Wanted a Christian America

Modern secularists love to present Franklin as a nonreligious Deist who wanted to keep Christianity out of the public domain. Such a view of Franklin, however, is based on selected quotations taken out of context and without regard for his changing views on God and Christianity as he matured. Such a view also ignores his Puritan heritage and his close friendship with Whitefield.

Franklin, like all the Founders, did not want an official, state church like the nations of Europe. He did however, want a society whose populace would be governed by Christian principles of virtue and morality. This was made clear in his letter to Whitefield, and in this sense, it is clear that Benjamin Franklin had a vision for a Christian America.

Remember Calvin Coolidge's history lesson, and warning, regarding the spirit that animated America's founding document

The Fourth of July in 1926 was the 150th anniversary of the signing of the Declaration of Independence. United States President Calvin Coolidge took the occasion to give a speech celebrating the charter.

In this time of poisonous partisanship, political turbulence and bewildering social change, this speech is a refreshing reminder of the principles that established this country.

After 150 years, America had showed itself to be respectably stable, Coolidge said. Time has proved "the value of our institutions and their dependability as rules for the regulation of human conduct and the advancement of civilization." The Fourth of July is meant "to reaffirm and reestablish those old theories and principles which time and the unerring logic of events have demonstrated to be sound. Amid all the clash of conflicting interests, amid all the welter of partisan politics, every American can turn for solace and consolation to the Declaration of Independence and the Constitution of the United States with the assurance and confidence that those two great charters of freedom and justice remain firm and unshaken." This is far less true 92 years after he spoke those words. The Constitution in particular has been shaken considerably.

President Coolidge then spoke about the spirit of the American Revolution. "[A] new civilization had come, a new spirit had arisen on this side of the Atlantic more advanced and more developed in its regard for the rights of the individual than that which characterized the Old World," he explained. "A separate establishment was ultimately inevitable. … The American Revolution represented the informed and mature convictions of a great mass of independent, liberty-loving, God-fearing people who knew their rights, and possessed the courage to dare to maintain them."

We naturally think of revolution as rebellion, but Coolidge argues convincingly that this was not what motivated America's Revolution. "[T]he Declaration of Independence was the result of the seasoned and deliberate thought of the dominant portion of the people of the Colonies," he said. "It had about it nothing of the lawless and disordered nature of a riotous insurrection. It was maintained on a plane which rises above the ordinary conception of rebellion. It was in no sense a radical movement but took on the dignity of a resistance to illegal usurpations. It was conservative and represented the action of the colonists to maintain their constitutional rights which from time immemorial had been guaranteed to them under the law of the land."

The Declaration bespeaks principles broader than just the secession of one people from another, Coolidge said. There is something about it that "has ever since caused it to be regarded as one of the great charters that not only was to liberate America but was everywhere to ennoble humanity. It was not because it was proposed to establish a new nation, but because it was proposed to establish a nation on new principles, that July 4, 1776, has come to be regarded as one of the greatest days in history."

The preamble of the Declaration lays out three of these principles: "the doctrine that all men are created equal, that they are endowed with certain inalienable rights, and that therefore the source of the just powers of government must be derived from the consent of the governed." These ideas had been around for millennia in various forms, but "had never been assembled before and declared in such a combination." Yet, Coolidge said, what truly made this extraordinary was the fact that this ideal was put into action—with a "duly authorized and constituted representative public body in its sovereign capacity, supported by the force of general opinion and by the armies of Washington already in the field. ... It was an assertion that a people had arisen determined to make every necessary sacrifice for the support of these truths and by their practical application bring the War of Independence to a successful conclusion and adopt the Constitution of the United States with all that it has meant to civilization."

Of all those principles, the one truly unique to America was "the doctrine of equality." Other nations had decided that the people should choose their own rulers; other nations had articulated what they considered to be inalienable rights. But equality "had not before appeared as an official political declaration of any nation. It was profoundly revolutionary. It is one of the cornerstones of American institutions."

And where did the understanding come from that "all men are created equal"? Coolidge documented how it came from America's religion. In his speech he tracks it through the colonial-era churches and the teachings of early American ministers. For example, as far back as 1710—early in the 18th century—an influential preacher named John Wise wrote, "Every man must be acknowledged equal to every man." The forceful preaching of men espousing this ideal, he said, "reached the neighborhood of Thomas Jefferson, who acknowledged that his 'best ideas of democracy' had been secured at church meetings."

"When we take all these circumstances into consideration," Coolidge said, "it is but natural that the first paragraph of the Declaration of Independence should open with a reference to nature's God and should close in the final paragraphs with an appeal to the Supreme Judge of the world and an assertion of a firm reliance on Divine Providence. Coming from these sources, having as it did this background, it is no wonder that Samuel Adams could say 'The people seem to recognize this resolution as though it were a decree promulgated from heaven.'

"No one can examine this record and escape the conclusion that in the great outline of its principles the Declaration was the result of the religious teachings of the preceding period." These principles "are found in the texts, the sermons, and the writings of the early colonial clergy who were earnestly undertaking to instruct their congregations in the great mystery of how to live. They preached equality because they believed in the fatherhood of God and the brotherhood of man. They justified freedom by the text that we are all created in the divine image …."

That is a remarkable truth. Yet we easily take for granted the blessing of living in a country that established it as a cornerstone principle, and that has striven ever since—unlike any other people in history—to live up to it.

America's founders used this belief as justification for establishing government "by the people." Anyone knowledgeable in the Bible can recognize that democratic, ground-up self-government is very different from the biblical model of government. The government the founders established certainly was more enduring than other forms this world has seen, as long as Americans were moral and religious. That no longer being the case, the problems and limitations associated with this form of government are becoming clearer all the time.

Still, this uncommon and revolutionary concept, established in the Declaration, of each and every person being created equal and endowed with God-given rights, is biblical, and beautiful, and extraordinarily powerful.

"In those days such doctrines would scarcely have been permitted to flourish and spread in any other country," President Coolidge continued. "This was the purpose which the fathers cherished. In order that they might have freedom to express these thoughts and opportunity to put them into action, whole congregations with their pastors had migrated to the Colonies. These great truths were in the air that our people breathed. Whatever else we may say of it, the Declaration of Independence was profoundly American."

Thus, Coolidge deduced, "In its main features the Declaration of Independence is a great spiritual document. It is a declaration not of material but of spiritual conceptions. Equality, liberty, popular sovereignty, the rights of man—these are not elements which we can see and touch. They are ideals. They have their source and their roots in the religious convictions. ... Unless the faith of the American people in these religious convictions is to endure, the principles of our Declaration will perish. We cannot continue to enjoy the result if we neglect and abandon the cause".

This is precisely what America is witnessing today. These religious convictions have been replaced with new principles of "morality": tolerating lawlessness, demanding government welfare, restricting freedoms in the name of enforcing liberal orthodoxy. And our departure from the Declaration's principles is accelerating.

"We are too prone to overlook another conclusion. Governments do not make ideals, but ideals make governments. This is both historically and logically true. Of course the government can help to sustain ideals and can create institutions through which they can be the better observed, but their source by their very nature is in the people. The people have to bear their own responsibilities. There is no method by which that burden can be shifted to the government. It is not the enactment, but the observance, of laws that creates the character of a nation."

How true this is. Modern society has somehow grown in its expectation that government should magically solve every problem and provide every need—and simultaneously in its contempt for government. We have abdicated our inescapable responsibility to embody the high ideals and strong character required of a truly strong nation.

How dangerous such abdication is. To forget this responsibility, and to lose sight of these foundational principles, invites disaster, Coolidge said: "A spring will cease to flow if its source be dried up; a tree will wither if its roots be destroyed."

Coolidge continued, "About the Declaration there is a finality that is exceedingly restful. It is often asserted that the world has made a great deal of progress since 1776, that we have had new thoughts and new experiences which have given us a great advance over the people of that day, and that we may therefore very well discard their conclusions for something more modern. But that reasoning cannot be applied to this great charter. If all men are created equal, that is final. If they are endowed with inalienable rights, that is final. If governments derive their just powers from the consent of the governed, that is final. No advance, no progress can be made beyond these propositions. If anyone wishes to deny their truth or their soundness, the only direction in which he can proceed historically is not forward, but backward toward the time when there was no equality, no rights of the individual, no rule of the people. Those who wish to proceed in that direction cannot lay claim to progress. They are reactionary.

Their ideas are not more modern, but more ancient, than those of the Revolutionary fathers."

How needed is such insight in today's America, which has grown almost unrecognizably so reactionary. Americans are replacing the revolutionary ideas that helped propel America to greatness with imported, tried-and-failed relics of ideas from other nations and ages. We are forcefully proving that not all change is progress, and that history is prophecy.

President Coolidge then built to his speech's powerful conclusion. It was only about three generations ago that America had a president who could articulate such moral clarity and provide such leadership. We have descended a long way since. I'll just allow his words to stand:

Under a system of popular government there will always be those who will seek for political preferment by clamoring for reform. While there is very little of this which is not sincere, there is a large portion that is not well informed. In my opinion very little of just criticism can attach to the theories and principles of our institutions. There is far more danger of harm than there is hope of good in any radical changes. We do need a better understanding and comprehension of them and a better knowledge of the foundations of government in general. Our forefathers came to certain conclusions and decided upon certain courses of action which have been a great blessing to the world. Before we can understand their conclusions we must go back and review the course which they followed. We must think the thoughts which they thought. Their intellectual life centered around the meeting-house. They were intent upon religious worship. While there were always among them men of deep learning, and later those who had comparatively large possessions, the mind of the people was not so much engrossed in how much they knew, or how much they had, as in how they were going to live. While scantily provided with other literature, there was a wide acquaintance with the Scriptures. Over a period as great as that which measures the existence of our independence they were subject to this discipline not only in their religious life and educational training, but also in their political thought. They were a people who came under the influence of a great spiritual development and acquired a great moral power.

No other theory is adequate to explain or comprehend the Declaration of Independence. It is the product of the spiritual insight of the people.

We live in an age of science and of abounding accumulation of material things. These did not create our Declaration. Our Declaration created them. The things of the spirit come first. Unless we cling to that, all our material prosperity, overwhelming though it may appear, will turn to a barren scepter in our grasp. If we are to maintain the great heritage which has been bequeathed to us, we must be like-minded as the fathers who created it. We must not sink into a pagan materialism. We must cultivate the reverence which they had for the things that are holy. We must follow the spiritual and moral leadership which they showed. We must keep replenished, that they may glow with a more compelling flame, the altar fires before which they worshiped.

The Bork Nomination

When Robert Bork was appointed to the U.S. Supreme Court by President Ronald Reagan, it created a firestorm in Congress, and he failed to get confirmed. Shortly thereafter, he wrote The Tempting of America, which I believe is the best book about constitutional law in a century—perhaps ever.

Mr. Bork believed the nation was more than halfway along in the destruction of our Constitution.

He was right! Our republic is in grave danger. We live today in a culture that is becoming much more anti-law and anti-God.

If the Constitution is to be rewritten, it should be done only by our legislative branch, or Congress, and the president, or the executive branch. If they err, these leaders are subject to the voters. But that is not true of the judicial branch—the courts. The U.S. Supreme Court justices are selected for life by the president.

Our forefathers designed the Constitution that way so the Supreme Court justices would not be so concerned about the people when unpopular judgments had to be made. The Supreme Court justices are subject only to constitutional law—not the voters!

Their job is to interpret the law—or better, to let the law interpret itself. They have no authority to rewrite the law. If they rewrite the law, it's almost impossible to correct the error.

In our history, there was a judge who wanted slavery. He kept searching the Constitution to support his belief. He found the phrase "substantive due process," and he twisted these words to show that slavery was constitutional.

It took a civil war to overturn that decision. That gives you some idea of how hard it is to change what judges do! Today judges used that same reasoning—"substantive due process"—to say that abortion is constitutional. Mr. Bork believed that reasoning to be a dangerous mistake, and so do I.

If the judges are not subject to constitutional law, they are subject to nothing and nobody!

Law schools routinely teach about being "legal realists." Like former Vice President Al Gore, they want an "evolving Constitution." But this reasoning gives the judges despotic powers. It also takes us away from the foundational law established by our forefathers.

Then why do our politicians allow it? The president and Congress often like the judges to do this if the decisions are favorable to their views and they know their views will not be approved by the voters. Still, the judges are taking power from the legislature and the executive branches as they rewrite the Constitution.

Our politicians simply lack the vision to see how disastrous this process is. It is based on selfish lawlessness—not law!

The Supreme Court justices are gaining dictatorial powers, and none of them were voted into their offices or approved by the people. The democratic process is being destroyed. That means we cannot maintain the rule of law.

Usually the people know very little about how the law works. But they know enough to lose respect for our governmental institutions. They also lose interest in the whole political system.

As a result, they end up doing what our predecessors in ancient Israel did. "In those days there was no king in Israel: every man did that which was right in his own eyes" (Judges 21:25). This is the history of our own people. And the book of Judges is a part of the biblical books called the former prophets. That means it is prophecy for this end time.

Today, we have no king or president or real authority figure that we look to for leadership. And that means we are a nation without strong leadership. The same is true of Britain.

No ship of state can find its way to a safe harbor without a captain to guide it. That is exactly the way it was in ancient Israel just before it was conquered! And that is exactly where America and Britain are today! There is no leader who can or will establish the rule of law. This sad state of affairs was also prophesied (Isaiah 3:1-5). In this prophecy, our leaders are likened to children!

What most people don't see is that we are destroying the rule of law. And history tells us that our republic cannot stand because of that evil.

Media and news personalities are a big part of the liberal culture—about 80 percent of them. The destroying of our constitutional republic would not be possible without their support. All too often they are deceived, and in turn they have the power to deceive our citizens.

Mr. Bork related how the Constitution is the big trump card in American politics. Today it is being used by the liberal culture to force their unlawful ideas on people!

The great heresy being taught in our law schools is that the judges are not bound by law. Some say the Constitution isn't even law!

That means we are being led by the human reasoning of a liberal culture.

That is often the opposite of establishing the rule of law. Again, history reveals that empires are destroyed if they fail to establish the rule of law. But the liberal culture often has contempt of history and our Founding Fathers. Liberals foolishly rely on their own reasoning, which is not grounded in foundational law.

The founders of the Constitution put in place the walls, roofs and beams of our Constitution, as Mr. Bork said. The judges' purpose is to preserve the architectural features—adding only filigree or ornamental work. Instead, the lawyers and judges are changing the very structure of our representative democracy.

The Constitution is being altered dramatically. And it is the foundation of our republic! We are experiencing a constitutional earthquake, and most of our people don't even know it—yet. Your future is being changed for you, and often you have no input.

This process is sure to lead to anarchy! That is why you and I should be deeply concerned.

Seeking Lawlessness

Why did our Founding Fathers work so hard to establish the Constitution? Because it was to be the supreme law of the land.

"A well-known Harvard law professor," Mr. Bork wrote, "turned to me with some exasperation and said, 'Your notion that the Constitution is in some sense law must rest upon an obscure philosophic principle with which I am unfamiliar.'"

But notice what the Constitution itself states: "This Constitution, and the laws of the United States which shall be made in pursuance thereof; and all treaties made, or which shall be made, under the authority of the United States, shall be the supreme law of the land; and the judges in every state shall be bound thereby, any thing in the Constitution or laws of any state to the contrary notwithstanding.

"The senators and representatives before mentioned, and the members of the several state legislatures, and all executive and judicial officers, both of the United States and of the several states, shall be bound by oath or affirmation, to support this Constitution; but no religious test shall ever be required as a qualification to any office or public trust under the United States."

A Harvard law professor is actually stating that the Constitution is not even law! That view comes from our most prestigious university. The very fact that he would even make that statement shows that we are already getting into extreme lawlessness!

The majority of our leaders now agree with the Harvard law professor. He made a statement that shows we are failing to establish the rule of law. The real issue here is lawlessness.

That means your future will be adversely affected.

In 2000, in a debate during the Democratic primaries, Vice President Gore was asked what sort of Supreme Court justices he would select if he were elected president. He responded, "I would look for justices of the Supreme Court who understand that our Constitution is a living and breathing document, that it was intended by our founders to be interpreted in the light of the constantly evolving experience of the American people."

Syndicated columnist Cal Thomas made this observation about that statement: "Mr. Gore's view of the Constitution, shared by most political liberals, is one of the most dangerous philosophies of our time. It establishes a class of philosopher-kings who determine the rights of the people and shreds the Constitution as a document that conforms people to unchanging principles that promote their own and the general welfare.

"A 'living' Constitution, notes constitutional attorney John Whitehead, means the Constitution is 'up for grabs,' and it becomes whatever the justices decide, not the people through their elected representatives ....

"The founders never intended the courts to be supreme. Their intention was that the law, rooted in objective and unchanging truth, would be preeminent" (Washington Times, March 8, 2000).

Law scholars today don't believe the Constitution was "rooted in objective and unchanging truth"—that is, they don't believe our founders established the rule of law. But that's just what the founders did. And now most lawyers and judges reject their foundational work.

Our views today reflect a deadly degeneration into lawlessness!

The liberal culture in politics wants a "living Constitution." Mr. Bork stated that many liberals imply the

Constitution is dead. They don't want unchanging truth, established 200 years ago, to direct their lives.

The liberal religious culture similarly wants a "living Bible." Modern religionists' "intelligence" demands that they adapt the Bible to modern times—even though every word was inspired by God (Matthew 4:4).

Most religions preach that God's law was done away, in spite of what Jesus said in Matthew 5:17-18: "Think not that I am come to destroy the law, or the prophets: I am not come to destroy, but to fulfil. For verily I say unto you, till heaven and earth pass, one jot or one tittle shall in no wise pass from the law, till all be fulfilled." Christ came to fulfill, or fill, the law to the full. He essentially was saying every t must be crossed and every i dotted. Still, many thought, and still think, that He came to destroy the law. They refuse to believe the truth!

Christians are supposedly people who follow Christ, the Lawgiver. That is how they got their name "Christian."

But whether secular or religious, we are racing into lawlessness, and our nation is plunging toward disaster. Any good history book will show us that! The Bible should be even more convicting. Study it and see the deadly danger of lawlessness.

When the new U.S. government was established, Benjamin Franklin said that we have

"a republic, *if* you can keep it."

It's all about either establishing the rule of law—or descending into lawlessness.

In an article posted at www.tedgunderson.com/articles/plansforcivilianinternment.htm, Mary Louise writes the following;

Along the Danube River in Austria about forty miles from Vienna, a prison camp called Stalag 17 was one of many prisoner of war facilities during WWII. Similar facilities exist in America, many in remote areas across our country adjacent to major highways, railroads and airports. The infrastructure for incarcerating and executing resisters and dissenters in the coming American Holocaust has already been set up, according to the 1968 government plans code-named Operation Cable Splicer and Operation Garden Plot.

Field manual 3-19.40 or FM 19-40 is the August 2001 version of military police internment/resettlement Operations. It supercedes the FM19-40 of February 1976 and FM 19-60 of May 1986 by order of the Secretary of the Army signed by administrative assistant, Joel B. Hudson.

Pending the approval of Army Chief of Staff, the military can detain and jail citizens en masse. Rex 84 called for many military bases to be closed and turned into prisons, based on the pretext that if a mass exodus of illegal aliens crossed the border; they would be quickly rounded up by FEMA. A more honest and realistic scenario would be the detention of Americans.

Under "Rex" the President could declare a state of emergency, empowering the head of FEMA to take control of the internal infrastructure of the U.S. and suspend the Constitution. The President could then invoke Executive Orders 11000 through 11004 which would draft all citizens into work forces under governmental supervision, empower the postmaster to register all men, women and children, seize all airports and aircraft, and seize all housing to establish forced relocation of all citizens.

Congressman Henry Gonzales clarified the question of the existence of civilian detention camps by stating, "The truth is – yes – you do have these standby provisions and the plans are here…whereby you could, in the name of stopping terrorism…evoke the military and arrest Americans and put them in detention camps."

Equipped with flexible "military operations in urban terrain" and "operations other than war" doctrine, lethal and "less-than-lethal" high-tech weaponry US armed forces and elite militarized police units are being trained to eradicate "disorder", "disturbance" and "civil disobedience" in America. The American corporate/military dictatorship has the power to enforce its definition of "disorder" and sees our Constitutional Re-

> public as a threat and any attempt to protect it as a "national security" requirement.
>
> Their rational for enacting such legislation is simple: self- preservation. They are systematically organizing themselves to protect their interests, profits and plots against the growing opposition to their criminal activities and are working to "suppress rebellion against the authority of the United States".
>
> A question that haunted me was how could Hitler rise to power with his satanic fascism and why did the German people allow it. I learned long ago that many Germans and Christians died along with the Jews, and what happened in Nazi Germany could happen in America if people were not vigilant. This time it will succeed on a grand scale unless multitudes of decent people refuse to accept or condone tyranny and death, while there is still time and while we still can."

Rome has a most interesting and somewhat complex strategy that she is using in her final crusade. Rome is using Islam, ecumenical jihad, and the threat of Islamic terror to set up totalitarianism in America and flooding the country with adherents to a belief that states the priesthood speaks for Almighty God in both spiritual and political matters. At the same time Rome is using the American military to crack open the Islamic world, pitting Shia against Sunni. At the same time a new and much bloodier version of the Holy Roman Empire is quietly being built using the economy to accomplish what panzers could not so that Rome can move into a region she has been unable to penetrate for over a thousand years.

In Pope Francis' visit to Israel, he stirred things up again by stopping unexpectedly and placing his hand on a pro Palestinain sign, bowed his head and prayed. All humble and holy like. Complete with sad looking face to add punch. A great actor and politician. This is the lasting image of his meddling. Francis wants Jerusalem and he can taste it and if it means calling his Muslim army to attack the Jews, for the greater glory of God then, the ends justify the means. The Jews will beg EU forces, led by Germany, to mediate. By that time the U.S. and Britain will have turned their faces away. The EU will then wipe out radical Islam and ally with Islam light.

Rome and Islam share many concepts. Both hate and abhor separation of church and state. Both hate and abhor any limiting of the birth rate. The more people, the more financial contributions.

Both share the same conceptual roots: Islam believes that Sharia law, in other words the Koran, interpreted by the Mullahs and Imams should rule society with no separation of church and state. In the end the Mullahs and Imams rule by fatwa's, and central to the main concept of jihad is first the submission of the soul to Allah through the Koran and obedience to the Mullahs, Imams and Mahdi's. Then, that Islam, which means submission [usually coerced], is spread externally by jihad, or holy war to the rest of the world ultimately under the control of the Koran and the Imams and Mullahs through Sharia law.

Romanism believes that the pope is the Vicar of Christ, and that he has been given the keys to the temporal and spiritual kingdom. Therefore he has the authority, it is believed, to rule both the spiritual and temporal realms. Submission to the papacy, the encyclicals, and rulings of the papacy is central. There is no separation of church and state, for the church rules the state. Through the Jesuits, the Dominicans, Franciscans, the military Order of Malta and the local priesthood in the confessional, [which is used as a vast system of espionage], keeps the papal world in submission. Crusades are launched, holy wars, to bring alien religions and dissenters into submission or extermination. Islam is very much a clone of the papacy.

Irish Author Alan O'Reilly offers this apt comparison of Romanism and Islam:

Anti-Semitism in the West often focuses on an alleged 'Jewish Conspiracy.'

There is no Jewish Conspiracy. Anti-Semitism stems from greed and jealousy.

It is common knowledge that the Jew is unusually gifted with respect to making money. God has given the Jew this ability to enable him to survive the millennia-long Diaspora. But the Gentile loves money. Greed and jealousy on his part toward the Jew therefore often follows.

It is true that some Jews have used their unusual money-making abilities for avaricious ends, e.g. international profiteering (Rothschild, Schiff) and even criminal ventures (Lansky, Siegel, Cohen etc.). - although the latter group is greatly outnumbered by Italian-Sicilian and Irish Catholics.

Of course, it is also regrettably true that some Jews have engaged in nefarious politics with globalist implications, e.g. Marx, Trotsky, though again, they are far outnumbered by Papists, especially the SJ.

But all such activities are entirely outwith the Jewish scriptures. If the Jew obeys his scriptures, he *cannot* engage in a conspiracy against his host community, his host nation and by extension, against any nation and therefore the world, as God's instructions to His people through the prophet Jeremiah show unequivocally.

"And seek the peace of the city whither I have caused you to be carried away captives, and pray unto the Lord for it: for in the peace thereof shall ye have peace" Jeremiah 29:7.

Historically, that instruction applied to the Babylonian Captivity under Nebuchadnezzar but in principle, it applies to the Diaspora.

However, a Muslim *can* engage in conspiracy, and indeed *must*, according to his belief system. Any non-Muslim country is perceived as being part of Dar-al-Harb, the House of War. Jihad, including conspiracy, must be mounted until that country, e.g. Britain, is forced into Dar-al-Islam, the House of Islam.

The same applies for the Catholic, whose belief system requires that the whole world be brought under the thralldom of the Pope of Rome. (Contemporary Marxists will basically fall into line with Papists, under the aegis of 'Liberation Theology.' Sinn Fein/IRA members Gerry Adams and Martin McGuinness are two examples.)

A Catholic, like a Muslim, *may* perceive his first loyalty to his host nation but he violates his own belief system in so doing and is therefore not a 'good' Catholic, or a 'good' Muslim. *Both Catholicism and Islam are church-state ideologies.* Judaism is also a church-state but only within the biblically ordained borders of the land of Israel - another reason why a scriptural Jew cannot engage in a global conspiracy.

These comments are apposite, as they apply to Britain but by extension to the USA or any non-Catholic nation:

"Let us never forget that whatever [Queen Elizabeth's] boasted authority may be it is as nothing and less than nothing compared to that of the Vicar of Christ"[i].

"The law of God that is the Pope's command will be or rather has been and is being carried into effect: the Parliamentary lie will be spit upon and trampled underfoot"[ii].

As is this, the substance of which had tragic consequences for the Jewish people. It is from another study I did.

Albert Close was a Protestant Christian historian. He revealed that when Oxford Don, Mr R.H. Crossman, was investigating the pre-war Hitlerian blood purges, he was told repeatedly, *"The pope [is] behind all the trouble"[iii]* [p 39].

Mr. Crossman attempted to broadcast this from Berlin in July 1934, via the BBC. The broadcast was suddenly cut off when he mentioned the pope. No explanation was ever given. The then BBC Chairman, Lord Reith, was part of the cover-up.

That BBC cover-up helped bring about World War 2. That war resulted in 55,000,000 dead, including 500,000 deaths from Britain and the Commonwealth (and 6,000,000 Jewish deaths).

It is no accident, that the present-day director-general of the BBC is Mark Thompson, who is a Catholic, as is Mark Byford, his deputy.

Thompson is said to be the most influential lay Catholic in Britain [iv]. No doubt he is. The BBC still portrays the pope as a man of God, not the antichrist (which he is).

In other words, Britain, Israel, the USA and the Jewish people have the same enemy as they have always had. Our national leaders do not understand this because, if not conspiratorial agents of the enemy themselves (which is entirely possible) then as St Paul revealed, Romans 11:25, they are conceited and ignorant - which adjectives are also apposite if they *are* enemy agents.

References:

[1] *Jesuit Plots From Elizabethan to Modern Times.* Albert Close, The Protestant Truth Society

[ii] *The 100 Most Influential Lay Catholics*, Ekklesia

[iii] The Catholic *Vindicator* cited in *No Pope Here*, by Dr. Ian R. K. Paisley, p.19 also, *The Popish Plot Exposed by Rome Herself,* Dr. Ian R. K. Paisley

[iv] *The Tablet*, July 16, 1851 cited in *No Pope Here,* Dr. Ian R.K. Paisley

W.G. (BILL) HEFNER
8TH DISTRICT, NORTH CAROLINA

2470 RAYBURN HOUSE OFFICE BUILDING
WASHINGTON, DC 20515
(202) 225-3715
FAX (202) 225-4036

COMMITTEES:
COMMITTEE ON APPROPRIATIONS
SUBCOMMITTEE ON DEFENSE
RANKING MEMBER
SUBCOMMITTEE ON MILITARY CONSTRUCTION

Congress of the United States
House of Representatives
Washington, DC 20515–3308

DISTRICT OFFICES:
P.O. BOX 385
101 UNION STREET, SOUTH
CONCORD, NC 28026
(704) 933-1615 or 786-1612
FAX (704) 782-1004

P.O. BOX 4220
123 S. MAIN STREET
CENTER COURT
SALISBURY, NC 28144
(704) 636-0838
FAX (704) 633-6271

P.O. BOX 1503
230 EAST FRANKLIN STREET
ROCKINGHAM, NC 28379
(910) 997-2070
FAX (910) 997-7987

March 24, 1997

Mr. Zell Setzer
P.O. Box 4198
Salisbury, NC 28145

Dear Mr. Setzer:

Enclosed is the information you requested pertaining to the Army's policy and guidance for establishing civilian inmate labor program and civilian prison camps on Army installations. This information has not yet been published (it is currently at the printers), however, it has been funded, staffed, and does reflect current Army policy. I hope you find this information useful.

With kindest regards, I am

Sincerely yours,

Bill Hefner

BILL HEFNER
Member of Congress

BH/ey

Enclosure

Rome's Link to Islam

Early on, around 400 A.D., the Vatican wanted Jerusalem because of the religious significance, but it was blocked by the Jews. Another problem facing the Vatican was the fact that true Christians were preaching in North Africa and Rome could not tolerate opposition. The Vatican had to create a weapon to eliminate both the Jews and true Christians who refused to accept Roman theology and control. Looking to North Africa they saw Arabs as a source of manpower.

A number of Arabs had become Romanists and reported to their leaders in Rome. St. Augustine, the man who invented the doctrine of, "Just Warfare", appeared on the scene and saw a way to build an army by creating a messiah for the Arabs.

Muhammed was 25 years old when he married a wealthy widow named Khadijah. She was about 40 at the time. Before Khadijah married Muhammed, according to the Jesuit Alberto Rivera, who claimed in 1980 while he was in training, that Cardinal Bea had taught that before she married Muhammed, she was a Papist who had given all of her wealth to the Catholic Church and retired to a convent. While there she was given a mission. Her job was to find a man who could be used by the Vatican to create a new religion for the children of Ishmael. She soon found Muhammed.

Khadijah had a cousin named Waraqua, who was a very faithful Catholic and had tremendous influence on Muhammed. The Vatican placed him in an important spot as Muhammed's advisor.

Muhammmed underwent intensive training under the guidance of Papists and was financed by the Vatican. Muhammed devoured the works of the warmonger, St. Augustine.

Under orders from the Vatican, Roman Catholic Arabs across North Africa began spreading the story of a great one who was about to rise up. Muhammed was being groomed to hate Jews and non-Catholic Christians. When Muhammed began to get strange, hallucinogenic ideas and dreams in a cave, it was his Catholic advisor Waraqua who became the translator and scribe. The writings were collected into what we call the Koran today.

With the help of the Vatican, Islam spread like wildfire. But eventually they could not be kept on a papal leash and Islamist hordes, who some 200 years later, became full of themselves and flush with victories, double-crossed the Vatican when the pope demanded Jerusalem as payback. The enmity has existed ever since.(From "The Prophet" Chick publications Chino, Ca. 1988 pp18-23)

After the Cairo conference on human population control in 1994, the papacy joined forces *culturally* at the urging of Opus Dei, with Islamic fundamentalism to bring down the U.S, eliminate separation of church and state and all remaining freedoms. The common ground here is opposition to abortion, which brought the two powers together to wage war on the West. At the same time the papacy is locked in a mortal struggle with Islam.

The threat of Islamic fundamentalist terrorism is causing the loss of all of the remaining freedoms with the erection of totalitarian systems within the American governmental system- the Department of Homeland Security, the National Intelligence Director, with de facto internal passports, and comprehensive surveillance, the Patriot Acts, which remove the remaining freedoms of the Bill of Rights. The relationship between those who are constantly watched and tracked, and those who watch and track them, is the relationship between masters and slaves.

At the same time, in order for the papacy to truly rule the world, the papacy must crack open and control the Islamic world and capture Jerusalem, the very thing that she sought to do in the crusades of the Middle Ages.

The Jesuits were expelled from Iraq in 1969 but made their way back into the country through U.S. Armed Forces chaplaincies. Fordham Jesuit Avery Cardinal Dulles said at a symposium in 2004, which pushed the Pentagon to justify the current Papal crusade, "There can be no abandoning of just-war principles…The infliction of harm has to be justified." www.Temple-News.com/media/paper143/news/2004/12/10/news/cardinal.colonel.seek.to.justify.war-827696.shtml

This sounds identical to what Francis Cardinal Spellman said about "preventive war" in reference to his crusade against the Buddhists in Vietnam and into which the U.S. was drawn and humiliated.

Unfortunately for the United States, the Vatican historically has always hated the guiding principles of the US. One has only to look at the fact that the Church backed the Axis powers in WWII, and then claimed to be a victim when it appeared Germany had lost. Operation Paperclip, which saved thousands of Nazi's from punishment by way of the Vatican ratlines, was run through the Franciscan [maybe this operation exposed the real reason for the pope's choice of names] and Dominican orders.

Rome is busily backing a newly resurgent Holy Roman Empire still in its infancy, which is, in turn, presently busy backing the moderate Arab countries in the same way they did in both World Wars. China has also, over the last several years, been the target of infiltration by the Jesuits in much the same way Japan was one hundred years ago. In this scenario a war could be launched on a global scale in which the Roman Church could finally, using secular and proxy armies, exterminate all opposition to her.

The first Crusades, besides being a total disaster, were launched for the express intent of enabling the relocation of the Papacy to Jerusalem.

World War III has already begun, Pope Francis reportedly said during a private meeting with a group of Jewish leaders held in his home on September 17, 2014.

Ronald S. Lauder, head of the Jewish group, explained the pope's statements: "Francis told us privately that he believes we are in World War III, but unlike the first two world wars, instead of happening all at once, this war is coming in stages. He said … now it is

Christians who are being annihilated and the world is silent."

Francis has reiterated his belief that the world is already in the early stages of World War III at least two other times. His belief is formed in part by ongoing conflicts in such places as Ukraine, Gaza, Afghanistan and regions of Africa. But nothing influences his assessment as much as the atrocities that the Islamic State terrorists are committing in Iraq and Syria—primarily against Christians.

In Iraq's Nineveh region alone, the Islamic State has driven around 200,000 Christians from their homes since early summer. Many of them now have only the clothes on their backs. The number of practicing Christians remaining in the city of Mosul is now thought to be zero—down from 10,000 at the beginning of the year. Similar exoduses are occurring in other parts of Iraq and in Syria.

Now, the pope says the violence must be stopped, even if that means by force.

"In these cases where there is an unjust aggression, I can only say that it is legitimate to stop the unjust aggressor," Francis said on September 15/2014. "I underscore the verb 'to stop.' I don't say 'bomb' or 'make war,' but to 'stop.' ... We must stop and think a little about the level of cruelty at which we have arrived. This should frighten us."

Francis is concerned in part because the Islamic State is only accelerating a trend that has long been underway. Before the birth of Islam, Catholicism was the dominant force in many Middle Eastern nations. Even a century ago, Christians made up over 30 percent of the Middle East's populations. Now that number is around 3 percent and quickly falling.

The Syriac and Chaldean Catholic churches of Syria and Iraq are viewed as integral bodies of the Catholic Church, and are in full communion with the bishop of Rome. The growing persecution they and other

Middle Eastern Christian groups are suffering is a festering wound for the Roman Catholic Church.

At present, Francis's calls for action against Christian-slaying Muslims remain fairly restrained. But Bible prophecy shows that the Vatican will soon go far beyond restrained statements to confront radical Islam.

The rising tide of Jihad is drowning the Middle East's Christians, but the Church will soon take violent action to reverse this trend. Look at the history of the Crusades. It shows that both Catholics and Muslims are fiercely determined to control the Holy Land and surrounding regions.

In the final crusade, the Roman Catholic Church will take its most drastic action yet against Islam.

In December 2014, U.S. President Barack Obama surprised the world by announcing that America would restore diplomatic ties with Cuba after 53 years of hostility. The terms of the deal completely favor Cuba. Cuba did not have to abandon communism or reform its dictatorial governance. The U.S. got nothing out of this deal.

What is this all about? We could write quite a bit about the president bypassing Congress and using yet another executive action to make this deal. We could say a lot about the dangers of America appeasing yet another regime that hates it. But the factor that is more significant than any of these issues is this: The deal was largely the handiwork of the Vatican.

Pope Francis played a vital role in the president's decision. "Pope Francis issued a personal appeal to me, and to Cuba's President Raúl Castro," President Obama said as part of his landmark announcement about it.

In early summer of 2014, the pope appealed to both leaders by letter, urging them to exchange prisoners and improve relations. The Vatican later hosted a clandestine meeting between the two sides in Rome. However, it was actually Francis's predecessor who put the plan into motion. In 2012, Pope Benedict XVI began pressuring the United States to normalize relations with Cuba. Francis carried on Benedict's efforts. After months of working behind the scenes, the momentous deal was sealed. Its announcement surprised the world.

So America has opened itself up to an unsavory regime just a short boat ride away. But this is about much, much more than that, especially when you understand the history of the Catholic Church and Cuba.

Cuba and the Holy Roman Empire

The Catholic Church's history with Cuba dates back hundreds of years. In 1492, Christopher Columbus was the one who claimed the Caribbean islands, including Cuba, for Spain, the champion of Catholicism. Spain was ruled by Ferdinand II, the king who expelled or forcefully converted Jews and Muslims and who established the Spanish Inquisition—which is why you find almost no Protestants in Spain today! Just one year later, Pope Alexander VI commanded Spain to conquer, colonize and catholicize the "pagans" of Cuba and the rest of the New World.

Meanwhile, Europe's Habsburg dynasty was becoming very powerful. Through marriage and inheritance, the Habsburg Empire extended into Spain in 1516. Soon, Spain was integrated into the empire. In the early 1500s, Charles V gained power over the Netherlands, Spain and Germany. In Rome in 1530, the pope crowned him emperor. He headed the fourth resurrection of the Holy Roman Empire.

Charles continued to work closely with the popes, and the Roman church steered his empire. By the end of the 1500s, Spain had become the richest country in the world.

Much of this wealth and power came from Spain's conquest of the New World. Fleets of ships laden with billions of dollars in gold and silver crossed the Atlantic. And Cuba played a vital role in its wealth. Havana, Cuba, was the primary port for shipping all the treasure Spain was confiscating and mining in the New World. Ships ferried tens of thousands of tons of silver and gold from North and South America to Havana and from Havana to Seville, Spain. There, the Spanish spent it on the Habsburg's struggle against the Ottoman Empire and its war with the major European powers of the day. It also helped to finance the Catholic Church's inquisitions as that church tried to extinguish all other religions in Europe.

For many years, not a single European power was strong enough to stop the mighty and wealthy Holy Roman Empire and its ambition to colonize and catholicize the New World. This is part of Cuba's heritage.

Modern Cuba is a Communist nation, but it has only been Communist for about 50 years—less than a lifetime. It has been a Catholic country for almost 500 years! Today, between 60 and 65 percent of Cubans say they are Catholic, so it's clear that the church's influence remains deeply entrenched.

Fidel Castro is close to death. And Raúl Castro is quite old. So the political equation could change radically in the next few years—or even months.

If enormous changes occur, the Vatican could gain real power in Cuba.

Cuba's Strategic Value

Many do not think the Caribbean is strategically important, but that's because the United States has dominated it for many decades. For the Catholic Spanish Empire, Cuba was the single strategic port that served two entire continents. For Napoleon, Haiti served as the basis of his empire in the New World. When he lost Haiti in a slave revolt, he gave up his ambition in the Western Hemisphere and sold off a massive chunk of territory in the Louisiana Purchase.

But there is a much more recent reminder of Cuba's strategic importance. If you are older, you probably remember late 1962, when the U.S. discovered that the Soviet Union was deploying missiles to Cuba. Sources told the Americans that some of the missiles were so big that the tractor trailers carrying them through Cuban towns had trouble making turns. The Soviets were fortifying Cuba with ballistic missiles equipped to carry nuclear warheads. And they were about to aim these deadly missiles at the American mainland from point-blank range.

Most authorities believe this was the closest the Cold War ever came to full-scale nuclear war.

The Soviets wanted to deploy and activate their missiles in Cuba without America finding out. With supersonic nuclear missiles only minutes away from America's cities, the Soviets could evade America's missile warning system and launch a surprise attack. I believe there is ample evidence that the Soviet leader Nikita Khrushchev would have attempted to destroy America at that time. What if Khrushchev had achieved his secret plan to surprise America? He would probably never have had a better opportunity to conquer America—and he knew it! After all, he did say that the Soviets would "bury" us. At the very least, the Soviet Union would have had the U.S. at nuclear gunpoint. America's foreign policy would have been neutralized.

However, something happened in Cuba. The Americans began hearing reports that missiles were coming in. But they needed confirmation. It was difficult to fly over Cuba, a hostile nation, without getting shot down. But somehow, the Soviet plan got out of phase. The missiles arrived and were out in the open before the antiaircraft batteries were fully operational. American spy planes spotted the missiles and brought home photographic proof of Cuba's nuclear buildup.

The Cuban Missile Crisis turned out to be a victory for America, a victory that could have easily been a crushing defeat. But it proved how strategic the Cuban islands are for anyone who wants to harm the U.S. With modern weapons, how easily and quickly an enemy force can strike America's military and its cities.

Who Does the U.S.-Cuba Thaw Benefit?

Where does the Vatican factor into all of this? One thing this Cuba deal has accomplished is that it has displayed to the world the kind of power Pope Francis has.

"Francis is a master of blending the spiritual with the political," wrote National Public Radio's Rome-based senior Europe correspondent, Sylvia Poggioli. "[He] has embraced the bully pulpit of the papacy, emerging as a daring, independent broker on the global stage" (Dec. 25, 2014).

What kinds of deals is Francis brokering? Who do they benefit? The Vatican claims that the U.S.-Cuba deal is "in the interest of the citizens of both countries." Is that true?

First, look at whether it was good for the people of Cuba.

Critics of American foreign policy in general and of the U.S. embargo of Cuba tend to romanticize Cuba's ruling regime. That is a serious error! Under the Castros, the people of Cuba have suffered political terror and human rights abuses. Fidel and Raúl Castro have run the nation as a totalitarian police state, and they continue to model it after the Soviet Union. Cubans are the only people in the Western Hemisphere who haven't been able to elect a leader in more than 55 years.

When Russia and Venezuela, the main sponsors of the Castro regime, started suffering in the last few months due to falling oil prices, it looked as if the Castro government could finally collapse. That could have paved the way for democracy to finally prevail for Cubans. What the Castro brothers needed in order to survive was an economic lifeline from their enemy, the United States. And that is exactly what the pope and President Obama delivered. The deal also gave their criminal government international legitimacy.

Anybody familiar with the Castro regime's track record knows that legitimizing and propping it up is not in the interest of the people of Cuba! The deal is based on hopes of some American leaders that the Cuban government will reform, but they required no change from it. And it is extremely rare for dictators to voluntarily loosen their power.

The normalization of relations, according to Rep. Ileana Ros-Lehtinen, a Florida Republican, "will embolden the Castro regime to continue its illicit activities, trample on fundamental freedoms, and disregard democratic principles."

This is a bad deal for the Cubans

Was it good for the people of the United States? Under the Castro regime, Cuba has acted as one of the Western Hemisphere's major sponsors of terrorism and drug trafficking. Legitimizing it is a victory for those who want to see America fall. Giving in to that Communist regime emboldens America's enemies.

It is also important that, as part of the deal, Cuba released Alan Gross, an American citizen wrongfully imprisoned for five years, and the U.S. released three Cuban spies. To U.S. enemies, this sends a clear message: A surefire way to win policy concessions from Washington, or to rescue your friends captured by the U.S., is to take American citizens hostage and hold them as long as necessary.

This places America's weakness on display for the world to see. It also potentially endangers Americans by putting a price on their heads.

For America, this was a disgraceful surrender. The president undid a strategy that the nation had been using for 53 years, a strategy that might have been on the verge of toppling one of the world's most renowned criminal regimes.

Florida Republican Sen. Marco Rubio said, "[T]he policy changes announced by President Obama will have far-reaching consequences for the American people. … There can be no doubt that the regime in Tehran is watching closely, and it will try to exploit President Obama's naivety as the Iranian leaders pursue concessions from the U.S. in their quest to establish themselves as a nuclear power."

Many American leaders like Rubio didn't like that Cuban deal, but the pope was not fazed by that. Modern leaders would—and should—object to this kind of deal even more forcefully if they knew anything about the Holy Roman Empire. For many, the fact that the pope endorsed this deal made it more palatable! This shows that they really don't understand anything about that Vatican-guided empire. It looks so righteous, so good. But look at the history of the Catholic Church! Not only has it authored a lot of foreign-policy nightmares throughout the ages, but conservative estimates say it has presided over the deaths of more than 50 million people! Why do so many just forget all about that?

The German Role

Pope Francis is from Argentina, but we shouldn't forget that the Vatican got involved in this deal as early as March 2012, when the church was led by Pope Benedict. He is the German pope emeritus, and he has friends in high places in Germany. We need to watch this carefully, because Bible prophecy shows clearly that America, Britain and the Jewish nation are in grave danger and will be double-crossed by a reconstituted German-led Holy Roman Empire.

How will this happen? I think Cuba could be a significant part of the strategy. Nobody would suspect the pope of doing anything malicious or double-crossing us or anything like that, but if you look at what the Bible says about the organization he leads, you see that it is not what it appears to be. Study the history of every single time the Roman church started guiding European politics. You see a lot of blood spilled every time!

Look at the two men who were the main players of this deal: the pope, and the U.S. president. And if they are working something out behind the scenes, like this Cuba thaw, then you have to believe there may be something really big going on.

Pope Francis has made clear that he wants to topple the global system of free-market capitalism.

"[S]ome people continue to defend trickle-down theories which assume that economic growth, encouraged by a free market, will inevitably succeed in bringing about greater justice and inclusiveness in the world," he wrote in *Joy of the Gospel* (Evangelii Gaudium), his November 2013 apostolic exhortation.

"This opinion … expresses a crude and naive trust in the goodness of those wielding economic power."

History shows that our free market has provided far more goodness than the Vatican has when it was powerful! Francis called free-market global capitalism "a new tyranny" and condemned it as "a financial system which rules rather than serves."

Which nation is the model of free-market global capitalism? The United States of America.

If Pope Francis is to be taken at his word, he could not possibly wish for the capitalist example nation to thrive, prosper and continue inflicting its "tyranny" on the world. If he is sincere in saying the capitalist system is a force of destruction, then he would feel not only justified, but obligated to use his influence to weaken it. And if decreasing U.S. power is among Francis's goals, he may have discovered that the current U.S. administration shares in it—to varying degrees on various policy points.

Bible prophecy discusses a massive double cross that the German-led European Union will commit against America. That double cross very well could include cyberattacks. It could knock out huge parts of our power grid and cause serious mayhem. That prophecy says those European nations are America's "lovers" right now, but that will not be the case for long!

Here is what Charles Krauthammer wrote January 1/2015: "Vladimir Putin has repositioned Russia as America's leading geopolitical adversary and the Castro's signed up for that coalition too. Cuba has reportedly agreed to reopen the Soviet-era Lourdes espionage facility, a massive listening post for intercepting communications."

That "massive listening post," so close to the U.S., could make the cyberwar far more dangerous!

When you consider what the Vatican is doing, you see how the Holy Roman Empire could also get control of that espionage facility.

Hackers recently attacked the U.S. Central Command Twitter page. This prompted Ron Fournier of the National Journal to say, "We can be brought to our knees over the Internet"!

Ezekiel 7:14 is an end-time prophecy indicating that will happen! Can you imagine America, the great superpower, being attacked, and not even responding?

Here is a critical point that most people overlook. George Friedman wrote in Stratfor's Geopolitical Weekly Dec. 23, 2014: "After the Soviet Union tried to deploy intermediate range ballistic missiles there, a new layer was created in which Cuba was a potential threat to the American mainland, as well as to trade routes."

The Bible prophesies of a deadly economic siege that is going to strike America. It is one third of the terrifying damage that will be suffered in the Great Tribulation. That siege is about somebody controlling "trade routes"—so it is not difficult to see how Cuba could play a strategic role in that.

The German-led European Union is the seventh and final resurrection of the Holy Roman Empire—that same Holy Roman Empire which, centuries ago, used Cuba so powerfully to fuel its wars. If the present resurrection were to move into Cuba again, it would be well positioned to make these kinds of attacks happen. The advantage is that it could do it in the cloak of secrecy, since Cuba is essentially a police state with tight controls on information. Think of the control that it could have. Think of how valuable Cuba has been to America's enemies in the past! You need to watch what is happening in Cuba.

Jeremiah 30 prophesies about God bringing the Great Tribulation on end-time Israel, which is modern-day America and Britain and Commonwealth and other countries.

The Bible shows that this will all happen quickly. And we are getting so close to this time!

The seventh resurrection of the Holy Roman Empire is apt to burst on the world scene in a few short years. It will have similar ambitions to what Charles V and the fourth resurrection had, and all its other resurrections. And that includes the sixth one under the political rule of Adolf Hitler!

The seventh head will cause many problems in this world.

So, does the present Pope Francis hold to the same vitriol against the government of the United States as his predecessors, Pope Leo XIII and pope Pius IX did?

Columnist Thomas D. Williams writes,

"In a peculiar, rambling essay, papal adviser Father Antonio Spadaro SJ has caricatured white southern evangelicals as well as conservative American Catholics as ignorant, theocratic, Manichean, war-mongering fanatics anxiously awaiting the apocalypse."

It is "these religious groups that are composed mainly of whites from the deep American South" that push conflicts and justify belligerence, while favoring the Old Testament "rather than be guided by the incisive look, full of love, of Jesus in the Gospels."

The article appeared in both Italian and English in the Vatican-vetted journal La Civiltà Cattolica, of which Father Spadaro is editor-in-chief. In it, the Jesuit priest says that U.S. Evangelicals and Catholics have engaged in "an ecumenism of conflict" that seeks to advance "a theocratic type of state."

Spadaro, a friend and counselor of Pope Francis, was assisted in drafting the essay by an Argentinian Presbyterian minister, Marcelo Figueroa, an old friend of the Pope's who was hand-picked by the pontiff as editor-in-chief of the Argentinean edition of the Vatican newspaper L'Osservatore Romano.

Conservative Christians, the article warns, are ultimately driven by "the desire for some influence in the political and parliamentary sphere and in the juridical and educational areas so that public norms can be subjected to religious morals."

But is this really so? The story that has dominated religious liberty discussions in the U.S. since 2011 has been that of the Little Sisters of the Poor, a group of Catholic nuns that was harassed by the Obama administration under the HHS mandate of the Affordable Care Act and made it all the way to the Supreme Court. Do Spadaro and Figueroa really believe that the good sisters were fighting for "some influence in the political and parliamentary sphere" rather than simply asking to live according to their religious beliefs?

The sweeping generalizations of Spadaro and Figueroa and their evident lack of familiarity with the complex religious landscape in the United States prompts concern about the quality of advice that Pope Francis is receiving from close advisers.

In point of fact, the United States is one of the most religiously diverse and pluralistic countries in the world, far more than any European nation, a fact of which the authors seem woefully ignorant. Christians make up over 70 percent of the population, and while the largest single group is the Roman Catholic Church, there are literally hundreds of other Christian denominations as well as the vast world of non-denominational Christianity.

Moreover, while Spadaro and Figueroa describe the influence of religion in American public life as a recent phenomenon, nothing could be further from the truth. They write that the American tendency to view the world in terms of good and evil and to mingle "politics, morals and religion" dates back to the beginning of the 20th century, with the publication of Lyman Stewart's 12-volume work, The Fundamentals. While this work did give the name to Christian fundamentalism in America, it was not nearly as influential as the authors seem to think.

It was the Frenchman Alexis de Tocqueville, perhaps the greatest commentator on religion in America of all time, who in the first half of the 19th century marveled at the unique role that religion played in the young United States—so different from that in his native Europe. Despite the age of the work, it aptly describes the historical place of religion in American society and its vibrant and permanent interaction with politics and public morality.

In his monumental 1835 classic, Democracy in America, Tocqueville observed: "Upon my arrival in the United States the religious aspect of the country was the first thing that struck my attention; and the longer I stayed there, the more I perceived the great political consequences resulting from this new state of things."

And in one of the most famous passages of that same work, the Frenchman described what he believed to be the source of America's "greatness" (his term).

> I sought for the greatness and genius of America in her commodious harbors and her ample rivers – and it was not there . . . in her fertile fields and boundless forests and it was not there . . . in her rich mines and her vast world commerce – and it was not there . . . in her democratic Congress and her matchless Constitution – and it was not there. Not until I went into the churches of America and heard her pulpits aflame with righteousness did I understand the secret of her genius and power. America is great because she is good, and if America ever ceases to be good, she will cease to be great.

The reason for this, Tocqueville argued, stems from the close interaction between moral principles and religious faith, and the need for a virtuous citizenry in a democratic state. "Lovers of liberty," he said, "should hasten to call religion to their aid, for they must know that one cannot establish the reign of liberty without that of mores, and mores cannot be firmly founded without beliefs."

Americans' willingness to bring their faith to bear on their moral decision-making should not be confused with the straw men drawn by Spadaro and Figueroa who long for a confessional, theocratic state. It is precisely the healthy secularism in the United States and the refusal of the founders to establish a state religion that has allowed faith to play such an important role in public life.

En route to Washington DC in 2008, Pope Benedict XVI told journalists that he was "fascinated" by the fact that the American Founders had intentionally created a secular state, not out of hostility toward religion, but out of respect for it and because they understood that religion can be lived authentically only under conditions of freedom.

Later in his trip, Benedict noted approvingly that, historically, Americans "do not hesitate to bring moral arguments rooted in Biblical faith into their public discourse." And upon his return to Italy, the Pope spoke of America as a model of "healthy secularism." He described it as a society "where the religious dimension, with the diversity of its expressions, is not only tolerated but appreciated as the nation's 'soul' and as a fundamental guarantee of human rights and duties."

To take issue with this singularly religious self-understanding, as Spadaro and Figueroa do, is to take issue with the United States itself. While the two men are of course free to do this, they should be aware that such blatant anti-Americanism will win them few friends and besmirches whatever other good work they may choose to do. While they obviously sought to harness their partisan critique to attack President Donald Trump and his chief strategist Steve Bannon, they have ended up attacking America itself.

After insulting American evangelicals, in fact, Spadaro and Figueroa go on to assail those "who profess themselves to be Catholic" but express themselves in ways "much closer to Evangelicals."

"They are defined as value voters as far as attracting electoral mass support is concerned," the authors continue, and share a dangerous "ecumenical convergence" with evangelicals over shared objectives "around such themes as abortion, same-sex marriage, religious education in schools and other matters generally considered moral or tied to values."

One can only wonder what the authors were thinking on penning these expressions, since Pope Francis himself has weighed in repeatedly on each of these very issues, insisting that the right to life and the nature of man-woman marriage are not merely religious issues, but should be enshrined in law.

"So great is the value of a human life, and so inalienable the right to life of an innocent child growing in the mother's womb, that no alleged right to one's own body can justify a decision to terminate that life," he said last year in a teaching letter on marriage and the family, called Amoris Laetitia.

In a bizarre irony, the authors rail against confusing the political and religious realms in the midst of their undeniably political—and indeed deeply partisan—screed.

How they could get away with publishing something so puerile, bigoted and tendentious in what was once considered a very serious academic journal is a mystery.

If by so doing the authors think they are acting like bridge-builders, to use one of the Pope's favorite images, they are sorely mistaken. They have erected a wall of prejudice and partisan narrow-mindedness that is all but impossible to scale.

Regardless of who the pope is, black or white, the U.S. has been used as an arm of the Jesuits. It has been transformed into a huge crime syndicate. As these Roman CFR wars spread, and the U.S. loses credibility and influence through internal treachery in Washington, the EU is stealthily being made over into another incarnation of Charlemagne's Holy Roman Empire of the German Nation. A new superpower is emerging, it will be a resurrection of the Nazi era and it will prove to be the nightmare outlined in Holy Writ. This time there will be no strong UK/US alliance to stop it.

A recent meeting in the spring of 2013 between the Iranian government and prominent leaders of the Taliban highlights the fight for control in the Hindu Kush, and how all eyes are distracted from the most dangerous player in the region. While nations such as Iran, Afghanistan and Pakistan fight to influence the Taliban in order to shore up their borders and counter U.S. influence, they underestimate the European presence. Bible prophecy tells us that this oversight will have a terrible cost attached, not only for the nations of the Middle East, but for the whole world.

The meeting in Iran, held from May 31 to June 2, highlighted how Iran is attempting to build its relationship with a group that it has long been at odds with. The misgivings between Iran and the Taliban have been slowly healing since the U.S. invasion of Afghanistan, when Iran started supporting and training the Taliban to fight U.S. troops. Iran and Afghanistan almost went to war in 1998 when the Taliban executed 11 Iranian diplomats. Coming together to hold diplomatic discussion is something that wouldn't have been considered in the days just before the U.S. invasion of Afghanistan in 2001. Now Iran is showing that it is open to discussion with old rivals.

To Iran, the Taliban is a tool by which it can exert influence over the region and counter the United States. By focusing so intently on the U.S., however, it is neglecting the more dangerous influence of Germany. German influence in the region is expanding, while the U.S. is becoming less of a threat. Germany understands what will happen as U.S. influence wanes. As German-Foreign-Policy.com explained (Aug. 1, 2012):

Experts are warning that a power vacuum could emerge in 2014 in Afghanistan, and that new proxy conflicts between foreign powers could occur. According to a recently published analysis by the government-financed German Institute of Global and Area Studies (giga), "apprehensions" have emerged that following a withdrawal of the majority of the Western occupation troops in about two years, the Taliban will take over control in Kabul and the country will again be plunged into chaos.

German policies and plans in the Middle East will not allow Germany's influence in the region to be undermined. If Germany lost its power in the region, it would lose its encirclement of the oil "golden triangle." To ensure it has quick access to the oil-rich Middle East, Germany maintains a presence in the region: Its navy is deployed in the Mediterranean, thus securing Suez, and patrols the coast of Lebanon, securing the Levant; the German military is in Sudan; its navy is off the Somali and Yemeni coastlines securing the Persian Gulf; and its military is active in Afghanistan. Germany imported 366 thousand barrels of oil per day from the Middle East in 2011. The European Union imports around 40 percent of its oil from the Middle East today.

German positioning in the Middle East helps it maintain access to Middle Eastern oil, thus offsetting its dependence on Russia, while at the same time placing German troops in positions capable of decisive military action if needed. Afghanistan is ideally situated as a base from which Germany could move against Iran. With 4,000 troops on the ground in Afghanistan now, and talks on how a military presence might remain post-2014, Germany is showing that it is unwilling to give up its position.

The only reason we can look at the Middle East and understand the real forces at play is because of Bible prophecy. Daniel 11:40 speaks of the king of the north (the German-led EU) coming against the king of the south (Iranian-led radical Islam) like a whirlwind.

How, exactly, has the king of the north surrounded the king of the south? Its troops haven't encircled Tehran. It doesn't have bases and aircraft carriers dotting Iran's borders. But it has made some very intelligent, very strategic deployments and deals that give it a presence all the way around Iran's sphere of influence.

Look at a world map—Iran and its allies are in the middle of a deadly circle!

Iran is spreading its influence westward into Egypt and Libya. But across Libya's western border lies Algeria. Germany recently crafted a deal that sends $10.5 billion worth of military hardware to that country. It also has a personnel carrier plant there. It has a deal to manufacture rifles in Algeria. Berlin has connections even within Egypt and has sold it hundreds of millions of dollars in armaments, including two attack submarines worth $700 million.

To the southwest, Germany has a handful of soldiers and police officers in Sudan, South Sudan, Uganda and the Democratic Republic of Congo.

Much closer to Iran, directly across the Persian Gulf, lie the Arabian Peninsula nations. Germany has sold $2.6 billion in weapons to Qatar, including dozens of Leopard II tanks. It has sold $9.3 billion in weapons to the United Arab Emirates and built a munitions factory there.

Germany is also working on some massive deals with Saudi Arabia. Among them: It is building a machine-gun factory there, and sending the Saudis 72 Eurofighters and somewhere between 270 and 800 Leopard II tanks.

There are also German military personnel in Djibouti and Somalia. In the Arabian Sea, the Bundeswehr has a frigate, maritime surveillance planes and 340 troops.

Look on the far side of Iran, and you see 4,400 German soldiers staying in its eastern neighbor, Afghanistan, even while American troops pull out. Washington is eager to get out—but Berlin has something else in mind.

Just north of Afghanistan is Uzbekistan. There, the German military operates an air base in Termez, with about 300 military staff plus transport aircraft.

The king of the north also has a strong presence to Iran's north. To the northwest, in the Mediterranean, lies Cyprus, a strategic military and intelligence asset. The terms that Germany dictated for Cyprus's economic bailout in mid-April basically gave the EU control of this island.

The Bundeswehr has deployed two anti-aircraft missile batteries in Turkey, along with 400 soldiers. In addition, it has developed the nation into a massive weapons export market, selling Turkey 715 tanks, 687 armored personnel carriers, 300 air defense missile systems, 197 ground survey radar units, eight frigates, two support ships and 15 submarines in the last two decades.

The German military has two patrol boats off Lebanon and up to 300 soldiers on the ground. It also has the largest contingent in Kosovo—1,249 soldiers—and a small presence in Bosnia and Herzegovina.

Germany is third in arms exporting behind the U.S. and Russia, and will probably become number one soon!

And this doesn't even touch the weapons industries and the land, sea and air power amassing inside Germany itself—or the deployments and power of its European, African and Middle Eastern allies—or the economic power of the European Union, which is dominated by Berlin.

Why is Germany so involved, stretching over the Middle East and much of the world? It is preparing for a whirlwind of destruction.

Germany has been at the heart of several resurrections of the "Holy" Roman Empire spanning more than

1,500 years. It thinks in terms of the Reich, which means empire.

The Allies never rooted out that deep feeling after World Wars I and II. After the Second World War, the Allies said, "It is our inflexible purpose to destroy German militarism and Nazism and to ensure that Germany will never again be able to disturb the peace of the world." But look at the map and you can see who is really preparing for war! Just as in 1870, 1914 and 1939, German militarism is about to again disturb the peace!

Germany has surrounded Iran and radical Islam, just as God prophesied it would. Soon that whirlwind is going to start rotating and whirling against the king of the south like a well-armed—probably nuclear-armed—vortex!

Right now, Iran is countering the U.S. and the EU- and trying to exert influence over its neighbors such as Afghanistan through forces like the Taliban and other terrorist organizations across the Middle East. Iran is well versed in gaining influence through the terrorists it sponsors. But, because it is so focused on its own ambitions, it fails to see that it is already caught in the German whirlwind.

As Dwight Eisenhower left office in January of 1961, he warned America against a military-industrial complex spinning out of control. This warning was almost completely ignored, of course, as the best warnings usually are.

Nonetheless, Eisenhower told us that the military-industrial complex would bankrupt the nation and subvert education in America. And then he did something that very few people remember: he expressed his concern that America's spiritual life would be undermined by the military-industrial complex:

(Its) total influence—economic, political, even spiritual—is felt in every city, every state house, every office of the federal government… we must not fail to comprehend its grave implications.

I'm almost tempted to call that speech prophetic. But prophetic or not, Ike nailed it. What he warned us about has happened. And perhaps nowhere have his "grave implications" been more apparent over recent years than in America's spiritual life.

Regardless of our many and varied beliefs, it is clear that the churches of America have always mattered a great deal. Tocqueville was struck by that fact back in the 1830s and it remains true in our time.

Churches are where the vast majority of Americans get their philosophical thought. Lord knows they can't get much of it from TV or from politicians. If the average American is going to sit still and listen to someone talk about things that matter, it will more than likely be in a church.

So, when a majority of American churches all pivot at once, it's an important event.

What Has Happened

Let me be blunt in defining this change: The US military, as Samuel Morse foresaw, joined with the church in promoting a joint righteousness, and the church became a cheerleader for the military.

I understand that this is a very stark statement, but it's something that I think all of us have noticed. We may use different words to describe it, but we all see it.

And what we have seen is church and state joining together in a type of partnership. This partnership filled churches and gave the US military a plentiful supply of recruits. Most importantly, it created a populace that reflexively supported the American war machine.

I view this as turning military service into a new type of sacrament, or at least a new standard of righteousness. Here are the specific things I see:

1/ American sporting events now begin with what are, essentially, worship services. God blessing America and the honor of the US military are mixed together, with swelling music, the singing of anthems, hands held over hearts, roaring airplanes, and more.

2/ The wounded soldier has become a new type of martyr.

3/ Soldiers in general have become the new missionaries, going to far-away, dangerous lands to spread "freedom," which has become a compliment or replacement for the gospel.

4/ Church services are now filled with state imagery. Flags are proudly displayed and politicians are prayed for.

5/ Veteran's Day, Memorial Day, and the 4th of July and have become holy days, complete with military guest speakers and ceremonies to praise soldiers.

6/ Local boys and girls who enlist in the military are praised from the pulpit.

7/ "Christ died for our sins and soldiers die for our freedoms" is now a widely accepted belief... the kind of thing people say "amen" to and feel righteous about.

None of these are "Jesus things." Changes like this have occurred in the past, but not in any periods we'd want to emulate.

The Grave Consequences

War is not our friend. It is not uplifting. It is not enlightening. And while most of us will maintain our right to self-defense, no one with any experience believes that killing other humans makes us better.

The American era of global hegemony is being destroyed in favour of trading Constitutional freedoms for security and to wage war. And it is all planned and manufactured. George W. Bush had been to Rome to see the Pope only a month or so prior to the World Trade Center attack. President Obama has had at least 3 audiences with the pope[s]. These meetings are in the form of a master and servant paradigm, as the various chess pieces are placed around the globe. Leviticus chapter 26, Deuteronomy chapter 28 and Ezekiel chapters 5-7 describes the end result.

This geo-political world view of a final push to rid the globe of heretics, infidels and sundry other individualists, was inadvertently alluded to by President Bush's "crusade" remark. The Vatican is busy folding the denominations of Christendom under her skirts under the banner of unity and has been doing so fervently since the 1980's, but unity without truth is whoredom.

The Bible is a history of a family God has chosen to establish righteous government on earth. All of the prophecies concerning the Houses of Israel and Judah and what this means for the world at large are playing out now in real time.

I am mourning for America, because she is dying. I am mourning for a nation that once knew such greatness but that has now fallen to depths that were once unimaginable. I am mourning for the death and destruction that are coming, and I am mourning for a future that our children and our grandchildren will never get to see. I am mourning for a nation that has refused to listen to the warnings and that now stands on the precipice of judgment. I am mourning for games that will never be played, for books that will never be finished, for family vacations that will never get to happen and for memories that will never be made. I am mourning for the economic depression that is coming, for the horror and suffering that friends and family will endure, and for the coming death of the country.

The Republic that trusted in God and stamped it indelibly as their motto, the very ones who God calls, 'My People', has come a long way from the faith of its fathers. We are no longer, "good".

Given our distorted view on what now constitutes the will of God, without the National repentance that Lincoln saw as the remedy for the nation in his days of war with the factions of Globalism and slavery, I doubt that God will allow the Republic 'under God' to survive.

Appendix

The legal justification of Papal claim to ownership of the North American colonies as an extension of the British Realm. King John I buys his 'salvation' through perpetual taxation to fill the Papacy's coffers

John I: Concession of England and her possessions in perpetuity to the Pope 1213

John, by the grace of God, king of England, lord of Ireland, duke of Normandy and Aquitaine, count of Anjou, to all the faithful of Christ who shall look upon this present charter, greeting.

We wish it to be known to all of you, through this our charter, furnished with our seal, that inasmuch as we had offended in many ways God and our mother the holy church, and in consequence are known to have very, much needed the divine mercy, and cannot offer anything worthy for making due satisfaction to God and to the church unless we humiliate ourselves and our kingdoms:-we, wishing to humiliate ourselves for Him who humiliated Himself for us unto death, the grace of the Holy Spirit inspiring, not induced by force or compelled by fear, but of our own good and spontaneous will and by the common counsel of our barons, do offer and freely concede to God and His holy apostles Peter and Paul and to our mother the holy Roman church, and to our lord pope Innocent and to his Catholic successors, the whole kingdom of England and the whole kingdom Ireland, with all their rights and appurtenances, for the remission of our own sins and of those of our whole race as well for the living as for the dead; and now receiving and holding them, as it were a vassal, from God and the Roman church, in the presence of that prudent man Pandulph, subdeacon and of the household of the lord pope, we perform and swear fealty for them to him our aforesaid lord pope Innocent, and his catholic successors and the Roman church, according to the form appended; and in the presence of the lord pope, if we shall be able to come before him, we shall do liege homage to him; binding our successors and our heirs by our wife forever, in similar manner to perform fealty and show homage to him who shall be chief pontiff at that time, and to the Roman church without demur.

As a sign, moreover, we will establish perpetual obligation and concession, we will establish that from the proper and especial revenues of our aforesaid kingdoms, for all the service and customs which we ought to render for them, saving in all things the penny of St. Peter, the Roman church shall receive yearly a thousand marks sterling, namely at the feast of St. Michael five hundred marks, and at Easter five hundred marks-seven hundred, namely, for the kingdom of England, and three hundred for the kingdom of Ireland-saving to us and to our heirs our rights, liberties and regalia; all of which things, as they have been described above, we wish to have perpetually valid and firm; and we bind ourselves and our successors not to act counter to them. And if we or any one of our successors shall presume to attempt this, whoever he be, unless being duly warned he come to his kingdom, and this senses, be shall lose his right to the kingdom, and this charter of our obligation and concession shall always remain firm.

Form of the oath of fealty

I, John, by the grace of God, 'king of England and lord of Ireland, from this hour forth will be faithful to God and St. Peter and the Roman church and my lord pope Innocent and his Successors who are ordained in a Catholic manner: I shall not bring it about by deed, word, consent or counsel, that they lose life or members or be taken captive, I will impede their being harmed if I know of it, and will cause harm to be removed from them if I shall be able: otherwise as quickly as I can I will intimate it or tell of it to such persons as I believe for certain will inform them. Any counsel which they entrust to me through themselves or through their envoys or through their letters, I will keep secret, nor will I knowingly disclose it to anyone to their harm. I will aid to the best of my ability in holding and defending against all men the patrimony of St. Peter, and especially the kingdom of England and the kingdom of Ireland. So may God and these holy Gospels aid me.

I myself bearing witness in the house of the Knights Templars near Dover, in the presence of master H., archbishop of Dublin; master J., bishop of Norwich; G., the son of Peter count of Essex, our justice; W., count of Salisbury, our brother; W. Marshall, count of Pembroke; R., count of Boulogne; W., count of Warren; S., count of Winchester; W., count of Arundel; W., count of Ferrieres; W, Briwer; Peter, son of Herbert; Warin, son of Gerold; on the 15th day of May, in the 14th year of our reign.

Stubb's Charters, p. 284, translated in Ernest F. Henderson, Select Historical Documents of the Middle Ages, (London: George Bell, 1910), pp. 430-431

Following pages 1891 encyclical of Pope Leo XIII

-

After Abraham Lincoln defeated the Jesuits and the globalist/feudalists of Europe under Pope Pius IX, the Jesuits renewed their effort to launch a religious, race and class war on U.S. soil under Pope Leo XIII. This encyclical is first and foremost addressed to the Jesuits and future popes. It was hidden in Quebec for over 120 years, until now. In 1983 Pope John Paul 2 claimed the U.S. for the Vatican when he symbolically kissed the tarmac in Washington D.C. In 2015 Pope Francis I, a Jesuit, came to Washington and Philadelphia and addressed the U.N. in N.Y. to deliver his marching orders. The U.S. Congress and the Administration, specifically those in the CFR [deep state] acted in concert to these orders

ENCYCLICAL.

A Letter From Pope Leo XIII to the Romish World.

Heretics Cut Off From the Church—They Have No Rights--Non-Romish Citizens of the United States Must Have No Privileges--All Papist Absolved from their Allegiance to the United States Government

ENCYCLICAL LETTER OF HIS HOLINESS LEO XIII, By Divine Providence Pope.

To the Jesuits, Patriarch, Primates, Archbishops, and other Ordinaries in Peace and Communion with the Apostolic See of the entire World.

For the Temporal Reign of the Future Popes, in the Land Discovered by Christopher Columbus, known as the United States of America.

Venerable Brethren: Greeting and the Apostolic Benediction, Leo, bishop and servant of the servants of God; be it remembered by posterity that he who is omnipotent in heaven and on earth, hath confided his church, which is one Holy Catholic, and Apostolical, and out of which there is no salvation, to one man upon earth, namely, to Peter, prince and apostles, and to the bishops of Rome, his successors, with full power to rule over it.

This pontiff alone hath been constituted head over all nations and kingdoms, and invested with power to destroy, to separate, to scatter, and subvert, to plant, build up, link together by mutual charity, in order to preserve the faithful in the spirit of unity, and surrender them whole and entire to their Saviour.

In order to fulfil the duties imposed on us by the divine goodness, we labor incessantly to maintain the unity of the Roman Catholic religion which God hath visited with heavy conflicts to the end, that His own may be tried, and for our correction; but the numbers and powers of the wicked have so far prevailed, that no portion of the earth has escaped their attempts to propagate their infectious and detested dogmas, being supported, among others, by that slave to every species of crime.

The American Republic under Protestant rulers is with the worst enemies of the church, where security is offered; this Republic having seized upon the lands discovered by Christopher Columbus a Catholic, and usurped the authority and jurisdiction of the supreme head of the church, the United States is filled with obscure heretics.

The Catholics have been oppressed, and the preachers of iniquity established.

The sacrifice of the mass, prayers, fastings, abstinence, celibacy and all the rites of Catholicity have been ignored by protestants.

The United States has been filled with books containing the most flagrant heresies of which the protestant version of the Bible is chief. And not content with adopting its false and impious doctrines, proselyting has been resorted to, to turn the Catholics from the one true Church. The whole Roman Catholic hierarchy and priesthood of the world, have been deprived of their livings by the Protestant heretics of America.

Courts have been set up and rendered decisions in ecclesiastical causes, and the people forbidden to acknowledge the authority of the Roman Church, or to obey its ordinances and cannonical decisions.

Naturalization oaths have been demanded in order that the subjects of the True Church might be made to subscribe to the United States Constitution, with its impious laws and nefarious teachings to compel them to renounce the true authority of the Catholic pontiff; to disacknowledge Him to be the head of both church and state, whereby those who have persevered in the faith have been compelled to suffer spiritual afflictions.

The Catholic bishops and clergy have been deprived of vast lands and this is known to all nations, and so clearly proved, that all palliation, argument, or protest on the part of the United States is unavailing.

We find, moreover, that impiety and crime have increased, that persecution against the religion of Rome has been redoubled by the Protestants dwelling in the United States of America.

With deep sorrow we are now constrained to have recourse to the arm of justice, and are obliged to take action against a nation that has rejected the Pope as head of all church and state governments.

In virtue, therefore, of the divine authority by which we have been placed on this Supreme throne of justice, an office so superior to our capability, we do, in the plenitude of apostolic power declare that all heretics and the encouragers of heresy, together with all adherents, have incurred the sentence of excommunication, and they are hereby cut off from the unity of the body of Jesus Christ.

Moreover, we proclaim the people of the United States of America to have forfeited all right to rule said Republic, and also all dominion, dignity and privileges appertaining to it. We likewise declare that all subjects of every rank and condition in the United States and every individual who has taken any oath of loyalty to the United States in any way whatever, may be absolved from said oath, as also from all duty, fidelity or obedience on or about the 5th of September, 1893, when the Catholic Congress shall convene at Chicago, Illinois, as we shall exonerate them from all engagements, and on or about the feast of Ignatius Loyola in the year of our Lord, 1893, it will be the duty of the faithful to exterminate all heretics found within the jurisdiction of the United States of America.

As the circulation of this bull, by sending to all places, would become a matter of difficulty, it is commanded that copies of it be taken and signed by jesuit notaries, subscribed by a bishop, and sealed with the seal of our court, they will then have the same power and efficacy as these presents here.

Given at St. Peters Rome, on the 25th of December, 1891, the fifteenth year of Our Pontificate. LEO XIII, POPE.

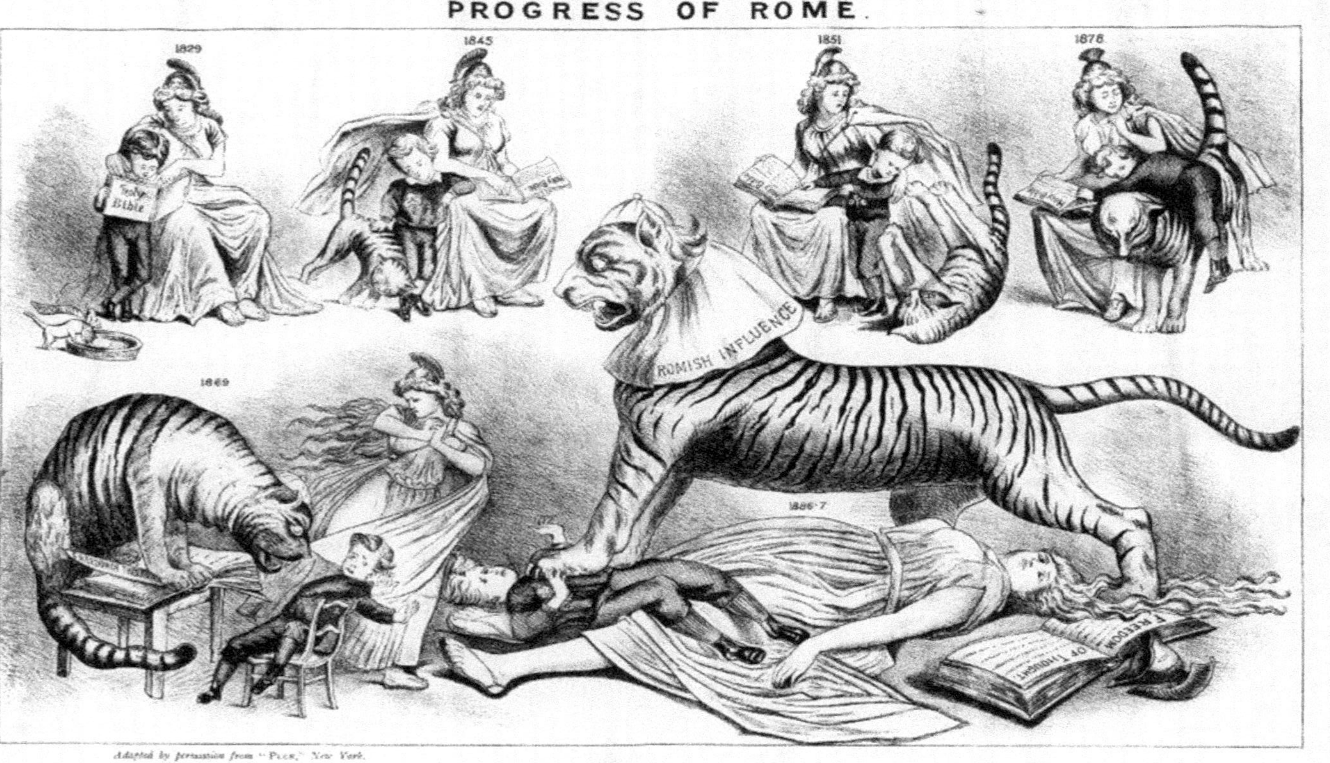

Adapted by permission from "Puck," New York.

1829 Catholic Emancipation.
1845 Maynooth Grant.
1851 Establishment of Romish Hierarchy in England.
1878 ditto ditto in Scotland.
1869 Overthrow of Protestant Church in Ireland.
1886-7 Dismemberment of the Empire and Destruction of Protestantism.

Supplement to Protestant Standard.

Photo: National Archives | HistoricCamdenCounty.com

WASHINGTON, D.C. (July 7, 1865) -- Dead on the gallows are Lincoln assassination conspirators Mary Surratt (left), the first woman ever put to death by the Federal Government, and Lewis Thornton Powell. Powell had attacked and attempted to assassinate Secretary of State William Seward at the same time John Wilkes Booth was shooting Lincoln.

THE PATRIOT

DETROIT, MICH., SATURDAY, FEB

POPE LEO'S

What Will Happen in the United States in

IC AMERICAN.

RUARY 25. 1893.

S DREAM.

1893 and '4 If His Dream Is Realized.

NO CHURCH NEED APPLY.

LITTLE JONATHAN. "Miss Columbia will not try your teaching, as it has proved to be so injurious in Dame Europa's school that our adopted children who left her don't care to learn under that system again."

THE INFALLIBLE ONE. "Oh, you Galileos, infidel vipers, I'll be revenged on you, for I keep the keys of heaven!"

Is America facing another Civil War?

A specter is haunting the United States—the specter of political violence. During the lead-up to the 2018 midterm elections, a mentally disturbed supporter of President Donald Trump was arrested on October 26 for sending pipe bombs to the addresses of prominent Democrats: Barack Obama, Hillary Clinton, George Soros, Eric Holder, John Brennan and Maxine Waters. Five days later, an agitated man carrying a "Trump is Satan" sign threatened to blow up a Republican Party office building in Traverse City, Michigan.

Gunshots were fired at a Republican Party office in Florida on October 29, the same day that actor James Cromwell told Variety magazine that there would be "blood in the streets" if Democrats did not stop President Trump.

Many Americans sense that this has been one of the most combative, even violent political climates in living memory. A Politico–Morning Consult poll conducted in late October found 58 percent of respondents consider political violence to be "widespread." One third blamed President Trump for the violence, while another third blamed Democrats in Congress. Almost two thirds thought the media was responsible for dividing the country.

Since Democrats failed to win back the Senate during midterm elections, violence may well worsen as leftists intensify their protests against Republicans, who control the presidency, the Supreme Court and the Senate.

"You cannot be civil with a political party that wants to destroy what you stand for," Hillary Clinton said on October 9. "I believe if we are fortunate enough to take back the House and/or the Senate, that's when civility can start again. But until then, the only thing that the Republicans seem to recognize and respect is strength."

An apparently growing number of Democrats believe they should unshackle themselves from human decency in their quest for power. For decades, leftists have been able to vote progressive policies into law via the ballot box. When the people and their congressional representatives have opposed those policies, they have used executive actions and Supreme Court rulings to push their agenda into law. But after being out of power for two years, many leftists are turning to 1960s-style rioting and protesting.

One third of Americans think a civil war is coming. Bible prophecy reveals they are right. But is this civil war coming because Republicans outmaneuvered Democrats in an election? What is the real cause? It is deeper than most people realize.

Enraged Democrats

Election exit polls show that 77 percent of Democrats support impeaching President Trump. The term "impeachment" is defined as "a charge of misconduct made against the holder of a public office" (Oxford English Dictionary). But impeachment does not remove an official from office. An impeached official must be convicted by a two-thirds vote in the Senate to be legally removed from office. This has never happened in American history. Now that Democrats have a slim majority in the House of Representatives, they have the power to impeach the president. But they control less than a majority of Senate seats, and would need 67 votes to convict the president.

Since they cannot convict, Democrats are wary of immediately pursuing impeachment. Instead, Democratic Rep. Nancy Pelosi plans to sue President Trump for his tax returns and support special counsel Robert Mueller's ongoing investigation into allegations that the Trump campaign coordinated with the Russian government prior to the 2016 elections. Democrats are expected to block Mr. Trump's legislative ambitions, scuttling his planned border wall with Mexico, his second major tax-cut package, and his trade policies.

Still, the biggest threat from America's growing political divide is politically motivated violence. Democrats in the House of Representatives plan to accuse President Trump of tax fraud or charge him for collusion with the Russian government. If this happens, then what would follow when Senate Republicans refuse to convict the president? If the Democrats' reaction to Justice Brett Kavanaugh's confirmation to the Supreme Court is a preview of things to come, left-wing protesters and activists may well riot.

Hillary Clinton said that civility could resume again when Democrats are back in power. Until then, the left will protest, riot, agitate, accuse, confront, scream, fight, kick and do whatever it takes to reclaim power.

The last time leftists resorted to these extreme tactics was in the 1960s and 1970s. During that era, the Black Panthers, the Weather Underground and other radical groups used terrorist tactics to fight the U.S. government. One presidential study pointed to a "crisis of violence" during the first 15 months of Richard Nixon's presidency, a period that included some 41,000 bomb threats and bombings. Meanwhile, radicals threatened to assassinate the president and burn down the houses of members of his cabinet.

Things have not gotten that bad during the first two years of Trump's presidency. Still, 1960s-style political violence has returned to America, and it is threatening to get much worse.

Violent Protests Prophesied

Some 2,500 years ago, God revealed an end-time prophecy to a Jewish slave named Ezekiel, who was being held captive in the Land of Babylon. "Moreover he said unto me, Son of man, eat that thou findest; eat this roll, and go speak unto the house of Israel" (Ezekiel 3:1).

This prophecy is addressed to "the house of Israel." It was not delivered to Israel in Ezekiel's day, because 10 of the 12 tribes of Israel were already in captivity in Assyria (while Ezekiel was in Babylon). Yet God had Ezekiel write down His message to Israel, foretelling of a future time when famine and war would devastate the cities of a rebellious Israelite nation.

"Moreover the word of the Lord came to me, saying, Son of man, eat thy bread with quaking, and drink thy water with trembling and with carefulness; And say unto the people of the land, Thus saith the Lord God of the inhabitants of Jerusalem, and of the land of Israel; They shall eat their bread with carefulness, and drink their water with astonishment, that her land may be desolate from all that is therein, because of the violence of all them that dwell therein. And the cities that are inhabited shall be laid waste, and the land shall be desolate; and ye shall know that I am the Lord" (Ezekiel 12:17-20).

This passage describes cities being laid waste "because of the violence of all them that dwell therein." This is describing a civil war that escalates into a foreign invasion. In Ezekiel 5, God reveals that one third of the nation's population will die from the pestilence, famine and violence that result from the civil war.

The pestilence, or plague of violence, will cause many health problems that lead to famine, sewage disposal will be disrupted. Gas lines will be broken. Jobs will be lost. Society will unravel and the collective panic will bring a stock market disaster! It will get so bad that violence and famine will take millions of lives!

Such devastation has never occurred in an Israelite nation from the time of Ezekiel until now. This is an end-time prophecy about the United States.

1960s Radicalism

It is easy for Democrats to blame political violence on President Trump, and it is easy for Republicans to blame leftist agitators in the streets. But the root cause of political violence in America stretches back decades.

The ideological conflict between Republicans and Democrats decreased after the U.S. Civil War ended in 1865. It continued narrowing—until the 1960s. That was when the cultural revolution struck America. As a result, the ideological conflict began increasing again. Today, direct opposition between America's two political parties is wider than at any point in the past 150 years.

The leaders of the modern Democratic Party were student radicals in the 1960s. And their ideological grandchildren—and in some cases their literal grandchildren—are the supporters of radical socialists like Sen. Bernie Sanders and newly elected Rep. Alexandria Ocasio Cortez.

Inspired by the writings of Communist philosophers like Antonio Gramsci and Herbert Marcuse, these radicals believe that utopia can happen only after an economic revolution. And economic revolution can happen only after a cultural revolution. So in addition to advocating socialist economic reforms, they have revolutionized views on sex, gender and race. Many of these student radicals flooded into two professions in particular: community organizing and academia. They accused America's system of individual liberty and constitutional checks and balances of being a mask for the power of wealthy, white European males.

The first generation in American history that could afford college education en masse learned in lecture halls dominated by socialists. These students were taught that traditional American principles like personal responsibility, individual liberty, free markets and limited government were racist and elitist. They were taught that the only way to create utopia on Earth was through democratic socialism. College students of the 1960s and 1970s absorbed these views not just because of youthful rebellion, but because they were specifically, explicitly targeted by socialists. This was a major step in revolutionizing American culture.

The ideological clash in America today is largely between the older generation and the younger generation. But how did this happen? How did a generation of Americans come to so radically reject their parents' values?

A New Generation

God delivered a sober warning to America's Israelite ancestors about teaching His laws to their children.

"Now therefore hearken, O Israel, unto the statutes and unto the judgments, which I teach you, for to do them, that ye may live, and go in and possess the land which the Lord God of your fathers giveth you. … Only take heed to thyself, and keep thy soul diligently, lest thou forget the things which thine eyes have seen, and lest they depart from thy heart all the days of thy life: but teach them thy sons, and thy sons' sons; Specially the day that thou stoodest before the Lord thy God in Ho-reb, when the Lord said unto me, Gather me the people together, and I will make them hear my words, that they may learn to fear me all the days that they shall live upon the earth, and that they may teach their children" (Deuteronomy 4:1, 9-10).

Americans do not reverence and obey God's Ten Commandments as they once did, and they have failed to teach their children about their nation's history with God. A USA Today poll found that only 1 in 6 Americans can even list the Ten Commandments. Adultery, fornication, divorce and other sins have destroyed families and created a generation that has lost faith in God. This generation is more likely to look to the federal government to give them their daily bread. The religious crisis America is suffering has created a spiritual vacuum that people are striving to fill with material pleasures and false ideas. Some turn to socialism and worship the state. Others turn to individualism and worship themselves. But the end result of this spiritual crisis will be social division, unrest and even violence as Americans clash with each other.

It is a fact that godless rationalism was behind the political violence of the 1960's. The present world crisis had already started prior to World War One, only most of the people were unaware of it. But men like Jesuit trained and educated Karl Marx and Lenin knew. This present world crisis resulted from the impact of science and technology – and the injection of godless 'German Rationalism' into the educational system. World Wars are the military expression of that crisis. Worldwide depressions are the economic expression. The so-called 'New Morality' is the moral expression. Universal desperation is the spiritual expression. This, in turn, has spawned riots, marches, civil disobedience and the collapse and breakdown of law and order.

Now many of the student radicals who caused so much violence in the 1960s have won control of the Democratic Party. They are pushing the nation into not only a cultural revolution or economic revolution, but into a violent revolution. This never would have happened if people had clung to God's law and taught their children to do the same.

Civil war is coming to America, not because one political party outmaneuvered another, but because, as Abraham Lincoln noted, the American people have turned away from God.

Many Americans are troubled by the divisions and hatreds being expressed right now, but they need to be a lot more concerned than they are! The problems are going to get worse and worse until people get the message, and they learn why these disasters are happening! Donald Trump's win is a prophetic sign of impending civil war and anarchy, followed by America's worst military defeat ever! But don't blame the politicians or the race-baiters or the professional rioters. This situation exists in America only because of the sins of the nation—of all Americans! We can no longer ignore what we have reaped by giving ourselves over to sin.

This is a reckoning!

God will allow the people of America to experience a second civil war for the same reason He allowed them to experience the first Civil War: to teach them the natural consequences of broken law. It will take real repentance to bring people back to God and end the "total crisis" that has gripped the nation.

Abraham Lincoln's Thanksgiving Day Proclaimation

Washington, D.C.
October 3, 1863

By the President of the United States of America.

A Proclamation.

The year that is drawing towards its close, has been filled with the blessings of fruitful fields and healthful skies. To these bounties, which are so constantly enjoyed that we are prone to forget the source from which they come, others have been added, which are of so extraordinary a nature, that they cannot fail to penetrate and soften even the heart which is habitually insensible to the ever watchful providence of Almighty God. In the midst of a civil war of unequalled magnitude and severity, which has sometimes seemed to foreign States to invite and to provoke their aggression, peace has been preserved with all nations, order has been maintained, the laws have been respected and obeyed, and harmony has prevailed everywhere except in the theatre of military conflict; while that theatre has been greatly contracted by the advancing armies and navies of the Union. Needful diversions of wealth and of strength from the fields of peaceful industry to the national defence, have not arrested the plough, the shuttle or the ship; the axe has enlarged the borders of our settlements, and the mines, as well of iron and coal as of the precious metals, have yielded even more abundantly than heretofore. Population has steadily increased, notwithstanding the waste that has been made in the camp, the siege and the battle-field; and the country, rejoicing in the consciousness of augmented strength and vigor, is permitted to expect continuance of years with large increase of freedom. No human counsel hath devised nor hath any mortal hand worked out these great things. They are the gracious gifts of the Most

High God, who, *while dealing with us in anger for our sins*, hath nevertheless remembered mercy. It has seemed to me fit and proper that they should be solemnly, reverently and gratefully acknowledged as with one heart and one voice by the whole American People. I do therefore invite my fellow citizens in every part of the United States, and also those who are at sea and those who are sojourning in foreign lands, to set apart and observe the last Thursday of November next, as a day of Thanksgiving and Praise to our beneficent Father who dwelleth in the Heavens. And I recommend to them that while offering up the ascriptions justly due to Him for such singular deliverances and blessings, they do also, with humble penitence for our national perverseness and disobedience, commend to His tender care all those who have become widows, orphans, mourners or sufferers in the lamentable civil strife in which we are unavoidably engaged, and fervently implore the interposition of the Almighty Hand to heal the wounds of the nation and to restore it as soon as may be consistent with the Divine purposes to the full enjoyment of peace, harmony, tranquillity and Union.

In testimony whereof, I have hereunto set my hand and caused the Seal of the United States to be affixed.

Done at the City of Washington, this Third day of October, in the year of our Lord one thousand eight hundred and sixty-three, and of the Independence of the United States the Eighty-eighth.

By the President: Abraham Lincoln

William H. Seward,
Secretary of State

Thomas Jefferson's original draft of the Declaration of Independence, 28 June, 1776 with hand-written corrections

A Declaration by the Representatives of United States of America, in General Congress Assembled

When, in the course of human events, it becomes necessary for a people to advance from that subordination in which they have hitherto remained, and to assume among the powers of the earth, the equal and independent station to which the laws of nature and of nature's god entitle them, a decent respect to the opinions of mankind requires that they should declare the causes which impel them to the change

We hold these truths to be [sacred and undeniable] selfevident, that all men are created equal and independent; that from that equal creation they derive in rights inherent and inalienables, among which are the preservation of life, and liberty and the pursuit of happiness; that to secure these ends, governments are instituted among men, deriving their just powers from the consent of the governed; that whenever any form of government shall become destructive of these ends, it is the right of the people to alter or to abolish it, and to institute new government, laying its foundation on such principles and organizing it's powers in such form, as to them shall seem most likely to effect their safety and happiness. prudence, indeed, will dictate that governments long established should not be changed for light and transient causes: and accordingly all experience hath shewn that mankind are more disposed to suffer while evils are sufferable, than to right themselves by abolishing the forms to which they are accustomed. But when a long train of abuses and usurpations, begun at a distinguished period, and pursuing invariably the same object evinces a design to [subject] reduce them to arbitrary power, it is their right, it is their duty, to throw off such government, and to provide new guards for their future security. --

Such has been the patient sufferance of these colonies; and such is now the necessity which constrains them to expunge their former systems of government. the history of his present majesty is a history of unremitting injuries and usurpations, among which no fact stands single or solitary to contradict the uniform tenor of the rest, all of which have in direct object the establishment of an absolute tyranny over these states. To prove this, let facts be submitted to a candid world, for the truth of which we pledge a faith yet unsullied by falsehood.

He has refused his assent to laws, the most wholesome and necessary for the public good:

He has forbidden his governors to pass laws of immediate and pressing importance, unless suspended in their operation till his assent should be obtained; and when so suspended, he has neglected utterly to attend to them.

He has refused to pass other laws for the accommodation of large districts of people unless those people would relinquish the right of representation [in the legislature], a right inestimable to them and formidable to tyrants only:

He has dissolved representative houses repeatedly, for opposing with manly firmness his invasions on the rights of the people.

[he has dissolved] he has refused for a long space of time, to cause others to be elected, whereby the legislative powers, incapable of annihilation, have returned to the people at large for their exercise, the state remaining in the meantime exposed to all the dangers of invasion from without, and convulsions within:

He has endeavored to prevent the population of these states; for that purpose obstructing the laws for naturalization of foreigners; refusing to pass others to encourage their migration hither, and raising the conditions of new appropriations of lands:

He has suffered the administration of justice totally to cease in some of these colonies, refusing his assent to laws for establishing judiciary powers:

He has made our judges dependent on his will alone, for the tenure of their offices, and the amount of their salaries.

He has erected a multitude of new offices by a self-assumed power, and sent hither swarms of officers to harrass our people, and eat out their substance.

He has kept among us, in times of peace, standing armies and ships of war:

He has affected to render the military, independent of and superior to civil power:

He has combined with others to subject us to a jurisdiction foreign to our constitutions, and unacknowledged by our laws; giving his assent to their pretended acts of legislation, for quartering large bodies of armed troops among us;

for protecting them, by mock trial, from punishment for any murders [which] they should commit on the inhabitants of these states; for cutting off our trade with all parts of the world;

for imposing taxes on us without our consent;

for depriving us of the benefits of trial by jury;

for transporting us beyond seas to be tried for pretended offenses;

for taking away our charters, and altering fundamentally the forms of our governments;

for suspending our own legislatures, and declaring themselves invested with power to legislate for us in all cases whatsoever;

he has abdicated government here, withdrawing his governors, and declaring us out of his alegiance and protection;

he has plundered our seas, ravaged our coasts, burnt our towns, and destroyed the lives of our people:

he is at this time transporting large armies of foreign mercenaries to compleat the works of death, desolation and tyranny, already begun with circumstances of cruelty and perfidy unworthy the head of a civilized nation:

he has endeavored to bring on the inhabitants of our frontiers the merciless Indian savages, whose known rule of warfare is an undistinguished destruction of all ages, sexes and conditions of existence:

he has incited treasonable insurrections of our fellow citizens with the allurements of forfeiture and confiscation of our property:

he has waged cruel war against human nature itself, violating it's most sacred rights of life and liberty in the persons of a distant people who never offended him, captivating and carrying them into slavery in another hemispere, or to incure miserable death in their transportation hither. This piratical warfare, the opprobium of infidel powers, is the warfare of the Christian king of Great Britain. [determined to keep open a market where MEN should be bought and sold,] he has prostituted his negative for suppressing every legislative attempt to prohibit or to restrain this execrable commerce [determining to keep open a market where MEN should be bought and sold]: and that this assemblage of horrors might want no fact of distinguished die, he is now exciting those very people to rise in arms among us, and to purchase that liberty of which he had deprived them, by murdering the people upon whom he also obtruded them: thus paying off former crimes committed against the liberties of one people, with crimes which he urges them to commit against the lives of another.

In every stage of these oppressions we have petitioned for redress in the most humble terms: our repeated petitions have been answered only by repeated injury. a prince, whose character is thus marked by every act which may define a tyrant, is unfit to be the ruler of a people who mean to be free. Future ages will scarce believe that the hardiness of one man, adventured within the short compass of twelve years only, on so many acts of tyranny without a mask, over a people fostered and fixed in principles of liberty.

Nor have we been wanting in attention to our British brethren. We have warned them from time to time of attempts by their legislature to extend an unwarrantable jurisdiction over these our states. we have reminded them of the circumstances of our emigration and settlement here, no one of which could warrant so strange a pretension: that these were effected at the expence of our own blood and treasure, unassisted by the wealth or the strength of Great Britain: that in constituing indeed our several forms of government, we had adopted one common king, thereby laying a foundation for perpetual league and amity with them: but that submission to their parliament was no part of our constitution, nor ever in idea, if history may be credited: and we appealed to their native justice and magnanimity, as well as to the ties of our common kindred to disavow these usurpations, which were likely to interrupt our correspondence and connections. They too have been deaf to the voice of justice and of consanguinity, and when occasions have been given them, by the regular course of their laws, of removing from their councils the disturbers of our harmony; they have by their free election re-established them in power. at this very time too they are permitting their chief magistrate to send over not only soldiers of our common blood, but Scotch and foreign mercenaries to invade and deluge us in blood. these facts have given the last stab to agonizing affection, and manly spirit bids us to renounce forever these unfeeling brethren. We must endeavor to forget our former love for them, and hold them, as we hold the rest of mankind, enemies in war, in peace friends. we might have been a free and a great people together; but a communication of grandeur and of freedom it seems is below their dignity. be it so, since they will have it: the road to [glory and] happiness [and to glory] is open to us too; we will climb it apart from them [in a seperate state] and acquiesce in the necessity which denounces [pronounces][our [everlasting Adieu!] eternal separation!

We, therefore, the representatives of the United States of America, in General Congress, assembled do , in the name, and by the authority of the good people of these states, reject and renounce the allegiance and subjection to the kinds of Great Britain and all others who may herafter claim by, through, or under them; we utterly dissolve and break off all political connection which may have heretofore subsisted between us and the people or parliament of Great Britain; and finally we do assert and declare these colonies to be free and independent states, and that as free and independent states they shall herafter have [full] power to levy war, conclude peace, contract alliances, establish commerce, and to do all other acts and things which independent states may of right do. And for the support of this declaration we mutually pledge to each other our lives, our fortunes and our sacred honor.

APPEAL TO HEAVEN